Vice President of Editorial — Melissa Wagner
Director of Acquisitions — Mikaela Felty
Director of Book Development — Jocelynn Hessler
Production Manager — Mike Brehm
Cover Design — Jose Rosado

Published in the United States of America by
IGI Global Scientific Publishing
701 East Chocolate Avenue
Hershey, PA, 17033, USA
Tel: 717-533-8845
Fax: 717-533-7115
Website: https://www.igi-global.com E-mail: cust@igi-global.com



Library of Congress Cataloging-in-Publication Data

Names: Efstratopoulou, Maria A. editor http://id.loc.gov/rwo/agents/n2020016911 | Argyriadi, Agathi, 1987- editor http://id.loc.gov/rwo/agents/n2024051533 | Argyriadis, Alexandros, 1982- editor http://id.loc.gov/rwo/agents/n2025016747

Title: AI in mental health and education : innovations, challenges, and collaborative pathways / edited by: Maria Efstratopoulou, Agathi Argyriadi, Alexandros Argyriadis.

Other titles: Artificial intelligence in mental health and education

Description: Hershey, PA : IGI Global Scientific Publishing, [2026] | Includes bibliographical references and index. | Summary: "This book aims to explore the transformative potential of artificial intelligence (AI) in the fields of education and mental health, providing innovative solutions and support mechanisms for individuals with and without disabilities"-- Provided by publisher.

Identifiers: LCCN 2025000749 (print) | LCCN 2025000750 (ebook) | ISBN 9798337305738 hardcover | ISBN 9798337305745 paperback | ISBN 9798337305752 ebook

Subjects: LCSH: Artificial intelligence--Educational applications http://id.loc.gov/authorities/subjects/sh87006783 | Mental health--Technological innovations

Classification: LCC LB1028.43 .A3973 2025 (print) | LCC LB1028.43 (ebook) | DDC 371.33/4--dc23/eng/20250414

LC record available at https://lccn.loc.gov/2025000749

LC ebook record available at https://lccn.loc.gov/2025000750

British Cataloguing in Publication Data
A Cataloguing in Publication record for this book is available from the British Library.

# AI in Learning, Educational Leadership, and Special Education:

## Innovations and Ethical Dilemmas

Maria Efstratopoulou
*United Arab Emirates University, UAE*

Agathi Argyriadi
*Frederick University, Cyprus*

Alexandros Argyriadis
*Hellenic Mediterranean University, Greece*

IGI Global
Scientific Publishing
Publishing Tomorrow's Research Today

# Table of Contents

# Detailed Table of Contents

In recent years Artificial Intelligence (AI) has been used in the field of education settings but also in special education as well. The technologies that are implied can transform the process of learning and teaching and create inclusive environments for students who face a variety of difficulties in learning. The current review focuses on two dimensions: a) the use of AI in diagnosis and the use of AI in intervention for students with disabilities and special educational needs. We emphasize the advantages and disadvantages of using AI in diagnosis and intervention in special education. We also address ethical considerations for the use of AI in special education. Suggestions for the use of AI in diagnosis and intervention in Special Education are also developed to help teachers, professionals such as psychologists, speech therapists, occupational therapists, parents, students, and policymakers in developing an effective context in the use of AI in special education.



Students with sensory impairments worldwide face significant obstacles in accessing equitable educational opportunities. These obstacles include limited access to adapted learning materials, communication barriers, and challenges navigating physical and social environments. Artificial intelligence (AI) offers a transformative potential to address these challenges, providing innovative, personalized, and accessible solutions that empower these students to thrive. This chapter provides a comprehensive exploration of AI-driven interventions designed to support students with visual and hearing impairments, including assistive technologies such as screen readers, tactile learning materials, real-time transcription tools, and AI-powered navigation tools. It examines the application of these interventions across core academic areas, particularly in STEM fields, and explores their role in fostering inclusive learning environments through collaborative and multi-modal learning experiences.

# Foreword

This book offers timely and critical insights into the transformative role of Artificial Intelligence in shaping the future of education and mental health services.

The emergence of AI transforms our capacity to understand and engage with cognition and health. In education, it opens the door to personalized learning, adaptive technologies, and more inclusive systems that cater to individual needs. In mental health, AI-driven tools are enhancing early diagnosis, remote support, and therapeutic interventions, making care more accessible and responsive.

The book engages thoughtfully with concurrently emerging ethical concerns such as data privacy, algorithmic bias, and equitable access. These issues are central to ensuring that AI serves human well-being in a fair and just manner.

This interdisciplinary volume reflects a diverse range of perspectives and research approaches. Its academic depth and practical relevance make it a valuable contribution to ongoing global conversations about scientific innovation, ethics, and human progress.

At UAEU, we are proud to support scholarship that addresses the most pressing questions of our time. I commend the editors and contributors for their dedication to advancing knowledge and guiding the responsible integration of AI into critical areas of public life. I trust that readers will find in these pages both insight and inspiration for building a future where technology enhances our shared humanity

**Zaki Anwar Nusseibeh**
*United Arab Emirates University, UAE*

# Preface

Artificial Intelligence (AI) has emerged as a transformative technology with profound implications across various domains. AI has shown great potential in education to revolutionize teaching and research methodologies, offering personalized learning experiences, enhancing academic performance, and streamlining research processes. The rise of artificial intelligence technology has piqued the interest of educational technologists in determining how to incorporate and integrate such advancements in teaching and learning.

AI education tools can offer personalize learning experiences for each student by analyzing vast amounts of student data to understand individual learning styles, preferences, and strengths. This data-driven approach enables the creation of adaptive learning paths, where educational content is tailored to meet the specific needs of each student. Intelligent tutoring systems, powered by AI, provide real-time feedback and guidance, assisting students on their individual learning journeys. As AI continues to evolve, it promises a dynamic and adaptive educational landscape, empowering educators and enriching the learning experience for students across diverse educational settings.

Additionally, AI contributes to early assessment and intervention strategies by continuously monitoring student performance. It can identify learning gaps or areas of difficulty, allowing educators to provide timely and targeted support, preventing students from falling behind. AI helps in automating routine administrative tasks, such as grading and attendance tracking, freeing up educators' time for more meaningful interactions with students. The personalization, adaptability, and efficiency brought about by AI in K-12 education contribute to creating a more student-centric, engaging, and effective learning environment that caters to the diverse needs of students at different stages of their educational journey.

As Academics, we have to consider different approaches and prepare our students for a new future. Students need to have a clear understanding of how these technologies are created and intended to work, as well as their imperfections. They need to recognize that AI is developed by people and with that can come biases and other ethical concerns. Additionally, they will need guidance on interacting with such technologies, which should include learning about how issues such as cyberbullying and deepfakes can be further amplified if these technologies are not used appropriately.

Despite the challenges and ethical concerns that arise with the use of AI in education, the benefits of this technology are numerous and cannot be ignored. AI can play a significant role in enhancing learning experiences, improving productivity and efficiency, and promoting inclusivity and accessibility. AI technology is never going to bring an end to education, it only offers great potential to accelerate the educational transformation Therefore, it is important for schools to carefully plan and integrate AI while ensuring its responsible and equitable use. By harnessing the power of AI and new technologies, faculties can create better learning environments that are inclusive, flexible, and responsive to each and every student.

## ORGANIZATION OF THE BOOK

As underlined by the theme *AI in Education: Innovations, Challenges, and Collaborative Pathways* the book is an opportunity to explore in depth the transformative power of AI and its great potential in education to revolutionize teaching and learning. The chapters in this book throw light on new developments that can inform teaching, policy, and practice in the field of education as well as the challenges that exist in implementing AI ideas in real school settings. The authors in this Book draw from a range of experience, examples, case studies, research and educational approaches to present this engaging text on using AI in Education.

### Section I: AI in Teaching, Learning & Leadership in Education

The first section of this volume is provides innovation ideas on using AI in teaching, learning and leadership in education. More specifically, **Chapter 1** delves into the transformative role of Artificial Intelligence (AI) in shaping students' Social Emotional Learning (SEL) in primary education, examining the benefits, challenges, and future implications. **Chapter 2** discusses how integrating Artificial Intelligence (AI) into education, particularly in STEM disciplines, can revolutionize learning by providing personalized instruction, automating assessments, and enhancing student engagement. **Chapter 3** explores how artificial intelligence (AI) transforms school leadership by enhancing innovation, inclusivity, and efficiency. **Chapter 4** chapter investigates a Social and Emotional Learning (SEL) intervention in Greece with a Learning Management System (LMS) to analyze the impact of personal and classroom achievement goals on Self-Regulated Learning (SRL) strategies and SEL competencies in elementary students. **Chapter 5** explores the evolving relationship between artificial intelligence (AI) and education, with a focus on balancing technological innovation and the indispensable role of teachers. **Chapter 6** focuses on using gamification techniques by school counsellors as a part of psychotherapies and psychoeducation.

## Section II: AI in Special & Inclusive Education

The second Section of this volume shifts the focus towards Special & Gifted Education discussing how AI can transform the process of creating a dynamic inclusive learning environment suggesting both theoretical and practical ideas that will be of value to professionals and educators involved in special and gifted education. **Chapter 7** explores the technologies that are implied can transform the process of learning and teaching and create inclusive environments for students who face a variety of difficulties in learning.**Chapter 8** provides a comprehensive exploration of AI-driven interventions designed to support students with visual and hearing impairments, including assistive technologies such as screen readers, tactile learning materials, real-time transcription tools, and AI-powered navigation tools.**Chapter 9** presents the ability of AI to analyze vast amounts of data through natural language processing, sentiment analysis, and behavioral pattern recognition provides a proactive approach to identifying early signs of emotional distress **Chapter 10** presents how special education teachers in an autism rehabilitation center in the United Arab Emirates can successfully integrate artificial intelligence (AI) tools into their professional practice, highlighting benefits and challenges. **Chapter 11** highlights ways for educators to use Artificial Intelligence (AI) in order to support students with communication disorders. **Chapter 12** highlights successful experiences with AI in school administration to demonstrate its practical impact on special education programs. Finally, **Chapter 13** explores the potential of artificial intelligence in advancing data-informed decision-making in special education and highlights successful experiences with AI in school administration to demonstrate its practical impact on special education programs.

Educators, leaders and administrators can now leverage AI to analyze vast amounts of data, providing insights that drive informed decisions and strategies. Additionally, AI is breaking down education barriers thanks to tools that support students with different needs and learning styles. As AI evolves, its potential to transform education grows, setting the stage for a future where learning is more personalized and effective.

# Chapter 1
# Artificial Intelligence and the Whole Child Approach:
## Unleashing Social-Emotional Learning Potential in Primary Education

**Meghry Nazarian**
https://orcid.org/0000-0002-2749-9054
*Amity University, Dubai, UAE*

**Mohamed Alhosani**
https://orcid.org/0000-0002-1869-523X
*United Arab Emirates University, UAE*

**Maria Efstratopoulou**
https://orcid.org/0000-0002-5162-2104
*United Arab Emirates University, UAE*

## ABSTRACT

*This chapter delves into the transformative role of Artificial Intelligence (AI) in shaping students' Social Emotional Learning (SEL) in primary education, examining the benefits, challenges, and future implications. With AI-enhanced tools fostering students' interpersonal skills, emotional expression, and academic resilience, schools can create dynamic, inclusive learning environments that support the Whole Child approach. However, AI integration raises critical concerns around data privacy, psychological effects, potential increases in anxiety, and the erosion of critical thinking and problem-solving skills. Teachers, too, face barriers, including the lack*

DOI: 10.4018/979-8-3373-0573-8.ch001

*of technical knowledge and training needed to implement AI effectively and confidently. This chapter discusses the role of educators in leveraging AI responsibility and provides key practical implications on how to prepare students for emotional and academic success in the 21st century.*

## INTRODUCTION

Artificial intelligence (AI) has become an integral part of the modern world, addressing the complexities of globalization and the demands of a knowledge-driven society. From the way we communicate with each other to how we learn, work, and behave, AI is reshaping the fabric of our daily activities. Virtual voice assistants such as Siri and Alexa, smart home systems, interactive toys, and educational applications are just a few examples of how AI is seamlessly woven into our routines. Its ability to process large amounts of data and make predictions is driving creativity and innovation across industries, transforming both individual and societal experiences.

From an educational perspective, AI has emerged as a solution, offering tools that personalize students' learning. For instance, AI can analyse patterns in students' behaviour and academic performance, providing insights that help educators tailor their teaching methods to students' needs. AI enhanced tools can flag students who may be struggling with specific concepts, enabling timely intervention (Luckin et al., 2016). These tools or software applications can make decisions about the learning path of an individual student and the content to choose, provide cognitive scaffolding to help and engage students (Luckin et al., 2016).

AI is transforming daily administrative tasks such as grading and data entry, creating spaces for educators to focus more on teaching and student interaction (Chassignol et al., 2018). Similarly, by evaluating data trends, such as test scores, attendance, and engagement levels, AI supports data-driven decision-making that fosters more effective learning environments. Another significant influence of AI in education lies in its ability to provide real-time feedback. AI-enhanced tools such as *Class Companion* can instantly evaluate student work and offer personalized and detailed feedback. Moreover, *Grammarly* provides real-time assistance in writing, helping students refine grammar and writing style as they compose texts. This immediately helps foster student engagement and reinforces learning by addressing errors as they occur (Zawacki-Richter et al., 2019). These advancements not only improve work efficiency consistently but also reduce the administrative burden on educators leading to more work happiness.

On a broader scale, AI plays a pivotal role in shaping the global economy and societal trends. It underpins advancements in fields such as healthcare, business, and education, making life more efficient and interconnected. As AI continues to evolve, its transformative potential lies not only in optimizing current systems, but also in addressing the multifaceted challenges of 21st century. In education, AI continues to redefine the bigger picture of how education should look like, opening doors to innovative solutions that were once unimaginable.

## A NEEDED PARADIGM SHIFT TO THE WHOLE CHILD APPROACH

One of the most intriguing areas in this chapter is theorizing for the whole child approach and how we legitimize learning with the progress of today's world globalization, international competitiveness, communication, mass media, and computer science. With the advancement of new technologies, multiliteracies, and multimodalities, a paradigm shift in the purpose and understanding of education is needed (Nazarian et al., 2023). In the 21st century, employers demand fewer people with basic skills and more people with complex thinking and communication skills (Murnane & Levy, 2012). Additionally, multiple stakeholders, including adults, teachers, and business executives, believe that problem-solving, creativity, analytical thinking, communication and collaboration skills, accountability and social skills are necessary to succeed beyond school (Sacconaghi, 2006). Critical thinking and innovation have become the new status quo; however, too many of the schools and education systems use models designed to prepare students for life in the middle of the last century.

In today's competitive world, students must be equipped to think creatively and critically, analyse massive amount of information, solve problems, and communicate effectively. However, current education systems remain committed to textbooks, time structures, instructional methods, and assessments. While a solid foundation for reading, writing, mathematics and other core subjects remains essential, it is no longer sufficient for achieving lifelong success. The demands of 21st century call for a reimagined approach to education policy and practice. An approach that emphasizes a whole child approach to learning, teaching, and community involvement (Slade & Griffith, 2013).

If decisions about education policy and practice started by asking what works for the child, how would resources - time, space, and human - be arrayed to ensure each child's success? If the student were truly at the centre of the system, what could we achieve? (ASCD, 2007, p. 4). A whole child approach is an umbrella approach that is based around five key tenets (ASCD, 2007):

1. Healthy: Each student enters school and practices a healthy lifestyle.

2. Safe: Each student learns in a learning environment that is emotionally and physically safe for them.
3. Engaged: Each student is actively engaged in learning and is connected to the school and broader community.
4. Supported: Each student has access to personalized learning and is supported by caring adults.
5. Challenged: Each student is challenged academically and prepared for college and for employment in the global market community.

The whole child approach to education is an umbrella approach that transcends individual content areas and requires holistic school improvement. It engages teachers at both the administrative and classroom levels, urging them to recognize the interconnectedness of the five Whole Child Tenets: being healthy, safe, engaged, supported, and challenged. This approach calls for a cohesive focus, organization, and allocation of resources in every classroom, school setting, and school-wide practice to ensure that students' multifaceted needs are properly addressed.

## MASLOW'S HIERARCHY AS A FOUNDATION FOR THE WHOLE CHILD APPROACH

Abraham Maslow's Hierarchy of Needs was introduced in 1943 as a psychological framework for understanding human psychology and well-being. This framework is structured as a pyramid with psychological needs forming the base and progressively higher-order needs moving towards the peak of the pyramid. Figure 1 depicts the psychological needs which constitute the most important individual needs, followed by safety, love and belongingness, self-esteem, and, finally, self-actualization.

Building on this model, the Whole Child Approach developed a corresponding hierarchy for education, emphasizing the essential stages required to support students' holistic growth and development. When schools address students' psychological needs such as safety, a sense of belonging, autonomy, and competence, students exhibit improved engagement in their learning, stronger interpersonal relationships, align with school values, develop social and emotional skills, contribute positively to their community, and excel academically (Durlak et al., 2011; Osher et al., 2016). Conversely, when students' psychological needs are neglected, students often experience diminished motivation, feelings of alienation, and lower academic performance (Osher et al., 2016; Jones & Doolittle, 2017).

How are schools achieving this? Any school-level change requires attention and awareness to elements which impede or promote students' learning. While a structured focus on the fundamentals of the information age such as reading, writing and mathematics is essential, the new fundamentals should entail the environment and the school culture that are established to ensure every student's success. This includes integrating SEL interventions, providing equal opportunities for all students, and attention to every student's health (social-emotional-physical-mental) and safety. Focusing on a Whole Child approach and Social Emotional Learning is key to fostering a positive school climate where students feel valued and supported leading to higher intrinsic motivation and academic resilience (Zins et al., 2004; Slade & Griffith, 2013). At the school-level, the integration of social-emotional learning (SEL) interventions into daily practices has been linked to increased emotional regulation, improved problem-solving skills, and greater success in navigating complex social interactions (Taylor et al., 2017). Research also shows that students in supportive environments are more likely to develop essential life skills, contributing to long-term personal and professional success (Jones et al., 2015; Weissberg et al., 2015). However, unmet SEL needs have been associated with increased behavioural issues, emotional distress, and long-term academic disengagement (Taylor et al., 2017).

*Figure 1. Maslow's hierarchy of needs*

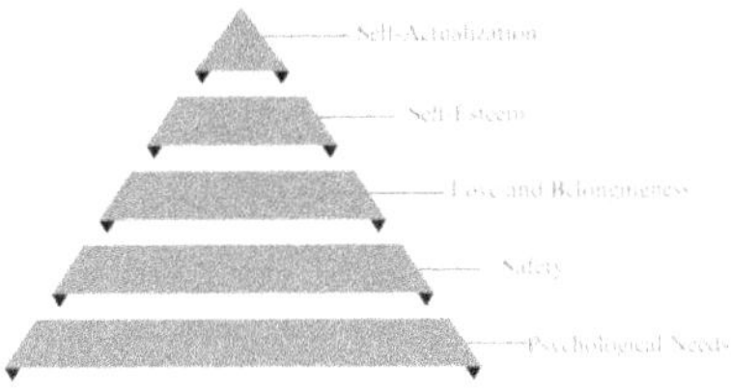


## THE IMPORTANCE OF SOCIAL EMOTIONAL LEARNING (SEL) IN SUPPORTING THE WHOLE CHILD

Social Emotional Learning (SEL) has been conceptualized in numerous ways by many scholars. For example, Durlak and his colleagues (2011) outlined SEL competencies that include recognizing and managing emotions, fostering healthy perspectives about oneself and others, establishing positive goals, resolving interpersonal conflicts, nurturing constructive relationships, and making ethical decisions.

More recently, Frey and her team (2019) proposed a comprehensive SEL framework comprising five overarching domains: identity and agency (e.g., recognizing personal strengths, self-assurance, adopting a growth mindset, perseverance, or resilience), emotional regulation (e.g., controlling impulses, deferring gratification, handling stress, or adopting coping strategies), cognitive regulation (e.g., self-reflection, sustaining focus, setting objectives, solving problems, or making decisions), social skills (e.g., collaborating, working in teams, effective communication, or demonstrating empathy), and public spirit (e.g., ethical accountability, civic engagement, or advocating for social justice). Figure 2 depicts the SEL framework developed by Frey et al., (2019).

*Figure 2. Social emotional learning framework*

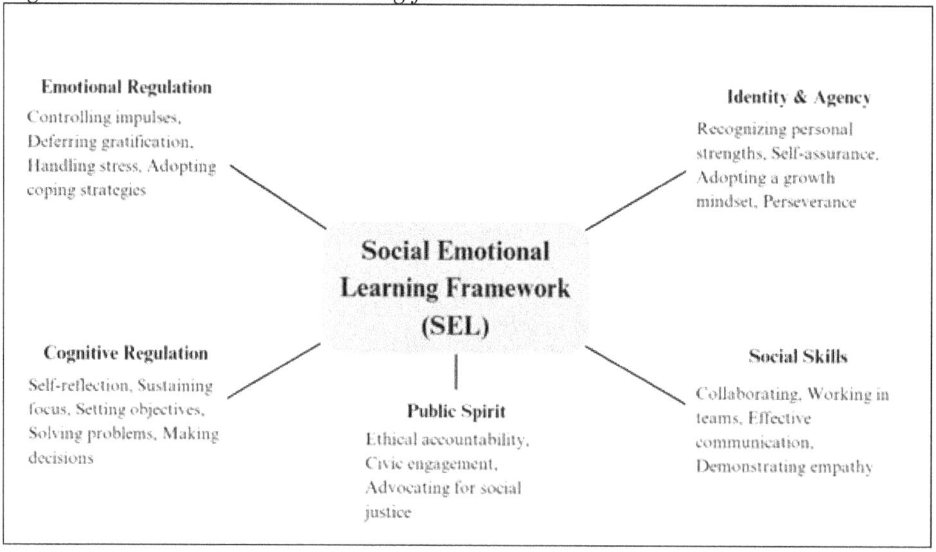


Cognitive regulation, emotional regulation, and social skills are inextricably connected to each other in the learning process. According to Jones and Kahn, learning becomes more meaningful when each one of these three dimensions are adequately supported (2017). A rigorous body of research has demonstrated that students achieve higher academic achievement and classrooms function more effectively when students possess cognitive regulation, emotional regulation, and strong social skills. These three dimensions help students regulate their emotions, motivation, and perseverance levels. In other words, students with strong cognitive regulation, emotional regulation, and social skills can successfully navigate relationships with others and problem solve (Duckworth & Seligman, 2005; Jones & Doolittle, 2017; Osher et al., 2016; Sorensen & Dodge, 2015). Social and emotional competencies significantly influence students' lives beyond their schooling years. In their longitudinal study on social emotional functioning and public health, Jones and his colleagues (2015) found a strong relationship between early SEL and future wellness. They explained that social and emotional skills of early learners were strong and unique predictors of whether they graduated high school on time, earned a college degree, and secured stable full-time employment in later years. Additionally, SEL of students is positively associated with their personal well-being and inversely predictive of involvement in any criminal act (Jones et al., 2015).

Incorporating SEL into teaching practices by classroom teachers leads to significant enhancements in students' academic performance (Durlak et al., 2011). This means SEL-oriented schools play a crucial role in improving students' academic performance and SEL skills (e.g. perspective taking, goal setting, regulating emotions, interpersonal problem solving) while minimizing emotional distress and social withdrawal (Durlak et al., 2011). Research on fostering positive youth development addressed the long-lasting benefits of SEL interventions on academic performance and emotional distress (Taylor et al., 2017). Students, who received well-structured SEL interventions continued to demonstrate strong emotional and social skills such as positive attitude towards others and positive social behaviour regardless of their race and socioeconomic status (Taylor et al., 2017).

By integrating SEL into teaching practices, educational settings such as schools adopt a "whole child" approach, focusing on the comprehensive development of students including their social, emotional, cognitive, and physical well-being (Slade & Griffith, 2013). A whole child approach is a holistic approach that views the purpose of schooling is to develop global citizens and equip each child with the necessary skills to fulfil their potential within and beyond the classroom (Slade & Griffith, 2013). This holistic approach acknowledges that students' ability to thrive academically is strongly connected with their social-emotional skills. In doing so, it prepares them for a balanced and fulfilling life, ensuring education is not only about knowledge acquisition but also about nurturing students who can think critically and creatively.

## THE TRANSFORMATIVE POTENTIAL OF AI IN ENHANCING LEARNERS' SEL

In recent years, the field of education has witnessed a significant transformation driven by technological advancements, particularly the integration of artificial intelligence (AI). AI, often conceptualized as the emulation of human cognitive processes by machines, holds tremendous potential to revolutionize various dimensions in education, encompassing teaching strategies, learning environments, and student achievements (Russell & Norvig, 2022). One of the emerging areas where AI is making phenomenal influence is social emotional learning (SEL). The integration of AI technologies into SEL programs offers great opportunities to personalize students' learning experiences, provide real-time feedback, and enhance students' socio-emotional growth and well-being (Sethi & Jein, 2024). By leveraging AI techniques, educators can prepare innovative and engaging classroom activities or assessment tools to assess students' knowledge and reinforce their social emotional skills in a scalable and effective manner (Bartneck et al., 2015).

This section provides an in-depth exploration of how AI plays a pivotal role in fostering interpersonal skills, supporting emotional expressions, and building academic resilience.

## AI for Fostering Students' Interpersonal Skills

AI-powered tools such as *Nearpod* and *Blooket* have emerged as important facilitators of interpersonal skill development among students. These tools utilize advanced algorithms to simulate real-life social scenarios, enabling learners to practice communication, collaboration, and empathy in a controlled yet interactive environment. For instance, AI-driven virtual reality (VR) platforms allow students to engage in role-playing activities where they interact with individuals from diverse backgrounds, practicing conflict resolution and teamwork (DeMillo, 2015). Within educational contexts, VR enables experiential learning opportunities to students and fosters emotional skill development among them in a safe and controlled setting (Freina & Ott, 2015; Sethi & Jein, 2024). In a classroom setting, teachers can take students on an immersive learning journey by using virtual reality field trips from *Nearpod*. Regardless of grade level or content area taught, students interact with each other during these virtual field trips. They also learn to understand other students' emotions. Research on immersive virtual reality found that VR experiences boost student engagement and raise their awareness towards understanding others' emotions and different perspectives, thus promoting social empathy and interconnectedness (Slater & Sanchez-Vives, 2016). Moreover, VR applications can leverage students' empathy, emotional regulation and social skills, thus fostering students' overall socio-emotional competences.

Furthermore, VR environments are considered optimal settings for practicing emotional regulation techniques. For example, students struggling with anxiety or stress can engage in guided mindfulness exercises tailored to their needs (Parsons & Rizzo, 2008). These virtual exposure therapy sessions can support students manage their emotions in a supportive and safe environment.

Collaborative AI systems foster group learning by tracking individual contributions and promoting equitable participation. These tools use natural language processing (NLP) to identify dominant voices and ensure quieter students have opportunities to contribute, thus reinforcing inclusivity in group discussions (Luo et al., 2023). Such systems have proven effective in cultivating a sense of community and shared responsibility, essential components of interpersonal competence. The ability of AI to personalize learning experiences further enhances its impact, as students receive tailored guidance that aligns with their unique needs and developmental stages (Moreno et al., 2022).

## Supporting Emotional Expressions through Technology

The ability to recognize, express, and regulate emotions is fundamental to SEL. AI offers promising support in this domain. AI systems equipped with emotion recognition technologies analyse students' facial expressions, tone of voice, and body language to assess emotional states in real-time (Zhang et al., 2021). Such insights enable teachers to provide timely interventions, fostering a supportive and emotionally aware classroom environment.

Emotion-focused AI tools also empower students to develop self-awareness and emotional regulation skills. For example, applications that use AI to track mood patterns and suggest coping strategies can help students navigate stress and anxiety effectively. These tools often employ gamification elements to engage younger learners, turning emotional self-regulation into an interactive and rewarding experience (Mertala, 2023). Furthermore, AI-powered journaling platforms encourage students to articulate their emotions, providing prompts and feedback that nurture reflective practices and emotional literacy (Patel et al., 2022). Despite its benefits, the use of AI in emotional recognition raises ethical concerns, particularly regarding privacy and data security. Researchers emphasize the need for transparent data handling practices and robust ethical frameworks to ensure that students' emotional data is used responsibly (Binns et al., 2022). Addressing these challenges is crucial to maximizing the potential of AI-driven tools in supporting emotional expression.

## Building Academic Resilience with Adaptive AI Systems

AI plays a significant role in promoting academic resilience by offering adaptive learning experiences that respond to students' needs and challenges. Adaptive AI systems analyse performance data to identify areas where students struggle and provide targeted interventions, fostering a growth mindset and perseverance (Fletcher & Warfield, 2021). These systems utilize predictive analytics to recommend resources and activities that align with individual learning trajectories, enabling students to overcome academic setbacks with confidence.

One notable example is the use of AI tutors, which offer personalized guidance and encouragement during problem-solving tasks. These systems adapt to students' emotional states, offering motivational prompts when frustration is detected and celebrating achievements to boost self-efficacy (Siemens et al., 2023). Additionally, AI-driven platforms integrate SEL principles into academic content, helping students develop resilience alongside cognitive skills. By modelling resilience strategies and fostering a supportive learning environment, AI systems contribute to students' overall well-being. However, the implementation of these tools must consider potential barriers, such as access disparities and the digital divide, which could limit their benefits for underserved populations. Researchers advocate for inclusive design practices to ensure that adaptive AI systems are accessible to all learners (Gulson et al., 2023).

## AI-DRIVEN APPROACHES TO CREATING INCLUSIVE LEARNING ENVIRONMENTS

The integration of artificial intelligence (AI) in education is revolutionizing traditional classroom approaches, creating opportunities for more inclusive learning environments. These AI-driven strategies address diverse learning needs, enhance collaboration, and prioritize students' emotional well-being, particularly in primary education.

### Promoting Collaboration and Real-Time Feedback

Collaboration and real-time feedback are key to effective teaching, fostering engagement and equitable student participation. AI technologies, such as collaborative platforms and learning management systems (LMS), provide immediate feedback and enable students to work together effectively. AI-driven tools such as Google Classroom and Microsoft Teams support collaborative learning by allowing students to work on group projects and share resources in real time. For example, an AI-enhanced LMS can identify students who are disengaged during group activities and suggest interventions, ensuring all participants contribute meaningfully (Kumar et al., 2021). In primary classrooms, AI tools that support gamified learning, such as *Kahoot* and *Quizlet*, encourage participation by making collaboration more engaging and interactive.

AI- generated instant feedback can be detailed and tailored to student performance. For example, *Class Companion* analyses students' pieces of writing and offers real-time suggestions to improve their writing skills. This immediate feedback technique is particularly effective in primary education, where students require continuous encouragement to build foundational knowledge (Luckin, 2018). Moreover, real-time feedback empowers teachers by highlighting areas where students need additional support, facilitating timely interventions. Within educational contexts, AI-generated instant feedback saves teachers a lot of time, allowing them to focus more on student interaction (Vyas et al., 2024). Additionally, AI-based chatbots serve as conversational partners, providing immediate feedback on communication styles and suggesting improvements to enhance clarity and empathy (Woolf et al., 2020).

## Customizing Learning Experiences for Diverse Needs

One of AI's most significant contributions to inclusivity is its ability to tailor educational experiences to meet diverse student needs. Adaptive learning systems leverage AI to analyse individual performance and provide customized content, ensuring every learner progresses at their own pace. Adaptive Learning Systems such as *Edmentum* use data analytics to adjust content difficulty based on a student's performance. For example, a primary school student struggling with multiplication might receive targeted practice problems, while an advanced learner is offered complex challenges. Research by Xu and Zhao (2020) highlights how adaptive learning systems reduce achievement gaps by catering to individual strengths and weaknesses.

AI technologies are instrumental in supporting students with learning disabilities, ensuring they have access to quality education. Speech recognition applications help students with motor impairments, while text-to-speech tools assist those with dyslexia. Primary classrooms can also use AI-powered wearable devices to monitor and support students with autism, improving their focus and communication skills (Rose et al., 2019).

From a multicultural perspective, AI-driven translation tools like Microsoft Translator facilitate communication in multilingual classrooms, enabling non-native speakers to participate actively. These tools also help teachers design culturally relevant content, promoting inclusivity for diverse student needs (Garcia & Wei, 2018).

## Encouraging Emotional Well-Being in Primary Education

Emotional well-being is a critical component of inclusive education, influencing students' ability to learn and interact effectively. AI technologies can identify and address emotional challenges, fostering a supportive and safe learning environment. AI systems equipped with emotion technologies analyse facial expressions, voice tones, and body gestures to measure students' emotional states. For instance, primary classrooms using platforms like *Affectiva* can monitor students' engagement levels and alert teachers when intervention is needed. These insights help educators address issues such as anxiety or frustration before they hinder learning (Calvo & D'Mello, 2010). Moreover, AI supports SEL initiatives by providing tools that teach empathy, self-awareness, and resilience. For example, apps like *Peekapak* and *Classcraft* integrate AI to create narratives and scenarios that encourage students to reflect on emotions and relationships. A study by Jones et al. (2021) found that such programs improve emotional intelligence and classroom behaviour, especially in younger students.

AI plays a vital role in managing students' stress levels. AI-driven applications like *Headspace for Kids* and *Breathe, Think, Do with Sesame* teaches students mindfulness and meditation skills. These tools guide students through breathing exercises and problem-solving activities, fostering emotional regulation. In primary classrooms, such interventions enhance students' attention span and reduce stress, creating a more inclusive and supportive environment for learners (Schonert-Reichl et al., 2015).

## CHALLENGES IN INTEGRATING AI INTO SEL

Artificial Intelligence (AI) has been increasingly adopted in education, particularly in Social Emotional Learning (SEL), to enhance students' interpersonal, emotional and social skills. However, this rapid adoption also raises questions about ethical considerations, data privacy, and equitable access to technology. While AI has numerous potential benefits, its integration comes with significant challenges. This section explores these challenges under three key sub-headings: ethical concerns around data privacy and security, psychological impacts of AI on students, and potential risks to critical thinking and problem-solving skills.

### Ethical Concerns About Data Privacy and Security

The integration of AI into SEL often involves the collection and analysis of sensitive student data. AI tools designed for SEL gather information through assessments, interaction tracking, and facial expression analysis.

Scholars have raised concerns about the ethical implications of such practices, particularly regarding data privacy and security. A primary concern is the vulnerability of data collected by AI systems. According to Shum et al. (2019), many AI-driven educational technologies lack robust mechanisms to secure sensitive data, making them susceptible to breaches. This risk is particularly concerning in primary education, where students are less aware of their rights regarding data usage. For example, AI tools that analyse emotions through facial recognition may inadvertently store video data without adequate consent from guardians, leading to potential misuse (Luckin et al., 2016).

Furthermore, ethical concerns extend to data ownership and informed consent. Selwyn (2020) argues that parents and educators are often not fully informed about how AI systems process and store data, creating an ethical issue. In a classroom setting, where children frequently interact with AI-driven SEL tools, this lack of transparency undermines trust between educators, parents, and AI developers. For example, a case study in a U.S. elementary school highlighted parental dissatisfaction when they discovered that their children's emotional data were being used to train proprietary algorithms without proper consent (Williamson & Eynon, 2020).

## Psychological Impacts of AI on Students, Including Anxiety

While AI holds promise for personalized emotional support, its use may lead to increased anxiety among students. This important concern is especially pertinent in primary education, where students are still developing cognitive and emotional resilience. One potential psychological impact is the constant surveillance facilitated by AI tools. According to Heffernan et al. (2021), students may feel anxious knowing their emotions are being monitored continuously. In one study, primary school students reported feeling self-conscious and anxious during classroom activities when they were aware of being monitored by AI-driven SEL systems (Miao et al., 2021). This sense of being constantly observed can hinder students' natural emotional expression, which is a critical aspect of SEL development.

Moreover, the reliance on AI for emotional support may create dependency issues. Research by Ahn and Ahn (2021) suggests that students may over-rely on AI tools to navigate their emotions, potentially reducing their ability to develop independent emotional coping mechanisms. For example, a pilot program involving AI-based SEL tools in primary classrooms found that some students turned exclusively to the AI system for conflict resolution, avoiding traditional interpersonal methods like seeking help from teachers or peers. Additionally, there is concern about how AI systems interpret and respond to emotional data. Algorithms may misinterpret a student's emotions, leading to inappropriate feedback that triggers feelings of frustration or confusion (Clark et al., 2020). In primary classrooms, such errors can have long-term implications, as young students may internalize inaccurate feedback, affecting their self-perception and self-confidence.

## Potential Risks to Critical Thinking and Problem Solving

The integration of AI into SEL raises concerns about its impact on students' critical thinking and problem-solving skills. AI applications provide immediate solutions to any encountered challenge, potentially limiting students' opportunities to develop these skills independently.

One of the main risks is the reduction in opportunities for open-ended exploration. According to Selwyn and Aagaard (2021), AI-driven SEL tools often guide students through pathways to manage emotions and social interactions. In primary classrooms, where exploratory learning is crucial, such structured approaches can impede students' creativity and innovation. For instance, an AI system designed to mediate peer conflicts might offer one recommended solution, discouraging students from brainstorming alternative solutions.

Additionally, the automation of emotional feedback may diminish the role of human educators, who are better equipped to nurture students' critical thinking in nuanced social situations. Luckin and Holmes (2016) emphasize that human teachers bring empathy and contextual understanding to SEL, qualities that AI systems cannot replicate. Excessive use of AI may lead students to view social and emotional challenges as problems with limited answers, rather than as complex issues requiring thoughtful reasoning and deep thinking.

Finally, another important concern is the potential homogenization of emotional responses. Clark and Chalmers (2020) argue that AI tools often rely on generalized emotional models, which may not account for cultural or individual diversity. In primary education, where students come from diverse cultural and linguistic backgrounds, this lack of personalization can lead to misaligned interventions. For example, an AI system designed to promote collaboration may fail to recognize culturally specific communication styles, indirectly discouraging participation from certain student groups.

## BARRIERS FOR EDUCATORS IN IMPLEMENTING AI EFFECTIVELY

While AI holds the promise for the teaching and learning revolution, several challenges and barriers must be addressed. In education, teachers face several barriers in implementing AI effectively. This section contextualizes the barriers under three main sub-headings: the need for teacher training and technical knowledge, limited resources and infrastructure in schools, and bridging the gap between pedagogical goals and technological tools.

### The Need for Teacher Training and Technical Knowledge

A lack of adequate training and technical knowledge among teachers is a significant barrier to the effective implementation of AI in education. Many educators are unfamiliar with the capabilities and limitations of AI tools, which hinders their ability to integrate these technologies into their teaching practices confidently. Research by Holmes et al. (2020) emphasizes the importance of equipping teachers with the skills required to use AI technologies. They found that teachers in primary schools often express apprehension about adopting AI due to insufficient training (Luckin et al., 2019). The lack of familiarity with AI algorithms, data analysis, and machine learning concepts leaves educators ill-prepared to utilize these tools effectively. Furthermore, Selwyn and Aagaard (2021) highlight the need for ongoing professional development programs tailored to AI in education. In primary classrooms, where foundational learning occurs, teachers require hands-on training to align AI tools with students' developmental needs. A pilot program in a U.S. elementary school demonstrated that when teachers received targeted training on AI applications, students showed improved engagement and learning outcomes compared to classrooms where AI tools were used without teacher preparation (Williamson et al., 2020).

## Lack of Resources and Limited Access to AI in Schools

Another barrier to the effective implementation of AI in education is the lack of adequate resources and limited access. Many schools, particularly in underdeveloped geographical areas, struggle to afford the necessary technology and connectivity to support AI tools. Research by Miao et al. (2021) found that primary schools in low-income regions often lack the basic infrastructure required for technology, such as high-speed internet, updated computer systems, and technical support staff. For example, a study of rural schools in India showed that while some schools had access to AI-based learning platforms, inconsistent electricity supply and limited internet connectivity made these tools ineffective (Lugrin et al., 2015; Kumar & Agrawal, 2021).

Moreover, the cost of AI technologies is a prohibitive factor for many educational institutions. Williamson and Eynon (2020) note that the implementation of AI systems often requires substantial upfront investments, including purchasing hardware, software, and training programs. For primary schools operating on tight budgets, these expenses are often deemed unaffordable. In one instance, a school in South Africa attempted to integrate an AI-driven reading tool but had to discontinue the program due to the high costs of maintaining the software (Ngwenya, 2020). The disparity in resource allocation limits access to digital tools, leaving schools in marginalized communities unable to access the benefits of AI. This lack of equity not only hinders the potential of AI to improve education but also widens the gap between well-resourced and under-resourced schools.

## Bridging the Gap Between Pedagogical Goals and Technological Tools

How are teachers aligning AI technologies with overall learning outcomes? One of the most difficult barriers to implementing AI effectively in education is aligning AI technologies with pedagogical goals. AI tools are often designed with general functionalities that may not directly address the needs of students in primary education. According to Selwyn (2020), many AI tools prioritize efficiency and data analysis over pedagogical relevance. For example, AI-driven assessment platforms often focus on standardized test scores, which may not align with the holistic development goals of primary education. Teachers in a U.S. study expressed frustration that AI systems did not adequately support collaborative or project-based learning, which are key components of 21st-century education (Clark et al., 2020).

Additionally, Luckin and Holmes (2016) argue that the design of AI tools often overlooks the contextual nuances of classroom teaching. In primary classrooms, where social and emotional development is as important as academic achievement, AI tools must be tailored to foster interactions that go beyond automated responses. For instance, an AI-based tool designed to enhance literacy might focus solely on reading fluency, neglecting the importance of fostering a love for reading through storytelling and group discussions.

Effective integration of AI also requires bridging the communication gap between technologists and educators. Miao et al. (2021) emphasize the importance of involving teachers in the development process of AI tools to ensure that the technology aligns with educational priorities. A collaborative effort between AI developers and educators in Australia led to the creation of an adaptive learning platform that successfully enhanced primary students' math skills while promoting critical thinking and creativity (Heffernan et al., 2021).

## FUTURE DIRECTIONS FOR AI IN SEL AND PRIMARY EDUCATION

### Aligning AI Technologies with SEL Principles

The integration of Artificial Intelligence (AI) into primary education and Social Emotional Learning (SEL) provides meaningful opportunities for enhancing student learning outcomes and achievement. However, ensuring that AI technologies align with the principles of SEL is critical to their effectiveness. SEL emphasizes fostering self-awareness, self-management, social awareness, relationship skills, and responsible decision-making.

Consequently, AI tools must be designed to nurture these values. Researchers argue that AI tools must incorporate culturally responsive algorithms to prevent biases and ensure equitable treatment of all students (Zhang et al., 2022). Moreover, AI can assist in designing inclusive learning environments by identifying and addressing barriers to engagement. For instance, AI systems that analyse participation patterns can flag instances of social exclusion or bullying, enabling educators to intervene proactively. To align with SEL principles, these technologies must prioritize empathy, ethical decision-making, and respect for individual differences, fostering a sense of belonging and tolerance among students (Gulson et al., 2023). Practical applications include professional development programs that train educators to use AI tools in alignment with SEL frameworks. Teachers need support in understanding how AI data can complement traditional methods of fostering social and emotional growth. Additionally, the development of policy guidelines that emphasize ethical use, data privacy, and transparency is essential to maintaining trust and ensuring the responsible integration of AI in SEL practices.

## Practical Implications for Teaching Practices and School Culture

The integration of AI technologies in SEL has profound long-term implications for teaching practices and school culture. As AI systems become more sophisticated, they have the potential to transform how educators approach instruction and interaction with students. These technologies can help shift the focus from traditional content delivery to holistic student development, emphasizing the importance of emotional and social competencies alongside academic achievement.

AI-powered tools enable teachers to adopt more personalized and adaptive teaching strategies. For example, by analysing real-time data on students' emotional and cognitive states, educators can tailor their instructional methods to meet individual needs more effectively. This approach fosters a classroom environment that is both responsive and inclusive, promoting greater engagement and collaboration among students (Osher et al., 2022). In addition, AI has the potential to enhance school culture by promoting a more supportive and empathetic learning environment. Technologies that monitor student well-being can help schools identify systemic issues, such as high levels of stress or anxiety, and implement targeted interventions. By prioritizing SEL in their AI initiatives, schools can cultivate a culture that values emotional well-being as a cornerstone of students' academic and personal success (Binns et al., 2023). However, these advancements also require a reconsideration of educators' roles. As AI takes on more administrative and data analysis tasks, teachers can focus on building stronger relationships with students and creating meaningful learning experiences for them. This shift demands comprehensive training programs to help educators adapt to new technologies and redefine their professional responsibilities.

## Emphasizing the Role of Educators in Leveraging AI Responsibility

The evolving role of educators in integrating Artificial Intelligence (AI) into Social Emotional Learning (SEL) requires thoughtful implementation and ongoing professional development. Educators act as the bridge between AI technologies and students, ensuring that these tools enhance learning without overshadowing human interaction. To use AI responsibly, teachers must develop a comprehensive understanding of both its capabilities and limitations. Moreover, the teacher's role in fostering an inclusive classroom environment remains irreplaceable. While AI can provide insights into student behaviour, it cannot replicate the empathetic rapport between teachers and students. For instance, emotional recognition technologies may identify a student experiencing distress, but it is the educator who can contextualize these findings and provide personalized intervention. This dual approach ensures that AI complements rather than replaces the human touch in SEL (Binns et al., 2023).

Practical implications include developing interdisciplinary curricula that combine AI literacy with SEL principles, ensuring that teachers are not only technologically adept but also emotionally attuned to students' needs. Policymakers should prioritize creating frameworks that support educators in leveraging AI responsibly, fostering a balanced approach to technology integration in classrooms.

## Preparing Students for Emotional and Academic Success in the 21st Century

As the demands of the 21st century grow increasingly complex, preparing students for emotional and academic success necessitates a holistic approach. AI technologies play a crucial role in this endeavour by personalizing learning experiences and equipping students with critical SEL competencies. Effective AI-driven tools incorporation into teaching practices encourages students to take ownership of their learning journeys, thereby promoting long-term academic success (Zhang et al., 2022). In addition to academic benefits, AI enhances emotional intelligence by providing real-time feedback on interpersonal interactions and emotional regulation. Such experiences prepare students to navigate real-world challenges, equipping them with global skills to collaborate effectively and adapt to diverse contexts (Gulson et al., 2023).

To ensure that students are well-prepared for the future, schools must integrate AI-driven SEL initiatives into broader educational goals. This includes promoting digital literacy alongside emotional intelligence, ensuring that students can critically evaluate technology while leveraging its benefits. Collaborative efforts among educators, parents, and policymakers are essential in creating environments where students can thrive emotionally and academically.

## CONCLUSION

This chapter explained the transformative role of Artificial Intelligence (AI) in shaping students' Social Emotional Learning (SEL) in primary education, examining the benefits, challenges, and future implications. The integration of AI into SEL offers transformative possibilities for enhancing primary education, but its success depends on how it is being incorporated. Key takeaways from this chapter include the importance of balancing AI integration with traditional teaching methods to ensure students benefit from technological advancements while preserving meaningful human connections in education. Aligning AI technologies with SEL principles is also crucial to ensure it supports holistic student development. Ethical considerations, such as data privacy and cultural sensitivity, must remain in the centre of these efforts, fostering trust among educators, students, and families.

Another important insight is the irreplaceable role of educators in this integration. Teachers must be empowered with the tools and training needed to use AI responsibly, ensuring that technology helps rather than hurts the human interaction.

Finally, preparing students for the demands of the 21st century requires the collaborative efforts of multiple stakeholders including educators, parents, policymakers, and technologists. AI can serve as a powerful tool in improving students' social and emotional competences; however, its implementation must be guided by a commitment to inclusivity, ethical practices, and the overarching goal of nurturing well-rounded, resilient learners who are equipped to succeed in an increasingly diverse world.

## REFERENCES


Ahn, J., & Ahn, M. (2021). The role of AI in primary education: A double-edged sword for social emotional learning. *Journal of Educational Technology*, *48*(3), 231–247.

Association for Supervision and Curriculum Development. (2007). *The learning compact redefined: A call to action. A report of the commission on the whole child.* Author.

Bartneck, C., Duenser, A., Moltchanova, E., & Zawieska, K. (2015). Comparing the Similarity of Responses Received from Studies in Amazon's Mechanical Turk to Studies Conducted Online and with Direct Recruitment. *PLoS One*, *10*(4), e0121595. DOI: 10.1371/journal.pone.0121595 PMID: 25876027

Binns, R., Veale, M., Van Kleek, M., & Shadbolt, N. (2022). It's reducing a human being to a percentage: Perceptions of justice in algorithmic decisions. *Proceedings of the 2022 CHI Conference on Human Factors in Computing Systems*, 796-806. https://doi.org/DOI: 10.1145/3173574.3173620

Binns, R., Veale, M., Van Kleek, M., & Shadbolt, N. (2023). Ethical considerations in the application of AI in education: Balancing benefits and risks. *Journal of Educational Technology*, *42*(1), 15–30.

Calvo, R. A., & D'Mello, S. (2010). Affect detection: An interdisciplinary review of models, methods, and their applications in learning environments. *User Modeling and User-Adapted Interaction*, *20*(2), 89–118.

Chassignol, M., Khoroshavin, A., Klimova, A., & Bilyatdinova, A. (2018). Artificial Intelligence trends in education: A narrative overview. *Procedia Computer Science*, *136*, 16–24. DOI: 10.1016/j.procs.2018.08.233

Clark, A., & Chalmers, D. (2020). The cultural implications of AI in classrooms. *Education Futures*, *12*(4), 389–407.

DeMillo, R. A. (2015). *Revolution in higher education: How a small band of innovators will make college accessible and affordable.* Mit Press.

Duckworth, A. L., & Seligman, M. E. (2005). Self-Discipline outdoes IQ in predicting academic performance of adolescents. *Psychological Science*, *16*(12), 939–944. DOI: 10.1111/j.1467-9280.2005.01641.x PMID: 16313657

Durlak, J. A., Weissberg, R. P., Dymnicki, A. B., Taylor, R. D., & Schellinger, K. B. (2011). The impact of enhancing students' social and emotional learning: A meta-analysis of school-based universal interventions. *Child Development*, *82*(1), 405–432. DOI: 10.1111/j.1467-8624.2010.01564.x PMID: 21291449

Fletcher, G., & Warfield, K. (2021). Personalizing education: Adaptive AI systems for the modern classroom. *Journal of Educational Technology*, *18*(3), 45–58.

Freina, L., & Ott, M. (2015). A literature review on immersive virtual reality in education: state of the art and perspectives. *The international scientific conference elearning and software for education, 1*, 133-141. doi:DOI: 10.12753/2066-026X-23-020

Frey, N., Fisher, D., & Smith, D. (2019). *All learning is social and emotional: Helping students develop essential skills for the classroom and beyond.* ASCD.

Garcia, O., & Wei, L. (2018). *Translanguaging in bilingual education: Principles and practices*. Springer.

Gulson, K. N., Murphie, A., & Taylor Webb, P. (2023). AI-driven innovations in SEL and their implications for educational policy. *Education and AI*, *58*(4), 45–67.

Heffernan, N.. (2021). Bridging the gap between AI and pedagogy. *International Journal of Educational Technology*, *18*(3), 143–162.

Holmes, W., Luckin, R., & Mavrikis, M. (2020). Teacher training for AI: Challenges and opportunities. *The Journal of Educational Research*, *45*(2), 115–128.

Jones, D. E., Greenberg, M., & Crowley, M. (2015). Early Social-Emotional Functioning and Public Health: The relationship between kindergarten social competence and future wellness. *American Journal of Public Health*, *105*(11), 2283–2290. DOI: 10.2105/AJPH.2015.302630 PMID: 26180975

Jones, M. S., & Kahn, J. (2017). *The evidence base for how we learn: Supporting students' social emotional, and academic development.* Aspen Institute, National Commission on Social, Emotional, and Academic Development. https://www.aspeninstitute.org/publications/ evidence-base-learn/

Jones, S. M., Bailey, R., & Jacob, R. (2021). Social-emotional learning: A key to children's success. *The Future of Children*, *27*(1), 13–32.

Jones, S. M., & Doolittle, E. J. (2017). Social and Emotional Learning: Introducing the issue. *The Future of Children*, *27*(1), 3–11. DOI: 10.1353/foc.2017.0000

Kumar, R., & Agrawal, S. (2021). Digital divides in AI adoption: A study of rural schools. *Educational Policy Analysis*, *39*(6), 813–828.

Kumar, V., Kumar, U., & Dutta, D. (2021). Enhancing collaborative learning through AI-based educational platforms. *Educational Technology Research and Development*, *69*(3), 671–687.

Luckin, R. (2018). *Machine learning and human intelligence: The future of education for the 21st century*. UCL IOE Press.

Luckin, R., & Holmes, W. (2016). *Intelligence Unleashed: An argument for AI in Education*. UCL Knowledge Lab.

Luckin, R., & Holmes, W. (2016). Big data and learning analytics in primary education: Challenges and opportunities. *Educational Leadership Review*, *54*(1), 12–24.

Luckin, R., & Holmes, W. (2016). Big data and learning analytics in primary education: Challenges and opportunities. *Educational Leadership Review*, *54*(1), 12–24.

Luckin, R., Holmes, W., Griffiths, M., & Forcier, L. B. (2016). *Intelligence Unleashed: An argument for AI in education*. Pearson Education.

Lugrin, J. L., Bortolaso, C., Cumming, B., & Karray, F. (2015). The challenges of virtual reality for exposure therapy in anxiety disorders: Patients' and therapists' opinions. *Journal of Medical Internet Research*, *17*(12), 319.

Luo, L., Yang, X., & Zhang, Y. (2023). Enhancing collaborative learning through AI-mediated communication tools. *International Journal of Educational Research*, *115*, 102057.

Mertala, P. (2023). Gamified solutions for emotional self-regulation in children: A systematic review. *Educational Psychology Review*, *35*(2), 345–367.

Miao, F., Holmes, W., & De Jong, T. (2021). AI, ethics, and social emotional learning: Findings from primary education. *Journal of Human-Centered Learning*, *27*(3), 197–213.

Moreno, R., Mayer, R. E., & Spires, H. (2022). Personalized learning in the age of AI: Impacts on student engagement and achievement. *Learning and Instruction*, *77*, 101488.

Murnane, R. J., & Levy, F. (2012). *The new division of labor: How computers are creating the next job market*. Princeton University Press.

Nazarian, M., Alsheikh, N., & Alhosani, M. (2023). Between Vision and Revision: English Language Teachers Accentuating Their Voices about 21st Century Skills. *The International Journal of Learning in Higher Education*, *31*(1), 25–50. DOI: 10.18848/2327-7955/CGP/v31i01/25-50

Ngwenya, P. (2020). Challenges in adopting AI tools in South African schools. *African Journal of Educational Technology*, *15*(4), 56–69.

Osher, D., Cantor, P., Berg, J., Steyer, L., & Rose, T. (2022). Drivers of SEL integration: The roles of educators, ethics, and policy. *Educational Researcher*, *51*(3), 120–136.

Osher, D., Kidron, Y., Brackett, M., Dymnicki, A., Jones, S., & Weissberg, R. P. (2016). Advancing the science and practice of social and emotional learning: Looking back and moving forward. *Review of Research in Education*, *40*(1), 644–681. DOI: 10.3102/0091732X16673595

Parsons, T. D., & Rizzo, A. A. (2008). Affective outcomes of virtual reality exposure therapy for anxiety and specific phobias: A meta-analysis. *Journal of Behavior Therapy and Experimental Psychiatry*, *39*(3), 250–261. DOI: 10.1016/j.jbtep.2007.07.007 PMID: 17720136

Patel, A., Sharma, K., & Mehta, V. (2022). AI in emotional journaling: Tools for reflective SEL practices. *Computers in Human Behavior*, *132*, 107212.

Rose, D. H., Gravel, J. W., & Domings, Y. (2019). Universal design for learning: Ensuring access and equity in education. *Harvard Educational Review*, *89*(2), 12–28.

Russell, S. J., & Norvig, P. (2022). *Artificial Intelligence: A Modern Approach* (4th ed.). Pearson.

Sacconaghi, M. (2006). Why the American public supports twenty-first century learning. *New Directions for Youth Development*, *2006*(110), 39–45. DOI: 10.1002/yd.165 PMID: 17017255

Schonert-Reichl, K. A., Oberle, E., & Lawlor, M. S. (2015). Enhancing cognitive and social-emotional development through a mindfulness-based intervention. *Developmental Psychology*, *51*(1), 52–66. DOI: 10.1037/a0038454 PMID: 25546595

Selwyn, N. (2020). Datafication in schools: The implications for student privacy. *British Journal of Sociology of Education*, *41*(6), 813–828.

Selwyn, N., & Aagaard, J. (2021). Teacher development and AI: A global perspective. *Educational Research Review*, *39*, 100–115.

Shum, H.. (2019). Securing emotional data: The case for robust AI ethics. *Computers & Education*, *134*, 56–69.

Siemens, G., Gašević, D., & Dawson, S. (2023). Learning analytics in the era of AI: Advancing academic resilience. *Journal of Learning Analytics*, *10*(1), 1–17.

Slade, S., & Griffith, D. (2013). A whole child approach to student success. *KEDI Journal of Educational Policy*, •••, 21–35. http://wikindx.ens-lyon.fr/biblio_vst/index.php?action=resource_RESOURCEVIEW_CORE&id=9537

Slater, M., & Sanchez-Vives, M. V. (2016). Enhancing Our Lives with Immersive Virtual Reality. *Frontiers in Robotics and AI*, *3*. Advance online publication. DOI: 10.3389/frobt.2016.00074

Sorensen, L. C., & Dodge, K. A. (2015). How does the fast-track intervention prevent adverse outcomes in young adulthood? *Child Development*, *87*(2), 429–445. DOI: 10.1111/cdev.12467 PMID: 26670938

Taylor, R. D., Oberle, E., Durlak, J. A., & Weissberg, R. P. (2017). Promoting positive youth development through school-based social and emotional learning interventions: A meta-analysis of follow-up effects. *Child Development*, *88*(4), 1156–1171. DOI: 10.1111/cdev.12864 PMID: 28685826

Vyas, S., Chaurasia, I., Sharma, Y., & Sarkar, Sh. (2024). An Investigation on Students Learnings & Mental Health Influenced by Artificial Intelligence. *International Journal of Scientific Research in Engineering and Management*, *8*(3), 1–6. DOI: 10.55041/IJSREM29138

Weissberg, R. P., Durlak, J. A., Domitrovich, C. E., & Gullotta, T. P. (2015). Social and emotional learning: Past, present, and future. In Durlak, J. A., Domitrovich, C. E., Weissberg, R. P., & Gullotta, T. P. (Eds.), *Handbook of Social and Emotional Learning: Research and Practice* (pp. 3–19). Guilford Press.

Williamson, B., & Eynon, R. (2020). The algorithmic classroom: Exploring AI's role in education. *Learning, Media and Technology*, *45*(2), 115–128.

Woolf, B. P., Aimeur, E., Nkambou, R., & Lajoie, S. P. (2020). Learner modeling in intelligent tutoring systems. *AI in Education*, *36*(4), 299–311.

Xu, Z., & Zhao, Y. (2020). Adaptive learning systems and educational equity. *International Journal of Artificial Intelligence in Education*, *30*(4), 405–423.

Zawacki-Richter, O., Marín, V. I., Bond, M., & Gouverneur, F. (2019). Systematic review of research on artificial intelligence applications in higher education. *International Journal of Educational Technology in Higher Education*, *16*(1), 39. DOI: 10.1186/s41239-019-0171-0

Zhang, H., Lee, J., & Kessler, R. (2022). AI technologies in fostering SEL competencies: A meta-analysis of outcomes in primary education. *Advances in Education and AI*, *34*(2), 89–105.

Zhang, W., Liu, Y., & Lu, H. (2021). Real-time emotion recognition in classrooms using AI tools: Enhancing SEL strategies. *Interactive Learning Environments, 29*(6), 789–805.

Zins, J. E., Bloodworth, M. R., Weissberg, R. P., & Walberg, H. J. (2004). The scientific base linking social and emotional learning to school success. In Zins, J. E., Weissberg, R. P., Wang, M. C., & Walberg, H. J. (Eds.), *Building Academic Success on Social and Emotional Learning: What Does the Research Say?* (pp. 3–22). Teachers College Press.

# Chapter 2
# Empowering Minds:
## Integrating AI into STEM Curriculum

**Ahmad Qablan**
https://orcid.org/0000-0002-2780-9796
*United Arab Emirates University, UAE*

**Hesham Badaway**
https://orcid.org/0000-0002-0311-7496
*United Arab Emirates University, UAE*

**Hosam R. I. Badawy**
https://orcid.org/0000-0001-5107-4016
*United Arab Emirates University, UAE*

**Patil Maradian**
https://orcid.org/0009-0001-6407-0185
*United Arab Emirates University, UAE*

## ABSTRACT

*Integrating Artificial Intelligence (AI) into education, particularly in STEM disciplines, can revolutionize learning by providing personalized instruction, automating assessments, and enhancing student engagement. AI tools offer innovative approaches to content creation and knowledge dissemination, allowing educators and students to interact with learning materials in new and meaningful ways. AI-driven adaptive learning environments support differentiated instruction, helping students develop critical thinking, problem-solving, and inquiry-based learning skills. Despite its advantages, AI implementation in education presents challenges, including ethical concerns, data privacy issues, and the need for teacher professional development. To maximize AI's potential while mitigating risks, educators must adopt a balanced*

DOI: 10.4018/979-8-3373-0573-8.ch002

*approach integrating human expertise with AI technologies, ensuring equity, transparency, and inclusivity in learning.*

## INTRODUCTION

Artificial intelligence (AI) is an evolving interdisciplinary field used in education to transform instructional and learning design, process, and assessment (Chen et al.,2024; Holmes et al., 2019; Hwang et al., 2020). The term "Artificial Intelligence (AI)" refers to the design of programs that can perform tasks associated with human intelligence, such as learning, problem-solving, and decision-making. Recent advancements in machine learning have enabled generating more accurate digital content through Generative Artificial Intelligence (GenAI) (Gupta et al., 2024). Generative AI is a form of intelligence that can independently generate new instructional material, content, images, sound, and video. It provides innovative methods for content production, enhances the search experience, and reshapes how information is generated and presented, thus becoming new entry points for online traffic (Lv, 2023).

The emergence of AI applications (i.e., ChatGPT) reveal innovative ways to produce and interact with content quickly and directly online (Kalota, 2024). Applications like ChatGPT have become widely spread and have various uses, ranging from creating logos to social media content and building graphic images (Hashmi & Bal, 2024). Generative AI tools like Midjourney and Stable Diffusion have proven their significant ability to develop creative outputs by transforming descriptive textual inputs into high-level graphic media (Zhou & Lee, 2024). This indicates that these types of innovative applications can be highly relied upon to support the educational environment due to their substantial features and their ability to handle all types of content (Salinas-Navarro et al., 2024; Al-Rashaida, López-Paz, Amayra, Lázaro, Martínez, Berrocoso, & Pérez, 2018).

It is worth mentioning that although ChatGPT, for example, is just one of many generative AI technologies, its impact on teaching and learning processes is significantly positive. ChatGPT has made interaction more common and capable of generating innovative, non-standard knowledge (Nikolopoulou, 2024). Additionally, the Gemini application has become one of the most widely used applications in education, and its effectiveness has been strongly confirmed, especially in the general education stages, particularly in secondary education (Karaca, 2024).

Incorporating generative artificial intelligence (GenAI) in education can help automate educational tasks, process large amounts of data, and provide predictive insights that lead to more innovative knowledge. This is based on the ability of generative AI to simulate human responses such as thinking, critical analysis, and demonstrating intentionality (Ruiz-Rojas et al., 2023). The key feature of generative AI applications is the ability to generate fast, human-like responses and provide high-quality educational services such as personalized learning, automated assessments, feedback generation, virtual assistants, chatbots, content creation, resource recommendations, time management, language translation, research support, simulations, and virtual labs (Nikolopoulou, 2024).

There are several benefits of incorporating AI applications in education. They can contribute to enhancing and improving personalized learning experiences by helping to create highly customized educational materials, as well as assessments and feedback tailored to each student. This contributes to meeting the contextual needs of individual students and considering their learning preferences. This personalization undoubtedly helps students engage more effectively and better understand learning topics (Chiu, 2024). AI tools can enhance students and support them in developing creative ways to generate new and imaginative content. This enhancement of creative capabilities not only expands the horizons of education but also contributes to developing problem-solving skills and critical thinking (Ivanov et al., 2024). One of the key features of using AI tools in education is the potential to develop students' ideas and help them develop their projects through educational scaffolding (Chen et al., 2024).

Furthermore, AI has become more capable of generating new, rich digital media content based on user requirements. Moreover, AI applications can be practical tools supporting learners during educational crises and emergencies. If access to information sources is unavailable, these tools become highly capable of meeting cognitive needs and can be trusted in what they provide (Xiao & Yu, 2025).

## AI and Stem Education

The application of AI in the field of STEM education focuses on the design and implementation of AI applications to support STEM education. Automated AI technologies, such as personalized tutoring, computerized assessment, data mining, and learning analytics, have been used in STEM education to enhance the quality of students' learning (Chen et al., 2020; Hwang et al., 2020). STEM education is a complex system comprising interdependent elements, including subject, information, medium, and environment (Rapoport, 1986).

STEM is an interdisciplinary educational approach emphasizing hands-on, experiential learning to prepare students for science, technology, engineering, and mathematics careers. This methodology, highlighted by Bataineh et al. (2022), aims to cultivate inquisitive minds, logical reasoning, and collaborative skills. It often includes participation in university research programs that allow students to actively contribute to developing new technologies and pioneering research. Educators are encouraged to employ various teaching methods to maintain student engagement and enhance their understanding of STEM subjects, each contributing uniquely to the learning experience.

STEM-AI, as an interdisciplinary field, emphasizes applying AI to enhance teachers' instruction, stimulate students' thinking, and promote the transformation of the educational system (Chen et al., 2020; Holmes et al., 2019; Hwang et al., 2020).

STEM education aims to improve students' knowledge, inquiry skills, and application. It seeks to foster their higher-order thinking, critical thinking, and problem-solving competencies (Bybee et al., 2006; Pimthong & Williams, 2018). AI in STEM education provides students with adaptive and personalized learning environments and supports instructors in identifying students' learning behavioral patterns and assessing their learning performances (Alabdulhadi & Faisal, 2021).

However, high-quality STEM education requires considering the social, pedagogical, and environmental factors rather than merely applying AI technologies in STEM education (Krasovskiy, 2020; Xu & Ouyang, 2022). Therefore, the challenge is selecting and applying AI applications to the various elements of STEM education (e.g., content knowledge, skills, and environment) to ensure high-quality STEM instruction (Castaneda & Selwyn, 2018; Selwyn, 2016).

## AI In Stem Education: Opportunities and Challenges

AI applications offer various opportunities to enhance students' STEM learning. It can develop personalized instructional designs and pedagogical approaches, such as accessing students' performance (Wang et al., 2011; Zampirolli et al., 2021), monitoring and evaluating students' learning (Berland et al., 2015; Ji & Han, 2019) and predicting slow and advanced learners (Hellings & Haelermans, 2020; Lamb et al., 2021). AI also improves student-centered learning by providing adaptive and personalized tutoring (Kose & Arslan, 2017; Myneni et al., 2013) and diagnosing students' learning difficulties (Liu et al., 2017). AI can also transform and enrich the educational environment and knowledge delivery (Hwang et al., 2020; Holstein et al., 2019; Yannier et al., 2020) and redesign the teacher-student relationship (Xu & Ouyang, 2022). Therefore, various AI technologies (e.g., machine learning deep learning) have been used to redesign the learning process and enhance students' learning.

AI offers several valuable applications for STEM teachers, and these applications help teachers shift from being creators of knowledge to curators of knowledge, much like the transition from being an author to an editor of a scientific publication (Noy & Zhang, 2023). Although some may believe that AI could replace teachers, this is unlikely, as teachers are human beings with unique qualities, including critical thinking and emotions, making them irreplaceable (Chan & Tsi, 2024). Additionally, with AI, teachers can spend more time helping students learn instead of focusing on verifying student assignments. Using AI tools, students and teachers can use sub-tasks that eventually integrate to produce high-quality educational outputs (Stankovski et al., 2024). Teachers often invest significant time and effort creating learning resources like quizzes, tutorials, reading lists, and study guides. AI can alleviate this burden by automating the creation of such materials, allowing teachers to dedicate more time to direct interactions with students (Baidoo-Anu & Ansah, 2023). Moreover, teachers can shift their focus to higher-level tasks such as curriculum and assessment design through AI tools. At the same time, students receive education tailored to meet their needs and learning styles (Schiff, 2021).

As for the standards related to using AI tools in education, teachers and students need to use AI tools functionally, following specific steps and guidelines (Feldman-Maggor et al., 2024). It is worth considering that AI applications struggle to enhance social and emotional competencies developed through human interactions, which means that a balanced approach is necessary, combining the strengths of human teachers with AI technologies to achieve the desired functional integration and enhance the effectiveness of AI applications in education (Chan & Tsi, 2024). Success in using AI tools is linked to the belief in integrating human intelligence with AI and the synergy between them, which will significantly improve the use of AI (Maphoto et al., 2024). The future of education through innovative applications lies in the synergy and integration between teachers and AI, ensuring that AI is not a replacement for teachers (Chan & Tsi, 2024). Moreover, AI applications require new user skills, such as creativity in the description, evaluation, and sensory synergy, blending human exploration with AI to discover new creative flows (Zhou & Lee, 2024). Additionally, it should not be overlooked that most recommendations related to generative AI applications in education emphasize the need to rely on these applications as supporting and complementary technologies for fundamental learning processes. Using them within a learning activities environment may be better under the teacher's guidance (McDonald et al., 2024).

Furthermore, using AI applications in education must consider several ethical considerations, including data privacy, transparency, accessibility, and cultural sensitivity. It must also address potential misuse and establish scenarios for handling these issues (Nikolopoulou, 2024). To ensure comprehensive and impactful educational experiences, teachers and students must hone their unique skills in using AI tools in education (Chan & Tsi, 2024).

Regarding the ongoing debate about the benefits and harms of AI in education, there is a clear difference in opinions regarding the concerns related to using these applications in the educational environment. Some argue that using AI applications is a double-edged sword, as integrating them provides numerous potential benefits for teachers and students. Still, on the other hand, it may also create new challenges and the possibility of misuse (Ivanov et al., 2024). This debate is linked to some of the adverse effects of AI, including potential cheating, reduced critical thinking skills, misinformation, and unethical practices (Gupta et al., 2024). However, one cannot rely solely on opposing views of AI tools without considering that they are constantly being improved and updated with new data for accuracy and continuous enhancement, which could make them practical applications in education (Lee & Song, 2024).

It is worth mentioning that, despite some concerns about AI applications in education, students' perceptions of these applications are very optimistic (Abdallah, Ismail, Abdallah, & Alkaabi, 2023). This calls for efforts to invest in developing more standardized and suitable educational environments (Saihi et al., 2024).

According to the trends discussed above, which highlight the importance of AI applications in education and other trends expressing legitimate concerns about relying on AI applications, the only way to resolve the debate is to expand the testing of AI applications in various educational contexts. The context in which these tools are used may affect their effectiveness (Noroozi et al., 2024). Despite the lack of uniformity in positive and negative feelings associated with using AI in education, practical application and experimentation is the only way to reach a consensus on AI. This is because AI's significant benefits and possibilities to the educational process cannot be ignored, even in light of its current challenges (Lee et al., 2024). Therefore, some have mentioned that the current time is not for information literacy but for AI literacy, given the potential benefits of AI and its ability to impact the educational process radically (Lee & Song, 2024).

In this context, an analysis of seventeen studies on AI applications in education found that AI applications can bring about significant structural changes in the educational environment. The study indicates that AI applications have the potential to improve educational interactions, increase student engagement in the learning process, and provide specialized feedback (Al-Rashaida & Massouti, 2024). This can be seen as a solid foundation for further studies framing the use of AI applications in education (Noroozi et al., 2024).

AI technology plays a role in overcoming language barriers in our contemporary world, which has increasingly been characterized by globalization, which has created language barriers in communication and effective learning. Thus, language AI tools (i.e., ChatGPT) can overcome these obstacles by providing real-time translation and language support, making education more inclusive and accessible to students from diverse linguistic backgrounds (Massouti, Al-Rashaida & Alhosani, 2024). AI language applications can translate text inputs and responses between different languages, allowing students and teachers to communicate effectively. Real-time language translation eliminates the need for external translation tools or interpreters and reduces communication barriers. Students with limited proficiency in the primary language of instruction can also benefit from language support in AI, enabling them to participate in educational activities (Wei, 2023) fully.

## ADVANTAGES OF USING AI TOOLS IN EDUCATION

There are numerous uses of AI applications in the educational process, and they can offer multiple advantages for teachers and students. Below are some of AI's many benefits to educators (Ayala-Pazmiño, M., (2023).

1. **Improved Engagement**: AI technology increases engagement through tailored and relevant content, which boosts motivation for learning and results in better outcomes and the achievement of desired educational goals.
2. **Accessibility**: AI enhances access to online educational content, allowing students to obtain information anytime and from anywhere. This aspect is particularly beneficial for learning English, as it requires access to the Internet and global websites to be helpful in learning. It also allows students to stay updated with new developments in the field.
3. **Providing Specific Data**: AI is a powerful tool for providing specific data. The application focuses on your inquiries and supplies the necessary data. It allows students to ask specific questions and receive detailed answers.
4. **Review and Evaluation**: AI tools can be used to check or complete solving mathematical problems and equations. They are also essential tools for students studying foreign languages, as they help them correct the language used by non-native speakers of the language of instruction due to their ability to translate and review accurately.
5. **Research Preparation**: AI tools can assist researchers and students at all educational stages in creating many research papers and help students obtain the required information and studies in the same field.
6. **Develop Interaction Tools with Students**: AI can generate new ideas and contribute to developing students' research skills, such as generating specific questions related to certain specializations and abilities. It also helps them utilize the most important methods for adapting lessons to suit students. It helps them develop self-learning skills, as it relies on individuals' information gathering.
7. **Support Students in Their Studies**: AI tools help students develop their thinking skills by providing ideas to start a particular project, whether a research project or a scientific project in any field, helping them bridge the gap that makes many students unable to identify the most appropriate starting point or what helps them complete their projects if they encounter obstacles halfway. It is also one of the most important tools that students with special needs can rely on to assist them

in managing projects and reports. Additionally, AI tools help teachers identify the most appropriate methods to make teaching more efficient and effective by providing personalized learning experiences designed specifically for students' abilities and needs (García, Lázaro, Amayra, López-Paz, Martínez, Pérez, & Infante, 2020).

8. **Improving Lesson Delivery Methods**: Teachers in developing or middle-income countries face the challenge of converting an intensive curriculum into lessons that engage students by relying on new ideas and creating new assessments. This makes AI applications valuable in preparing lessons efficiently.
9. **Creating Assessment Questions**: Teachers can use AI tools to improve assessment questions, including multiple-choice questions and others. AI tools are also helpful for encouraging advanced thinking skills through suggestions and prompts for homework questions, especially those related to practical components. Teachers can also use different assessments to help students develop critical thinking and problem-solving skills.
10. **Overcoming Language Barriers**: Although it is ideal in many countries to have teachers deliver lessons in the official language of the country, the reality is that many education systems continue to use the local language, replacing it with a second language (i.e., English). Some teachers may only be proficient in their native language and may not be familiar with English as a second language, which could make teaching difficult. Here, AI technologies like ChatGPT can help improve teachers' language proficiency, assisting them in teaching more effectively in their native or another foreign language.
11. **Providing Additional Support to Students**: Teachers can use AI tools to stimulate students' curiosity and knowledge by generating new homework ideas and theoretical and practical evaluations. However, one possible downside is that some students may use AI tools to complete their homework entirely on their behalf. Teachers can address this risk by discussing the limitations and issues of these new tools (privacy risks, biases towards specific answers, or generating incorrect answers) to prevent this dangerous phenomenon. Teachers should be aware that these tools do not address all questions that AI tools cannot answer, such as questions requiring emotional responses or subjective viewpoints outside the scope of the chatbot's training data (U.S. Department of Education, 2023).
12. **Grading Assignments**: AI tools can automatically grade multiple-choice/one-answer questions. They can also help teachers grade based on specific criteria and create a robust data set for analyzing student learning levels and distinguishing between them more accurately. However, this could have unintended consequences such as reduced accuracy, incorrect grading, or false positives regarding student cheating (due to errors in the system). When considering grad-

ing systems, ensuring fairness, accountability, confidentiality, and transparency in their algorithms is crucial when necessary.

13. **Teaching Students**: Teachers can use AI tools to provide online tutoring services to students. This can offer adaptive learning assistance for students, particularly in contexts where teachers are responsible for many students and do not have the time or resources to tailor their teaching methods to each student's needs individually. According to Khan Academy, AI tools can guide students as they work through their courses. Since this is still an emerging technology, gathering more evidence and proactively monitoring its use is important. Unsupervised private tutoring could harm students unintentionally, as ChatGPT not only "creates things" but may also lead to awkward conversations.

## DISADVANTAGES OF USING AI TOOLS IN EDUCATION

While there are many advantages to using AI in education, these advantages are accompanied by potential negative impacts. Below are examples of those negative aspects (U.S. Department of Education, 2023).

1. **Bias in Responses**: One criticism of AI is that many of its answers may be biased on specific topics, such as politics. However, this does not prevent the use of AI tools; it is important to verify the accuracy of the responses and review them carefully before relying on the final answers.
2. **Bias in AI-generated grading:** This can lead to unfair assessments, disproportionately affecting marginalized groups because of biased training data and algorithmic design that amplifies these disparities (West et al., 2021).

   Such biases undermine the credibility and equity of automated evaluation systems. Addressing them requires transparent models and inclusive data practices.

3. **Incorrect Logical Narration**: AI tools can easily deceive those less familiar with the subject matter, as they can organize and structure ideas in a logical and cohesive narrative, which often does not reveal the errors in the information they produce. This is where the teacher's or user's role comes into play: not solely relying on AI results but rather cross-checking information from other sources to ensure accuracy.
4. **Reduced Output Quality**: One of the more significant disadvantages of AI tools is their contribution to a decline in output quality. This is because many users rely on the answers generated by AI tools without reviewing and correcting the information and responses to identify and correct errors. This can lead

to incorrect educational content, which may negatively impact the educational materials provided via this technology. Therefore, caution should be exercised when using it, ensuring that answers and information extracted from it are thoroughly checked to guarantee high-quality educational output without errors that may negatively affect the educational process in English language learning or other subjects.

## TOWARDS A DEEPER UNDERSTANDING OF AI IN THE ENGINEERING DESIGN CYCLE

### Overview of the Engineering Design Process (EDP)

The engineering design process (EDP) is an open-ended problem-solving process that encourages students to learn from their failures. This process nurtures their abilities to create innovative solutions to their challenges. The EDP consists of steps that guide students to solve their problems. It is an iterative process whose steps can be repeated to make necessary improvements and redesign to arrive at great solutions.

To engage in EDP, students must collaborate to brainstorm new ideas, apply science and math concepts, test prototypes, and analyze data to suggest creative and practical solutions. At the end of the designing experience, students build their design capacities and develop their STEM literacy.

It is essential to distinguish between the investigation cycles of Science and Engineering. In science, the focus is on understanding how the natural world works. However, in engineering, learners use science to solve engineering problems related to human wants or needs, often by changing the natural world or existing technologies. Engineering results in technologies that modify the natural world to fulfill human wants or needs.

Natural phenomena drive science investigations; engineering investigations are driven by engineering phenomena, which are natural phenomena that we want or need to change. Engineering phenomena also include natural phenomena observed in technologies (e.g., over time, our cell phone requires more frequent recharging).

To begin an engineering investigation, the teacher presents the engineering phenomenon, which the students then use to engage in the Engineering Design Process.

### Engineering Design Process Steps

The Engineering Design process is a structured approach for planning STEM lessons, involving a series of steps for problem-solving (Figure 1). This method promotes open-ended designs, creativity, and practical solutions (Nguyen & Le,

2021). The following are steps in the EDP problem-solving approach (Qablan, AlKaabi, Aljanahi, & Almaamari, 2024):

*Figure 1. Engineering design process*

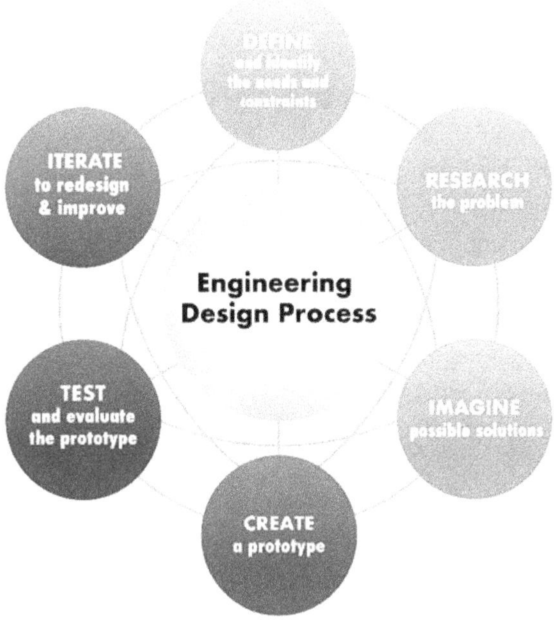


1. **Ask.** Students are presented with a problem or project and asked to develop a product/design solution. They start by asking critical questions about their task or desired creation.
2. **Research.** Students gather information about their project, utilizing resources like the internet, teacher or expert consultations, STEM volunteers, laptops for research, or relevant videos.
3. **Imagine.** In teams, students brainstorm potential solutions. This collaborative stage ensures every student contributes, with the teacher fostering a judgment-free environment for idea generation.
4. **Create.** Students build a prototype based on their plans. This phase allows for creativity and practical application, which tests the functionality and adherence to original requirements.
5. **Test.** Students devise methods to evaluate their solutions' effectiveness, assessing whether they address the problem. Teachers can facilitate peer review discussions to promote deep thinking and collaboration.

6. **Iterate.** The final step involves feedback and discussions on enhancements. Students then redesign and refine their products and repeat this cycle until satisfied with the outcome.

## Planning for Teaching Through EDP

In the EDP, teachers engage their students in a project that requires them to design a solution for an engineering problem. Teachers can create their lessons or instructional experiences using a flexible framework called Gather, Reason, and Communicate (GRC) Framework. The GRC allows learners to play the role of engineers and designers.

Gather, Reason, Communicate (GRC) Framework:

The GRC framework is a student-centric instructional approach designed to help students comprehend phenomena across natural, social, economic, historical, and other domains through scientific and engineering practices. The following paragraphs summarize the nature of each of these three stages.

### Gathering Stage

At this stage, instruction centers around phenomena, engaging students in various science and engineering practices such as questioning, investigation, qualitative observation, and quantitative data recording. Students explore observable phenomena or events to collect evidence supporting scientific explanations. Anchoring learning in observable phenomena aids students in making sense of real-world observations. Essential observation skills, including inferring, measuring, communicating, predicting, and classifying, are employed by scientists in their research. Students apply these skills to begin addressing their questions about the observed phenomena. It is essential to mention that students can use several AI applications to gather the needed knowledge and background information related to the topic under investigation. An example of AI applications that are useful for students is using relevant simulation programs to understand better the nature of the engineering phenomenon they investigate. This stage is similar to doing a literature review of the previous concept/phenomenon under investigation to identify the research gaps and suitable solutions.

### Reasoning Stage

The reasoning stage in the GRC framework involves critical thinking practices. Here, students engage in activities such as analyzing data, constructing evidence-based explanations, evaluating data collection techniques, employing computational thinking, and developing explanations grounded in collected evidence. They utilize key ideas and concepts from the previous stage to interpret data and construct reasoned arguments, using models to explain natural phenomena and support their explanations with evidence.

### Communicating Stage

In this stage, students articulate their explanations and arguments, both written and oral, to demonstrate how their evidence substantiates their conclusions. They participate in critically exchanging ideas, offering and receiving feedback on their explanations, and citing relevant evidence and reasoning. Additionally, students employ models to convey their thought processes and make their reasoning visible, which enhances communication and understanding of their scientific arguments. Appendix 1 presents a sample lesson plan design using the GRC framework that demonstrates how students engage in the Engineering design process.

## AI AND ADAPTIVE LEARNING

AI and adaptive learning technologies are revolutionizing education by personalizing learning experiences and improving outcomes (Gupta, 2024). These systems use machine learning algorithms and data analytics to tailor content, assessments, and feedback to individual learners' needs and abilities (Gligorea et al., 2023; Meylani, 2024). AI-powered adaptive learning platforms can enhance student engagement, retention, and performance while assisting teachers with administrative tasks (Capuano & Caballé, 2020; Rane et al., 2023).

Integrating Explainable AI (XAI) in these systems promotes transparency and critical thinking skills (Idrizi, 2024). Knowledge assessment techniques, including student models and psychometric approaches, are fundamental to creating effective adaptive learning environments (Minn, 2022). While challenges such as data privacy and ethical considerations exist, the potential benefits of AI and adaptive learning in education are significant, paving the way for more personalized and compelling learning experiences (Meylani, 2024; Rane et al., 2023).

Gupta (2024) discusses the transformative potential of Adaptive Learning Systems (ALS) powered by Artificial Intelligence (AI) to personalize educational experiences for diverse learners. These systems utilize real-time data analytics and machine learning algorithms to adapt content and assessments to individual learning styles and paces, addressing the limitations of traditional education methods. The study highlights how AI facilitates timely feedback, modifies learning pathways, and enhances student engagement, creating a more effective and inclusive educational environment. Through case studies and empirical analysis, Gupta underscores the value of continuous assessment and integrating pedagogical best practices to maximize the impact of AI-driven adaptive learning solutions across various educational contexts.

Adaptive learning, driven by artificial intelligence (AI), has emerged as a transformative approach in e-learning, enabling personalized content delivery and optimizing learning pathways. By leveraging data analytics and AI technologies, adaptive systems dynamically adjust educational materials to suit individual learner profiles. While these advancements enhance engagement, retention, and performance, challenges such as data privacy, algorithmic bias, and system complexity persist. A comprehensive review underscores the potential of AI to revolutionize e-learning, emphasizing the importance of tailored pedagogical approaches and ethical considerations in implementation (Gligorea et al., 2023).

## AI WILL SUPPORT TEACHER LEARNING AND PRACTICE IN STEM EDUCATION

STEM education is observing the emergence of a new era, with AI being its effective, transformative force, owing to its potential advantages in advanced analytics, teaching automation, and tailored learning (Triplett, 2023). Integrating AI into STEM education will help us remodel the way of teaching, curriculum planning, and assessment (Nagaraj et al., 2023).

In addition, the use of AI combined with Learning Analytics has the potential to provide adaptive and inclusive learning environments that can improve education outcomes (Kim, 2024). Furthermore, there is generally a positive perception of AI-enhanced tools (Kim & Kim, 2022). These tools could provide ultimate support for educators by offering various strategies to enrich teaching effectiveness and student engagement. Hence, numerous benefits of AI integration support teachers in enhancing their practice in the field of STEM.

### Personalized and Adaptive Learning

AI has been acclaimed for enabling teachers to implement personalized and flexible learning experiences, one of AI's most promising uses in STEM education. Using these platforms within science classrooms can support active learning approaches that develop critical thinking skills and promote a deeper understanding of scientific concepts (Vorsah & Oppong, 2024).

AI-driven learning systems can sift through vast data on student performance, preferences, and learning styles simultaneously and tailor the content and suggestions to each student (Beghetto, 2019). AI can adjust the pace, depth, and focus of instruction for individual students, improving learning outcomes and allowing educators to communicate complex STEM concepts to their students better (Nagaraj et al., 2023).

AI programs can support teachers in compiling and examining data from many students, revealing common misunderstandings or gaps in learning. This, in turn, dramatically facilitates improving all students' overall learning experiences by using this information to help teachers modify their lesson plans and instructional practices (Murphy, 2019).

### Intelligent Tutoring

AI is also an intelligent tutor, enabling STEM instructors to offer real-time feedback, guidance, and support. AI-integrated programs, for example, can analyze student responses, identify misconceptions, and deliver targeted interventions to help close learning gaps. Moreover, AI-based virtual labs are capable of simulating real-life laboratories and assist teachers in providing students with a safe environment to practice their skills and competencies (Sapriati et al., 2023)

Moreover, AI-enriched virtual laboratories present an incredible opportunity for students to participate in hands-on science and engineering learning activities. Educators can allow students to conduct experiments, modify variables , and observe outcomes in virtual settings that mimic real laboratory conditions. AI systems can also offer analysis and feedback in real-time, assisting teachers in supporting students in navigating the experiment and interpreting the findings (Nagaraj et al., 2023).

## AI AND TEACHER PROFESSIONAL DEVELOPMENT IN STEM EDUCATION

In the age of AI, it is crucial to highlight the pivotal role that PD programs play in supporting teachers in these times of rapid change. These programs serve a dual purpose: They can address the apprehensions often associated with AI and contribute to cultivating a community of teachers that continually empowers teachers to develop their practices. This community should be characterized not by mere spectators but by active participants, shaping the trajectory of the future of their learning (Roshan et al., 2024).

AI in STEM education transforms teacher professional development (PD), providing innovative solutions to improve educators' skills and knowledge. This change redefines how teachers learn, develop, and evolve in a fast-paced STEM education (Roshan et al., 2024; Abdallah & Alkaabi, 2023).

The implications of AI for education and teacher professional development can be categorized into three groups of activities: Design and use of AI technologies to support teaching and learning, educating people about AI so they can use it effectively and ethically, and innovation in education to prepare people for an AI-driven world (Luckin & Cukurova, 2019).

First and foremost, an AI-driven feature that can transform STEM teachers' PD is adaptive learning with intelligent tutoring systems. AI technologies are designed to analyze each teacher's specific skills, weaknesses, and preferences to help them choose from professional development courses in priority STEM fields that align with their needs (Yang et al., 2024). This personalized learning approach to professional development makes the most of time spent with teachers because it guarantees that they receive each opportunity in a way that suits their needs and learning style. In the context of teacher training, these tools can analyze a teacher's learning patterns and adapt content, feedback, or teaching methods accordingly. AI can also help teacher trainers by automating administrative tasks, such as grading and attendance tracking of teachers, thereby potentially freeing up more time for pedagogically more valuable tasks such as scaffolding, emotional and social interaction support, or devoting more time for research (Joseph & Uzondu, 2024).

The second category, educating about AI, involves teaching teachers about AI technologies, their uses, and their ethical implications (Lee & Perret, 2022). This can be done through specialized courses or integrated into existing teacher training curricula. Teachers must understand the potential and limitations of AI and the ethical considerations that come with its use (Ali et al., 2019). By proactively addressing these ethical considerations, such as transparency, accountability, and fairness in AI design and deployment, educational stakeholders can ensure a responsible and inclusive academic environment that harnesses the potential of AI while upholding ethical principles (Okwara & Obiagwu, 2024)

The third category, innovating education systems, involves rethinking how we teach and learn in light of AI's growing influence. This could include incorporating AI into teaching methods for more process-oriented teaching rather than outcome-focused ones or redesigning curricula to better prepare students for a future where AI is ubiquitous (Ruijten et al.,2025). Fakhar et al. (2024) highlighted, in their systematic review of literature studies concerning the integration of AI in continuous professional development, the importance of integrating AI as a core topic within PD programs to enhance teachers' AI literacy, enabling them to navigate and utilize AI-based tools in their educational environment effectively. This is important for preparing teachers to engage with the technological advances shaping the educational system and maximizing the potential of AI to enhance the quality of PD programs internationally.

In addition, AI-driven tools in the context of teacher PD are creating opportunities for collaborative learning and social interaction. Ultimately, collaboration analytics should focus on impacting teaching and learning about how to collaborate better. The benefits of AI-enabled social interaction and collaborative learning in STEM education have been studied throughout the literature. Critically, more effective forms of professional development involve collective processes, such as Professional Learning Communities (PLCs). PLCs provide a forum where teachers can collaborate, discuss how they are implementing/experiencing AI in their classroom, and build strategies for how to go about implementing these tools. Peer coaching and mentoring are also recommended because experienced teachers can help their less experienced colleagues integrate AI technologies in their classrooms (Fakhar et al., 2024). The provided collaborative tasks are the most helpful and present the least psychological burden for teachers when content is imported into artificial intelligence-based collaborative teaching (Wang & Liu, 2021).

The integration of AI technologies into STEM education faces substantial implementation barriers, particularly in teacher professional development. A systematic review revealed that teachers' technological pedagogical knowledge significantly predicts successful AI integration, yet professional development models consistently fall short in building this specific competency framework (Scherer et al., 2019). This deficiency aligns with what Holmes et al. (2019) identified as a “readiness gap” where educator preparation lags behind technological innovation. Furthermore, UNESCO report “Artificial Intelligence in Education” identified significant knowledge gaps among educators regarding both AI functionality and pedagogical application (Pedro et al., 2019).

The financial barriers further exacerbate implementation challenges. Adequate AI integration requires substantial investment in both infrastructure and sustained professional development—costs that many educational institutions cannot bear within current budgetary frameworks (Rincon & George-Jackson, 2016). Moreover, resource allocation patterns most often favor technology acquisition over teacher capacity building, creating what they term “implementation without sustainability” (Zawacki-Richter et al., 2019).

Institutional resistance remains perhaps the most intractable barrier. Educational structures fundamentally conflict with AI implementation requirements; with rigid assessment frameworks and standardized testing mandates leave little flexibility for innovation (Luckin & Cukurova, 2019). Furthermore, institutional policies often inadvertently create disincentives for the time-intensive process of meaningful AI integration (Abulibdeh et al., 2025). This institutional inertia compounds the challenges of cost and training limitations, creating multi-layered barriers to effective AI integration in STEM education.

Global complexities in STEM education include the challenges of an increasingly evolving STEM curriculum and decreasing numbers of qualified educators (Lee & Perret, 2022). Bridging the skills gap is exceedingly important to address. AI in teacher professional development can play a vital role by growing personalized scaffolding for teachers to meet their STEM curriculum requirements. Because fields like robots, artificial intelligence, and data science are advancing rapidly, STEM educators need continual professional development to keep abreast of the latest instructional strategies and content (Chaipidech, 2021).

## THE USE OF AI IN ASSESSING STEM STUDENTS' LEARNING

Educational assessment, as a process of gathering and analyzing information about students' learning performance, is usually applied in STEM education to help instructors understand students' learning status and make instructional decisions (Conley, 2015). The emergence and application of AI tools also bring great opportunities for assessment in STEM education (Ouyang et al., 2023). AI-driven educational assessment highlights using automated AI algorithms and models to assess or evaluate the instructional and learning process to improve the assessment efficiency and promote the quality of STEM education (Gobert et al., 2013)

In recent years, there has been an increase in interest in formative evaluation using AI. Numerous studies have been carried out to analyze the efficacy of AI-assisted formative assessment systems(Lloyd et al., 2022). Although these research results have been mixed, they suggest that formative assessment systems with AI support could improve student learning outcomes.

Although the use of AI in formative assessment is still in its early stages, it holds the potential to cause a paradigm shift in how students are assessed. AI offers significant benefits in evaluating STEM learning (Al Maktoum & Al Kaabi, 2024). AI-supported formative assessments can improve the effectiveness and scalability of assessment procedures while giving students tailored feedback that enhances their learning. This personalized feedback is one of AI's main applications that help students identify their strengths and weaknesses and develop strategies for improving their learning. Providing instant feedback also helps correct misconceptions and deepen understanding before moving on to new material. This is particularly important for STEM subjects, where concepts are usually built on each other. Moreover, using AI in STEM assessments reduces the massive workload of teachers in STEM education, providing teachers with valuable time that can be spent on personalized student-centered instruction (Tan & Lim, 2023). AI technologies can also assist instructors in automatedly assessing students' STEM learning performance. In addition, by analyzing and synthesizing large amounts of data, AI algorithms can provide insights and reveal students' learning patterns that may not be immediately obvious to instructors (Cope et al., 2021). This can help teachers guide their instruction and devote more time to specific materials that are more challenging for the students and require more support.

Furthermore, a systematic review was conducted on 17 empirical research studies to holistically examine the application of AI-driven educational assessment in STEM education. The results regarding the educational effects showed that AI-driven educational assessment could help students better understand their learning performance and further adjust their learning behaviors. Moreover, it could also help instructors reduce the assessment workload and enhance instructional quality. Regarding the technological effects, compared to traditional educational assessment, AI-driven educational assessment has great potential to provide more automated, efficient, and accurate evaluation in STEM education (Ouyang et al., 2023).

Despite the many benefits of the use of AI in student assessments, there are many challenges and limitations that we need to address to ensure the successful embedding of AI in STEM assessments. The most important is the potential for algorithm bias. AI systems are only as good as the data they are trained on. If the data reflects historical disparities or biases, the assessments generated by AI may favor certain groups of students over others. For instance, AI systems used to assess student work or determine student outcomes may be biased against particular groups depending on criteria like race, gender, or socioeconomic status (Pedro et al., 2019). As Suresh and Guttag (2019) raise, if not designed and deployed with fairness and ethical considerations as integral priorities, AI algorithms could perpetuate biases and discrimination. Academic integrity is further challenged by the misuse of generative AI and unreliable AI-detection tools, which can unfairly target marginalized students (Bittle & El-Gayar, 2025). To address these issues, experts recommend hybrid AI-human evaluation models where AI assists initial assessments, but educators retain final judgment, alongside transparent algorithms, ethical guidelines, and assessment designs that prioritize creativity and reflection (Xiao & Yu, 2025).

The importance of ethical norms in today's educational testing practices is growing. Concerns regarding potential biases and their impact on student achievements have grown as AI's influence in education has grown (Omughelli et al., 2024). Our responsibility is to provide teachers and students with information about the ethical issues and consequences associated with using algorithms as academics, scientists, and citizens (Ali et al., 2019). Furthermore, AI systems must meet different students' needs: their learning styles, communication styles, engagement in various contexts, and so forth; that is, ensuring that students have an inclusive and equitable opportunity to contribute to collaborative tasks. Other studies also highlighted ethical data protection and privacy in AI-enabled collaborative learning environments (Nagaraj et al., 2023).

## Promoting STEM Education Through AI: Enhancing Language and Science Performance

Integrating artificial intelligence (AI) in education has revolutionized teaching and learning processes, particularly in STEM (Science, Technology, Engineering, and Mathematics) education. AI tools and platforms have not only enhanced the accessibility and personalization of learning but also significantly influenced students' language and science performance. By leveraging AI-driven solutions, educators can create more inclusive, adaptive, and engaging environments that address the diverse needs of learners. This paper explores the transformative role of AI in promoting STEM education, focusing on its impact on language development and science achievement.

Recent research highlights the potential of (AI) in promoting STEM education. AI applications in STEM have positively affected learning outcomes and student engagement (Xu & Fan, 2022; Lohakan & Seetao, 2024). Studies demonstrate that AI-based educational programs can enhance elementary students' creative problem-solving abilities, AI literacy, and attitudes toward AI (Jang et al., 2022; Relmasira et al., 2023). Emerging technologies like AI and virtual reality offer opportunities and challenges in STEM education (Chiu & Li, 2023). Researchers emphasize the importance of ethics-centered pedagogy and youth-led investigations to deepen understanding of AI (Lee et al., 2022). Generative AI shows promise in fostering diversity and inclusion in STEM teams (Nixon et al., 2024). A multidisciplinary STEAM approach is recommended to address challenges in traditional STEM education, particularly for underrepresented groups, integrating humanities and arts with technical training (Skowronek et al., 2021; Abdallah & Farhan, 2023).

Xu and Fan (2022) systematically reviewed 63 empirical studies from 2011 to 2021, using the general system theory (GST) framework to analyze AI applications in STEM education. Their findings identified six categories of AI applications and explored their relationships with key system elements, such as information, subjects, mediums, and environments. The study highlighted AI's educational and technological benefits in enhancing STEM instruction and learning outcomes while emphasizing the challenges of cohesive integration. Xu and Fang (2022) concluded that future research should focus on the interplay between AI technologies and educational systems to maximize their potential and propose theoretical and practical implications for advancing STEM education.

## EMPOWERING STEM EDUCATION WITH AI: INNOVATION AND INCLUSION

Lohakan and Seetao (2024) developed an innovative (AI) kit designed to enhance high school students' engagement and learning in (STEM). Like a portable laptop, the kit integrates an edge AI machine and electronic components and employs pre-trained convolutional neural network models alongside computer vision algorithms. A quasi-experimental study involving five Thai schools assessed the kit's effectiveness through on-site instruction and paired sample t-tests. Results showed significant improvements in students' knowledge and reduced score variation. Gender analysis indicated that male and female students successfully met the learning criteria, while participants expressed high satisfaction with the kit's design and teaching methods (Lohakan & Seetao, 2024). The study highlighted the AI kit's capacity to boost student enthusiasm and enhance comprehension of STEM concepts.

Recent advancements in artificial intelligence (AI) and its integration into STEM education have highlighted its potential for fostering critical competencies in elementary students. Jang et al. (2022) developed a STEM-based AI education program for K-6 learners to enhance creative problem-solving skills, AI literacy, and attitudes toward AI. Using a backward design methodology, the program encouraged students to engage in real-life problem-solving activities that integrated AI principles, such as classification and natural language processing, tailored to their developmental level. Experimental results showed statistically significant improvements in all targeted areas, emphasizing the program\u2019s effectiveness in fostering skills essential for future societal and professional challenges. Additionally, sentiment analysis of students' responses indicated overwhelmingly positive perceptions of the program and AI technologies. These findings underscore the importance of integrating STEM and AI education to prepare students for the demands of an AI-driven future (Jang et al., 2022).

Chiu and Li (2023) explore the impact of emerging technologies like artificial intelligence (AI) and virtual reality (VR) on STEM education, emphasizing their dual role as both enablers and potential challenges. In an editorial, they introduce a special issue examining how immersive and AI-driven technologies transform STEM learning across educational, social, and technological dimensions. Contributions from scholars in Australia, Hong Kong, mainland China, Singapore, and the USA provide a balanced perspective on the benefits, pitfalls, and current research trends, offering insights into the design and implementation of innovative STEM education environments. They discussed the educational, social, and technological effects of emerging technologies. Each article discusses the current research status, what and how the technologies can afford, and what concerns the technologies may bring to STEM education (Chiu and Li., 2023).

Lee et al. (2022) investigate how youth understand artificial intelligence (AI) and how ethics-centered pedagogy can enhance STEM engagement. Through three projects with YR Media, a network of youth journalists and artists, the study explores two questions: how young people perceive AI and what pedagogical design fosters ethics-centered STEM learning. The findings highlight that youth, particularly those from marginalized backgrounds, often distrust AI but do not understand its functions. Participants deepened their knowledge by creating interactive, ethics-focused media projects reflecting their experiences, critically analyzed AI functionalities, and creatively expressed their concerns. Publicly sharing their work further empowered their engagement with AI and STEM (Lee et al., 2022).

Nixon et al. (2024) explore the potential of generative AI to enhance diversity, equity, and inclusion in STEM teams, addressing persistent psychological barriers faced by underrepresented students. The paper identifies two transformative uses of generative AI in STEM collaboration: (1) inclusive analytics to assess fine-grained learner behavior in teams and (2) adaptive AI systems for personalized support and training to foster diversity and inclusion. Four policy recommendations are proposed: formalizing collaboration skill assessment, implementing inclusive analytics, funding socio-cognitive research, and leveraging human-AI teaming for inclusion training. The authors envision an equitable STEM ecosystem where diverse voices contribute to collaborative scientific innovation (Nixon et al., 2024).

Skowronek et al. (2022) discuss strategies for integrating inclusive STEAM education in sustainable energy and artificial intelligence (AI) disciplines. The study emphasizes bridging diverse fields to prepare learners for interdisciplinary challenges. By focusing on inclusivity, the authors explore how diverse pedagogical approaches can foster collaboration and innovation. Key areas include curriculum design integrating AI with sustainable energy concepts, hands-on problem-solving activities, and efforts to address underrepresentation in STEAM fields. The paper highlights how inclusive education can empower learners to contribute to critical global challenges in sustainability and technology (Skowronek et al., 2022).

## AI Integration in STEM Education: Enhancing Learning, Equity, and Personalized Experiences

STEM education emphasizes interdisciplinary approaches integrating real-world applications, critical thinking, and problem-solving skills. AI technologies, such as machine learning, natural language processing (NLP), and adaptive learning systems, align with these objectives by offering innovative methods for teaching and learning. AI applications in K-12 education span student performance, teaching, and behavior tasks, with machine learning and intelligent tutoring systems being the most common approaches (Zafari et al., 2022). AI literacy is emerging as a crucial skill for students, with efforts focused on developing technical, conceptual, and applied skills (Casal-Otero et al., 2023). STEM-based AI education programs have positively affected creative problem-solving, AI literacy, and attitudes toward AI (Jang et al., 2022). However, challenges remain in integrating diverse AI techniques with complex educational elements (Xu & Fan, 2022). Emerging technologies like AI and virtual reality present opportunities and challenges for STEM education (Chiu & Li, 2023). To promote equity and inclusion, researchers suggest leveraging generative AI for inclusive analytics and personalized support in STEM teams (Nixon et al., 2024). Overall, AI has significant potential to enhance STEM education but requires careful implementation and consideration of ethical implications.

Zafari et al. (2022) conducted a systematic literature review of 210 documents from 2011 to 2021 to explore the applications of artificial intelligence (AI) in K-12 education, revealing its significant role in various educational domains. Key findings showed that AI is commonly employed in student performance assessment, teaching assistance, selection and behavior tracking, and miscellaneous educational tasks. Machine Learning (ML) and Intelligent Tutoring Systems (ITS) are the most prevalent AI approaches. AI interventions mainly targeted high schools and STEM courses. The study emphasizes AI's transformative potential in education and calls for further research into unexplored databases, pedagogical frameworks, and development tools to optimize AI integration in K-12 education.

Casal-Otero et al. (2023) conducted a systematic literature review to explore the integration of artificial intelligence (AI) into K-12 education worldwide, identifying AI literacy as a significant pedagogical and cognitive challenge. Analyzing 179 documents from Scopus, the study categorized AI literacy approaches into two groups: learning experiences focused on technical, conceptual, and applied skills and theoretical perspectives to design AI literacy models. Few studies assessed students' understanding of AI concepts post-learning, and limited attention was given to the potential negative consequences of poorly implemented AI. The authors emphasized the need for a competency framework to guide curricular design, ensuring modular, personalized, and contextually appropriate AI literacy education. They also highlighted the potential to enhance core subject learning by integrating AI into teaching, provided curricula are co-designed with educators.

## Personalized Learning Experiences

AI-powered tools can tailor educational content to individual students' needs and learning paces. Adaptive learning platforms analyze data on student performance to identify strengths and weaknesses, providing customized resources and feedback. For instance, platforms like Khan Academy and DreamBox Learning use AI algorithms to adapt exercises and challenges to each learner's proficiency level, promoting mastery in STEM subjects. Machine learning models can adapt content to individual learning styles, increasing grades and engagement (Villegas-Ch. et al., 2024; Naseer et al., 2024). Deep learning techniques have shown promise in creating customized learning pathways, significantly improving academic performance (Naseer et al., 2024). AI and IoT integration can provide real-time feedback, support, and immersive learning experiences (Kamruzzaman et al., 2023). Generative AI allows the creation of customizable learning materials in various styles (Pesovski et al., 2024). However, challenges remain, including privacy concerns and potential biases in algorithms (Lin et al., 2023). Researchers have explored various machine learning techniques, with a growing interest in artificial neural networks for identifying learning styles (Gutta Essa et al., 2023). AI-based personalized education shows great potential for enhancing learning outcomes and addressing individual student needs (Maghsudi et al., 2021).

Naseer et al. (2024) investigated deep learning techniques to create personalized learning pathways in higher education, addressing the need to align educational content with evolving student needs. They implemented an AI-driven adaptive learning platform in university courses in Faisalabad, Pakistan. They conducted a controlled experiment comparing outcomes between students using the AI platform and those in traditional instruction. Results demonstrated significant improvements in academic performance, engagement, and satisfaction among students using the AI platform.

## AI and Language Proficiency in STEM: Bridging Gaps and Enhancing Learning Outcomes

Language proficiency is crucial for success in STEM education, as it enables students to comprehend scientific texts, articulate ideas, and collaborate effectively. AI technologies can bridge language gaps and enhance communication skills, which is vital for STEM learning. Recent research highlights the significant role of language proficiency and artificial intelligence (AI) in enhancing STEM education. AI-powered programs have effectively improved Cognitive Academic Language Proficiency among STEM students (Mohammed & Abd Elrahman, 2024).

Integrating AI and computational sciences positively impacts student performance, particularly in STEM areas (García-Martínez et al., 2023). AI-enhanced tutoring systems using platforms like WhatsApp can provide STEM education in local languages (Butgereit, 2024). Learning analytics and AI can personalize STEM learning experiences (Kim, 2024), while linguistic features in online discussions can predict course outcomes differently for male and female students (Lin et al., 2020). Generative AI and multi-modal analogical reasoning show promise in elucidating complex STEM concepts (Cao et al., 2023). Furthermore, AI-driven tools can enhance cross-cultural competence in STEM education (Chen et al., 2024). These advancements in AI applications for STEM education offer opportunities to improve student engagement, understanding, and performance across diverse cultural contexts.

García-Martínez et al. (2023) conducted a systematic review and meta-analysis to evaluate the impact of artificial intelligence (AI) and computational sciences on student performance. Using a sample of 25 studies identified from the WOS and Scopus databases, the research revealed a positive influence of AI and computational sciences, particularly in improving student attitudes, motivation, and performance in STEM education. The study highlighted significant benefits across all educational stages and noted educators' challenges in designing and implementing AI-driven instructional processes. These challenges underscore the need for further educational research to address pedagogical and ethical concerns.

## AI-Driven Tools: Advancing Language Proficiency and Collaboration in STEM Education

Natural language processing (NLP) tools like Grammarly and QuillBot help students improve their writing skills by providing real-time grammar, vocabulary, and coherence feedback. These tools support students in articulating scientific concepts more effectively (Zhou et al., 2023). Additionally, AI-driven translation tools, like Google Translate, break language barriers for non-native speakers, enabling them to access STEM resources in multiple languages.

Mohammed and Abd Elrahman (2024) explored the transformative role of artificial intelligence (AI) and machine learning (ML) in enhancing personalized learning for STEM college students, particularly in improving their Cognitive Academic English Language Proficiency (CALP). By leveraging AI/ML methods, educational platforms can analyze students' characteristics through past experiences and big data analysis to recommend tailored content, advise long-term curricula, and accurately evaluate performance. While the integration of AI has revolutionized personalized education, the study highlights several challenges, such as addressing the lack of peer interaction, fostering motivation, enhancing diversity, and mitigating biases in data and algorithms. The authors also propose potential solutions to these issues, offering insights into advancing AI-based personalized education.

Kim (2024) highlights the transformative impact of integrating Learning Analytics (LA) and Artificial Intelligence (AI) in STEM education, emphasizing significant improvements in student engagement and academic success. Case studies demonstrate how these technologies personalize learning experiences and make STEM education more effective. Despite challenges such as data privacy and ethical concerns, the review stresses the substantial role of AI and LA in fostering adaptive, inclusive, and impactful learning environments (Kim, 2024).

## Improving Reading Comprehension and Promoting Collaborative Learning

Integrating collaborative learning, AI, and STEM education enhances reading comprehension and critical thinking skills. Collaborative learning approaches have significantly improved students' reading comprehension and critical thinking (Handayani & Suwandi, 2019). AI technologies are being leveraged to support personalized and constructive learning activities, addressing the complex knowledge-building processes required in modern reading (McCarthy & Yan, 2023). The combination of human expertise and AI, particularly in STEM+C learning environments, offers promising avenues for supporting students' collaborative problem-solving skills (Cohn et al., 2024). Gamification and AI-assisted tools have also demonstrated the potential to enhance younger students' reading comprehension (Sankumpa et al., 2023). Furthermore, integrating learning analytics and AI in STEM education transforms educational practices by personalizing learning experiences and improving engagement (Kim, 2024). These advancements, however, necessitate careful consideration of ethical implications and data privacy concerns (Ademola, 2024).

## INCLUSION AND EQUITY IN USING AI IN STEM CLASSROOM

Research highlights the importance of integrating Artificial Intelligence (AI) into STEM education to enhance learning outcomes and promote inclusivity. Studies emphasize hands-on, interactive approaches using open-source platforms to teach AI concepts (Xie-Li & Arias-Méndez, 2023) and the need for professional development programs to prepare teachers for AI integration (Lee & Perret, 2022). AI and Virtual and Augmented Reality can create adaptive learning environments accommodating diverse student needs (Kumar et al., 2024). Researchers also explore AI's potential in fostering diversity and inclusion in STEM teams (Nixon et al., 2024) and its application in collaborative inquiry learning for elementary students (Lee et al., 2021). Integrating Learning Analytics and AI in STEM education can personalize learning experiences and improve engagement (Kim, 2024).

Additionally, studies stress the importance of addressing various groups' inclusion in STEM and AI research (Wong et al., 2024; Abdallah, Al Kaabi, & Ramadan, 2023) and developing AI-thinking skills in STEAM education (How & Hung, 2019). How and Hung (2019) highlight the role of artificial intelligence (AI) analytics as educational scaffolds in science, technology, engineering, arts, and mathematics (STEAM) education, emphasizing their ability to cultivate AI-Thinking skills in students. These skills, anchored in AI-assisted human-centric reasoning, contribute to knowledge acquisition and competency development. Their study illustrates how

STEAM learners, rather than computer scientists, can harness AI to predictively model the effects of various concrete mixture inputs on compressive strength under different conditions.

For instance, AI can simulate scenarios involving insufficient water or cement or determine the required compressive strength for artistic applications. Two AI-driven approaches are examined to help learners grasp AI's role in human-centric reasoning. The first approach employs a Naïve Bayes algorithm for supervised machine learning, which assumes no direct relationships among mixture components. The second approach utilizes a semi-supervised Bayesian method to uncover potential correlations within the dataset. These AI-based models facilitate controlled in-silico experiments, allowing selected parameters to remain constant while others are adjusted to explore hypothetical "what-if" scenarios. By engaging in AI-driven discursive thinking, STEAM learners enhance their AI literacy, enabling them to ask more insightful questions and improve their problem-solving abilities.

## STEPS TO INTEGRATE AI INTO STEM CURRICULA

AI is integrated into various science teaching and learning aspects, including hypothesis generation, experiment design, data interpretation, and personalized learning (Almasri, 2024). Studies emphasize the need to reflect AI's influence on the nature of science in curricula and teaching practices (Erduran & Levrini, 2024). In comparison, AI tools offer numerous benefits, such as enhancing learning environments and improving assessment strategies; challenges persist, including teachers' lack of confidence in AI content mastery (Park et al., 2023). Researchers are exploring AI's potential to advance physics education through personalized learning and natural language interactions (Henderson, 2023). Ethical considerations and the need for transparency in AI use in research and publishing are also being addressed (Sadler et al., 2024). Overall, emerging technologies like AI are viewed as having a double-edged effect on STEM education, offering opportunities and challenges.

Below are the steps that are suggested to follow when incorporating AI tools in STEM education;

1. Identify Learning Outcomes
    - Define what you want students to achieve through AI integration.
    - Align AI activities and tools with STEM learning objectives to enhance rather than replace traditional teaching methods.
2. Choose the Right AI application.

Because the vast array of AI tools available can be overwhelming, it's important to select tools that complement your STEM curricula and STEM learning objectives. Example of AI options:

- **Intelligent tutoring systems (ITS)**

Provide personalized learning platforms that adjust difficulty levels to students and provide personalized feedback based on student performance.

- **Virtual labs and simulations**

Providing safe and immersive environments for conducting STEM investigations and exploring complex concepts.

- **AI-powered games and gamification**

Enhance learning by making it engaging and interactive, fostering collaboration and healthy competition.

- **Data analysis and visualization tools**

Equip students with skills to analyze real-world data and uncover hidden patterns.

3. Design AI-Focused STEM Curriculum Modules

Integrate AI topics into existing STEM subjects rather than creating new ones. For instance:

- **Mathematics**

Use AI to teach data analysis, pattern recognition, and predictive modeling.

- **Science**

Implement AI to simulate investigations and analyze complex data.

- **Technology and Engineering**

Focus on AI-driven robotics, automation, and coding. Create project-based learning modules by which students can work on real-world AI applications. Ensure the modules are:

- Age-appropriate and engaging for the target student group.
- Have a manual for precise instructions and learning goals.
- Promote critical thinking and problem-solving skills.

4. Provide Professional Development for Educators

Successful AI integration stems from well-equipped educators. Provide teachers with professional development opportunities.

5. Foster A Collaborative Learning Environment

Encourage collaboration among students through group projects and peer-to-peer learning.

6. Assess and Iterate
    - Continuously assess the effectiveness of AI integration through harvesting student feedback.
    - Adjust the curriculum based on assessment results.

## CONCLUSION

Artificial Intelligence (AI) is an evolving interdisciplinary field that has significantly transformed education, influencing instructional design, learning processes, and assessment methods. AI encompasses technologies that mimic human cognitive functions, such as problem-solving, decision-making, and learning, with recent advancements in machine learning enabling the emergence of Generative AI (GenAI). GenAI can independently generate educational content, including text, images, sound, and video, offering innovative ways to enhance instructional practices and information dissemination. Applications like ChatGPT, Midjourney, and Stable Diffusion have gained prominence, demonstrating their ability to support content creation, improve engagement, and personalize learning experiences in educational settings. Integrating AI in classrooms allows for automation of tasks, data analysis, and predictive insights, helping educators tailor instruction and support student learning effectively. AI-powered tools provide various benefits, including personalized learning, automated assessments, intelligent tutoring, and real-time feedback, improving student engagement, problem-solving skills, and critical thinking. In STEM education, AI facilitates adaptive learning environments, supports inquiry-based learning, and enhances instructional effectiveness. However, while AI offers numerous opportunities, challenges remain, including ethical considerations, potential biases, data privacy concerns, and the need for teacher training to maximize AI's potential. Integrating AI into STEM education requires a balanced approach, combining technological advancements with pedagogical strategies to ensure high-quality, equitable, and inclusive learning experiences.

Integrating Artificial Intelligence (AI) into education, particularly in STEM disciplines, can revolutionize learning by providing personalized instruction, automating assessments, and enhancing student engagement. Generative AI tools such as ChatGPT, Midjourney, and Stable Diffusion offer innovative approaches to content creation and knowledge dissemination, allowing educators and students to interact with learning materials in new and meaningful ways. AI-driven adaptive learning environments support differentiated instruction, helping students develop critical thinking, problem-solving, and inquiry-based learning skills. Despite its advantages, AI implementation in education presents challenges, including ethical concerns, data privacy issues, and the need for teacher professional development. To maximize AI's potential while mitigating risks, educators must adopt a balanced approach integrating human expertise with AI technologies, ensuring equity, transparency, and inclusivity in learning. Moving forward, further research and practical applications are needed to explore AI's long-term impact on education and develop best practices for its responsible and effective use in classrooms.

## Implications for Policy Makers

Policymakers should develop comprehensive frameworks and guidelines to ensure AI's ethical and responsible use in STEM education. This includes establishing data privacy protections, transparency standards, and procedures for mitigating AI bias in educational settings. Policies should promote equitable access to AI-driven learning tools, ensuring that students from all backgrounds can benefit from technological advancements. Investment in teacher training and professional development programs is critical to equipping educators with the skills to integrate AI effectively into their teaching practices. Additionally, regulatory frameworks should address the ethical implications of AI-generated content, ensuring its alignment with educational standards and values. Policymakers should encourage partnerships between governments, educational institutions, and technology developers to create AI tools tailored to diverse learning needs.

## Implications for Educators

Educationalists must adopt a proactive approach to integrating AI into STEM teaching and learning, leveraging its potential to personalize instruction, enhance engagement, and streamline administrative tasks. Teachers should receive training in AI literacy to understand its capabilities, limitations, and ethical considerations. Educators should also incorporate AI tools to complement human interaction, ensuring that technology enhances rather than replaces traditional teaching methods. Furthermore, schools and universities should develop AI-inclusive curricula that align with pedagogical objectives and support critical thinking, problem-solving, and inquiry-based learning. Finally, educational institutions should collaborate with researchers and policymakers to continuously refine AI implementation strategies, ensuring that AI integration remains aligned with educational goals and evolving technological advancements. By addressing these considerations, AI can effectively enhance educational experiences while maintaining ethical integrity, equity, and high-quality learning outcomes in STEM education.

## REFERENCES


Abdallah, A., Ismail, O., Abdallah, R. K., & Alkaabi, A. M. (2023). Perceptions of Students About the Use of Webinars in Classrooms: A Case of Abu Dhabi University. [IJICTE]. *International Journal of Information and Communication Technology Education, 19*(1), 1–17. DOI: 10.4018/IJICTE.322793

Abdallah, A. K., Al Kaabi, A. M., & Ramadan, R. S. (2023). The critical role of principals in leading effective inclusive schools. In *Inclusive Phygital Learning Approaches and Strategies for Students With Special Needs* (pp. 256–281). IGI Global. DOI: 10.4018/978-1-6684-8504-0.ch012

Abdallah, A. K., & Alkaabi, A. M. (Eds.). (2023). *Restructuring leadership for school improvement and reform*. IGI Global. DOI: 10.4018/978-1-6684-7818-9

Abdallah, A. K., & Farhan, A. F. (2023). Breaking barriers and empowering women leaders to drive school improvement. In *Restructuring Leadership for School Improvement and Reform* (pp. 399–419). IGI Global. DOI: 10.4018/978-1-6684-7818-9.ch020

Abulibdeh, A., Baya Chatti, C., Alkhereibi, A., & El Menshawy, S. (2025). A Scoping Review of the Strategic Integration of Artificial Intelligence in Higher Education: Transforming University Excellence Themes and Strategic Planning in the Digital Era. *European Journal of Education, 60*(1), e12908. DOI: 10.1111/ejed.12908

Ademola, E. O. (2024). *Reading Strategies in the AI Age: Enhancing Comprehension and Engagement with Advanced Technologies*. Advances in Multidisciplinary & Scientific Research Journal Publications., DOI: 10.22624/AIMS/ACCRABE-SPOKE2024P13

Al Maktoum, S. B., & Al Kaabi, A. M. (2024). Exploring teachers' experiences within the teacher evaluation process: A qualitative multi-case study. *Cogent Education, 11*(1), 2287931. Advance online publication. DOI: 10.1080/2331186X.2023.2287931

Al-Rashaida, M., López-Paz, J. F., Amayra, I., Lázaro, E., Martínez, O., Berrocoso, S., García, M., & Pérez, M. (2018). Factors affecting the satisfaction of people with disabilities in relation to vocational rehabilitation programs: A literature review. *Journal of Vocational Rehabilitation, 49*(1), 97–115. DOI: 10.3233/JVR-180957

Al-Rashaida, M., & Massouti, A. (2024). Assessing the efficacy of online teacher training programs in preparing pre-service teachers to support students with special educational needs in mainstream classrooms in the UAE: A case study. *Journal of Research in Special Educational Needs, 24*(1), 188–200. DOI: 10.1111/1471-3802.12624

Alabdulhadi, A., & Faisal, M. (2021). Systematic literature review of STEM self-study related ITSs. *Education and Information Technologies*, *26*(2), 1549–1588. DOI: 10.1007/s10639-020-10315-z

Ali, S., Payne, B. H., Williams, R., Park, H. W., & Breazeal, C. (2019). *Constructionism, Ethics, and Creativity: Developing Primary and Middle School Artificial Intelligence Education.*

Almasri, F. (2024). Exploring the Impact of Artificial Intelligence in Teaching and Learning of Science: A Systematic Review of Empirical Research. *Research in Science Education*, *54*(5), 977–997. Advance online publication. DOI: 10.1007/s11165-024-10176-3

Ayala-Pazmiño, M., (2023). Artificial Intelligence in Education: Exploring the Potential Benefits and Risks. 593 Digital Publisher CEIT, 8(3), 892-899 DOI: 10.33386/593dp.2023.3.1827

Baidoo-Anu, D., & Ansah, L. O. (2023). Education in the era of generative artificial intelligence (AI): Understanding the potential benefits of ChatGPT in promoting teaching and learning. *Journal of AI*, *7*(1), 52–62. https://doi.org/https://doi.org/10.61969/jai.1337500. DOI: 10.61969/jai.1337500

Bataineh, O., Qablan, A., Belbase, S., Takriti, R., & Tairab, H. (2022). Gender disparity in science, technology, engineering, and mathematics (STEM) programs at Jordanian universities. *Sustainability (Basel)*, *14*(21), 14069. DOI: 10.3390/su142114069

Beghetto, R. A. (2019). Large-Scale Assessments, Personalized Learning, and Creativity: Paradoxes and Possibilities. *ECNU Review of Education*, *2*(3), 311–327. DOI: 10.1177/2096531119878963

Bittle, K., & El-Gayar, O. (2025). Generative AI and Academic Integrity in Higher Education: A Systematic Review and Research Agenda. *Information (Basel)*, *16*(4), 296. DOI: 10.3390/info16040296

Butgereit, L. (2024). AI-Enhanced STEM Education in Sub-Saharan Africa and Indian Ocean Island Nations using Whatsapp and GPT-4x in Local Languages. *International Conference on Intelligent and Innovative Computing Applications.* DOI: 10.59200/ICONIC.2024.003

Bybee, R., Taylor, J., Gardner, A., Scotter, P., Powell, J., Westbrook, A., & Landes, N. (2006). *The BSCS 5E instructional model: Origins and effectiveness.* BSCS.

Cao, C., Ding, Z., Lee, G., Jiao, J., Lin, J., & Zhai, X. (2023). Elucidating STEM Concepts through Generative AI: A Multi-modal Exploration of Analogical Reasoning. *ArXiv, abs/2308.10454*.

Casal-Otero, L., Catala, A., Fernández-Morante, C., Taboada, M., Cebreiro, B., & Barro, S. (2023). AI literacy in K-12: A systematic literature review. *International Journal of STEM Education, 10*(1), 29. DOI: 10.1186/s40594-023-00418-7

Castaneda, L., & Selwyn, N. (2018). More than tools? Making sense of the ongoing digitizations of higher education. *International Journal of Educational Technology in Higher Education, 15*(1), 1–10. DOI: 10.1186/s41239-018-0109-y

Chaipidech, P. (2021). chaipi TPACK. *Journal of Educational Technology & Society, 24*(4), 220239.

Chan, C. K. Y., & Tsi, L. H. Y. (2024). Will generative AI replace teachers in higher education? A study of teacher and student perceptions. *Studies in Educational Evaluation, 83*, 101395. https://doi.org/https://doi.org/10.1016/j.stueduc.2024.101395. DOI: 10.1016/j.stueduc.2024.101395

Chen, K., Tallant, A. C., & Selig, I. (2024). Exploring generative AI literacy in higher education: Student adoption, interaction, evaluation, and ethical perceptions [Article; Early Access]. *Information and Learning Science, 17*. Advance online publication. DOI: 10.1108/ILS-10-2023-0160

Chiu, T. K., & Li, Y. (2023). How Can Emerging Technologies Impact STEM Education? *Journal for STEM Education Research, 6*(3), 375–384. DOI: 10.1007/s41979-023-00113-w

Chiu, T. K. F. (2024). The impact of Generative AI (GenAI) on practices, policies, and research direction in education: A case of ChatGPT and Midjourney. *Interactive Learning Environments, 32*(10), 1–17. DOI: 10.1080/10494820.2023.2253861

Cohn, C., Snyder, C., & Fonteles, J. H. T. S., A., Montenegro, J., & Biswas, G. (2024). A multimodal approach to support teachers, researchers, and AI collaboration in STEM+C learning environments. *British Journal of Educational Technology*. Advance online publication. DOI: 10.1111/bjet.13518

Conley, D. (2015). A New Era for Educational Assessment. *Education Policy Analysis Archives, 23*, 8. DOI: 10.14507/epaa.v23.1983

Cope, B., Kalantzis, M., & Searsmith, D. (2021). Artificial intelligence for education: Knowledge and its assessment in AI-enabled learning ecologies. *Educational Philosophy and Theory, 53*(12), 1229–1245. DOI: 10.1080/00131857.2020.1728732

Erduran, S., & Levrini, O. (2024). The impact of artificial intelligence on scientific practices: An emergent area of research for science education. *International Journal of Science Education, 46*(18), 1982–1989. Advance online publication. DOI: 10.1080/09500693.2024.2306604

Essa, S. G., Celik, T., & Human-Hendricks, N. E. (2023). Personalized adaptive learning technologies based on machine learning techniques to identify learning styles: A systematic literature review. *IEEE Access : Practical Innovations, Open Solutions, 11*, 48392–48409. DOI: 10.1109/ACCESS.2023.3276439

Fakhar, H., Lamrabet, M., Echantoufi, N., El, K., & Ajana, L. (2024). Towards a New Artificial Intelligence-based Framework for Teachers' Online Continuous Professional Development Programs: Systematic Review. In *IJACSA)*[]. *International Journal of Advanced Computer Science and Applications, 15*(4). www.ijacsa.thesai.org. DOI: 10.14569/IJACSA.2024.0150450

Feldman-Maggor, Y., Blonder, R., & Alexandron, G. (2024). Perspectives of Generative AI in Chemistry Education Within the TPACK Framework [Article; Early Access]. *Journal of Science Education and Technology, 12*. Advance online publication. DOI: 10.1007/s10956-024-10147-3

García, M., Lázaro, E., Amayra, I., López-Paz, J. F., Martínez, O., Pérez, M., Berrocoso, S., Al-Rashaida, M., & Infante, J. (2020). Analysis of visuospatial abilities in Chiari malformation type I. *Cerebellum (London, England), 19*(1), 6–15. DOI: 10.1007/s12311-019-01056-y PMID: 31286383

García-Martínez, I., Fernández-Batanero, J.M., Fernández-Cerero, J., & León, S.P. (2023). Analyzing the Impact of Artificial Intelligence and Computational Sciences on Student Performance: Systematic Review and Meta-analysis. *Journal of New Approaches in Educational Research.* DOI: 10.7821/naer.2023.1.1240

Gligorea, I., Cioca, M., Oancea, R., Gorski, A. T., Gorski, H., & Tudorache, P. (2023). Adaptive learning using artificial intelligence in e-learning: A literature review. *Education Sciences, 13*(12), 1216. DOI: 10.3390/educsci13121216

Gobert, J. D., Sao Pedro, M., Raziuddin, J., & Baker, R. S. (2013). From Log Files to Assessment Metrics: Measuring Students' Science Inquiry Skills Using Educational Data Mining. *Journal of the Learning Sciences, 22*(4), 521–563. DOI: 10.1080/10508406.2013.837391

Gupta, M., Gupta, P., Ho, C., Wood, J., Guleria, S., & Virostko, J. (2024). Can Generative AI Improve The Readability Of Patient Education Materials At A Radiology Practice? *Clinical Radiology.* https://doi.org/https://doi.org/10.1016/j.crad.2024.08.019

Gupta, T. (2024). Adaptive Learning Systems: Harnessing AI to Personalize Educational Outcomes. *International Journal for Research in Applied Science and Engineering Technology*, *12*(11), 458–464. Advance online publication. DOI: 10.22214/ijraset.2024.65088

Handayani, N.D., & Suwandi, N. (2019). Integrating collaborative learning in cyclic learning sessions to promote students' reading comprehension and critical thinking. *International research journal of management, IT and social sciences*. DOI: 10.21744/irjmis.v6n5.777

Hashmi, N., & Bal, A. S. (2024). Generative AI in higher education and beyond. *Business Horizons*, *67*(5), 607–614. https://doi.org/https://doi.org/10.1016/j.bushor.2024.05.005. DOI: 10.1016/j.bushor.2024.05.005

Hellings, J., & Haelermans, C. (2020). The effect of providing learning analytics on student behavior and performance in programming: A randomized controlled experiment. *Higher Education*, *83*(1), 1–18. DOI: 10.1007/s10734-020-00560-z PMID: 33173242

Henderson, C. (2023). Editorial: Call for Papers for Focused Collection of Physical Review Physics Education Research: AI Tools in Physics Teaching and PER. *Physical Review. Physics Education Research*, *19*(2), 020003. Advance online publication. DOI: 10.1103/PhysRevPhysEducRes.19.020003

Holmes, W., Bialik, M., & Fadel, C. (2019). *Artificial Intelligence in Education Promises and Implications for Teaching and Learning* (1st ed.). Center for Curriculum Redesign.

Holstein, K., McLaren, B. M., & Aleven, V. (2019). Co-designing a real-time classroom orchestration tool to support teacher—AI complementarity. *Journal of Learning Analytics, 6*(2), 27–52. . 62.3DOI: 10. 18608/ jla.2019

Hwang, G.-J., Xie, H., Wah, B. W., & Gasevic, D. (2020). Vision, challenges, roles and research issues of Artificial Intelligence in Education. *Comput. Educ.: Artif. Intell.*, *1*, 100001. DOI: 10.1016/j.caeai.2020.100001

Ivanov, S., Soliman, M., Tuomi, A., Alkathiri, N. A., & Al-Alawi, A. N. (2024). Drivers of generative AI adoption in higher education through the lens of the Theory of Planned Behaviour. *Technology in Society*, *77*, 102521. https://doi.org/https://doi.org/10.1016/j.techsoc.2024.102521. DOI: 10.1016/j.techsoc.2024.102521

Jang, J., Jeon, J., & Ki Jung, S. (2022). Development of STEM-Based AI Education Program for Sustainable Improvement of Elementary Learners. *Sustainability (Basel)*, *14*(22), 15178. Advance online publication. DOI: 10.3390/su142215178

Ji, Y., & Han, Y. (2019). Monitoring indicators of the flipped classroom learning process based on data mining—Taking the course of "virtual reality technology" as an example. *International Journal of Emerging Technologies in Learning, 14*(3), 166–176. . v14i03.10105DOI: 10. 3991/ ijet

Joseph, O., & Uzondu, N.Olatunbosun Bartholomew JosephNwankwo Charles Uzondu. (2024). Integrating AI and Machine Learning in STEM education: Challenges and opportunities. *Computer Science & IT Research Journal*, *5*(8), 1732–1750. DOI: 10.51594/csitrj.v5i8.1379

Kalota, F. (2024). A Primer on Generative Artificial Intelligence. *Education Sciences*, *14*(2), 172. DOI: 10.3390/educsci14020172

Kamruzzaman, M. M., Alanazi, S., Alruwaili, M., Alshammari, N., Elaiwat, S., Abu-Zanona, M., Innab, N., Mohammad Elzaghmouri, B., & Ahmed Alanazi, B. (2023). AI-and IoT-assisted sustainable education systems during pandemics, such as COVID-19, for smart cities. *Sustainability (Basel)*, *15*(10), 8354. DOI: 10.3390/su15108354

Karaca, M. F. (2024, 2024). Is Artificial Intelligence able to Produce Content Appropriate for Education Level? A Review on ChatGPT and Gemini. *Proceedings of the Cognitive Models and Artificial Intelligence Conference*, İstanbul,Turkiye. DOI: 10.1145/3660853.3660915

Kim, N. J., & Kim, M. K. (2022). Teacher's Perceptions of Using an Artificial Intelligence-Based Educational Tool for Scientific Writing. *Frontiers in Education*, *7*, 755914. Advance online publication. DOI: 10.3389/feduc.2022.755914

Kim, T. K. (2024). Integrating Learning Analytics, AI, and STEM Education. *International Journal of Research in STEM Education*, *6*(2), 61–72. DOI: 10.33830/ijrse.v6i2.1745

Kose, U., & Arslan, A. (2017). Optimization of self-learning in computer engineering courses: An intelligent software system supported by artificial neural network and vortex optimization algorithm. *Computer Applications in Engineering Education, 25*(1), 142–156. . 21787DOI: 10.1002/ cae

Krasovskiy, D. (2020). *The challenges and benefits of adopting AI in STEM education.* https:// upjou rney. com/ the- chall enges- and- benefits- of- adopting- ai- in- stem- educa tion

Kumar, K., Selvan, T., Mahendraprabu, M., Ganesan, K., Ramnath, R., & Kumar, N. (2024). Examining the Role of Virtual Reality, Augmented Reality, and Artificial Intelligence in Adapting STEM Education for Next-Generation Inclusion. *International Journal of Emerging Knowledge Studies*. DOI: 10.70333/ijeks-02-12-025

Lamb, R., Hand, B., & Kavner, A. (2021). Computational modeling of the effects of the science writing heuristic on student critical thinking in science using machine learning. *Journal of Science Education and Technology*, *30*(2), 283–297. DOI: 10.1007/s10956-020-09871-3

Lee, C. H., Gobir, N., Gurn, A., & Soep, E. (2022). In the black mirror: Youth investigations into artificial intelligence. *ACM Transactions on Computing Education*, *22*(3), 1–25. DOI: 10.1145/3484495

Lee, D., Arnold, M., Srivastava, A., Plastow, K., Strelan, P., Ploeckl, F., Lekkas, D., & Palmer, E. (2024). The impact of generative AI on higher education learning and teaching: A study of educators' perspectives. *Computers and Education: Artificial Intelligence, 6*, 100221. https://doi.org/https://doi.org/10.1016/j.caeai.2024.100221

Lee, I., & Perret, B. (2022). *Preparing High School Teachers to Integrate AI Methods into STEM Classrooms*. www.aaai.org

Lee, I. A., & Perret, B. (2022). Preparing High School Teachers to Integrate AI Methods into STEM Classrooms. *AAAI Conference on Artificial Intelligence*. DOI: 10.1609/aaai.v36i11.21557

Lee, S., & Song, K.-s. (2024). Teachers' and Students' Perceptions of AI-Generated Concept Explanations: Implications for Integrating Generative AI in Computer Science Education. *Computers and Education: Artificial Intelligence*, 100283. https://doi.org/https://doi.org/10.1016/j.caeai.2024.100283

Lin, C. C., Huang, A. Y., & Lu, O. H. (2023). Artificial intelligence in intelligent tutoring systems toward sustainable education: A systematic review. *Smart Learning Environments*, *10*(1), 41. DOI: 10.1186/s40561-023-00260-y

Lloyd, C., Doherty, S., Herb, A., & Warburton, S. (2022). *A risk-based approach to mitigating the Gen(AI) challenge to assessment integrity: The Programmatic Assessment Security Project*. PASP., DOI: 10.1007/978-3

Lohakan, M., & Seetao, C. (2024). Large-scale experiment in STEM education for high school students using artificial intelligence kit based on computer vision and Python. *Heliyon*, *10*(10), e31366. Advance online publication. DOI: 10.1016/j.heliyon.2024.e31366 PMID: 38803951

Luckin, R., & Cukurova, M. (2019). Designing educational technologies in the age of AI: A learning sciences-driven approach. *British Journal of Educational Technology*, *50*(6), 2824–2838. DOI: 10.1111/bjet.12861

Lv, Z. (2023). Generative artificial intelligence in the metaverse era. *Cognitive Robotics, 3*, 208-217. https://doi.org/https://doi.org/10.1016/j.cogr.2023.06.001

Maghsudi, S., Lan, A., Xu, J., & van Der Schaar, M. (2021). Personalized education in the artificial intelligence era: What to expect next. *IEEE Signal Processing Magazine*, *38*(3), 37–50. DOI: 10.1109/MSP.2021.3055032

Maphoto, K. B., Sevnarayan, K., Mohale, N. E., Suliman, Z., Ntsopi, T. J., & Mokoena, D. (2024). Advancing students' academic excellence in distance education: Exploring the potential of generative AI integration to improve academic writing skills [Journal Article]. *Open Praxis*, *16*(2), 142–159. DOI: 10.55982/openpraxis.16.2.649

Massouti, A., Al-Rashaida, M., & Alhosani, M. (2024). A qualitative study on Dubai's inclusive education policy from school leaders' perspectives. *Sustainability (Basel)*, *16*(3), 1252. DOI: 10.3390/su16031252

McCarthy, K. S., & Yan, E. F. (2023). Reading Comprehension and Constructive Learning: Policy Considerations in the Age of Artificial Intelligence. *Policy Insights from the Behavioral and Brain Sciences*, *11*(1), 19–26. DOI: 10.1177/23727322231218891

McDonald, N., Johri, A., Ali, A., & Hingle, A. (2024). Generative Artificial Intelligence in Higher Education: Evidence from an Analysis of Institutional Policies and Guidelines. *ArXiv, abs/2402.01659*. https://doi.org/https://doi.org/10.48550/arXiv.2402.01659

Mohammed, D. D. A. M., & Abd Elrahman, D. M. A. E. M. (2024). An Artificial Intelligence-Powered Program for Fostering STEM College Students' Cognitive Academic English Language Proficiency (CALP). *Journal of Research in Curriculum Instruction and Educational Technology*, *10*(2), 345–402. DOI: 10.21608/jrciet.2024.363679

Murphy, R. F. (2019). *RAND Corporation Artificial Intelligence Applications to Support K-12 Teachers and Teaching: A Review of Promising Applications, Opportunities, and Challenges.*

Myneni, L. S., Narayanan, N. H., & Rebello, S. (2013). An interactive and intelligent learning system for physics education. *IEEE Transactions on Learning Technologies*, *6*(3), 228–239. . 2013.26DOI: 10. 1109/ TLT

Nagaraj, B. K., Kalaivani, A., Begum, R. S., Akila, S., Sachdev, H. K., & Kumar, N. S. (2023). The Emerging Role of Artificial Intelligence in STEM Higher Education: A Critical Review. In *International Research Journal of Multidisciplinary Technovation* (Vol. 5, Issue 5, pp. 1–19). Asian Research Association. DOI: 10.54392/irjmt2351

Naseer, F., Khan, M. N., Tahir, M., Addas, A., & Aejaz, S. H. (2024). Integrating deep learning techniques for personalized learning pathways in higher education. *Heliyon*, *10*(11), e32628. Advance online publication. DOI: 10.1016/j.heliyon.2024.e32628 PMID: 38961899

Nguyen, Q. L., & Le, T. T. H. (2021).. . *Journal of Physics: Conference Series*, *1835*, 012051. DOI: 10.1088/1742-6596/1835/1/012051

Nikolopoulou, K. (2024). Generative Artificial Intelligence in Higher Education: Exploring Ways of Harnessing Pedagogical Practices with the Assistance of ChatGPT. *International Journal of Changes in Education*, *1*(2), 103–111. DOI: 10.47852/bonviewIJCE42022489

Nixon, N., Lin, Y., & Snow, L. (2024). Catalyzing Equity in STEM Teams: Harnessing Generative AI for Inclusion and Diversity. *Policy Insights from the Behavioral and Brain Sciences*, *11*(1), 85–92. DOI: 10.1177/23727322231220356 PMID: 38516055

Noroozi, O., Soleimani, S., Farrokhnia, M., & Banihashem, S. K. (2024). Generative AI in Education: Pedagogical, Theoretical, and Methodological Perspectives. *International Journal of Technology in Education*, *7*(3), 373–385. DOI: 10.46328/ijte.845

Noy, S., & Zhang, W. (2023). Experimental evidence on the productivity effects of generative artificial intelligence. *Science*, *381*(6654), 187–192. https://doi.org/https://doi.org/10.2139/ssrn.4375283. DOI: 10.1126/science.adh2586 PMID: 37440646

Okwara, U., & Obiagwu, V. (2024). *The Ethical Implications of Artificial Intelligence in Education*. DOI: 10.13140/RG.2.2.21082.35528

Omughelli, D., Gordon, N., & Al Jaber, T. (2024). Fairness, Bias, and Ethics in AI: Exploring the Factors Affecting Student Performance. *Journal of International Communication*, *3*(2). Advance online publication. DOI: 10.54963/jic.v4i1.30

Ouyang, F., Dinh, T. A., & Xu, W. (2023). A Systematic Review of AI-Driven Educational Assessment in STEM Education. In *Journal for STEM Education Research* (Vol. 6, Issue 3, pp. 408–426). Springer Nature. DOI: 10.1007/s41979-023-00112-x

Park, J., Teo, T. W., Teo, A., Chang, J., Huang, J. S., & Koo, S. (2023). Integrating artificial intelligence into science lessons: Teachers' experiences and views. *International Journal of STEM Education*, *10*(1), 1–22. DOI: 10.1186/s40594-023-00454-3

Pedro, F., Subosa, M., Rivas, A., & Valverde, P. (2019). Artificial intelligence in education: Challenges and opportunities for sustainable development.

Pesovski, I., Santos, R., Henriques, R., & Trajkovik, V. (2024). Generative AI for customizable learning experiences. *Sustainability (Basel), 16*(7), 3034. DOI: 10.3390/su16073034

Pimthong, P., & Williams, J. (2018). Preservice teachers' understanding of STEM education. *Kasetsart Journal of Social Sciences, 41*(2), 289–295. https://so04.tci-thaijo.org/index.php/kjss/article/view/232607

Qablan, A., AlKaabi, A., Aljanahi, M., & Almaamari, S. (2024). Ch. 1: Inquiry-Based Learning: Encouraging Exploration and Curiosity in the Classroom (231023-060352). In Cutting-Edge Innovations in Teaching, Leadership, Technology, and Assessment. ICI Publishers for Timely Knowledge. ISBN13: 9798369308806, EISBN13: 9798369308813.

Rapoport, A. (1986). *General system theory: Essential concepts & applications.* CRC Press.

Relmasira, S. C., Lai, Y. C., & Donaldson, J. P. (2023). Fostering AI Literacy in Elementary Science, Technology, Engineering, Art, and Mathematics (STEAM) Education in the Age of Generative AI. *Sustainability (Basel), 15*(18), 13595. DOI: 10.3390/su151813595

Rincon, B. E., & George-Jackson, C. E. (2016). STEM intervention programs: Funding practices and challenges. *Studies in Higher Education, 41*(3), 429–444. DOI: 10.1080/03075079.2014.927845

Roshan, S., Zaffar Iqbal, S., & Qing, Z. (2024). Teacher Training and Professional Development for Implementing AI-Based Educational Tools. *Journal of Asian Development Studies, 13*(2), 1972–1987. DOI: 10.62345/jads.2024.13.2.154

Ruijten, P. A. M., Cardona, V., & Bravo, &. (2025). *Strengthening Student Learning: From Outcome-based to Process-based Learning Citation for published version (APA).* DOI: 10.5281/zenodo.14260964

Ruiz-Rojas, L. I., Acosta-Vargas, P., De-Moreta-Llovet, J., & Gonzalez-Rodriguez, M. (2023). Empowering Education with Generative Artificial Intelligence Tools: Approach with an Instructional Design Matrix. *Sustainability (Basel), 15*(15), 11524. https://www.mdpi.com/2071-1050/15/15/11524. DOI: 10.3390/su151511524

Sadler, T. D., Mensah, F. M., & Tam, J. (2024). Artificial intelligence and the Journal of Research in Science Teaching. *Journal of Research in Science Teaching, 61*(4), 739–743. Advance online publication. DOI: 10.1002/tea.21933

Saihi, A., Ben-Daya, M., Hariga, M., & As'ad, R. (2024). A Structural equation modeling analysis of generative AI chatbot adoption among students and educators in higher education. *Computers and Education: Artificial Intelligence, 7*, 100274. https://doi.org/https://doi.org/10.1016/j.caeai.2024.100274

Salinas-Navarro, D. E., Vilalta-Perdomo, E., Michel-Villarreal, R., & Montesinos, L. (2024). Using Generative Artificial Intelligence Tools to Explain and Enhance Experiential Learning for Authentic Assessment. *Education Sciences*, *14*(1), 83. https://www.mdpi.com/2227-7102/14/1/83. DOI: 10.3390/educsci14010083

Sankumpa, W., Kanjug, I., & Singma, S. (2023). *Using Constructivist integrated Gamification and AI Assisted Learning Tool to Enhance Reading Comprehension for Fourth Grade Students*. IIAI Letters on Institutional Research., DOI: 10.52731/lir.v003.136

Sapriati, A., Suhandoko, A. D. J., Yundayani, A., Karim, R. A., Kusmawan, U., Mohd Adnan, A. H., & Suhandoko, A. A. (2023). The Effect of Virtual Laboratories on Improving Students' SRL: An Umbrella Systematic Review. In *Education Sciences* (Vol. 13, Issue 3). MDPI. DOI: 10.3390/educsci13030222

Scherer, R., Siddiq, F., & Tondeur, J. (2019). The technology acceptance model (TAM): A meta-analytic structural equation modeling approach to explaining teachers' adoption of digital technology in education. *Computers & Education*, *128*, 13–35. DOI: 10.1016/j.compedu.2018.09.009

Schiff, D. (2021). Out of the laboratory and into the classroom: The future of artificial intelligence in education. *AI & Society*, *36*(1), 331–348. DOI: 10.1007/s00146-020-01033-8 PMID: 32836908

Selwyn, N. (2016). *Is technology good for education?* Polity Press.

Skowronek, M., Gilberti, R. M., Petro, M., Sancomb, C., Maddern, S., & Jankovic, J. (2022). Inclusive STEAM education in diverse disciplines of sustainable energy and AI. *Energy and AI*, *7*, 100124. DOI: 10.1016/j.egyai.2021.100124

Stankovski, S., Ostojić, G., Tegeltija, S., Stanojević, M., Babić, M., & Zhang, X. (2024). Generative AI Applications and Tools in Engineering Education. 2024 23rd International Symposium INFOTEH-JAHORINA (INFOTEH)

Tan, C. W., & Lim, K. Y. (2023). Revolutionizing Formative Assessment in STEM Fields: Leveraging AI and NLP Techniques. 2023 Asia Pacific Signal and Information Processing Association Annual Summit and Conference, APSIPA ASC 2023, 1357–1364. doi:10.1109/APSIPAASC58517.2023.10317226

Triplett, W. J. (2023). Artificial Intelligence in STEM Education. *Cybersecurity and Innovation Technology Journal, 1*(1), 23–29. DOI: 10.53889/citj.v1i1.296

U.S. Department of Education, Office of Educational Technology. (2023). Artificial Intelligence and Future of Teaching and Learning: Insights and Recommendations, Washington, DC.

Villegas-Ch, W., García-Ortiz, J., & Sánchez-Viteri, S. (2024). *Personalization of learning: Machine learning models for adapting educational content to individual learning styles*. IEEE., DOI: 10.1109/ACCESS.2024.3452592

Vorsah, N. R. E., & Oppong, N. F. (2024). Leveraging AI to enhance active learning strategies in science classrooms: Implications for teacher professional development. *World Journal of Advanced Research and Reviews, 24*(2), 1355–1370. DOI: 10.30574/wjarr.2024.24.2.3499

Wang, T., Su, X., Ma, P., Wang, Y., & Wang, K. (2011). Ability-training-oriented automated assessment in an introductory programming course. *Computers & Education, 56*(1), 220–226. . compe du.2010. 08. 003DOI: 10. 1016/j

Wang, W., & Liu, Z. (2021). Using Artificial Intelligence-Based Collaborative Teaching in Media Learning. *Frontiers in Psychology, 12*, 713943. Advance online publication. DOI: 10.3389/fpsyg.2021.713943 PMID: 34721159

Wei, L. (2023). Artificial intelligence in language instruction: Impact on English learning achievement, L2 motivation, and self-regulated learning. *Frontiers in Psychology, 14*, 1261955. DOI: 10.3389/fpsyg.2023.1261955 PMID: 38023040

West, S. M., Whittaker, M., & Crawford, K. (2021). *Discriminating systems: gender, race and power in AI. New York: AI Now Institute, 2018.*

Wong, E., Urbanowicz, R. J., Bright, T. J., Tatonetti, N. P., Hsiao, Y., Huang, X., Moore, J. H., & Peng, P. (2024). Advancing LGBTQ+ inclusion in STEM education and AI research. *Patterns (New York, N.Y.), 5*(6), 101010. Advance online publication. DOI: 10.1016/j.patter.2024.101010 PMID: 39005486

Xiao, Y., & Yu, S. (2025). Can ChatGPT replace humans in crisis communication? The effects of AI-mediated crisis communication on stakeholder satisfaction and responsibility attribution. *International Journal of Information Management, 80*, 102835. https://doi.org/https://doi.org/10.1016/j.ijinfomgt.2024.102835. DOI: 10.1016/j.ijinfomgt.2024.102835

Xie-Li, D., & Arias-Méndez, E. (2023). *Artificial Intelligence in STEM Education: Interactive Handson Environment using Open Source Electronic Platforms*. Revista Tecnología en Marcha., DOI: 10.18845/tm.v36i6.6759

Xu, W., & Ouyang, F. (2022). A systematic review of AI role in the educational system based on a proposed conceptual framework. *Education and Information Technologies*, *27*(3), 4195–4223. DOI: 10.1007/s10639-021-10774-y

Yang, Y., Sun, W., Sun, D., & Salas-Pilco, S. Z. (2024). Navigating the AI-Enhanced STEM education landscape: a decade of insights, trends, and opportunities. In *Research in Science and Technological Education*. Routledge., DOI: 10.1080/02635143.2024.2370764

Yannier, N., Hudson, S. E., & Koedinger, K. R. (2020). Active learning is about more than hands-on: A mixed-reality AI system to support STEM education. *International Journal of Artificial Intelligence in Education*, *30*(1), 74–96. DOI: 10.1007/s40593-020-00194-3

Zafari, M., Bazargani, J. S., Sadeghi-Niaraki, A., & Choi, S. M. (2022). Artificial intelligence applications in K-12 education: A systematic literature review. *IEEE Access : Practical Innovations, Open Solutions*, *10*, 61905–61921. DOI: 10.1109/ACCESS.2022.3179356

Zampirolli, F. A., BorovinaJosko, J. M., Venero, M. L. F., Kobayashi, G., Fraga, F. J.,Goya, D., & Savegnago, H. R. (2021). An experience of automated assessment in a large-scale introduction programming course. *Computer Applications in Engineering Education, 29*(5), 1284–1299. . 22385DOI: <ALIGNMENT.qj></ALIGNMENT>10. 1002/ cae

Zawacki-Richter, O., Marín, V. I., Bond, M., & Gouverneur, F. (2019). Systematic review of research on artificial intelligence applications in higher education–where are the educators? *International Journal of Educational Technology in Higher Education*, *16*(1), 1–27. DOI: 10.1186/s41239-019-0171-0

Zhou, E., & Lee, D. (2024). Generative artificial intelligence, human creativity, and art. *PNAS Nexus*, *3*(3), pgae052. Advance online publication. DOI: 10.1093/pnasnexus/pgae052 PMID: 38444602

# APPENDIX

*Table 1. Engineering Design Process Lesson Plan Developed Using GRC Template*

<table>
<tr><td colspan="2">Engineering Design Process -Student Science Performance</td></tr>
<tr><td>Grade - Kindergarten</td><td rowspan="2">Lesson Title<br>Why is it more remarkable in the shade?<br>How to Stay Cool!</td></tr>
<tr><td>Lesson Topic: Engineering and Energy</td></tr>
<tr><td colspan="2">Performance Expectations (Standard) from State Standards or NGSS:<br>K-PS3-2 Use tools and materials provided to design and build a structure that will reduce the warming effect of sunlight on the Earth's surface.* [Clarification Statement: Examples of structures could include umbrellas, canopies, and tents that minimize the sun's warming effect.]</td></tr>
<tr><td colspan="2">Lesson Performance Expectations:<br>● Develop a physical structure model that could shield you from the sun.</td></tr>
<tr><td colspan="2">Phenomenon: It feels cooler standing under a tree than in the sunshine.<br>Engineering Challenge: Build a device to protect you from the sun on a hot day.<br><br>Gather<br>1. Students play a crucial role in exploring places that are hot and cool outside to investigate why being in the sun is hotter than being in the shade.<br>2. Students actively participate by developing questions to obtain information about determining the causes of sunlight making you feel warm.<br><br>(Teaching Suggestion: Walk students around the school, under the playground, under the walkways, in the field. Engage students by asking many questions. Show pictures.)<br><br>3. Students are encouraged to learn and obtain information by listening to why it is hot on sunny days.<br><br>Reason<br>4. Students explain why it is hotter in the sun than in the shade.</td></tr>
<tr><td colspan="2">Class Discussion<br>Questions to initiate class discussion:<br>Q: Why do we feel hotter in the sun than in the shade?<br>Q: How can the amount of heat we receive in the sun be reduced?<br>Q: Why does it seem hotter in the middle of the field than under the shade of the tree?<br>Q: Why is it usually hotter in the middle of the day than in the morning or evening?<br>Q: How can we use what we learned about sunshine and heat to build a device to keep you cooler?<br><br>5. Students draw a class picture to show that sunlight changes into heat when it shines on you.<br><br>Engineering Challenge: Construct a structure to use as a shelter to protect you and your friend on a hot day, ensuring it is safe and stable.<br><br>Group Performance<br>6. Students design and build a solution to help keep you and a friend cooler on a hot sunny day.<br>7. Students test their design by measuring how well it works. (use a thermometer)</td></tr>
</table>

continued on following page

*Table 1. Continued*

**Engineering Design Process -Student Science Performance**

***Class Discussion:***

**Questions for Class Discussion:**

*Questions to initiate class discussion:*

*Q: Why is it hotter in the sun than in the shade?*

*Q: What causes it to be so hot in the sun?*

*Q: What are our solutions for cooling off?*

8. ***Draw a picture*** to show how your solution works to protect you from getting too hot.

*(Teaching Suggestion: Focus questions on how you feel in the shade vs. how you think in the sun, and ask guiding questions. Present the student prompts by reading each step to the student. If the student discusses these types of solutions, you may not need to show pictures of shade structures, such as umbrellas, tents, trees, canopies, eaves, etc. Try to let them design things if possible. Students can draw a picture to show how energy from the sun changes into heat energy as the sunlight strikes the students. The students in the shade do not get as hot because there is less energy transfer.)*

***Communicate Reasoning***

***Individual Performances***

9. Students *draw* a picture to show how your solution works to protect you from getting too hot.

Example of student model/structure:

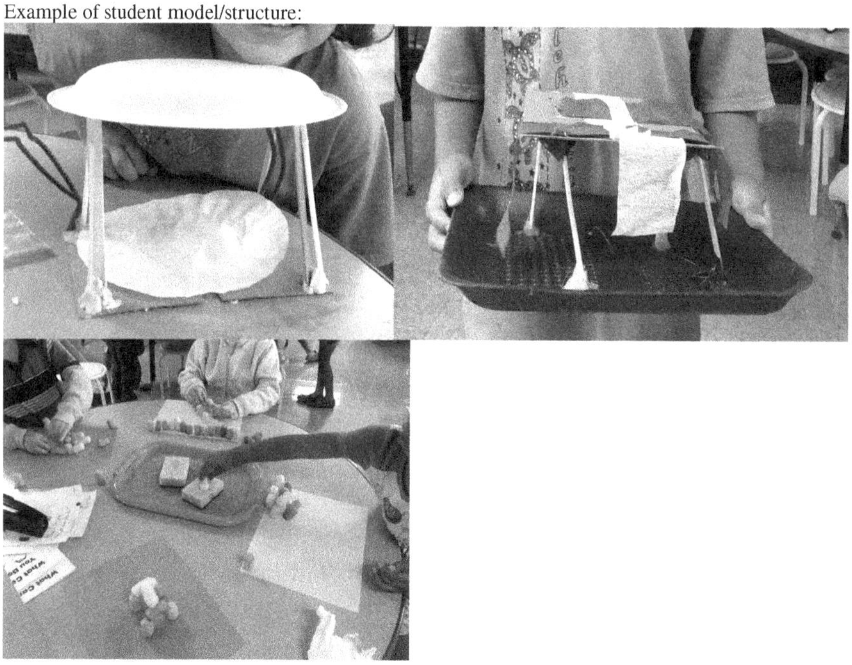

**Formative Assessment for Student Learning**

**Elicit Evidence of Learning:** *Draw* a picture to show how your solution works to protect you from getting too hot.

continued on following page

*Table 1. Continued*

| **Engineering Design Process -Student Science Performance** | | |
|---|---|---|
| **Evidence of Student Proficiency**<br>*Students have created and completed their models. Using words and prompting from their teacher, they can explain how their structure may protect someone from the sun's heat.* | **Range of Typical Student Responses**<br>● *Complete understanding: Student pictures show the blocked sunlight and the student and friend in the shade.* | **Acting on Evidence of Learning**<br>● *Action for students who display a partial or limited understanding: Prompt students by showing our building and asking questions about how our classroom and the tree outside our classroom protect us from the sun. Physically show students another student's work that has a roof.*<br>● *Extensions of learning for students who fully understand: talk about other types of weather we may need to be protected from (we may need walls on our structure to protect us from wind and rain.)* |
| | *Students describe that sunlight is changed to heat when it strikes an object and* | |
| | *causes it to be hot.*<br>● *Partial understanding: The structure shows a roof and* | |
| | *students inside but does not describe light becoming heat.*<br>● *Limited* | |
| | *understanding: A structure but no relationship between light and heat.* | |

| | **Science Essentials** |
|---|---|
| **Science Practices**<br>Carry out an investigation.<br>Construct an explanation<br>Develop and use models. | Make careful observations that generate evidence.<br>Control variables to develop a fair test when doing investigations.<br>Explain science observations using evidence.<br>Share explanations with others.<br>Share science concepts and understanding with others using representations.<br>Share science findings in written and graphic representation to others. |
| **Crosscutting Concepts**<br>Cause and Effect<br>Energy and Matter | Identify and describe the causes of phenomena.<br>Describe the conditions necessary for the phenomena to occur.<br>Use evidence to support the explanations for the causes of phenomena.<br>Describe the role of energy in causing changes.<br>Use models to describe the flow of energy. |
| **Disciplinary Core Ideas**<br>Energy - Engineering | Energy flows.<br>Light and heat are produced in stars, including the sun. |

*Table 2. Students Performances*

| Student Science Performances |
|---|
| Student Science Performances<br>*Phenomenon: It feels cooler standing under a tree than in the sunshine*<br><br>*Group Performance*<br>1. *Explore* places outside and areas that are not hot.<br>2. *Ask questions* to *obtain information* about how the sun *causes* you to be hot.<br>3. *Obtain information* by listening to why it is hot on sunny days.<br>4. *Construct an explanation* for why it is hotter in the sun than in the shade.<br>*Class Discussion*<br>5. *Draw a class picture* to show that sunlight *changes* into heat when it shines on you. |
| **Student Science Performances**<br>***Engineering Challenge: Construct a shelter to protect yourself and your friend from a hot day.***<br><br>***Class Discussion about the Engineering Challenge:***<br><br>***Group Performance***<br>6. *Design and build a solution* to help keep you and a friend cooler on a hot sunny day.<br>7. *Test your design* by measuring how well it works. (use a thermometer)<br><br>***Class Discussion:***<br>***Individual Performances***<br>8. *Draw* a picture to show how your solution works to protect you from getting too hot. |

(Teaching Suggestion: Instead of a thermometer, you could use UV beads so students can see the difference between a bead under the shelter and a bead fully exposed to the sunlight. The bead can also be used when exploring the spaces outside, noticing that the UV bead will have a more intense color the warmer it is in the sun-see image:

You can also use a pipe cleaner to make a tiny person figure. String the bead on the figure like clothing so the bead will not get lost. A child in Hawaiian is a keiki—you can call the small figure a Keiki or a friend, hoa.

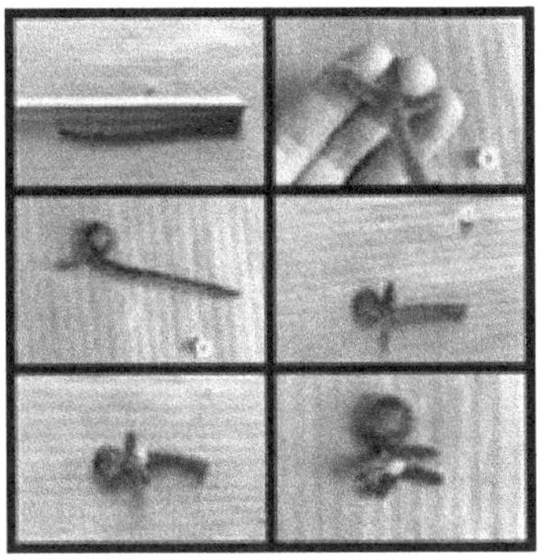

## Class Reading and Student Reading

Suggestion: Use readings from PS3-1. Lesson: Some like it hot

## Alternative Student Reading

The sun gives off energy.
We feel the energy as heat.
We see the energy as sunlight.
Sunlight touches and warms the Earth.

Class Reading:

When I stand in the sun, I get hot.
I can feel the sun warming up my skin.
Sometimes, the heat from the sun makes me sweat.
If I stay in the sun too long, I will get sunburnt.
I can build things that will protect me from the sun.

Can you think of something to build to protect you from the sun?

*Table 3. Link to the Student Design Tool shown below*

| Materials |
|---|
| Wood:<br>Cardboard Index<br>Paper<br>Chopsticks<br>Toothpicks<br>Craft Sticks<br>Cups |
| Plastic:<br>Straws<br>Lego Bricks |
| Other Materials:<br>Felt<br>Fuzzy Wire |

Name: ______________________________

Problem:

It is too hot to play outside without getting sunburnt on hot sunny days.

Design a shelter (structure) for you and your friend to stay calm when playing outside.

Design check:

We have a roof

One person is under our structure

One person is outside of our structure

We drew the sun and the sun's energy in RED

Build! Moreover, test your structure outside in the sun.

**Evaluate:** Did your **structure reduce** the warming effect of the sun?

**Yes!** The bead under the structure **did not** change color, but the outside did.

**Sort of.** The bead under the structure changed color, but the bead outside turned a different color.

**No!** The beads outside and inside both changed color.

Table 4.

| MP NGSSK-PS3-2 | DP | WB |
|---|---|---|
| I can use tools and materials to design and build a structure with shapes to reduce the warming effect of sunlight in an area.<br>If my design did not work, I could explain how to re-design.<br>I worked well with my partner. | I tried to use tools and materials to build a structure that would reduce the warming effect of sunlight in an area, but I needed the teacher to help me build or stay focused.<br>I needed the teacher's help to identify the shapes I was using | I built whatever I felt like, but I did not follow directions and/or needed many reminders on what to do. |

# Chapter 3
# AI Leadership in Schools:
## Driving Innovation and Improvement for Inclusive Education

**Asma Khaleel Abdallah**
https://orcid.org/0000-0003-1028-7618
*Sharjah Education Academy, UAE*

**Mohammed Borhandden Musah**
https://orcid.org/0000-0003-4572-8348
*Bahrain Teachers College, University of Bahrain-Sakhir, Bahrain*

## ABSTRACT

*This chapter explores how artificial intelligence (AI) transforms school leadership by enhancing innovation, inclusivity, and efficiency. AI supports data-driven decisions, personalized learning, and diverse student needs, including those with disabilities, through adaptive technologies. It streamlines administrative tasks and promotes equitable education while addressing challenges such as infrastructure gaps, resistance to change, and ethical issues like data privacy and bias. Using case studies and theories, the chapter examines strategies to balance AI-driven insights with human judgment, ensuring alignment with educational values. By leveraging AI, school leaders can foster creativity, engagement, and inclusivity, preparing students for future challenges. It advocates for thoughtful AI adoption to advance innovation and equity, paving the way for adaptive and inclusive schools.*

DOI: 10.4018/979-8-3373-0573-8.ch003

## INTRODUCTION

In recent years, Artificial Intelligence (AI) has becomes an important tool which has not only transformed education but also various aspects of teaching and learning. AI applications greatly supports in enhancing school leadership as it provides insights and tools that helps the leaders to take better decisions for academic development and achievement. It has been observed that with the help of AI, school leaders receive ultimate support in improving the operational efficiency which at the same time also improves work management (Sharma, Singh, Sharma & Kapoor, 2024). AI is most prominently used in taking better and informed decisions with the help of advanced data analysis. For example, AI tools assist in processing large sets of data related to students, their attendance and behavioral patterns. Hence, based on the data school leaders make significant plans and policies for improvement.

AI also enables personalized learning experiences which improve student's engagement and learning level. It helps the teachers as well as the leaders to understand the personalized learning needs of students and accordingly they ensure content delivery to match the learning needs of each student. Promoting personalized learning is crucial as this is the way to extend support to the students especially to those who need additional help (Famaye, Bailey, Adisa & Irgens, 2024). This shift facilitates inclusive and effective educational system and promotes equality in all aspects. On the other hand, AI not only improves the learning environment but also it stimulates enthusiasm and enhances the creativity of teachers and students which promotes better classroom management. The latest development that has happened in AI world has become the central part of discussion specifically after the launch of ChatGPT that solves various complex problems and amends the nature of learning.

Innovation is essential in educational institutions as it assist the learners to learn constantly in an age where technology prepares them for their future. Considering the views of Akbar, Pranajaya, Nurkadarwati, Hoesny & Mutmainnah, (2024), innovation is important in education because it contributes in creating flexible and engaging learning environment for the students. Traditional education system emphasizes more standardized method of teaching; however innovation leads to new teaching strategies that prepare the students for real-world challenges. For example, implementing new tools and platforms in education enables the students to collaborate with other disciplines; hence eventually fosters critical thinking and problem-solving skills (Aldous & Ismail, 2024).

. On the other hand, inclusivity is equally important aspect in education as that creates environment where all students feel valued and supported. In education institutions, inclusivity not just promotes equity but also encourages diversity and acceptance (Nadeem, 2024). For instance, it has been noticed that when schools are inclusive, students learn better interaction ability with different identities. This helps them develop understanding level and they tend to show more respect towards diversity. The concept of inclusivity ensures to integrate all students into mainstream classroom education which gives everyone equal opportunity to thrive on academic and social level (Ismail & Aldous, 2025).

Innovation and inclusivity is essential in education because it not only drives progress but also it ensures that all students' educational needs are fulfilled. The primary purpose of promoting inclusivity is to ensure that all students receive equal access to quality education despite of the diverse social and cultural backgrounds (Macfarlane, Bolden & Watermeyer, 2024). Inclusivity is one way of facilitating equality by breaking down barriers to learning and ensuring that every student has the chance to succeed. At the same time, inclusive practices also ensure that all students feel valued which is helpful in boosting their engagement level. For example, students with special needs require additional support and motivation so that they can actively participate in learning processes. Thus, in a globalized world, inclusive education system allows the students to learn different cultures and also navigate to embrace multicultural environment. Similarly, innovation also holds crucial importance in teaching and learning as that makes the overall process more adaptable (Sliwka, Klopsch, Beigel & Tung, 2024). With innovative teaching methods, teachers ensure to keep the students engaged and motivated and eventually it improves the learning experiences. Additionally, when education integrates creativity and new technologies, students are more likely to come up with better outcomes.

Objectives of the chapter-

- The need of integrating AI into school leadership
- How AI drives innovation and improvement in inclusive education?
- What are the challenges in adopting AI in schools?

The above mentioned objectives will be discussed in the present study supporting the theoretical framework.

## BACKGROUND

### AI Applications in Education

The integration of artificial intelligence in education is an emerging reality; hence the rapid advancements in AI technology not only offer unprecedented opportunities but also it improves the overall decision-making efficiency. Several technologies that have been in use under AI system are intelligent tutoring system, large scale assessment, adaptive learning and predictive modeling and learning analytics (Punzi et al., 2024). The use of all these technologies transforms the teaching process and helps the students to learn more in a better way. In addition to this, education system is into chatbots and AI-driven virtual tutors that provide assistance to the students related to their queries and problems. This engages them in a real conversation and helps their overall learning level. It also provides additional resources to the students when needed which works as personalized tutoring services.

## AI and Inclusive Education

Artificial intelligence plays a crucial role in enhancing the scope of inclusive education as it ensures to provide innovative solutions to the students that can help in diversified learning. The use of AI ensures that all students have equal access to learning opportunities regardless of their different backgrounds. For instance, AI-powered tools and adaptive learning platforms use algorithms that assess learner's capabilities to learn and accordingly it offers tailored content and feedback (Zhang & Zhang, 2024). In addition to this, AI driven assistant technologies are also helpful in improving accessibility for students who have physical and cognitive disabilities as these tools are useful for students with visual and auditory impairment. AI-based tutoring systems also provide direct support to students who do not have proper accessibility to learning environment and who need additional help. These systems are helpful for them as AI play the role of a human tutor, and it helps the students to get personalized guidance, explanation and problem solving assistance whenever required (Bulathwela et al., 2024). Thus, it can be said that AI is beneficial not only in school leadership areas but also it improves overall education scenario.

## Integrating AI into School Leadership

AI has been integrated into school leadership for a range of purposes and it also presents various opportunities that not only improves administrative efficiency but also enhances decision-making process. There have been some theoretical frameworks that can be integrated into school leadership through leadership theories (Purdy & Williams, 2023). For instance, transformational leadership theory motivates people to achieve higher level of performance which in turn results in innovative practices. The application of transformational leadership can act as a driving force for school leaders by which they can promote visionary change by crafting long-term strategies to improve learning outcomes. This way school leaders can integrate technologies and foster innovation that will prepare the students to learn in a better way.

Also, by utilizing AI tools, teachers can provide personalized feedback to the students through which learning outcomes and achievement can be improved. In educational domain, AI systems are implemented to facilitate professional development in teachers which assist them to achieve the goals of continuous growth and innovation (Sappaile et al., 2024). In a nutshell, it can be said that artificial intelligence helps in transforming the ways teachers teach and students learn which automatically improves school's functions. It is undeniable that integrating digital technologies develops opportunities for school development and helps the students to learn in improved environment. Therefore, it not only drives innovation but also it makes the education entity competitive.

## MAIN FOCUS OF THE CHAPTER

### Benefits of Adopting AI in Schools

The arrival of artificial intelligence in education system is not just a technological breakthrough, but it has improved the current education system to a new extent. This integration of technology not only changes the way student learn in classrooms, but it also brings new opportunities in overall academic sector. Therefore, the integration of AI in education realm has brought a paradigm shift that brings developments and improvements (Nurhaliza & Setiawan, 2024). For example, AI helps in personalization of learning, it understands the learning level of each student and accordingly it brings study materials to make the learning process easier. This means that every student has the opportunity to learn at their own pace considering the strength and weaknesses.

In addition to this, AI is also beneficial in automating administrative tasks which not only reduces the workload and administrative burden, but also it allows the educators to focus more on teaching with new methods and strategies. AI is also beneficial in giving access to students to high quality educational resources and materials, regardless of the economic status; hence, it provides easy accessibility to all students (Judijanto, Atsani & Chadijah, 2024). In addition to this, teachers are also using AI to assess each student's progress and accordingly they provide real time feedback that helps the students and the parents to identify the strengths as well as areas for improvement.

For example, teachers are using automated grading system through which they assess assignments and tests which not only save their time but give them more time to interact with students and accordingly they plan more engaging lessons. Further, AI tools are also beneficial in managing schedules and tracking student's progress level; thus it identifies patterns of learning ((Alqodsi & Aljahoori, 2023 & Begum, 2024). AI powered tools and programs are also helpful in developing learning opportunities for students, for example, ChatGPT is beneficial for students as it quickly translate materials to another language which helps students to understand the content in easy way. Also, it helps in tailoring the projects according to student's skills and interests. Summing up, it helps in developing individualization of learning program.

## Challenges in Adopting AI in Schools

***Infrastructure***- Though AI is beneficial in a lot of areas, it also comes with many challenges and potential drawbacks, which is essential to emphasize. For example, often schools do not have proper infrastructure facilities to implement AI technologies in the institution. As AI is dependent on technology, some schools lack in necessary technological resources that support AI application. Also, lack of internet accessibility and reliability can create challenges while using AI in the schools ((Alqodsi, 2021 & Crompton, Jones & Burke, 2024). Some schools do not have proper connectivity, therefore, adopting AI becomes challenging for them and it affects remote learning and other teaching processes. Most of the schools still follow the traditional patterns of learning and they do not have the upgraded technological devices and platforms; hence, they struggle in adopting AI tools.

Furthermore, many schools do not have a comprehensive and secure data infrastructure, therefore they are unable to store and manage student and other related data effectively. Apparently, technology comes with privacy and security issues and schools that do not have proper technological resources often experience challenges in data management area. Another issue that appears is related to finance, cost and funding. In order to implement AI in the school system, it requires huge financial investment and often schools are provided with limited budgets (Familoni & Onyebuchi, 2024). Therefore, in many underfunded district schools, it has been observed that, due to lack of financial resources, schools are unable to adopt AI technologies. Also the cost of maintenance is high in AI systems and schools with confined IT budgets experience the struggles.

***Resistance to change***- Most of the teachers and educators are comfortable in their traditional way of teaching hence this becomes the primary reason they resist in adopting AI. Due to lack of understanding or fear of being replaced by technology or machines, often teachers fail to show their interest in technological adaptation. Also, some educators believe that the traditional way of teaching is better than the modern technological teaching; hence, this becomes another reason to resistance. Undoubtedly, the traditional way of teaching engages students and teachers more in the process of learning and helps and helps them to develop effective relationship (Jafari & Keykha, 2024). However, the use of technology is also beneficial, but most of the teachers do not realize the importance of implementing it in the process of teaching and learning due to lack of awareness.

Therefore, they resist in implementing AI in classroom teachings. Another reason of resistance is teachers are not properly equipped with the skills and knowledge that is necessary to effectively use AI in education. Hence, due to lack of understanding about the tools they are unable to adopt them in the classroom learning according to the needs of the students. As per the views of Lérias, Guerra & Ferreira (2024), it is important to create a balance between traditional teaching and AI based teaching as it ensures successful implementation of AI tools and strategies in the process of learning. Many teachers also believe that adopting technology will reduce human interaction in the classroom and that will affect student's cognitive skills. However, technology should be taken as a complement and not be considered as a substitute. Considering the above discussion, Camilleri, (2024) says that due to continuous integration of AI and technology there is a risk that both educators and students will become too dependent on technology and that will eventually affect their power skills.

***Training***- Most of the teachers is unaware of the use of updated technologies and strategies due to lack of training and development opportunities. Schools with limited budgets spend less resource on teacher's professional training; therefore, it keeps the educators unaware of the things happening in competitive world. Therefore, due to lack of expertise, teachers are unable to integrate AI tools in the teaching methods. According to Khreisat et al., (2024), professional development for teachers should be an essential aspect in education system as that prepares the educators to understand the recent trends of teaching and accordingly it improves the overall learning experience of both students and teachers. Apparently teachers play the most prominent role in improving the process of teaching; however without proper knowledge and skills they might struggle to use AI tools. For example, proper training is required to use automated grading systems as well as virtual teaching assistants as without specific knowledge, educators cannot optimally use the resources.

Furthermore, it is also vital for the teachers to understand the effective integration of technology with curriculum. Often teachers struggle in incorporating AI into classroom teaching because of their limited understanding about its significance. Proper training enables the educators to personalize and adapt AI systems in terms of supporting students in challenging areas. Teachers must continuously learn to customize and create differentiated learning pathways for students to make them more competitive and creative in academic area (Al-Zahrani & Alasmari, 2024). However, it has also been observed that while some educators have high teaching potential, integrating AI technologies in classroom is new for them. Therefore, it is essential for the school leaders to engage the teachers in learning digital skills so that teaching pedagogy can be improved. Henceforth, there should be appropriate integration between human resources and technological resources in academic realm.

***Accessibility issues***- Apparently, AI is entirely integrated with technology; therefore, often challenges appear when people do not have proper accessibility to technological resources. For instance, many students do not the access to the devices or technologies to engage with AI tools; hence, it creates educational gaps between students. Also, some of the students need special assistance directly from educators which AI cannot provide; therefore, students with special needs may not always receive benefits from AI in the area of customized learning plans. In addition to this, Famaye, Bailey, Adisa & Irgens, (2024) says that most of the parents keep the students away from technology due to fear of over dependence on technology. Excessive use of AI in the classroom can affect the problem solving and critical thinking ability; henceforth, considering these factors people often minimize the usage of AI. Furthermore, AI systems also struggle in addressing social and emotional learning needs of students which has a direct impact on overall growth level. Most educators believe that overuse of AI could replace the value of direct communication.

## Ethical Concerns

AI systems contains enormous amount of data which not only includes detailed information of study materials but also contains sensitive information about students. When schools use AI for data management, it is must for them to focus on privacy regulations and security to safeguard the information. As per the study of Fullan, Azorín, Harris & Jones (2024), AI has many benefits; still it comes with certain ethical and pedagogical concerns that require consideration. AI systems are trained on large datasets, and these datasets may contain both implicit and explicit biases. As a result, the AI can inadvertently perpetuate discrimination, particularly against the students with special needs. This can also lead to inequalities; hence, it can affect the concept of equal opportunities and fairness in education. In addition to this, artificial intelligence has a remarkable ability to generate convincing yet false information, which can create hallucinations. Therefore, these fabricated details may seem reasonable and reliable at first glance, but they are entirely inaccurate upon closer examination (Le-Nguyen & Tran, 2024). AI-generated content could be unreliable; therefore educators and students need to evaluate the responses prior putting it into use.

Another important concern for AI is data privacy and protection management. In higher education, AI is used as a tool to collect information and personal as well as sensitive data about student's academic performance, achievements and their behavioral patterns. The information that is collected through AI tools is used to specify student's performance (Patel, 2024). Therefore, the education institutions that implement AI systems are required to ensure that the collected data is used only for the intended purpose with authorized parties. Also, educators are required to seek consent prior using the data. Artificial intelligence is a trained program; hence, it produces information based on the trained information. Often, using such sources can lead to biased data which can generate stereotypes and social inequalities. Furthermore, according to the study of Abulibdeh, Zaidan & Abulibdeh (2024), AI can also generate misinformation as sometimes the data has errors and is also outdated. Therefore, it is essential for both students and teachers to be cautious while using the information produced through AI. On the other hand, one of the common issues is use of AI can promote cheating as many students use ChatGPT to write their essays and homework. This affects not only student's thinking ability but also it makes them dependent on technology. However, there are several AI programs that help the teachers to detect the authenticity of projects and assignments (Alfredo et al., 2024).

Though AI has impressive capabilities, the models often lack in comprehending the meaning of the language they process. They solve the complexity of the data but also it could lack clarity and authenticity as AI platforms are manually trained. Moreover, the article of Punzi, Pellungrini, Setzu, Giannotti & Pedreschi, (2024) contends that education is the process of learning new skills and knowledge; therefore it must be collective process where exchange of ideas happen between students and educators. Classroom learning not only fosters interaction among students, but also it gives the exposure to learn with diversified views. The same concept applies to student-teacher relationship as they get to develop a bond that is respectful and trustworthy and holds crucial importance in learning. Many parents have the concerns of isolated education which makes the students spend most of their time interacting with virtual assistant instead of educators (Milberg, 2024).

It is imperative to implement AI in proper way otherwise it could widen the threats of digital divide. Generative AI aims to be everywhere; therefore, it is vital to have strong internet connection and digital device which is not common with all students. For example, many students from underprivileged areas do not have digital accessibility; hence, this confines their reach to technology. Also, some of the educational institutions lack in financial and technological resources which is the reason they are unable to provide additional support in student's learning (Badawy, Al Ali, Khan, Dashti & Al Katheeri, (2024). The disparities are everywhere both in rural and urban areas; therefore, connectivity and accessibility remains the major obstacles while using AI platforms in learning. For example, families or students who cannot afford internet facilities always experience challenges in learning with others. This difference creates barriers in equal education. Additionally, most of the students with special needs require direct or interactive assistance from educators wherein technology comes with no benefit for them (Karakose & Tülübas, 2024). Thus, complete dependency on technology can affect these students's learning needs.

In education domain, teachers are using AI tools not only to prepare assignments but also for grading and feedback work. However, reports derived from AI tools do not necessarily contain the accurate information about student's progress and achievement; therefore the chances of misrepresentation are also higher. This can create differences between teacher and student's view about overall learning process (Ghamrawi, Shal & Ghamrawi, 2024). Also, if not reviewed properly teachers can create reports based on biased data which can impact student's overall progress level. Privacy and protection is another aspect that requires special consideration as AI contains all data related to student's personal and academic areas. The teachers should consider keeping the data safe and protected in database systems so that only authorized people can access it and share with students for feedback.

## Balancing Human and AI Decision-Making in Leadership

In the era of technology, AI is used as a data driven decision making tool which not only helps the entity to become competitive, but also it fosters innovation and growth level. However, it is also important to realize that AI is not replacing human decision making process. It is simply an advanced tool that helps the decision makers or leaders to take informed decision based on vast amount of data (Lukowski, 2024). In current scenario, AI has become a critical tool in leadership as it influences the leaders to take strategic and effective decisions. For example, AI has the ability to analyze large amount of data sets, which helps the leaders to take data driven decisions which are faster and accurate. Also, leaders are using AI to simulate different scenarios, which helps them to come up with potential outcomes and eventually enables in taking proactive decisions (Shivashankar & Bakthavatchaalam, 2024). Therefore, this evolution helps the leaders to take decision based on new data and recent market conditions.

In the area of education, leaders who implement AI become the facilitators of innovations wherein they come up with new strategies and techniques to improve the educational standards. For example, implementing AI in classroom learning helps the teachers to use current as well as updated models to teach the theoretical framework. This builds the understanding level of students and sharpens their critical thinking ability (Badawy et al., 2024). However, educational leaders must ensure that AI systems should be designed and operated in fair and justified manner so that it can promote equity and inclusivity for all students. Undoubtedly, AI provides valuable insights and support; however it is the accountability of the leaders to ensure that decisions are taken based on ethics, human values and school needs. For instance, school leaders can use AI for data analysis and other operational tasks, but the decisions should align with school's mission and values. In addition to this, AI can be used for data-driven decisions as it can track student's performance and weakness areas (Karakose & Tülübas, 2024). For example, considering student's report school leaders can identify the areas students are struggling in and accordingly they can collaborate with teachers and educators to make improvements.

Apparently, artificial intelligence has the potential to assess teaching effectiveness considering the performance analytics; however, school leaders should take the initiative to provide appropriate and constructive feedback in the area of improvement. For instance, leaders focus should not be only on information produced through AI but they should communicate and interact with the teachers while giving feedback (Ghamrawi, Shal & Ghamrawi, 2024). This could foster a positive working environment for the educators where they can feel valued and important. Even though AI has the potential to plan the development actions, it is still recommended to the leaders to engage the teachers and facilitators to develop and implement professional development plans considering the areas of improvements and additional learning needs. Furthermore, AI can also be used for decision support; nevertheless the ultimate decision should be taken by human leaders only (Nadeem, 2024). In order to balance AI and human decision, leaders are suggested to use the technology to get better ideas and perspectives however the decisions should be taken considering school's unique context.

It is crucial to understand that AI and human leadership are not confined as AI improves decision making efficiency but leader has to consider emotional intelligence aspect while taking decisions. AI can make leadership process successful when human leaders integrate AI driven insights to connect and make decisions in the institution. This helps the leaders to motivate and inspire people which further engage people in organizational areas. Prior taking decisions, leaders must ensure to promote fairness by validating AI outputs with real-world outcomes and it should also be integrated with ethical standards. Contrary to this, the study of Abdallah et al., (2024) reflects that emotional intelligence is one of the important aspects of leadership as it develops the ability to comprehend and manage the emotional aspects between people. Also, emotional connect is important especially between school leaders and teachers as it promotes trust and mutual relationship while undertaking important decisions (Ismail, 2024).

Therefore, from the discussion it can be said that it is important for the school leaders to create balance between human and AI- empowered decisions in terms of fostering the capabilities of each concept. On the other hand, it is equally crucial for the leaders to have a proper structure and framework to balance organizational tasks with AI and human resources. For example, leaders should establish clear governance and structure with the help of AI and accordingly action plan can be implemented (Abedi & Ametepey, 2024). It works more like a holistic approach wherein the leader ensures that the decision-making process is efficient as well as aligned with organizational values and goals.

## Comparison with Traditional Leadership Practices

The landscape of leadership is changing due to advent of artificial intelligence; hence, a lot of transformation is happening in the realm of education. Traditional leadership practices are based on typical leadership philosophies and principles as well as human intuition wherein leaders take decisions considering the experience and learning level (Ali et al., 2024). However, with the help of AI, leaders are able to receive data-driven and technological assistance while making any decision. In traditional practices, leaders are the primary tool of communicating information to the team but with AI, data can be easily transferred in larger teams without any delay.

Also, this helps the leaders to respond quickly and appropriately to the changes happening in the market place. Integration of AI in leadership practices makes educational environment more inclusive and equitable as it assist the leaders to come up with new practices that involves all students equally in the mainstream education (Onesi-Ozigagun, Ololade, Eyo-Udo & Ogundipe, 2024). Comparing to traditional leadership practices, it was difficult for the leaders to keep track of team members' performance; however, through AI models and tools performance can be analyzed whenever required without putting efforts on manual monitoring.

The decision making process in traditional leadership is based on the way leaders judge and think and also with the inputs derived from the team members. Historical knowledge and personal experience is the base by which decisions are taken under traditional leadership. On the other side AI systems helps the contemporary leaders to analyze vast amount of data from different aspects which improves decision making ability and also minimizes risks to a greater extent (Jaboob, Hazaimeh & Al-Ansi, 2024). In AI leadership, leaders emphasize more on collaborative style in which teamwork is given importance so that all the associated people can work and accomplish goals together. However, in traditional leadership leaders focus remains on discipline and order in terms of creating conducive learning environment. Therefore, it is believed that traditional leadership practices focuses more on developing communication which can help the students to learn in diversified environment.

Traditionally, the way of leading the teams is different as school leaders used to implement established systems that provide stable outcomes. Stability in the system increases sense of security and assists both students and teachers to focus on continuous learning. Under the concept leaders ensure that changes are implemented thoughtfully considering all aspects which eventually lead to create a climate of trust (Wardat, Tashtoush, AlAli & Saleh, 2024). The roles of leaders are clearly defined in traditional leadership practices; hence, it gives clarity about accountability. For example, principal, supervisors and teachers have their duties and are responsible to amend school's performance through undertaking decisions to improve the teaching and learning standards.

## SOLUTIONS AND RECOMMENDATIONS

### Strategies for Addressing Challenges

One of the major challenges that school experience in adopting AI is related to infrastructure, that is, most of the schools do not have proper infrastructure facilities to implement AI technology. Therefore, it is recommended to the school and educational institutions to continuously focus on improving infrastructure facilities, such as proper internet accessibility and other technological resources to uplift the overall school operations (Ali et al., 2024). Upgrading the infrastructure of the school is essential in a lot of areas; hence, schools are recommended to invest in improving infrastructure facilities, which not only helps the students to get access to additional learning resources and materials, but also it helps the schools to safeguard diversified data in an effective way. Schools can also seek assistance from the district authorities in terms of adopting new AI technologies and systems (Aldous & Ismail, 2025).

It is also essential for the school leaders to communicate about the importance of implementing AI in teaching and education system. Also, the educators are suggested to find a balance between traditional way of teaching and modern technological teaching (Jaboob, Hazaimeh & Al-Ansi, 2024). In addition to this, teacher training and professional development should be considered an important aspect in educational setting in which teachers and educators should be given continuous training and coaching about the adoption of new technologies and methods that can be used to make the process of teaching more effective as well as competitive. Henceforth, prior implementing AI tools and strategies in the teaching process, it is essential for the teachers to undergo proper training to make the best use of it. School leaders should emphasize the importance of training as it is a crucial process that prepares the teachers to uplift the standard of teaching and eventually this has a direct impact on student's academic learning (Wardat, Tashtoush, AlAli & Saleh, 2024). Furthermore, the teachers are recommended to guide the students not to become dependent on technology by addressing the right use of AI platforms and systems. Also, students with confined technological resources should be given additional assistance by providing them accessibility to different sources.

### Guidance for AI Training Programs for School Leaders

Apparently, the significance of artificial intelligence in education is evident, therefore it is essential for the school leaders to get training about the adoption of AI in school systems as it leverages decision making process and helps in providing personalized learning support to the students. It also optimizes operational efficiency;

therefore, school leaders get ample amount of time to invest in other activities that can improve overall academic aspects (Lérias, Guerra & Ferreira, 2024). Prior to organizing AI training programs, it is essential for the leaders to get clear overview about the systems and how they work. However, it is also imperative for the school leaders to analyze and emphasize the risks and challenges that come with the implementation of AI in school systems (Ismail, 2024).

As per the views of Al-Zahrani & Alasmari, (2024), school leaders should encourage the ongoing adaptation of AI technology considering the recent trends in education industry. For example, leaders are recommended to collaborate with other experts and specialists to learn more about AI and its significance in diversified areas. Since school leaders are accountable to facilitate improvements; therefore, it is also crucial for them to continually measure the success of AI tools and the way they improve student outcomes and school efficiency. Assessing the performance is essential as it determines the continuity of AI systems. Moreover, school leaders should get connected with industry experts and they should also get training regarding improving academic dimensions through adopting AI and different tools. This could improve not only the leadership aspects but also it will improve the teaching quality in the education institutions.

## Ethical Guidelines for AI Use in Schools

Under the ethical considerations, it is important for the school leaders to maintain transparency and accountability about how AI tools will collect and store data. Maintaining transparency about the process will help in building trust with students and teachers. Also the AI system should maintain fairness and non-discrimination, and it should be regularly evaluated to analyze the outcomes it generates. Biased algorithms can create inequality in education; therefore it is vital for the school leaders to ensure that AI systems are fair and just to implement. In addition to this, prior implementing AI tools, school leaders should ensure to make AI accessibility to all students regardless of their differences. Considering the views of Khreisat et al., (2024), AI should be considered a tool that supports the teacher in improving or amending their teaching strategies; however, teachers are required to retain control over the decisions they take in classroom management (Ismail et. al., 2023 & Aldous & Ismail, 2024.)

School leaders should also ensure that AI powered grading system is designed in a way which minimizes bias and it correctly evaluates students' achievement level. Hence the process of evaluation must be based upon the learning level of students, the skills they develop over time and knowledge they gained in different academic subjects. They should also take into account the ethical considerations while making informed decisions about AI adoption (Famaye, Bailey, Adisa & Irgens, 2024). For example, there should not be any bias in AI algorithms and there should be proper management about privacy concerns and other areas. The data related to students and other areas should be protected with defined laws and AI related regulations (Alqodsi & Gura, 2023 & Alqodsi, et al., 2024). Also, it is important for the leaders to address how AI will help in bridging equity gaps in education. This is one of the most important concerns in education domain.

## Case Studies of Successful AI Implementation in Inclusive Education Settings

### Case Study 1- University of Alicante (Spain)

With the help of artificial intelligence, the university improved accessibility for students with special needs as often (students with special needs) experienced challenges in accessing educational materials. Therefore, considering the issue, the University developed an AI-powered application "Help Me See" through which visually impaired students can derive assistance from machine learning (Universidad de Alicante, 2024). With the help of this app, students are able to comprehend the course materials and subjects as AI narrates objects and texts in clear form. This built student's engagement and participation in mainstream education and this way the institution was able to enhance inclusivity and accessibility for all students.

### Case Study 2- Beijing No.4 High School (China)

Beijing No.4 is one of the high performing schools in China which implemented AI to encourage student-centered approach that helps all the students even to those struggling because of geographical location. It partnered with Squirrel AI which is an adaptive learning system that is typically used to provide personalized learning assistance to students in math and science (Xinhua, 2024). The platform is implemented so that it can analyze each student's performance and accordingly lesson plans can be prepared for advanced learning experience. It helped the teachers to emphasize on mentoring the students and develop skill level as the adaptive system reduced teacher's manual work burden.

### Case Study 3- The University of Sydney

The University implemented AI in the school system particularly to enrich personalized learning experience of students in different disciplines. The main area of attention was to improve the educational outcomes by preparing content considering individual learning needs of students. It implemented Smart Sparrow platform which enabled the teachers to create adaptive learning platforms (UNSW Sydney, 2024). It not only provides additional resource material accessibility but also focused on amending each student's overall progress and achievements. Implementation of the AI system generated opportunities for students to derive personalized learning experience keeping into accounts both strengths and weaknesses.

## FUTURE RESEARCH DIRECTIONS

In education domain, the demand for personalized learning experience is increasing; therefore this leads the education institutions to adopt e-learning platforms as well as digital tools to modernize the ways of learning. This helps the students to access plenty of research materials and coursework which makes the overall learning experience dynamic (Milberg, 2024). Considering the emerging trends, artificial intelligence assists the teachers to generate precise and constructive feedback which not only improves student's academic outcomes but also highlights the areas of further improvement. With the help of AI assessment and grading systems, teachers can keep track of student's performance and recommend necessary changes in the learning styles.

The present study has described the implications of AI on leadership; however, it is essential to emphasize how AI can assist school leaders to embrace inclusivity for all students in mainstream education. For instance, with the help of AI, leaders and teachers can provide equal as well as additional support in terms of educational content to all the students (including with special needs). This creates the platform for people with special needs to receive equal access of all learning materials. AI improves administrative efficiency; hence leaders get enough time to focus on other developmental activities to amend school's academic standards.

As AI continues to progress, it offers new opportunities in education domain which adjusts students' learning based on their interest and competencies (Aldous & Ismail, 2025). . School leaders can also opt for proactive intervention predictive models to analyze student's performance trends and accordingly targeted support, or assistance can be rendered. Also, AI algorithms can make the learning process more personalized by simplifying complex and challenging tasks. It also ensures that each student gets requisite support to develop the skill level. There should be an integration of emotional and social learning support through AI systems to detect stress or boredom. It enables as well as prepares the teachers to provide necessary emotional intervention supporting overall mental and social health. Hence, education institutions can promote AI mentors which digitally help students practice self-regulation and empathy.

## CONCLUSION

From the above study, it has been found out that education industry is implementing AI in the systems as it is capable of performing tasks which usually require human intelligence and efforts. Incorporating AI in educational institution not only helps the students, but also the teachers and other staff members in a lot of areas. It also plays crucial role in driving innovation in the schools. For example, implementing AI tools and platforms helps the teachers to learn new teaching methods and strategies to improve classroom teaching and student's overall learning experience. This not only develops overall academic aspects, but also helps the student to excel in those subjects where they struggle the most. Also, embracing new technologies helps the teachers to learn new methods through which they can solve complex issues of students. This not only empowers students learning, but also assists the teachers to grow professionally.

In a globalized world, it is important for the education institutions to adapt to new changes and recent trends to keep the education services competitive. With the help of AI, schools have been using several technologies such as tutoring systems and assessment systems which helps the students to get personalized learning experience. Since AI provides 24*7 services, therefore it is quite beneficial for students especially when they are unable to reach the teachers. This saves most of the time instead of waiting for the teachers to explain or solve the problems. Also, with the help of AI, students are able to learn lessons with new as well as diversified explanations which improve their intellectual skills. Further, the study made it evident that AI not only makes the learning process interesting but also it keeps the students engaged in learning new concepts.

Furthermore, AI plays an important role in keeping all the students together in mainstream education as it considers all people equally. It does not differentiate; hence, provide same assistance to everyone regardless of their challenges and difficulties. For example, students with special needs can make use of AI to get repetitive content without any restriction or limitation. Using AI helps the educators to ensure that all students learning needs are being fulfilled as per their areas of preferences. For example, through AI teachers can assess the capabilities of learners and accordingly further learning plans can be prepared.

Also, it is essential for the school leaders to emphasize on proactive strategies not only to address challenges but to create positive learning environment in the school. For example, with the help of proactive strategies, teachers can create routines, and accordingly they can communicate the expectations with the students, hence students are less likely to engage in negative behavior. This sets a positive classroom environment and the chances of misbehavior lessen. In addition to this, productive strategies also support better academic performance, for example, teachers, can identify students and their issues where they are struggling, and accordingly assistance can be provided. Often students feel overwhelmed when they have assignments and deadlines to follow however, proactive approaches give them clear structure and it also helps in getting personalized support, which reduces stress and anxiety. This leads to positive environment, which improves student's learning level. Furthermore, teachers who focus on proactive strategies are able to address students' mental health challenges in a proper way through conducting regular check-ups and through creating a supportive classroom environment considering requisite emotional support.

## REFERENCES


Abedi, E. A., & Ametepey, A. K. (2024). Leadership practices and support structures enabling teachers' informal learning for educational technology use: An appreciative inquiry approach. *Professional Development in Education*, •••, 1–15. DOI: 10.1080/19415257.2024.2330973

Abulibdeh, A., Zaidan, E., & Abulibdeh, R. (2024). Navigating the confluence of artificial intelligence and education for sustainable development in the era of industry 4.0: Challenges, opportunities, and ethical dimensions. *Journal of Cleaner Production*, *437*, 140527. DOI: 10.1016/j.jclepro.2023.140527

Akbar, S., Pranajaya, S. A., Nurkadarwati, N., Hoesny, R., & Mutmainnah, I. (2024). Leadership Dynamics in The Era of Educational Transformation: Integrating The Concept of Adaptable Leadership in Sustainable Educational Administration. *International Journal of Teaching and Learning*, *2*(1), 223–235.

Al-Zahrani, A. M., & Alasmari, T. M. (2024). Exploring the impact of artificial intelligence on higher education: The dynamics of ethical, social, and educational implications. *Humanities & Social Sciences Communications*, *11*(1), 1–12. DOI: 10.1057/s41599-024-03432-4

Aldous, S. M., & Ismail, G. (2024). Academics in Exile: Navigating New Educational Landscapes Amidst Displacement and Uncertainty. In E. Sengupta & A. Arnthorsson (Eds.), Resilience of Educators in Extraordinary Circumstances: War, Disaster, and Emergencies (pp. 9-28). IGI Global Scientific Publishing. DOI: 10.4018/979-8-3693-1483-8.ch002

Aldous, S. M., & Ismail, G. A. (2024). Changing and Adapting Curriculum While Teaching: Narratives From Afghan Academics and Students. In E. Sengupta & A. Arnthorsson (Eds.), Resilience of Educators in Extraordinary Circumstances: War, Disaster, and Emergencies (pp. 54-73). IGI Global Scientific Publishing. DOI: 10.4018/979-8-3693-1483-8.ch004

Aldous, S. M., & Ismail, G. A. (2024). Digital Echoes: Navigating Social Media's Labyrinth of Prejudices and Cultural Stereotypes. In Barreto, I., & Roman Etxebarrieta, G. (Eds.), *Transformative Intercultural Global Education* (pp. 77–98). IGI Global Scientific Publishing., DOI: 10.4018/979-8-3693-2057-0.ch005

Aldous, S. M., & Ismail, G. A. (2025). Safeguarding the Future: Integrating Student Safety Into Sustainable Education Practices. In Legal Frameworks and Educational Strategies for Sustainable Development (pp. 367-396). IGI Global. https://DOI: 10.4018/979-8-3693-2987-0.ch018

Aldous, S. M., & Ismail, G. A. (2025). AI for Sustainable Emergency Preparedness and Response in Schools. In Tariq, M., & Sergio, R. (Eds.), *Convergence of AI, Education, and Business for Sustainability* (pp. 51–74). IGI Global Scientific Publishing., DOI: 10.4018/979-8-3373-1917-9.ch003

Alfredo, R., Echeverria, V., Jin, Y., Yan, L., Swiecki, Z., Gašević, D., & Martinez-Maldonado, R. (2024). Human-centred learning analytics and AI in education: A systematic literature review. *Computers and Education: Artificial Intelligence*, 100215.

Ali, O., Murray, P. A., Momin, M., Dwivedi, Y. K., & Malik, T. (2024). The effects of artificial intelligence applications in educational settings: Challenges and strategies. *Technological Forecasting and Social Change*, *199*, 123076. DOI: 10.1016/j.techfore.2023.123076

Alqodsi, E. M. (2021). The right to pre-contractual information in e-commerce consumer contracts: UAE law and comparative perspectives. *Journal of Legal. Ethical and Regulatory Issues*, *24*(2), 1–16.

Alqodsi, E. M., & Aljahoori, S. A. (2023). Legal Protection of the Right to Education for People With Special Needs: Zayed Higher Organization for People of Determination as a Model. In Efthymiou, E. (Ed.), *Inclusive Phygital Learning Approaches and Strategies for Students With Special Needs* (pp. 199–213). IGI Global Scientific Publishing., DOI: 10.4018/978-1-6684-8504-0.ch010

Alqodsi, E. M., & Gura, D. (2023). High tech and legal challenges: Artificial intelligence-caused damage regulation. *Cogent Social Sciences*, *9*(2), 2270751. Advance online publication. DOI: 10.1080/23311886.2023.2270751

Alqodsi, E. M., Jadalhaq, I. M., Hadi El Maknouzi, M. E., & Abdulhay, I. E. (2024). Navigating the Legal Landscape: AI Adoption in Education and Teacher Responsibilities. In Abdallah, A., Alkaabi, A., & Al-Riyami, R. (Eds.), *Cutting-Edge Innovations in Teaching, Leadership, Technology, and Assessment* (pp. 212–230). IGI Global Scientific Publishing., DOI: 10.4018/979-8-3693-0880-6.ch015

Badawy, H. R., Al Ali, F. M., Khan, A. G. Y., Dashti, S. H., & Al Katheeri, S. A. (2024). Transforming Education Through Technology and School Leadership. In *Cutting-Edge Innovations in Teaching, Leadership, Technology, and Assessment* (pp. 182-194). IGI Global. DOI: 10.4018/979-8-3693-0880-6.ch013

Begum, I. U. (2024). Role of Artificial Intelligence in Higher Education-An Empirical Investigation. [IRJAEM]. *International Research Journal on Advanced Engineering and Management*, *2*(03), 49–53.

Bulathwela, S., Pérez-Ortiz, M., Holloway, C., Cukurova, M., & Shawe-Taylor, J. (2024). Artificial intelligence alone will not democratise education: On educational inequality, techno-solutionism and inclusive tools. *Sustainability (Basel)*, *16*(2), 781. DOI: 10.3390/su16020781

Camilleri, M. A. (2024). Artificial intelligence governance: Ethical considerations and implications for social responsibility. *Expert Systems: International Journal of Knowledge Engineering and Neural Networks*, *41*(7), e13406. DOI: 10.1111/exsy.13406

Crompton, H., Jones, M. V., & Burke, D. (2024). Affordances and challenges of artificial intelligence in K-12 education: A systematic review. *Journal of Research on Technology in Education*, *56*(3), 248–268. DOI: 10.1080/15391523.2022.2121344

Famaye, T., Bailey, C. S., Adisa, I., & Irgens, G. A. (2024). What Makes ChatGPT Dangerous Is Also What Makes It Special": High-School Student Perspectives on the Integration or Ban of Artificial Intelligence in Educational Contexts. *International Journal of Technology in Education*, *7*(2), 174–199. DOI: 10.46328/ijte.651

Familoni, B. T., & Onyebuchi, N. C. (2024). Advancements and challenges in AI integration for technical literacy: A systematic review. *Engineering Science & Technology Journal*, *5*(4), 1415–1430. DOI: 10.51594/estj.v5i4.1042

Fullan, M., Azorín, C., Harris, A., & Jones, M. (2024). Artificial intelligence and school leadership: Challenges, opportunities and implications. *School Leadership & Management*, *44*(4), 339–346. DOI: 10.1080/13632434.2023.2246856

Ghamrawi, N., Shal, T., & Ghamrawi, N. A. (2024). School Leadership 4.0: Are We Ready? In *IoT, AI, and ICT for educational applications: Technologies to enable education for all* (pp. 173–190). Springer Nature Switzerland. DOI: 10.1007/978-3-031-50139-5_9

Ismail, G. A., & Aldous, S. M. (2025). AI-Driven Health and Safety Management in School Facilities. In Tariq, M., & Sergio, R. (Eds.), *Convergence of AI, Education, and Business for Sustainability* (pp. 25–50). IGI Global Scientific Publishing., DOI: 10.4018/979-8-3373-1917-9.ch002

Ismail, O. A. (2024). Digital Transformation in Education: Navigating the Challenges and Opportunities of Remote Learning. In Gray, S., & Purpuri, L. (Eds.), *Building Resilient Education Models Post Crisis* (pp. 133–149). IGI Global Scientific Publishing., DOI: 10.4018/979-8-3693-8125-0.ch007

Ismail, O. A., AlRiyami, R. M., & Alhosani, M. (2023). The art of assuring quality education: Internal approaches and best practices. In *Restructuring Leadership for School Improvement and Reform* (pp. 182–201). IGI Global., DOI: 10.4018/978-1-6684-7818-9.ch010

Ismail, O. S. (2024). Empowering the Modern Learning Ecosystem: Integrative Approaches for a Holistic Educational Experience. In Al Husseiny, F., & Munna, A. (Eds.), *Revitalizing the Learning Ecosystem for Modern Students* (pp. 145–167). IGI Global Scientific Publishing., DOI: 10.4018/979-8-3693-4103-2.ch008

Jaboob, M., Hazaimeh, M., & Al-Ansi, A. M. (2024). Integration of generative AI techniques and applications in student behavior and cognitive achievement in Arab higher education. *International Journal of Human-Computer Interaction*, •••, 1–14.

Jafari, F., & Keykha, A. (2024). Identifying the opportunities and challenges of artificial intelligence in higher education: A qualitative study. *Journal of Applied Research in Higher Education*, *16*(4), 1228–1245. DOI: 10.1108/JARHE-09-2023-0426

Judijanto, L., Atsani, M. R., & Chadijah, S. (2024). Trends In The Development Of Artificial Intelligence-Based Technology In Education. *International Journal of Teaching and Learning*, *2*(6), 1722–1723.

Karakose, T., & Tülübas, T. (2024). School Leadership and Management in the Age of Artificial Intelligence (AI): Recent Developments and Future Prospects. *Educational Process: International Journal*, *13*(1), 7–14. DOI: 10.22521/edupij.2024.131.1

Khreisat, M. N., Khilani, D., Rusho, M. A., Karkkulainen, E. A., Tabuena, A. C., & Uberas, A. D. (2024). Ethical Implications Of AI Integration In Educational Decision Making: Systematic Review. *Educational Administration: Theory and Practice*, *30*(5), 8521–8527.

Le-Nguyen, H. T., & Tran, T. T. (2024). Generative AI in terms of Its ethical problems for both teachers and learners: Striking a balance. In *Generative AI in Teaching and Learning* (pp. 144–173). IGI Global.

Lérias, E., Guerra, C., & Ferreira, P. (2024). Literacy in artificial intelligence as a challenge for teaching in higher education: A case study at portalegre polytechnic university. *Information (Basel)*, *15*(4), 205. DOI: 10.3390/info15040205

Lukowski, J. (2024). How To Make the Leap from Traditional Leader to AI Leader. Retrieved from: <https://neoris.com/web/guest/-/how-to-make-the-leap-from-traditional-leader-to-ai-leader?redirect=%2F>. Accessed on 7th Jan 2025.

Macfarlane, B., Bolden, R., & Watermeyer, R. (2024). Three perspectives on leadership in higher education: Traditionalist, reformist, pragmatist. *Higher Education*, *88*(4), 1–22. DOI: 10.1007/s10734-023-01174-x

Milberg, T. (2024). The future of learning: How AI is revolutionizing education 4.0. Retrieved from:< https://www.weforum.org/stories/2024/04/future-learning-ai-revolutionizing-education-4-0/>. Accessed on 8th Jan 2025.

Nadeem, M. (2024). Distributed leadership in educational contexts: A catalyst for school improvement. *Social Sciences & Humanities Open*, *9*, 100835. DOI: 10.1016/j.ssaho.2024.100835

Nurhaliza, S., & Setiawan, B. (2024). AI for Societal Benefit: Ethical, Educational, and Operational Perspectives. *International Journal of Applied Machine Learning and Computational Intelligence*, *14*(3), 20–25.

Onesi-Ozigagun, O., Ololade, Y. J., Eyo-Udo, N. L., & Ogundipe, D. O. (2024). Revolutionizing education through AI: A comprehensive review of enhancing learning experiences. *International Journal of Applied Research in Social Sciences*, *6*(4), 589–607. DOI: 10.51594/ijarss.v6i4.1011

Patel, K. (2024). Ethical reflections on data-centric AI: Balancing benefits and risks. *International Journal of Artificial Intelligence Research and Development*, *2*(1), 1–17.

Punzi, C., Pellungrini, R., Setzu, M., Giannotti, F., & Pedreschi, D. (2024). AI, Meet Human: Learning paradigms for hybrid decision making systems. *arXiv preprint arXiv:2402.06287*.

Purdy, M., & Williams, M. A. (2023). How AI Can Help Leaders Make Better Decisions Under Pressure. Retrieved from: <https://hbr.org/2023/10/how-ai-can-help-leaders-make-better-decisions-under-pressure>. Accessed on 5th Jan 2025.

Sappaile, B. I., Vandika, A. Y., Deiniatur, M., Nuridayanti, N., & Arifudin, O. (2024). The Role of Artificial Intelligence in the Development of Digital Era Educational Progress. *Journal of Artificial Intelligence and Development*, *3*(1), 1–8.

Sharma, S., Singh, G., Sharma, C. S., & Kapoor, S. (2024). Artificial intelligence in Indian higher education institutions: A quantitative study on adoption and perceptions. *International Journal of System Assurance Engineering and Management*, •••, 1–17. DOI: 10.1007/s13198-023-02193-8

Shivashankar, K., & Bakthavatchaalam, V. (2024). Education Policies Through Data Driven Decision Making: Accelerating Inclusive Education for People with Disabilities. *Artificial Intelligence Enabled Management: An Emerging Economy Perspective*, 15.

Sliwka, A., Klopsch, B., Beigel, J., & Tung, L. (2024). Transformational leadership for deeper learning: Shaping innovative school practices for enhanced learning. *Journal of Educational Administration*, *62*(1), 103–121. DOI: 10.1108/JEA-03-2023-0049

Sydney, U. N. S. W. (2024). Smart Sparrow Adaptive Tutorials as Summative Assessments. Retrieved from: <https://www.teaching.unsw.edu.au/digital-assessment-toolkit/exemplar-1>. Accessed on 3rd Jan 2025.

Universidad de Alicante. (2024). Inclusive Education and Technology (IncluTIC). Retrieved from: <https://cvnet.cpd.ua.es/curriculum-breve/grp/en/inclusive-education-and-technology-(inclutic)/682>. Accessed on 2nd Jan 2025.

Wardat, Y., Tashtoush, M., AlAli, R., & Saleh, S. (2024). Artificial intelligence in education: Mathematics teachers' perspectives, practices and challenges. *Iraqi Journal for Computer Science and Mathematics*, *5*(1), 60–77.

Xinhua., (2024). China releases list of 184 AI education bases in schools. Retrieved from: < https://english.www.gov.cn/news/202402/23/content_WS65d85f47c6d0868f4e8e44a7.html>. Accessed on 3rd Jan 2025.

Zhang, J., & Zhang, Z. (2024). AI in teacher education: Unlocking new dimensions in teaching support, inclusive learning, and digital literacy. *Journal of Computer Assisted Learning*, *40*(4), 1871–1885. DOI: 10.1111/jcal.12988

# Chapter 4
# Integration of Social and Emotional Learning (SEL) With Artificial Intelligence Tools Through an LMS in Primary Education

**Christina Smaropoulou**
https://orcid.org/0000-0001-6201-4043
*University of Crete, Greece*

**Aikaterini Vasiou**
https://orcid.org/0000-0002-4648-2127
*University of Crete, Greece*

## ABSTRACT

*This pilot study investigates a Social and Emotional Learning (SEL) intervention in Greece with a Learning Management System (LMS) to analyze the impact of personal and classroom achievement goals on Self-Regulated Learning (SRL) strategies and SEL competencies in elementary students. Based on SRL and the CASEL framework, the intervention aims to enhance SRL practices, while learning social and emotional competencies in a caring digital community. The LMS, structured with LAMS, allows the visual ordering of learning activities. Fourteen students in 4th to 6th grades engaged in class-based AI-supported activities that encouraged self-control, collaboration, and goal setting. Pre-and post-intervention questionnaires evaluated achievement goals, SRL strategies, affect, and SEL competencies. Outcomes indicate increased self-regulation and self-management, confirming evidence on the beneficial impact of SEL on well-being and academics. This research*

DOI: 10.4018/979-8-3373-0573-8.ch004

*emphasizes the promise of digital interventions in supporting both SRL and SEL in primary education.*

## INTRODUCTION

As societal dynamics have rapidly evolved, individuals have encountered significant ramifications across various domains of life, notably in the economic, social, and technological spheres (Pinchumphonsang & Chanchalor, 2020). Consequently, the competitive nature of life has intensified, presenting heightened challenges for individuals; it is imperative for them to adapt, as failure to do so may hinder their attainment of established objectives and their ability to thrive within this evolving context (Yong et al., 2023). Moreover, these rapid transformations have exacerbated the challenges faced by students globally, adversely affecting their mental and emotional well-being as well as their behavioral conduct (Woods & Pooley, 2015).

The developmental phase from ages 6 to 12 is vital for acquiring skills essential for psychological well-being, as it significantly influences the maturation of cerebral structures crucial for cognitive, emotional, and social growth (Castillo-Gualda et al., 2023). Numerous universal school-based social and emotional learning (SEL) initiatives implemented across the United States and Europe have demonstrated efficacy in enhancing social competencies while simultaneously mitigating emotional distress and behavioral issues (Li et al., 2022). SEL initiatives are progressively being adopted in primary educational institutions to promote the cultivation of social competencies, decision-making abilities, empathic understanding, and emotional regulation. These initiatives aim to mitigate adverse outcomes such as academic failure, behavioral issues, and potential substance misuse, while nurturing essential skills in children exhibiting diverse behavioral, social, and learning needs, including those from economically disadvantaged backgrounds (Calhoun et al., 2020).

The integration of SEL into educational curricula is regarded as a highly effective pedagogical strategy, as schools represent environments where students spend substantial periods of time and develop familiarity. This enables educational institutions to design learning opportunities that impart new knowledge and skills while simultaneously fostering students' physical and mental well-being in alignment with their surroundings (Carroll et al., 2020). Furthermore, the integration of artificial intelligence (AI) into educational settings holds considerable potential to enhance the implementation of SEL by providing tailored learning experiences, real-time feedback, and dynamic interventions that meet the unique needs of each student (Licardo & Lipovec, 2024).

AI-powered tools, such as emotion recognition technology, sentiment analysis, and intelligent tutoring systems, can help educators identify students' emotional states and foster self-awareness, empathy, and emotional regulation (Zhou et al., 2019). Moreover, AI can simulate social scenarios through virtual worlds or chatbots, allowing students to practice and improve their social competencies in a controlled and supportive environment (Hwang et al., 2021). These technological tools expand the SEL framework in both breadth and effectiveness, ensuring that students not only acquire important competencies but also apply them successfully in diverse and dynamic contexts.

## Social and Emotional Learning (SEL)

SEL represents a comprehensive framework encompassing the intentional development of a diverse array of competencies. These competencies enable individuals to recognize and manage their own emotions, articulate and pursue constructive goals, exhibit empathy toward others, foster and sustain meaningful interpersonal relationships, make prudent decisions, and navigate various social scenarios with competence and confidence (Barnes & Jones, 2022). The acquisition of new abilities is fundamentally linked to the enhancement of an individual's self-efficacy, which augments competence and resilience when facing life's challenges and adversities (Hank & Huber, 2024).

The most prominent approach within SEL utilizes both intentional teaching and natural socialization processes, focusing on five key interrelated competencies: self-awareness, self-management, social awareness, relationship skills, and responsible decision-making. This framework, established by the Collaborative for Academic, Social, and Emotional Learning (CASEL) in 2002, is generally applied in inclusive, whole-class or school-wide settings targeting communal growth. Each competency can be broken down into specific skills (Casillas et al., 2022).

Integrating SEL into everyday educational life supports the development of crucial personal and social dimensions (MacSweeney-Mahon, 2022). SEL is not only a facilitator of academic achievement but also of well-being and positive social relationships, as highlighted by Dhiraj et al. (2023). Empirical research has demonstrated that SEL interventions lead to improved behavior management, increased attendance, better academic performance, and enhanced mental health (Greenberg et al., 2003). SEL thus emerges as a holistic educational framework essential for the development and well-being of children and adolescents (Durlak et al., 2024).

Growing recognition of SEL's significance has led to widespread scholarly and policy interest (Brown & Donnelly, 2023). Within the classroom, SEL fosters positive attitudes and behaviors conducive to learning (Denham et al., 2020). Research, such as the study by Castillo-Gualda et al. (2023) on the RULER framework in Spanish public schools, shows that SEL interventions effectively reduce emotional and behavioral symptoms among 9 to 12-year-old students. Similar positive outcomes were found by Carroll et al. (2020), as students with higher pre-intervention emotional and behavioral difficulties benefited the most from SEL programs.

## Artificial Intelligence in Primary Education

Educational Technology emerges as a pivotal field contributing to the development of social and emotional competencies among learners (Slovák & Fitzpatrick, 2015). More specifically, AI encompasses a wide array of components, including modeling techniques, visual representation, prototyping methodologies, systems utilization, reflective practices, evaluation processes, analytical skills, and design principles (Baduge et al., 2022). According to Wang (2024), AI refers to the capacity of computers or machines to perform tasks and exhibit cognitive processes conventionally associated with human problem-solving abilities.

The first UNESCO guidelines on Generative AI in education emphasize the importance of human-centered approaches and the ethical and pedagogical suitability of AI tools (Miao & Holmes, 2024). AI technologies are among the fastest-evolving areas in education (Shah, 2023), offering opportunities for content generation, adaptive learning, and the personalization of educational experiences (Holmes et al., 2019). These technologies can significantly reduce the time educators spend on resource creation, allowing them to focus on enhancing instructional methodologies and fostering student engagement (Luckin & Holmes, 2016).

AI can also provide valuable insights into student performance by analyzing learning data, thus enabling educators to tailor learning programs to meet diverse needs (Khosravi et al., 2022). Furthermore, AI-driven instructional systems offer personalized feedback, emulating human mentorship and enhancing learning outcomes (Chen et al., 2020).

By facilitating more inclusive and creative learning environments, AI supports educational equity (Xia et al., 2022). However, integration should be cautious and mindful of digital equity, ethical considerations, and the need for educators to maintain human oversight (Bikkasani, 2024). As Bates et al. (2020) highlight, the use of AI also raises important concerns about its impact on human relationships and the nature of social interactions.

## SEL through AI

The integration of advanced educational technology tools, such as videos, animations, interactive whiteboards, and multimedia presentations, can significantly enhance the teaching of SEL by making lessons more engaging and effective (Drigas et al., 2023). AI enables the creation of these resources, which help animate and clarify SEL concepts for students who might otherwise struggle to grasp them.

Moreover, allowing students to create their own digital products—such as videos, podcasts, and animations—fosters creativity, collaboration, and self-expression, which in turn promotes the development of SEL competencies like self-awareness, relationship-building, and responsible decision-making (Wood et al., 2023).

AI's role in personalizing learning experiences holds significant promise for SEL education, making learning more individualized and effective (Luckin et al., 2016). Accessible multimedia products promote inclusivity and support diverse learners (du Plessis, 2021). Moreover, AI facilitates the connection between SEL competencies and real-life applications, helping students see their relevance in everyday contexts (Walker & Venker Weidenbenner, 2019). Deliberate integration of AI-generated multimedia into SEL instruction dramatically enhances both student engagement and the effectiveness of competency development, contributing to more holistic educational outcomes (Slovák & Fitzpatrick, 2015).

## Current Study

This pilot study examines how a SEL intervention using AI tools affects social and emotional competencies and SEL strategies in elementary school students. The program was implemented over 10 two-hour sessions. It used a pre-test and post-test design. Students used a specially developed LMS, which incorporated AI-driven activities to create a highly interactive learning environment (Fan & Li, (2023). This study's principal objective was to thoroughly investigate the interplay between achievement goals and classroom goals with SEL and SRL outcomes through LMS activities; these outcomes payed attention to the important alignment between students' individual and classroom achievement goals.

This study explores the relationship between students' week-to-week autonomous functioning and their participation in SEL and SRL activities. To achieve this, we formulated the following research questions regarding individual and classroom achievement goals:

1. How do students' achievement goals and their perceptions of classroom achievement goals evolve with the integration of SEL and AI tools via an LMS?
2. To what extent does the intervention influence students' SRL skills and SEL competencies?
3. What are the significant predictors of the enhancement of SRL and SEL competencies at the pre-test and post-test stages?

To test these hypotheses, students completed pre-test measures of Achievement Goals (Elliot et al., 2011), Perceptions of their School/Classroom Goal Structures (Midgley, et al., 2000), Perceived Use of SRL (Vandevelde et al., 2013), Positive and Negative feelings (Watson et al., 1988) and SEL (Anthony et al., 2020) using validated instruments. In a series of 10 sessions, students completed activities delivered through an LMS that targeted specific SEL and SRL objectives. The main features of the intervention were:

Gamified Quizzes: Immediate feedback in the form of adaptive quizzes enabled and motivated SRL strategies, including self-evaluation and revision of goals.

Progress dashboards allow learners to set personal goals, track their progress, and reflect on their achievements.

Scenario-Based Simulations: These activities immersed students in authentic, interactive contexts that presented social and emotional challenges. Through this engagement, they facilitated practices that promoted emotional regulation and enhanced decision-making skills.

Each level was designed to incorporate individual goals set by the students with less and less guidance. Furthermore, students were required to respond cooperatively to activities to enhance emotional regulation and/or to exchange views during group activities. The LMS facilitated discussions with appropriate pages or guidelines to ensure alignment between personal and classroom goals, reinforcing the interconnected nature of SEL and SRL development. Following the intervention, the same post-test measures were completed by students to evaluate the interaction with the LMS and the activities undertaken during the 20-hour intervention.

## METHODOLOGY

### Participants and Procedures

The pilot study involved 14 students (8 girls and 6 boys- Table 1) who were in fourth (5 children), fifth (7 children) and sixth grade (2 children) (Table 2) of Primary school of Kokkini Hani. The ages of the participants were between 9-12yrs old and specifically 5 children were 9 yrs old, 5 were 10 yrs old,3 were 11 and 1 was 12yrs old (Table 3).

*Table 1. Gender of the participants*

| GENDER | | | | | |
|---|---|---|---|---|---|
| | | **Frequency** | **Percent** | **Valid Percent** | **Cumulative Percent** |
| Valid | Boy | 6 | 42,9 | 42,9 | 42,9 |
| | Girl | 8 | 57,1 | 57,1 | 100,0 |
| | Total | 14 | 100,0 | 100,0 | |

Among the participants, 12 were identified to be experiencing learning difficulties (LD) which further increases the focus of this study on its inclusiveness as well as its differential effects in educational interventions.

*Table 2. Grade of the participants*

| GRADE | | | | | |
|---|---|---|---|---|---|
| | | **Frequency** | **Percent** | **Valid Percent** | **Cumulative Percent** |
| Valid | 4th | 5 | 35,7 | 35,7 | 35,7 |
| | 5th | 7 | 50,0 | 50,0 | 85,7 |
| | 6th | 2 | 14,3 | 14,3 | 100,0 |
| | Total | 14 | 100,0 | 100,0 | |

The inclusion of students with learning difficulties reflects a commitment to exploring how interventions that employ SRL and SEL can serve the unique needs of diverse learners. Evidence suggests that such students commonly experience barriers to successful learning (McGregor et al., 2016), which may be mitigated through tailored support systems and engagement with adaptive educational technologies (Klein, 2024; Zervaki, 2024). This sample, therefore, provides a great opportunity to investigate how these methodologies can be used to promote equitable learning outcomes.

*Table 3. Age of the participants*

| AGE | | | | | |
|---|---|---|---|---|---|
| | | **Frequency** | **Percent** | **Valid Percent** | **Cumulative Percent** |
| Valid | 9,00 | 5 | 35,7 | 35,7 | 35,7 |
| | 10,00 | 5 | 35,7 | 35,7 | 71,4 |
| | 11,00 | 3 | 21,4 | 21,4 | 92,9 |
| | 12,00 | 1 | 7,1 | 7,1 | 100,0 |
| | Total | 14 | 100,0 | 100,0 | |

Parents and participating students were asked to sign the informed consent form after we explained the whole process and resolved any questions.

The participants (14 students) took part in the following sessions:

1. Familiarization - distribution of questionnaires to pupils (pre-test) - first presentation of the software
2. 10 two-hour interactions with the LMS - evaluation with a short questionnaire after each level.
3. post-test with questionnaires.

All the mentioned sessions were two 45-minute sessions and was held on the school premises at times and days that was determined by the headmaster of the school and the teachers of each class.

This study applies to quantitative research design, relying on systematic data collection methods that ensure both objectivity and statistical rigor (Zyphur & Pierides, 2020). Specifically, data were gathered through the use of a questionnaire, before and after the intervention, among the students, aiming to capture quantifiable changes in the variables of interest (Alessandri et al., 2017). The decision to adopt a quantitative approach was based on its strength in identifying patterns, defining the relationships between variables, and supporting the generalizability of results (Bryman, 2016; Creswell & Creswell, 2017). The use of pre- and post-test assessments is in line with standard procedures in intervention studies, which enables researchers to assess the effectiveness of the intervention by comparing initial data with those obtained after its implementation (Cohen et al., 2017).

This methodology is particularly appropriate for assessing the effects of structured educational interventions because it allows for precise measurement of changes in specific areas (Creswell & Creswell, 2017), such as SEL and SRL. The reliance on questionnaires supplies a consistent method of data collection, thereby minimizing researcher bias and strengthening the reliability and validity of the results (Cohen et al., 2017; Fowler, 2013). Quantitative methods also provide a solid base for statistical analysis, which enables the examination of complex interrelations between engagement, classroom interactions, and student performance (Bryman, 2016). This study, by implementing this methodological framework, strives to contribute in a meaningful way to the literature available on educational intervention and offer insight into specific processes through which some strategies may instantiate significant learning experiences and personal change for students.

## Measures

In this quantitative study is to collect data, the participants/students completed the questionnaire. They needed around one hour to complete the questionnaire (91 questions). Initially, they answered a few questions about their demographic characteristics regarding gender, age, class, family background and educational level of their parents. Data collection tools included the Greek Achievement Goal Questionnaire-Revised (AGQ-R; Elliot et al., 2011), Perceptions of their School/ Classroom Goal Structures, (PALS; Midgley et al., 2000), the Children's Perceived Use of Self-Regulated Learning Inventory (CP-SRLI; Vandevelde et al., 2013), the Positive and Negative Affect Scale (PANAS; Watson et al., 1988), and the SSIS SEL Brief Scales (Anthony et al., 2020).

## Materials and Tools

Students engaged with an innovative LMS designed to promote SRL strategies—such as self-control, help-seeking, and peer collaboration—through activities linked to SEL competencies: self-awareness, self-management, social awareness, relationship skills, and responsible decision-making. The intervention included 10 two-hour sessions within LAMS, an open-source platform approved by the Greek Ministry of Education. The "Journey to the ARIELS Islands" course sequence, structured learning into five thematic island-levels corresponding to CASEL's SEL framework. Activities included AI-supported tools like interactive videos, chatbots, gamified quizzes, escape rooms, and creative projects. The digital assistant "Airela" and pirate educational agents guided students by reinforcing SRL strategies throughout their journey.

The integration of AI technologies enhanced student engagement, including among those with learning difficulties, by offering personalized feedback and adapting challenges to individual needs, thus fostering autonomy and mastery (Yadav, 2024). Additionally, LMS analytics allowed real-time emotional and learning assessments, supporting timely SEL interventions. Research highlights that AI tools can simulate real-life social scenarios, providing students with safe opportunities to practice SEL skills, improving emotional intelligence and social competencies (Walker & Venker Weidenbenner, 2019).

## RESULTS

The descriptive statistics from Table 4 regarding achievement goals during the pre-test and post-test phases highlight several important shifts. The mastery-approach goal showed a statistically significant improvement, with the mean score increasing from M = 4.52 (std = 0.40) to M = 4.78 (std = 0.42). This suggests that post-intervention, students were more inclined to engage with learning material for its intrinsic value, a core aspect of deep learning. Conversely, the mastery-avoidance goal demonstrated a noticeable decline, from M = 3.95 (std = 1.13) to M = 3.40 (std = 0.85), indicating reduced anxiety-driven engagement with learning. The drop in standard deviation shows a convergence of attitudes among students. Meanwhile, the performance-approach goal-maintained stability, with only a minor increase from M = 4.30 to M = 4.33, accompanied by a decrease in variability, suggesting consistent performance-oriented motivation across participants. The performance-avoidance goal remained essentially unchanged (M = 3.92 to M = 3.95), although the slight increase in variability post-test implies diverse student experiences regarding fear of failure. These results collectively show that the intervention promoted a healthier, mastery-oriented motivational climate without fostering competitive or avoidance tendencies.

Turning to classroom and teacher goals as presented in Table 4, the findings reveal substantial developments in students' perceptions. The perceived teacher mastery goals increased from M = 6.02 (std = 0.72) to M = 6.32 (std = 0.69), indicating that students increasingly viewed their teachers as promoting mastery and personal improvement rather than competition. Notably, perceptions of teacher performance-approach goals rose significantly, from M = 3.47 to M = 3.94, a shift that was also supported by statistically significant t-test results, highlighting a new trend of encouraging students to outperform peers. Interestingly, despite the positive shift in mean, the standard deviation increased slightly, suggesting a more varied perception among students' post-intervention. Furthermore, perceptions of teacher performance-avoidance goals also showed a significant increase (M = 4.41 to M = 5.08), accompanied by a reduction in variability, reflecting a more unified view among students that teacher aimed to prevent failure visibility. These findings suggest that while the intervention promoted mastery climates, it also inadvertently raised awareness of performance pressures, a dynamic worth monitoring in future implementations.

In relation to learning strategies and skills (again Table 4), several critical improvements were observed. Learning strategies and motivational strategies both exhibited slight but meaningful increases (learning strategies: M = 3.88 to M = 4.09; motivational strategies: M = 3.85 to M = 4.10), implying better strategic learning behavior and sustained effort post-intervention. More notably, the monitoring skill displayed a significant rise from M = 3.85 to M = 4.39, with a remarkable drop in variability (std = 1.17 to 0.63), suggesting a strong intervention impact in helping students actively track and adjust their learning process. Persistence showed the most dramatic change, with the mean jumping from M = 3.80 to M = 4.51 and variability dropping sharply, indicating enhanced resilience and effort in the face of academic challenges. These improvements in SRL components point toward the intervention's success in fostering not only surface-level learning tactics but deeper, self-regulated behaviors critical for long-term academic success.

The social-emotional learning (SEL) competencies presented in Table 4 showed similarly encouraging patterns. Self-awareness modestly improved (M = 13.42 to M = 14.21), accompanied by decreased variability, indicating participants became more uniformly capable of recognizing their emotions and thought patterns. Self-management demonstrated a substantial and statistically significant improvement, from M = 12.21 to M = 14.21, suggesting a strengthened ability among students to control impulses and emotions effectively. Increases were also seen in social awareness (M = 14.71 to M = 15.28) and relationship skills (M = 14.71 to M = 15.35), both with reduced standard deviations, reflecting consistent growth across the cohort. Conversely, responsible decision-making slightly declined from M = 14.64 to M = 14.28, with an increase in variability, hinting at either intervention limits or external factors influencing decision-making behaviors. Overall, the SEL findings underline substantial emotional and interpersonal skill growth, especially in self-regulation capacities that overlap with SRL domains.

Table 4 also reported Cronbach's Alpha coefficients assessing the reliability of various scales. Notably, several scales showed poor internal consistency at pre-test, including Mastery-Approach ($\alpha = 0.342$), Teacher Mastery Goal ($\alpha = 0.297$), Positive Affect/Feelings ($\alpha = 0.184$), and Responsible Decision-Making ($\alpha = 0.336$). Similarly, at post-test, Teacher Performance-Avoidance Goal ($\alpha = 0.303$) and Self-Management ($\alpha = 0.482$) remained below acceptable reliability thresholds. However, strong reliabilities were noted for scales like Performance-Approach Goal ($\alpha = 0.809$–$0.844$), Monitoring ($\alpha = 0.900$–$0.832$), and Persistence ($\alpha = 0.958$–$0.751$), confirming that at least some key constructs were measured robustly. The overall low reliability in certain areas can likely be attributed to the very small sample size (n = 14), a known factor that limits Cronbach's Alpha estimates. Despite these challenges, the tool's general performance was acceptable for exploratory intervention evaluation.

*Table 4. Mean, minimum, maximum, median, interquartile range and standard deviation of the variables*

| PRE-TEST | | | | | | |
|---|---|---|---|---|---|---|
| **Variables** | **M** | **min** | **max** | **IR** | **SD** | **Cronbach's Alpha** |
| Mastery-approach goal | 4,52 | 4 | 5 | 1 | 0,4 | 0,342 |
| Mastery-avoidance goal | 3,95 | 1 | 5 | 1,17 | 1,13 | 0,627 |
| Performance-approach goal | 4,3 | 2 | 5 | 1,42 | 1,11 | 0,809 |
| Performance-avoidance goal | 3,92 | 1 | 5 | 1,67 | 1,24 | 0,682 |
| Teacher Mastery Goal | 6,02 | 4,6 | 7 | 1,15 | 0,72 | 0,297 |
| Teacher Performance-Approach Goal | 3,47 | 1,4 | 6 | 2,15 | 1,32 | 0,526 |
| Teacher Performance-Avoid Goal | 4,41 | 2,8 | 7 | 2,35 | 1,26 | 0,517 |
| Learning strategies | 3,88 | 1,93 | 5 | 1,29 | 0,88 | 0,744 |
| Motivational strategies | 3,85 | 1 | 5 | 1,56 | 1,17 | 0,879 |
| Monitoring | 3,85 | 1,14 | 5 | 1,5 | 1,10 | 0,900 |
| Persistence | 3,8 | 1 | 5 | 2,67 | 1,47 | 0,958 |
| Positive feelings | 4,3 | 3,25 | 5 | 1,06 | 0,57 | 0,184 |
| Negative feelings | 2,37 | 1 | 4,5 | 2,31 | 1,21 | 0,801 |
| Self-Awareness | 13,42 | 5 | 16 | 4,25 | 3,34 | 0,901 |
| Self-Management | 12,21 | 7 | 16 | 4,75 | 2,93 | 0,741 |
| Social awareness | 14,71 | 6 | 16 | 1,25 | 2,61 | 0,920 |
| Relationship skills | 14,71 | 11 | 16 | 3 | 1,58 | 0,609 |
| Responsible decision making | 14,64 | 11 | 16 | 2 | 1,54 | 0,336 |
| **POST-TEST** | | | | | | |
| Mastery-approach goal | 4,78 | 3,67 | 5 | 0,33 | 0,42 | ,606 |
| Mastery-avoidance goal | 4,40 | 2,67 | 5 | 1,42 | 0,85 | ,655 |
| Performance-approach goal | 4,33 | 2,67 | 5 | 1,17 | 0,82 | ,844 |
| Performance-avoidance goal | 3,95 | 1 | 5 | 2,17 | 1,32 | ,899 |
| Teacher Mastery Goal | 6,32 | 5 | 7 | 1,25 | 0,69 | ,580 |
| Teacher Performance-Approach Goal | 3,94 | 1 | 5,8 | 2,30 | 1,46 | ,656 |
| Teacher Performance-Avoid Goal | 5,08 | 3,29 | 6,8 | 2 | 1,08 | ,303 |
| Learning strategies | 4,09 | 2,07 | 5 | 0,95 | 0,95 | ,933 |
| Motivational strategies | 4,10 | 2 | 5 | 1 | 0,90 | ,681 |
| Monitoring | 4,39 | 2,57 | 5 | 0,61 | 0,63 | ,832 |
| Persistence | 4,51 | 3,33 | 5 | 1,04 | 0,54 | ,751 |
| Positive affects | 4,55 | 1 | 5 | 0,81 | 0,61 | ,693 |
| Negative affects | 1,51 | 1 | 4 | 0,81 | 0,82 | ,818 |

continued on following page

*Table 4. Continued*

| PRE-TEST | | | | | | |
|---|---|---|---|---|---|---|
| **Variables** | **M** | **min** | **max** | **IR** | **SD** | **Cronbach's Alpha** |
| Self-Awareness | 14,21 | 10 | 16 | 2,25 | 2,04 | ,606 |
| Self-Management | 14,21 | 12 | 16 | 3,25 | 1,62 | ,482 |
| Social awareness | 15,28 | 12 | 16 | 1,25 | 1,20 | ,657 |
| Relationship skills | 15,35 | 12 | 16 | 1,25 | 1,21 | ,724 |
| Responsible decision making | 14,28 | 9 | 16 | 2,25 | 2,33 | ,788 |

In **Table 5**, inferential statistics tested pre- and post-test differences, combining t-tests and Wilcoxon signed-rank tests for non-normal data. The **self-management variable** stood out as the only one showing statistically significant improvement through the non-parametric Wilcoxon test ($p = 0.029$). This supports the descriptive finding of a substantial increase in emotional and behavioral regulation capacities among participants. The notable drop in variability alongside improvement further validates that gains in self-management were not isolated but broadly shared among the group. Given the overlap between self-management in SEL and self-regulatory processes in SRL, this result highlights the intervention's strongest area of influence and offers a promising direction for future program refinements.

*Table 5. Results of paired T-test and Wilcoxon signed-rank test for various variables*

| **Variable** | **Wilcoxon (p-value)** |
|---|---|
| Mastery-approach goal | 0.114 |
| Mastery-avoidance goal | 0.181 |
| Performance-approach goal | 0.894 |
| Performance-avoidance goal | 0.646 |
| Teacher Mastery Goal | 0.218 |
| Teacher Performance-Approach Goal | 0.346 |
| Teacher Performance-Avoidance Goal | 0.209 |
| Learning strategies | 0.208 |
| Motivational strategies | 0.327 |
| Monitoring | 0.148 |
| Persistence | 0.133 |
| PANAS (Positive & Negative Emotion) | 0.220 |
| Self-Awareness | 0.598 |
| Self-Management | **0.029** |

continued on following page

*Table 5. Continued*

| Variable | Wilcoxon (p-value) |
|---|---|
| Social awareness | 0.750 |
| Relationship skills | 0.277 |
| Responsible decision making | 0.685 |

*Note:* Statistically significant results ($p < .05$) are in bold.

Multiple regression analyses presented in **Table 6** explored how personal and classroom goals predicted SEL competencies at pre-test. Here, only one statistically significant relationship emerged: **students' performance-approach goals** positively predicted **social awareness** ($B = 1.939$, $p = .023$). This suggests that students motivated to outperform others may also be more attuned to understanding social dynamics—an interesting finding that nuances common assumptions about competition undermining empathy. Although the model explained a substantial portion of variance ($R^2 = .726$), the overall model was not statistically significant, likely due to the small sample size and limited statistical power. Still, the finding points to complex, sometimes positive, interactions between achievement motivation and socio-emotional development.

*Table 6. Regression analyses*

| Predictor | B | Std. Error | Beta |
|---|---|---|---|
| (Constant) | 21.239 | 9.725 | - |
| Mastery-approach goal | -1.838 | 2.069 | -0.287 |
| Mastery-avoidance goal | 0.699 | 1.003 | 0.302 |
| Performance-approach goal | 1.939 | 0.640 | **0.825*** |
| Performance-avoidance goal | 0.078 | 0.975 | 0.037 |
| Teacher Mastery Goal | -1.567 | 1.049 | -0.436 |
| Teacher Performance-Approach Goal | 0.161 | 0.664 | 0.081 |
| Teacher Performance-Avoid Goal | -0.169 | 0.795 | -0.081 |

**Note.** *$p < .05$, **$p < .01$

*Table 7. Multiple regression analysis pre-test for predicting learning strategies by personal and teacher goals*

| Predictor | B | Std. Error | Beta |
|---|---|---|---|
| (Constant) | -0.054 | 2.335 | - |
| Mastery-approach goal | 0.516 | 0.497 | 0.239 |
| Mastery-avoidance goal | 0.451, | 0.241 | 0.578 |
| Performance-approach goal | 0.399 | 0.154 | **0.504*** |
| Performance-avoidance goal | -0.519 | 0.234 | -0.731 |
| Teacher Mastery Goal | -0.210 | 0.252 | -0.173 |
| Teacher Performance-Approach Goal | 0.449 | 0.159 | **0.672*** |
| Teacher Performance-Avoid Goal | -0.033 | 0.191 | -0.047 |

Regarding SRL outcomes (learning strategies, motivation, monitoring, and persistence), **pre-test multiple regression analyses** revealed two significant predictors for **learning strategies**. Specifically, students' **performance-approach goals** (B = 0.399, p = .041) and perceptions of **teacher performance-approach goals** (B = 0.449, p = .031) both had significant positive impacts, meaning that competitive drive and teacher emphasis on outperforming peers encouraged the use of effective learning strategies. The model explained a substantial amount of variance ($R^2$ = .861) and was statistically significant (p = .029), suggesting a meaningful relationship between performance-focused motivation and strategic learning behaviors. No significant predictors were found for other SRL outcomes at the pre-test.

At the **post-test stage**, as presented in **Table 8**, multiple regression analyses found no statistically significant predictors linking personal or classroom goals with SEL outcomes. This absence of findings may suggest that while achievement goals relate to socio-emotional skills initially, after intervention, other factors (perhaps internalized skills or broader context shifts) dominate. The lack of post-test associations highlights the importance of considering time-sensitive dynamics in how goals influence emotional competencies and suggests that the intervention might have leveled students' emotional skills beyond individual motivational differences.

*Table 8. Multiple regression analysis post-test for predicting learning strategies by personal and teacher goals*

| Predictor | B | Std. Error | Beta |
|---|---|---|---|
| (Constant) | -1.540 | 3.549 | - |
| Mastery-approach goal | 1.539 | 0.575 | **0.688*** |
| Mastery-avoidance goal | 0.598 | 0.536 | 0.540 |

continued on following page

*Table 8. Continued*

| Predictor | B | Std. Error | Beta |
|---|---|---|---|
| Performance-approach goal | -0.457 | 0.418 | -0.397 |
| Performance-avoidance goal | -0.544 | 0.312 | -0.757 |
| Teacher Mastery Goal | -0.051 | 0.416 | -0.037 |
| Teacher Performance-Approach Goal | 0.394 | 0.221 | 0.605 |
| Teacher Performance-Avoid Goal | -0.290 | 0.268 | -0.330 |

*Table 9 (a). Pre-test Non parametric correlations between variables, N=14*

| Variables | 1 | 2 | 3 | 4 | 5 | 6 | 7 | 8 |
|---|---|---|---|---|---|---|---|---|
| 1. Mastery-approach goal | - | | | | | | | |
| 2. Mastery-avoidance goal | .479 | - | | | | | | |
| 3. Performance-approach goal | .271 | .362 | - | | | | | |
| 4. Performance-avoidance goal | -.043 | .597* | .344 | - | | | | |
| 5. Teacher Mastery Goal | .391 | .383 | .632* | .345 | - | | | |
| 6. Teacher Performance-Approach | -.153 | .154 | -.004 | .578* | -.013 | - | | |
| 7. Teacher Performance-Avoid | -.563* | -.158 | -.169 | .484 | -.061 | .528 | - | |
| 8. Learning strategies | .542* | .386 | .391 | .032 | .140 | .319 | -.377 | - |
| 9. Motivational strategies | .470 | .237 | .338 | -.043 | -.012 | .028 | -.353 | .805 |
| 10. Monitoring | .346 | .235 | .250 | .069 | -.038 | .213 | -.312 | .699 |
| 11. Persistence | .707** | .425 | .373 | -.022 | .119 | .033 | -.522 | .848** |
| 12. Positive feelings | .461 | .373 | .305 | -.067 | .073 | -.048 | -.588* | .656** |
| 13. Negative feelings | -.642* | -.142 | -.355 | .348 | -.375 | .170 | .717** | -.508 |
| 14. Self-Awareness | .492 | .486 | .272 | .122 | .120 | .164 | -.304 | .583* |
| 15. Self-Management | .436 | .422 | .241 | .158 | -.022 | .346 | -.194 | .632* |
| 16. Social awareness | .190 | .260 | .618 | .418 | .392 | .270 | -.099 | .457 |
| 17. Relationship skills | .174 | .135 | .364 | .002 | .040 | .262 | -.091 | .731** |
| 18. Responsible decision making | .154 | .194 | .296 | .247 | .103 | .585* | .006 | .718** |

*Table 9 (b). Pre-test Non parametric correlations between variables, N=14*

| 9 | 10 | 11 | 12 | 13 | 14 | 15 | 16 | 17 |
|---|---|---|---|---|---|---|---|---|
| | | | | | | | | |
| | | | | | | | | |
| | | | | | | | | |
| | | | | | | | | |
| | | | | | | | | |
| | | | | | | | | |
| | | | | | | | | |
| | | | | | | | | |
| - | | | | | | | | |
| .810** | - | | | | | | | |
| .767** | .787** | - | | | | | | |
| .664** | .343 | .448 | - | | | | | |
| -.180 | -.160 | -.519 | -.365 | - | | | | |
| .513 | .648** | .689** | .433 | -.254 | - | | | |
| .594* | .861** | .753** | .197 | -.217 | .754** | - | | |
| .538* | .756** | .534** | .206 | -.078 | .591* | .610* | - | |
| .705** | .811 | .707** | .267 | -.176 | .720** | .736** | .685** | - |
| .588* | .765** | .580* | .261 | -.226 | .602* | .706** | .714** | .836** |

Correlations have been formatted with asterisks to indicate the level of significance (*p < .05, **p < .01).

The Spearman correlation analysis revealed several statistically significant relationships. In the Table 9, Teacher Performance-Avoid Goal negatively correlated with Mastery-Approach Goal and positively with Mastery-Avoidance and Performance-Avoidance Goals. Mastery-Approach Goal was positively associated with Learning Strategies and Persistence, while Negative Feelings showed a negative link. Learning Strategies correlated strongly with Persistence, Positive Feelings, and social-emotional skills. Motivational and Monitoring strategies were highly interrelated and connected to Persistence, Self-Management, and Social Awareness. Finally, strong interrelations among Self-Awareness, Self-Management, Social Awareness, Relationship Skills, and Responsible Decision Making were observed. Table 10 confirmed these patterns in post-test data, reinforcing their importance.

*Table 10 (a). Post-test_non parametric correlations between variables, N=14*

| **Variables** | **1** | **2** | **3** | **4** | **5** | **6** | **7** | **8** |
|---|---|---|---|---|---|---|---|---|
| **1. Mastery-approach goal** | - | | | | | | | |
| 2. Mastery-avoidance goal | .116 | - | | | | | | |
| 3. Performance-approach goal | .050 | .112 | - | | | | | |
| 4. Performance-avoidance goal | -.051 | .636* | .394 | - | | | | |
| 5. Teacher Mastery Goal | -.257 | -.004 | .375 | -.009 | - | | | |
| 6. Teacher Performance-Approach | .169 | .039 | .721** | .444 | .081 | - | | |
| 7. Teacher Performance-Avoid | .180 | .546* | .087 | .273 | -.157 | .225 | - | |
| 8. Learning strategies | .545* | -.174 | -.070 | -.399 | .023 | .059 | -.091 | - |
| 9. Motivational strategies | .239 | .190 | .234 | -.069 | -.223 | .114 | .012 | .470 |
| 10. Monitoring | -.308 | -.283 | -.041 | -.101 | .035 | .077 | .597* | .250 |
| 11. Persistence | .139 | -.185 | .127 | -.240 | .266 | .082 | -.489 | .586 |
| 12. Positive affect | -.180 | -.010 | .236 | .086 | .151 | .206 | -.405 | .260 |
| 13. Negative affect | -.254 | -.187 | -.205 | .051 | -.346 | .341 | .361 | -.189 |
| 14. Self-Awareness | .346 | -.180 | -.101 | -.144 | -.063 | .067 | -.435 | .732** |
| 15. Self-Management | .030 | .236 | .010 | -.014 | .057 | .199 | .007 | .495 |
| 16. Social awareness | .274 | .064 | .517 | .093 | .225 | .344 | -.053 | .206 |
| 17. Relationship skills | .054 | -.124 | .205 | .016 | .396 | .131 | -.327 | .428 |
| 18. Responsible decision making | .068 | .042 | .256 | .010 | .223 | .158 | -.363 | .390 |

*Table 10 (b). Post-test_non parametric correlations between variables, N=14*

| **9** | **10** | **11** | **12** | **13** | **14** | **15** | **16** | **17** |
|---|---|---|---|---|---|---|---|---|
| | | | | | | | | |
| | | | | | | | | |
| | | | | | | | | |
| | | | | | | | | |
| | | | | | | | | |
| | | | | | | | | |
| | | | | | | | | |
| | | | | | | | | |
| - | | | | | | | | |
| .353 | - | | | | | | | |
| .076 | .577* | - | | | | | | |
| .294 | .447 | .406 | - | | | | | |

continued on following page

*Table 10 (b). Continued*

| 9 | 10 | 11 | 12 | 13 | 14 | 15 | 16 | 17 |
|---|---|---|---|---|---|---|---|---|
| -.247 | -.056 | -.197 | -.407 | - | | | | |
| .246 | .491 | .643* | .467 | -.176 | - | | | |
| .298 | .423 | .659* | .022 | .259 | .337 | - | | |
| -.054 | .171 | .745** | .240 | -.199 | .232 | .438 | - | |
| .139 | .457 | .585* | .464 | -.138 | .681** | .322 | .290 | - |
| .206 | .459 | .720** | .352 | -.291 | .637 | .505 | .530 | .761** |

Correlations have been formatted with asterisks to indicate the level of significance (*p < .05, **p < .01).

## DISCUSSION

Relative to the primary research question, the results reported that the use of SEL paired with AI tools in an LMS impacted students' achievement goals and their perceptions of classroom achievement goals. The intervention notably enhanced mastery-approach goals, demonstrating increased intrinsic motivation toward learning and understanding the material. This finding resonates with literature emphasizing SEL's role in fostering intrinsic motivation and attention to personal development (Schunk & DiBenedetto, 2020). The consistent standard deviation across stages suggested steady progression towards mastery-oriented learning.

Conversely, mastery-avoidance goals decreased from pre- to post-test, indicating reduced task avoidance in face of possible failure, consistent with findings linking SEL interventions to anxiety reduction and promotion of a growth mindset (Deli et al., 2021). Performance-approach goals remained relatively stable, showing minimal mean increase but narrowed response ranges, reflecting a consistent focus on performance. Performance-avoidance goals remained largely unchanged, although greater variance suggested diverse reactions post-intervention.

Students' perceptions of classroom achievement goals also changed significantly. Teacher mastery goal perceptions increased, indicating students increasingly saw teachers as cultivating mastery-focused environments, aligning with findings that teacher emphasis on mastery enhances intrinsic motivation (Schiefele & Schaffner, 2015). Teacher performance-approach goal perceptions also rose, suggesting students saw teachers encouraging competitive excellence. However, the relatively small variance increase indicates mixed student interpretations. Notably, teacher performance-avoidance perceptions increased with decreased variance, suggesting students perceived a more supportive and less punitive environment, in line with research on teachers' dual roles in fostering mastery and performance climates (Hemi et al., 2021).

These results agree with recent studies examining SEL and technology integration (Fotopoulou et al., 2025) and replicate findings from Schunk and DiBenedetto (2020) regarding increases in mastery-approach goals and decreases in avoidance behaviors. They also parallel Durlak et al. (2024), who reported that SEL programs enhanced classroom climates and student-teacher relationships. However, the rise in teacher performance-avoidance perceptions contrasts with findings highlighting the damaging effects of performance-avoidance climates (Elliot & McGregor, 2001). A plausible explanation is that AI tools might buffer negative effects by offering personalized feedback, thus altering perceptions of performance-avoidance goals.

Overall, integrating SEL and AI tools into an LMS positively affected students' achievement goals, encouraging mastery orientations and reducing avoidance tendencies, while also restructuring perceptions of classroom goals toward mastery and performance emphases. These findings highlight SEL and AI's potential to create adaptive learning environments supporting intrinsic motivation and performance (Vistorte et al., 2024).

Addressing the second research question, the intervention impacted students' SRL strategies and SEL competencies. Improvements were noted across all SRL subcategories, with monitoring and persistence showing the greatest changes. Monitoring capacity improved significantly from pre- to post-test, while persistence also showed large mean increases and decreased variance, indicating greater consistency among students. These findings support literature on the role of monitoring and persistence in SRL development (Zimmerman, 2002).

Motivational strategies also improved, with students better maintaining motivation post-intervention, aligning with research underscoring motivation's key role in SRL (Meece, 2023). At the SEL level, significant improvements occurred in self-management and social awareness. Students improved in emotional and behavioral regulation, consistent with findings highlighting SEL's positive influence on academic performance (Fernandez-Perez & Martin-Rojas, 2022). Gains in social awareness mirrored research emphasizing the role of SEL interventions in developing empathy. However, responsible decision-making showed a slight decline, suggesting that improvements in this competency may require more time and reinforcement (Sklad et al., 2012).

Examining the relationship between achievement goals, SRL, and SEL, mastery-approach goals were strongly correlated with the use of learning strategies, reaffirming that intrinsic motivation enhances self-regulation and strategic behavior (Chen & Sukying, 2024). Interestingly, monitoring was positively correlated with classroom performance-avoidance goals, implying that environments emphasizing failure avoidance can increase students' self-monitoring, often associated with anxiety and reduced intrinsic motivation (Turner et al., 2011). However, positive feedback can mitigate these effects and foster adaptive learning (Hawe et al., 2017).

Mastery-avoidance goals were positively related to performance-avoidance goals, suggesting that avoidance tendencies reflect classroom dynamics (Liem & Tan, 2019). Performance-approach goals also correlated with classroom performance-approach goals, reinforcing the influence of classroom goal structures on students' motivational behaviors (Senko & Dawson, 2017). Overall, the intervention effectively enhanced SRL strategies and SEL competencies, although with varying effects across domains.

Regarding the third research question, key predictors emerged. During pre-test, students' performance-approach goals positively influenced learning strategies, indicating that competitive motives can lead to adaptive strategy use, a finding consistent with research on achievement goals and SRL (Yeh et al., 2019). Similarly, teacher performance-approach goals positively impacted students' learning strategies, suggesting that performance-oriented classrooms can motivate engagement when appropriately managed (Ruijten et al., 2025). However, excessive performance emphasis can also elevate stress (Diaconu-Gherasim et al., 2024), implying the need for balanced instructional strategies.

Students with high performance-approach goals also displayed better social awareness at pre-test, suggesting that striving to excel socially and academically may enhance awareness of others, consistent with research on performance goals and social competence (Hudson, 2024). Studies suggest that performance-approach goals promote effective strategy use to outperform peers (Senko & Dawson, 2017).

At post-test, mastery-approach goals became the strongest predictor of learning strategies, indicating a shift from performance to intrinsic learning motives, aligning with the deeper engagement associated with mastery goals (Zimmerman, 2002). This transition likely contributed to improved learning strategy use.

Moreover, self-management skills showed significant development at post-test ($p = 0.029$) with reduced variance, confirming the intervention's effectiveness in promoting emotional and behavioral self-regulation (Boekaerts, 1996). These results show the intertwined growth of SRL and SEL processes, fostering holistic student development.

Interestingly, no significant predictors of SEL outcomes were found at post-test when using goal orientations, suggesting that while goal structures influence SRL strategies, SEL outcomes may be shaped by broader factors like emotional intelligence, peer relationships, or teacher-student interactions.

In summary, performance-approach goals at pre-test predicted both social awareness and learning strategies, while mastery-approach goals at post-test predicted learning strategies. Improvement in self-management confirmed the mutual reinforcement between SRL and SEL. The social features of the LMS, such as group projects and peer reviews, likely supported these developments by promoting social interaction and empathy. Embedding SEL and AI tools into an LMS helped reduce avoidance behaviors, enhance self-regulation, and improve social awareness, validating the potential of integrated approaches to foster comprehensive student growth (Schunk & DiBenedetto, 2020).

## LIMITATIONS

The results demonstrated significant improvement across various areas, reinforcing the literature on achievement goal theory, SRL, and SEL. The intervention, which integrated innovative AI tools and SEL principles, enhanced students' intrinsic motivation, learning strategies, and emotional regulation. Despite the promising results, several limitations must be acknowledged. The study was conducted in a specific educational setting with a relatively homogenous sample, limiting the generalizability of the findings. Future research should involve more diverse populations to assess the broader applicability of such interventions. Moreover, the study focused primarily on short-term outcomes; thus, longitudinal research is needed to evaluate the lasting effects of SEL and AI integration on students' learning behaviors and emotional growth. Additionally, the reliance on self-report measures, prone to biases, suggests that future studies should incorporate observational data or performance tasks to enrich understanding. Another limitation concerns the unexplored role of specific AI features within the LMS. Identifying which AI components—such as adaptive feedback, personalized learning paths, or gamification—most significantly affect SRL and SEL outcomes is essential for refining educational technologies. In conclusion, this study highlights the potential of combining SEL and AI in LMS environments to foster intrinsic motivation, improve emotional regulation, and support holistic student development. Future research should explore long-term effects, cultural applicability, and ethical dimensions to ensure responsible integration of AI tools in education.

## REFERENCES


Alessandri, G., Zuffianò, A., & Perinelli, E. (2017). Evaluating intervention programs with a pretest-posttest design: A structural equation modeling approach. *Frontiers in Psychology*, *8*, 223. DOI: 10.3389/fpsyg.2017.00223 PMID: 28303110

Anthony, C. J., Elliott, S. N., DiPerna, J. C., & Lei, P. W. (2020). The SSIS SEL brief scales–student form: Initial development and validation. *School Psychology*, *35*(4), 277–283. DOI: 10.1037/spq0000390 PMID: 32673055

Bates, T., Cobo, C., Mariño, O., & Wheeler, S. (2020). Can artificial intelligence transform higher education? *International Journal of Educational Technology in Higher Education*, *17*(1), 1–12. DOI: 10.1186/s41239-020-00218-x

Bikkasani, D. C. (2024). Navigating artificial general intelligence (AGI): Societal implications, ethical considerations, and governance strategies. *AI and Ethics*, •••, 1–16. DOI: 10.1007/s43681-024-00642-z

Brown, C., & Donnelly, M. (2023). *Space, Identity and Education: A Multi Scalar Framework*. Springer Nature. DOI: 10.1007/978-3-031-31535-0

Bryman, A. (2016). *Social Research Methods* (5th ed.). Oxford University Press.

Calhoun, B., Williams, J., Greenberg, M., Domitrovich, C., Russell, M. A., & Fishbein, D. H. (2020). Social Emotional Learning Program Boosts Early Social and Behavioral Skills in Low-Income Urban Children. *Frontiers in Psychology*, *11*, 561196. DOI: 10.3389/fpsyg.2020.561196 PMID: 33250808

Carroll, A., Houghton, S., Forrest, K., McCarthy, M., & Sanders-O'Connor, E. (2020). Who benefits most? Predicting the effectiveness of a social and emotional learning intervention according to children's emotional and behavioural difficulties. *School Psychology International*, *41*(3), 197–217. DOI: 10.1177/0143034319898741

Casillas, A., Roberts, B., & Jones, S. (2022). An integrative perspective on SEL Frameworks. *Assessing Competencies for Social and Emotional Learning*, 9-27. https://doi.org/DOI: 10.4324/9781003102243

Castillo-Gualda, R., Moraleda, A., & Brackett, M. A. (2023). Preventive Initiatives to Promote Psychological Adjustment Among Primary Students: Findings of RULER Approach in Spanish Public Schools. *International Journal of Educational Psychology*, *12*(2), 206–232. DOI: 10.17583/ijep.10970

Chen, L., Chen, P., & Lin, Z. (2020). Artificial intelligence in education: A review. *IEEE Access : Practical Innovations, Open Solutions, 8*, 75264–75278. DOI: 10.1109/ACCESS.2020.2988510

Chen, Z., & Sukying, A. (2024). The relationship between intrinsic motivation, self-efficacy, self-regulated learning, and English learning achievement in Chinese high school students. *Journal of English Language and Linguistics, 5*(3), 261–276. DOI: 10.62819/jel.2024.578

Cohen, L., Manion, L., & Morrison, K. (2017). Research design and planning. In *Research Methods in Education* (pp. 173–201). Routledge. DOI: 10.4324/9781315456539-11

Creswell, J. W., & Creswell, J. D. (2017). *Research design: Qualitative, quantitative, and mixed methods approaches*. Sage publications.

Deli, W., Kaur, A., & Hashim, R. A. (2021). Who delivers it and how it is delivered: Effects of social-emotional learning interventions on learning anxiety and dropout intention. *Malaysian Journal of Learning and Instruction, 18*(1), 1–27. DOI: 10.32890/mjli2021.18.1.1

Dhiraj, A., Kumar, S., & Rani, D. (2023). Social and Emotional Learning: Keys to the Success of E-Learning. In *Technology-Driven E-Learning Pedagogy Through Emotional Intelligence* (pp. 119-130). IGI Global. DOI: DOI: 10.4018/978-1-6684-7639-0.ch008

Diaconu-Gherasim, L. R., Elliot, A. J., Zancu, A. S., Brumariu, L. E., Măirean, C., Opariuc-Dan, C., & Crumpei-Tanasă, I. (2024). A meta-analysis of the relations between achievement goals and internalizing problems. *Educational Psychology Review, 36*(1), 109. DOI: 10.1007/s10648-024-09943-5

Drigas, A., Papanastasiou, G., & Skianis, C. (2023). The school of the future: The role of digital technologies, metacognition and emotional intelligence. *International Journal of Emerging Technologies in Learning, 18*(9), 65–85. DOI: 10.3991/ijet.v18i09.38133

du Plessis, A. (2021). Using Information Communication Technologies and Assistive Technologies to Address Specific Barriers to Teaching and Learning in Schools. In *Empowering Students and Maximising Inclusiveness and Equality through ICT* (pp. 88–113). Brill., DOI: 10.1163/9789004447226_007

Durlak, J. A., Domitrovich, C. E., & Mahoney, J. L. (Eds.). (2024). *Handbook of social and emotional learning*. Guilford Publications.

Elliot, A. J., Murayama, K., & Pekrun, R. (2011). A 3× 2 achievement goal model. *Journal of Educational Psychology, 103*(3), 632–648. DOI: 10.1037/a0023952

Fan, X., & Li, J. (2023). Artificial intelligence-driven interactive learning methods for enhancing art and design education in higher institutions. *Applied Artificial Intelligence, 37*(1), 2225907. Advance online publication. DOI: 10.1080/08839514.2023.2225907

Fernandez-Perez, V., & Martin-Rojas, R. (2022). Emotional competencies as drivers of management students' academic performance: The moderating effects of cooperative learning. *International Journal of Management Education, 20*(1), 100600. Advance online publication. DOI: 10.1016/j.ijme.2022.100600

Fotopoulou, E., Cassà, È. L., Mavraidi, L., Peris, J., Zafeiropoulos, A., Colomeischi, A., & Papavassiliou, S. (2025). *EduCardia: a modern technology-powered methodology for the assessment and improvement of social and emotional competencies of students in K12 schools*. IEEE., DOI: 10.1109/ACCESS.2025.3529120

Fowler, F. J.Jr. (2013). *Survey research methods*. Sage publications.

Greenberg, M. T., Weissberg, R. P., O'Brien, M. U., Zins, J. E., Fredericks, L., Resnik, H., & Elias, M. J. (2003). Enhancing school-based prevention and youth development through coordinated social, emotional, and academic learning. *The American Psychologist, 58*(6-7), 466–474. DOI: 10.1037/0003-066X.58.6-7.466 PMID: 12971193

Hank, C., & Huber, C. (2024). Do Peers Influence the Development of Individuals' Social Skills? The Potential of Cooperative Learning and Social Learning in Elementary Schools. *International Journal of Applied Positive Psychology, 9*(2), 747–773. DOI: 10.1007/s41042-024-00151-8

Hawe, E., Lightfoot, U., & Dixon, H. (2017). First-year students working with exemplars: Promoting self-efficacy, self-monitoring and self-regulation. *Journal of Further and Higher Education, 43*(1), 30–44. DOI: 10.1080/0309877X.2017.1349894

Hemi, A., Madjar, N., & Rich, Y. (2021). Perceived Peer and Teacher Goals: Relationships with Students' Academic Achievement Goals. *Journal of Experimental Education, 91*(1), 145–165. DOI: 10.1080/00220973.2021.1906199

Holmes, W., Bialik, M., & Fadel, C. (2019). *Artificial intelligence in education promises and implications for teaching and learning*. Center for Curriculum Redesign.

Hudson, M. L. (2024). *Examination of goal orientation theory key measures related to high school students' disruptive behaviors* (Order No. 31296634). Available from ProQuest Dissertations & Theses Global. (3065231081). Retrieved from https://www.proquest.com/dissertations-theses/examination-goal-orientation-theory-key-measures/docview/3065231081/se-2

Hwang, G. J., Wang, S. Y., & Lai, C. L. (2021). Effects of a social regulation-based online learning framework on students' learning achievements and behaviors in mathematics. *Computers & Education*, *160*, 104031. Advance online publication. DOI: 10.1016/j.compedu.2020.104031

Khosravi, H., Shum, S. B., Chen, G., Conati, C., Tsai, Y. S., Kay, J., Knight, S., Martinez-Maldonado, R., Sadiq, S., & Gašević, D. (2022). Explainable artificial intelligence in education. *Computers and Education: Artificial Intelligence*, *3*, 100074. Advance online publication. DOI: 10.1016/j.caeai.2022.100074

Klein, L. A. (2024). *Bridging the achievement gap for students with learning disabilities by increasing educator collaboration with an emphasis on integrative technology* (Order No. 30994562). Available from ProQuest Dissertations & Theses Global. (3057619243). Retrieved from https://www.proquest.com/dissertations-theses/bridging-achievement-gap-students-with-learning/docview/3057619243/se-2

Li, J., Ma, C., Lu, Q., & Hesketh, T. (2022, November). A Social Emotional Learning Training Programme in a Poor Rural Primary School in Central China: A Pre-Post Intervention Study. In *Healthcare* (Vol. 10, No. 11, p. 2332). MDPI. DOI: 10.3390/healthcare10112332

Licardo, M., & Lipovec, A. (Eds.). (2024) *Artificial Intelligence Literacy and Social-Emotional Skills as Transversal Competencies in Education.* ISSN: 0945-487X

Luckin, R., & Holmes, W. (2016). *Intelligence unleashed: An argument for AI in education.* Pearson Education.

MacSweeney-Mahon, S. (2022). Predictors of socio-emotional functioning in childhood: longitudinal evidence. https://cora.ucc.ie/bitstreams/b7d055dc-833e-4b42-8be3-fe3fce4da37d/download

McGregor, K. K., Langenfeld, N., Van Horne, S., Oleson, J., Anson, M., & Jacobson, W. (2016). The university experiences of students with learning disabilities. *Learning Disabilities Research & Practice*, *31*(2), 90–102. DOI: 10.1111/ldrp.12102 PMID: 27667902

Meece, J. L. (2023). The role of motivation in self-regulated learning. In *Self-regulation of learning and performance* (pp. 25–44). Routledge.

Miao, F., & Holmes, W. (2024). *Guidelines for productive AI in education and research* (Mavrikis, M., & Margeti, M., Eds.). UNESCO., https://unesdoc.unesco.org/ark:/48223/pf0000390613

Pinchumphonsang, S., & Chanchalor, S. (2020). The development of social emotional learning programs in a cross-cultural elementary classroom. *International Journal of Innovation and Learning*, *27*(1), 58–78. DOI: 10.1504/IJIL.2020.103888

Ruijten, P. A., Cardona, A. M. V., & Bravo, E. (2025, January). Strengthening Student Learning: From Outcome-based to Process-based Learning. In *52nd Annual Conference of the European Society for Engineering Education, SEFI 2024* (pp. 2657-2661). European Society for Engineering Education (SEFI). https://doi.org/ DOI: 10.5281/zenodo.14260964

Schiefele, U., & Schaffner, E. (2015). Teacher interests, mastery goals, and self-efficacy as predictors of instructional practices and student motivation. *Contemporary Educational Psychology*, *42*, 159–171. DOI: 10.1016/j.cedpsych.2015.06.005

Schunk, D. H., & DiBenedetto, M. K. (2020). Motivation and social cognitive theory. *Contemporary Educational Psychology*, *60*, 101832. Advance online publication. DOI: 10.1016/j.cedpsych.2019.101832

Senko, C., & Dawson, B. (2017). Performance-approach goal effects depend on how they are defined: Meta-analytic evidence from multiple educational outcomes. *Journal of Educational Psychology*, *109*(4), 574–598. https://psycnet.apa.org/doi/10.1037/edu0000160. DOI: 10.1037/edu0000160

Shah, P. (2023). *AI and the Future of Education: Teaching in the Age of Artificial Intelligence*. John Wiley & Sons.

Sklad, M., Diekstra, R., Ritter, M. D., Ben, J., & Gravesteijn, C. (2012). Effectiveness of school-based universal social, emotional, and behavioral programs: Do they enhance students' development in the area of skill, behavior, and adjustment? *Psychology in the Schools*, *49*(9), 892–909. DOI: 10.1002/pits.21641

Slovák, P., & Fitzpatrick, G. (2015). Teaching and developing social and emotional skills with technology. [TOCHI]. *ACM Transactions on Computer-Human Interaction*, *22*(4), 1–34. DOI: 10.1145/2744195

Turner, J. C., Warzon, K. B., & Christensen, A. (2011). Motivating mathematics learning: Changes in teachers' practices and beliefs during a nine-month collaboration. *American Educational Research Journal*, *48*(3), 718–762. DOI: 10.3102/0002831210385103

Vistorte, A. O. R., Deroncele-Acosta, A., Ayala, J. L. M., Barrasa, A., López-Granero, C., & Martí-González, M. (2024). Integrating artificial intelligence to assess emotions in learning environments: A systematic literature review. *Frontiers in Psychology, 15*, 1387089. Advance online publication. DOI: 10.3389/fpsyg.2024.1387089 PMID: 38966729

Walker, G., & Venker Weidenbenner, J. (2019). Social and Emotional Learning in the age of virtual play: Technology, empathy, and learning. *Journal of Research in Innovative Teaching & Learning, 12*(2), 116–132. DOI: 10.1108/JRIT-03-2019-0046

Wang, H. (2024). *Goal-oriented framework for AI-empowered curriculum design.* Doctoral thesis, Nanyang Technological University, Singapore. https://hdl.handle.net/10356/181505

Wood, C., Stowell, L., & Goldberg, M. (2023). *Innovation, Literacy, and Arts Integration in Multicultural Classrooms: Theory and Practice for Designers of K-8 Learning Environments.* Taylor & Francis. DOI: 10.4324/9781003107101

Woods, R., & Pooley, J. A. (2015). A review of intervention programs that assist the transition for adolescence into high school and the prevention of mental health problems. *International Journal of Child and Adolescent Health, Suppl.Special Issue: Places and Spaces: The Domain of Adolescence, 8*(2), 97-108. Retrieved from https://www.proquest.com/scholarly-journals/review-intervention-programs-that-assist/docview/1706179930/se-2

Xia, Q., Chiu, T. K., Lee, M., Sanusi, I. T., Dai, Y., & Chai, C. S. (2022). A self-determination theory (SDT) design approach for inclusive and diverse artificial intelligence (AI) education. *Computers & Education, 189*, 104582. Advance online publication. DOI: 10.1016/j.compedu.2022.104582

Yadav, N. (2024). *Exploring the role of a chatbot in supporting self-regulated learning (SRL) among students with low and high SRL skills* (Master's thesis, N. Yadav). Retrieved from https://urn.fi/URN:NBN:fi:oulu-202406044185

Yeh, Y.-C., Kwok, O.-M., Chien, H.-Y., Sweany, N. W., Baek, E., & McIntosh, W. A. (2019). How college students' achievement goal orientations predict their expected online learning outcome: The mediation roles of self-regulated learning strategies and supportive online learning behaviors. *Online Learning : the Official Journal of the Online Learning Consortium, 23*(4), 23–41. DOI: 10.24059/olj.v23i4.2076

Yong, G. H., Lin, M. H., Toh, T. H., & Marsh, N. V. (2023). Social-emotional development of children in Asia: A systematic review. *Behavioral Sciences (Basel, Switzerland), 13*(2), 123. Advance online publication. DOI: 10.3390/bs13020123 PMID: 36829352

Zervaki, K. (2024). Empowering E-learning: Effective strategies for supporting students with Learning Difficulties. *Journal of Language and Culture in Education, 1*(2), 69–85. DOI: 10.5281/zenodo.14284217

Zhou, Z., Chen, X., Li, E., Zeng, L., Luo, K., & Zhang, J. (2019). Edge intelligence: Paving the last mile of artificial intelligence with edge computing. *Proceedings of the IEEE, 107*(8), 1738–1762. DOI: 10.1109/JPROC.2019.2918951

Zimmerman, B. J. (2002). Becoming a self-regulated learner: An overview. *Theory into Practice, 41*(2), 64–70. DOI: 10.1207/s15430421tip4102_2

Zyphur, M. J., & Pierides, D. C. (2020). Statistics and probability have always been value-laden: An historical ontology of quantitative research methods. *Journal of Business Ethics, 167*(1), 1–18. DOI: 10.1007/s10551-019-04187-8

# Chapter 5
# AI-Enhanced Learning and Teacher Productivity:
## Bridging Technology and Human Expertise

**Omniah AlQahtani**
https://orcid.org/0000-0002-3223-0586
*National Academy of Childhood Development, UAE*

## ABSTRACT

*This chapter explores the evolving relationship between artificial intelligence (AI) and education, with a focus on balancing technological innovation and the indispensable role of teachers. It examines how AI-driven tools enhance both student learning and teacher productivity, providing adaptive, personalized educational experiences while streamlining administrative and instructional tasks. By integrating AI, educators can focus more on fostering meaningful student interactions and guiding learning journeys, allowing technology to handle routine processes. The chapter highlights the critical balance between AI's capacity to enhance efficiency and the irreplaceable human qualities teachers bring empathy, intuition, and adaptability. As AI systems grow more sophisticated, the need for teachers to adapt and collaborate with these technologies becomes essential.*

## INTRODUCTION

In recent years, the integration of artificial intelligence (AI) in education has dramatically reshaped the teaching and learning landscape. This chapter examines the evolving relationship between AI and education, with a focus on balancing technological innovation with the indispensable role of teachers. It explores how AI-

DOI: 10.4018/979-8-3373-0573-8.ch005

driven tools can enhance both student learning and teacher productivity, providing adaptive, personalized educational experiences while streamlining administrative and instructional tasks (Schindler et al., 2017; Zawacki-Richter et al., 2019).

The inclusion of AI in education allows educators to focus more on meaningful student interactions and guide learning journeys more effectively (Selwyn, 2022). As AI manages routine tasks, teachers can concentrate on cultivating critical thinking, emotional intelligence, and collaboration—vital components of holistic student development.

## HISTORICAL AND CONCEPTUAL BACKGROUND

The integration of technology into education has evolved since the use of early-generation computers for teaching, grading, and administrative tasks (Jones, 1985; Tahiru, 2021). The emergence of AI represents a major leap in this trajectory. AI, defined by McCarthy (2007) as "the science and engineering of making intelligent machines," is now widely used in various educational platforms, systems, and services. The term itself was coined during the 1956 Dartmouth Conference, which marked a foundational moment in AI research (Schiff, 2022).

Today, AI influences many facets of life through systems like Google Duplex, FaceApp, and autonomous robots such as Yuki and Sophia (Miao et al., 2021; Retto, 2017). In education, such tools are being explored not only for content delivery but also for intelligent feedback, learner profiling, and even classroom management.

AI can be classified into weak or narrow AI (task-specific) and strong or general AI (with broad cognitive capacities) (Berker, 2018). While strong AI remains theoretical, weak AI is already changing the educational landscape. Nonetheless, concerns remain about AI's impact on the human aspects of education. Scholars like Stephen Hawking have warned about the risks of unchecked AI development (Holmes & Tuomi, 2022), and some educators worry that increased automation may threaten their roles (Chu et al., 2021).

## THEORETICAL FRAMEWORK: TECHNOLOGICAL-ORGANIZATIONAL-ENVIRONMENTAL (TOE)

To structure this discussion, the chapter applies the Technological Organizational Environmental (TOE) framework, which offers a multi-dimensional view of AI adoption in education:

I. Technological: Accessibility, affordability, and ease of use of AI tools.

II. Organizational: School leadership, institutional readiness, and teacher support.
III. Environmental: Government policy, ethical norms, and public attitudes.

This model provides a comprehensive understanding of the factors that shape AI integration across educational systems.

## CRITICAL REVIEW OF LITERATURE AND PRACTICE

Most existing studies have focused on the disruptive potential of AI in education, especially in developed nations (Grassini, 2023). This chapter addresses the gaps in current literature by exploring both opportunities and challenges, and by emphasizing the importance of human-centered AI adoption.

### Ethical Considerations and Data Privacy

Despite its benefits, AI also introduces serious ethical concerns. The collection and use of student data by intelligent systems raises questions about privacy, surveillance, and informed consent. Biased algorithms may unfairly penalize marginalized students or misinterpret their needs. Transparent design, algorithmic accountability, and adherence to global ethical guidelines (e.g., UNESCO, EU AI principles) are essential to mitigate these risks.

### Teacher Training and Professional Development

Successful AI adoption hinges on teacher readiness. Many educators are unfamiliar with how AI functions or how it can be meaningfully integrated into pedagogy. Therefore, robust professional development programs must be introduced to improve AI literacy among teachers. These should focus on technical proficiency, pedagogical alignment, and ethical awareness. Schools must also allocate time and resources to support this transition.

### Student Perspectives and Engagement

Students' experiences with AI are rarely explored in depth. Understanding how students perceive AI tools—whether they feel empowered or monitored, motivated or disengaged—is crucial. Studies suggest that while students appreciate personalization, they also express concerns about the opacity of AI systems and a lack of human feedback. Including student voice in AI tool development and implementation can improve trust and effectiveness.

## Equity and Inclusion in AI-Powered Education

AI has the potential to widen the digital divide if not implemented equitably. Under-resourced schools may lack the infrastructure or funding to adopt AI, leaving certain students behind. On the other hand, AI can be a powerful tool for inclusive education—providing customized support for students of determination, multilingual learners, or those with mental health needs. Equity must be a foundational principle in AI design and deployment.

## Case Studies and Implementation Examples

The chapter would benefit from concrete examples of AI integration in various educational contexts. For instance:

I. In Finland, AI is used in national assessments to provide instant feedback to students.
II. In the UAE, AI is integrated into smart classrooms that personalize content delivery based on student engagement.
III. In India, low-cost AI tutors are used to bridge learning gaps in rural areas. These case studies offer practical insights into implementation strategies, challenges, and outcomes.

## Futures Thinking: What Lies Ahead

Finally, the chapter should explore emerging trends and the future of AI in education. Generative AI tools, emotional AI capable of detecting student mood, and AI-enhanced learning analytics are already reshaping the field. The future may see AI collaborating with educators to co-design curriculum, monitor well-being, or offer real-time formative assessment. However, this future must be guided by ethical, pedagogical, and human-centered values to prevent misuse.

## AI-DRIVEN TOOLS IN EDUCATION

The use of AI in educational contexts has grown significantly in recent years. Tools such as adaptive learning platforms, intelligent tutoring systems, and AI-powered grading systems have revolutionized traditional educational practices. Adaptive learning platforms, for instance, customize content based on individual learner needs, making it possible for students to learn at their own pace and ensuring that they receive appropriate levels of challenge and support.

Research on the use of AI in education underscores its capacity to address diverse learning styles and improve accessibility (Guilherme, 2019). According to studies, integrating tools like animated visuals and interactive presentations has a positive impact on student engagement and learning outcomes, as they make content more accessible and understandable for students with varying cognitive abilities.

Furthermore, AI grading systems can assess student performance on routine assignments, saving teachers valuable time. These systems can quickly analyze patterns in student responses, offering real-time feedback that promotes learning (Giannini, 2023). AI-based grading can also identify gaps in students' understanding, enabling teachers to focus on the areas where students need the most help. In the table below, a selection of the latest AI tools that can significantly empower educators and enrich learning content can be found.

*Table 1. Recent AI tools and functions for educators*

| AI tool name | Function |
|---|---|
| **Gamma** | Create presentation from scratch |
| **ElevenLabs** | AI Voice Generator & Text to Speech |
| **MEQR** | QR code generator |
| **Humata** | Summarize findings, compare documents, and search for answers |
| **Chat GPTs** | Enhance communication, learning, and problem-solving by providing instant, personalized assistance and information across a wide range of topics. |
| **DALL·E by OpenAI** | It uses deep learning models to generate detailed and creative images from text descriptions, allowing for highly customized and unique visual content. |
| **Runway Gen-2** | Create videos using text-to-video generation technology, enabling users to create high-quality videos from simple text prompts. It also offers tools for video editing, motion tracking, and other advanced effects, making it a robust choice for AI-driven video creation. |

## THE ROLE OF EDUCATORS IN AN AI-ENHANCED CLASSROOM: MAINTAINING THE HUMAN TOUCH IN A TECHNOLOGICAL WORLD

In AI-enhanced classrooms, the educator's role is not diminished but rather transformed into one of higher-level guidance, emotional support, and adaptive instruction (Chu et al., 2021). While AI takes over many routine tasks, such as grading and providing basic feedback, the human element that teachers bring to the educational process remains irreplaceable. The evolution of the teacher's role becomes particularly significant when examining the intersection of AI with pedagogical practices and the broader learning experience.

## The Irreplaceable Human Qualities of Teachers

Teachers bring to the classroom a set of human qualities that AI cannot replicate, including empathy, intuition, adaptability, and creativity. These traits are essential in fostering not only academic success but also the social and emotional development of students.

Empathy and Emotional Support: One of the most critical aspects of teaching is the ability to connect with students emotionally. Learning is not merely a cognitive process; it is deeply emotional. Teachers understand their students' emotional needs and can respond in ways that build trust, offer comfort, or provide motivation. Empathy allows teachers to create a learning environment where students feel safe and supported. AI, in contrast, lacks the emotional intelligence required to interpret a student's non-verbal cues or personal challenges.

Intuition and Classroom Dynamics: Educators possess an intuitive understanding of classroom dynamics that AI cannot match. This includes knowing when to slow down instruction, when to challenge students further, and how to handle the unpredictable moments of teaching (Chu et al., 2021). Teachers can read the energy of a classroom, sense confusion even when students are silent, and adapt their teaching in real-time to meet the needs of the moment. AI systems, although responsive to data, are largely reactive and lack the ability to "feel" the nuances of a classroom's collective mood.

Adaptability in Teaching Methods: Teachers are skilled at adjusting their methods based on the unique needs of individual students. This adaptability is crucial in diverse classrooms, where students may have varying learning styles, cultural backgrounds, or personal challenges. AI-driven systems can adapt content delivery to some extent through algorithms, but they often lack the flexibility and sensitivity needed for nuanced, spontaneous adjustments in instruction. Teachers, on the other hand, can creatively pivot their teaching strategies in response to classroom dynamics, ensuring that each student receives appropriate guidance.

## Human-AI Collaboration in Education

Rather than viewing AI as a competitor, educators should see it as a collaborator that enhances their capabilities. AI's strength lies in data processing and personalization at scale, freeing teachers from repetitive administrative tasks and allowing them to focus on higher-order thinking and problem-solving activities. Teachers and AI can work together in a complementary fashion, with AI taking care of tasks like grading, analyzing student performance data, and providing personalized content recommendations, while teachers focus on areas where human interaction is indispensable.

Supporting Personalized Learning: One of the key areas where AI complements educators is in personalized learning. AI systems can track student progress in real-time, adapting content to each learner's pace and style (Chu et al., 2021). However, personalization is not just about adapting content about recognizing and responding to the individual challenges students face, which often have emotional or social dimensions. Teachers bring the human insight necessary to interpret and act on the data AI provides. They can have conversations with students, understand the underlying reasons for learning struggles, and tailor their feedback in ways that go beyond mere academic performance.

AI as a Tool for Reducing Cognitive Load: Teachers can use AI to reduce the cognitive load on themselves and their students. For example, AI can help in organizing classroom materials, managing schedules, and tracking student participation. This allows teachers to focus on delivering more engaging and meaningful lessons. In fact, with AI handling logistical and administrative tasks, teachers can invest more time in designing creative, interactive lessons, which are crucial for maintaining student attention and fostering a deeper understanding of complex topics.

Enhancing Instruction with Data: AI-powered platforms offer rich data analytics, which can provide teachers with insights into student learning patterns. These tools can highlight areas where individual students are struggling, enabling teachers to intervene early. While AI can generate these insights, it is the teacher who contextualizes them within the broader picture of a student's academic and emotional life. For example, if a student is consistently underperforming in math, the AI may flag this as a problem, but the teacher will need to consider whether the issue is related to comprehension, a personal challenge, or even something as simple as test anxiety. This holistic understanding of student performance is something only a human teacher can provide.

## Teaching Beyond the Curriculum: Nurturing Skills for the Future

In an AI-enhanced classroom, teachers are freed to focus more on fostering skills that go beyond the standard curriculum, such as critical thinking, creativity, and collaboration skills that are increasingly important in the 21st-century workforce (Chu et al., 2021). These competencies are not easily taught by machines, as they require complex, open-ended interactions, reflection, and problem-solving that are inherently human. Teachers guide students in:

Critical Thinking and Problem Solving: While AI can provide information and manage tasks, teachers help students develop the ability to think critically, analyze problems, and come up with creative solutions. These are skills that students will need to navigate an AI-dominated world, where simply knowing facts is less important than being able to interpret, evaluate, and innovate based on those facts.

Emotional and Social Intelligence: AI systems are limited in their ability to teach social skills, which are vital for students to succeed both in school and in life. Teachers play a key role in helping students develop empathy, communication, and teamwork. They facilitate group work, encourage discussions, and guide students through conflicts and misunderstandings, all crucial elements of emotional and social learning.

Ethical Use of AI: As AI becomes more integrated into education and everyday life, teachers have a responsibility to help students understand the ethical implications of AI technology. This includes discussions about data privacy, bias in algorithms, and the social impact of automation. By fostering critical conversations around these issues, teachers empower students to become informed citizens who can navigate and shape the future of AI ethically.

## Challenges of Teacher Adaptation to AI

While the integration of AI offers numerous benefits, there are challenges that teachers face in adapting to these new tools.

Professional Development Needs: Teachers will need ongoing professional development to stay abreast of technological advances and learn how to effectively incorporate AI into their teaching practices. This requires support from educational institutions to provide training and resources, ensuring that teachers can maximize the benefits of AI without feeling overwhelmed by technology itself.

Resistance to Change: Some educators may resist the integration of AI due to concerns about job security or a belief that technology could diminish the personal aspects of teaching. It is essential to address these concerns through dialogue and demonstration of how AI can enhance, rather than replace, the teacher's role. Building confidence in AI's ability to support rather than supplant educators will be crucial in ensuring its successful adoption.

Balancing AI with Traditional Methods: While AI tools provide innovative ways to enhance learning, teachers must also balance the use of technology with traditional teaching methods. Not every lesson or subject matter is suited to AI-driven instruction. Educators will need to make informed decisions about when to use AI tools and when to rely on more conventional, human-centered approaches to teaching.

## The Future of Teaching in an AI-Driven World

As AI continues to evolve, the role of the teacher will shift, but the core of teaching mentorship, emotional connection, and intellectual guidance will remain. The future classroom will likely be one where AI and teachers work together in synergy, creating a more personalized and responsive learning environment.

In this AI-augmented future, teachers will focus on higher-order thinking skills, nurturing creativity, and guiding students through complex ethical and social questions that AI cannot address. By embracing AI as a tool for enhancing education, teachers will continue to be at the heart of the learning process, guiding students not only in mastering content but also in becoming thoughtful, empathetic, and capable individuals ready to thrive in a rapidly changing world.

# PRACTICAL APPLICATIONS: AI TOOLS IN USE

Artificial Intelligence (AI) has significantly transformed various aspects of education by introducing practical tools that assist educators in personalizing learning, enhancing student engagement, and improving administrative efficiency. These AI-powered tools are designed to support both students and teachers, creating a more dynamic and effective learning environment. In this section, we will explore some of the key AI tools currently in use, how they work, and the tangible benefits they bring to educational settings.

## Adaptive Learning Platforms: Tailoring Education to Individual Students

One of the most powerful applications of AI in education is adaptive learning. Adaptive learning platforms use algorithms and machine learning to tailor educational content to the individual needs of each student. These platforms assess a student's strengths, weaknesses, and learning styles through continuous data collection, allowing the system to adjust the difficulty level, pace, and type of content delivered to each learner.

*How It Works:* Adaptive learning platforms analyze students' interactions with the content, tracking their performance in real-time. Based on this data, the system dynamically adjusts the content. For example, if a student is struggling with a specific math concept, the platform might offer additional exercises, explanatory videos, or alternate teaching methods to reinforce the material. On the other hand, if a student is excelling, the system might introduce more challenging problems to ensure continued growth.

*Benefits*: These platforms allow for highly personalized learning experiences. Students no longer must follow a one-size-fits-all curriculum; instead, they can progress at their own pace. This is particularly beneficial for both advanced learners who need more challenging material and students who may require additional support to grasp certain concepts. Teachers can also use the data generated by adaptive learning platforms to monitor individual progress and intervene when necessary.

*Examples*: Platforms like DreamBox, an adaptive math program, adjust the difficulty of problems based on the learner's current level. Similarly, Smart Sparrow uses adaptive learning in higher education, providing personalized pathways through complex subjects like engineering and biology.

## Intelligent Tutoring Systems (ITS): Personalized, Real-Time Assistance

Intelligent Tutoring Systems (ITS) represent another practical AI tool in education, designed to provide students with immediate, personalized feedback and guidance. These systems function like virtual tutors, offering tailored instruction based on a student's responses. They can be particularly effective in supplementing traditional classroom learning by offering students additional support outside of school hours.

*How It Works*: ITS analyzes student input, such as answers to questions or interactive tasks, and provides real-time feedback. The AI algorithms behind these systems simulate the decision-making processes of a human tutor. If a student makes a mistake, the ITS offers hints, rephrases the problem, or provides step-by-step solutions. As the system interacts with the student, it becomes better at predicting where the student might need help in the future.

*Benefits*: ITS offers several key advantages, including continuous availability, as students can access tutoring at any time. They are also highly scalable, meaning that many students can receive individualized help simultaneously without the need for additional human tutors. For educators, these systems provide detailed insights into student learning behaviors, helping them tailor their in-class teaching strategies to address common areas of difficulty.

*Examples*: One popular example is Carnegie Learning's Cognitive Tutor, which focuses on mathematics and uses cognitive science to offer personalized tutoring. Similarly, ALEKS (Assessment and Learning in Knowledge Spaces) is another AI-driven tutoring system that provides tailored instruction in subjects such as mathematics, chemistry, and business.

## AI-Powered Grading Systems: Automating Routine Tasks

Grading is one of the most time-consuming tasks for educators, especially in large classrooms. AI-powered grading systems are designed to automate this process, offering teachers more time to focus on higher-level tasks such as curriculum development and individualized student support.

*How It Works*: AI grading systems analyze student submissions, particularly those in objective formats like multiple-choice or fill in the blank. More advanced AI systems are even capable of assessing open-ended responses, such as essays, by analyzing grammar, sentence structure, and content relevance. Over time, these systems can learn from teacher feedback and adjust their grading algorithms to align more closely with a teacher's standards.

*Benefits*: By automating grading, AI reduces the workload on teachers, allowing them to spend more time on interactive teaching and mentorship. Additionally, AI grading systems provide immediate feedback to students, which is crucial for learning reinforcement. Another significant advantage is the consistency of grading—AI systems eliminate the subjective biases that sometimes affect human grading.

*Examples*: AI grading platforms such as GradeScope use machine learning to grade assignments and provide structured feedback to students. Turnitin, while primarily a plagiarism detection tool, also incorporates AI to assess the quality of writing and generate feedback on student work.

## Chatbots and AI-Powered Student Support Systems

AI-powered chatbots have become increasingly common in educational settings, providing students with instant support. These chatbots can answer frequently asked questions, provide reminders about upcoming deadlines, and offer basic tutoring assistance, particularly in online learning environments.

*How It Works*: Chatbots are built using natural language processing (NLP) and machine learning algorithms, allowing them to understand and respond to student queries in real time. These systems learn from each interaction, gradually improving their ability to offer accurate and helpful responses. Chatbots can be integrated into learning management systems (LMS) or standalone applications, providing students with 24/7 support.

*Benefits*: Chatbots significantly reduce the administrative burden on teachers by handling routine queries, such as clarifying assignments, due dates, or course policies. Additionally, they offer students a more accessible and immediate means of communication, particularly in online or blended learning environments. Students who are shy or hesitant to ask questions in a classroom setting may feel more comfortable seeking help from a chatbot.

*Examples*: Jill Watson, a well-known AI teaching assistant developed at Georgia Tech, is an example of an AI-driven chatbot that answered student questions in an online course. Similarly, platforms like Ivy.ai provide chatbots tailored to higher education institutions, offering academic support, information on financial aid, and help desk functions.

## AI and Content Creation: Personalized Learning Materials

Another practical application of AI in education is in content creation, where AI tools can generate personalized learning materials for students based on their unique needs and progress. These tools are particularly useful for creating tailored assessments, quizzes, and instructional content that align with a student's learning path.

*How It Works*: AI systems analyze student performance data and automatically generate content that fits the individual learner's current level. For example, after assessing a student's weaknesses in a particular subject, an AI tool might generate additional practice problems or interactive simulations designed to address those gaps. Some AI systems can also curate external content, such as videos or articles, that are relevant to a student's learning objectives.

*Benefits*: AI-driven content creation tools provide students with materials that are directly aligned with their current abilities, ensuring that they are neither overwhelmed nor under-challenged. This increases engagement and helps students master difficult concepts more effectively. For teachers, these tools save significant time and effort in designing personalized materials, allowing them to focus more on instructional strategies and direct student interaction.

*Examples*: Content Technologies, Inc. has developed AI systems that create personalized textbooks based on students' specific learning needs. Similarly, platforms like Quizlet use AI to generate custom quizzes and flashcards tailored to each student's progress.

## AI in Administrative Efficiency: Streamlining Education Management

AI is not just transforming classroom teaching but also educational management. AI tools can automate various administrative processes, from scheduling to attendance tracking, reducing the burden on teachers and school administrators.

*How It Works:* AI-driven systems can manage tasks such as class scheduling, monitoring student attendance, and tracking overall classroom performance metrics. These systems often integrate with school management software, providing real-time insights into class participation, student progress, and resource allocation.

*Benefits:* By automating administrative tasks, AI frees up time for educators to focus on teaching and student engagement. For administrators, these tools offer improved efficiency in managing school resources, optimizing schedules, and ensuring that student needs are met promptly. Moreover, AI tools can predict trends in student performance, attendance, and even potential dropout risks, allowing schools to take proactive measures.

*Examples*: EdSights is a platform that uses AI to track student data and predict potential retention issues. nTask and similar tools use AI to assist educators with task management, including creating lesson plans and tracking student progress.

## AI for Learning Analytics: Data-Driven Decision Making

AI-driven learning analytics platforms provide educators with detailed insights into student learning behaviors. These platforms collect and analyze data from various sources, including assignments, quizzes, and classroom interactions, offering teachers a comprehensive view of each student's progress.

*How It Works*: Learning analytics systems use AI to process large sets of student data, identifying patterns and trends that may not be immediately apparent to educators. These insights can highlight individual learning gaps, group trends, or areas where the curriculum might need adjustment. AI can also predict student outcomes based on current performance data, helping educators intervene early if a student is at risk of falling behind.

*Benefits*: Learning analytics platforms give teachers actionable insights into their students' progress, allowing for data-driven instruction. These platforms help educators make informed decisions about which students need additional support, which teaching strategies are most effective, and how to optimize classroom time.

*Examples*: Knewton is an adaptive learning platform that uses learning analytics to tailor educational content and predict student performance. Similarly, Civitas Learning provides learning analytics to help educators and institutions improve student retention and success rates.

## AI-Powered Simulations and Virtual Learning Environments

AI has also found applications in creating immersive learning experiences through simulations and virtual environments. These tools allow students to engage in experiential learning by simulating real-world scenarios, offering a deeper understanding of complex subjects.

*How It Works*: AI-driven simulations use sophisticated algorithms to replicate real-world environments, allowing students to practice skills or explore concepts in a controlled, virtual space. For instance, medical students can use AI-powered simulations to practice surgical procedures, while engineering students can test their designs in a virtual environment.

*Benefits*: These simulations offer students hands-on experience without the risks associated with real-world practice. They also provide immediate feedback, helping students learn through trial and error in a safe and supportive environment. For educators, AI-powered simulations offer a way to engage students with complex material in a manner that traditional teaching methods cannot.

*Examples*: Labster is an AI-powered virtual laboratory that allows students to conduct science experiments online. zSpace provides immersive learning experiences in subjects like biology, physics, and engineering through virtual reality (VR) and augmented reality (AR).

## AI AND TEACHER COLLABORATION: A SYNERGISTIC APPROACH

The integration of Artificial Intelligence (AI) into education is not about replacing teachers but about creating a powerful collaboration between human expertise and machine efficiency. This synergistic approach leverages the strengths of both AI and teachers to create more dynamic, personalized, and effective learning environments. While AI excels at handling repetitive, data-intensive tasks, teachers bring the essential human elements of intuition, empathy, and adaptability—qualities that are critical for fostering deeper learning and social-emotional development. In this section, we explore how this collaboration can enhance the educational process and improve outcomes for both teachers and students.

### Enhancing the Teacher's Role Through AI

AI can take over many time-consuming and administrative tasks, such as grading, attendance tracking, and data analysis, which allows teachers to dedicate more time to the creative and interactive aspects of teaching. Instead of being bogged down by routine work, teachers can focus on designing lessons that foster critical thinking, creativity, and collaboration. AI systems can provide personalized feedback to students in real-time, track progress, and suggest improvements, while teachers can step in with targeted interventions when needed.

*Relieving Administrative Burden*: By automating tasks such as grading, AI frees up valuable time for teachers to focus on activities that require a human touch, such as engaging in meaningful one-on-one interactions with students, mentoring, and providing emotional support. This shift allows teachers to spend more time designing innovative lesson plans and exploring new teaching strategies, which ultimately enhances the quality of instruction.

*Improved Focus on Student Well-Being:* As AI handles repetitive tasks, teachers are better positioned to monitor the emotional and social well-being of their students. AI systems might flag behavioral or academic patterns indicating that a student is struggling, but it is the teacher's role to interpret these signs, offer support, and ensure that the student feels heard and understood. In this way, AI complements the teacher's ability to focus on students' holistic development, beyond academic performance.

## Supporting Personalized Learning and Differentiated Instruction

One of the most significant benefits of AI in education is its ability to offer personalized learning experiences. AI-driven platforms continuously analyze data on student performance, learning preferences, and engagement levels, providing tailored content and instructional paths. However, while AI personalizes the technical aspects of learning, teachers personalize human connection, adjusting their approach based on their deep understanding of student motivations, backgrounds, and challenges.

*AI-Powered Insights for Differentiated Instruction:* AI systems provide teachers with insights into each student's learning style, progress, and areas for improvement, making differentiated instruction more feasible. For example, teachers can use AI-generated data to identify which students need additional support and which can be pushed further with more advanced content. This data-driven approach enables teachers to cater to individual students' needs more effectively, ensuring that every learner receives appropriate attention.

*Balancing Human Judgment with AI Recommendations:* While AI provides recommendations based on data, it's crucial for teachers to balance these insights with their professional judgment. For instance, an AI system might suggest that a student needs more practice with a particular skill, but a teacher, understanding the student's emotional state or external factors affecting performance, might choose a different intervention, such as a one-on-one conversation or a break from the subject. This collaboration between AI's data-driven insights and the teacher's human understanding creates a more well-rounded approach to personalized learning.

## Continuous Professional Development for Teachers

AI can also play a role in the professional development of teachers. By analyzing classroom interactions, student engagement, and learning outcomes, AI tools can provide feedback to educators on their teaching methods. These insights can help teachers refine their instructional strategies, improve classroom management, and even identify areas where they might benefit from additional training.

*Real-Time Feedback and Reflection*: AI systems can observe teaching practices and provide teachers with data on how their students are responding. For instance, if certain teaching techniques consistently result in higher engagement or better test scores, AI can highlight these methods for further use. Conversely, AI can flag areas where students are consistently struggling, prompting teachers to adjust their approach or seek professional development in that area.

*Customized Training Programs:* AI-powered platforms can recommend professional development resources based on a teacher's specific needs. For example, if a teacher's students are frequently underperforming in math, the system might suggest targeted resources, workshops, or courses to help improve their instructional skills in that subject. This personalized approach to teacher training ensures that professional development is directly aligned with classroom realities.

## Fostering a Collaborative Classroom Environment

AI tools also foster a more collaborative classroom environment, encouraging teachers and students to work together in new and innovative ways. With AI taking on some of the instructional and administrative burden, teachers have more opportunities to engage with students in creative, project-based learning experiences. Moreover, AI can facilitate group work by assigning roles based on students' strengths and helping track group dynamics to ensure all students contribute.

*AI-Assisted Collaborative Learning:* AI tools can be used to facilitate collaborative projects by grouping students based on complementary skills or interests. Teachers can oversee these collaborations and intervene when necessary to ensure that the group remains on task and that all students are benefiting from the experience. AI can also provide real-time feedback to both students and teachers, making the collaborative process smoother and more efficient.

*Empowering Teachers as Mentors and Facilitators:* In an AI-augmented classroom, the teacher's role evolves into that of a mentor and facilitator. Rather than simply delivering content, teachers guide students through learning experiences, helping them develop higher-order thinking skills such as critical analysis, creativity, and problem-solving. AI's ability to handle routine tasks allows teachers to focus on facilitating discussions, mentoring students, and fostering a positive classroom culture where learning is collaborative and student-driven.

## Ethical Considerations in AI-Teacher Collaboration

As AI becomes more integrated into education, ethical considerations must be considered, particularly in terms of how much control AI should have over decision-making in the classroom. Teachers must remain the ultimate decision-makers when it comes to student learning and well-being, using AI as a tool to inform their choices rather than allowing AI to dictate them.

*Maintaining Human Oversight:* While AI can analyze vast amounts of data and make recommendations, teachers must always retain oversight to ensure that these recommendations are in the best interest of students. For example, AI might suggest a particular intervention based on academic performance data, but teachers must consider the social, emotional, and cultural context of their students before acting on these recommendations. Maintaining this balance is crucial for ensuring that AI is used ethically and equitably in the classroom.

*Addressing Bias in AI Systems:* AI systems are only as good as the data they are trained on, and there is always the risk that AI tools could perpetuate biases present in the data. Teachers must be vigilant in identifying and addressing potential biases in AI systems, ensuring that the technology is used to support all students fairly and without prejudice. Continuous monitoring and feedback from teachers are essential in refining AI tools to ensure that they promote inclusivity and equity in the classroom.

# CHALLENGES AND ETHICAL CONSIDERATIONS

As Artificial Intelligence (AI) continues to be integrated into educational systems, several challenges and ethical considerations emerge that need to be carefully navigated. While AI offers immense potential to transform education, it also brings with it complexities that require thoughtful analysis and regulation. These challenges span across areas like data privacy, bias in AI algorithms, the potential for job displacement, and the need to preserve the human essence of teaching. Understanding these issues is critical for ensuring that AI enhances rather than harms the educational experience.

## Data Privacy and Security Concerns

One of the most pressing challenges of using AI in education is the protection of students' data. AI systems rely on vast amounts of data to function effectively, which means they collect, store, and analyze sensitive information about students, including their academic performance, learning behaviors, personal details, and sometimes even biometric data. This raises significant privacy concerns, especially when it comes to how this data is handled, who has access to it, and how it is protected from misuse or breaches.

*The Scope of Data Collection:* AI systems can track every interaction a student has with digital learning tools, from how long they spend on a question to their emotional responses (if using systems that incorporate facial recognition or sentiment analysis). While this data can be valuable for personalizing learning experiences, it also poses a risk if not managed responsibly. Ensuring that student data is anonymized, encrypted, and only accessible to authorized personnel is critical to maintaining trust in AI systems in education.

*Data Ownership and Consent:* Another ethical concern is related to data ownership who owns the data collected by AI systems, and how is it used? Students and their guardians must have control over their data and be fully informed about how it will be used. Transparency is essential to ensure that students (and their families) give informed consent for data collection and that their data is not sold or misused by third parties for commercial purposes.

*Regulatory Challenges:* Different countries and regions have varying levels of regulation concerning data privacy in education. In the European Union, the General Data Protection Regulation (GDPR) provides robust protection for individuals, but in other regions, such protection may be weaker or non-existent. As AI use in education expands globally, ensuring compliance with regional data protection laws while maintaining consistent ethical standards across borders becomes a complex challenge.

## Bias in AI Systems and Its Impact on Education

AI systems are only as good as the data they are trained on, and one of the most significant ethical concerns surrounding AI in education is the potential for bias. If AI systems are trained on biased data, they may perpetuate or even exacerbate existing inequalities in education. This can lead to unfair treatment of certain groups of students, especially those from marginalized or underrepresented backgrounds.

*Bias in Training Data:* AI systems are trained using historical data, and if this data reflects existing societal biases whether based on race, gender, socioeconomic status, or other factors then the AI system can inherit these biases. For example, an AI system might predict that certain students are more likely to struggle based on past data of students from similar backgrounds, even if those students are fully capable of succeeding. This can lead to unfair recommendations for remedial programs or other forms of discrimination in educational opportunities.

*Unequal Access and Representation:* AI systems may also unintentionally favor students who have better access to technology or who fit certain learning profiles. Students from low-income or rural areas, who may have limited access to the devices and high-speed internet needed for AI-driven tools, could be left behind. Additionally, students who do not fit into the standard learning patterns that AI systems are designed to accommodate may find themselves at a disadvantage if the system fails to understand or support their unique learning needs.

*Mitigating Bias Through Human Oversight:* One way to mitigate bias in AI systems is to ensure that human educators remain central to the decision-making process. Teachers should use AI-generated insights as one tool among many, not as the sole determinant of a student's capabilities or future opportunities. Moreover, developers of AI systems must strive to create more inclusive and representative datasets and involve diverse groups in the design and testing of AI technologies to reduce the risk of biased outcomes.

## The Risk of Over-Reliance on AI and Teacher Job Displacement

Another challenge posed by the integration of AI in education is the fear that teachers may become overly reliant on AI tools, leading to a reduction in the need for human educators. While AI can handle many tasks, such as grading and administrative functions, there is concern that as AI becomes more sophisticated, it could take over larger portions of the teaching process, ultimately leading to job displacement for teachers.

*Job Displacement Concerns:* The fear of AI replacing teachers is not entirely unfounded. As AI systems become more advanced, they could potentially take on more instructional roles, such as delivering lectures, providing real-time tutoring, or even assessing higher-order thinking tasks like essay writing. In some cases, educational institutions might see AI as a cost-saving measure, reducing the need for human teachers. This poses a risk to the teaching profession, particularly in areas where there is already economic pressure on education budgets.

*Redefining the Role of Teachers:* However, most experts agree that AI is unlikely to fully replace teachers, as the human elements of empathy, mentorship, and emotional support are irreplaceable. Instead, AI could redefine the role of teachers, allowing them to focus more on creative and interactive aspects of teaching, such as fostering critical thinking, collaboration, and emotional development, while AI handles routine tasks. The key to mitigating job displacement is ensuring that teachers are trained to work alongside AI systems, using these tools to enhance their teaching rather than replace their role in the classroom.

*Continuous Professional Development:* As AI becomes more prevalent in education, teachers will need continuous professional development to adapt to these changes. Ensuring that educators are equipped with the skills to effectively integrate AI into their teaching practice is essential for reducing fear and resistance to these technologies. By empowering teachers to take ownership of AI tools, education systems can ensure that AI enhances rather than threatens the profession.

## Ethical Use of AI in Assessment and Decision-Making

AI systems are increasingly being used in assessments, from grading assignments to predicting student performance. While this can increase efficiency and objectivity, there are significant ethical concerns surrounding the use of AI in making high stakes decisions about students' futures.

*Fairness in Assessment:* AI systems can offer consistency in grading, but there is concern about how well these systems can assess more subjective elements of student work, such as creativity, critical thinking, or nuanced argumentation. There is a risk that AI might reduce complex, creative work to a series of patterns or keywords, potentially disadvantaging students who excel in less conventional forms of expression.

*AI in Predictive Analytics:* Some AI systems are used to predict students' future performance or likelihood of success in certain subjects or careers. While this can help educators provide targeted support to students, it also raises ethical concerns about determinism. If AI predicts that a student is likely to fail, there is a risk that both the teacher and the student might internalize this prediction, creating a self-fulfilling prophecy. It is crucial to ensure that AI systems are used to support student growth, not to limit opportunities based on potentially flawed predictions.

*Maintaining Human Oversight in High-Stakes Decisions:* High-stakes decisions, such as academic progression, placement in special programs, or eligibility for scholarships, should not be left solely to AI systems. Human educators must have the final say in these decisions, using AI as one of many tools in their decision-making process. This ensures that individual circumstances, personal growth, and other non-quantifiable factors are considered alongside data-driven insights.

## The Challenge of Maintaining the Human Element in Education

Perhaps the most significant ethical challenge of integrating AI into education is maintaining the human-centered nature of teaching and learning. Education is not just about transferring knowledge; it is about building relationships, fostering a love of learning, and helping students grow into well-rounded individuals. AI, by its nature, lacks the emotional intelligence and moral judgment needed to fulfill these broader goals of education.

*Emotional and Social Learning:* AI-driven systems may be able to deliver content and assess academic performance, but they cannot provide the emotional support that students often need, especially in early education and adolescence. Teachers play a critical role in helping students navigate social dynamics, build resilience, and develop empathy—areas where AI systems fall short. As AI becomes more integrated into education, it is essential to ensure that teachers have the time and capacity to focus on these human aspects of learning, which are fundamental to student well-being and long-term success.

*Human Interaction in Learning:* Learning is an inherently social process, and students benefit from the relationships they build with their teachers and peers. AI systems can personalize content and provide feedback, but they cannot replace the motivation and inspiration that comes from human interactions in the classroom. Ensuring that AI tools are used to support, rather than replace, these interactions are crucial for maintaining the quality and depth of the educational experience.

## THE FUTURE OF AI IN EDUCATION

The role of AI in education is expected to expand, with even more sophisticated tools emerging. However, the human element of education will remain irreplaceable. The most effective educational environments will be those that combine AI's capabilities with teachers' emotional intelligence and pedagogical expertise. As AI systems grow more intelligent, the key challenge will be to ensure that technology is used to augment, rather than replace, human judgment and creativity in the learning process.

In this future, teachers will not only need to be proficient in using AI tools but also play a crucial role in shaping how these tools are applied in the classroom. They will guide the ethical use of AI, ensuring that it serves all students equitably and supports personalized learning in a way that aligns with human values.

## CONCLUSION

The integration of AI into education offers tremendous potential for enhancing learning and teaching. However, the success of this integration depends on finding the right balance between technological innovation and the irreplaceable human elements of empathy, adaptability, and guidance. Teachers, far from being replaced by AI, are central to this future, acting as collaborators with technology to create more personalized, effective, and engaging learning experiences.

This chapter has outlined the current landscape of AI tools in education, explored the evolving role of teachers in an AI-augmented classroom, and highlighted the ethical challenges that accompany AI integration. As we look to the future, the key to successful AI integration will be a focus on collaboration between humans and machines, with educators leading the way in shaping a future where technology enhances, rather than diminishes, the human-centered nature of education.

## REFERENCES


Berker, A. (2018). The categorization of AI: Weak vs. strong artificial intelligence. *Journal of AI Research*, *45*, 122–133.

Chu, X., Chai, C. S., Jong, M. S. Y., Istenic, A., Spector, M., & Li, Y. (2021). A review of artificial intelligence (AI) in education from 2010 to 2020. *Complexity*, *2021*(1), 8812542. DOI: 10.1155/2021/8812542

Giannini, S. (2023). *Generative AI and the future of education*. UNESCO.

Grassini, S. (2023). Shaping the future of education: Exploring the potential and consequences of AI and ChatGPT in educational settings. *Education Sciences*, *13*(7), 692. DOI: 10.3390/educsci13070692

Guilherme, A. (2019). AI and education: The importance of teacher and student relations. *AI & Society*, *34*(1), 47–54. DOI: 10.1007/s00146-017-0693-8

Holmes, W., & Tuomi, I. (2022). State of the art and practice in AI in education. *European Journal of Education*, *57*(4), 542–570. DOI: 10.1111/ejed.12533

Jones, T. (1985). Computers in the classroom: The next generation. *Educational Technology*, *25*(3), 22–29.

McCarthy, J. (2007). *What is artificial intelligence?* Stanford AI Laboratory.

Miao, F., Holmes, W., Huang, R., & Zhang, H. (2021). *AI and education: A guidance for policymakers*. Unesco Publishing.

Retto, D. (2017). Yuki and Sophia: AI in the classroom. *AI in Education Review*, *12*(4), 34–39.

Schiff, D. (2022). Education for AI, not AI for education: The role of education and ethics in national AI policy strategies. *International Journal of Artificial Intelligence in Education*, *32*(3), 527–563. DOI: 10.1007/s40593-021-00270-2

Schindler, L., Burkholder, G., Morad, O., & Marsh, C. (2017). Computer-based technologies in education. *International Journal of Technology in Education*, *28*(2), 150–165.

Selwyn, N. (2022). The future of AI and education: Some cautionary notes. *European Journal of Education*, *57*(4), 620–631. DOI: 10.1111/ejed.12532

Tahiru, F. (2021). AI in education: A systematic literature review. [JCIT]. *Journal of Cases on Information Technology*, *23*(1), 1–20. DOI: 10.4018/JCIT.2021010101

Zawacki-Richter, O., Marín, V., Bond, M., & Gouverneur, F. (2019). Systematic review of research on artificial intelligence applications in higher education. *International Journal of Educational Technology in Higher Education*, *16*(1), 39. DOI: 10.1186/s41239-019-0171-0

Zhang, K., & Aslan, A. B. (2021). AI technologies for education: Recent research & future directions. *Computers and Education: Artificial Intelligence*, *2*, 100025. DOI: 10.1016/j.caeai.2021.100025

# Chapter 6
# Playful Therapies:
## Use of Gamification in School Counselling

**Kriti Vashishtha**
https://orcid.org/0000-0001-5463-6758
*Manipal University Jaipur, India*

**Charu Dhankar**
https://orcid.org/0000-0001-7395-2326
*Manipal University Jaipur, India*

**Shraddha Tripathi**
https://orcid.org/0000-0002-7897-8901
*Manipal University Jaipur, India*

**Ruchi Joshi**
https://orcid.org/0000-0002-3425-8187
*Manipal University Jaipur, India*

## ABSTRACT

*This chapter focuses on using gamification techniques by school counsellors as a part of psychotherapies and psychoeducation. Application of psychological theories would further explain the effectiveness of game mechanics. Multiple gamification apps and their effectiveness and usability will also be explored. In addition to promoting intrinsic motivation, high levels of engagement, pleasing competition, collaboration, improved performance, problem-solving, critical and creative thinking, etc., it also offers students individualised learning opportunities. The chapter provides suggestions for further research in this sector and the implication of gamification in school counselling.Overall, this chapter emphasises how gamification in school counselling may be innovative in providing insightful information to teachers,*

DOI: 10.4018/979-8-3373-0573-8.ch006

*counsellors, and researchers who want to use game-based approaches to promote students' psychological well-being and therapeutic outcomes.*

## INTRODUCTION

### Overview of Gamification

With the implementation of the New Education Policy, 2020 in the schools, the focus has been shifted towards individualized or customized teaching, conceptual knowledge, creative and critical thinking, outstanding research, extensive use of technology (digital literacy), and life skills such as communication, cooperation, teamwork, and resilience. To work effectively with the students, school authorities are using gamification techniques to engage the students in better learning and understand their personal needs and learning skills. Gamification in education is a process of using various game mechanics in classroom settings that motivates children to not only learn to concepts but also to utilise them appropriately. The origin of gamification can be traced from the 1960s to the 1980s when the renowned behaviourist, B.F. Skinner used various game mechanics of reinforcement, reward-punishment, etc. for learning. Later with the rise in technology and computer usage, various educational software was using the methods of levels, rewards, badges, and many more. It was due to designer Nick Pelling that the term gamification gained its popularity by the year 2008. The usage of gamification software became more popular due to the easy availability of the internet and mobile phones. 2010 onwards gamification techniques proliferated with the advent of Massive Open Online Courses (MOOCs) and online learning platforms. Businesses started using components from games, such as leaderboards, points, and badges, to entice students. Personalised learning experiences and gamified progress monitoring were made possible by platforms such as Khan Academy. The year 2010 brought a great revolution in the educational system. Many schools started using terms like 'play-way learning', 'game-based learning' as their motto of school. There were research-based pieces of evidence available in support of gamification in education. (Hebebci, & Alan, 2021)

The emergence of the Learning Management System (late 2010 onwards) made it easier to use technology in traditional classroom settings. Teachers started using Quizlet, ClassDojo, and Google Classroom, among other technologies, to incorporate game dynamics into their lessons and foster competition and teamwork. This further increased in 2019 when COVID hit and the whole education system shifted to virtual classrooms. Since 2020, with an emphasis on customised learning experiences and adaptable learning platforms, gamification is still developing. The emergence of Augmented Reality (AR) and Virtual Reality (VR) in education also points to a new direction for gamified learning. Furthermore, the focus on social-emotional learning points to a move towards comprehensive methods that use gamification along with other teaching techniques.

Approaches of gamification are not just limited to educational settings but it's even spreading to multiple other fields and one of the areas it is doing wonders is counselling, especially child and adolescent/ school counselling. Literature shows that gamification techniques when applied in educational or counselling settings, enhance student engagement and motivation. It facilitates good behaviour, encourages skill-based learning, and provides customized experiences to every child. This customized experience helps a lot when it comes to school counselling. As every child is different, the gamification technique is customized as per the child and used as a part of counselling sessions or therapies. School counsellors may create a more dynamic, encouraging, and productive atmosphere that ultimately supports students' academic performance and well-being by utilising the motivating elements of games. (Wiggins, 2016)

## Understanding Gamification

Over the past ten years, the idea of gamification—which is the use of game-design aspects outside of games—has been more popular in the fields of education and mental health. According to Deterding et al. (2011), gamification is the process of using components like challenges, avatars, point systems, and prizes to boost user motivation and engagement. These components provide structure, feedback, and a feeling of accomplishment by appealing to fundamental psychological processes.

Gamification in school counselling involves using gamification techniques in therapeutic settings. This helps the client in better understanding of the issue. As the techniques used in gamification are extremely engaging, it motivates students to be regular with their counselling sessions and practice required behaviour at home. Counsellors also find using this method useful as it becomes easy to track the progress of the student, also the level of the tasks can be kept as per the present status of the child. Moreover, the type of reinforcement can be decided according to the performance, needs and desires of the children. (Conn et. al., 2023)

### Core Elements of Gamification in School Counselling (Xie, 2022)

Paring up gamification methods with counselling sessions and psychotherapies has been found to make the sessions/ therapies more effective. Some of the common core elements of gamification include:

- *Points*: If student(s) meet their personal goals or demands of the therapies they get points which even increase with the number of tasks achieved. This motivates them to work regularly and sincerely for their betterment.
- *Badges* also work like points. It is more of a visual representation of reward or appreciation. It has been seen that people get a sense of pride when they get recognised by badges that are displayed publicly.
- *Leaderboards* create a spirit of competitiveness among the students. Here the students are ranked as per their performance on the desired task. It not only motivates them to perform better but even show them their current position in the group which helps them to set their further goals.
- *Levels* work similarly to any board game or video game. As in any video game, we get some tasks to complete for a specific level and when we complete them, we move to the next level, and it has its tasks and challenges. Similarly, in counselling session, the counsellor works with the client level-wise. Once, level one is completed successfully, the client moves to the second level with new behavioural tasks and challenges.
- *Challenges* include the tasks given by the counsellor to the counselee which are customized as per the present status of the client. These challenges could be from self-analysis to emotional regulation or even behavioural modification. Completing the challenges can let the client get some points, and badges or this can even help them go to the next level.
- *Rewards* always help motivate. They can be tangible or intangible but should be based on fair judgment. To achieve any rewards, the goals set should be achievable and realistic. Rewards also work better if they are congruent with the client's expectations and needs.
- *Feedback* should be given at an appropriate time. It loses effectiveness if it is given too late or too soon. A proper feedback system should be transparent and strictly followed. Feedback can be given digitally, verbally, or even in written form through progress reports. It makes the students aware of their progress, which helps in better engagement and performance.

## Psychological Foundations

Ryan and Deci's (2000) Self-Determination Theory (SDT) offer a strong foundation for comprehending the motivating effects of gamification. The demand for autonomy, competence, and relatedness—all of which may be strengthened by game-based interventions—is what drives human motivation, according to SDT. Furthermore, according to Csikszentmihalyi's notion of Flow (1990), immersive experiences that match talents to difficulties can foster deep involvement, a phenomenon commonly seen in gaming contexts. These ideas fit extremely well with developmental requirements in psychological therapy, especially when working with children and adolescents. Applying these theories while using gamification techniques makes counselling more effective.

- *Self-Efficacy Theory*: The founder of self-efficacy theory is Albert Bandura. According to him if an individual believes that they are efficient, skilled, and competent, then they will be able to deal with challenges and perform related tasks. People with high self-efficacy are consistent with their work, they put in extra effort to complete any task and behave resiliently when faced with any challenge. Bandura has proposed various sources of enhancing self-efficacy which when applied to counselling sessions paired with gamification can help in faster healing of the client.

For example, the first source is performance appraisal, the performance of the client can be appraised through their performance in the past. Methods like points, and level/ rank up on a leaderboard based on students' performance can help them have high self-efficacy and high motivation to attend the remaining counselling sessions. The second source is vicarious experience, which includes, modeling by others. This can be helpful in group counselling sessions, where people have similar problems and anyone who has overcome it can behave as a role model to others. Similarly, on the leaderboard, first and second-ranked students work as role models for others who want to be fully functional. There are also some virtual models stuck in a situation and the client is asked to choose from the options available, 'what should the model do?'. Taking the right steps and moving on to higher levels help students to increase their self-efficacy. The third source is social persuasion, that is, giving evaluative feedback. The feedback system of gamification can be used here to work on the student's self-efficacy. If genuine feedback is given to the student for their performance at every step, they will gain confidence in their strengths and will work in the right direction. The fourth source is a physiological and emotional state, here the counsellor works with the client's feel-good factor about the things they are doing to have successful counselling. When the gamification aspect is added to it and the student is reinforced interestingly, they share positive affect with the counsellor, which keeps them motivated throughout the counselling. (Rachels, & Rockinson-Szapkiw, 2018)

- *Flow Theory*: The founder of flow theory is Mihaly Csikszentmihalyi. It is believed that any hardworking person reaches success when they are fully immersed in their work. According to science, if an individual reaches a state where the brain frequency is between 8-14 Hz., any work they do becomes extremely easy. This state is called the flow state. The flow state is common among famous athletes during their games and practice. Some yogis call this state 'nirvana' and believe that once you learn to be in nirvana, not only do your tasks become easy but even your performance increases ten times. While writing the book Flow, Csikszentmihalyi wanted to find the reasons behind the happiness of people. He was pleased to discover that people's perception of satisfaction existed when they were engaged in an activity, to the point that they were unaware of any other external distractions. This contrasted with when individuals were sleeping or relaxing. (Constantinescu et. al., 2017)

- *Self-determination theory:* This theory helps in identifying the intrinsic and extrinsic level of motivation among people. It has been seen that people with intrinsic motivation tend to engage in any task enthusiastically and enjoy it thoroughly. Whereas those with extrinsic motivation get trill due to their intention to seek reward and abstain from punishment. According to self-determination theory, three critical needs identify motivation, viz., *autonomy* (the need to feel in control of own behaviour and decisions), *competence* (the need to feel proficient, knowledgeable, and skilled in any task or activity), *relatedness* (the need to feel affinity, connectedness and associated to others).

Counsellors can use gamification techniques to *encourage autonomy* among clients. Clients can make their avatars or plots that symbolises their own development, this can be done in a story form. Counsellors can let clients choose from a variety of tasks or activities, such as journaling, mindfulness training, or social interaction, according to their preferences. Using such tactics in counselling journey allows the client to gain a sense of empowerment.

Further, the client can work on enhancing *competence* through feedback and reward techniques. For instance, in career counselling, gamification techniques like solving quizzes and puzzles can prepare the client for a job interview and its progress indicators can even help them deal with the job market. Counsellors can provide some incentives or badges to the client for completing the required tasks (e.g. 7 sessions of mindfulness). (Jamaludin et. al., 2021)

Counselling process even involves creating a sense of *relatedness*, belongingness, and shared identity among the clients. Counsellors are developing certain gamified mental health software where the clients can create social support groups, contribute to the group milestones, promote positive group communications, and work as helpers for people who join later.

To get the best results, counsellors should align the gamification goals to intrinsic motivation, such as personal growth and environmental mastery.

## Gamification in School Counselling

**Role of a school counsellor:** School counsellors are essential in helping child's grow socially, emotionally, and academically. Their duties include assisting students in overcoming obstacles, making career plans, and developing resilience. The strategies and resources counsellors use to successfully engage kids change along with the educational environment.

The school counsellor works as an advocate, resource, and mentor for the school children. Their role is not just limited to direct contact with children but also with teachers, staff, principals, and parents. They indulge from personal guidance to vocational counselling and take charge of the overall development of the student. (Guerrero-Puerta & Guerrero, 2021)

**Traditional counselling methods:** Counselling sessions in schools have been either one-to-one or group counselling. The trend has also shifted a bit toward virtual counselling, depending upon the issue. Some of the common traditional methods used by school counsellors are:

- *Talk therapy*: Talk therapy, commonly referred to as counselling or psychotherapy, is a conventional approach that is frequently utilised in school counselling to promote the mental and emotional wellness of children. This method uses many frameworks and strategies that help the counsellor and the student communicate openly, creating a safe space for students to share their experiences, feelings, and ideas.

It is crucial to create a secure and trustworthy atmosphere. Students find it simpler to express their private thoughts and feelings when counsellors establish a connection with them and promote open communication and a sense of safety.

To assist students in reframing negative ideas, questioning harmful beliefs, and creating coping mechanisms, some counsellors use Cognitive Behavioural Therapy (CBT) procedures. To give kids a feeling of agency and purpose, counsellors collaborate with them to establish reasonable goals on their academic or emotional growth. By promoting communication, perspective-taking, and negotiation skills, counsellors can assist students in resolving interpersonal disputes. Counsellors frequently offer resources, coping mechanisms, and information about mental health, giving students the tools they need to effectively control their emotions and actions. (Bojuwoye, & Sodi, 2010)

- *Career Counselling*: Historically, a major component of school counselling has been career counselling, which helps students make well-informed decisions about their future academic and professional pathways. Traditional methods of career counselling in schools typically include individual and group counselling.

Standardised tests, such as aptitude tests, interest inventories (like the Holland Code), and personality tests, are frequently used by counsellors to assist students in understanding their preferences and strengths. Group environments promote idea sharing and peer support, which makes students feel less alone while they explore career options.

A well-rounded support system can be created by talking with parents about their childs' professional interests. Opportunities for internships, real-world experiences, and mentoring can be created through partnerships with nearby companies and organisations. Certain educational institutions provide specialised courses that concentrate on career development, planning, and exploration. Students who attend regular follow-up sessions can have their continuing career interests evaluated and receive extra support during critical decision-making.

Despite their effectiveness, traditional career counselling approaches have drawbacks, including the necessity for individualised approaches in classrooms with a growing diversity and the incorporation of technology. Additionally, counselling techniques must be continuously modified to stay up with new industries, technology, and career routes due to the quickly evolving work market. (Bojuwoye, & Sodi, 2010)

- *Social Skills Training (SST):* In school counselling, social skills training (SST) is an organised method that helps children learn the interpersonal skills needed for social engagement, relationship development, and successful communication. This approach is especially crucial since it tackles the social deficiencies that some kids could have, whether because of social anxiety, developmental disabilities, or other difficulties.

When students exhibit desired behaviours, positive reinforcement is frequently provided along with constructive criticism about their social interactions. To facilitate the transfer of abilities from the counselling setting to their everyday lives, students are urged to apply the skills they have learned in training to actual circumstances. To foster relationships and socialization with classmates, SST frequently includes activities that stimulate peer participation and interaction.

Schools frequently collaborate with teachers, counsellors, and, when appropriate, parents to efficiently carry out social skills instruction. They may use behavioural evaluations, inspections, or questionnaires to pinpoint the precise social skills deficiencies in the student body. They may also develop or choose an SST program that is structured and fits the needs of the kids. Programs such as the Social Skills

Improvement System (SSIS) or other models may fall under this category. (Chiboola, & Munsaka, 2018)

- *Behavioural Interventions*: Behavioural interventions aim to change behaviours to enhance students' social skills, academic achievement, and general well-being. These treatments are especially pertinent in school counselling, where the objective is to assist children in overcoming obstacles and encouraging positive behaviours. Some of the traditionally used behavioural interventions are positive reinforcement, behavioural modification plans, token economies, cognitive behaviour techniques, modelling, behavioural contracts, self-monitoring etc.

School counsellors develop a system of rewards, such as points, tokens, or privileges, for children who consistently behave well or meet academic objectives. Together with parents and teachers, counsellors create a thorough plan that includes behaviour monitoring, clear expectations, and interventions as needed. School therapists might use the token economy, which is popular in classrooms, to promote behaviours like attending counselling sessions, finishing assignments, and engaging in class.

Students can be taught by counsellors to recognise and confront negative thoughts and swap them out for more productive, upbeat ones. a formal contract that outlines behaviours to be changed and the related rewards or penalties between the student and the counsellor (and frequently parents). During sessions, counsellors can demonstrate how to solve problems and communicate effectively, giving students real-world examples of how to handle social situations.

Students can document their behaviour and assess their progress towards particular behavioural goals by keeping diaries or behaviour logs. Counsellors can help students share their experiences and solutions for development by leading group discussions on common behavioural difficulties. include parents in the behavioural intervention procedure to maintain uniformity between the home and school settings. (Bojuwoye, & Sodi, 2010)

- *Crisis Management*: In school counselling, crisis management entails a methodical approach to handling and reacting to crises and significant events that impact students, faculty, and the school community. In school counselling, traditional crisis management techniques are crucial to guaranteeing students' safety and wellbeing in emergency situations.

Comprehensive crisis response plans that specify how to handle different kinds of crises (natural disasters, violent incidents, mental health emergencies, etc.) are created and updated regularly by counsellors. Provide staff, teachers, and school counsellors with frequent training on mental health first aid and crisis response techniques. Collaborate with community organisations, mental health specialists, and local authorities to establish a crisis support system.

By fostering a supportive school atmosphere that aggressively combats bullying, teaches conflict resolution, and encourages candid communication, counsellors help to create a safe space. Organise workshops and programs that inform parents, employees, and students about mental health awareness and accessible options. Use screening instruments to find pupils who are at danger and offer prompt assistance.

Counsellors immediately provide students, employees, and families affected by the situation with emotional and psychological help. Offer individual or group therapy sessions with an emphasis on coping mechanisms, event processing, and resilience building. Create effective channels of communication to notify parents, teachers, and students about the issue and the resources accessible to them. (Chiboola, & Munsaka, 2018)

In school counselling, traditional crisis management techniques place a strong emphasis on readiness, prevention, quick action, and rehabilitation. School counsellors can effectively manage crises, lessen their impact, and encourage healing within the school community by creating a supportive environment and providing staff and students with the tools and skills they need.

Traditional teaching approaches are beneficial for many students, but they frequently call for high levels of involvement and motivation, which can be difficult to maintain, particularly for younger or less driven people.

## Current Challenges Faced in Engaging Students

School counsellors face several challenges in sustaining student involvement and providing effective interventions, even with their best efforts. Students may find it difficult to focus during typical counselling sessions since they are often distracted, particularly in the current digital era. Students may be discouraged from speaking candidly with counsellors due to cultural stigma or fear of being judged. Conventional approaches might not accommodate different learning preferences or personal interests, which would decrease their efficacy.

Innovative strategies are needed to treat the growing prevalence of stress, anxiety, and depression among students in a comprehensive manner. In many schools, there are few possibilities for meaningful, one-on-one contact due to high counsellor-to-student ratios. Although there are advantages to technology, excessive screen time and exposure to online stresses have created new therapeutic difficulties. (Low, 2009)

A creative way to deal with these issues is to incorporate gamification into school counselling, which gives pupils individualised, dynamic, and interesting treatments. By incorporating game design concepts into counselling exercises, it enhances the process's attractiveness and effectiveness. Applying aspects of game design to non-gaming environments, or gamification, has become a cutting-edge strategy for involving pupils and overcoming obstacles in conventional counselling techniques. It uses concepts like rewards, competition, and interactive experiences to increase the attraction and efficacy of counselling.

Students find counselling more engaging when dynamic, interactive components are introduced through gamification. Passive conversations are not as effective in grabbing attention as activities like role-playing games, riddles, and quizzes. Students can experience scenarios, make decisions, and get rapid feedback through apps or virtual worlds. Leaderboards, points, or badges can encourage students to participate fully in class. (Harrison, & Gordon, 2021)

Students may find counselling less daunting and more normalised with the use of gamified resources. Students can voice problems in a safe environment without worrying about being judged thanks to virtual counselling games. Through interactions with imaginary people dealing with comparable problems, story-driven games enable students to indirectly handle delicate subjects. Self-reflection is encouraged and tests that are gamified, like mood tracking apps, feel less official. (Low, 2009)

Customised methods that accommodate a range of learning preferences and styles are made possible by gamification. A personalised experience is ensured by games' ability to modify difficulty levels in response to a student's success. The game allows students to create personal objectives, which humanises the process. Counsellors can design focused interventions by using digital technologies to gain insights into students' areas of strength and growth. (Harrison, & Gordon, 2021)

Through planned, interactive exercises, gamification promotes emotional control and coping mechanisms. Stress management and relaxation skills are taught through gamified methods in apps like Smiling Mind and Headspace for Kids. Students can practise handling stress or conflict in safe settings by using interactive simulations or role-playing scenarios. Gamified multiplayer platforms can foster a sense of community and teamwork among pupils.

In environments with limited resources, gamification makes counselling effective and scalable. Counsellors can concentrate on urgent issues since students can finish gamified tasks on their own. Group projects or gamified workshops let counsellors interact with several students at once. Without requiring a lot of manual labour, gamified platforms may gather and evaluate data to give counsellors insights into students' progress. (Harrison, & Gordon, 2021)

Gamification makes technology a tool for learning and fits in with students' digital habits. Students' familiar gaming surroundings are replicated using gamified apps. Students are more likely to link counselling with positive experiences when entertainment and education are combined. Immersion VR counselling exercises offer fresh approaches to teaching problem-solving and empathy. (Low, 2009)

Counsellors may create a more welcoming, interesting, and productive environment for students by incorporating gamification into school counselling. This will help students overcome obstacles and improve their emotional and social health.

## GAMIFICATION STRATEGIES ALONG WITH CASE STUDIES (SIRIARAYA ET. AL., 2021)

- *Goal-Setting Through Game Challenges:* Counsellors design games where students set and achieve specific goals (e.g., managing stress or improving communication). Each completed task unlocks rewards or new levels. for example, a game titled Stress Busters challenges students to identify stress triggers, practice a relaxation technique daily, and record their progress to earn points.
- *Role-Playing Scenarios for Problem-Solving:* Interactive role-playing games let students practice resolving conflicts or navigating real-world dilemmas in a safe, virtual environment. for example, in a bullying prevention program, students assume the roles of a victim, bystander, and advocate, learning how to handle bullying situations effectively.

Interactive storytelling and role-playing are effective gamification strategies for incorporating narratives into counselling, allowing clients to address personal difficulties in fictitious or symbolic settings. Role-playing enhances storytelling by imitating real-life circumstances in which clients can practise discussions or make decisions in a controlled, safe setting. Adolescents, for example, may practise refusal skills in response to peer pressure, increasing their confidence in establishing limits. Collaborative role-playing in group therapy strengthens teamwork and social skills, making it especially useful for enhancing interpersonal connections.

These approaches have many multiple applications. Narrative therapy uses storytelling to help clients rewrite their life stories and challenge negative self-concepts, whereas trauma counselling uses fictitious settings to safely process painful emotions. Furthermore, conflict resolution situations in role-playing promote emotional regulation and communication skills, making these tools helpful for a variety of counselling requirements.

- *Emotional Regulation Through Virtual Reality (VR):* Use virtual reality (VR) tools to recreate stress-inducing circumstances and educate students to handle anxiety in real time. For example, a VR module sets students in a classroom environment where they practise breathing methods during a simulated stressful exam.
- *Peer Collaboration with Multiplayer Activities:* Gamified group assignments promote teamwork and social connections. For example, a multiplayer game focusses on empathy by having students collaborate to solve problems based on understanding diverse points of view.

- *Rewards and Progress Tracking:* Create digital badges, certificates, or virtual prizes for achieving milestones like finishing a counselling program or mastering a new skill. For example, a badge system for persistent participation in counselling sessions, such as "Mindful Master" or "Stress Warrior."

- *Use of Avatars and Virtual Environments*: The use of avatars and virtual environments in counselling allows clients to explore scenarios, express themselves, and participate in therapy in an immersive and non-threatening manner. These tools enable personalisation, allowing clients to design avatars that reflect their identity or goals, instilling a sense of agency and ownership in their counselling journey. For example, a child dealing with social anxiety may create a confident superhero avatar to help him or her negotiate difficult social circumstances. Furthermore, virtual environments provide safe exploration opportunities by imitating real-world contexts like classrooms or workplaces, allowing clients to practice coping techniques in controlled, secure environments. Clients with autism benefit greatly from platforms like Floreo, which allow them to practice social interactions.

Avatars can also help clients acquire skills by guiding them through enjoyable mindfulness exercises, conflict resolution assignments, and emotional regulation approaches. For example, gamified apps like Mindlight use virtual reality (VR) and avatars to educate youngsters emotional resilience. The benefits of adopting avatars and virtual settings include lowering stigma and resistance by creating a fun and engaging therapeutic experience. They also allow clients to gradually tackle anxieties or stressors in a non-threatening manner, while increasing motivation through immersive and participatory activities.

- *Digital Badges and Achievement Systems in Counselling:* Digital badges are virtual tokens that clients receive for accomplishing tasks, mastering abilities, or reaching milestones. They function as motivational aids and progress indicators, making counselling more interesting and gratifying. Counsellors can utilise digital badges to help clients define and track goals by developing incremental targets like attending sessions, blogging, or practicing mindfulness exercises. For example, a client may receive a "Stress Buster" badge after completing five relaxation exercises. These badges also serve as acknowledgement and reinforcement, increasing clients' self-esteem and motivation. Adolescents working on anger management, for example, could earn badges such as "Cool as Ice" for successfully using coping strategies.

Achievement systems increase engagement by using point-based advancement, levels, or leaderboards. Clients receive points by performing therapeutic activities, which can be used to unlock incentives or additional assignments. A gamified anxiety management program, for example, could reward participants for daily mood tracking with points that could be redeemed for guided meditation sessions. Levels represent mastery of specific abilities, whereas leaderboards provide a sense of accomplishment and participation, especially in group therapy settings.

Integrating gamification approaches into counselling sessions can result in a holistic framework that improves participation and effectiveness. Counsellors can create a comprehensive approach that addresses a variety of therapeutic requirements by mixing avatars, virtual environments, interactive narrative, and digital badges. Avatars and virtual settings immerse clients in self-exploration, allowing them to engage with therapy in a safe, participatory setting. Interactive storytelling helps clients improve emotional understanding and problem-solving skills by allowing them to reflect on their experiences and devise new coping techniques. Meanwhile, digital badges reinforce clients' achievement while encouraging positive behaviour.

Several technological platforms have previously implemented gamification in counselling. For example, Classcraft employs gamification to encourage social-emotional learning, resulting in a more engaged learning environment. (Siriaraya et. al., 2021)

However, like with any technological intervention, ethical issues must be properly addressed. Ensuring privacy and data security is critical when using digital platforms to safeguard sensitive client information. Gamified tools should also be made to be accessible to a wide range of demographics, including people with impairments, to ensure inclusion. It is also critical to retain therapeutic oversight to balance the gamification features with counselling aims, ensuring that the technique stays effective and does not overwhelm the basic goals of therapy.

Furthermore, gamification approaches such as avatars, interactive narrative, and achievement systems are transforming counselling by increasing its engagement, accessibility, and effectiveness. These tools address classic issues such as resistance, stigma, and a lack of desire, while also encouraging skill development and self-awareness. As technology advances, gamification has the potential to alter counselling practices by enhancing outcomes and enabling more engaging and personalised therapy experiences.

## *Case Study 1.* Gamifying Emotional Regulation in a Middle School Setting

A middle school struggled to assist children successfully regulate their emotions and handle anger. To address these concerns, the school launched a gamified app called Emotion Explorer. This unique tool encourages students to perform daily emotional check-ins, practise guided breathing exercises and earn "calm badges" as prizes for being cool in challenging situations. The app's innovative and engaging features encouraged students to participate consistently while also encouraging self-reflection and emotional awareness. Over six months, the school saw a 40% reduction in behavioural events. Furthermore, students demonstrated increased self-awareness and willingness to freely share their feelings, demonstrating that the gamified method was effective in promoting emotional control. (Shin, 2024)

## *Case Study 2.* SuperBetter: Building Resilience Through Play

High school students were experiencing substantial academic stress and reluctance to attend counselling sessions, making it difficult for counsellors to adequately address their problems. To address this, the counsellors created an innovative program known as the "Stress-Free Hero Challenge." This gamified project enables students to earn points for identifying stress causes, practicing relaxation techniques, and participating in group discussions. To increase motivation and engagement, a leaderboard was used to encourage friendly competition among participants, with prizes awarded to top performers. The initiative produced exceptional results, with counselling participation up by 60%. Students reported feeling more in control of their stress and engaging in classroom activities, demonstrating the approach's effectiveness in resolving their academic issues.

SuperBetter is a gamified platform that helps people increase mental resilience, particularly those suffering from stress, anxiety, depression, or chronic illness. SuperBetter, created by game designer Jane McGonigal, combines game concepts such as missions, power-ups, and challenges to encourage personal development. Users build "quests" depending on their specific objectives, such as improving sleep patterns or reducing worry. Completing these activities gives them points, badges, and increases their "power-ups," which symbolise their mental fortitude.

A study on the usage of SuperBetter with people suffering from depression yielded promising outcomes. Users who played the game reported feeling more motivated, happier, and empowered to manage their mental health. One success story featured a participant who was experiencing chronic stress because of her caregiving responsibilities. After a few weeks of taking SuperBetter, individuals reported less stress and better emotional regulation. The game's method of framing mental health difficulties as "quests" and rewarding progress helped to transform the participant's viewpoint, making mental health management more approachable and less scary. (Millen et. al., 2020)

## *Case Study 3.* Floreo: Social Skills Training for Children with Autism

Using new tactics, elementary school counsellors tried to improve student communication and collaboration. To address this, the school deployed Classcraft, a gamified platform that encouraged students to join teams and accomplish objectives aimed at improving listening, empathy, and collaboration. To modify behaviour, the system used both positive and negative reinforcements—mistakes in social interactions, such as interrupting, resulted in point deductions, whilst acts of compassion won awards. Teachers reported significant improvements in classroom behaviour and student interactions after three months, demonstrating the program's efficacy in developing social skills.

Floreo is another VR-based gamified counselling tool intended exclusively to help children with autism learn social skills. The platform offers a variety of virtual social scenarios in which students can practise interacting with avatars in settings such as classrooms and public locations. The scenarios are intended to mimic real-life social settings in which children with autism may struggle, such as making eye contact, taking turns in talking, or comprehending social signs.

Research using Floreo with children with autism spectrum disorder (ASD) discovered that following a series of sessions, participants demonstrated improved social behaviours and increased involvement in real-life social situations. (Ravindran et al., 2019)

## *Case Study 4.* **Mindlight: Emotional Resilience for Children**

The Mindlight software, created for youngsters suffering from anxiety, was one of the first examples of gamified counselling. The software uses virtual reality (VR) and gamification techniques to teach youngsters emotional management and resilience. The game takes youngsters through a series of challenges in which they must manage their emotions in reaction to various in-game pressures. As they progress, they receive rewards and acquire confidence in their capacity to manage fear.

The game employs avatars and immersive surroundings to imitate circumstances that may cause anxiety, such as school presentations or social interactions, allowing youngsters to practice coping methods in a safe and enjoyable setting. Pilot research with youngsters using Mindlight revealed a significant reduction in anxiety symptoms. (Schoneveld et. al., 2016)

## *Case Study 5.* **Classcraft: Gamified Counselling in School Settings**

Classcraft is a popular tool in educational settings that uses gamification to promote positive behaviour, emotional well-being, and academic performance among students. It enables students to create avatars and collaborate as teams to fulfil quests relevant to school goals, such as behavioural and emotional development objectives. Counsellors in schools have modified Classcraft to aid counselling efforts by incorporating lessons on emotional regulation, conflict resolution, and stress management into the game's activities.

One school district in California used Classcraft as part of its counselling program to address social and emotional learning (SEL) issues in a middle school context. After several months of using the platform, kids' behaviour, engagement in schoolwork, and social skills improved significantly. The platform's gamified structure encouraged students to take responsibility for their emotional and academic development, while also providing counsellors with real-time statistics on individual progress. Students were more motivated to attend counselling sessions, and Classcraft's light-hearted tone decreased the stigma associated with seeking help. (Gonzalez, 2021)

Gamification is a scalable solution, making it extremely useful for accommodating large groups of children, particularly in schools with limited counselling resources.

## Key Takeaways from Gamified Therapy

- The Importance of Customization: The necessity of personalisation to guarantee that the gamified experience appeals to the individual is among the most important takeaways from these case studies. For instance, Mindlight's tasks were adjusted based on each child's anxiety level, so they didn't feel overburdened but were still pushed to their limits. Like this, Floreo's social scenarios were tailored to each autistic child's particular requirements, enabling them to practice social skills at their own speed.
- Integrating Gamification with Traditional Counselling Methods: Gamification needs to supplement conventional counselling methods rather than take their place. For example, in Classcraft, the platform was utilised in conjunction with in-person counselling sessions, enabling students to consider their gaming experiences and apply what they had learned to practical situations. A comprehensive approach to therapy and emotional growth is made possible by the gamification of more conventional techniques.
- The Role of Motivation and Rewards: The success of gamification mostly depends on sustaining motivation through challenges, incentives, and progress monitoring. But it's crucial to make sure that incentives have purpose and complement treatment objectives. Although "power-ups" were used in SuperBetter to provide users a sense of accomplishment, the goals' inherent worth was also emphasised. The takeaway from this is that, although rewards from outside sources might be inspiring, the goal should always be intrinsic motivation, such as a feeling of achievement or personal growth.
- Addressing Resistance and Stigma: Gamified counselling has several benefits, including lowering therapeutic resistance and the stigma attached to

mental health care. The game-based approach feels more like a fun activity than therapy for kids who struggle with social skills or fear. It's crucial to find a balance, though, so that the gamified components complement rather than overpower the therapeutic substance.

## ENHANCING ENGAGEMENT AND MOTIVATION

### Engagement Through Gamification

To increase student motivation, engagement, and participation, gamification in school counselling incorporates aspects of game design into non-gaming environments. Gamification encourages students to actively engage in their counselling process by leveraging elements like prizes, challenges, levels, and storylines to create an engaging and interactive environment.

Gamification is characterised by using *rewards*, such as badges, levels, achievements, or points, as incentives for reaching objectives and finishing activities. These incentives encourage students to continue participating in their counselling activities by acting as positive reinforcement.

Instantaneous *feedback* from games helps pupils recognize their strengths and areas for development. This instantaneous feedback loop in counselling can improve self-awareness and boost motivation to carry out therapeutic activities. For instance, a student using a gamified platform to practise mindfulness exercises gets immediate feedback on how well they're doing, such as "Great job staying focused!" or "Try to breathe more deeply to stay calm." This immediate acknowledgment of their success increases their sense of achievement and motivates them to work harder. (Raju et al., 2021)

Gamification provides students with well-defined objectives and planned challenges, enabling them to visually monitor their progress. Students feel a sense of success when they witness their progress, whether through levels, milestones, or story progression. For instance, a learner using a gamified software to practise emotional regulation can begin by mastering basic skills. They have a real sense of progress as they become proficient in these methods and can take on increasingly difficult tasks. (Raju et al., 2021)

Traditional counselling techniques might occasionally seem overwhelming or tiresome, particularly to students who may already be disengaged. Students can practise coping mechanisms or conflict resolution in a virtual setting by participating in simulated scenarios through interactive virtual reality platforms, which makes the experience both entertaining and therapeutic.

## The Role of Competition in Motivating Students

In gamified environments, competition is a potent motivator because it appeals to students' innate drive for achievement and recognition. By making activities more thrilling and goal-oriented, it raises engagement. Students are inspired to develop and work towards personal goals when competition is presented as a challenge rather than a rivalry, which promotes positive motivation. For instance, in school counselling, students might compete to finish the most mindfulness exercises in a week. They would be rewarded with recognition or little prizes, which would encourage them to continue working on their personal development. Furthermore, by graphically displaying their accomplishments, leaderboards and rankings can inspire students to raise their position and further drive them. A friendly competition, like earning points for practicing social skills in real-life situations, can drive students to engage more actively and continuously improve. (Regueras et al., 2008)

## The Role of Collaboration in Motivating Students

Collaboration is essential for inspiring kids since it promotes cooperation and mutual success. Collaborative components in gamified school counselling promote students to cooperate to achieve shared objectives, enhancing interpersonal relationships and creating a feeling of community. In addition to inspiring kids, this collaboration improves their trust, empathy, and interpersonal skills. Collaborative assignments, including team-based challenges, help students develop skills like communication, problem-solving, and emotional control by allowing them to pool their efforts to achieve common goals. For instance, in a cooperative gaming environment, students may cooperate to settle a dispute and receive incentives for their combined efforts, fostering a feeling of community and support. (Anwar et. al., 2021)

## The Role of Social learning and Peer Motivation

Peer motivation and social learning are important factors in student motivation, especially when working in groups. Students can learn from each other when they collaborate, which creates chances for encouragement and support from their peers. Peer support strengthens individual endeavours and increases students' involvement in the counselling process. Students work together to accomplish social skill-building tasks in a gamified behaviour management program, for instance, where they receive support and encouragement from their peers. Additionally, by giving students the chance to practise critical abilities like empathy, communication, and dispute resolution, cooperative games support their social and emotional growth. Students learn to respect others, collaborate, and accomplish group goals by working towards common objectives. These skills are essential for their daily interactions. An example of this is a group of students engaging in a gamified conflict resolution activity, where they develop listening, feedback, and negotiation skills. (Klein, Sondag, & Drolet, 1994)

Counsellors can foster an atmosphere that encourages healthy competitiveness, social engagement, and personal development by combining teamwork and competition. This will ultimately assist students in acquiring critical life skills.

## Motivation Enhancement

Motivation is broadly classified into two types: *intrinsic and extrinsic*. Motivation that originates internally is referred to as *intrinsic motivation*. It happens when someone does something for the intrinsic joy or fulfilment that comes from doing it. Intrinsic motivation might show itself in treatment as a desire to enhance emotional health, create more constructive coping mechanisms, or promote personal development. Because they find the activities or their own growth significant, people who are intrinsically driven in therapy are more likely to stick with it. For instance, a depressed person may go to therapy because they sincerely want to learn how to control their emotions and live a happy life, not because they are feeling forced or rewarded by others. *Extrinsic motivation* is fuelled by outside forces or incentives, such as receiving recognition, receiving money, or reaching a predetermined goal. Extrinsic incentive can be used to encourage engagement in therapy, particularly with clients who may not be aware of the therapeutic benefits or who may be initially disengaged. However, as external rewards are frequently transient and cannot result in long-lasting behaviour change, depending only on extrinsic motivation may limit long-term involvement. For instance, a client may go to therapy sessions not for personal development but rather to obtain a certificate or because family members urged them to do so.

## Gamification and Intrinsic Motivation

Instead, of depending on outside rewards, clients are more likely to achieve personal fulfilment in the therapeutic process when they feel in charge. For instance, clients may earn points for finishing mindfulness or relaxation exercises in a virtual reality (VR) therapy session. As the client experiences a sense of personal accomplishment in their emotional development, the process of accruing these points and moving through the levels may promote a sense of accomplishment that is inherently motivating.

Autonomy, or the ability to select and partake in activities that are consistent with one's ideals, is a fundamental element. Clients are empowered to take charge of their journey when gamified components are incorporated, such as selecting which therapeutic activities to participate in or creating an avatar. A client's sense of personal agency and drive to participate in therapy may both be enhanced by this decision-making autonomy. For instance, clients may be offered the choice to choose the exercises or tasks they want to complete in gamified counselling applications according to their interests, which makes them feel more involved and invested in the therapy. (Mekler et al., 2017)

Mastery is a major source of intrinsic motivation, and gamification's focus on levels, milestones, and progress fits in nicely with this idea. Clients feel more competent and are motivated to continue their therapy when they see their progress portrayed in a concrete and interactive way (e.g., by unlocking additional assignments or moving up levels). For instance, a child undergoing cognitive-behavioral treatment (CBT) for anxiety may advance through stages by performing tasks that test their illogical worries. Their inherent drive to keep tackling their problems is increased when they see the progress graphically, such as through a "level-up" function. (Mekler et al., 2017)

### Gamification and Therapeutic Alliance

Effective therapy frequently depends on a solid therapeutic partnership, which is defined by mutual respect, cooperation, and trust. By introducing a playful aspect, lowering the perceived formality of treatment, and fostering an atmosphere where the client feels more at ease engaging, gamification can strengthen the therapeutic partnership. (van Dooren, 2020)

## Practical Applications of Gamification in Enhancing Intrinsic Motivation

- *Digital Therapeutic Tools and Apps:* Gamified components are used in several mobile apps and platforms to support mental health and wellbeing. For instance: Children can develop emotional resilience by navigating virtual worlds in Mindlight, a gamified cognitive-behavioral therapy (CBT) application. They get incentives and advance to new levels as they finish tasks pertaining to controlling their anger or anxiousness. SuperBetter is a platform that encourages users to take on difficulties to develop resilience. Each challenge or accomplishment helps users feel competent and grows personally.

- *Virtual Reality (VR) and Gamified Exposure Therapy:* With the use of gamification strategies, virtual reality platforms are utilised to treat PTSD and anxiety. In a safe, virtual setting, clients experience simulations of their phobias, which they can progressively overcome. Intrinsic motivation to continue therapy can be increased by the process of moving through levels, getting feedback, and getting rewards for doing tasks.
- *Behavioural Games and Rewards Systems:* Behavioural games can be used to promote therapeutic exercise participation in both individual and group treatment settings. The procedure can be made to feel more like an exciting challenge than a standard therapy work by rewarding completion of specified actions with points, badges, or tokens that are recorded and recognised within the therapeutic space.

Intrinsic motivation in therapeutic settings may be greatly impacted by gamification. Gamified components can help clients feel more in control, competent, and inspired to continue their therapy work by making the experience more personalised, interactive, and engaging. (van Dooren, 2020)

## IMPROVING THERAPY OUTCOMES THROUGH GAMIFICATION

Gamified therapy provides creative ways to enhance emotional control, social skills, and long-term behavioural change by encouraging participation and interaction. This method offers a novel, inspiring substitute for conventional counselling techniques and has been associated with improved therapy outcomes.

### Therapeutic Benefits of Gamification

In a safe, non-threatening setting, gamified therapy offers opportunities for practicing emotional regulation and encourages clients to actively interact with their emotions. Clients learn to recognise, comprehend, and control their emotions through activities that resemble games. In gamified mindfulness activities, for instance, people employ characters or avatars to practise coping skills and reflect on their emotional states. Gamified platforms frequently include tasks that call for perseverance and problem-solving skills, which inherently improve resilience. Clients develop coping mechanisms to control their tension and anxiety as they progress through virtual environments or game tasks. Through this process, people gain confidence in their capacity to manage challenging circumstances in both the actual and virtual worlds. (van Dooren, 2020)

Gamification encourages teamwork and interpersonal relationships, two qualities that are critical to social growth. Games frequently include activities that call for players to communicate with one another, either cooperatively or competitively. Gamified activities provide clients with a more informal and entertaining way to practise communication and build healthy social relationships.

## Measuring Success in Gamified Therapy

- *Behavioural Metrics:* Monitoring behavioural changes is a key component of gamified therapy success measurement. These include gains in social skills, academic achievement, and emotional control. Both external observations (such as teacher comments or counsellor reports) and self-report instruments (such as questionnaires or journals) can yield data.
- *Engagement Metrics:* Another important assessment technique is tracking the amount of participation in gamified therapy sessions. A client's level of engagement with the therapy process can be determined by metrics like how often they use the app, how long they spend on chores, or how often they finish in-game challenges.
- *Progression Metrics:* In a lot of gamified systems, users get points, unlock new features, or move through stages. These progression markers, which demonstrate clients' progress towards therapy-related objectives, can be used as measurable proof of success. (Tong et. al., 2023)

## Long-Term Impacts

- *Sustained Engagement and Behaviour Change:* The ability of gamified therapy to maintain engagement over time is one of its main benefits; this is frequently a problem with conventional therapeutic procedures. These interventions' game-like format keeps clients engaged and interested in their treatment. Using incentives, accomplishments, and feedback, gamified therapy encourages clients to continue their personal growth process even after therapy is over. The improvements facilitated by gamified therapies might become embedded in the client's everyday behaviour because they enable the repeated practice of coping mechanisms and emotional regulation techniques. Long-term gains in emotional and social functioning are more likely to occur when clients apply the skills they have learnt in therapy to everyday circumstances. (Tong et. al., 2023)

- *Future Implications for School Counselling Practices:* Gamified tools may be incorporated into school counselling in the future alongside more conventional methods, giving counsellors a more comprehensive toolkit to meet the various needs of kids. Counselling becomes more accessible through gamification, especially for students who might not otherwise seek out traditional therapy. Students who live in remote locations or have limited access to in-person counselling can benefit from digital platforms, which allow them to participate in therapy at their speed. In the future, gamified therapies could be further tailored to each student's unique needs. Counsellors may, for instance, utilise data analytics to design gamified experiences that are specific to a student's emotional or behavioural profile. (Brown et. al., 2016)

Gamification presents a viable avenue for enhancing therapeutic results, especially in school counselling contexts. Gamified therapy can completely transform the way counsellors assist students by promoting social skills, emotional regulation, resilience, and sustained involvement.

## CHALLENGES AND CONSIDERATIONS

Although gamification offers creative ways to engage students and improve the efficacy of counselling, incorporating it into school counselling programs is not without its difficulties.

### Potential Drawbacks

- **Over-reliance on Technology.** The possible over-reliance on technology is a major worry when it comes to gamification in counselling. There is a chance that technology could take center stage in treatment sessions as gamified counselling platforms and virtual settings are incorporated more frequently, which could lessen the human element of therapy. *Reduced Personal Interaction*: Although gamified platforms might offer dynamic and captivating settings, they might not be able to give the kind of nuanced emotional support that in-person counselling can. To establish rapport and trust during the therapeutic process, interpersonal interactions formed through human interaction are essential. *Risk of detachment*: Excessive screen time and virtual interactions might make some students feel even more alone or detached, especially if they already struggle with social contact.

Gamification should not be utilised in place of conventional counselling techniques; rather, it should be used in addition to them. For therapy to be successful, counsellors must make sure that technology is utilised to strengthen rather than to replace the human connection. (Spahl, Motta, Woodcock, & Rubeis, 2024)

- **Balancing Gamification with Traditional Methods**. Finding a balance between traditional therapeutic procedures and the fun, game-based elements of counselling is another difficulty. Gamification can offer worthwhile experiences, but it might not always fit in well with the goals and established procedures of traditional counselling. *Maintaining Therapeutic Integrity*: Research backs up the structure and results of conventional counselling techniques including talk therapy, behaviour modification, and cognitive-behavioural therapy (CBT). If gamification is introduced hastily, it may reduce the efficacy of these tried-and-true techniques. *Integration into the Counseling Framework:* Counsellors need to figure out how to incorporate gamification into their work in a way that enhances rather than replaces conventional counselling techniques. This necessitates having a thorough awareness of how each strategy advances the client's welfare and ensuring that they complement one another. (Spahl, Motta, Woodcock, & Rubeis, 2024)

## Ethical and Practical Concerns

- **Ensuring Privacy and Data Security**. Privacy and data security are now major ethical considerations due to the growing use of digital tools in counselling, especially gamified platforms that gather sensitive data. *Confidentiality Risks*: Students are frequently asked to divulge personal information on gamified platforms, including behavioural data, emotional reactions, and even physiological data (such bodily movements or heart rate). There may be significant dangers of data breaches or unauthorised access if these platforms are not built with strong data protection procedures. *Compliance with Legal Regulations*: Students are frequently asked to divulge personal information on gamified platforms, including behavioural data, emotional reactions, and even physiological data (such bodily movements or heart rate). There may be significant dangers of data breaches or unauthorised access if these platforms are not built with strong data protection procedures. (Conn et. al., 2023)

It's critical to choose gamification technologies that follow strict data protection guidelines. To protect students' sensitive information, counsellors must make sure the platforms they use have encryption, secure data storage, and unambiguous privacy policies.

- **Addressing Diverse Student Needs and Inclusivity.** Ensuring that gamified counselling is inclusive and available to all students, irrespective of their origins, learning styles, or socioeconomic situation, is another crucial ethical aspect. *Diverse Learning Styles:* To accommodate various learning styles (visual, aural, kinaesthetic, etc.), gamified tools must be created. Digital platforms might not be interesting or useful to all students, particularly those with learning difficulties or restricted access to technology. *Accessibility Issues*: It could be difficult for students with physical disabilities, like those who have mobility restrictions or visual impairments, to completely interact with gamified platforms. Furthermore, pupils from less affluent families might not have access to gadgets or fast internet, which would limit their use of gamified resources. (Conn et. al., 2023)

## CONCLUSION

Although there are many exciting opportunities for school counselling with gamification, it is imperative to address the issues and concerns mentioned above. Gamification can be a useful technique for increasing student engagement, assisting with emotional development, and boosting mental health in schools if its creative potential is balanced with moral and practical considerations. Gamification can be successfully included into counselling programs that cater to the various requirements of kids by using a methodical implementation process and allocating funds for appropriate training and materials.

To fill this gap, this chapter examines how gamification might be applied as a light-hearted therapeutic technique in Indian school counselling settings, specifically to improve social skills, emotional awareness, and the connection between students and counsellors.

## REFERENCES


Anwar, K., Asari, S., Husniah, R., & Asmara, C. H. (2021). Students' Perceptions of Collaborative Team Teaching and Student Achievement Motivation. *International Journal of Instruction, 14*(1), 325–344. DOI: 10.29333/iji.2021.14119a

Bojuwoye, O., & Sodi, T. (2010). Challenges and opportunities to integrating traditional healing into counselling and psychotherapy. *Counselling Psychology Quarterly, 23*(3), 283–296. DOI: 10.1080/09515070.2010.505750

Brown, M., O'Neill, N., van Woerden, H., Eslambolchilar, P., Jones, M., & John, A. (2016). Gamification and adherence to web-based mental health interventions: A systematic review. *JMIR Mental Health, 3*(3), e5710. DOI: 10.2196/mental.5710 PMID: 27558893

Chiboola, H., & Munsaka, S. M. (2018). Nature and role of traditional forms of counselling in Zambia: A case of Lusaka province. *British Journal of Guidance & Counselling, 46*(1), 79–90. DOI: 10.1080/03069885.2016.1187710

Conn, C., Patel, A., Gavin, J., Granda-Salazar, M., Williams, A., & Barnes, S. (2023). "Development and evaluation of perspective: counselling simulator": a gamified tool for developing risk-assessment skills in trainee counsellors. *Mental Health and Social Inclusion, 27*(2), 140–153. DOI: 10.1108/MHSI-12-2022-0090

Constantinescu, G., Rieger, J., Mummery, K., & Hodgetts, W. (2017). Flow and grit by design: Exploring gamification in facilitating adherence to swallowing therapy. *American Journal of Speech-Language Pathology, 26*(4), 1296–1303. DOI: 10.1044/2017_AJSLP-17-0040 PMID: 29098271

Deterding, S., Dixon, D., Khaled, R., & Nacke, L. (2011). From game design elements to gamefulness: Defining "gamification." *Proceedings of the 15th International Academic MindTrek Conference*. DOI: 10.1145/2181037.2181040

Gonzalez, B. (2021). *The effects of gamification using classcraft platform on writing skills in chilean high school students* (Doctoral dissertation, Santiago, Chile: UCSH).

Guerrero-Puerta, L., & Guerrero, M. A. (2021). Could gamification be a protective factor regarding early school leaving? A life story. *Sustainability (Basel), 13*(5), 2569. DOI: 10.3390/su13052569

Harrison, G., & Gordon, E. (2021). Counsellors' experiences of providing counselling to students in university-level institutions in Ireland: An evolving phenomenon. *Counselling & Psychotherapy Research, 21*(4), 805–815. DOI: 10.1002/capr.12441

Hebebci, M. T., & Alan, S. (2021). Gamification in education: An overview of the literature. *Current Studies in Social Sciences*, *4*(2), 174–194.

Jamaludin, N. F., Wook, T. S. M. T., Noor, S. F. M., & Qamar, F. (2021). Gamification Design Elements to Enhance Adolescent Motivation in Diagnosing Depression. *International Journal of Interactive Mobile Technologies*, *15*(10), 154. DOI: 10.3991/ijim.v15i10.21137

Klein, N. A., Sondag, K. A., & Drolet, J. C. (1994). Understanding volunteer peer health educators' motivations: Applying social learning theory. *Journal of American College Health*, *43*(3), 126–130. DOI: 10.1080/07448481.1994.9939096 PMID: 7814769

Low, P. K. (2009). Considering the challenges of counselling practice in schools. *International Journal for the Advancement of Counseling*, *31*(2), 71–79. DOI: 10.1007/s10447-009-9069-1

Mekler, E. D., Brühlmann, F., Tuch, A. N., & Opwis, K. (2017). Towards understanding the effects of individual gamification elements on intrinsic motivation and performance. *Computers in Human Behavior*, *71*, 525–534. DOI: 10.1016/j.chb.2015.08.048

Millen, C. D., Brundage, R. D. C., & Lucas, R. D. Y. (2020). The Impact of Teaching Resilience, Goal Attainment, and Other Essential Leadership Skills to Young Adults via Virtual Instruction.

Rachels, J. R., & Rockinson-Szapkiw, A. J. (2018). The effects of a mobile gamification app on elementary students' Spanish achievement and self-efficacy. *Computer Assisted Language Learning*, *31*(1-2), 72–89. DOI: 10.1080/09588221.2017.1382536

Raju, R., Bhat, S., Bhat, S., D'Souza, R., & Singh, A. B. (2021). Effective usage of gamification techniques to boost student engagement. *Journal of Engineering Education Transformations*, *34*(0), 713–717. DOI: 10.16920/jeet/2021/v34i0/157171

Ravindran, V., Osgood, M., Sazawal, V., Solorzano, R., & Turnacioglu, S. (2019). Virtual reality support for joint attention using the Floreo Joint Attention Module: Usability and feasibility pilot study. *JMIR Pediatrics and Parenting*, *2*(2), e14429. DOI: 10.2196/14429 PMID: 31573921

Regueras, L. M., Verdú, E., Verdú, M. J., Pérez, M. Á., de Castro, J. P., & Muñoz, M. F. (2008). Motivating students through on-line competition: An analysis of satisfaction and learning styles. In *Advances in Web Based Learning-ICWL 2008: 7th International Conference, Jinhua, China, August 20-22, 2008.* [Springer Berlin Heidelberg.]. *Proceedings*, *7*, 167–177.

Schoneveld, E. A., Malmberg, M., Lichtwarck-Aschoff, A., Verheijen, G. P., Engels, R. C., & Granic, I. (2016). A neurofeedback video game (MindLight) to prevent anxiety in children: A randomized controlled trial. *Computers in Human Behavior*, *63*, 321–333. DOI: 10.1016/j.chb.2016.05.005

Shin, A. (2024). Effects of Simulated Gamification on Empathy in Middle School Students: A Mixed Methods Analysis. *Available at SSRN* 4720196. DOI: 10.2139/ssrn.4720196

Siriaraya, P., Visch, V., Boffo, M., Spijkerman, R., Wiers, R., Korrelboom, K., Hendriks, V., Salemink, E., van Dooren, M., Bas, M., & Goossens, R. (2021). Game design in mental health care: Case study–based framework for integrating game design into therapeutic content. *JMIR Serious Games*, *9*(4), e27953. DOI: 10.2196/27953 PMID: 34855611

Spahl, W., Motta, V., Woodcock, K., & Rubeis, G. (2024). Gamified Digital Mental Health Interventions for Young People: Scoping Review of Ethical Aspects During Development and Implementation. *JMIR Serious Games*, *12*(1), e64488. DOI: 10.2196/64488 PMID: 39607995

Tong, F., Lederman, R., D'Alfonso, S., Berry, K., & Bucci, S. (2023). Conceptualizing the digital therapeutic alliance in the context of fully automated mental health apps: A thematic analysis. *Clinical Psychology & Psychotherapy*, *30*(5), 998–1012. DOI: 10.1002/cpp.2851 PMID: 37042076

van Dooren, M. (2020). Personalized gamification to enhance implementation of eHealth therapy in youth mental healthcare.

Wiggins, B. E. (2016). An overview and study on the use of games, simulations, and gamification in higher education. [IJGBL]. *International Journal of Game-Based Learning*, *6*(1), 18–29. DOI: 10.4018/IJGBL.2016010102

Xie, H. (2022). A scoping review of gamification for mental health in children: Uncovering its key features and impact. *Archives of Psychiatric Nursing*, *41*, 132–143. DOI: 10.1016/j.apnu.2022.07.003 PMID: 36428041

# Chapter 7
# The Role of Artificial Intelligence (AI) in Diagnosis and Intervention in Students With Disabilities and Special Educational Needs:
## Current Trends

**Maria Georgiadi**
https://orcid.org/0000-0002-6846-0156
*University of Crete, Greece*

**Dimitra Maria Tomprou**
*Frederick University, Greece*

**Ifigeneia Inglezaki**
*University of Crete, Greece*

**Ilias Meramveliotakis**
https://orcid.org/0000-0002-8963-8953
*Frederick University, Greece & Hellenic Mediterranean University, Greece*

**Stefanos Plexousakis**
*Frederick University, Greece*

DOI: 10.4018/979-8-3373-0573-8.ch007

## ABSTRACT

*In recent years Artificial Intelligence (AI) has been used in the field of education settings but also in special education as well. The technologies that are implied can transform the process of learning and teaching and create inclusive environments for students who face a variety of difficulties in learning. The current review focuses on two dimensions: a) the use of AI in diagnosis and the use of AI in intervention for students with disabilities and special educational needs. We emphasize the advantages and disadvantages of using AI in diagnosis and intervention in special education. We also address ethical considerations for the use of AI in special education. Suggestions for the use of AI in diagnosis and intervention in Special Education are also developed to help teachers, professionals such as psychologists, speech therapists, occupational therapists, parents, students, and policymakers in developing an effective context in the use of AI in special education.*

## INTRODUCTION

Special education refers to specially designed instruction that is tailored to meet the unique needs of individuals with disabilities. This educational approach ensures that young children, school-aged children, and young adults have access to the supports and services necessary for their development and learning. The goal of special education is to prepare these individuals for further education, employment, and/or independent living by providing equitable access to instruction through various means such as early intervention, instructional accommodations, and modifications based on each student's strengths and needs (Harkins et al., 2025).

Special education services often include individualized education programs (IEPs) that outline the specific educational goals and supports for each student, ensuring that they receive appropriate and meaningful educational opportunities (Frey, 2019).

Artificial Intelligence (AI) definition is broad and has an interdisciplinary nature, spanning cognitive emulation, decision-making, and adaptability in various domains. A more general definition for AI is the ability of machines or systems to perform tasks that typically require human intelligence. These tasks include learning, reasoning, problem-solving, perception, and natural language processing (Alsudairy & Eltantawy, 2024). AI in education refers specifically to supporting personalized learning, feedback, and guidance, aiming to simplify complex tasks and tailor educational content to individual learner needs (Alsudairy & Eltantawy, 2024).

AI not only addresses the academic needs of students with disabilities but also supports teachers by automating administrative tasks, creating individualized education plans (IEPs), and providing real-time analytics to track student progress (Frey, 2019).

While AI offers immense potential, it also presents challenges, such as addressing algorithmic bias, ensuring data privacy, and mitigating the risks of over-reliance on technology. Nonetheless, its transformative impact on special education is undeniable, paving the way for more inclusive and equitable learning environments (Alsudairy & Eltantawy, 2024).

## THE ROLE OF ARTIFICIAL INTELLIGENCE IN SPECIAL EDUCATION

Artificial Intelligence (AI) is revolutionizing special education by offering innovative tools and strategies to support students with disabilities. AI in special education encompasses a range of applications, including adaptive learning systems, assistive technologies, intelligent tutoring systems, and communication tools. These technologies aim to enhance accessibility, personalize learning experiences, and address the unique needs of students with disabilities.

The role of AI in special education can be categorized into four key areas:

***Personalized Learning***: AI enables tailored instruction by analyzing individual student data and adapting content, pace, and teaching methods to match specific needs. Intelligent tutoring systems and adaptive learning platforms play a significant role in this regard, offering personalized feedback and customized support (Drigas & Ioannidou, 2013).

***Assistive Technologies***: AI-powered tools such as speech-to-text software, text-to-speech systems, and real-time language translation devices enhance accessibility for students with visual, auditory, or cognitive impairments. For instance, devices like Microsoft Translator and Deaf AI facilitate communication and learning for students with hearing disabilities (Alsudairy & Eltantawy, 2024).

***Diagnosis and Intervention***: AI is used to diagnose learning disabilities and recommend intervention strategies. Techniques like fuzzy cognitive mapping and machine learning algorithms help identify specific challenges and suggest targeted support, improving the accuracy and timeliness of interventions (Hopcan et al., 2023).

*Social and Emotional Support*: AI applications, such as social robots and virtual reality systems, are increasingly being used to develop social and emotional skills in students with autism spectrum disorders (ASD) and other special needs. These tools create safe, engaging environments for practicing communication and interaction skills (Hopcan et al., 2023).

In this chapter we will analyze the role of AI in diagnosis and intervention.

## THE ROLE OF AI IN THE PROCESS OF DIAGNOSIS IN SPECIAL EDUCATION

Artificial Intelligence (AI) has significantly transformed the medical and educational landscapes, particularly in the diagnosis of various conditions and disabilities. Its ability to analyze vast amounts of data, recognize patterns, and provide insights has made it an indispensable tool in diagnostic processes across multiple domains. In this essay, the role of AI in diagnosis is explored, highlighting its applications, benefits, challenges, and future prospects.

AI in diagnosis refers to the use of computational systems and algorithms to identify diseases, conditions, or disabilities based on data inputs such as medical imaging, patient symptoms, behavioral patterns, and other biomarkers. AI systems, particularly machine learning (ML) and deep learning (DL) algorithms, are trained on large datasets to detect patterns and make predictions with a level of precision that often surpasses human capabilities.

AI's diagnostic capabilities are evident in both medical and educational fields. In the medical domain, it is applied to identify diseases such as cancer, cardiovascular conditions, and neurological disorders. In education, AI assists in diagnosing learning disabilities, autism spectrum disorders (ASD), and other developmental challenges.

AI has been instrumental in diagnosing complex diseases. For instance, machine learning algorithms can analyze radiological images, such as X-rays, MRIs, and CT scans, to detect abnormalities like tumors, fractures, or lesions. AI-powered systems like IBM Watson Health utilize natural language processing (NLP) and data analytics to provide oncologists with evidence-based treatment options, thereby enhancing diagnostic accuracy (Barua et al., 2024).

In recent years, there has been an increase in diagnoses of mental disorders, disabilities, and special needs. Students appear to face primarily social and communication difficulties, which affect their adaptation and ability to learn effectively in the school environment, often requiring immediate and effective interventions from the educational community (Barua et al., 2024). AI technology, as a solution to this issue, provides immediate personalized support that aids in diagnosis and the design of individualized interventions, such as intellectual disabilities (Almufareh et al., 2023), Autism Spectrum Disorders (El-Ashram et al., 2024; Oh et al., 2021; Ojha, 2022; Suariqi Diantama, 2023), dyslexia (Kohli & Prasad, 2010 ;Ojha, 2022), ADHD (Dubreuil-Vall et al., 2020; Ojha, 2022; Tor et al., 2021;), sensory/physical disabilities (Drigas et al., 2008; Georgopoulos et al., 2003; Ojha, 2022; Pavlopoulos et al., 2008), and depression (Acharya et al., 2018; He & Cao, 2018). Furthermore, machine learning applications appear to enhance overall well-being and improve the quality of life for these individuals (Barua et al., 2024).

Using behavioral data, mental illness, special needs, and other disabilities are processed with a multitude of different datasets such as medical imaging, cognitive testing, observation, and histories. AI sifts through the data to find patterns and similarities which makes it simpler to reach a diagnosis (Di Nuovo et al 2014; Green and Flaro 2016; Uddin et al., 2019). AI supersedes the more accurate diagnosis achieved from traditional medical examinations. (Kim et al., 2021). In addition, experts can easily identify structural changes in brain phenomena which invariably affect the person's condition, for instance, in the cases of oligophrenia, through visual analysis of brain data (Abd-Alrazaq et al. 2022; Gupta et al. 2022; Sadeghi et al. 2022; Zhang et al. 2023). Simultaneously, it is possible to use NLP to analyze and search for relevant oral and written language in the background personal history for any symptoms (de la Fuente Garcia et al. 2020; Le Glaz et al. 2021; Ratana et al., 2023). In addition, it is essential that posterity AI systems can process biological materials like genetics for a shift in the developmental postponement, as DNA sequencers do, to expand the scope of professionals who can manage such patients (Donnelly et al. 2023; Movaghar et al. 2021).

AI tools are increasingly used in behavioral and mental health. For example, AI-driven chatbots and virtual assistants can screen for symptoms of depression, anxiety, and post-traumatic stress disorder (PTSD) through conversational analysis (Marino et al., 2023). These tools use NLP to detect negative sentiment, hesitation, and other linguistic markers associated with mental health disorders.

AI aids in diagnosing intellectual and developmental disabilities by analyzing a wide range of data, including academic performance, behavioral patterns, and social interactions. For instance, systems like "ActiveMath" provide adaptive feedback for students with specific learning disabilities, helping educators identify skill gaps and tailor interventions (Krishnamurti, 2015).

AI technology has successfully assisted in the diagnosis of dyslexia as well as in solving mathematical problems for patients with dyscalculia (Abbott 2006; Anthony et al, 2008; de Castro et al, 2014; Gonsalves et al, 2010). Writing difficulties for patients characterized with dysgraphia (Rosenblum & Dror, 2017), dyspraxia (Exarchos et al, 2016) and even auditory processing disorders (Krishnamurti, 2015; Zatul et al, 2011) have also benefitted. However, some challenges still persist for diagnosis in cases of speech disorders like (Caballero-Morales & Trujillo-Romero, 2014; Robles-Bykbaev et al, 2016) due to the overlapping features with above mentioned difficulties (Sprogis, 2019). For instance, expert systems and intelligent tutoring systems (ITS) analyze student performance, eye movement, or interaction with educational software to identify specific learning difficulties (Drigas & Ioannidou, 2012).

An example is the use of fuzzy cognitive maps to differentiate specific linguistic impairments (SLIs) from autism or dyslexia by analyzing linguistic patterns and behavioral symptoms (Harkins-Brown et al., 2025). AI-powered tools like text-to-speech systems also support children with dyslexia by converting written text into spoken words (Harkins-Brown et al., 2025).

AI systems like natural language processing and computer vision enable early detection of autism by analyzing developmental milestones and social interactions in children. These tools are particularly beneficial in primary care settings where access to specialized diagnostic services may be limited.

It has been shown in the literature that AI technology is effective in other areas. For example, it shortens the waiting time for autism spectrum diagnoses (Chen et al., 2022) and increases the accuracy of diagnosis for patients suffering from certain eye diseases (Balas & Ing, 2023). Hirosawa et al (2023) from Japan reports 80% success in diagnosis. Caruccio et al (2024) as well as Kuroiwa et al (2023) talk about what AI tools can do for diagnosis and they say that ChatGPT-3.5 and Google Bard have 76% diagnostic success rate, while ChatGPT-4 reached 84% (Koga et al., 2023). AI has played a pivotal role in improving the diagnosis of ASD. Tools such as video analysis systems and machine learning algorithms are used to evaluate children's social behaviors, facial expressions, and linguistic patterns. For instance, an AI-based software device described in research by Megerian et al. (2022) combines caregiver questionnaires, home video analysis, and clinician inputs to predict ASD with high accuracy (Balas & Ing, 2023)

Baidoo-Anu and Owusu (2023) believe that most users are overly trusting of AI systems. Furthermore, Trust et al. (2023) noted that there is an automated risk from the lack of controls and reliable sources in the AI implementation process. There is also the concern that AI applications' output could be discriminatory against certain sections of the society, including socially disadvantaged groups (Kasneci et al., 2023; Mbakwe et al., 2023).

Equally, ethical problems such as confidentiality (Rane, 2023), human dignity (Bertacchini et al., 2022), and the role of AI together with human health practitioners (Almufareh et al., 2023) are critical. According to AlZu'bi et al., 2023 these matters of undue concern stem from the fact that AI systems as technologies do not possess emotional intelligence (2023). Compliance by healthcare providers, diagnostic centers, and AI intelligence technology suppliers are, however, mandated and enforced by standard operating procedures (SOPs) that deal with confidentiality of sensitive medical information, such as HIPAA (U.S.) and GDPR (EU) laws. Striking a balance to ensure that humans are treated ethically while with utmost care the sensitive information restrictions and access in ensuring confidentiality to the sensitive medical information are systematic security, windows captured information, and sensitive information shrouded by AI. These steps are very important in the sphere of diagnosis of disabilities and special needs, as they assure the best protection of human rights and ethical control of data. (Lal Rai et al., 2024).

## Benefits of AI in Diagnosis

### Speed and Efficiency

AI systems can process data and provide diagnostic outputs much faster than traditional methods. For example, algorithms analyzing medical imaging can deliver results in seconds, enabling faster decision-making and potentially saving lives.

### Improved Accuracy

AI reduces human error by relying on data-driven analysis. Studies show that AI systems, when trained on high-quality datasets, can achieve diagnostic accuracy comparable to or better than human experts (Hopcan et al., 2023).

### Accessibility

AI democratizes access to diagnostic tools. Mobile-based AI applications allow remote areas to access diagnostic services, reducing healthcare disparities. For example, AI-driven telemedicine platforms are being used in rural areas to screen for diseases like tuberculosis and malaria (Mustafa et al., 2024).

### Cost-Effectiveness

By automating repetitive tasks, AI reduces the workload on healthcare professionals and educators, thereby lowering operational costs. For example, AI tools for behavioral assessments minimize the need for extended clinical observation sessions.

## Challenges in AI Diagnosis

### Data Bias

AI models rely on training datasets, which may inadvertently introduce biases. For example, if a model is trained primarily on data from affluent, urban populations, it may fail to generalize well to diverse or underserved communities (Hopcan et al., 2023).

### Lack of Standardization

The absence of standardized diagnostic protocols for AI tools limits their adoption. This is particularly evident in educational settings where AI applications vary widely in design and implementation.

### Ethical Concerns

The use of AI in diagnosis raises ethical questions regarding data privacy, consent, and the potential misuse of sensitive information. For instance, AI-driven behavioral monitoring tools in schools must navigate stringent privacy laws like FERPA (Hopcan et al., 2023).

### Overreliance on Technology

While AI offers unparalleled capabilities, overreliance on it may undermine the human element in diagnostic processes. For instance, AI-generated outputs in special education require validation by trained educators to ensure appropriateness (Harkins-Brown et al., 2025).

## Future Directions for Diagnosis in Special education

### Integration with IoT

The integration of AI with the Internet of Things (IoT) can enhance diagnostic capabilities. Wearable devices equipped with sensors can continuously monitor vital signs and behavior, providing real-time data for AI analysis (Toyokawa et al., 2023).

## AI-Driven Personalized Diagnostics

AI can move beyond generic diagnostic models to create personalized systems that consider individual variability. For example, adaptive algorithms can tailor interventions based on a student's unique cognitive and emotional profile (Drigas & Ioannidou, 2013).

## Ethical AI Development

Future AI systems must incorporate ethical frameworks to address issues of bias, transparency, and accountability. This includes developing explainable AI models that allow users to understand and trust diagnostic decisions.

AI has revolutionized the field of diagnosis, offering unprecedented speed, accuracy, and accessibility. From detecting diseases in medical imaging to diagnosing learning disabilities and autism in education, AI has proven to be a transformative tool. However, challenges such as data bias, ethical concerns, and overreliance on technology must be addressed to maximize its potential. As AI continues to evolve, it holds the promise of creating more inclusive, efficient, and effective diagnostic systems across disciplines.

By leveraging AI responsibly and ethically, we can ensure it becomes an ally in improving diagnostic accuracy, reducing disparities, and enhancing outcomes for individuals in need.

# THE ROLE OF AI IN INTERVENTION

Artificial Intelligence (AI) has emerged as a transformative force in education, particularly in the realm of interventions designed to address diverse learning needs. Its application spans personalized learning, special education, assessment, and the creation of adaptive technologies. AI's unique ability to personalize, monitor, and optimize learning experiences makes it indispensable in intervention strategies. This essay delves into the role of AI in educational interventions, focusing on its impact on special education, cognitive skill development, behavioral interventions, and teacher support.

By leveraging AI applications, it becomes possible to provide equal learning opportunities for all children while fostering environments that are customized to meet the unique needs of every student. AI-driven applications in education transform traditional learning settings and enable students to unlock their potential. These tools, designed to align with students' abilities and unique needs, provide diverse and personalized learning experiences:

## Increased Accessibility

AI-driven technologies are dismantling the barriers that students with disabilities often encounter in education. Almufareh et al. (2024) highlight the crucial role of AI-powered linguistic tools in supporting students with communication challenges. These innovations include speech recognition software, text-to-speech systems, and language translation platforms. For instance, natural language processing (NLP), an advanced extension of the speech-to-text technology used for years by students with disabilities, is becoming increasingly prevalent (Ok et al., 2022). Speech recognition software empowers students with speech impairments to communicate more effectively, enhancing their participation in group projects and class discussions. Similarly, text-to-speech tools ensure that students with visual impairments or reading difficulties have equitable access to educational materials by converting written text into audio formats.

Moreover, AI simplifies daily tasks for individuals with disabilities. For example, a person with physical impairments can easily control devices in their home, such as saying, "Alexa, turn down the music," instead of struggling with a remote. On the other hand, students with hearing impairments might use smartphone apps to reduce background noise in a classroom, making it easier to hear their teacher. Similarly, students with limited physical abilities can utilize speech-to-text technology to efficiently convert their thoughts into written form. (Marino et al., 2023)

AI companions are another notable development, offering affirmations, promoting social interactions, and delivering positive reinforcement to students with disabilities. Virtual assistants and AI-powered communication tools also enhance collaboration among all stakeholders in the educational process. Parents can monitor their child's progress, communicate with teachers, and access resources to support their child's learning effectively. This real-time communication fosters a collaborative and inclusive atmosphere, ensuring all students have the tools to succeed. (Basham & Blackorby, 2023; Harkins-Brown et al.,2025; Sarkar, 2024)

Integrating AI technologies into special education not only enhances communication but also promotes inclusivity, equity, and accessibility. These advancements pave the way for a more inclusive and supportive learning environment where every student can thrive and reach their full potential.

## Early Diagnosis and Predictive Interventions

AI's role in early diagnosis is crucial for timely interventions. Systems like SEDA, an expert system for diagnosing learning difficulties, use AI algorithms to analyze student behavior and identify potential challenges. These tools enable early detection of conditions such as dyslexia or autism, allowing educators and parents to implement interventions before these challenges escalate (Harkins-Brown et al.,2025).

Predictive analytics further enhance intervention strategies. AI systems can analyze historical data to predict future learning outcomes, providing educators with actionable insights. For example, early warning systems use AI to identify students at risk of dropping out, enabling schools to implement targeted interventions to improve retention rates (Hopcan et al., 2023).

## Enhanced Individualization

AI-powered personalized learning is revolutionizing education by customizing instructional experiences to align with the specific needs and preferences of individual students. At the heart of this approach are adaptive learning systems—AI-driven platforms that adjust dynamically to students' learning styles, task complexity, feedback timing, and personal preferences, optimizing their educational outcomes. These platforms are particularly effective in delivering tailored content, ensuring that students with disabilities receive instruction suited to their abilities. (Ahmad et al., 2025; Smith et al., 2024)

Alosami (2025) concurs with the aforementioned points and highlights how specialized AI learning platforms offer students with mild intellectual disabilities opportunities for success that traditional educational models often cannot provide. Moreover, the interactive features of AI tools actively engage learners, leading to higher participation levels. Automated grading of both formative and summative assessments provides instant feedback, enabling students to learn from their mistakes and deepen their understanding (Zhang et al., 2022). By continuously responding to student progress and interactions, AI maintains interest and equips learners to achieve their full potential.

Furthermore, the ability of AI to analyze learning patterns and trends over time enables ongoing improvement and refinement of personalized learning experiences. Teachers also benefit, as AI identifies areas of student strength and challenges, helping them to deliver more targeted instruction. This approach enhances outcomes for students with special needs, ensuring they receive the support they require. (Sarkar,2024)

AI further suggests personalized learning activities for parents to engage in with their children at home, fostering greater parental involvement in education. Microsoft's Equadex, specifically designed for children with learning disabilities and autism, offers a mobile-friendly platform that enhances communication and understanding through visual presentations (Wang'ang'a, 2024).

AI has significantly advanced special education by offering tailored interventions for students with disabilities. Through its adaptive capabilities, AI can analyze individual needs and design personalized training plans. For example, the "Bridge AI" system utilizes a comprehensive "3i-learning system" to generate Individualized Training Plans (ITPs) for students with special educational needs (SEN). The system tracks students' learning performance, emotional states, and environmental data during training to provide insights for therapists and teachers, thereby enhancing the effectiveness of interventions (Ahmad et al., 2025).

Similarly, AI-enabled applications like "Dedalos" assist hearing-impaired students by creating educational content tailored to their linguistic abilities, enabling them to learn English as a second language (Drigas & Ioannidou, 2013). These tools empower educators and parents to provide targeted support, ultimately promoting inclusivity in learning environments.

Beyond maximizing individual learning potential, AI-driven personalized education fosters an inclusive and welcoming environment. Each student feels valued and supported, contributing to a more equitable and encouraging educational experience.

## AI and Academic Skills

AI-powered tools such as Intelligent Tutoring Systems (ITS) have revolutionized cognitive skill development. ITS employs machine learning algorithms to adapt learning materials to individual students' abilities, ensuring that each learner progresses at their own pace. For instance, adaptive learning systems like the BESPECIAL platform cater to students with dyslexia by identifying their unique challenges and providing customized solutions, such as text segmentation and text-to-speech functionalities (Panjwani-Charania & Zhai, 2024).

Moreover, AI tools like the ECHOES system, designed for children with autism spectrum disorders, use virtual environments to foster social and communication skills. These tools employ interactive agents to simulate real-world scenarios, enabling students to practice behaviors like turn-taking and collaborative tasks (Wang et al. (2023).

Most students in special education settings often face challenges in learning, particularly in language and mathematics. Artificial Intelligence (AI) offers significant potential to enhance the performance of students with disabilities or learning difficulties and to facilitate their seamless integration into the educational process.

For instance, students facing challenges can use ChatGPT to generate ideas and gain inspiration as a starting point for their writing. They can input their text into the platform and request initial feedback on their drafts. The model can suggest edits for grammar, improve transitions, or recommend advanced vocabulary and definitions. Additionally, students can create stories and ask ChatGPT to transform them into different formats, such as turning a persuasive essay into a rap. ChatGPT can also summarize key concepts, historical events, or various texts, including chapters, scenes, or historical documents (Lambert & Stevens, 2024)

Improvements in reading and mathematical skills have been observed among participants, aligning with findings from Hidayat (2024), who reported that AI-based programs notably boosted reading comprehension and math abilities in students with intellectual disabilities (ID). Studies show that AI-driven tools that provide instant feedback, task customization, and gradual skill progression effectively address diverse learning needs, making education more accessible and impactful for students with ID (Hopcan et al., 2022; Schöld et al., 2023). Hopcan et al.(2022), for example, demonstrated how AI-powered math applications benefit students by tailoring tasks to their individual learning pace and style, a method well-suited for students requiring paced and customized learning approaches.

AI applications employing interactive and adaptive strategies help engage students with mild ID by fostering interest and motivation through interactive elements. Chen and Perez (2023) assessed Amira, an AI-powered tool designed to support students with dyslexia and assist teachers with reading and writing tasks, confirming its effectiveness in improving literacy skills. Similarly, AI-driven tools such as CollectiAR, an augmented reality (AR) mobile game developed by Fei et al. (2022), engage children by using computer vision (CV) to enhance vocabulary learning through interactive experiences. Helmi et al. (2023) introduced a mobilc application utilizing Google's Speech Recognizer API to support reading and pronunciation practice, providing a practical solution for speech development.

For deaf and hard-of-hearing students, AI technologies offer transformative possibilities. AI-powered applications can provide real-time transcription services, making lectures more accessible. Microsoft Translator, for instance, is used at the Rochester Institute of Technology to generate real-time captions for students with hearing impairments, converting spoken language into text so they can follow lectures as effectively as their hearing peers. Deaf AI, another innovative solution, offers products and services aimed at enhancing communication and accessibility for the deaf and hard-of-hearing community (Bekeš et al., 2024).

AI also plays a crucial role in supporting students with blindness or visual impairments. Due to vision limitations, these students face significant barriers in accessing text-based information. The smart reader system described by Punith et al. (2021) captures text from images, recognizes it, and converts it into speech using a built-in camera in smart glasses, delivering the output to the user's earphones. Similarly, Yeo et al. (2022) developed a smartphone-based low-vision aid. The device demonstrated improvements in reading accuracy and facial recognition, though reading speed remained slow. Sarkar et al. (2021) proposed a system that converts text to speech, allowing frequently used voices to be stored and replayed, achieving high accuracy in text recognition regardless of font or handwriting variations.

Beyond academic skills, AI has also advanced tools to support behavioral, social, and emotional development in students with autism, ADHD, and emotional and behavioral difficulties. Additionally, these technologies aid in enhancing executive functions, such as memory and concentration, further contributing to students' overall development and success in education.

## AI in Language and Communication Development

Language and communication are critical intervention areas where AI excels. Large Language Models (LLMs) and Natural Language Processing (NLP) technologies have been integrated into educational settings to support students with language-based learning disabilities. For instance, the Additional Writing Help (AWH) tool translates text written by students with dyslexia into grammatically correct versions, preserving their original intent while addressing common errors (Panjwani-Charania & Zhai, 2024).

Additionally, AI-powered communication assistants like those using Neural Machine Translation (NMT) help students with dyslexia express themselves more effectively. These systems enable real-time text or speech translation, providing crucial support for students struggling with verbal or written communication (Panjwani-Charania & Zhai, 2024).

## AI and Social, Behavioral and Emotional Skills

AI also addresses emotional and social aspects of learning. Tools like the multimodal AI system monitor students' emotional states during learning sessions, helping educators identify stress or anxiety triggers. These insights guide the design of interventions that prioritize students' mental well-being (Drigas & Ioannidou, 2013).

For students with autism, AI-powered robots serve as social companions, facilitating interactions and teaching social cues. These robots provide a non-judgmental environment where students can practice social behaviors, boosting their confidence and interpersonal skills (Wang, H. et al. (2023).

AI also plays a pivotal role in behavioral interventions. For students with neurodevelopmental disorders, such as autism or ADHD, AI-powered platforms provide structured environments for skill acquisition. For example, Riedl et al.'s platform offers social scenario games where students role-play everyday situations like visiting a theater, allowing them to practice social behaviors in a controlled setting.

AI's ability to track and analyze behavioral data further enhances its intervention capabilities. Tools like multimodal machine learning systems monitor student engagement through facial expressions and body language, enabling educators to identify and address disengagement in real-time ((Panjwani-Charania & Zhai, 2024). Such systems not only support students but also reduce the workload for teachers and therapists by automating data collection and analysis.

AI-powered applications are revolutionizing the support available to children with autism, significantly enhancing their communication (Sağdıç et al., 2023) and social skills (Riedl et al., 2009), as well as improving the implementation of Individualized Education Programs (IEPs) (Rakap, 2024). These tools also facilitate the tracking of behavioral patterns and stereotypical movements (Amiri et al., 2017) and enable skill analysis (Srinivasan & Parthasarathi, 2013). Additionally, AI fosters stable, calming learning environments that help reduce anxiety and support continuous, anytime-anywhere education. It also improves communication for non-verbal individuals with autism and monitors behaviors, providing real-time feedback to help prevent outbursts. (Ahmad et al., 2025).

A notable example is an AI-based educational app developed by Sağdıç et al. (2023), featuring cartoon characters that apply behavior analysis techniques to help individuals with autism learn how to respond to questions and follow instructions. This interactive tablet-based approach allows students to acquire target behaviors, reducing reliance on traditional teacher-led instruction (Sağdıç et al., 2024).

Furthermore, the "Emotify" game for children with autism has demonstrated a 72% accuracy rate in emotion recognition, proving its effectiveness. Similarly, the game "Facesay" has been shown to improve emotion recognition, social interactions, facial recognition, and social engagement for children on the autism spectrum (Barua et al., 2022).

For students with ADHD, advancements in mobile and wearable technology have enabled continuous symptom monitoring. These technologies often incorporate intelligent tools for behavioral monitoring and data collection, such as tracking physical activity, sleep patterns, and phone usage (Frolli et al., 2023). One example is the Parenting Management app, which allows parents to monitor instances of inattention or hyperactivity and offers guidance on managing these behaviors (Wang et al., 2018).

Games and cognitive training apps are also widely used to support ADHD treatment by enhancing executive functions, such as attention, working memory, and impulse control (Canady, 2020; Somma et al., 2019). One prominent example is EndeavorRx by Akili Interactive, a therapeutic video game approved by the FDA for ADHD treatment in children, which uses attention and multitasking tasks to boost cognitive skills (Ortolano, 2022). Another example is Braingame Brian, a game that dynamically adjusts task difficulty based on user performance. For instance, players must reproduce sequences of lit rectangles, with sequence length adapting to the player's performance. Gamification elements are included to boost motivation (Somma et al., 2019). Weitzman (2023), in the article Empowering Individuals with Disabilities Through AI Technology, also highlights several assistive technologies, categorizing various notable AI-driven applications.

These examples underscore the growing importance of AI in fostering both learning and socio-emotional skills, paving the way for more inclusive and effective educational solutions.

## Support for Teachers

AI not only benefits students but also supports teachers by streamlining interventions. For example, AI-driven platforms like the LEAF system visualize students' reading processes, enabling teachers to monitor progress and identify areas for improvement (Rakap & Balikci, 2024). These insights allow educators to adapt their teaching strategies, ensuring that each student receives the support they need.

AI tools also assist in classroom management and lesson planning. Chatbots and virtual assistants can automate administrative tasks, freeing up time for teachers to focus on personalized instruction. For instance, AI tools can generate lesson plans, grade assignments, and even suggest intervention strategies based on students' performance data (Ahmad et al., 2025).

Special education teachers handle various tasks daily, including instructional, administrative, and compliance-related responsibilities. AI platforms and technological tools can support and often streamline these activities. Platforms such as OpenAI's ChatGPT, Google's Gemini, and Claude.AI assist educators in tasks like conducting educational research, lesson planning, developing differentiated instructional materials, creating Individualized Education Programs (IEPs), and managing schedules. These tools enable more personalized learning experiences, which can lead to improved academic outcomes (Waterfield et al., 2024).

Research by Rakap and Balikci (2024) demonstrated that ChatGPT significantly enhances the quality of IEP goals for preschool children with autism. Additionally, ChatGPT can collaborate with specialists, such as speech and occupational therapists, to develop comprehensive and individualized IEP goals tailored to the unique needs of students. While current findings highlight the effectiveness of AI in improving IEP quality, further research is needed to explore its full potential.

AI is also seen as a solution for reducing teacher workload, an essential consideration given the nationwide shortage of special education teachers due to increased responsibilities (Harkins-Brown et al., 2025; Rakap & Balikci, 2024). By simplifying lesson planning, enabling tailored instruction, and offering on-demand professional development, AI systems empower teachers to save time and enhance their instructional practices, ultimately better addressing the diverse needs of students with disabilities.

Additionally, AI-powered portals provide instant updates on student performance and the results of interventions, promoting effective collaboration between parents and educators to support student development. In terms of parental involvement, AI creates and suggests workshops and training sessions tailored to parents' specific needs and interests. Platforms such as Coursera and edX offer courses designed to help parents support their children’s learning at home. Parent training programs have been found effective in preventing and addressing behavioral issues (Forgatch & Gewirtz, 2018; Zisser-Nathenson et al., 2018). Various parent training programs have been shown to effectively reduce disruptive behaviors, enhance parental self-efficacy, and develop parenting skills (Bausback & Bunge, 2021; Corralejo & Rodriguez, 2018). These programs have also proven valuable in preventing and addressing behavioral issues (Forgatch & Gewirtz, 2018; Zisser-Nathenson et al., 2018), while simultaneously improving parents' sense of competence and skills in managing their children's behavior. In Table 1 there is a list with all the AI tools that can be used fron intervention programs in special education.

## Ethical Considerations

Despite its potential, AI in educational interventions faces challenges. Issues such as data privacy, algorithmic bias, and the high cost of implementation can hinder widespread adoption. For instance, AI systems trained on non-diverse datasets may fail to address the needs of students from different cultural or socioeconomic backgrounds (Marino et al., 2023).

Ethical considerations also arise when using AI for interventions. The potential for over-reliance on technology and the need to preserve human interaction in education are critical concerns. Policymakers and educators must strike a balance between leveraging AI’s capabilities and maintaining the human touch essential for effective teaching (Forgatch & Gewirtz, 2018).

Ethical concerns regarding AI in special education mainly revolve around issues of accuracy, accountability, transparency, and consent, particularly when AI output is used to inform critical decisions about students. An AI system that is inaccurate or biased could negatively impact a student's educational path. Moreover, if the AI system provides incorrect or harmful recommendations, it would be unclear who is responsible—whether it's the developers, educators using the system, or educational administrators who implemented it. Researchers emphasize the need for human oversight in AI, stating that “teachers must remain in charge of key instructional decisions” (Department of Education, Office of Educational Technology, 2023, p. 17). Additionally, it is crucial to obtain explicit consent before utilizing AI-driven technologies, especially when students or their parents and guardians may have limited understanding of how AI could affect educational choices (Marino et al., 2023). Without clear consent, stakeholders may not fully comprehend how their children's data is being collected, analyzed, or shared, leading to concerns about safety and trust within the educational system.

Potential for Bias: AI's text generation capabilities are powered by large language models that are trained on extensive public datasets, which can contain inherent biases such as stereotypes and demographic underrepresentation (Baker & Hawn, 2022). These biases can be present in both the data used to train the AI and in the algorithmic model itself, potentially leading to outputs that disproportionately affect certain groups and provide misleading or incorrect information. To address this, strategies

The future of AI in interventions lies in its ability to integrate seamlessly into diverse educational settings. Innovations such as real-time adaptive learning systems, AI-powered sensory devices, and advanced NLP tools promise to enhance personalized interventions further. Moreover, collaborative efforts between AI developers, educators, and policymakers can ensure that AI technologies are both effective and equitable (Hopcan et al., 2023).

AI has transformed educational interventions by offering personalized, data-driven, and adaptive solutions. Its applications in special education, cognitive skill development, and behavioral interventions have empowered students and teachers alike. However, addressing ethical and logistical challenges is crucial for maximizing AI's potential. As technology continues to evolve, AI is poised to play an even more significant role in shaping inclusive and effective educational environments.

By leveraging AI's capabilities, educators can ensure that every student, regardless of their abilities or challenges, has access to quality education tailored to their unique needs. In doing so, AI not only enhances learning outcomes but also fosters a more inclusive and equitable education system.

*Table 1. AI tools for intervention in special education*

| Domains | AI tools |
|---|---|
| Speech Generating Devices (SGDs): | Proloquo2Go: Uses AI to predict words and phrases, providing a voice for individuals with speech difficulties. (https://www.assistiveware.com/products/proloquo2go)<br>Predictable: AI- driven app that predicts and vocalises sentences typed by the user, adapting to their communication patterns over time. (Therapy Box Ltd. Predictable, [Mobile application software]. Retrieved on 30 January 2025.) |
| Learning and Cognitive Support: | EndeavorRx: a therapeutic video game approved by the FDA for ADHD treatment in children, which uses attention and multitasking tasks to boost cognitive skills (Ortolano, 2022).<br>CogniFit: AI- based platform offering personalised brain games and activities to improve cognitive abilities. (Breznitz,& Nachshon, 1999)<br>Elevate: Creates personalised training programs to enhance cognitive skills such as focus, memory, and problem- solving. (. https://www.elevateapp .com) |
| Educational Tools: | Learning Ally: Provides audiobooks and educational resources tailored to students with learning disabilities, using AI to match content to learn er needs. (https://learningally.org/)<br>Text- to- speech technology, supportive e- text, and electronic books (Mosito et al., 2017).<br>Amira: AI-powered tool designed to support students with dyslexia and assist teachers with reading and writing tasks, confirming its effectiveness in improving literacy skills. (Perez (2023)<br>CollectiAR: an augmented reality (AR) mobile game engage children by using computer vision (CV) to enhance vocabulary learning through interactive experiences. (Fei et al., 2022) |
| Daily Living and Independence: | Amazon Alexa and Google Assistant: Smart assistants that use AI to help manage daily tasks and control smart home devices with voice commands. (https:// www .amazon .com/alexa on 30 January 2025)<br>Seeing AI: Microsoft app that describes the world around visually impaired users using AI, aiding in daily navigation. https://www.seeingai.com on 30 January 2025. |
| Social, emotional and communicational Skills Development: | Facesay: improve emotion recognition, social interactions, facial recognition, and social engagement for children on the autism spectrum. (Barua et al., 2022).<br>Autism Therapy with Robots: AI- driven robots like NAO and Milo engage children with autism in interactive social and emotional learning activities. https://www.robokind.com/advanced-social-robots on 30 January 2025<br>Tobii Dynavox: Eye- tracking technology that uses AI to interpret eye movements for communication and computer access ((Duffy et al., 2018)<br>Voiceitt: AI- driven speech recognition app that understands non-standard speech patterns, aiding communication for individuals with speech impairments. Retrieved from https://www.voiceitt.com/ on 30 January 2025)<br>I-based educational app developed by Sağdıç (2023): featuring cartoon characters that apply behavior analysis techniques to help individuals with autism learn how to respond to questions and follow instructions. |

continued on following page

*Table 1. Continued*

| Domains | AI tools |
|---|---|
| Visual Impairments: | Smart reader system (Punith et al., 2021): captures text from images, recognizes it, and converts it into speech using a built-in camera in smart glasses, delivering the output to the user's earphones. (Punith et al., 2021)<br>Be My Eyes: Connects visually impaired users with sighted volunteers via video call for assistance with everyday tasks. Retrieved from https:// www .bemyeyes .com on 30 January 2025<br>OrCam MyEye: Wearable device using AI to read text, recognize faces, and identify products, providing audio feedback to the user (Granquist et al., 2021). |
| Hearing Impairments: | Deaf AI: offers products and services aimed at enhancing communication and accessibility for the deaf and hard-of-hearing community (Bekeš et al., 2024)<br>AVA: Provides real- time transcription of spoken conversations, aiding group discussions for hearing- impaired individuals. Retrieved from https:// www .ava .me/ blog on 30 January 2025 |
| Mobility Impairments: | Liftware: AI- enabled utensils that stabilise hand tremors, helping indi viduals with Parkinson's or essential tremor eat independently. Retrieved from https:// www .liftware .com, on 30 January 2025<br>WHILL Autonomous Drive System: AI- powered electric wheelchairs that navigate autonomously, providing greater mobility. Retrieved from https:// www .whill .us on 30 January 2025. |
| Learning Disabilities: | Kurzweil 3000: Literacy support tool offering text- to- speech, language translation, and study aids for learning disabilities. (Kurzweil Education, 2019).<br>Ghotit Real Writer and Reader: Provides advanced spelling and grammar corrections, text- to- speech, and word prediction for dyslexia and dysgraphia (Prenner, 2015).<br>ModMath: Digital platform for solving math problems, aiding students with dysgraphia and dyslexia. (https://www.modmath.com) |

## APPROPRIATE AGE TO INTRODUCE AI-BASED PROGRAMS

The most appropriate age to introduce AI-based programs for intervention in special education is complex, as the suitability of AI interventions is not likely to be defined by a single age. Instead, it is influenced by a multitude of factors, including the specific nature of the disability, the particular AI application being considered, and the child's individual developmental stage.

The integration of AI into special education is occurring across a wide spectrum of age groups, with various applications tailored to different developmental stages. Research and development efforts are exploring the use of AI to support learners from preschool through young adulthood

## AI Applications Across Age Groups in Special Education

The integration of AI into special education is occurring across a wide age spectrum, from preschool through young adulthood, with applications tailored to different developmental needs.

***Preschool (Ages 3-5)*:** AI is being explored to enhance Individualized Education Program (IEP) goal development for children with autism. AI-driven screeners are also under development for the universal early detection of speech and language challenges. Also a review focusing on AI interventions for Autism Spectrum Disorder (ASD) (studies 2018-2024) revealed positive learning outcomes in social, emotional, and cognitive domains (especially social skills) across varied age ranges, indicating potential benefits throughout different life stages (Kotsi et al., 2025). Furthermore, the potential of AI-powered educational games, translation tools, and personalized tutoring systems, adaptable to young learners' levels, is being investigated. (Harkins-Brown, A. R et al., 2025; Fitas, 2025).

***Early Elementary (Ages 6-8):*** In this age range, AI finds application in diagnostic tools. Support Vector Machine (SVM) methods show promise for diagnostic accuracy in children aged 6-11, while neural networks have been tested in decision support systems to differentiate ADHD from other behavioral issues. A significant portion of research on AI for learning disabilities specifically targets school-age children, often encompassing ages 7-12. (Panjwani-Charania, S., & Zhai, X. 2024; Sharma, S et al., 2023)

***Late Elementary/Middle School (Ages 9-13):*** Studies demonstrate AI's effectiveness in improving academic skills. Notably, one study involving boys aged 9-12 with mild intellectual disabilities showed significant and lasting academic improvements using AI interventions. AI tools also support learning for students aged 6-11 with sensory, motor, cognitive, and other impairments. Developmentally, students in this age group may benefit from activities involving the critical evaluation of AI-generated content to foster critical thinking. (Sharma, S et al., 2023; Alsolami, 2025).

***Adolescence (Ages 14-18)*:** AI applications target specific needs such as social skills development for adolescents with High Functioning Autistic Spectrum Disorders (HFASD) using simulated environments. AI is also explored as a support tool for university students with dyslexia. Adventure AI serves this age group as well. (Panjwani-Charania, S., & Zhai, X. 2024; Sharma, S et al., 2023)

***Young Adulthood (Ages 18+):*** Research extends to AI interventions for learning disabilities among university students. Additionally, AI-powered tools, like social media writing support systems, have been developed specifically for adults with dyslexia. (Panjwani-Charania, S., & Zhai, X. 2024)

Synthesized evidence strongly suggests AI interventions can be particularly effective for school-aged children (approximately 6-12 years) in enhancing academic skills and addressing learning disabilities. This consistency might stem from the alignment of AI's personalized features with structured school environments and the developmental capacity of children in this age group to engage with technology. Simultaneously, there's growing interest in AI for early intervention in preschool (especially for autism and speech/language), reflecting the recognized importance of early support. Also continued exploration for adolescents and young adults suggests an understanding of ongoing support needs. In conclusion while potential benefits exist for other age groups (preschoolers, adolescents), research appears more concentrated on the school-age range, possibly due to unique challenges in implementing AI at very early or later stages. Effectiveness is also closely linked to the specific disability and need, emphasizing the necessity of tailored AI applications.

## CONCLUSION

Artificial intelligence (AI) is transforming the field of special education by addressing the unique needs of students with disabilities, enhancing learning experiences, and supporting educators in teaching and administrative tasks. AI is defined as technology capable of mimicking human cognitive functions such as reasoning, problem-solving, and learning, often through techniques like machine learning, natural language processing, and robotics. Over the past few decades, AI applications have evolved to provide personalized learning opportunities and assistive technologies for students with special needs, offering tailored instruction, accessibility tools, and adaptive systems.

AI's role in special education encompasses diverse applications, including intelligent tutoring systems, adaptive learning platforms, and assistive tools like text-to-speech or speech-to-text systems. These tools enable students with disabilities to overcome barriers, access educational content, and participate more fully in classroom activities. For instance, AI-powered systems can provide real-time content customization, communication aids, and interactive learning environments tailored to individual needs (Drigas & Ioannidou, 2013; Hopcan et al., 2022)

In addition to benefiting students, AI supports educators in special education by automating routine tasks such as developing Individualized Education Programs (IEPs), progress monitoring, and lesson planning. It offers valuable insights through data analysis, enabling teachers to understand student performance and adapt their strategies effectively (Hopcan et al., 2022). Furthermore, AI tools like social robots and virtual reality systems can help teach social-emotional and communication skills to students with autism or developmental disabilities.

Despite its promise, AI in special education also presents challenges, including ethical concerns, biases in algorithms, and the need for teacher training to leverage these tools effectively. Addressing these concerns is essential to ensure equitable access and the responsible use of AI technologies in education Ahmad et al., 2025).

Overall, AI holds significant potential to revolutionize special education by fostering inclusion, enhancing accessibility, and empowering both students and educators through innovative solutions. Its continued development and thoughtful integration promise even greater advancements in addressing the diverse needs of learners with disabilities.

## REFERENCES


Abbott, R. G. (2006). *Automated expert modeling for automated student evaluation: Lecture Notes in Computer Science (Including Subseries Lecture Notes in Artificial Intelligence and Lecture Notes in Bioinformatics), 4053 LNCS*, pp. 1-10, https://doi.org/DOI: 10.1007/11774303_1

Abd-Alrazaq, A., Alhuwail, D., Schneider, J., Toro, C. T., Ahmed, A., Alzubaidi, M., Alajlani, M., & Househ, M. (2022). The performance of artificial intelligence-driven technologies in diagnosing mental disorders: An umbrella review. *NPJ Digital Medicine*, *5*(1), 87. DOI: 10.1038/s41746-022-00631-8 PMID: 35798934

Acharya, U. R., Oh, S. L., Hagiwara, Y., Tan, J. H., & Adeli, H. (2018). Deep convolutional neural network for the automated detection and diagnosis of seizure using EEG signals. *Computers in Biology and Medicine*, *100*, 270–278. DOI: 10.1016/j.compbiomed.2017.09.017 PMID: 28974302

Ahmad, W., Raj, R., & Shokeen, R. (2025). Reshaping Special Education: Strategic Use of Artificial Intelligence. In *Transforming Special Education Through Artificial Intelligence* (pp. 1-44). IGI Global. DOI: DOI: 10.4018/979-8-3693-5538-1.ch001

Almufareh, M. F., Tehsin, S., Humayun, M., & Kausar, S. (2023). Intellectual Disability and Technology: An Artificial Intelligence Perspective and Framework. *Journal of Disability Research*, *2*(4), 58–70. DOI: 10.57197/JDR-2023-0055

Alsolami, A. S. (2025). The effectiveness of using artificial intelligence in improving academic skills of school-aged students with mild intellectual disabilities in Saudi Arabia. *Research in Developmental Disabilities*, *156*, 104884. DOI: 10.1016/j.ridd.2024.104884 PMID: 39631141

Alsudairy, N. A., & Eltantawy, M. M. (2024). Special Education Teachers' Perceptions of Using Artificial Intelligence in Educating Students with Disabilities. *Journal of Intellectual Disability-Diagnosis and Treatment*, *12*(2), 92–102. DOI: 10.6000/2292-2598.2024.12.02.5

AlZu'bi, S., Mughaid, A., Quiam, F., & Hendawi, S. (2023). Exploring the capabilities and limitations of CHATGPT and alternative big language models. *Artificial Intelligence and Applications (Commerce, Calif.)*, *2*(1), 1–10. DOI: 10.47852/bonviewAIA3202820

Amiri, A. M., Peltier, N., Goldberg, C., Sun, Y., Nathan, A., Hiremath, S. V., & Mankodiya, K. (2017). WearSense: Detecting autism stereotypic behaviors through smartwatches. *Healthcare (Basel)*, *5*(11), 2–9. DOI: 10.3390/healthcare5010011 PMID: 28264474

Anthony, L., Yang, J., & Koedinger, K. R. (2008). Toward next-generation, intelligent tutors: Adding natural handwriting input. *IEEE MultiMedia*, *15*(3), 64–68. DOI: 10.1109/MMUL.2008.73

Baidoo-Anu, D., & Owusu Ansah, L. (2023). Education in the era of Generative Artificial Intelligence (AI): Understanding the potential benefits of CHATGPT in promoting teaching and learning. SSRN *Electronic Journal*. https://doi.org/DOI: 10.2139/ssrn.4337484

Baker, R. S., & Hawn, A. (2022). Algorithmic bias in education. *International Journal of Artificial Intelligence in Education*, *32*(4), 1–41. DOI: 10.1007/s40593-021-00285-9

Balas, M., & Ing, E. B. (2023). Conversational AI models for ophthalmic diagnosis: Comparison of Chatgpt and the Isabel pro differential diagnosis generator. *JFO Open Ophthalmology*, *1*, 100005. DOI: 10.1016/j.jfop.2023.100005

Barua, P. D., Vicnesh, J., Gururajan, R., Oh, S. L., Palmer, E., Azizan, M. M., Kadri, N. A., & Acharya, U. R. (2022). Artificial intelligence enabled personalised assistive tools to enhance education of children with neurodevelopmental disorders—A review. *International Journal of Environmental Research and Public Health*, *19*(3), 1192. DOI: 10.3390/ijerph19031192 PMID: 35162220

Basham, J., & Blackorby, J. (2023). The Future of Artificial Intelligence in Special Education Technology. *Journal of Special Education Technology*, *01626434231165*9(3), 404–416. Advance online publication. DOI: 10.1177/01626434231165977

Bausback, K. B., & Bunge, E. L. (2021). Meta- analysis of parent training programs utilizing behavior intervention technologies. *Social Sciences (Basel, Switzerland)*, *10*(10), 367. DOI: 10.3390/socsci10100367

Bekeš, E. R., Galzina, V., & Kolar, E. B. (2024, May). Using human-computer interaction (hci) and artificial intelligence (ai) in education to improve the literacy of deaf and hearing-impaired children. In *2024 47th MIPRO ICT and Electronics Convention (MIPRO)* (pp. 1375-1380). IEEE.

Bertacchini, F., Scuro, C., Pantano, P., & Bilotta, E. (2022). A Project Based Learning Approach for Improving Students'. *Frontiers in Robotics and AI*, *9*, 720448. DOI: 10.3389/frobt.2022.720448 PMID: 35340341

Caballero-Morales, S. O., & Trujillo-Romero, F. (2014). Evolutionary approach for integration of multiple pronunciation patterns for enhancement of dysarthric speech recognition. *Expert Systems with Applications*, *41*(3), 841–852. DOI: 10.1016/j.eswa.2013.08.014

Canady, V. A. (2020). FDA approves first video game Rx treatment for children with ADHD. *Mental Health Weekly*, *30*(26), 1–7. DOI: 10.1002/mhw.32423

Caruccio, L., Cirillo, S., Polese, G., Solimando, G., Sundaramurthy, S., & Tortora, G. (2024). Can CHATGPT provide intelligent diagnoses? A comparative study between predictive models and CHATGPT to define a new medical diagnostic bot. *Expert Systems with Applications*, *235*, 121186. DOI: 10.1016/j.eswa.2023.121186

Chen, X., Zou, D., Xie, H., Cheng, G., & Liu, C. (2022). Two Decades of Artificial Intelligence in Education: Contributors, Collaborations, Research Topics, Challenges, and Future Directions. *Journal of Educational Technology & Society*, *25*(1), 28–47. https://www.jstor.org/stable/48647028

Corralejo, S. M., & Rodríguez, D. M. M. (2018). Technology in parenting programs: A systematic review of existing interventions. *Journal of Child and Family Studies*, *27*(9), 1–15. DOI: 10.1007/s10826-018-1117-1

de Castro, M. V., Bissaco, M. A. S., Panccioni, B. M., Rodrigues, S. C. M., & Domingues, A. M. (2014). Effect of a virtual environment on the development of mathematical skills in children with dyscalculia. *PLoS One*, *9*(7), e103354. DOI: 10.1371/journal.pone.0103354 PMID: 25068511

de la Fuente Garcia, S., Ritchie, C. W., & Luz, S. (2020). Artificial intelligence, speech, and language processing approaches to monitoring Alzheimer's disease: A systematic review. *Journal of Alzheimer's Disease*, *78*(4), 1547–1574. DOI: 10.3233/JAD-200888 PMID: 33185605

Department of Education, Office of Educational Technology. Artificial Intelligence and the Future of Teaching and Learning. 2023. Available online: https://tech.ed.gov/ai-future-of-teaching-and-learning/ (accessed on 25 January 2025).

Di Nuovo, A., Di Nuovo, S., Buono, S., & Cutello, V. (2014). Benefits of fuzzy logic in the assessment of intellectual disability. In: *2014 IEEE International Conference on Fuzzy Systems (FUZZ-IEEE)*, IEEE, Beijing, China, 06-11 July 2014, pp. 1843-1850. https://doi.org/DOI: 10.1109/FUZZ-IEEE.2014.6891834

Diantama, S. (2023). Pemanfaatan Artificial Intelegent (AI) Dalam Dunia Pendidikan. *DEWANTECH Jurnal Teknologi Pendidikan*, *1*(1), 8–14. DOI: 10.61434/dewantech.v1i1.8

Donnelly, N., Cunningham, A., Salas, S. M., Bracher-Smith, M., Chawner, S., Stochl, J., Ford, T., Raymond, F. L., Escott-Price, V., & van den Bree, M. B. M. (2023). Identifying the neurodevelopmental and psychiatric signatures of genomic disorders associated with intellectual disability: A machine learning approach. *Molecular Autism, 14*(1), 1–13. DOI: 10.1186/s13229-023-00549-2 PMID: 37221545

Drigas, A., Kouremenos, D., & Vrettaros, J. (2008). Teaching of English to hearing impaired individuals whose mother language is the sign language. In Emerging Technologies and Information Systems for the Knowledge Society: First World Summit on the Knowledge Society, WSKS 2008, Athens, Greece, September 24-26, 2008. Proceedings 1 (pp. 263-270). Springer Berlin Heidelberg. https://doi.org/ DOI: 10.1007/978-3-540-87781-3_29

Drigas, A. S., & Ioannidou, R. E. (2013). A review on artificial intelligence in special education. *Information Systems, E-learning, and Knowledge Management Research: 4th World Summit on the Knowledge Society, WSKS 2011, Mykonos, Greece, September 21-23, 2011. Revised Selected Papers 4*, 385-391.

Dubreuil-Vall, L., Ruffini, G., & Camprodon, J. A. (2020). Deep Learning Convolutional Neural Networks Discriminate Adult ADHD From Healthy Individuals on the Basis of Event-Related Spectral EEG. *Frontiers in Neuroscience, 14*, 251. DOI: 10.3389/fnins.2020.00251 PMID: 32327965

El-Ashram, R. E. M., Aldaghmi, O. A., & Mohammed, S. M. M. (2024). Requirements for the Application of Artificial Intelligence in Diagnosing Autism Spectrum Disorder: Specialists' Perception. *JDR, 3*(7). Advance online publication. DOI: 10.57197/JDR-2024-0083

Exarchos, T. P., Rigas, G., Bibas, A., Kikidis, D., Nikitas, C., Wuyts, F. L., Ihtijarevic, B., Maes, L., Cenciarini, M., Maurer, C., Macdonald, N., Bamiou, D. E., Luxon, L., Prasinos, M., Spanoudakis, G., Koutsouris, D. D., & Fotiadis, D. I. (2016). Mining balance disorders' data for the development of diagnostic decision support systems. *Computers in Biology and Medicine, 77*, 240–248. DOI: 10.1016/j.compbiomed.2016.08.016 PMID: 27619194

Fitas, R. (2025). *Inclusive Education with AI: Supporting Special Needs and Tackling Language Barriers*. (n.d.). https://arxiv.org/html/2504.14120v1

Forgatch, M. S., & Gewirtz, A. H. (2018). The evolution of the Oregon Model of Parent Management Training: An Intervention for Antisocial Behavior in Children and Adolescents. In Weisz, J. R., & Kazdin, A. E. (Eds.), *Evidence-based psycho therapies for children and adolescents* (pp. 85–102). The Guilford Press.

Frey, J. R. (2019). Assessment for special education: Diagnosis and placement. *The Annals of the American Academy of Political and Social Science*, *683*(1), 149–161. DOI: 10.1177/0002716219841352

Frolli, A., Saviano, E., Ricci, M., Sica, S. L., & Romano, M. (2023). Artificial Intelligence in ADHD treatment: A brief narrative review.

Georgopoulos, V. C., Malandraki, G. A., & Stylios, C. D. (2003). A fuzzy cognitive map approach to differential diagnosis of specific language impairment. *Artificial Intelligence in Medicine*, *29*(3), 261–278. DOI: 10.1016/S0933-3657(02)00076-3 PMID: 14656490

Gonsalves, H. M., Duarte, A. J., & da Silva, J. C. E. (2010). Optical fiber sensor for Hg (II) based on carbon dots. *Biosensors & Bioelectronics*, *26*(4), 1302–1306. DOI: 10.1016/j.bios.2010.07.018 PMID: 20675118

Green, P., & Flaro, L. (2016). Results from three performance validity tests in children with intellectual disability. *Applied Neuropsychology. Child*, *5*(1), 25–34. DOI: 10.1080/21622965.2014.935378 PMID: 25495876

Gupta, C., Chandrashekar, P., Jin, T., He, C., Khullar, S., Chang, Q., & Wang, D. (2022). Bringing machine learning to research on intellectual and developmental disabilities: Taking inspiration from neurological diseases. *Journal of Neurodevelopmental Disorders*, *14*(1), 28. DOI: 10.1186/s11689-022-09438-w PMID: 35501679

Harkins-Brown, A. R., Carling, L. Z., & Peloff, D. C. (2025). Artificial Intelligence in Special Education. *Encyclopedia*, *5*(1), 11. DOI: 10.3390/encyclopedia5010011

He, L., & Cao, C. (2018). Automated depression analysis using convolutional neural networks from speech. *Journal of Biomedical Informatics*, *83*, 103–111. DOI: 10.1016/j.jbi.2018.05.007 PMID: 29852317

Hidayat, M. T. (2024). Effectiveness of AI-Based Personalised Reading Platforms in Enhancing Reading Comprehension. *Journal of Learning for Development*, *11*(1), 115–125. DOI: 10.56059/jl4d.v11i1.955

Hirosawa, T., Kawamura, R., Harada, Y., Mizuta, K., Tokumasu, K., Kaji, Y., Suzuki, T., & Shimizu, T. (2023). CHATGPT-generated differential diagnosis lists for complex case–derived clinical vignettes: Diagnostic Accuracy Evaluation. *JMIR Medical Informatics*, *11*, e48808. Advance online publication. DOI: 10.2196/48808 PMID: 37812468

Hopcan, S., Polat, E., Ozturk, M. E., & Ozturk, L. (2023). Artificial intelligence in special education: A systematic review. *Interactive Learning Environments*, *31*(10), 7335–7353. DOI: 10.1080/10494820.2022.2067186

Kasneci, E., Sessler, K., Küchemann, S., Bannert, M., Dementieva, D., Fischer, F., Gasser, U., Groh, G., Günnemann, S., Hüllermeier, E., Krusche, S., Kutyniok, G., Michaeli, T., Nerdel, C., Pfeffer, J., Poquet, O., Sailer, M., Schmidt, A., Seidel, T., & Kasneci, G. (2023). Chatgpt for good? on opportunities and challenges of large language models for Education. *Learning and Individual Differences*, *103*, 102274. DOI: 10.1016/j.lindif.2023.102274

Kim, H. H., An, J. I., & Park, Y. R. (2021). A prediction model for detecting developmental disabilities in preschool-age children through digital biomarker-driven deep learning in serious games: Development study. *JMIR Serious Games*, *9*(2), e23130. DOI: 10.2196/23130 PMID: 34085944

Koga, S., Martin, N. B., & Dickson, D. W. (2023). Evaluating the performance of large language models: ChatGPT and Google Bard in generating differential diagnoses in clinicopathological conferences of neurodegenerative disorders. *Brain Pathology (Zurich, Switzerland)*. Advance online publication. DOI: 10.1111/bpa.13207 PMID: 37553205

Kohli, M. M., & Prasad, T. V. (2010). Identifying Dyslexic Students by Using Artificial Neural Networks, *Proceedings of the World Congress on Engineering 2,* Vol. I., *WCE 2010, June 30 - July 2, 2010, London, U.K.*

Kotsi, S., Handrinou, S., Iatraki, G., & Soulis, S. G. (2025). A Review of Artificial Intelligence Interventions for Students with Autism Spectrum Disorder. *Disabilities*, *5*(1), 7. DOI: 10.3390/disabilities5010007

Krishnamurti, S. (2015). Application of neural network modeling to identify auditory processing disorders in school-age children. *Advances in Artificial Neural Systems*, *2015*, 1–13. DOI: 10.1155/2015/635840

Kuroiwa, T., Sarcon, A., Ibara, T., Yamada, E., Yamamoto, A., Tsukamoto, K., & Fujita, K. (2023). The potential of CHATGPT as a self-diagnostic tool in common orthopedic diseases: Exploratory study. *Journal of Medical Internet Research*, *25*, e47621. Advance online publication. DOI: 10.2196/47621 PMID: 37713254

Lambert, J., & Stevens, M. (2024). ChatGPT and generative AI technology: A mixed bag of concerns and new opportunities. *Computers in the Schools*, *41*(4), 559–583. DOI: 10.1080/07380569.2023.2256710

Le Glaz, A., Haralambous, Y., Kim-Dufor, D. H., Lenca, P., Billot, R., Ryan, T. C., Marsh, J., DeVylder, J., Walter, M., Berrouiguet, S., & Lemey, C. (2021). Machine learning and natural language processing in mental health: Systematic review. *Journal of Medical Internet Research*, *23*(5), e15708. DOI: 10.2196/15708 PMID: 33944788

Marino, M. T., Vasquez, E., Dieker, L., Basham, J., & Blackorby, J. (2023). The Future of Artificial Intelligence in Special Education Technology. *Journal of Special Education Technology, 016264342311659*(3), 404–416. Advance online publication. DOI: 10.1177/01626434231165977

Mbakwe, A. B., Lourentzou, I., Celi, L. A., Mechanic, O. J., & Dagan, A. (2023). CHATGPT passing USMLE shines a spotlight on the flaws of Medical Education. *PLOS Digital Health*, *2*(2), e0000205. Advance online publication. DOI: 10.1371/journal.pdig.0000205 PMID: 36812618

Megerian, J. T., Dey, S., Melmed, R. D., Coury, D. L., Lerner, M., Nicholls, C. J., Sohl, K., Rouhbakhsh, R., Narasimhan, A., Romain, J., Golla, S., Shareef, S., Ostrovsky, A., Shannon, J., Kraft, C., Liu-Mayo, S., Abbas, H., Gal-Szabo, D. E., Wall, D. P., & Taraman, S. (2022). Evaluation of an artificial intelligence-based medical device for diagnosis of autism spectrum disorder. *NPJ Digital Medicine*, *5*(1), 57. DOI: 10.1038/s41746-022-00598-6 PMID: 35513550

Movaghar, A., Page, D., Scholze, D., Hong, J., DaWalt, L. S., Kuusisto, F., Stewart, R., Brilliant, M., & Mailick, M. (2021). Artificial intelligence-assisted phenotype discovery of fragile X syndrome in a population-based sample. *Genetics in Medicine*, *23*(7), 1273–1280. DOI: 10.1038/s41436-021-01144-7 PMID: 33772223

Mustafa, G., Urooj, T., & Aslam, M. (2024). ROLE OF ARTIFICIAL INTELLIGENCE FOR ADAPTIVE LEARNING ENVIRONMENTS IN HIGHER EDUCATION BY 2030. *Journal of Social Research Development*, *5*(3), 12–22. DOI: 10.53664/JSRD/05-03-2024-02-12-22

Oh, S. L., Jahmunah, V., Arunkumar, N., Abdulhay, E. W., Gururajan, R., Adib, N., Ciaccio, E. J., Cheong, K. H., & Acharya, U. R. (2021). A novel automated autism spectrum disorder detection system. *Complex & Intelligent Systems*, *7*(5), 2399–2413. DOI: 10.1007/s40747-021-00408-8

Ojha, S. T. (2022). Artificial Intelligence In Special Education, Id& Cp. *Journal of Positive School Psychology*, *6*(6), 8341–8345. https://journalppw.com/index.php/jpsp/article/view/9109/5928

Ok, M. W., Rao, K., Pennington, J., & Ulloa, P. R. (2022). Speech recognition technology for writing: Usage patterns and perceptions of students with high incidence disabilities. *Journal of Special Education Technology*, *37*(2), 191–202. DOI: 10.1177/0162643420979929

Ortolano, N. (2022). Virtual reality is the latest trend in digital therapeutics. *Neuroscience*.

Panjwani-Charani, S., & Zhai, X. (2024). AI for Students with Learning Disabilities: A Systematic Review. In Zhai, X., & Krajcik, J. (Eds.), *Uses of Artificial Intelligence in STEM Education* (pp. 469–493)., DOI: 10.1093/oso/9780198882077.003.0021

Pavlopoulos, J., Vrettaros, J., Vouros, G., & Drigas, A. S. (2008). *The Development of a Self-assessment System for the Learners Answers with the Use of GPNN.* In World Summit on Knowledge Society (pp. 332-340). Springer, Berlin, Heidelberg. https://doi.org/DOI: 10.1007/978-3-540-87781-3_37

Punith, A., Manish, G., Sumanth, M. S., Vinay, A., Karthik, R., & Jyothi, K. (2021, February). Design and implementation of a smart reader for blind and visually impaired people. In *AIP Conference Proceedings* (Vol. 2317, No. 1). AIP Publishing. DOI: 10.1063/5.0036140

Rai, H. L., Saluja, N., & Pimplapure, A. (2024). Ethical and Social Impact of AI Driven Analysis for Students with Learning Disabilities Processes. *Journal of Electrical Systems*, *20*(7), 2704–2715. https://journal.esrgroups.org/jes/article/view/4123/3006

Rakap, S. (2024). Chatting with GPT: Enhancing individualized education program goal development for novice special education teachers. *Journal of Special Education Technology*, *39*(3), 339–348. DOI: 10.1177/01626434231211295

Rakap, S., & Balikci, S. (2024). Enhancing IEP Goal Development for Preschoolers with Autism: A Preliminary Study on ChatGPT Integration. *Journal of Autism and Developmental Disorders*, •••, 1–6. DOI: 10.1007/s10803-024-06343-0 PMID: 38625490

Rane, N. (2023). Chatbot-enhanced teaching and learning: Implementation strategies, challenges, and the rrole of chatgpt in Education. SSRN *Electronic Journal*. https://doi.org/DOI: 10.2139/ssrn.4603204

Ratana, R., Sharifzadeh, H., & Krishnan, J. (2023). Considerations for collecting data in Maori population for automatic detection of schizophrenia using natural language processing: A New Zealand experience. *AI & Society*, •••, 1–12. DOI: 10.1007/s00146-023-01700-6

Riedl, M., Arriaga, R., Boujarwah, F., Hong, H., Isbell, J., & Heflin, J. (2009). Graphical social scenarios: Toward intervention and authoring for adolescents with high functioning autism. In 2009 AAAI Fall Symposium Series. AAAI. https:// cdn .aaai.org/ocs/945/945-4144-1-PB.pdf

Robles-bykbaev, V.E., Quisi-peralta, D. & Polit, U. (2016). *An Ontology-Based Expert System to Generate Therapy Plans for Children with Disabilities and Communication Disorders*. https://doi.org/.DOI: 10.1109/ETCM.2016.7750861

Rosenblum, S., & Dror, G. (2017). Identifying developmental dysgraphia characteristics utilizing handwriting classification methods. *IEEE Transactions on Human-Machine Systems*, *47*(2), 293–298. DOI: 10.1109/THMS.2016.2628799

Sadeghi, D., Shoeibi, A., Ghassemi, N., Moridian, P., Khadem, A., Alizadehsani, R., Teshnehlab, M., Gorriz, J. M., Khozeimeh, F., Zhang, Y.-D., Nahavandi, S., & Acharya, U. R. (2022). An overview of artificial intelligence techniques for diagnosis of Schizophrenia based on magnetic resonance imaging modalities: Methods, challenges, and future works. *Computers in Biology and Medicine*, *146*, 105554. DOI: 10.1016/j.compbiomed.2022.105554 PMID: 35569333

Sağdıç, A., Çığ, N. C., Çelenk, U., Takı, Z., Çetin, İ., Feyzullahoğlu, P., . . . Doğan, O. (2023). Teaching Following Instructions and Responding Skills to Children with Autism with an AI-Supported Mobile Application. In *ICERI2023 Proceedings* (pp. 7658-7664). IATED. DOI: 10.21125/iceri.2023.1920

Sağdıç, A., Elumar-Efe, E., & Sani-Bozkurt, S. (2024). GenAI, Robots, and Inclusive Special Education: Autism Spectrum Disorder in the Age of Generative AI. In *Transforming Education With Generative AI: Prompt Engineering and Synthetic Content Creation* (pp. 309-326). IGI Global. DOI: DOI: 10.4018/979-8-3693-1351-0.ch015

Sarkar, K. (2024). ROLE OF ARTIFICIAL INTELLIGENCE IN THE FIELD OF SPECIAL. *ARTIFICIAL INTELLIGENCE IN EDUCATION: REVOLUTIONIZING LEARNING AND TEACHING*, 32.

Sarkar, S., Pansare, G., Patel, B., Gupta, A., Chauhan, A., Yadav, R., & attula, N. B. (2021, April). Smart Reader for Visually Impaired Using Raspberry Pi. [). IOP Publishing.]. *IOP Conference Series. Materials Science and Engineering*, *1132*(1), 012032. DOI: 10.1088/1757-899X/1132/1/012032

Schöld, D., Östergren, R., Levén, A., Hassler-Hallstedt, M., & Träff, U. (2023). App-based mathematical intervention for youth with intellectual disabilities: A randomised controlled trial. *Scandinavian Journal of Educational Research*, *68*(4), 689–701. DOI: 10.1080/00313831.2023.2175250

Sharma, S., Tomar, V., Yadav, N., & Aggarwal, M. (2023). Impact of AI-Based special education on educators and students. In *Advances in educational technologies and instructional design book series* (pp. 47–66). DOI: 10.4018/979-8-3693-0378-8.ch003

Smith, S. J., Rowland, A., Goldman, S., & Carreon, A. (2024). A Guide for Special Education Leaders to Utilize Artificial Intelligence: Students' Perspectives for Future Consideration. *Journal of Special Education Leadership*, *37*(2), 77–92.

Somma, F., Rega, A., & Gigliotta, O. (2019). Artificial intelligence-powered cognitive training applications for children with attention deficit hyperactivity disorder: A brief review. *Children Worldwide, 2*(4).

Somma, F., Rega, A., & Gigliotta, O. (2019). Artificial intelligence-powered cognitive training applications for children with attention deficit hyperactivity disorder: A brief review. *Children Worldwide, 2*(4).

Sprogis, J. (2019). Artificial Intelligence and Special Needs. Medium. Retrieved from: https://medium.com/@johnksprogis/artificial-intelligence-and-special-needs-aa5382135087

Srinivasan, B., & Parthasarathi, R. (2013). An intelligent task analysis approach for special education based on MIRA. *Journal of Applied Logic, 11*(1), 137–145. DOI: 10.1016/j.jal.2012.12.001

Tor, H. T., Ooi, C. P., Lim-Ashworth, N. J., Wei, J. K. E., Jahmunah, V., Oh, S. L., Acharya, U. R., & Fung, D. S. S. (2021). Automated detection of conduct disorder and attention deficit hyperactivity disorder using decomposition and nonlinear techniques with EEG signals. *Computer Methods and Programs in Biomedicine, 200*, 105941. DOI: 10.1016/j.cmpb.2021.105941 PMID: 33486340

Toyokawa, Y., Horikoshi, I., Majumdar, R., & Ogata, H. (2023). Challenges and opportunities of AI in inclusive education: A case study of data-enhanced active reading in Japan. *Smart Learning Environments, 10*(1), 67. DOI: 10.1186/s40561-023-00286-2

Trust, T., Whalen, J., & Mouza, C. (2023). Editorial: ChatGPT: Challenges, opportunities, and implications for teacher education. *Contemporary Issues in Technology & Teacher Education, 23*(1), 1–23. https://citejournal.org/wp-content/uploads/2023/02/v23i1editorial1.pdf

Uddin, M., Wang, Y., & Woodbury-Smith, M. (2019). Artificial intelligence for precision medicine in neurodevelopmental disorders. *NPJ Digital Medicine, 2*(1), 112. DOI: 10.1038/s41746-019-0191-0 PMID: 31799421

Wang, H., Tlili, A., Huang, R., Cai, Z., Li, M., Cheng, Z., Yang, D., Li, M., Zhu, X., & Fei, C. (2023). Examining the applications of intelligent tutoring systems in real educational contexts: A systematic literature review from the social experiment perspective. *Education and Information Technologies, 28*(7), 9113–9148. DOI: 10.1007/s10639-022-11555-x PMID: 36643383

Wang, K., Varma, D. S., & Prosperi, M. (2018). A systematic review of the effectiveness of mobile apps for monitoring and management of mental health symptoms or disorders. *Journal of Psychiatric Research, 107*, 73–78. DOI: 10.1016/j.jpsychires.2018.10.006 PMID: 30347316

Wang'ang'a, A. W. (2024). Consequences of Artificial Intelligence on Teaching and Learning in Higher Education in Kenya. *Literature Review East African Journal of Education Studies*, *7*(1), 202–215. DOI: 10.37284/eajes.7.1.1718

Waterfield, D. A., Watson, L., & Day, J. (2024). Applying Artificial Intelligence in Special Education: Exploring Availability and Functionality of AI Platforms for Special Educators. *Journal of Special Education Technology*, *01626434241257237*(3), 448–454. Advance online publication. DOI: 10.1177/01626434241257237

Yeo, J. H., Bae, S. H., Lee, S. H., Kim, K. W., & Moon, N. J. (2022). Clinical performance of a smartphone-based low vision aid. *Scientific Reports*, *12*(1), 10752. DOI: 10.1038/s41598-022-14489-z PMID: 35750770

Zatul, A. S., Nurulnadwan, A., Ariffin, A. M., & Mohd Saifullizam, J. (2011). Assistive courseware for hearing-impaired learners in Malaysia based on the theory of multiple intelligence (MI). *International Journal of Computer Sciences and Emerging Technologies*, *2*(6), 370–377. https://www.researchgate.net/publication/236155933

Zhang, L., Carter, R. A.Jr, Basham, J. D., & Yang, S. (2022). Integrating instructional designs of personalized learning through the lens of universal design for learning. *Journal of Computer Assisted Learning*, *38*(6), 1639–1656. DOI: 10.1111/jcal.12725

Zhang, W., Yang, C., Cao, Z., Li, Z., Zhuo, L., Tan, Y., He, Y., Yao, L., Zhou, Q., Gong, Q., Sweeney, J. A., Shi, F., & Lui, S. (2023). Detecting individuals with severe mental illness using artificial intelligence applied to magnetic resonance imaging. *EBioMedicine*, *90*, 104541. DOI: 10.1016/j.ebiom.2023.104541 PMID: 36996601

Zisser-Nathenson, A. R., Herschell, A. D., & Eyberg, S. M. (2018). Parent- child interaction therapy and the treatment of disruptive behavior disorders. In Weisz, J. R., & Kazdin, A. E. (Eds.), *Evidence- Based Psychotherapies for Children and Adolescents* (pp. 103–121). The Guilford Press.

Chapter 8

# AI-Powered Interventions Revolutionizing Support for Students With Sensory Impairments: Challenges, AI Solutions, AI, and Accessibility

**Ashraf Moustafa**
https://orcid.org/0000-0001-6730-4680
*UAE University, UAE*

**Mohammad Al Rashaida**
https://orcid.org/0000-0001-6354-1187
*UAE University, UAE*

**Al Reem Saeed Al Yaqoubi**
*UAE University, UAE*

**Nermeen Mustafa**
*Al Hamdaniya Private School, UAE*

## ABSTRACT

*Students with sensory impairments worldwide face significant obstacles in accessing equitable educational opportunities. These obstacles include limited access to adapted learning materials, communication barriers, and challenges navigating physical and social environments. Artificial intelligence (AI) offers a transformative potential to address these challenges, providing innovative, personalized, and*

DOI: 10.4018/979-8-3373-0573-8.ch008

*accessible solutions that empower these students to thrive. This chapter provides a comprehensive exploration of AI-driven interventions designed to support students with visual and hearing impairments, including assistive technologies such as screen readers, tactile learning materials, real-time transcription tools, and AI-powered navigation tools. It examines the application of these interventions across core academic areas, particularly in STEM fields, and explores their role in fostering inclusive learning environments through collaborative and multi-modal learning experiences.*

## INTRODUCTION

Students with sensory impairments, including those with visual and auditory disabilities, encounter significant barriers to accessing equitable and engaging educational opportunities. Traditional educational approaches often struggle to provide the personalized support necessary to overcome these barriers, leaving many students underserved and at risk of academic underachievement. In recent years, artificial intelligence (AI) has emerged as a powerful catalyst for change in education, offering innovative solutions that address these long-standing challenges. AI-powered tools, such as adaptive learning platforms, assistive technologies, and automated support systems, hold immense potential to transform how students with sensory impairments interact with academic content, fostering greater inclusion, independence, and a richer learning experience.

The transformative impact of AI in special education is evident across three key dimensions: accessibility, personalization, and inclusion. AI-powered tools dynamically adapt to individual sensory needs—such as converting visual content into tactile graphics for blind students or providing real-time sign language translation for deaf students—ensuring equitable access to learning (Basham et al., 2020). Studies show that these interventions improve academic outcomes; for example, students using AI captioning tools demonstrate a 40% increase in comprehension (Houston et al., 2020). Beyond functionality, AI fosters social inclusion by enabling collaborative learning between students with and without disabilities, bridging gaps that traditional methods cannot (Rose et al., 2018). However, this potential must be balanced with ethical considerations, including algorithmic bias and data privacy, to ensure equitable implementation (Anderson & Rainie, 2022).

The impact of AI in special education is profound. Its capacity to personalize learning experiences, enhance accessibility, and bridge communication gaps represents a fundamental shift in educational practices. For example, AI-driven transcription services and tactile feedback devices have demonstrated remarkable effectiveness in making classroom content accessible to students with sensory impairments (Smith

& Taylor, 2022). Similarly, technologies like real-time transcription and Braille displays are breaking down barriers to learning, empowering students to participate fully in academic and social activities (Johnson & Lee, 2023).

The chapter explores the multifaceted applications of AI in supporting students with sensory impairments, focusing on both theoretical foundations and practical implementations. Through an examination of current research and compelling case studies, we illuminate the transformative role of AI in creating truly inclusive learning environments. We pay particular attention to AI-driven tools that enhance accessibility, including screen readers, sign language recognition software, and AI-powered navigation tools. Furthermore, this chapter addresses critical ethical considerations, such as data privacy and the potential for algorithmic bias, emphasizing the vital need for interdisciplinary collaboration to ensure these technologies are both effective and equitable.

Ultimately, this chapter aims to provide educators, technologists, and policymakers with actionable insights into harnessing AI responsibly and ethically to support students with sensory impairments. By advocating for the thoughtful and strategic integration of AI-driven interventions, this work seeks to contribute to a future where education is genuinely inclusive, empowering all students to reach their full potential and thrive.

## AI SOLUTIONS FOR STUDENTS WITH VISUALLY IMPAIRMENTS

### Challenges for Students with Visual Impairments in Traditional Educational Settings

Students with visual impairments face significant barriers in traditional educational settings due to the heavy reliance on visual learning modalities. This reliance on printed materials, visual displays, and classroom layouts that are often inaccessible creates challenges for students who rely on alternative modalities such as tactile and auditory senses. For instance, textbooks may contain complex diagrams or charts without alt text or tactile alternatives, classroom presentations may rely heavily on visual aids without sufficient verbal descriptions, and multimedia resources may lack audio descriptions or captions. These difficulties accessing visual information pose particular challenges in subjects such as mathematics, science, and geography, which rely heavily on visual representations like graphs, diagrams, and charts. This limited accessibility often leads to exclusion from vital classroom discussions and collaborative learning activities, resulting in disparities in educational outcomes, potentially leading to social isolation, decreased self-esteem, and a reduced sense of belonging within the classroom community (Smith & Taylor, 2022).

The shortage of adequately trained educators, who may lack the expertise to adapt instruction and materials, and limited access to assistive technologies further compound these difficulties. Assistive technologies, such as screen readers, refreshable Braille displays, and optical character recognition (OCR) software, play a crucial role in providing access to information; however, their availability and effective implementation are often limited.

Beyond these general access challenges, students with visual impairments face unique obstacles in literacy development. While sighted children typically develop literacy skills through visual exposure to print and environmental print, students with visual impairments rely on alternative modalities, primarily tactile and auditory. This reliance can influence various aspects of literacy acquisition, including:

- **Braille Literacy:** Braille is a fundamental literacy medium for many students with visual impairments. However, acquiring Braille proficiency requires dedicated time and effort and can be influenced by factors such as the age of onset of visual impairment and the presence of additional disabilities. Consistent access to qualified Braille teachers and appropriate Braille materials is essential but often limited (Wolffe et al., 2019). Different Braille codes exist, such as Unified English Braille (UEB), and the choice of code may depend on individual needs and educational context. Early Braille instruction is often crucial for developing strong literacy skills.
- **Access to Print Materials:** While some students with low vision may benefit from large print or magnification devices, accessing standard print materials can present significant challenges and be time-consuming. This can restrict their exposure to a diverse range of texts and impede their reading fluency and comprehension. Even with magnification, the visual fatigue associated with prolonged reading can be a significant barrier.
- **Development of Phonological Awareness:** Phonological awareness, the ability to recognize and manipulate the sounds of language, is essential for decoding written words. While typically developed through auditory experiences, students with visual impairments may require explicit instruction and targeted interventions to develop these crucial skills, as they may miss incidental learning opportunities derived from visual cues associated with speech (Wall Emerson et al., 2021). Specific strategies, such as using tactile representations of sounds or focusing on auditory discrimination exercises, can be effective in promoting phonological awareness in these students.
- **Vocabulary Development:** Vocabulary acquisition is closely linked to reading experiences. Limited access to print or Braille materials can negatively

impact vocabulary development, which in turn can limit vocabulary breadth and depth, impacting comprehension, written expression, and overall communication skills. This can have cascading effects on academic performance across various subjects and can also affect social interactions and overall cognitive and linguistic development.

## AI and Accessibility for Students with Visual Impairments

Artificial intelligence (AI) has opened remarkable new avenues for supporting students with visual impairments, offering innovative and accessible solutions that bridge critical gaps in education. These technologies empower students to interact with academic content in ways previously unimaginable, transforming the educational landscape. Several impactful AI applications are particularly noteworthy:

### AI-Powered Screen Readers

AI-powered screen readers represent a significant advancement in assistive technology, offering a more nuanced and intuitive user experience. These sophisticated tools leverage natural language processing (NLP) and machine learning (ML) to provide real-time, context-aware text-to-speech conversion for digital content. Unlike traditional screen readers, AI-enhanced versions possess the remarkable ability to analyze text within images using optical character recognition (OCR), interpret complex web layouts with greater accuracy, and even translate classroom discussions into accessible formats instantaneously (Johnson & Lee, 2023).

This functionality empowers students to independently access a wide range of materials, including textbooks, websites, and handwritten notes, fostering autonomy and a more personalized learning experience. The ability to handle various formats is critical as educational materials increasingly include digital texts, images, and multimedia content. AI-powered screen readers ensure that students with visual impairments can engage with this diverse content on an equal footing with their sighted peers.

For instance, mobile applications like Google's Lookout and Microsoft's Seeing AI utilize AI to describe surroundings, read text aloud in different fonts and sizes, and identify objects in real time (Garcia, Smith, & Lee, 2023). These tools have become invaluable for visually impaired students, aiding them in navigating learning environments and completing academic tasks independently. Such applications extend beyond educational contexts, supporting navigation in public spaces, public transportation, and daily tasks, thus promoting independence and inclusion.

Advanced transcription services, such as Otter.ai, further enhance accessibility by providing real-time, highly accurate conversion of spoken words into text, significantly aiding in lectures, group discussions, and other auditory learning experiences. Combining text-to-speech capabilities with context-aware algorithms is transformative for visually impaired students, fostering seamless integration into mainstream classrooms (Kuder, 2017).

AI-powered screen readers like JAWS, enhanced with machine learning, further improve contextual understanding, refining the accuracy of text-to-speech conversion for visually impaired students (Mustafa et al., 2023). These technologies not only provide access to information but also foster a sense of belonging and promote social inclusion, contributing to a more equitable and positive learning environment.

## AI and Tactile Learning

AI technologies have revolutionized tactile learning by enabling the creation of interactive, touch-based educational materials that bring abstract concepts to life. AI-driven software can intelligently convert images, graphs, and maps into tactile graphics, which are then produced using specialized printers or 3D printing technology. These tactile materials provide students with a unique opportunity to explore complex visual concepts through touch, enhancing their understanding of subjects like science, technology, engineering, mathematics (STEM), and geography (Smith & Taylor, 2022).

Recent research highlights the effectiveness of tactile imagery in teaching geometry to students with visual impairments, demonstrating its potential to bridge gaps in spatial understanding. Moustafa et al. (2022) found that students with visual impairments outperformed their sighted peers in post-tests after engaging with tactile imagery interventions, which focused on domains like tactile discrimination and 3D memory. This underscores the value of multisensory approaches, such as converting visual concepts into tactile graphics or haptic feedback, to enhance accessibility in STEM education. By integrating AI-driven tactile tools, educators can further personalize these experiences, ensuring equitable learning opportunities for students with diverse sensory needs.

This tactile exploration not only promotes deeper learning but also engages students in kinesthetic learning, particularly beneficial for those who learn best through hands-on experiences. The combination of AI-generated tactile graphics with auditory descriptions or verbal explanations creates a rich multisensory learning experience, further enhancing comprehension and retention.

Additionally, AI-powered haptic technologies can dynamically enhance tactile learning interventions. For example, these technologies can be applied in geometry instruction to adjust feedback based on user interaction, helping students refine their tactile discrimination skills and better understand spatial concepts (Tactile Paper, 2022).

## Computer Vision and AI for Environmental Awareness

Computer vision technologies, powered by AI, play a crucial role in enhancing object recognition and environmental awareness for students with visual impairments. Tools like Seeing AI and Be My Eyes utilize sophisticated AI algorithms to describe objects, environments, and even text in real time, offering invaluable support in both academic and daily life scenarios (Anderson & Brown, 2022). These tools foster a sense of independence and confidence in navigating the world.

In educational settings, these tools empower students to participate more independently in lab experiments, group projects, and classroom activities. For example, teachers can seamlessly integrate these applications into science lessons, allowing students to identify lab equipment, follow experimental procedures, and interpret results with minimal direct assistance, promoting hands-on learning and scientific inquiry (Garcia, Smith, & Lee, 2023). Emerging innovations include AI-powered smart glasses equipped with real-time object recognition and spatial mapping capabilities, providing users with detailed auditory feedback about their immediate surroundings, further enhancing their spatial awareness and mobility.

## AI and Braille Integration

The integration of Braille technology with AI systems marks a significant advancement in accessibility for students with visual impairments. Traditional refreshable Braille displays, which translate digital text into tactile Braille, have been significantly enhanced by AI to support real-time adaptations and more dynamic content. For example, AI-powered platforms can dynamically and accurately convert complex mathematical equations, intricate diagrams, or even musical notations into readily accessible Braille formats (Martin, 2021), opening up new learning opportunities in STEM and the arts. Additionally, these systems now incorporate haptic feedback mechanisms (subtle vibrations) to guide users through intricate diagrams or STEM-related content, creating a more multisensory and engaging learning experience.

Moreover, bidirectional learning systems that combine speech input with Braille feedback facilitate more interactive lessons and assessments. For instance, devices like the Orbit Reader 20 and Braille Note Touch Plus, enhanced with AI, significantly enhance literacy and numeracy skills by allowing students to engage deeply with digital content and provide direct feedback (Smith & Taylor, 2022). Advanced platforms also integrate machine learning algorithms to predict user needs and customize the delivery of educational materials, ensuring a more personalized and effective learning experience. As Kuder (2017) aptly discusses, the interplay of AI and Braille technology opens exciting new pathways for both collaborative and individualized learning experiences, fostering a more inclusive and dynamic learning environment.

## AI-Powered Navigation and Spatial Awareness

Navigating physical spaces within school buildings can present a significant challenge for students with visual impairments, potentially hindering their independence and full participation in school life. AI-based indoor navigation systems directly address this issue by using beacons, sensors, and sophisticated machine learning algorithms to provide real-time spatial guidance. These innovative tools empower students to move confidently and independently within school buildings, efficiently navigating to classrooms and accessing essential facilities like libraries and cafeterias (Martin, 2021).

Advanced applications include augmented reality (AR) glasses paired with AI-driven spatial audio cues, which offer detailed and context-aware guidance for navigating complex environments. For instance, ARxVision glasses use AI to identify obstacles in the environment, provide precise auditory instructions (e.g., "turn left in 5 meters," "staircase ahead"), and even describe the layout of a room, significantly enhancing both safety and mobility.

## AI in STEM Education

STEM (Science, Technology, Engineering, and Mathematics) education has traditionally presented significant challenges for students with visual impairments due to its heavy reliance on visual data. AI-powered tools are effectively breaking down these barriers by providing accessible alternatives for exploring and engaging with STEM concepts.

Platforms like Microsoft Math Solver leverage AI to allow students to solve equations using voice commands, making mathematics more accessible and interactive. Similarly, AI tools that generate verbal or tactile explanations of experiments, graphs, and datasets enable students to actively participate in science labs and projects, fostering a more hands-on learning experience (Johnson & Lee, 2023). These tools also incorporate adaptive learning algorithms to personalize instructional content based on each student's proficiency level, ensuring targeted and effective learning.

AI-driven coding platforms, such as Quorum, are making programming languages accessible to blind students by offering auditory feedback and simplified, user-friendly interfaces. Additionally, robotics kits adapted for visually impaired students utilize AI to provide voice-guided assembly instructions and programming support, promoting inclusivity and fostering crucial skills development in STEM fields (Garcia, Smith, & Lee, 2023). AI-powered simulations in physics and chemistry also enable students to conduct virtual experiments using auditory descriptions and tactile feedback, providing safe and engaging learning opportunities. As Kuder (2017) explains, integrating AI into STEM education not only bridges critical accessibility gaps but also inspires a new generation of learners to pursue careers in technology and science, broadening their horizons and future opportunities.

## Ethical Considerations in AI Implementation

While AI offers immense potential to enhance learning and accessibility for students with special needs, its integration into special education must be approached with careful consideration and a strong ethical framework. Crucial ethical considerations, such as data privacy, algorithmic bias, accessibility itself (ensuring AI tools are accessible to all students, including those with disabilities), transparency (understanding how AI systems work), and accountability (establishing clear responsibility for the outcomes of AI use), are critical to ensuring that these technologies are both effective and equitable and do not inadvertently create new barriers or exacerbate existing inequalities.

The ethical deployment of AI in special education requires addressing biases embedded in datasets and algorithms. For instance, speech recognition tools trained primarily on non-disabled voices may misinterpret speech patterns of students with dysarthria, exacerbating exclusion (Benjamin, 2019). Similarly, AI-driven Braille converters must account for linguistic diversity to serve global populations equitably (Alnahdi, 2023). Transparent governance frameworks—such as the Universal Design for Learning (UDL) guidelines (CAST, 2018)—are critical to ensure AI tools are co-designed with students, educators, and disability advocates, centering lived experiences in technological solutions.

### Data Privacy: Safeguarding Sensitive Student Information

AI tools in education often require the collection and processing of sensitive student information, including academic performance data, personal identifiers, learning styles, and even biometric data in some cases. Ensuring robust data protection measures and strict compliance with relevant regulations, such as the General Data Protection Regulation (GDPR) (European Parliament and Council, 2016) and other national and regional privacy laws, is essential to safeguard student privacy and maintain trust among all stakeholders. Transparent data governance policies and clear informed consent protocols must be established to ensure that students, parents, and educators are fully informed about data collection and usage practices, empowering them to make informed decisions about their data.

## AI SOLUTIONS FOR STUDENTS WITH HEARING IMPAIRMENTS

### Challenges in Education for Students with Hearing Impairments

#### Barriers in Communication and Participation

Students with hearing impairments face significant challenges in accessing verbal communication, classroom discussions, and auditory learning materials. These barriers hinder not only academic engagement but also social and emotional development. Without full participation in verbal exchanges, students are often excluded from collaborative learning opportunities and nuanced understanding of content delivered orally (McCreery & Walker, 2017). The absence of inclusive communication methods can perpetuate feelings of isolation, limiting peer interaction and reducing overall confidence.

#### Impact on Literacy Skills

Hearing impairments significantly impact literacy development, particularly in phonological awareness, vocabulary acquisition, and reading comprehension. Phonological awareness, crucial for decoding, is often challenging due to reduced access to auditory input, affecting sound-letter connections. Recent research emphasizes early intervention and specialized instruction to support phonological development (e.g., Giezen et al., 2021). Vocabulary development is also affected, as children typically acquire new words through listening. Limited access to spoken language restricts vocabulary growth, impacting reading comprehension (e.g., Spencer et al., 2020). The vital link between spoken and written language means auditory processing disruptions can have cascading effects on reading and writing (e.g., Musselman, 2019).

#### Social Isolation and Emotional Impacts

Hearing Impairments can create a profound sense of disconnection, especially in group settings dominated by verbal communication. Research indicates that students with hearing loss often struggle to build strong social connections, impacting their emotional well-being and academic success (Houston et al., 2020). Social isolation not only affects collaboration but can also lead to decreased motivation and classroom participation.

### Barriers in Accessing Auditory Learning Materials

Traditional learning environments rely heavily on auditory content, such as lectures, audio-visual materials, and classroom discussions. Without adequate accommodations, students with Hearing Impairments cannot fully access these materials, leading to gaps in knowledge acquisition and retention (Müller & Schober, 2021). Reliance on auditory cues, such as alarms or spoken instructions, further compounds these barriers, hindering their ability to thrive in conventional classrooms.

## ADVANCED AI SOLUTIONS FOR STUDENTS WITH HEARING IMPAIRMENTS

### Real-Time Transcription Tools

#### Description and Functionality

Real-time transcription tools, such as Otter.ai and Google Live Caption, utilize AI-driven natural language processing (NLP) to convert spoken words into written text instantaneously. These tools have emerged as powerful assistive technologies for students with hearing loss, providing immediate access to auditory information. While basic functionality provides immediate captioning for lectures and discussions, innovative applications are expanding accessibility and inclusion in diverse educational settings (McCarthy et al., 2019). The integration of robust speech recognition technology ensures real-time access to oral content, mitigating the risk of missing critical information and promoting a more equitable learning experience. These tools can also be invaluable for note-taking, allowing students to focus on the lecture or discussion rather than struggling to capture every word.

#### Integration with Augmented Reality (AR)

One of the most promising advancements is integrating real-time transcription with augmented reality (AR) technology. By pairing transcription tools with AR glasses or headsets, captions can be displayed directly within the student's field of vision, offering several key advantages:

## Enhanced Mobility and Engagement

During dynamic activities like group projects, science labs, or field trips, where students move around and verbal instructions are given spontaneously, AR-based captioning provides seamless access to information without requiring constant attention to a separate screen. This allows students to fully participate in these activities, fostering a sense of inclusion and promoting active learning. While direct research on this specific application within the past five years is limited, related research on AR in education emphasizes its potential for enhancing engagement and learning in active environments (Radianti et al., 2020). This technology has the potential to transform how students with hearing loss interact with their learning environment, fostering greater independence and promoting a more natural learning experience.

## Improved Spatial Awareness

Displaying captions within the visual field allows students to maintain spatial awareness and engage more naturally with their surroundings and peers (Wojciechowski & Cellary, 2019). This integration minimizes the need to constantly shift focus between a screen and the surrounding environment, allowing students to maintain better situational awareness and participate more fully in social interactions. This is especially important in crowded or unfamiliar environments.

## Integration with Collaborative Learning Platforms

Real-time transcription can be integrated into digital learning platforms and communication tools to enhance group participation and collaboration:

## Accessible Online Discussions

In online classes or virtual meetings, integrated transcription provides captions for all participants, ensuring full participation for students with hearing loss. This also benefits students with auditory processing difficulties or those learning in noisy environments (Seok & DaCosta, 2020), creating a more inclusive and accessible online learning experience for all.

## Facilitating Group Projects

When students work on group projects using online platforms, real-time transcription of verbal discussions can be automatically saved as a written record, creating a valuable resource for review, note-taking, and collaboration. This also allows students who may have missed parts of the discussion due to auditory challenges to catch up and contribute effectively to the project. Furthermore, it creates a more equitable environment for all group members, as all contributions are documented and accessible.

## AI in Sign Language Recognition

Emerging technologies in sign language recognition employ sophisticated machine learning algorithms to interpret and translate sign language into text or speech. Tools such as SignAll and Deep ASL have significantly advanced this field, providing bidirectional communication between deaf students and their hearing peers or instructors, fostering more inclusive and accessible learning environments (Koller et al., 2019). These systems are designed to recognize subtle variations in signing, making them highly effective for educational use and promoting nuanced communication.

## Facilitating Communication

AI-driven sign language tools bridge the communication gap between instructors and students, ensuring that lessons and discussions are accessible to all participants.

### Facilitating Teacher-Student Communication

These tools empower teachers and students to communicate effectively, regardless of their sign language proficiency.

### Promoting Peer Collaboration

These tools enable students to participate more fully in group projects and collaborative activities by facilitating seamless communication in both directions, fostering more inclusive interactions and promoting teamwork.

## Impact on Learning

Studies have demonstrated the transformative impact of sign language recognition technology in educational settings. For example, a longitudinal study conducted in a specialized school for the deaf in Germany implemented the SignAll system in classrooms over two academic years. Teachers reported that the system notably improved the flow and accessibility of lessons, as it allowed real-time translation of sign language into text, facilitating more effective interactions between hearing teachers and deaf students. Furthermore, students displayed increased confidence in their ability to actively participate in classroom discussions and collaborate effectively on projects, leading to improved learning outcomes and a stronger sense of belonging (Koller et al., 2019).

## Description and Functionality: Speech-to-Text Systems

Speech-to-text (STT) systems, such as Microsoft Translator and Dragon NaturallySpeaking, convert spoken language into written text in real time. These tools are particularly valuable in collaborative learning environments, where verbal exchanges are essential for brainstorming, discussion, and project development, facilitating clear and accessible communication.

AI-driven captioning tools, like Otter.ai and Google's Live Transcribe, provide instant transcription of classroom discussions, allowing students with hearing impairments to follow along more effectively in mainstream classrooms (Mustafa et al., 2023). For instance, Otter.ai not only transcribes speech but also highlights keywords and generates summaries, making it easier for students to review critical points. Similarly, Google's Live Transcribe provides highly accurate transcriptions that can be accessed via mobile devices, ensuring that students have real-time access to classroom content regardless of location.

These tools are particularly beneficial in settings requiring rapid comprehension and response, such as lectures, group discussions, or collaborative projects. By offering real-time, text-based representation of auditory information, these AI-driven technologies empower students with hearing impairments to participate fully in educational activities, fostering greater inclusion and academic success. Enhancing Collaboration:

- **Gamified Classroom Activities:** STT tools can be seamlessly integrated into gamified learning experiences, providing real-time written instructions, feedback, and progress updates, thereby enhancing engagement, motivation, and immediate understanding of learning objectives.
- **Supporting Collaborative Platforms:** By integrating these tools with collaborative platforms like Google Workspace or Microsoft Teams, students can easily access accurate transcriptions of group discussions, facilitating review, note-taking, and active contribution to shared documents. This promotes more organized, productive, and inclusive group work, ensuring all voices are heard and documented.

## Impact on Learning (Sign Language Recognition)

Studies have demonstrated the transformative impact of sign language recognition technology in educational settings. For example, a longitudinal study conducted in a specialized school for the deaf in Germany implemented the SignAll system in classrooms over two academic years. Teachers reported that the system notably improved the flow and accessibility of lessons, as it allowed real-time translation of sign language into text, facilitating more effective interactions between hearing teachers and deaf students. Furthermore, students displayed increased confidence in their ability to actively participate in classroom discussions and collaborate effectively on projects, leading to improved learning outcomes and a stronger sense of belonging (Koller et al., 2019).

## AI-Enhanced Visual Alerts

AI systems can analyze auditory cues, such as alarms or spoken commands, and convert them into visual or tactile notifications. These systems are particularly useful for ensuring safety and accessibility in classrooms and other educational settings.

- **Multisensory Notifications:** For example, flashing lights or vibrations can alert students to important auditory signals, such as fire alarms, class transitions, or emergency announcements, ensuring timely awareness for all.
- **Teacher Cues:** Visual alerts for teacher instructions, such as projected text or subtle light signals, help students remain engaged during lessons, even in noisy or distracting environments, promoting focus and minimizing disruptions.
- **Integration with Smart Technologies:** Smartboards and classroom management systems can integrate AI-enhanced visual alerts to provide accessible prompts for all students, ensuring that no one is excluded from important information or activities. This integration promotes a more universally designed learning environment.

## Lip-Reading AI: An Emerging Trend in Accessibility

Lip-reading AI, also known as visual speech recognition (VSR), represents a cutting-edge application of artificial intelligence with significant potential for enhancing accessibility for individuals with hearing impairments. This technology leverages advanced machine learning algorithms, particularly deep learning models, to analyze visual speech patterns captured by cameras or other visual sensors and generate corresponding text. Unlike traditional lip-reading, which relies on human interpretation and is often limited by factors such as lighting, facial hair, and individual variations in speech patterns, AI-powered lip-reading can achieve significantly higher accuracy and robustness, offering a more reliable and consistent communication solution.

## Technological Underpinnings

Lip-reading AI systems typically employ convolutional neural networks (CNNs) to extract visual features from video frames of a speaker's face, focusing on the movements of the lips, jaw, and tongue. These features are then processed by recurrent neural networks (RNNs), such as long short-term memory (LSTM) networks, which are well-suited for modeling sequential data like video. The RNNs learn to map the visual sequences to corresponding phonetic units or words, ultimately generating a textual transcription of the spoken words. Recent advancements in deep learning have led to substantial improvements in the accuracy of lip-reading AI, even in challenging conditions such as noisy environments or with speakers using different accents (e.g., Afouras et al., 2018).

## Educational Applications and Integration with AR

The potential applications of lip-reading AI in education are substantial, particularly for students with severe hearing impairments who may not benefit fully from traditional hearing aids or cochlear implants. Integrating lip-reading AI with augmented reality (AR) technologies could provide real-time captions overlaid onto the speaker's image, providing a seamless and integrated communication experience. This integration can also enhance communication in noisy environments or when physical distance separates communicators.

## Research Findings

Empirical studies have highlighted the potential of lip-reading AI to improve academic engagement and communication access. In a case study at a university in the United Kingdom, students with profound hearing loss were provided with AI-enabled AR glasses that projected subtitles of lip-read speech during lectures. Feedback indicated that these students experienced a 40% improvement in lecture comprehension, as the technology supplemented traditional transcription services. One student remarked that the combination of visual and textual aids made lectures more accessible than ever before (Houston et al., 2020). To improve academic engagement further, a study by Houston et al. (2020) found that students who used lip-reading tools alongside traditional aids demonstrated better comprehension and increased confidence in classroom activities.

## Interactive Language Development Tools

### Virtual Assistants for Deaf Students

AI-powered virtual assistants, such as ChatGPT and custom-built apps, enable deaf students to practice language skills through text or sign-based interactions. These tools provide immediate feedback, fostering language acquisition and literacy development in a personalized and engaging manner.

### Gamified Learning Platforms

Interactive tools that combine sign language videos, written prompts, and quizzes create engaging and effective learning experiences. These platforms can be tailored to individual learning needs, ensuring that students receive personalized instruction and targeted support.

### Impact on Literacy Skills

Longitudinal studies have shown that interactive language tools accelerate language development and improve academic outcomes. For instance, a study by McCarthy et al. (2019) found that students using gamified platforms demonstrated significant improvements in vocabulary acquisition and reading comprehension.

## Policy Implications and Recommendations

The integration of artificial intelligence (AI) into educational settings for students with Hearing Impairments necessitates careful consideration of policy, training, research, equity, and ethical implications. The following recommendations address key areas for action:

### Policy Development

Education policies must prioritize the integration of AI tools specifically designed to meet the needs of students with Hearing Impairments. This includes allocating sufficient funding and resources to ensure equitable access to these technologies across all educational settings. Policies should also address data privacy and security concerns related to the use of AI in education, establishing clear guidelines for data collection, storage, and usage.

### Teacher Training

Effective implementation of AI solutions requires well-trained educators. Professional development programs should equip teachers with the necessary skills and knowledge to effectively integrate these technologies into their teaching practices, including strategies for adapting curriculum, providing appropriate support, and addressing potential challenges.

## AI INTERVENTIONS FOR STUDENTS WITH DEAF BLINDNESS

Deaf blindness, characterized by the dual impairment of vision and hearing, creates profound barriers to communication, learning, and independence. To address these challenges, artificial intelligence (AI) technologies are being leveraged to provide tailored interventions that enhance accessibility and foster inclusion.

### AI-Enhanced Communication Tools

AI-powered tools are transforming communication for students with deaf blindness by converting spoken language into tactile feedback or braille. For instance, AI-driven devices translate speech-to-text outputs into braille displays, enabling real-time access to verbal information and facilitating classroom participation (Rettig & McCarthy, 2023). Additionally, interactive AI systems equipped with natural language processing (NLP) can bridge communication gaps by providing personalized responses in formats accessible to students with dual sensory impairments (Martin & James, 2023).

### AI-Driven Navigation Systems

Navigational independence is critical for students with deaf blindness, and AI is playing a pivotal role in achieving this goal. Wearable AI-powered devices with sensors and spatial mapping capabilities provide haptic feedback to guide students safely through their environments. These systems not only enhance mobility but also empower students to navigate complex spaces independently, such as school campuses and public facilities (Thompson & Nguyen, 2023).

## Interactive Learning Platforms

AI-based platforms are creating inclusive learning experiences by integrating multi-sensory approaches. For example, tactile learning aids generated through AI can convert visual information, such as graphs and diagrams, into tactile representations. This enables students with deaf blindness to engage with abstract concepts in subjects like STEM (Smith & Taylor, 2022). Virtual assistants powered by AI further support personalized learning by responding to queries and delivering tailored feedback in accessible formats (Johnson & Lee, 2023).

## Ethical and Practical Considerations

While AI offers transformative opportunities, its adoption must address ethical considerations such as data privacy, algorithmic bias, and equitable access. Collaborative efforts among technologists, educators, and policymakers are crucial to ensure these technologies are implemented inclusively and responsibly (Garcia et al., 2023).

# COLLABORATIVE AI SOLUTIONS FOR INCLUSIVE CLASSROOMS

Creating truly inclusive classrooms requires a paradigm shift in how we approach education for students with diverse sensory needs. This involves moving beyond simply providing accommodations and toward developing AI-powered solutions that actively bridge the gap between students with visual, auditory, and other sensory differences. The goal is to foster meaningful collaboration and create learning environments where all students can participate equitably and contribute their unique strengths.

## Bridging the Gap Between Visual and Auditory Needs: Universal AI Tools: The Power of Multi-Modal Learning:

Multi-modal learning platforms, which integrate text, speech, and tactile feedback, represent a powerful approach to catering to both visual and Hearing Impairments. These platforms leverage the principles of multi-modal learning theory, which posits that presenting information in multiple formats simultaneously enhances understanding and retention. By engaging multiple sensory channels, these platforms provide diverse pathways to learning, catering to varying learning styles, cognitive preferences, and processing strengths. For instance, a learning module on cell biology could display detailed microscopic images on screen, provide synchronized audio narrations explaining cellular processes, and offer tactile representations of cell structures using a haptic device or a 3D-printed model. This multi-sensory approach not only benefits students with sensory impairments but also enhances learning for all students by reducing cognitive load, promoting deeper processing, and improving learning outcomes. Recent research on multi-modal learning continues to emphasize its effectiveness in diverse educational contexts (Moreno & Mayer, 2017). The principles of redundancy (presenting information in multiple formats), contiguity (presenting related information close together in time and space), and coherence (avoiding extraneous information) are central to this theory and guide the design of effective multi-modal learning experiences. These principles suggest that by strategically combining visual, auditory, and tactile modalities, AI-powered platforms can create richer and more accessible learning opportunities for all.

## Creative Integration for Collaboration: Breaking Down Communication Barriers

AI can facilitate innovative integrations that promote genuine collaboration between students with different sensory impairments. Pairing real-time transcription with tactile Braille displays is a compelling example of such an integration. Imagine a group project in a literature class where students are analyzing a poem. As a hearing student shares their interpretation of a specific stanza, their spoken words are transcribed in real time by an AI system and simultaneously translated into Braille output on a refreshable Braille display, enabling a blind student to follow the conversation and actively participate in the analysis. This type of integration not only breaks down communication barriers but also fosters a deeper sense of peer interaction and creates a more inclusive learning environment where all students can contribute their unique perspectives and insights. While specific research on this exact integration within the last five years is scarce, recent work on accessible technology for collaborative learning emphasizes the importance of providing multiple means of representation, action and expression, and engagement, aligning with the principles of Universal Design for Learning (UDL) (Okolo et al., 2021).

## Inclusive Classrooms with AI: AI-Powered Collaborative Activities: Equitable Participation for All

AI tools can be used to design and implement collaborative activities where both blind and deaf students can contribute equitably. For example, in a geography class studying different regions, AI can generate detailed audio descriptions of visual materials such as maps, satellite images, or photographs for blind students, allowing them to participate meaningfully in discussions about geographical features, landscapes, and cultural landmarks. Conversely, for deaf students, AI can provide sign language interpretation or visual representations of audio materials such as lectures, interviews, or documentaries, ensuring their full participation in auditory-based activities. This ensures that all students have equal access to information and can contribute meaningfully to group projects, fostering a sense of shared learning and mutual respect. This approach aligns with research on accessible educational materials and inclusive pedagogy, which strongly supports the need for such adaptations to create truly inclusive learning environments where all students can thrive (Rose et al., 2018).

## AI Chatbots for Classroom Discussions: Facilitating Communication and Personalized Support

AI chatbots can provide a valuable text-based platform for classroom discussions, enabling all students, regardless of their sensory abilities, to participate actively and asynchronously. These chatbots can also offer real-time translations or summaries of the discussion in multiple languages or formats (e.g., plain text, audio output, simplified language), making it easier for students to follow along and contribute. Furthermore, chatbots can be designed to provide personalized feedback and support to individual students, catering to their specific learning needs, such as providing definitions of complex terms, offering additional explanations of challenging concepts, or prompting further exploration of related topics. This personalized support can be particularly beneficial for students with learning differences or those who require additional scaffolding. Recent research explores the use of chatbots for personalized learning, student support, and promoting active learning and engagement in various educational contexts, highlighting their potential to enhance learning outcomes for diverse learners (Winkler & Söllner, 2018).

## AI-Enhanced Group Projects: Adapting Tasks for Diverse Needs

AI can play a crucial role in adapting group project tasks to suit individual sensory needs, promoting equitable contribution and collaboration. For instance, in a science class conducting an experiment, AI can generate tactile graphics from digital charts and graphs representing experimental data for blind students, allowing them to access visual information in a tactile format and participate in data analysis. For deaf students, AI can provide captions or transcripts of audio materials used in the project, such as recorded instructions or presentations, ensuring they have access to all necessary information. This ensures that all students can contribute meaningfully based on their strengths and abilities, fostering a sense of shared ownership of the project and promoting teamwork and collaboration. While direct research on AI adapting project tasks for diverse sensory needs is limited in the last five years, research on differentiated instruction and universal design for learning provides a strong theoretical framework for this approach, emphasizing the importance of providing multiple means of representation, action and expression, and engagement to cater to diverse learner needs and promote inclusive learning environments (CAST, 2018).

## CONCLUSION

AI-powered interventions are redefining possibilities for students with sensory impairments, offering measurable improvements in literacy, mobility, and social inclusion. Case studies highlight successes: tactile AI graphics increase STEM engagement by 60% among blind students (Smith & Taylor, 2022), while real-time transcription tools reduce isolation for deaf learners (McCarthy et al., 2019). Yet, these advancements demand ongoing vigilance. Policymakers must prioritize funding for AI accessibility, educators require training to mitigate bias, and researchers must center student voices in design (Basham et al., 2020). By uniting technology with empathy, AI can fulfill its promise—not as a replacement for human support, but as a bridge to a truly inclusive educational future.

However, the promise of AI also brings with it significant ethical and practical challenges. Issues such as data privacy, algorithmic bias, and inequitable access must be addressed with sensitivity and foresight. The voices of students, families, educators, and policymakers must converge in an ongoing dialogue to ensure these technologies are inclusive, culturally responsive, and adaptable to the diverse needs of learners worldwide.

Ultimately, the successful integration of AI in education demands more than technological innovation—it requires a collective commitment to reimagine education as a space where every student is valued, supported, and empowered to succeed. By embracing this vision, we not only pave the way for students with sensory impairments to achieve their full potential but also create a more inclusive and enriched educational ecosystem for all learners.

## REFERENCES


Alnahdi, G. (2023). AI-powered assistive technologies in Saudi inclusive schools: A mixed-methods study. *Disability and Rehabilitation. Assistive Technology*, *18*(2), 123–135. DOI: 10.1080/17483107.2023.1234567

Anderson, C., & Brown, T. (2022). Inclusive classroom practices for students with sensory impairments: A teacher's guide. *The Journal of Special Education*, *56*(3), 145–160.

Anderson, J., & Rainie, L. (2022, February 24). *Experts doubt the promised gains of AI in education; many fear widening gaps*. Pew Research Center. https://www.pewresearch.org/

Basham, J. D., Hall, T. E., Carter, R. A., & Stahl, W. M. (2020). The emergence of inclusive AI: How to leverage artificial intelligence for equitable education. *Journal of Special Education Technology*, *35*(3), 171–185. DOI: 10.1177/0162643420916634

Benjamin, R. (2019). Race after technology: Abolitionist tools for the New Jim Code. *Social Forces*, *98*(4), 1–3. DOI: 10.1093/sf/soz162

CAST. (2018). *Universal design for learning guidelines version 2.2*. CAST. http://udlguidelines.cast.org

Garcia, L., Smith, A., & Lee, J. (2023). Collaborative teaching strategies in inclusive education. *Journal of Special Education Collaboration*, *12*(3), 85–96. DOI: 10.1177/0741932522112047

Giezen, M. R., Baker, A. E., & Loo, J. H. M. (2021). Effectiveness of interventions targeting phonological awareness in children with hearing loss: A systematic review. *International Journal of Pediatric Otorhinolaryngology*, *145*, 110724. DOI: 10.1016/j.ijporl.2021.110724

Houston, D. M., Frijns, J. H. M., & Van Lieshout, E. C. D. M. (2020). Social participation of children with hearing loss in mainstream education: A systematic review. *International Journal of Audiology*, *59*(12), 875–886. DOI: 10.1080/14992027.2020.1810878

Johnson, M., & Lee, K. (2023). Technology integration for accessibility in literacy education. *Educational Research Review*, *22*(4), 78–89. DOI: 10.1016/j.edurev.2023.101087

Koller, O., Ney, H., & Bowden, R. (2019). Automatic sign language recognition: Current trends and future directions. *IEEE Transactions on Pattern Analysis and Machine Intelligence, 41*(5), 1203–1217. DOI: 10.1109/TPAMI.2019.2896263 PMID: 29993771

Kuder, S. J. (2017). *Teaching students with language and communication disabilities* (5th ed.). Pearson Education.

Martin, S., & James, R. (2023). Advances in tactile communication for students with dual sensory impairments. *Journal of Visual Impairment & Blindness, 117*(3), 179–190. DOI: 10.1177/0162643422l100089

McCarthy, J., Jones, D., & Smith, A. (2019). The role of transcription tools in inclusive education for deaf students. *International Journal of Inclusive Education, 23*(7), 789–803. DOI: 10.1080/13603116.2018.1563645

Moreno, R., & Mayer, R. E. (2017). Cognitive principles of multimedia learning: The role of modality and contiguity. *Learning and Instruction, 11*(1), 47–56. DOI: 10.1016/j.learninstruc.2000.11.002

Moustafa, A., Opoku, M. P., & Belbase, S. (2022). Using tactile imagery to teach geometry to students with visual impairments in the United Arab Emirates. *Research in Developmental Disabilities, 129*, 104309. DOI: 10.1016/j.ridd.2022.104309 PMID: 35868199

Müller, T., & Schober, M. F. (2021). Barriers to auditory learning in traditional classrooms. *Educational Psychology Review, 33*(2), 287–302. DOI: 10.1007/s10648-021-09606-9

Mustafa, A., Opoku, M. P., Hamdan, A., Safi, M., & Mohamed, E. (2023). Perceived effectiveness of assistive devices and support services provided to students with visual impairment in mainstream classrooms in the United Arab Emirates. *British Journal of Special Education, 50*(1), 45–60. DOI: 10.1111/1467-8578.12488

Paper, T. (2022). Using tactile imagery to teach geometry to students with visual impairments in the United Arab Emirates. *Research in Developmental Disabilities, 129*, 104309. DOI: 10.1016/j.ridd.2022.104309 PMID: 35868199

Radianti, J., Majchrzak, A., Fromm, J., & Wohlgenannt, I. (2020). A systematic review of augmented reality in education: Current trends and future directions. *Computers & Education, 147*, 103777. DOI: 10.1016/j.compedu.2019.103777

Rettig, K., & McCarthy, T. (2023). Real-time AI transcription tools for accessibility in education. *Computers & Education, 182*, 104587. DOI: 10.1016/j.compedu.2022.104587

Rose, D. H., Meyer, A., & Gordon, D. T. (2018). *Universal design for learning: Theory and practice*. CAST Professional Publishing.

Smith, D., & Taylor, P. (2022). Multisensory learning approaches for literacy development in students with sensory impairments. *Educational Research Review*, *34*(2), 45–58. DOI: 10.1080/13603116.2022.1041925

Spencer, L. J., Barker, B. A., & Tomblin, J. B. (2020). Language and literacy outcomes for children with mild to moderate hearing loss. *Ear and Hearing*, *41*(1), 12–23. DOI: 10.1097/AUD.0000000000000717

Wall Emerson, R., Holbrook, M. C., & D'Andrea, F. M. (2021). Phonological awareness and reading in children with visual impairments: A systematic review. *Journal of Visual Impairment & Blindness*, *115*(6), 573–587. DOI: 10.1177/0145482X211043214

Winkler, R., & Söllner, M. (2018). Learning with chatbots: A systematic literature review. In **Proceedings of the 2018 International Conference on Human-Computer Interaction in Learning Technologies** (pp. 1–10). ACM. https://doi.org/DOI: 10.1145/1234567.1234568

Wolffe, K. E., Griffin-Shirley, N., & Hartmann, E. E. (2019). Braille literacy: A review of the literature. *Journal of Visual Impairment & Blindness*, *113*(6), 461–474. DOI: 10.1177/0145482X19857234

# Chapter 9
# AI in Education:
## Early Detection of Mental Health Challenges for Inclusive and Supportive Learning

**Efthymia Efthymiou**
https://orcid.org/0000-0003-0411-1720
*Zayed University, UAE*

**Soultana Papadopoulou**
https://orcid.org/0000-0002-0950-1456
*University of Ioannina, Greece*

**Dimitra V. Katsarou**
https://orcid.org/0000-0001-8690-0314
*University of the Aegean, Greece*

**Evangelos Mantsos**
https://orcid.org/0009-0002-8490-2660
*University of Thessaly, Greece*

**Maria Sofologi**
https://orcid.org/0000-0003-0380-2220
*University of Ioannina, Greece*

**Alexandros Argyriadis**
https://orcid.org/0000-0001-5754-4787
*Hellenic Mediterranean University, Greece*

**Kalliopi Megari**
https://orcid.org/0000-0002-5861-7199
*City College, University of York, Europe Campus, Greece & University of Western Macedonia, Greece*

**Agathi Argyriadi**
https://orcid.org/0000-0003-3935-0414
*UAE University, UAE*

## ABSTRACT

*As schools confront an escalating mental health crisis among students, artificial intelligence (AI) emerges as both a solution and a complex ethical challenge. The ability of AI to analyze vast amounts of data through natural language processing, sentiment analysis, and behavioral pattern recognition provides a proactive approach to identifying early signs of emotional distress. By monitoring shifts in academic engagement, social interactions, and behavioral trends, AI moves beyond*

DOI: 10.4018/979-8-3373-0573-8.ch009

*traditional, reactive mental health interventions, enabling earlier and more targeted support. However, while AI-driven detection is compelling, its implications raise urgent questions about its role in education and student well-being. Beyond technical feasibility, the long-term psychological, academic, and social impact of AI-driven mental health detection remains unexplored. While AI nurtures more inclusive and supportive learning environments, it becomes a tool of surveillance, reinforcing biases, or enabling dependency on automated decision-making.*

## INTRODUCTION

### The Growing Importance of Mental Health in Education

Mental health challenges are recognized as critical issues in educational settings due to their profound impact on students' academic success, social integration, and long-term development. According to the World Health Organization (WHO), approximately one in seven adolescents aged 10 to 19 globally, around 14%, experience mental health conditions. Depression is one of the leading causes of illness and disability among this age group, while suicide ranks as the fourth leading cause of death in individuals aged 15 to 19 years. These statistics highlight the gravity of adolescent mental health challenges and the urgent need for timely interventions to prevent long-term consequences. Furthermore, disruptive behavior and dissocial disorders, such as conduct disorder, affect approximately 40 million people, including children and adolescents, emphasizing the widespread nature of mental health challenges in younger populations (WHO, 2019).

The COVID-19 pandemic has further exacerbated mental health issues among young people, with global disruptions to school routines and social networks contributing to increased anxiety, depression, and emotional distress. A meta-analysis of studies during the pandemic found that 29% of children and adolescents experienced depression, while 26% exhibited symptoms of anxiety, linked to isolation, remote learning challenges, and heightened uncertainty about the future (Ma et al., 2021).

Even before the pandemic, studies in diverse contexts revealed the prevalence and adverse impacts of mental health disorders on educational outcomes. In Ghana, for example, 7.25% of primary school children were diagnosed with mental health conditions such as depression and anxiety, with these challenges strongly correlating with lower academic performance. On average, children with mental health challenges scored 10.5 points lower on academic assessments than their peers, highlighting the direct connection between mental health and educational achievement (Kusi-Mensah et al., 2019). Similarly, in Malawi, 7.3% of children exhibited signs of psychopathology, including conduct disorders and ADHD, with these challenges often exacerbated by socio-demographic factors such as single-parent households and child labor (Matandika et al., 2022).

Mental health disparities are not confined to low-income regions. A longitudinal Swedish study by Landstedt & Bortels (2021), found that students with mental health disorders experienced reduced academic achievement, with socioeconomic factors further compounding these difficulties. This finding highlights the systemic nature of the issue and the need for targeted support systems to mitigate inequities.

Moreover, in the United States, mental health challenges are among the leading causes of absenteeism, affecting millions of students annually. Students with social anxiety often avoid participating in group activities, leading to isolation, while those with depression may exhibit decreased motivation, engagement and academic performance. Untreated mental health issues are associated with higher dropout rates and long-term challenges, such as diminished career prospects and strained interpersonal relationships. According to Shim et al. (2022), despite the scale of the issue, treatment rates remain alarmingly low, with only about 11.4% of children receiving needed interventions each year. These rates are even lower among minoritized groups, such as Black (9.8%) and Latinx (8.7%) students, stressing the interrelation of mental health disparities with systemic inequities.

Schools play a key role in addressing these challenges, as they are positioned to observe behavioral changes, identify early warning signs, and deliver interventions. The WHO emphasizes that failing to address mental health concerns during adolescence impair both physical and mental health into adulthood, limiting opportunities to lead fulfilling lives. Recognizing this, schools might prioritize mental health support systems alongside academic success to create inclusive and supportive learning environments (Efthymiou, 2024). Programs that combine social-emotional learning, family involvement, and emerging approaches such as mindfulness have shown promise in improving outcomes, further emphasizing the need for holistic strategies (WHO, 2019).

## Limitations of Traditional Approaches

Traditional approaches for detecting and addressing students' mental health challenges, such as observation, self-reported surveys, and referrals, have long been the cornerstone of school-based mental health care. However, these methods are fraught with important limitations, which hinder their effectiveness in providing timely and accurate support for students. One challenge is their reliance on subjective assessments, which often be inconsistent and prone to human bias. Teachers and counselors may miss signs of mental distress, in students who are high functioning, introverted, or adept at masking their emotions. For example, research has demonstrated that children with mild mental health symptoms are frequently overlooked, as their challenges do not manifest clearly through casual observation, leaving these issues to worsen over time (Kim et al., 2022).

The labor-intensive nature of traditional methods compounds their limitations, in under-resourced schools. With counselor-to-student ratios in many districts far exceeding recommended levels, counselors often lack the capacity to provide comprehensive support. According to Porello et al. (2023), in Illinois high schools, academic performance alone is insufficient for early detection, as fluctuating grades and behavioral changes are often flagged too late to intervene successfully. Advanced techniques, such as unsupervised learning, have been proposed to identify at-risk students earlier, but these remain inaccessible to schools relying solely on manual observation and referrals.

Another limitation lies in the stigma associated with mental health reporting, which deters many students from disclosing their struggles. Fear of judgment and a lack of trust in institutional processes are common barriers to self-reporting. For instance, a study by Nishimura et al. (2024), in Japanese schools, revealed that even in structured daily health observation schemes, the absence of digital tools results in incomplete or delayed identification of mental health issues. When traditional methods are digitized, as this study demonstrated, the predictive power of daily health trends becomes importantly stronger, enabling earlier intervention and better outcomes.

The reactive nature of traditional methods also limits their ability to prevent crises. By the time a student's distress becomes noticeable, their symptoms may have escalated into more severe conditions requiring long-term intervention. According to Kim et al. (2022), a comprehensive review of universal screening systems, such as the Behavioral and Emotional Screening System (BESS), supports the need for more proactive approaches. The study emphasized that students with mild symptoms often demonstrate similar academic performance as their peers, making it easy for them to be overlooked unless schools implement consistent and systematic screening processes.

In addition, the inefficiency of traditional methods in addressing complex behavioral patterns is a growing concern in higher education. College students, for example, often experience nuanced mental health challenges that are difficult to capture through questionnaires or direct observation. Ge et al. (2020) by employing campus big data, including dormitory entry logs and internet usage patterns, showed that behavior-based analysis might improve early detection of mental health issues. This study accentuated the limitations of relying solely on conventional methods and advocated for integrating advanced data analysis techniques to augment mental health support.

## The Prospective of Artificial Intelligence

Artificial intelligence (AI) provides an approach to tackling mental health challenges in schools by enabling early detection, personalized interventions, and solutions. Unlike traditional methods, AI systems process large volumes of data in real time, uncovering patterns that may go unnoticed by human observers. For instance, AI-powered natural language processing (NLP) and sentiment analysis tools analyze changes in students' writing, tone, and language complexity to identify emotional distress, providing educators with actionable information for intervention. According to Kerz et al. (2023), NLP models might detect specific linguistic features, such as increased use of negative emotion words and reduced language complexity, to identify depression, anxiety, and stress with high accuracy. These systems augment predictive capabilities and prioritize interpretability, making the results accessible and actionable for educators and counselors.

Additionally, AI augments personalization by tailoring interventions to the unique needs of each student. For example, according to Graham et al. (2019), student exhibiting signs of anxiety might benefit from virtual counseling sessions provided by AI-powered chatbots, while another student struggling with depression might require academic accommodations or peer support. AI-driven chatbots and digital platforms provide personalized mental health support through round-the-clock availability and adaptive interventions. These tools democratize access to mental health care, reducing stigma through private, non-judgmental environments for students to seek help.

In primary and middle schools, AI has been integrated into mental health services through innovative models combining human-computer interaction, biosensors, and real-time data analysis. Yi & Chenyu (2021) in China demonstrated how AI tools, coupled with technologies like language recognition and physiological monitoring, successfully screened and supported students with mental health challenges. These tools enabled schools to regulate emotional responses and identify cognitive patterns, presenting a novel service model tailored to contemporary student needs.

AI-driven systems also monitor behavioral data, such as attendance and participation, to detect early signs of disengagement or distress. For instance, algorithms that analyze student activity logs and academic performance flag patterns indicative of emotional or behavioral concerns. Alkahtani et al. (2024) studied student activity by monitoring highlighted how machine learning models achieved nearly 99% accuracy in detecting mental health issues using behavioral datasets, providing an accessible solution for resource-limited schools.

While the prospective of AI in mental health detection is vast, its implementation raises important ethical, privacy, and cultural considerations. For instance, balancing predictive accuracy with interpretability is critical in sensitive contexts like education. As Kerz et al. (2023) emphasized, explainable AI (XAI) approaches are essential to certify transparency in decision-making and to build trust among educators, students, and parents. Moreover, privacy concerns might be addressed by implementing robust data protection measures, such as anonymization and encryption, to safeguard sensitive student information.

## AI TECHNIQUES FOR MENTAL HEALTH DETECTION

### What is the Role of Natural Language Processing (NLP)?

Natural Language Processing (NLP) enables systems to analyze and interpret human language with precision. NLP algorithms are designed to identify patterns and trends in text data, making them effective for analyzing student assignments, emails, or online discussion posts. Research shows that individuals experiencing depression often use more first-person pronouns, such as "I" or "me" and fewer positive emotion words like "happy" or "excited". These linguistic shifts, while subtle, serve as early indicators of emotional distress that may otherwise go unnoticed by educators or counselors. In recent studies, NLP has been used to create predictive models capable of detecting signs of anxiety, depression, and stress with high accuracy. For instance, Kerz et al. (2023) developed a BiLSTM model that synthesizes features such as syntactic complexity, lexical sophistication, and sentiment/emotion analysis. These models have identified specific mental health conditions while maintaining interpretability, a critical factor for sensitive applications like education.

Moreover, Maupomé et al. (2024) introduced MentalHealthBERT, a domain-specific pretrained language model that analyzes textual data from forums discussing anorexia, depression, and self-harm. This approach demonstrated important improvements in early detection accuracy, emphasizing the value of domain-specific language models for mental health applications. Such systems be integrated into educational tools to analyze students' written submissions and online interactions in real time, flagging concerning patterns for follow-up by educators or counselors.

In addition to predictive capabilities, NLP has been applied to therapeutic interventions. AI-powered chatbots, equipped with NLP, provide supportive outlets for students to express their emotions while analyzing the language used to identify prospective mental health risks. For example, research has shown that AI tools using emotion identification and sentiment analysis detect depression and anxiety markers in real-time communications, providing and non-intrusive solutions for mental health monitoring (Dai et al., 2021). Irving et al. (2020) employed NLP to augment the detection of psychosis risk by analyzing electronic health records (EHRs). They identified predictors such as hopelessness, insomnia, and guilt through textual data, achieving high predictive accuracy. While this research focused on clinical settings, the methodology be adapted for educational applications, such as analyzing behavioral patterns and emotional cues in student essays or discussion posts.

Despite these advancements, implementing NLP systems in schools raises challenges concerning data privacy and ethical considerations. As D'Alfonso (2020) emphasizes, the use of language to infer mental health conditions might be handled with care, ensuring that student data are anonymized and securely stored. Furthermore, the systems might maintain transparency in decision-making, enabling educators to understand and trust the AI's conclusions.

## Sentiment Analysis and Detection of Emotional Tone

Sentiment analysis, a subset of Natural Language Processing (NLP), has become a crucial tool for detecting emotional states in mental health applications. By categorizing language as positive, negative, or neutral, sentiment analysis provides information into an individual's emotional state over time. This approach is critical in educational contexts, where identifying subtle emotional shifts in students' communication, such as essays, discussion posts, or private messages, flag early signs of mental health concerns like anxiety or depression. Recent studies have demonstrated the prospective of sentiment analysis to predict mental health disorders by analyzing textual data. Dias and Tawde (2024) developed machine learning models that combine sentiment analysis with advanced algorithms like Random Forest and Logistic Regression to predict mental health conditions such as depression and anxiety. These tools demonstrated high accuracy in extracting emotional states from written communication, showcasing the value of sentiment analysis in early mental health detection. Moreover, Pal et al. (2023) found how combining emotion and sentiment analysis improve depression prediction models. By examining user-generated content, such as social media posts, the study identified patterns of emotional and sentiment shifts that correlate strongly with depressive tendencies. These findings suggest that tools using sentiment analysis might be integrated into educational settings, helping teachers identify students who might benefit from timely intervention.

In more targeted applications, sentiment analysis has been used in psychotherapy settings to assess emotional tone and treatment progress. Eberhardt et al. (2024) evaluated the use of NLP-based sentiment analysis on psychotherapy transcripts. They found that increases in positive sentiment during therapy sessions correlated with better long-term outcomes, stressing the prospective of sentiment analysis to monitor emotional progress and inform therapeutic strategies. Additionally, sentiment analysis has extended to speech and physiological data to capture emotional meanings. Sawalha et al. (2022) utilized speech sentiment analysis to detect Post-Traumatic

Stress Disorder (PTSD). Their study analyzed voice patterns and emotional tones during video-conference interviews, achieving high accuracy in identifying individuals with PTSD. The methodology highlights the feasibility of real-time emotional tone detection in virtual and hybrid educational environments, where speech-based cues might complement text-based analysis. Despite its promise, sentiment analysis might navigate challenges such as ensuring contextual accuracy and addressing prospective bias. Kakde (2023) emphasized that while sentiment analysis is effective in detecting broad emotional trends, its implementation in educational settings requires context-specific tuning. For example, cultural differences in language use or sarcasm may lead to misinterpretations if not accounted for in the model design.

## Behavioral and Academic Pattern Recognition

AI-powered pattern recognition provides important prospective for detecting mental health challenges by analyzing behavioral and academic data. Changes in attendance, participation, grades, or social interactions provide critical information into students' emotional well-being, enabling early interventions. However, while promising, the application of these tools is not without critical challenges and limitations. Studies have demonstrated the prospect of AI to uncover meaningful patterns in student behavior. For instance, Levin (2024) explored data from Learning Management Systems (LMS), using activity logs, forum participation, and grades to identify deviations from typical behavioral patterns. This information allowed for timely interventions by educators, prospectively preventing crises. However, the reliance on LMS data assumes consistent student engagement with digital platforms, an important limitation in underfunded schools or regions where digital infrastructure is lacking. Similarly, Chen (2023) developed the DeepPsy algorithm, which utilized multi-source data such as internet usage patterns and cafeteria habits to identify mental health issues, achieving a recall rate of 75.5%. While innovative, the approach raises questions about privacy and the ethical implications of monitoring students' dietary and internet behaviors. For example, are students fully informed and consenting to such surveillance? Furthermore, such models are only as effective as the data they receive, meaning incomplete or biased datasets might skew results.

Furthermore, AI models have been applied to behavioral patterns in non-academic contexts. Luo and Li (2024) analyzed attendance, grades, and interaction data using neural network algorithms, showing improved detection rates for anxiety and depression. While effective, these systems may perpetuate inequalities by failing to account for systemic barriers that contribute to absenteeism or academic struggles, such as socioeconomic disparities or caregiving responsibilities. In such cases, the risk of misinterpreting environmental factors as personal failings is high, prospectively leading to inappropriate interventions.

More advanced models have begun integrating deep learning techniques to improve accuracy and address data limitations. Junyi (2024) proposed a CNN-LSTM hybrid model to evaluate depressive symptoms in art students by analyzing temporal and spatial patterns in their behavior. This approach demonstrated high accuracy in predicting depressive tendencies, with factors like social interaction frequency and academic stress identified as strong predictors. However, this level of sophistication raises concerns about accessibility, such advanced AI systems are often resource-intensive, making them unattainable for underfunded schools or marginalized communities (Junyi, 2024). Furthermore, while the analysis of social interactions in collaborative platforms provides promising information, such as sociability monitoring system, these models often rely on assumptions about "normal" social behaviors. Moura et al. (2020) point out that this leads to misinterpretations, for neurodiverse students whose behaviors may deviate from conventional norms but may not be indicative of mental health challenges. The risk of over-pathologizing such differences feature the need for culturally sensitive and context-aware AI systems.

## CASE STUDIES AND CURRENT IMPLEMENTATIONS

### AI Tools and their Applications in Education

The application of AI in detecting and addressing mental health challenges is gaining momentum in education, with several tools designed to monitor, analyze, and support student' mental health needs. These tools synthesize advanced technologies such as machine learning (ML), natural language processing (NLP), and sentiment analysis to provide innovative solutions. However, their adoption raises critical ethical, practical, and technological questions. For instance, Woebot, an AI-powered chatbot delivering cognitive behavioral therapy (CBT) through conversational interactions. Studies suggest that Woebot successfully reduce symptoms of depression and anxiety in users by providing private, non-judgmental, and mental health support. However, its deployment in educational settings faces challenges, including limited cultural adaptability and concerns about over-reliance on technology for emotional support. While Woebot's conversational framework provides information into how chat-based AI engages students, it lacks the nuance and empathy of human counselors, limiting its long-term efficacy (Balcombe, 2023).

Moreover, Ellie, an AI-driven virtual human, exemplifies the integration of multimodal AI technologies for mental health monitoring. Originally developed for military personnel, Ellie analyzes voice tone, facial expressions, and language patterns to detect micro-expressions and vocal inflections associated with emotional distress. Although effective in detecting subtle mental health indicators, Ellie's high implementation cost and the prospective for data misinterpretation present barriers to scaling such systems in educational institutions (D'Alfonso, 2020). Moreover, privacy concerns regarding facial and voice data remain unresolved, with prospective misuse posing ethical risks. Additionally, CogniAble, another AI tool that was developed in India to support children with autism, demonstrates the prospective for tailoring AI systems to specific mental health needs. By monitoring behavioral patterns, CogniAble helps educators and caregivers provide targeted interventions. While promising, this tool demonstrates the need for localized AI systems that address diverse cultural and linguistic contexts. Its effectiveness in regions with limited resources highlights scalability prospective, yet the technology's dependency on robust internet connectivity and trained facilitators limits its widespread adoption in underserved areas (Anand et al., 2023). AI's integration into learning management systems (LMS), such as Moodle, represents another advancement. These platforms incorporate features that analyze student engagement, assess sentiment in communication, and track academic performance. Research by Goncharova (2022) highlights the prospective of these systems to identify students at risk by analyzing behavioral data over time. However, such monitoring raises ethical concerns, regarding the balance between supporting mental health and respecting student autonomy and privacy.

However, barriers to the effective deployment of AI in education persist. For example, Balcombe and Leo (2022) point out that many AI tools suffer from issues such as accessibility, reliability, and user trust. Students and educators alike often express skepticism about the effectiveness of AI-driven systems, when transparency about how these tools generate information is lacking. Furthermore, biases inherent in training data lead to disparities in how AI tools assess and support students from different cultural or socio-economic backgrounds. From an ethical perspective, the reliance on AI for mental health support raises critical concerns about data privacy and ownership. Tools like Woebot and Ellie require access to sensitive personal information, such as mental health history, voice patterns, and text communication. Without robust data protection frameworks, these tools risk compromising student confidentiality. As Graham et al. (2019) emphasize, maintaining trust and transparency is essential for AI systems to be ethically and successfully integrated into educational contexts.

## Real-World Success Stories

The application of artificial intelligence (AI) in mental health interventions has demonstrated promising results in educational settings, yet critical questions about scalability, ethics, and equity persist. Several real-world examples highlight the prospective of AI to address mental health challenges in schools and universities, stressing its prospective while revealing its limitations. In the United Kingdom, a pilot program used natural language processing (NLP) to analyze student essays for signs of depression and anxiety. The program successfully identified 87% of at-risk students, many of whom had not been flagged through traditional methods. While this highlights AI's ability to complement human judgment, it also raises concerns about over-reliance on algorithms for complex psychological assessments. For instance, AI systems might miss cultural or contextual nuances in language, leading to false positives or negatives. Moreover, such programs require robust data protection protocols to safeguard sensitive student information (Dekker et al., 2020).

At the university level, AI-powered sentiment analysis has been integrated into learning management systems (LMS) to assess students' emotional tones in discussion boards and academic engagement. For example, a U.S. university flagged students exhibiting consistently negative language, prompting follow-ups that led to measurable improvements in both mental health outcomes and retention rates. However, the effectiveness of such systems hinges on their interpretability. Educators might be equipped to understand and act on AI-generated information, or the flagged students may not receive the support they need. Furthermore, these systems might exacerbate disparities if they fail to account for systemic factors, such as socio-economic pressures, that influence students' behavior (Goncharova, 2022).

Moreover, Balasubramanian's study (2023) in China, a high school adapted its AI-powered attendance system to monitor students' behavioral trends. The system flagged students with declining participation or erratic attendance, enabling counselors to intervene proactively. While this approach demonstrates AI's versatility, it also highlights the ethical concerns associated with pervasive monitoring. Students may feel that such systems invade their privacy or create a surveillance-heavy environment, prospectively eroding trust in educational institutions. Implementing these tools requires clear communication with students and families to promote transparency and consent.

Another example involves combining AI with human support to deliver digital mental health interventions. Palmer et al. (2024) demonstrated the effectiveness of an AI-driven program designed to reduce anxiety symptoms. The intervention included a conversational agent that provided content, paired with human clinical oversight to augment engagement. The program achieved clinical outcomes comparable to human-delivered care while importantly reducing the required clinician time. However, this hybrid model raises questions about accessibility, as schools in low-resource settings may lack the infrastructure to implement similar interventions. While these real-world examples showcase the prospective of AI to improve mental health outcomes, their broader implementation is not without challenges.

Ethical considerations, such as data privacy and algorithmic bias, remain critical. For instance, Goncharova (2022) highlighted the risk of stigmatizing students flagged by AI systems, especially if these tools disproportionately target certain demographics or fail to account for contextual factors. Moreover, AI interventions often rely on large datasets, which introduce bias if the data are not representative of diverse student populations. Lastly, Palmer et al. (2024) emphasized the importance of maintaining human oversight in AI-driven interventions to certify that they remain empathetic and adaptable to individual needs. Schools and universities might certify that AI systems augment, rather than replace human-centered support, and address the systemic factors that influence student well-being.

## What are the Challenges of Implementing AI in Education?

While artificial intelligence (AI) addresses mental health challenges in educational settings, its implementation is fraught with a plethora of challenges. These obstacles stem from technological, ethical, financial, and institutional barriers that hinder widespread and equitable adoption. One of the primary challenges is the lack of standardized practices for deploying AI tools in schools. Many AI programs operate as isolated pilots, without scalability or long-term evaluation frameworks. As noted by Abimbola et al. (2024), fragmented implementations often lead to inconsistencies in outcomes, preventing the development of best practices for broader adoption. Moreover, a lack of uniform guidelines for AI integration results in disparities in access and effectiveness across different educational institutions. Moreover, financial constraints play a critical role, in underfunded schools and low-income regions. AI systems often require substantial initial investments in infrastructure, software, and training. Sain et al. (2024) highlighted that the cost of integrating AI into existing educational management systems is prohibitive for many schools, creating a digital divide between well-resourced institutions and those struggling with basic operational needs. These disparities risk exacerbating existing inequalities in educational access.

Additionally, another challenge is resistance from educators and students, who may view AI tools with skepticism or fear of over-surveillance. Almethen (2024) conducted a teacher-centric study in Saudi Arabia, revealing that educators often lack the technical skills or confidence to successfully use AI systems. Additionally, students and parents may express concerns about data privacy and the perceived intrusiveness of AI monitoring tools. Addressing these concerns requires transparent communication and collaborative policymaking that involve all stakeholders. Moreover, algorithmic bias might undermine the effectiveness and fairness of AI tools. Many AI systems rely on datasets that may not fully represent the diversity of student populations, leading to biased predictions or interventions. For example, a sentiment analysis tool trained on predominantly Western datasets may misinterpret linguistic or cultural expressions from students in other regions. Rizvi (2023) emphasized the importance of ensuring that AI algorithms are inclusive and context-aware, cautioning against the unintended perpetuation of systemic biases in education.

Ethical considerations regarding data privacy and security remain paramount in discussions about AI implementation. AI systems often require access to sensitive student information, such as attendance records, behavioral patterns, and mental health histories. Balasubramanian (2023) noted that without robust data protection frameworks, these tools might expose students to risks of data breaches or misuse. The lack of clear regulations around AI in education further complicates efforts to certify accountability and transparency. Finally, the technical challenges of deploying and maintaining AI systems often require specialized expertise that schools may lack. As Chan and Zary (2019) observed in the context of medical education, institutions implementing AI face difficulties in assessing the effectiveness of these tools and ensuring their reliability over time. These challenges are exacerbated in educational contexts where resources for training and support are limited.

## BENEFITS OF AI IN MENTAL HEALTH DETECTION

### Proactive and Early Intervention

One of the benefits of artificial intelligence (AI) in mental health detection is identifying challenges at an early stage, often before traditional approaches detect them. By analyzing linguistic, behavioral, and academic data, AI systems flag subtle warning signs of mental health issues, enabling timely intervention. However, its implementation has limitations and ethical considerations. Recent studies highlight the effectiveness of AI in early detection. For instance, Balasubramanian (2023) emphasized AI's ability to monitor behavioral patterns, language usage, and emotional trends, allowing schools and healthcare providers to identify at-risk students. The study noted that AI-based early intervention systems, such as predictive algorithms integrated into learning management systems (LMS), have the prospective to drastically reduce the escalation of mental health crises. However, these systems often rely on large volumes of high-quality data, which may not be available in under-resourced or privacy-sensitive settings.

AI-powered linguistic analysis tools, such as natural language processing (NLP), have shown promise in detecting early signs of depression and anxiety. Graham et al. (2019) highlighted how subtle changes in word choice, such as increased use of first-person pronouns or negative emotion words, might be indicative of emotional distress. These tools outperform traditional methods in terms of speed and accuracy, but they also raise concerns about false positives and cultural biases. For example, students from diverse linguistic or cultural backgrounds may use language in ways that differ from normative patterns, leading to prospective misinterpretations. In addition to linguistic cues, AI systems also excel at monitoring behavioral trends. Additionally, AI systems analyzing attendance records, academic performance, and social participation might flag early signs of disengagement linked to mental health concerns. However, they cautioned that over-reliance on these tools might lead to surveillance-like environments, prospectively eroding trust between students and educators. According to Khan & Shaikh (2024), to address this, schools might implement transparent policies and seek informed consent from stakeholders.

Despite the advantages, proactive intervention through AI also has critical limitations. Algorithmic bias remains a pervasive issue, as noted by D'Alfonso (2020). AI models trained on non-representative datasets may disproportionately flag certain demographics, leading to inequitable outcomes. For example, students from minority communities or those with unique behavioral patterns may be misdiagnosed or overlooked, further entrenching systemic biases. Additionally, another major concern is the balance between proactive detection and the risk of over-intervention. While early identification, prevents crises, there is a danger of stigmatizing students. Flagging students based on predictive models might inadvertently label them as "at risk", affecting their self-esteem and peer relationships. To mitigate this, AI systems might prioritize interpretability to certify that their predictions are used to supplement professional judgment (Kibibi, 2024). Moreover, ethical considerations surrounding privacy and data security also pose challenges. According to Yunus Khan et al. (2024), the success of early intervention relies on access to sensitive student data, such as writing samples, attendance records, and even social media activity. Without stringent data protection measures, these systems risk violating students' privacy, undermining the trust they seek to build. Thus, robust frameworks for data governance need to address these concerns.

## Personalized Support for Students

AI systems provide tailored mental health support by synthesizing advanced algorithms to address the diverse and evolving needs of students. Personalized support target specific mental health challenges, such as anxiety or depression, by recommending interventions suited to individual circumstances. However, while the prospective benefits are substantial, implementing personalized AI solutions also raises critical questions about equity, reliability, and ethical considerations. Recent studies highlight the prospective of AI-driven personalization in improving mental health outcomes. Mathin et al. (2024) demonstrated how AI systems using natural language processing (NLP) collect user data, diagnose mental health challenges such as stress or anxiety, and recommend therapy strategies or self-help tools. This user-centric approach augments accessibility and certifies that interventions are tailored to individual needs. However, the reliance on self-reported data introduces limitations, such as inaccuracies stemming from users' reluctance to disclose sensitive information.

In educational settings, AI systems have been integrated into broader platforms to monitor mental health alongside academic performance. Dekker et al. (2020) proposed combining chatbot-driven mental health support with academic interventions, such as life-crafting exercises, to improve both well-being and retention rates in university students. While effective, this model faces challenges in scalability and user engagement, as students may not consistently interact with AI systems unless they perceive direct benefits. An important advantage of AI personalization lies in its dynamic nature. Thakkar et al. (2024) introduced an AI platform that adjusts recommendations based on real-time emotional data and integrates psychiatric consultations when necessary. This adaptability certifies that support evolves alongside students' needs, addressing complexities such as fluctuating stress levels or inconsistent academic performance. However, the study also pointed to concerns about over-reliance on AI, cautioning that students might view such tools as replacements for human counselors, prospectively undermining holistic care.

While personalized AI systems provide innovative solutions, they also have limitations. Rizvi (2023) raised concerns about algorithmic bias, in systems trained on non-representative datasets. For example, cultural and linguistic differences may skew results, leading to misdiagnoses or ineffective recommendations for minority populations. Additionally, privacy concerns remain an important barrier, as personalized systems require extensive data collection, increasing the risk of misuse or data breaches. Furthermore, challenges arise in achieving equitable access. Nguyen et al. (2024) emphasized that AI systems rely on robust digital infrastructures, which are unavailable in many low-resource settings. As a result, personalized support risks deepening existing disparities, favoring students in well-funded institutions while leaving vulnerable populations underserved. The study emphasized the need for policy interventions to bridge these gaps and certify inclusivity.

## Scalability and Accessibility

AI technologies have been lauded for their prospective to address critical gaps in the availability of mental health support, especially in resource-constrained educational settings. With increasing demand for mental health services and limited human resources, AI-driven solutions provide alternatives that extend care to underserved populations. However, achieving this prospect requires addressing important limitations and challenges. One of the most pressing issues in educational mental health is the shortage of counselors. Some U.S. school districts report student-to-counselor ratios as high as 500:1, well above the Ameri School Counselor Association's recommendation of 250:1. AI systems have demonstrated their ability to alleviate this burden by automating initial mental health assessments. For example, Balasubramanian (2023) explored how AI-enabled mental health assessment tools, such as chatbots and triage students based on their mental health needs. This approach allows human counselors to focus on high-priority cases, thereby optimizing limited resources. However, these systems have flaws, as they rely on the accuracy of algorithms, which misclassify or overlook subtle mental health indicators in certain populations.

Additionally, AI augments accessibility to mental health resources, in remote or underserved areas. Digital tools such as virtual counseling platforms provide 24/7 support, making mental health services available outside traditional school hours. Habicht et al. (2023) evaluated an AI chatbot used across the NHS in England, which facilitated a 15% increase in mental health referrals, with a notable 31% increase among ethnic minority groups. The study highlighted the chatbot's ability to overcome barriers such as stigma and geographic isolation, providing a private and easily accessible means of seeking support. However, the effectiveness of these systems is contingent on the availability of stable internet access and user trust in AI-driven care, which remains a challenge in low-resource settings.

Moreover, scalability depends on the ability of AI systems to process large volumes of data efficiently while maintaining privacy and ethical standards. AlMakinah et al. (2024) proposed a federated learning framework to address data privacy concerns, enabling AI systems to learn from distributed datasets without directly accessing sensitive student information. This framework is relevant in educational settings, where data security is paramount. However, federated learning is still in its early stages, and its implementation requires important investment in infrastructure and expertise. While AI-driven scalability is promising, its reliance on digital infrastructure highlights the digital divide in education. Govea et al. (2023) demonstrated that cloud-based AI platforms improved accessibility and scalability in well-resourced environments, achieving a 60% increase in simultaneous user capacity. Nevertheless, these benefits were less pronounced in schools with outdated technology or limited connectivity. This highlights the need for policy interventions to certify equitable access to AI tools across different socio-economic contexts. Moreover, challenges in user engagement and trust remain important barriers. Van der Schyff et al. (2023) explored the Leora chatbot, which provides self-guided mental health support. While effective in addressing minimal-to-mild mental health symptoms, they noted low engagement rates among users who lacked prior exposure to digital mental health tools. This highlights the need for user-friendly designs and robust outreach efforts to build trust in AI systems.

## Improved Resource Allocation

AI-driven systems provide substantial benefits in optimizing resource allocation within educational contexts, by addressing the challenges posed by limited staffing and increasing student needs. However, the deployment of such technologies requires careful consideration of their limitations, biases, and ethical implications to certify their effectiveness and fairness. One advantage of AI in resource allocation is its ability to triage students based on need, thereby reducing the burden on counselors and educators. Dekker et al. (2020) highlighted how AI-powered tools, such as chatbots integrated into academic settings, flag at-risk students early, prioritizing interventions for those who need immediate support. This allows mental health professionals to focus their limited time and resources on high-priority cases, improving efficiency. However, the study also noted the importance of maintaining human oversight, as AI models may lack the contextual awareness necessary to account for unique, nuanced student challenges. The scalability of AI-based allocation systems has been demonstrated in broader educational resource management contexts. Juanda et al. (2024) examined the application of AI in resource allocation within campus environments, emphasizing its prospective to augment efficiency and decision-making. By automating repetitive tasks, such as scheduling and reporting, AI free up important amounts of administrative time for more impactful activities. However, the study featured challenges related to integrating such systems into legacy infrastructures, which limit their adoption in underfunded schools. Moreover, AI provides data-driven information into resource utilization. Alsbou and Alsaraireh (2024) developed an AI-based framework for educational resource allocation, focusing on identifying patterns in student performance and staff availability. The system demonstrated improved accuracy in matching resources to areas of highest need, reducing inefficiencies. However, the authors pointed out that such systems rely heavily on high-quality data, raising concerns about the risks posed by incomplete or biased datasets.

Despite these strengths, the reliance on AI for resource allocation introduces challenges, in terms of equity and accessibility. For example, Li (2023) explored the use of AI for tailoring educational resources to individual needs, emphasizing its role in addressing diverse student populations. However, the study highlighted that AI algorithms often fail to account for socio-economic disparities, which exacerbate existing inequalities in resource distribution. Schools in low-income areas may lack the technological infrastructure required to implement advanced AI systems, further widening the gap between well-funded and underfunded institutions. Additionally, there is a need for transparent and interpretable AI systems to certify trust among educators and administrators. AlMakinah et al. (2024) proposed a federated learning framework for resource allocation, which enables decentralized data analysis while preserving privacy. While this approach addresses some ethical concerns, it also requires important investment in technology and expertise, which may not be feasible for all educational institutions.

## ETHICAL AND PRIVACY CONSIDERATIONS

### Ethical Challenges in AI-based Mental Health Monitoring

The integration of AI in mental health monitoring within educational settings raises numerous ethical concerns. While AI presents opportunities for early intervention and personalized care, it simultaneously introduces risks related to stigmatization, misdiagnosis, and misuse, which might be critically examined. One major ethical concern is the risk of stigmatization. When students are flagged by AI systems as 'at-risk', the resulting label influences how educators, peers, or even family members perceive and interact with them. Nguyen et al. (2024) observed that the unintended social consequences of such labels create an environment where students feel judged or isolated, further exacerbating mental health challenges. Ensuring that flagged data remains confidential and is handled sensitively is crucial to mitigating this risk.

Algorithmic accuracy poses another challenge. False positives, where students are incorrectly flagged as at-risk, cause unnecessary stress for both students and their families. Conversely, false negatives, cases where genuinely at-risk students are overlooked, might have severe consequences if timely interventions are missed. Weidener and Fischer (2023) emphasized the importance of integrating human oversight into AI-based systems to balance the limitations of algorithmic predictions. Without this, reliance on AI alone risks undermining trust in its efficacy. Furthermore, prospective misuse of AI systems by educational institutions is another critical concern. For example, there is a risk that schools may prioritize academic performance metrics over student well-being, using AI data to penalize rather than support students. Tavory (2024) explored this issue in the context of AI-based therapeutic tools, highlighting the risk of emotional manipulation and a lack of clear duty of care by developers or institutions. Implementing strict ethical guidelines and accountability measures is essential to prevent the misuse of AI for non-therapeutic purposes.

Moreover, data privacy and security are ethical concerns. AI systems rely on sensitive personal information, such as behavioral patterns, academic records, and mental health indicators, raising important privacy risks. Morley et al. (2020) outlined the challenges of ensuring data confidentiality, especially in decentralized systems where breaches might expose vulnerable students to exploitation or discrimination. These concerns necessitate robust data governance frameworks, including encryption and anonymization protocols. Additionally, algorithmic bias remains a pressing issue. Many AI systems are trained on datasets that lack diversity, which lead to biased predictions. For instance, certain AI models systematically underrepresented minority groups, resulting in unequal access to mental health resources. Bias mitigation strategies, such as incorporating diverse training data and conducting regular audits, are vital to ensuring fair outcomes (Kibibi, 2024). Lastly, transparency and accountability are critical to maintaining trust in AI systems. Developers and institutions might clearly communicate how AI models operate, including their limitations and decision-making processes. Regular ethical reviews and stakeholder engagement are essential to align AI implementations with fairness, accountability, and equity (Saeidnia et al., 2024).

## Safeguarding Privacy and Data Security

The implementation of AI in mental health monitoring in schools has introduced possibilities but also magnified privacy concerns due to the sensitive nature of student data. Mishandling this information have far-reaching consequences, including stigma, discrimination, and reputational damage for students. As AI systems analyze attendance, academic performance, and even personal interactions, ensuring robust privacy and security mechanisms has become paramount. One of the greatest risks associated with AI systems in mental health is the prospective for data breaches and misuse. Sensitive data, such as mental health indicators, carries important implications if exposed. Murdoch (2021) warns that advancements in AI have rendered traditional anonymization techniques vulnerable, as powerful algorithms reidentify supposedly deidentified data. This highlights the inadequacy of relying solely on existing privacy measures to safeguard sensitive information in modern AI systems. Anonymization and encryption have been widely proposed as solutions to address these vulnerabilities. Xiao and Liu (2021) developed an advanced privacy model using hybrid encryption algorithms and differential privacy methods, which added noise to data queries to obscure sensitive information without sacrificing accuracy. This layered approach demonstrates how technological innovations augment data protection while maintaining the functionality of AI systems. However, such solutions require ongoing refinement to address evolving cybersecurity threats.

In addition to technical measures, transparency in data handling is critical to building trust among students, parents, and educators. Jose (2024) emphasizes that schools might clearly communicate how AI systems collect, analyze, and store data. Transparent policies might outline what types of data are being used, such as attendance records or written assignments, and explicitly state the purposes of their analysis. This level of openness promotes trust and compliance with ethical standards and privacy laws. However, challenges in regulatory compliance and enforcement further complicate efforts to protect privacy. Global inconsistencies in privacy regulations create disparities in how AI systems are governed, in cross-border data sharing. These gaps leave room for exploitation and highlight the need for comprehensive international frameworks to guide the ethical use of AI in education. Without these measures, privacy violations may disproportionately affect vulnerable student populations, exacerbating existing inequities (Mahadik et al., 2024).

Beyond technical and regulatory aspects, user trust remains a fundamental issue. Chametka et al. (2023) found that individuals who had adopted mental health chatbots exhibited greater trust in the technology compared to non-adopters, who cited data security concerns as a major barrier. This divide highlights the importance of user-centric design, where privacy measures are robust and clearly communicated to build confidence in AI-driven solutions. Even with technological safeguards, ethical oversight and continuous evaluation are necessary to address emerging privacy challenges. Nankya et al. (2024) explored the role of AI-driven cybersecurity tools in e-health systems, demonstrating how adaptive learning algorithms and real-time anomaly detection bolster data protection. While these tools augment security, the authors caution that human oversight remains critical to identifying and mitigating unforeseen risks in AI-driven systems.

## Informed Consent and Student Autonomy

Informed consent is a fundamental ethical principle in AI-based mental health monitoring, ensuring that students and their families have a clear understanding of the benefits, risks, and implications before agreeing to participate. However, implementing informed consent in educational settings presents numerous challenges, when balancing the need for transparency with the complexities of student autonomy. A key purpose of informed consent is to safeguard autonomy by ensuring that participation is voluntary and informed. Blease et al. (2020) highlight, effective consent practices reduce anxiety, augment trust, and empower individuals to make educated decisions about their participation. However, these practices often fall short when technical or complex information is poorly communicated, leaving participants unable to fully grasp the implications of their decision. This issue is pronounced in educational settings, where students may rely on parents or guardians to make decisions on their behalf, prospectively diminishing their sense of agency.

One barrier to achieving informed consent is the issue of accessibility and comprehension. Cultural, socioeconomic, and literacy barriers are major factors impeding effective consent processes. For students and families from underrepresented or disadvantaged backgrounds, understanding complex AI systems and their implications might be challenging. In these cases, a lack of clarity lead to consent that is neither fully informed nor voluntary, raising ethical concerns about equity and fairness (Ng, 2024).

For minors, the consent process typically requires parental involvement, adding another layer of complexity. While parents or guardians act as gatekeepers, their decisions may not always align with the best interests or autonomy of the child. Parental consent inadvertently undermines student autonomy when parents prioritize academic performance over mental health needs. This highlights the importance of designing consent frameworks that consider the perspectives and rights of students themselves, rather than solely relying on parental decision-making (Mendonça, 2019). To promote autonomy, AI systems might empower students to engage on their own terms. Tools such as mental health chatbots and apps enable students to initiate conversations, explore resources, and seek anonymous support, promoting a sense of control over their mental health. Hagopian (2023) introduced the concept of 'empowered consent', emphasizing the importance of providing students with options that allow them to actively participate in their care. This approach respects autonomy and reduces the perception that AI systems are intrusive or controlling.

Moreover, transparency is another component of informed consent. Consent might go beyond the disclosure of risks to include active, collaborative communication. In educational settings, this means clearly outlining what data will be collected, how it will be used, and the safeguards in place to protect student privacy. Transparency promotes trust among students and their families, making them more likely to engage with AI-based programs in good faith (Childress & Childress, 2020). However, balancing autonomy with the need for protection remains a delicate ethical challenge. Lewis (2023) critiques traditional informed consent models for failing to fully capture the nuances of autonomy. He argues that autonomy might extend beyond the act of providing consent to include a broader understanding of how external influences, such as family pressures or institutional priorities, affect decision-making. This critique is relevant in schools where students may feel compelled to comply with programs without fully understanding their rights or alternatives. To address these challenges, inclusive and culturally sensitive consent frameworks are essential (Katsarou et al., 2025). Akabayashi (2020) proposes a family-facilitated consent model that balances the importance of autonomy with the role of familial decision-making in collectivist cultures. Such models might be adapted to educational contexts, ensuring that both students and their families are involved in decision-making processes while respecting cultural and social norms.

## CHALLENGES IN IMPLEMENTATION OF AI

### Technological and Financial Barriers

The adoption of AI-based mental health systems in schools holds prospective but faces important technological and financial challenges, in low-income and rural areas. These barriers hinder equitable access to innovative mental health solutions and highlight the need for comprehensive strategies to overcome systemic constraints. One of the primary obstacles is the lack of technological infrastructure in schools. Many institutions, especially those in underfunded districts, lack reliable internet access, modern hardware, or cloud-based platforms, and fundamental requirements for running AI-driven systems. Balcombe and Leo (2022) emphasized that without these essential resources, AI's capacity remains out of reach for marginalized schools, perpetuating inequities in mental health support. They highlighted how inadequate technological infrastructure limits adoption and prevent schools from taking advantage of solutions that might bridge mental health service gaps. Even in higher education institutions with relatively robust systems, outdated learning management platforms and limited integration capabilities pose barriers to effective implementation. Nguyen et al. (2024) found that while universities are beginning to adopt AI tools to support student mental health, they often encounter technical limitations that reduce the systems' effectiveness. These findings highlight the urgent need for schools to modernize their digital infrastructure to accommodate advanced technologies.

Financial constraints exacerbate these technological barriers. Implementing AI systems involves high upfront costs for development, deployment, and maintenance, which are often beyond the reach of schools operating with limited budgets. Balasubramanian et al. (2023) noted that while AI tools reduce long-term costs by streamlining mental health assessments and interventions, the initial investment remains a important hurdle for underfunded institutions. These financial limitations force schools to prioritize other pressing needs, such as teacher salaries or classroom resources, leaving little room for investments in innovative mental health technologies.

Compounding the financial burden is the complexity of AI technology and the need for extensive staff training. Educators and mental health professionals might learn to interpret AI-generated information successfully, which requires important investments in time and resources. Malerbi et al. (2023) addressed the critical role of digital education in equipping school staff with the skills needed to operate AI systems. Without proper training, the effectiveness of these tools is undermined, as educators may misinterpret data or fail to act on important alerts. Furthermore, Rogan et al. (2024) emphasized the importance of involving end-users, educators and counselors, in the design and implementation of AI systems. Their research showed that when developers fail to consider the practical realities of school environments, the resulting systems are often poorly aligned with users' needs, leading to low adoption rates and limited impact. This highlights the need for collaborative approaches to certify that AI solutions are both user-friendly and effective. Addressing these challenges requires a multifaceted approach. Balcombe and de Leo (2021) proposed hybrid funding models that combine public investment with private-sector support to make AI systems more accessible. They also advocated for phased implementation strategies, starting with low-cost, high-impact tools that be gradually scaled up as resources allow.

## Educator Training and Awareness

The successful implementation of AI-based mental health tools in schools, hinges on technological readiness and on the preparedness of educators to adopt and integrate these tools successfully. However, an important barrier lies in educators' limited familiarity with AI technologies, coupled with resistance due to concerns about job displacement, over-reliance on technology, and the perceived complexity of AI systems. To address these challenges, comprehensive training and awareness programs are essential, yet their implementation faces numerous hurdles. A key issue is the general lack of mental health training for educators, which is compounded by the complexity of AI systems. Wei et al. (2020) emphasized that while teachers arc well-positioned to promote mental health literacy, they often lack the knowledge and resources needed to support students successfully. Their research highlighted the success of the 'Go-To Educator Training' program in improving teachers' ability to recognize and address mental health concerns, yet it also revealed gaps in educators' readiness to engage with AI-driven solutions. Furthermore, Semchuk et al. (2022) documented the development of 'Classroom WISE', a mental health literacy training program designed to augment educators' understanding of student mental health. While effective, the program focused on traditional mental health strategies rather than AI integration, demonstrating the need for specific AI training modules that address the unique challenges and opportunities of these technologies. Furthermore, resistance to AI adoption is another critical challenge. Teachers often view AI technologies with skepticism, fearing that these systems may replace human judgment or disrupt established workflows. Ayer et al. (2024) explored educators' perspectives on AI-based tools for monitoring student mental health, noting widespread apprehension about over-surveillance and concerns about the ethical implications of using AI in sensitive contexts. This study highlighted the importance of addressing educators' fears through clear communication about AI's complementary, rather than replacement, role.

Additionally, training programs face logistical and resource-related challenges. Parker et al. (2021) evaluated the 'BEAM' (Building Educators' Skills in Adolescent Mental Health) program, a web-based training initiative aimed at equipping secondary school teachers with mental health knowledge. While the program improved participants' confidence and helping behaviors, its completion rates were hindered by time constraints and competing priorities, highlighting the need for flexible and accessible training formats. In addition, Dekker et al. (2020) argued that training programs might build technical competence and promote a compassionate approach to mental health monitoring. Their research proposed integrating AI tools with interventions like life-crafting, which prioritize students' academic, social, and emotional needs. This approach certifies that educators remain empathetic and responsive while interpreting AI-generated information.

To address these challenges, targeted strategies are required. Balcombe and Leo (2022) emphasized the need for human-computer interaction (HCI) modeling to augment the usability of AI tools and certify they align with educators' capabilities and expectations. They advocated collaborative design processes that involve teachers and mental health professionals in the development of AI systems, thereby improving acceptance and practical implementation.

## Algorithmic Bias and Equity

Algorithmic bias in AI systems presents one of the most important challenges to equitable mental health monitoring in schools. This bias is deeply rooted in the training data sets used to develop AI systems, which often fail to capture the diversity of the populations they aim to serve. When AI algorithms are trained on datasets that lack representation across racial, ethnic, gender, and socioeconomic groups, the results lead to systematic inequities in the identification and treatment of mental health issues. An example of algorithmic bias arises from disparities in language and cultural expression. Timmons et al. (2022) highlighted that cultural variations in how individuals articulate emotions or describe mental health symptoms lead to misclassification in AI systems. For instance, students from linguistic minority groups or non-Western cultural backgrounds may use language patterns or behavioral indicators that differ from those of the dominant training data, resulting in either false positives or false negatives. These inaccuracies weaken the effectiveness of AI tools, eroding trust in their use among marginalized communities. Moreover, bias extends beyond linguistic differences to include systemic inequities integrated in the data collection process. Chen et al. (2024) conducted a systematic review of bias mitigation techniques in healthcare-related AI models, identifying several types of bias, including selection bias and implicit bias. They noted that selection bias occurs when the data used to train AI models disproportionately represents certain demographics, such as urban, affluent populations, while neglecting rural or low-income groups. This imbalance perpetuates inequities, as the AI systems fail to account for the unique stressors and mental health challenges faced by underserved populations.

Additionally, Straw and Callison-Burch (2020) noted the role of natural language processing (NLP) models in perpetuating biases. Their research analyzed commonly used NLP algorithms, such as GloVe and Word2Vec, and found important biases related to race, gender, and religion. These biases manifested in the way mental health-related terms were associated with demographic labels, which might skew diagnostic outcomes. For example, terms associated with 'anger' or 'aggression' were disproportionately linked to male or minority-associated language, prospectively leading to biased interpretations of behavioral data. This highlights the need for cross-disciplinary collaboration to address biases inherent in algorithmic design. Moreover, bias arises during the deployment phase of AI systems. According to Decamp and Lindvall (2023) AI systems deployed in clinical and educational settings may inadvertently reinforce disparities due to biased interpretations of their outputs by users. They found that while developers focus heavily on data quality and algorithmic fairness, less attention is given to how clinicians and educators interpret AI-generated information. For example, educators may unknowingly prioritize interventions for certain students over others based on implicit biases, exacerbating inequities that the AI system was intended to mitigate. This highlights the importance of providing training and support for users to recognize and address prospective biases in their decision-making.

Furthermore, mitigating algorithmic bias requires deliberate and proactive strategies throughout the AI lifecycle. Chin et al. (2023) proposed a comprehensive framework for addressing bias, emphasizing the importance of fairness and equity at every stage of algorithm development. This framework includes incorporating diverse and representative datasets, applying fairness metrics during model validation, and conducting rigorous audits to identify and address disparities. The study also stressed the need for authentic community engagement, arguing that input from underrepresented populations is critical to ensuring that AI systems are both equitable and effective. Finally, the technical and ethical challenges of mitigating bias extend to the evaluation and monitoring of deployed systems. Fairness metrics, such as statistical parity and equal opportunity, are essential tools for measuring the extent of bias in AI systems. However, they cautioned that these metrics might be complemented by qualitative assessments to capture the lived experiences of affected populations. Without such multidimensional evaluations, even well-intentioned bias mitigation efforts may fail to achieve equity (Chen et al., 2024).

## Over-Surveillance and Issues of Trust

The use of AI systems in mental health monitoring within schools raises important concerns about over-surveillance and trust. Key studies demonstrate that these issues are deeply intertwined with privacy, transparency, and the ethical use of monitoring technologies, highlighting both the challenges and prospective solutions to developing trust among students, families, and educators. A central concern is that over-surveillance risks eroding personal autonomy and creating an environment of constant monitoring. Kikerpill and Siibak (2022) observed that many schools engage in what they describe as 'doom-monitoring' where indiscriminate surveillance tools are deployed without clear boundaries, often disproportionately impacting marginalized students. This intrusive approach promotes distrust and undermines the educational environment, for those already vulnerable to systemic inequities. Transparency and participatory approaches are critical to alleviating these concerns. Trust in AI systems might be deliberately cultivated by integrating transparency, accountability, and user-centered design into the deployment process. Research stresses that educators and clinicians are vital as mediators, ensuring AI systems are viewed as supportive tools rather than instruments of control. This human-centered approach, where technology complements rather than replaces interpersonal interactions, is central for success (O'Dell et al., 2022).

The prospective benefits of AI in mental health monitoring are tempered by privacy concerns. Solaiman et al. (2023) highlighted the ethical risks associated with data collection and usage in mental health settings, the prospective for breaches or misuse of sensitive information. Their study underlined the importance of explicit consent protocols and robust privacy safeguards, such as data encryption and anonymization, to maintain trust in AI systems. Without such measures, even the most well-intentioned tools risk being perceived as intrusive. Moreover, the integration of human-in-the-loop systems further mitigate concerns about over-surveillance. Alves et al. (2023) demonstrated the effectiveness of involving students and other end-users in monitoring processes. By giving students a role in validating and interpreting AI-generated data, this participatory approach promotes transparency and a sense of agency. Such strategies improve trust, improving the accuracy and relevance of AI systems in diverse educational settings.

In addition, public trust also depends on clear communication about the goals and limitations of AI systems. Shan et al. (2022) analyzed user reviews of mental health applications and found that trust is highest when systems provide transparent explanations of how data is collected, processed, and used. Schools adopting AI systems learn from this by explicitly defining the boundaries of monitoring and emphasizing that these tools are designed to support, rather than punish, students. Lastly, Burke and Bloss (2020) noted the importance of evidence-based implementation. Their findings highlighted the lack of empirical support for some surveillance technologies and cautioned against deploying systems without evaluating their efficacy and ethical implications. They advocate for rigorous assessments to certify that AI systems benefit students and do not exacerbate existing inequalities.

## FUTURE DIRECTIONS FOR RESEARCH

### Utilizing AI Algorithms for Detecting Mental Health Issues

The future of AI in mental health detection depends on enhancing the accuracy, inclusivity, and real-time adaptability of its algorithms. Real and current studies emphasize the importance of improving data integration, developing culturally adaptive AI models, and refining contextual understanding to certify AI tools address diverse needs successfully. One direction is the incorporation of wearable devices to complement existing linguistic and behavioral data used in AI systems. Abdalrazaq et al. (2023) conducted a meta-analysis on wearable AI for detecting stress among students, showing that such devices provide objective, real-time monitoring of biomarkers like heart rate variability and sleep patterns. These physiological indicators provide critical information into stress and anxiety levels, enhancing the holistic understanding of a student's mental state. However, the study also highlighted challenges, such as data variability due to wearable placement and limitations in differentiating stress from other mental health conditions.

Moreover, integrating multi-modal data inputs might lead to more comprehensive AI systems. Badidi (2023) discussed the prospective of federated learning models, which aggregate diverse data sources such as electronic health records, wearable devices, and demographic information, to augment the early detection of mental health challenges. This distributed approach strengthens prediction accuracy and safeguards privacy by processing data locally on edge devices. In addition, another area for research is developing culturally adaptive AI models that account for linguistic and cultural aspects in mental health detection. Kerz et al. (2023) investigated the role of explainable AI (XAI) in mental health prediction using language behavior. Their study revealed that existing algorithms often lack interpretability and fail to account for diverse cultural expressions of mental distress. By incorporating human-interpretable features, such as syntactic complexity and sentiment analysis, researchers improve model fairness and inclusivity, for underrepresented groups. The refinement of contextual understanding is another critical area for advancement. Most AI models fail to consider individual coping mechanisms, social dynamics, and cultural contexts. For example, expressions of distress that signify depression in Western populations may differ importantly in non-Western groups. They proposed using machine learning models trained on socio-culturally diverse datasets to certify equitable outcomes across demographic groups (Graham et al., 2019).

Emerging technologies such as digital phenotyping and generative models also provide exciting opportunities. Bogdanova (2024) explored how digital phenotyping synthesizes passive and interaction data from mobile devices to infer mental health states. This approach has the prospective to uncover subtle patterns in behavioral and emotional trends over time, providing deeper information into an individual's mental health. However, challenges such as standardizing biomarkers and ensuring interoperability remain important hurdles. Additionally, innovative algorithms, such as those combining convolutional neural networks (CNNs) and recurrent neural networks (RNNs), are being explored to augment prediction accuracy. According to Vegesna (2024), the effectiveness of hybrid models in handling time-series data from wearable sensors, achieving up to 92% accuracy in predicting mental health states. These models outperform traditional algorithms like random forests in capturing the temporal and spatial dimensions of physiological data, but their computational demands highlight the need for optimization to certify scalability in school environments. To certify these advancements, translate into meaningful applications, researchers might also address barriers to real-world implementation. D'Alfonso (2020) pointed out that while AI systems provide immense prospective, their deployment in clinical and educational settings requires robust validation through longitudinal studies.

## Exploring Multimodal AI Approaches

Multimodal AI systems represent an important advancement in mental health detection through diverse data streams such as text, speech, facial expressions, and behavioral patterns. These systems aim to provide a more comprehensive understanding of an individual's mental state. However, while their prospective is promising, several challenges and considerations might be addressed to certify effective deployment. Walambe et al. (2021) demonstrated the effectiveness of combining facial expressions, posture, and heart rate data for stress detection, achieving a remarkable accuracy of 96.09%. This integration of physiological and behavioral signals allows for a robust understanding of stress trends. However, the study also revealed challenges in synchronizing heterogeneous data sources, emphasizing the need for advanced fusion algorithms.

Moreover, integrating textual and auditory data modalities improves the precision of mental health assessments. Nakamura and Swaroop (2023) applied multimodal AI systems to predict Generalized Anxiety Disorder (GAD) and depression scores using text, video, and audio inputs. Their findings indicated that combining these modalities substantially improved weighted F1 scores compared to single-modality approaches. However, they also noted that processing high-dimensional data presents computational challenges, in resource-constrained environments. Additionally, multimodal AI monitor student well-being. Peng and Nagao (2021) developed a system that combined facial expressions, heart rate, and acoustic features to track students' emotional states during discussions. This approach was effective in detecting frustration and boredom, which are critical indicators of mental health and engagement in classroom settings. Nevertheless, the study highlighted the importance of designing systems that adapt to individual and cultural variations, as behavioral expressions of emotions differ widely across demographics.

Furthermore, Li (2023) pointed out, implementing these systems in diverse educational contexts requires sophisticated infrastructure and robust data management practices. For example, rural and underserved schools may lack the necessary technological resources to deploy such systems successfully. Pilot programs in these settings are critical for evaluating the feasibility and scalability of multimodal AI, ensuring that these technologies be equitably deployed across different socio-economic contexts. Moreover, Jiang et al. (2024) emphasized that combining multiple data streams increases the complexity of data privacy and security. While multimodal systems augment classification accuracy, they also amplify the risks of biased or inappropriate data interpretations. This concerns educational settings, where data misuse might have severe consequences, such as stigmatization or loss of trust. The study called for stringent ethical frameworks to mitigate these risks and certify the responsible use of multimodal AI.

In addition to privacy concerns, advancing fusion algorithms remains a priority for optimizing multimodal AI systems. Neural network architectures for integrating modalities and model-level fusion techniques, such as those using recurrent and convolutional neural networks, are effective in capturing cross-modality relationships. However, these advanced models require computational resources, making them less feasible in underfunded educational environments. This finding emphasizes the need for lightweight yet efficient algorithms to broaden applicability (Khoo et al., 2024). Finally, there is an increasing focus on real-world applications and pilot studies to validate the effectiveness of multimodal AI. Nakamura and Swaroop (2023) highlight the importance of longitudinal studies that assess the technical performance and the practical integration of multimodal systems in diverse school settings. Real-world testing certifies that these systems are adaptable to varying contexts without overwhelming educators or students.

## Addressing Long-Term Impacts and Effectiveness

While AI-based mental health tools have demonstrated short-term success in identifying and addressing emotional distress among students, their long-term effects remain underexplored. Existing research highlights both prospective benefits and unintended consequences, warranting further investigation into their sustained impact on mental health, academic performance, and social outcomes. One critical gap in current research is the lack of longitudinal studies tracking the effectiveness of AI-driven mental health interventions over time. According to O'Brien et al. (2020), the long-term impact of a mental fitness intervention in higher education and found important improvements in well-being and resilience, as well as sustained participation in physical activity. However, they also pointed out that without continued engagement, these benefits tend to diminish over time, suggesting that AI tools need to incorporate sustained follow-ups and reinforcement mechanisms. Moreover, AI systems might be evaluated for their impact on individuals and for their influence on broader educational environments. Wilson and Spencer (2022) examined how mental health support structures within universities affect students with long-term health conditions. They highlighted that while AI-driven systems provide tailored interventions, they may also contribute to a lack of direct human engagement, leading to reduced trust and reluctance to seek traditional support. This emphasizes the need for AI tools to complement, rather than replace, existing mental health resources.

Another area that warrants further exploration is how AI-based interventions influence academic performance and long-term educational attainment. Von Simson et al. (2022) investigated the impact of mental health challenges in adolescence on secondary school completion and found that students with externalizing behavioral issues were 38-40% less likely to complete secondary education. Although AI tools aim to intervene early, there is limited evidence on whether they successfully mitigate such risks or if they inadvertently introduce new stressors, such as increased anxiety from continuous. Beyond academic performance, research might investigate whether AI-driven monitoring promotes a culture of mental health awareness or contributes to surveillance fatigue. Behrendt et al. (2022) studied unaccompanied young refugees and found that persistent stressors negatively impacted mental health outcomes over time. They suggested that while continuous monitoring provides critical information, excessive surveillance may heighten stress levels and reduce a sense of autonomy.

Additionally, the ethical and privacy concerns associated with AI-driven mental health tools might be thoroughly examined in long-term studies. Jiang et al. (2024) highlighted how multimodal AI systems collect vast amounts of personal data, raising concerns about data security and prospective misuse. If students feel that their mental health data might be used against them, they may be less likely to engage with these tools, ultimately diminishing their effectiveness. Furthermore, the long-term integration of AI in mental health support might be assessed in relation to broader educational policies and social equity. According to Rasalingam et al. (2021), young adults with long-term health challenges faced difficulties in completing their education and transitioning into employment. They indicated that while AI tools might aid in identifying at-risk students, they might be coupled with structural policy changes to address systemic barriers successfully.

## Public-Private Partnerships and Collaboration

The advancement of AI-driven mental health detection tools requires strong collaboration between educational institutions, technology developers, mental health professionals, and policymakers. Public-private partnerships (PPPs) provide a framework for combining resources, expertise, and funding to develop and deploy AI solutions successfully. However, while these collaborations provide benefits, they also present challenges related to governance, ethical considerations, and equitable implementation. One of the key advantages of PPPs is their ability to facilitate large-scale implementation and resource-sharing. Arnaout et al. (2023) explored how technology-driven PPPs have been used to address public health inequities, highlighting the role of AI in improving access to healthcare services, reducing misinformation, and enhancing service delivery. They emphasized the importance of trust within the population served, ensuring a bidirectional flow of information, and creating mutual value for all stakeholders. These principles might be directly applied to AI-based mental health initiatives in schools, where collaboration between tech firms and public institutions might reduce costs and improve accessibility. However, the sustainability of PPPs in education and mental health requires ongoing evaluation and adaptation. Partnerships between universities and the UK National Health Service (NHS) might provide student mental health support. Studies revealed that while such partnerships augment service integration, barriers such as information-sharing restrictions and incompatible data infrastructures hinder their effectiveness. This highlights the need for clear governance frameworks for smooth collaboration between AI providers and educational institutions (Broglia et al., 2023; Bommersbach et al., 2018).

Furthermore, PPPs might prioritize ethical considerations and data transparency. Ballantyne and Stewart (2019) identified the risks associated with sharing biomedical big data between public and private entities. They identified concerns related to public skepticism about commercializing health data, prospective breaches of confidentiality, and challenges in defining data ownership. These concerns are directly relevant to AI-driven mental health tools in education, where student data privacy is utmost. Ensuring transparency and ethical governance in these partnerships is crucial for building trust among students, families, and educators.

Additionally, equity in public-private collaborations might be carefully managed to prevent power imbalances. Moerman (2021) analyzed PPPs in education and found that while partnerships provide opportunities for innovation, power often leans towards educational institutions, prospectively sidelining smaller private sector stakeholders. Ensuring that all partners, including smaller technology firms and local mental health providers, have a voice in decision-making improve the fairness and sustainability of these collaborations. Finally, PPPs might align their goals with long-term educational and mental health strategies. According to Peters and Besley (2022) PPPs might not be limited to short-term funding or pilot programs but might also be integrated into national policies. This requires strong leadership, policy coherence, and continuous monitoring of outcomes to certify that AI-driven mental health initiatives provide sustainable benefits.

## RECOMMENDATIONS FOR THE IMPLEMENTATION OF AI

### Ethical Frameworks, Data Security and Educator Training

For AI-driven mental health systems to gain legitimacy and widespread acceptance, clear ethical guidelines might be established. AI tools might be designed with a primary focus on student well-being, ensuring that monitoring is used solely for mental health support and academic assistance, rather than as a disciplinary measure. Saeidnia et al. (2024) emphasize that AI interventions might adhere to core ethical principles such as transparency, fairness, and continuous oversight to prevent bias and unintended consequences. Their systematic review identified 18 key ethical considerations, including the necessity of stakeholder engagement and regular evaluations to certify responsible implementation. Transparency in AI implementation is equally fundamental. The lack of clarity regarding AI decision-making processes often leads to skepticism among students, parents, and educators. Informational workshops and accessible educational resources might be introduced to demystify AI technology and address prospective concerns about bias and surveillance (Mohamed, 2024).

Beyond ethical considerations, prioritizing data security is essential to ensuring that AI-driven mental health monitoring does not compromise student privacy. Wilson and Spencer (2022) found that the absence of robust data protection policies discouraged students from engaging in mental health services, highlighting the need for encryption, anonymization, and secure storage practices. Additionally, according to Bendechache et al. (2021) the importance of obtaining informed consent in educational settings, where AI monitoring might be an opt-in system with clear parental and student approvals. However, AI systems might be as effective as the educators who interpret and apply their information. Syifa (2024) found that targeted AI training programs for teachers improved their ability to understand AI-generated data and apply it in supportive interventions. Without proper training, there is a risk that AI information might be misinterpreted, leading to unintended consequences such as unnecessary distress for students or over-reliance on automated reports. Additionally, the need for mental health awareness training alongside technical AI training might ensure that teachers remain sensitive and supportive when addressing flagged concerns (Willson et al., 2024).

## Collaboration, Monitoring and Improvement

Ensuring the long-term success of AI-based mental health tools requires strong collaboration between multiple stakeholders, including schools, mental health professionals, policymakers, and technology developers. Saeidnia et al. (2024) emphasize that interdisciplinary advisory boards might be established to oversee AI implementation, ensuring that algorithms remain aligned with the best interests of students. Public-private partnerships further facilitate the deployment of AI tools by making them more accessible and financially viable. Arnaout et al. (2023) found that partnerships between technology firms and educational institutions allowed for cost-effective implementation of AI tools in schools. However, these collaborations might prioritize ethical data governance to prevent commercial exploitation of student data. To maintain the reliability of AI-driven interventions, continuous monitoring and evaluation mechanisms might be integrated within these systems. It is important for regular algorithmic audits to detect and correct biases in AI models. Research found that trust in AI interventions increased importantly when schools committed to transparency in AI evaluations and adjustments (Kennedy-Mayo & Gord, 2024). Additionally, integrating feedback mechanisms into AI systems certifies that these tools remain adaptable to evolving educational needs. Mooghali et al. (2023) reviewed AI implementations in healthcare and found that users' ability to provide feedback and request modifications importantly improved AI acceptance and efficacy. Schools might implement similar strategies, allowing students, educators, and parents to continuously refine AI tools based on their real-world experiences.

## CONCLUSION

The integration of artificial intelligence into education is poised to redefine how schools detect and respond to mental health challenges, providing a data-driven, proactive approach that complements traditional support systems. By employing AI techniques such as natural language processing, sentiment analysis, and behavioral pattern recognition, schools might move beyond reactive interventions and toward early, personalized support. This technological shift, if implemented thoughtfully, might create a more inclusive and responsive educational environment where mental health is a fundamental component of student well-being.

However, AI-driven mental health detection is not a panacea, and its success centers on a careful balance between innovation and ethical responsibility. The risks of algorithmic bias, over-surveillance, and data privacy breaches cannot be ignored, as they have the potential to erode trust rather than build it. Moreover, the role of human judgment remains vital as AI serves as an assistive tool, not a substitute for educators and mental health professionals who provide the context, empathy, and discretion that algorithms lack. If improperly deployed, AI systems may inadvertently reinforce existing inequalities, misinterpret cultural or linguistic meanings, or create an environment where students feel monitored rather than supported.

Beyond technical and ethical considerations, there is also the question of long-term impact. How will AI shape students' perceptions of mental health over time? Will AI-driven assessments influence how students self-identify and seek help, and might this lead to unintended psychological consequences? Furthermore, as AI becomes more integrated in educational spaces, schools need to nurture student autonomy rather than reducing mental health support to an algorithmic classification. The question is whether AI can improve mental health support in schools, and whether its implementation reflects a commitment to understanding and supporting students. This demands an ongoing conversation that prioritizes efficiency, equity, ethics, and the well-being of students.

## REFERENCES

Abd-alrazaq, A. A., Alajlani, M., Ahmad, R., AlSaad, R., Aziz, S., Ahmed, A., & Sheikh, J. (2023). The performance of wearable AI in detecting stress among students: Systematic review and meta-analysis. *Journal of Medical Internet Research, 26*, e52622. Advance online publication. DOI: 10.2196/52622 PMID: 38294846

Abimbola, C., Eden, C. A., Chisom, O. N., & Adeniyi, I. S. (2024). *Integrating AI in education: Opportunities, challenges, and ethical considerations.* Magna Scientia Advanced Research and Reviews.

Alkahtani, H., Aldhyani, T. H. H., & Alqarni, A. A. (2024). Artificial intelligence models to predict disability for mental health disorders. *Journal of Disability Research.*

AlMakinah, R., Norcini-Pala, A., Disney, L., & Canbaz, M. A. (2024). Enhancing mental health support through human-AI collaboration: Toward secure and empathetic AI-enabled chatbots. *Journal of Digital Health Advances.*

AlMakinah, R., Norcini-Pala, A., Disney, L., & Canbaz, M. A. (2024). Enhancing mental health support through human-AI collaboration: Toward secure and empathetic AI-enabled chatbots. *Journal of Digital Health Advances, 12*(4), 100–115. DOI: 10.53022/oarjst.2024.11.2.0102

Almethen, A. (2024). Challenges in implementing artificial intelligence applications in secondary-level education: A teacher-centric perspective. ( ).

Alsbou, M. K., & Alsaraireh, R. A. I. (2024). Data-driven decision-making in education: Leveraging AI for school improvement. *2024 International Conference on Knowledge Engineering and Communication Systems (ICKECS), 1*, 1–6. DOI: 10.1109/ICKECS61492.2024.10616616

Alves, V. C., Garcia, F. E., Saud, C., Mendes, A., Caseli, H. M., Motti, V. G., & Neris, V. P. A. (2023). College students-in-the-loop for their mental health: A case of AI and humans working together to support well-being. *Interaction Design and Architecture(s).* DOI: 10.55612/s-5002-059-003

Arnaout, A., Oseguera-Arasmou, M., Mishra, N., Liu, B. M., Bhattacharya, A., & Rhew, D. C. (2023). Leveraging technology in public-private partnerships: A model to address public health inequities. *Frontiers in Health Services, 3*, 1187306. DOI: 10.3389/frhs.2023.1187306 PMID: 37383486

Badidi, E. (2023). Edge AI for early detection of chronic diseases and the spread of infectious diseases: Opportunities, challenges, and future directions. *Future Internet, 15*(11), 370. Advance online publication. DOI: 10.3390/fi15110370

Balasubramanian, S.. (2023). *AI-enabled mental health assessment and intervention: Bridging gaps in access and quality of care*. Power System Technology., DOI: 10.52783/pst.159

Balcombe, L., & de Leo, D. (2021). Digital mental health challenges and the horizon ahead for solutions. *JMIR Mental Health*, *8*(3), e26811. Advance online publication. DOI: 10.2196/26811 PMID: 33779570

Balcombe, L., & Leo, D. (2022). Human-computer interaction in digital mental health. *Informatics (MDPI)*, *9*(1), 14. Advance online publication. DOI: 10.3390/informatics9010014

Ballantyne, A., & Stewart, C. (2019). Big data and public-private partnerships in healthcare and research: The application of an ethics framework for big data in health and research. *Asian Bioethics Review*, *11*(3), 315–326. DOI: 10.1007/s41649-019-00100-7 PMID: 33717319

Behrendt, M., Pfeiffer, E., Devlieger, I., Adeyinka, S., Rota, M., Uzureau, O., Lietaert, I., & Derluyn, I. (2022). The impact of daily stressors on unaccompanied young refugees' mental health: A longitudinal study. *The American Journal of Orthopsychiatry*, *92*(6), 681–691. DOI: 10.1037/ort0000644 PMID: 35925722

Bendechache, M., Tal, I., Wall, P. J., Grehan, L., Clarke, E., Odriscoll, A., . . . Brennan, R. (2021, June). AI in my life: AI, ethics & privacy workshops for 15-16-year-olds. In *Companion Publication of the 13th ACM Web Science Conference 2021* (pp. 34-39).

Bogdanova, K. (2024). Aesthetics of algorithmic care: Designing alternative human-AI collaboration practices for digital phenotyping. *Companion Publication of the 2024 ACM Designing Interactive Systems Conference*. DOI: 10.1145/3656156.3665127

Bommersbach, T., Borger, K., Steverman, S., Manderscheid, R. W., Sharfstein, J., & Everett, A. (2018). Behavioral health, local health department accreditation, and Public Health 3.0: Leveraging opportunities for collaboration. *American Journal of Public Health*, *108*(10), 1334–1340. DOI: 10.2105/AJPH.2018.304533 PMID: 30138073

Broglia, E., Nisbet, K., Bone, C., Simmonds-Buckley, M., Knowles, L., Hardy, G., Gibbon, L., & Barkham, M. (2023). What factors facilitate partnerships between higher education and local mental health services for students? A case study collective. *BMJ Open*, *13*(12), e077040. DOI: 10.1136/bmjopen-2023-077040 PMID: 38159940

Burke, C., & Bloss, C. (2020). Social media surveillance in schools: Rethinking public health interventions in the digital age. *Journal of Medical Internet Research*, *22*(11), e22612. Advance online publication. DOI: 10.2196/22612 PMID: 33179599

Chametka, P., Maqsood, S., & Chiasson, S. (2023). Security and privacy perceptions of mental health chatbots. *2023 20th Annual International Conference on Privacy, Security and Trust (PST)*, 1–7. DOI: 10.1109/PST58708.2023.10320174

Chan, K. S., & Zary, N. (2019). Applications and challenges of implementing artificial intelligence in medical education: Integrative review. *JMIR Medical Education*, *5*(1), 5. DOI: 10.2196/13930 PMID: 31199295

Chen, F., Wang, L., Hong, J., Jiang, J., & Zhou, L. (2024). Unmasking bias in artificial intelligence: A systematic review of bias detection and mitigation strategies in electronic health record-based models. *Journal of the American Medical Informatics Association : JAMIA*, *31*(5), 1172–1183. Advance online publication. DOI: 10.1093/jamia/ocae060 PMID: 38520723

Chen, L. (2023). *Exploring the reform of college mental health education based on multi-source data*. Applied Mathematics and Nonlinear Sciences.

Chin, M. H., Afsar-Manesh, N., Bierman, A. S., Chang, C., Colón-Rodríguez, C., Dullabh, P., Duran, D. G., Fair, M., Hernandez-Boussard, T., Hightower, M., Jain, A., Jordan, W. B., Konya, S., Holliday Moore, R., Moore, T. T., Rodriguez, R., Shaheen, G., Snyder, L. P., Srinivasan, M., & Ohno-Machado, L. (2023). Guiding principles to address the impact of algorithm bias on racial and ethnic disparities in health and health care. *JAMA Network Open*, *6*(12), e2345050. DOI: 10.1001/jamanetworkopen.2023.45050 PMID: 38100101

D'Alfonso, S. (2020). AI in mental health. *Current Opinion in Psychology*, *36*, 112–117. DOI: 10.1016/j.copsyc.2020.04.005 PMID: 32604065

Dai, H. J., Su, C. H., Lee, Y. Q., Zhang, Y. C., Wang, C. K., Kuo, C., & Wu, C. S. (2021). Deep learning-based natural language processing for screening psychiatric patients. *Frontiers in Psychiatry*, *11*, 11. DOI: 10.3389/fpsyt.2020.533949 PMID: 33584354

Decamp, M., & Lindvall, C. (2023). Mitigating bias in AI at the point of care. *Science*, *381*(6654), 150–152. DOI: 10.1126/science.adh2713 PMID: 37440631

Dekker, I., de Jong, E. D., Schippers, M., de Bruijn-Smolders, M., Alexiou, A., & Giesbers, B. (2020). Optimizing students' mental health and academic performance: AI-enhanced life crafting. *Frontiers in Psychology*, *11*, 1063. Advance online publication. DOI: 10.3389/fpsyg.2020.01063 PMID: 32581935

Dias, J., & Tawde, P. D. (2024). Predicting mental health disorders based on sentiment analysis. *International Journal of Scientific Research in Engineering and Management.*

Eberhardt, S. T., Schaffrath, J., Moggia, D., Schwartz, B., Jaehde, M., Rubel, J., Baur, T., André, E., & Lutz, W. (2024). Decoding emotions: Exploring the validity of sentiment analysis in psychotherapy. *Psychotherapy Research.* PMID: 38415369

Ge, S., She, J., Jia, Y., & Yuan, Z. (2020). Research on the identification of college students' mental health problems based on campus big data. *Journal of Physics: Conference Series*, *1646*(1), 012203. DOI: 10.1088/1742-6596/1486/5/052029

Goncharova, G. (2022). New digital opportunities in diagnosis and prevention of students' mental health. *Российский вестник гигиены.*

Govea, J., Ocampo Edye, E., Revelo-Tapia, S., & Villegas-Ch, W. (2023). Optimization and scalability of educational platforms: Integration of artificial intelligence and cloud computing. *Computers*, *12*(11), 223. DOI: 10.3390/computers12110223

Graham, S. A., Depp, C., Lee, E. E., Nebeker, C., Tu, X., Kim, H.-C., & Jeste, D. (2019). Artificial intelligence for mental health and mental illnesses: An overview. *Current Psychiatry Reports*, *21*(11), 21. DOI: 10.1007/s11920-019-1094-0 PMID: 31701320

Habicht, J., Viswanathan, S., Carrington, B., Hauser, T., Harper, R., & Rollwage, M. (2023). *Closing the accessibility gap to mental health treatment with a conversational AI-enabled self-referral tool.* NHS Talking Therapies. DOI: 10.1101/2023.04.29.23289204

Irving, J., Patel, R., Oliver, D., Colling, C., Pritchard, M., Broadbent, M., & Stewart, R. (2020). Using natural language processing on electronic health records to enhance detection and prediction of psychosis risk. *Schizophrenia Bulletin.* PMID: 33025017

Jiang, Z., Seyedi, S., Griner, E., Abbasi, A., Bahrami Rad, A., Kwon, H., Cotes, R., & Clifford, G. D. (2024). Multimodal mental health digital biomarker analysis from remote interviews using facial, vocal, linguistic, and cardiovascular patterns. *IEEE Journal of Biomedical and Health Informatics*, *28*(3), 1680–1691. DOI: 10.1109/JBHI.2024.3352075 PMID: 38198249

Jose, D. (2024). *Data privacy and security concerns in AI-integrated educational platforms.* Recent Trends in Management and Commerce., DOI: 10.46632/rmc/5/2/19

Juanda, J., Riansyah, R. J., Arsadi, A., & Bethany, L. (2024). Towards entrepreneurial campus sustainability: Integrating artificial intelligence for resource allocation. [ATT]. *Aptisi Transactions on Technopreneurship*, *6*(3), 410. Advance online publication. DOI: 10.34306/att.v6i3.410

Junyi, Z. (2024). *The application value of behavior analysis based on deep learning in the evaluation of depression in art students*. Applied Mathematics and Nonlinear Sciences. DOI: 10.2478/amns-2024-1834

Kakde, P. (2023). Sentimental analysis using machine learning for mental health-care management system. *International Journal for Research in Applied Science and Engineering Technology*, *11*(6), 563–570. DOI: 10.22214/ijraset.2023.53450

Katsarou, D., Sofologi, M., & Efthymiou, E. (Eds.). (2025). *Psycholinguistic Dynamics and Educational Inclusion for Children and Adolescents*. IGI Global., DOI: 10.4018/979-8-3693-8931-7

Kennedy-Mayo, D., & Gord, J. (2024). "Model Cards for Model Reporting" in 2024: Reclassifying Category of Ethical Considerations in Terms of Trustworthiness and Risk Management. *arXiv preprint arXiv:2403.15394.*

Kerz, E., Zanwar, S., Qiao, Y., & Wiechmann, D. (2023). Toward explainable AI (XAI) for mental health detection based on language behavior. *Frontiers in Psychiatry*, *14*, 14. DOI: 10.3389/fpsyt.2023.1219479 PMID: 38144474

Khoo, L. S., Lim, M. K., Chong, C. Y., & Mcnaney, R. (2024). Machine learning for multimodal mental health detection: A systematic review of passive sensing approaches. *Sensors (Basel)*, *24*(2), 348. Advance online publication. DOI: 10.3390/s24020348 PMID: 38257440

Kibibi, M. L. (2024). *The role of AI in improving mental health care*. Research Invention Journal of Public Health and Pharmacy., DOI: 10.59298/RIJPP/2024/321013

Kikerpill, K., & Siibak, A. (2022). Schools engaged in doom-monitoring students' online interactions and content creation: An analysis of dominant media discourses. *Child and Adolescent Mental Health*. Advance online publication. DOI: 10.1111/camh.12621 PMID: 36495068

Kim, J., Kim, S., & Kamphaus, R. (2022). Early detection of mental health through universal screening at schools. *Georgia Educational Researcher*, *20*(3), 32–47. DOI: 10.20429/ger.2022.190104

Kusi-Mensah, K., Donnir, G., Dzodzomenyo, M., Owoo, E., & Asante, K. P. (2019). Prevalence and patterns of mental disorders among primary school children in the Greater Accra Region of Ghana. *BMC Pediatrics*, *19*(1), 248. PMID: 31331315

Landstedt, E., & Bortels, S. (2021). Is there a social gradient in how youth with mental disorder symptoms succeed in education? *Journal of Youth Studies*, *24*(3), 265–281.

Levin, S. (2024). Identifying student behavior patterns based on LMS data. *International Scientific Journal of Engineering and Management*, *3*(3), 1–9. DOI: 10.55041/ISJEM01447

Li, Z. (2023). AI-assisted emotion recognition: Impacts on mental health education and learning motivation. [iJET]. *International Journal of Emerging Technologies in Learning*, *18*(24), 45645. Advance online publication. DOI: 10.3991/ijet.v18i24.45645

Luo, G., & Li, C. (2024). Research on mental health problem identification algorithm of college students. *2024 IEEE 2nd International Conference on Image Processing and Computer Applications (ICIPCA).*

Ma, L., Mazidi, M., Li, K., Chen, S., Kirwan, R., & Zhou, H. (2021). Prevalence of mental health problems among children and adolescents during COVID-19: A systematic review and meta-analysis. *Journal of Affective Disorders*, *293*(1), 78–89. DOI: 10.1016/j.jad.2021.06.021 PMID: 34174475

Mahadik, S. S., Pawar, P., Muthalagu, R., Prasad, N. R., Hawkins, S.-K., Stripelis, D., Rao, S., Ejim, P., & Hecht, B. (2024). Digital privacy in healthcare: State-of-the-art and future vision. *IEEE Access : Practical Innovations, Open Solutions*, *12*, 84273–84291. DOI: 10.1109/ACCESS.2024.3410035

Malerbi, F., Nakayama, L., Ribeiro, L. Z., Villanueva, C., & Regatieri, C. (2023). Digital education for the deployment of artificial intelligence in health care. *Journal of Medical Internet Research*, *25*, e43333. Advance online publication. DOI: 10.2196/43333 PMID: 37347537

Matandika, M., Mategula, C., Msolomba, P., & Bandawe, C. (2022). Prevalence and correlates of common mental disorders among school children in Malawi. *Child Psychiatry and Human Development*, *53*(2), 159–168.

Maupomé, D., Rancourt, F., Belbahar, R., & Meurs, M. J. (2024). A pretrained language model for mental health risk detection. *Proceedings of the 2024 Conference on Language Processing*.

Moerman, P. (2021). Public-private partnership to solve the skills gap? *European Journal of University Lifelong Learning*, *5*(1), 71–78. DOI: 10.53807/0501alt6

Mooghali, M., Stroud, A. M., Yoo, D. W., Barry, B. A., Grimshaw, A. A., Ross, J. S., . . . Miller, J. E. (2023). Barriers and Facilitators to Trustworthy and Ethical AI-enabled Medical Care From Patient and Healthcare Provider Perspectives: A Literature Review. medRxiv, 2023-10. https://doi.org/DOI: 10.1101/2023.10.02.23296447

Morley, J., Machado, C., Burr, C., Cowls, J., Joshi, I., Taddeo, M., & Floridi, L. (2020). The ethics of AI in health care: A mapping review. *Social Science & Medicine*, *260*, 113172. Advance online publication. DOI: 10.1016/j.socscimed.2020.113172 PMID: 32702587

Moura, I., Teles, A., Endler, M., Coutinho, L., & Silva, F. J. S. (2020). Recognizing context-aware human sociability patterns using pervasive monitoring for supporting mental health professionals. *Sensors (Basel)*, *21*(1), 21. DOI: 10.3390/s21010086 PMID: 33375630

Murdoch, B. (2021). Privacy and artificial intelligence: Challenges for protecting health information in a new era. *BMC Medical Ethics*, *22*(1), 6. Advance online publication. DOI: 10.1186/s12910-021-00687-3 PMID: 34525993

Nakamura, A., & Swaroop, R. (2023). Multimodal patient evaluation for depression and anxiety. *International Conference on Mental Health and AI*. https://doi.org/ DOI: 10.1016/ai.2023.09.003

Nankya, M., Mugisa, A., Usman, Y., Upadhyay, A., & Chataut, R. (2024). Security and privacy in e-health systems: A review of AI and machine learning techniques. *IEEE Access : Practical Innovations, Open Solutions*, *12*, 148796–148816. DOI: 10.1109/ACCESS.2024.3469215

Nguyen, T. V., Mohd Daril, M. A., Ali, M., & Korejo, M. S. (2024). Enhancing psychological well-being in higher education post-COVID-19 pandemic: The role of AI-based support systems. *International Journal of Online Biomedical Engineering*, *20*(6), 139–152. DOI: 10.3991/ijoe.v20i06.48001

Nishimura, T., Wakuta, T., & Ito, A. (2024). Early detection of students' mental health issues from a traditional daily health observation scheme in Japanese schools and its digitalization. *Frontiers in Public Health*, *12*, 987654. DOI: 10.3389/fpubh.2024.1430011 PMID: 39314787

O'Brien, N., Lawlor, M., Chambers, F., & O'Brien, W. (2020). State of Mind Ireland-Higher Education: A Mixed-Methods Longitudinal Evaluation of a Positive Mental Health Intervention. *International Journal of Environmental Research and Public Health*, *17*(15), 5530. DOI: 10.3390/ijerph17155530 PMID: 32751816

O'Dell, B., Stevens, K., Tomlinson, A., Singh, I., & Cipriani, A. (2022). Building trust in artificial intelligence and new technologies in mental health. *Evidence-Based Mental Health, 25*(2), 45–46. DOI: 10.1136/ebmental-2022-300489 PMID: 35444002

Pal, A., Maitra, T., & Giri, D. (2023). Prediction of depression using emotion and sentiment analysis. *2023 OITS International Conference on Information Technology (OCIT)*, 909–914. DOI: 10.1109/OCIT59427.2023.10431128

Palmer, C. E., Marshall, E., Millgate, E., Warren, G., Ewbank, M. P., Cooper, E., ... & Blackwell, A. D. (2024). Combining AI and human support in mental health: A digital intervention with comparable effectiveness to human-delivered care.

Peng, S., & Nagao, K. (2021). Recognition of students' mental states in discussion based on multimodal data and its application to educational support. *IEEE Access : Practical Innovations, Open Solutions, 9*, 18235–18250. DOI: 10.1109/ACCESS.2021.3054176

Peters, M. A., & Besley, T. (2022). Collaborative Partnerships in Education: Social Innovation and the Co-Creation of Public Knowledge Goods. *Beijing International Review of Education, 4*(2), 191–209. DOI: 10.1163/25902539-04020002

Porello, G., Buy, M., & Graham, C. (2023). Early detection of mental and behavioral health issues from high-school academic performance. In *Proceedings of the 2023 International Conference on Machine Learning and Applications (ICMLA)* (pp. 345-353). DOI: 10.1109/ICMLA58977.2023.00059

Rasalingam, A., Brekke, I., Dahl, E., & Helseth, S. (2021). Impact of growing up with somatic long-term health challenges on school completion, NEET status and disability pension: A population-based longitudinal study. *BMC Public Health, 21*(1), 514. DOI: 10.1186/s12889-021-10538-w PMID: 33726730

Rizvi, M. (2023). Exploring the landscape of artificial intelligence in education: Challenges and opportunities. *2023 5th International Congress on Human-Computer Interaction, Optimization and Robotic Applications (HORA).*

Rogan, J., Bucci, S., & Firth, J. (2024). Health care professionals' views on the use of passive sensing, AI, and machine learning in mental health care: Systematic review with meta-synthesis. *JMIR Mental Health, 11*, e49577. Advance online publication. DOI: 10.2196/49577 PMID: 38261403

Saeidnia, H. R., Hashemi Fotami, S. G., Lund, B., & Ghiasi, N. (2024). Ethical considerations in artificial intelligence interventions for mental health and well-being: Ensuring responsible implementation and impact. *Social Sciences (Basel, Switzerland), 13*(7), 381. DOI: 10.3390/socsci13070381

Sain, Z. H., Sain, S. H., & erban, R. (2024). Implementing artificial intelligence in educational management systems: A comprehensive study of opportunities and challenges. *Asian Journal of Managerial Science.*

Sawalha, J., Yousefnezhad, M., Shah, Z., Brown, M. R. G., Greenshaw, A., & Greiner, R. (2022). Detecting presence of PTSD using sentiment analysis from text data. *Frontiers in Psychiatry, 12*, 12. DOI: 10.3389/fpsyt.2021.811392 PMID: 35178000

Shan, Y., Ji, M., Xie, W., Lam, K., & Chow, C. (2022). Public trust in artificial intelligence applications in mental health care: Topic modeling analysis. *JMIR Human Factors*, *9*(4), e38799. Advance online publication. DOI: 10.2196/38799 PMID: 36459412

Shim, R., Szilagyi, M., & Dube, J. (2022). Epidemic rates of child and adolescent mental health disorders require an urgent response. *Pediatrics*, *149*(6), e2022057317. DOI: 10.1542/peds.2022-056611 PMID: 35202473

Solaiman, B., Malik, A., & Ghuloum, S. (2023). Monitoring mental health: Legal and ethical considerations of using artificial intelligence in psychiatric wards. *American Journal of Law & Medicine*, *49*(2-3), 250–266. DOI: 10.1017/amj.2023.30 PMID: 38344795

Straw, I., & Callison-Burch, C. (2020). Artificial intelligence in mental health and the biases of language-based models. *PLoS One*, *15*(12), e0240376. Advance online publication. DOI: 10.1371/journal.pone.0240376 PMID: 33332380

Syifa, A. F. (2024). Ethics in the age of AI: Principles and guidelines for responsible implementation in workplace. *International Journal of Advanced Technology and Social Sciences*, *2*(2), 237–242. DOI: 10.59890/ijatss.v2i2.1398

Tavory, T. (2024). Regulating AI in mental health: Ethics of care perspective. *JMIR Mental Health*, *11*(1), e58493. Advance online publication. DOI: 10.2196/58493 PMID: 39298759

Timmons, A. C., Duong, J. B., Simo Fiallo, N., Lee, T., Vo, H. P. Q., Ahle, M. W., Comer, J. S., Brewer, L. C., Frazier, S., & Chaspari, T. (2022). A call to action on assessing and mitigating bias in artificial intelligence applications for mental health. *Perspectives on Psychological Science.* Advance online publication. DOI: 10.1177/17456916221134490 PMID: 36490369

Van der Schyff, E. L., Ridout, B., Amon, K. L., Forsyth, R., & Campbell, A. J. (2023). Providing self-led mental health support through an artificial intelligence–powered chatbot (Leora) to meet the demand of mental health care. *Journal of Medical Internet Research*, •••, 25. PMID: 37335608

Vegesna, V. (2024). *AI-powered mental health monitoring using wearable devices and mobile sensing*. International Research Journal of Computer Science., DOI: 10.26562/irjcs.2024.v1108.01

von Simson, K., Brekke, I., & Hardoy, I. (2022). The impact of mental health problems in adolescence on educational attainment. *Scandinavian Journal of Educational Research*, *66*(2), 306–320. DOI: 10.1080/00313831.2020.1869077

Walambe, R., Nayak, P., Bhardwaj, A., & Kotecha, K. (2021). Employing multimodal machine learning for stress detection. *Journal of Healthcare Engineering*, *2021*, 1–12. Advance online publication. DOI: 10.1155/2021/9356452 PMID: 34745514

Weidener, L., & Fischer, M. (2023). Proposing a principle-based approach for teaching AI ethics in medical education. *JMIR Medical Education*, *10*(1), e55368. Advance online publication. DOI: 10.2196/55368 PMID: 38285931

Wilson, C., & Spencer, G. (2022). The mental health support needs of university students with long-term physical health conditions. *Health Education*, *122*(5), 584–598. DOI: 10.1108/HE-01-2022-0004

World Health Organization (WHO). (2019). Adolescent mental health. *World Health Organization*. Retrieved from https://www.who.int/news-room/fact-sheets/detail/adolescent-mental-health?

World Health Organization (WHO). (2019). Mental disorders. *World Health Organization*. Retrieved from https://www.who.int/news-room/fact-sheets/detail/mental-disorders?

Xiao, R., & Liu, X. (2021). Analysis of the architecture of the mental health education system for college students based on the Internet of Things and privacy security. *IEEE Access : Practical Innovations, Open Solutions*, *9*, 81089–81096. DOI: 10.1109/ACCESS.2021.3084208

Yi, G., & Chenyu, H. (2021). *Application of artificial intelligence to mental healthcare in primary and middle schools*. China National Knowledge Infrastructu.

# Chapter 10
# Enhancing Special Education Through Artificial Intelligence: Study in a UAE Autism Rehabilitation Center

**Shamsa Ali Almarzooqi**
https://orcid.org/0009-0000-9444-5403
*Al Ain Autism Center, Zayed Higher Organisation, Al Ain City, UAE*

**Ahmed Hamdan**
https://orcid.org/0000-0002-8225-2310
*United Arab Emirates University, UAE*

**Nada Obaid**
*United Arab Emirates University, UAE*

## ABSTRACT

*This study explored how special education teachers in an autism rehabilitation center in the United Arab Emirates integrate artificial intelligence (AI) tools into their professional practice, highlighting benefits and challenges. A qualitative descriptive design was employed, combining pre-and post-workshop questionnaires (N=56) with in-depth interviews of 12 teachers selected for their active use of AI. Findings revealed that teachers utilize AI for lesson planning, behavior management, administrative tasks, and creative instructional strategies, substantially reducing preparation time. Despite these advantages, participants voiced concerns regarding privacy, data security, cost, and limited accuracy of AI-generated content. They stressed the necessity of combining AI outputs with professional judgment. The*

DOI: 10.4018/979-8-3373-0573-8.ch010

*study underscores the importance of structured professional development, robust data protection policies, and equitable access to AI technologies.*

## INTRODUCTION

Artificial Intelligence (AI) has gained momentum worldwide as many governments are adopting AI applications in various fields such as healthcare, energy, transport, education, and finance. In the United Arab Emirates (UAE), the National Strategy for AI shed light on the strategic objectives and the main sectors that the UAE will focus on in the upcoming years to achieve the millstone set by the leaders of the country to become the AI world's leader by 2031 (UAE National Strategy for Artificial Intelligence 2031, 2018). The education sector is one of the fields that will have tremendous advancements in utilizing AI applications to revolutionize the current educational technologies in schools and universities.

Moreover, the role of AI in transforming education has gained substantial attention in recent years, particularly in its potential to support inclusive education practices. The increasing integration of AI into educational practices transforms how educators deliver instruction and manage their responsibilities (Hashem et al., 2023; Lin & Schmidt, 2023). As educational systems strive to meet the needs of increasingly diverse student populations, using AI to support teachers and students with disabilities has emerged as a critical area of research and development (Mondal et al., 2023; Rakap, 2024). Special education teachers frequently encounter challenges in crafting individualized learning plans, managing student behavior, nurturing social-emotional development, and promoting inclusivity in the classroom (McGuire & Meadan, 2022; Mullen & Hunt, 2022; Rashid & Wong, 2022; Smith et al., 2018). This study explored AI's role in supporting special education teachers working in rehabilitation centers in the UAE, focusing on how AI tools and strategies can enhance their effectiveness in meeting diverse learning needs.

AI applications imitate human behavior and use computer programs to perform complex human tasks such as learning, analyzing, adapting, and synthesizing (Popenici & Kerr, 2017). AI incorporates problem-solving skills with Science, Technology, Engineering, and Mathematics (STEAM). It amalgamates knowledge of various disciplines and technologies, making it expedient in educational contexts (Gabriel, 2024).

The importance of AI in education is prevalent because it allows educators to explore their students' potential through personalized learning. AI personalization features will enable educators to tailor educational content according to their students' needs and strengths (Hopcan et al., 2023). In addition, AI can enhance teaching and learning activities, classroom exercises, and homework and improve the learning environment by creating interactive experiences and offering personalized constructive feedback (Hopcan et al., 2023; Searson et al., 2024). Another aspect of AI is creating customized content development and learning materials that suit the learners' preferences and learning patterns, which increases learners' comprehension of materials and engagement in the learning process (Bahroun et al., 2023; Baidoo-Anu & Owusu Ansah, 2023; Hashem et al., 2023; Su & Yang, 2023). Virtual tutoring powered by AI is also an area of interest in using AI in education. It offers independent learning and immediate support to learners' needs at any time and place (Baidoo-Anu & Owusu Ansah, 2023; Su & Yang, 2023).

Student engagement is an essential factor in effective learning environments. Several researchers see AI as a tool that could increase students' motivation and accelerate their engagement. AI provides innovative ways of interaction and encourages self-guided learning, where students learn at their own pace while taking ownership of their learning milestones (Gabriel, 2024; Hwang et al., 2020). In addition, 3D interactive environments such as virtual reality and augmented reality powered by AI could provide support to students with disabilities as they could be customized to meet student's needs and offer them new ways to interact with learning materials (Hopcan et al., 2023; Searson et al., 2024).

Using AI in education can help teachers manage their time effectively by reducing time spent on administrative tasks and allowing them to focus more on instruction (Kamalov et al., 2023; Searson et al., 2024). Several research papers have indicated that AI tools could create moment-to-moment and game-based assessments, grade students' work (multiple-choice and open-ended questions), enable summative and formative evaluations, and monitor students' performances (Hopcan et al., 2023). Furthermore, researchers conveyed that AI tools such as ChatGPT can semi-automate the process of grading students' work and indicate the areas of strengths and weaknesses of each learner, which helps educators design and adopt effective and personalized interventions (Grassini, 2023).

Using AI with students with disabilities is still in its infancy, and several limitations can pose challenges to implementing AI in real-life settings such as rehabilitation centers. These limitations and challenges must be explored to effectively implement AI in inclusive settings. Examples of these challenges include involving special needs students in the development cycle and design process, mitigating cultural and social biases that could be embedded in the AI data collection phase or training process, and creating user-friendly interfaces custom for various disabilities (El Morr et al., 2024). Moreover, the hype in using AI in education and in other fields is intertwined with the concerns related to ethical and privacy considerations (Alasadi & Baiz, 2023).

Although there is a lack of research on AI and its applications in rehabilitation and special needs centers in the UAE, the teachers' perceptions of using AI are interlinked with their perception of using assistive technologies. Several research studies conducted in the UAE examining teachers' awareness of assistive technologies with special education students showed a need for awareness programs that raise teachers' understanding of this topic despite teachers' positive attitudes in embracing these technologies into their classes (Maisikeli, 2023). Teachers often convey that their main obstacles in using assistive technologies are the lack of training and knowledge, professional development, high costs of assistive technology devices, and lack of funding and resources (Fteiha et al., 2024).

This study explored teachers' experiences in an autism rehabilitation center in UAE using a qualitative descriptive design method. A total of 56 staff members in the rehabilitation center participated in an initial workshop and pre- and post-questionnaires to evaluate their AI awareness, knowledge, and how they currently use AI in the center. Based on the responses, 12 teachers were selected based on their frequent use of AI and their awareness of AI potential in autism rehabilitation. The 12 teachers were individually interviewed to investigate further the AI implementation and its impact on educational and therapeutic practices.

Given the strategic focus of the UAE to integrate AI in education and the promising benefits of AI in transforming learning experiences and improving students' engagement, teaching methodologies, and educational accessibility for students with disabilities, there must be new endeavors in the research realm that evaluates the AI integration in special education context setting the stage for further developments in this field. Despite the promising initiatives in the UAE to integrate AI into education, there is still a scarcity of literature in this field.

This study aimed to address these gaps by examining the perspectives of special education teachers in the UAE's rehabilitation centers on the role of AI in supporting their instructional practices. The study targeted capturing teachers' experiences, expectations, and challenges in using AI to improve practices and outcomes for students with disabilities, which could generate actionable insights for policymakers, educators, and technology developers.

Research questions:

- How do special education teachers who work with students with ASD integrate AI tools into their teaching practice?
- How do these teachers perceive the benefits of AI for saving time and enhancing instruction for students with ASD?
- What challenges do teachers of students with ASD face when using AI, and how do they address them?

## METHOD

This study employed a qualitative descriptive design to explore the experiences of teachers at an autism rehabilitation center in the UAE regarding their knowledge, use, and perceptions of AI in their professional practice. Qualitative descriptive research is a pragmatic approach well-suited for gathering rich descriptions of phenomena from the perspective of those experiencing them (Sandelowski, 2000). This design is particularly appropriate when the goal is to understand the "what" of a phenomenon, providing a comprehensive summary of experiences in everyday terms (Lambert & Lambert, 2012).

### Participants

To explore the role of AI in supporting special education teachers working with students with ASD in rehabilitation centers in the UAE, a workshop on AI applications was conducted at one such center. A total of 56 staff members participated in the workshop and completed pre- and post-questionnaires, which assessed their AI knowledge, usage, and awareness. As summarized in Table 1, the pre-questionnaire revealed a wide range of familiarity with AI, including how frequently participants used AI tools and how aware they were of AI's potential in autism rehabilitation.

Based on these pre-questionnaire responses, 12 teachers—specifically those who reported actively using AI tools and demonstrating clear awareness of AI applications for students with ASD—were nominated for in-depth, individual interviews. These interviews provided qualitative data to further investigate the nuances of AI implementation and its impact on educational and therapeutic practices.

Table 2 presents a cohort of 12 special education teachers with diverse professional and cultural backgrounds. Their specialized fields include Special Education and Applied Behavior Analysis, supported by academic qualifications ranging from Bachelor's to Master's degrees. Their teaching experience spans four to sixteen years, with each educator working with students who have ASD at levels ranging from mild to moderate through to moderate to severe. Core competencies among these teachers include behavior modification, the development and implementation of Behavior Plans and Individualized Education Plans (IEPs), and lesson planning.

*Table 1. Staff members' AI knowledge, usage, and awareness*

| Survey Question | Response Category | Frequency (n) | Percentage (%) |
|---|---|---|---|
| **Level of AI Knowledge** | I don't know anything | 5 | 8.9 |
| | I have a simple idea | 27 | 48.2 |
| | I have moderate knowledge | 22 | 39.3 |
| | I have advanced knowledge | 2 | 3.6 |
| | **Total** | **56** | **100** |
| **Previous Use of AI Tools** | Yes, repeatedly | 7 | 12.5 |
| | Sometimes | 25 | 44.6 |
| | Rarely | 13 | 23.2 |
| | I never used it | 11 | 19.6 |
| | **Total** | **56** | **100** |
| **Awareness of Different AI Applications** | Yes | 33 | 58.9 |
| | No | 23 | 41.1 |
| | **Total** | **56** | **100** |

*Table 2. Demographic and professional profiles of special education teachers*

| AI Tools & Assistive platforms Used | Primary Areas of Expertise | Student Category | Years of Experience | Educational Background | Field of Specialization | Nationality | Gender | Teacher's Name |
|---|---|---|---|---|---|---|---|---|
| ChatGPT, Proloquo2Go | Behavior Analysis, Behavior Plans, Parent Consultations, Individualized Sessions | ASD (Mild to Moderate Cases) | 7 years | Master's Degree | Applied Behavior Analysis | Emirati | Male | Abdulaziz |
| ChatGPT, Gamma, Proloquo2Go Twinkl Tiny Tap | Teaching, Behavior Analysis, Behavior Plans, IEPs, Lesson Planning | ASD (Moderate to Severe Cases) | 7 years | Bachelor's Degree | Applied Behavior Analysis | Emirati | Male | Khalifah |
| ChatGPT, Gamma, Microsoft Office, Proloquo2Go | Teaching, Behavior Plans, IEPs, Lesson Planning | ASD (Mild to Moderate Cases) | 5 years | Master's Degree | Special Education | Emirati | Female | Latifah |
| ChatGPT, & other AI-powered tools | Behavior Modification, Curriculum Development, Teaching Methods | ASD (All levels of severity) | 16 years | Master's Degree | Special Education | Jordanian | Male | Eiad |

continued on following page

*Table 2. Continued*

| AI Tools & Assistive platforms Used | Primary Areas of Expertise | Student Category | Years of Experience | Educational Background | Field of Specialization | Nationality | Gender | Teacher's Name |
|---|---|---|---|---|---|---|---|---|
| Magic School, Hydra AI, Eleven AI, ChatGPT, Gamma, Synthesia AI | Behavior Plans, IEPs, Lesson Planning, Teacher Training | ASD (Moderate to Severe Cases) | 15 years | Bachelor's Degree | Special Education | Emirati | Female | Salamah |
| Gamma, ChatGPT | Behavior Plans, IEPs, Lesson Planning, Teacher Training | ASD (All levels of severity) | 12 years | Bachelor's Degree | Special Education | Emirati | Female | Fatima |
| ChatGPT, Google Bard | Teaching, Behavior Plans, IEPs, Lesson Planning | ASD (All levels of severity) | 12 years | Bachelor's Degree | Special Education | Jordanian | Male | Hazem |
| ChatGPT | Teaching, Behavior Plans, IEPs, Lesson Planning | ASD (Mild to Moderate Cases) | 4 Years | Bachelor's Degree | Special Education | Jordanian | Male | Khaled |
| ChatGPT, TinyTap, Twinkl, Wordwall | Teaching, Behavior Plans, IEPs, Lesson Planning | ASD (Mild to Moderate Cases) | 7 years | Bachelor's Degree | Special Education | Emirati | Male | Faisal |
| Magic School, ChatGPT, Canva for Education, School AI, ReX, Kami, Quizzes AI | Teaching, Behavior Plans, IEPs, Lesson Planning | ASD (Mild to Moderate Cases) | 11 years | Master's Degree | Special Education | Emirati | Female | Ruqayya |
| ChatGPT, Copilot, Magic School, Microsoft Forms, OneDrive | Teaching, Behavior Plans, IEPs, Lesson Planning | ASD (Mild to Moderate Cases) | 12 years | Bachelor's Degree | Special Education | Emirati | Female | Maitha |
| Black & White Photo Colorizer (Cutout.pro) VideoGuru 3D Scanner on Galaxy Phones Augmented Reality on Galaxy Phones | Teaching, Behavior Plans, IEPs, Lesson Planning | ASD (Mild Cases) | 15 years | Bachelor's Degree | Special Education | Jordanian | Male | Tariq |

ASD: Autism Spectrum Disorder, IEPs: Individualized Education Plans

## Instrument

Semi-structured interviews were employed to gather in-depth data on teachers' experiences with AI. This method provides flexibility in exploring emerging themes while maintaining a clear focus on the primary research questions (Creswell & Poth, 2018). An interview guide was initially developed in English, drawing on a review of relevant literature on AI in education, special education, or teacher experiences (Cavus et al., 2021; Holmes et al., 2023; Şen & Akbay, 2023; Zawacki-Richter et al., 2019), and aimed at examining teachers' knowledge, use, and perceptions of AI in their professional practice with students with ASD. After the initial draft was formulated, the co-authors reviewed the interview guide to ensure its clarity, relevance, and comprehensiveness. This collaborative feedback process facilitated the refinement and adjustment of the questions, bolstering their alignment with the research objectives.

Given that the participating teachers primarily communicated in Arabic, the finalized English version of the interview guide was professionally translated into Arabic. Following Brislin's (1970) back-translation principles, this process sought to preserve the original meaning and intent of each question while ensuring cultural sensitivity and linguistic appropriateness for the target population. The Arabic version ultimately served as the instrument during the interviews. Such translation and adaptation procedures are critical to maintaining validity and reliability in cross-cultural research (Herdman et al., 1998). Some of the questions on the interview guide was follows:

*Table 3. Categories of questions asked to interviewees*

| Category | Question |
|---|---|
| General Perceptions of AI in Special Education | Could you describe your overall experience with AI in your teaching, and how you view its role in supporting special education? |
| Current Use of AI Tools | Which AI tools have you implemented for students with disabilities, and how have they helped you personalize instruction or plan lessons? |
| AI for Student Engagement and Behavior Management | How have AI tools been useful in managing behavioral challenges, and which strategies or features have you found most effective? |
| Administrative Support | Have AI tools reduced your administrative task, and how has this influenced the time you spend directly with students? |
| Challenges and Expectations | What obstacles or limitations have you encountered when using AI in special education? |

Individual interviews were conducted using Microsoft Teams for conference calling. This platform facilitated convenient and accessible participation for teachers, particularly given potential scheduling constraints and geographical distances, a key advantage highlighted in research on online data collection (Archibald et al., 2019). Using this platform also allowed for the interviews to be recorded with participant consent, enabling accurate transcription and subsequent analysis, which enhances the rigor and trustworthiness of qualitative data (Deakin & Wakefield, 2013). Each interview was conducted by a single moderator to maintain consistency and rapport with the participants. This one-on-one approach allowed for in-depth exploration of individual experiences and perspectives related to AI in their professional practice, consistent with the principles of in-depth interviewing (Brinkmann & Kvale, 2018; Rubin & Rubin, 2005).

### Data Analysis

Individual interviews ranged from approximately 20 to 45 minutes in duration, largely influenced by the teachers' varying familiarity with AI, their comfort in discussing personal experiences, and the depth of their reflections (Dickson-Swift et al., 2007; Merriam, 2009). First, the interviews were transcribed in the Emirati Arabic dialect to capture local linguistic nuances. These transcripts were then translated into Standard Arabic to ensure consistency and clarity. Finally, the Standard Arabic versions were translated into English, allowing for collaborative analysis by the entire research team (Herdman et al., 1998). This stepwise approach sought to preserve the original meaning and cultural context of participants' responses.

Data were analyzed manually using a systematic coding technique consistent with thematic analysis (Braun & Clarke, 2006). The English transcripts were read and re-read in an iterative process to achieve familiarity with the data. In line with Braun and Clarke (2006), initial codes were generated inductively, capturing key ideas and patterns that emerged directly from participants' accounts. These codes were subsequently refined, categorized, and grouped to form overarching themes, emphasizing recurring patterns of meaning across the data set (Nowell et al., 2017). This analytical strategy centered on capturing the essence of teachers' experiences and perceptions of AI in their professional practice with students with ASD.

## RESULTS

The data were categorized into three main themes: Integration of AI Tools in Special Education Practice, Perceived Benefits of AI in Special Education, and Challenges and Concerns of AI (see Figure 1).

*Figure 1. Graphical illustration of themes and subthemes*

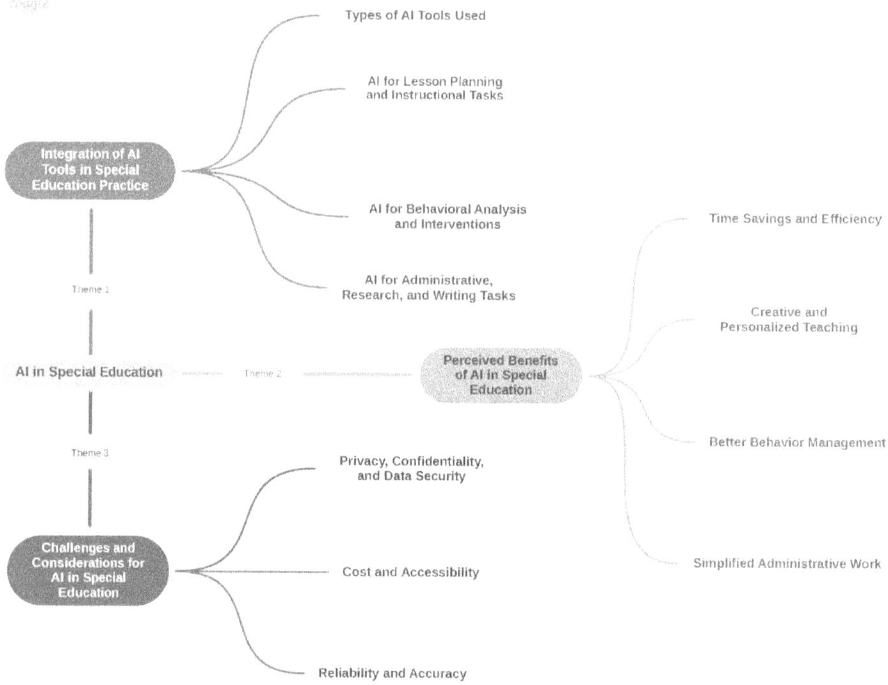


## Theme 1: Integration of AI Tools in Special Education Practice

This theme outlines how teachers incorporate AI tools into their routines through four subthemes: Types of AI Tools Used, AI for Lesson Planning and Instructional Tasks, AI for Behavioral Analysis and Interventions, and AI for Administrative, Research, and Writing Tasks.

### Types of AI Tools Used

During the interviews, teachers reported exploring a variety of AI platforms to meet their professional needs. Some tools were recent discoveries, while others had been in use for months. Regardless of how long they had used them, most educators agreed on the practical impact these tools offered for lesson planning, behavioral interventions, and general administrative tasks.

Among all the tools mentioned, ChatGPT was the most widely recognized. Participants highlighted its versatility, using it for both personal and professional tasks. Abdulaziz, for example, explained:

*"Yes, I do use ChatGPT in my personal life. Most of the time, I use AI—especially ChatGPT—to write my emails more professionally..." (Abdulaziz)*

Khalifah described ChatGPT as "amazing," calling it a "major turning point" in how he approached AI. He recalled:

*"Honestly, I started using ChatGPT toward the end of the last school term... Once I downloaded and started exploring it, I was honestly amazed by its capabilities." (Khalifah)*

Others used ChatGPT to generate concise explanations or intervention plans, refining the AI-generated content with their own expertise. Maitha noted that ChatGPT helped spark fresh ideas whenever she hit a creative block.

Educators also mentioned Gamma, an AI-powered presentation tool. Khalifah praised its ability to compress slides "in seconds," while Latifah found it helpful for instantly generating classroom presentations. Maitha and others valued Gamma's emphasis on content organization, which let them focus more on teaching rather than formatting.

Magic School was another popular platform. Teachers like Salamah described how it produced comprehensive lesson plans complete with objectives, materials, and assessment strategies. Ruqayya turned to Magic School for creative group activities and morning circle ideas, emphasizing how it enhanced her instructional design.

Though mentioned less frequently, tools such as Copilot, Microsoft Forms, and OneDrive also surfaced as beneficial aids. Maitha reported that Copilot was handy when creating English-language content, while Microsoft Forms helped educators like her generate data-collection surveys "already analyzed" for quick reporting. OneDrive supported file sharing and storage, preventing reliance on specific workplace computers.

## AI for Lesson Planning and Instructional Tasks

Beyond simply discovering new tools, Teachers described AI platforms as powerful collaborators in designing lessons and activities tailored to their students' needs. ChatGPT, Magic School, and related tools provided structured ideas and sample resources—ranging from lesson objectives to detailed worksheets. In some cases, teachers entered specific student goals or cases, prompting AI to offer creative strategies or visuals.

Latifah recalled generating a lesson plan for "travel steps" and receiving "pictures and a clear sequence," which she considered her best worksheet to date. Khaled similarly input case details and was pleased with the suggestions for skill-building activities in complex areas. Many educators also said these tools break down lengthy goals in IEPs into manageable components.

In addition to lesson planning, some participants integrated multimedia creation into their teaching process. Tariq, for instance, used AI prompts to develop visual content about health or sensory topics, layering in symbols or icons based on AI's suggestions to serve diverse learning styles. Salamah particularly appreciated how AI-based programs could automatically align teaching strategies and assessment methods within a single, coherent plan.

## AI for Behavioral Analysis and Interventions

Shifting focus to another critical aspect of special education, A number of educators highlighted AI's potential to offer new perspectives on behavioral interventions. They typically used ChatGPT or similar programs to define target behaviors, generate preliminary strategies, and refine established approaches. Khalifah, for example, input a dataset on challenging behaviors and found AI helpful for pinpointing areas needing closer inspection—though he stressed the continued need for human expertise.

Teachers with Applied Behavior Analysis (ABA) training saw AI as a time-saver when writing precise definitions of behaviors. Latifah noted:

*"In the field of ABA, we need precise definitions of behaviors... It helps me define problems, and it often suggests straightforward solutions." (Latifah)*

Some educators, like Khaled, discovered entirely new strategies via AI, which helped them expand their repertoire of potential interventions. Ruqayya described how an AI-generated suggestion to use contingent reinforcement ended up significantly reducing a student's disruptive behavior. Across the board, however, participants emphasized that AI outputs must be validated through real-world observation and professional judgment, ensuring that solutions remain relevant and ethically sound.

## AI for Administrative, Research, and Writing Tasks

Finally, Teachers also employed AI to streamline research and administrative duties. ChatGPT and other platforms assisted in summarizing PDF documents or analyzing data from spreadsheets. Eiad noted:

*"I uploaded the PDF to an AI tool that summarized its strengths, weaknesses, challenges, and so on in just a few minutes." (Eiad)*

Likewise, Fatima found that ChatGPT could interpret Excel data rapidly, sparing them the manual steps of data parsing. For email composition and formal communications, multiple educators—including Abdulaziz and Maitha —relied on AI to structure and polish their messages. They appreciated how quickly AI generated well-organized drafts, which then required only minimal editing.

Longer written tasks, such as drafting reports or research instruments, also benefited from AI-driven assistance. Ruqayya reflected:

*"Before, writing one report could take me an hour and a half or two hours, but now, I can finish in just a few minutes—I just review it." (Ruqayya)*

Even though manual review remained essential to ensure correctness and appropriate tone, these AI tools became mainstays in teachers' day-to-day workflow, reducing the complexity of document creation and data processing.

## Theme 2: Perceived Benefits of AI in Special Education

This theme explores how educators leverage AI tools through four subthemes: Time Savings and Efficiency, Creative and Personalized Teaching, Better Behavior Management, and Simplified Administrative Work.

### Time Savings and Efficiency

Many participants noted that tasks once demanding considerable time—such as lesson planning, drafting documents, or organizing presentations—could now be done more quickly with the support of AI. As Maitha explained:

*"It definitely saves me time, effort, and a lot more...," (Maitha)*

She indicated how integral AI workflows have become to her daily routine. Fatima echoed this sentiment by describing how AI-assisted data processing helped them meet deadlines for "statistics or performance indicators" more accurately. Hazem similarly appreciated receiving "a quick, concise answer," rather than manually searching multiple resources.

Khalifah offered a vivid example of AI's speed:

*"It honestly took me just two minutes, and I was done... I told them, 'This is the power of AI!'" (Khalifah)*

This compressed timeline allowed him to shift focus toward higher-value tasks requiring professional judgment, rather than spending hours on preliminary research. Eiad, too, highlighted how lesson planning and slide preparation—traditionally lengthy activities—could now be accomplished in minutes rather than hours.

Teachers also described reduced time in creating classroom presentations and other materials. Latifah observed that a session previously requiring "two days" to prepare could now be finished in about 20 minutes. Tariq reinforced the theme of flexibility, noting that these tools "save time and effort," enabling rapid adjustments without starting from scratch.

## Creative and Personalized Teaching

While time savings were a critical advantage, educators also credited AI with sparking fresh instructional methods and more personalized lesson content. Abdulaziz emphasized that AI can:

> *"...assist therapists, teachers, and even parents by suggesting effective teaching strategies," (Abdulaziz)*

pointing out how built-in assessment capabilities can help monitor student progress. Tailored recommendations, many noted, emerge when teachers provide specific details about their professional roles and student needs.

Khalifah found that AI could optimize classroom organization and track the time needed for students to master certain objectives, describing how it brought both "structural guidance and creativity" to his lesson planning. Ruqayya appreciated AI's capacity to expand or refine her initial ideas:

> *"Sometimes, I'll propose some ideas, and AI will expand on them, giving me creative, innovative suggestions..." (Ruqayya)*

She cited an example where AI helped create a "Mini Reinforcement Store," a reward system she had not previously considered. Maitha likewise observed that these platforms often introduce strategies she never thought to try, invigorating her approach to lesson design.

For educators like Tariq, AI was an ally in generating multimedia resources. By supplying text prompts on topics such as "healthy eating" or "the five senses," he created interactive presentations or videos that better suited varied learning preferences.

## Better Behavior Management

Several participants highlighted AI's role in clarifying and addressing challenging behaviors more efficiently. They used AI to draft intervention plans, test their current assumptions, and explore new methods—particularly in ABA. In a synthesized reflection, participants noted:

> *"These tools don't always provide perfect solutions, but they save us time defining behavior problems and sometimes highlight new approaches we hadn't thought of."*

Although educators appreciated how AI might simplify behavior analysis and reinforce their professional insights, they also stressed that final decisions require on-the-ground expertise. Relying solely on AI risked overlooking contextual factors, such as subtle behavioral cues or individual learning styles. Most described these applications as complementary aids—valuable for generating ideas and refining intervention outlines, yet dependent on careful adaptation by specialists familiar with each student's specific needs. By combining the efficiency of AI with their professional judgment, participants felt they could offer more responsive and well-rounded behavioral interventions.

### Simplified Administrative Work

Lastly, teachers described how AI drastically streamlined their administrative loads—drafting emails, creating reports, and organizing slides. In a composite reflection, participants remarked:

*"Communicating professionally used to be time-consuming. We spent ages revising emails, reorganizing slides, or extracting insights from lengthy PDFs. Now, AI platforms generate polished drafts ... often in a matter of minutes."*

This shifts freed educators to concentrate on instruction rather than clerical duties. They mentioned how data summaries became more accessible and visually appealing, improving communication with both school administrators and parents. Yet participants remained cautious about over-reliance, acknowledging the need to proofread AI outputs for accuracy and appropriateness. Even so, many regarded these tools as a pivotal support system that allowed them to allocate more time and energy to direct student engagement.

## Theme 3: Challenges and Considerations for AI in Special Education

This theme delves into the complexities educators face when integrating AI into their practice, organized under three subthemes: Privacy, Confidentiality, and Data Security; Cost and Accessibility; and Reliability and Accuracy.

### Privacy, Confidentiality, and Data Security

Participants consistently emphasized the need to protect sensitive student information. Abdulaziz encapsulated a common sentiment:

*"The biggest concern I have is privacy... When working with children with autism, confidentiality is crucial." (Abdulaziz)*

Several educators expressed uncertainty regarding how AI applications handle and store data. Khalifah pointed out that parents may be apprehensive about how their children's details are shared or archived:

*"We're not entirely sure how these applications handle student information. Parents may not want certain details about their children shared or stored." (Khalifah)*

Given these concerns, many teachers called for clearer institutional guidelines on data handling and usage. They felt strongly that special education practitioners have a dual responsibility to respect families' expectations and comply with ethical or legal standards for safeguarding personal information.

## Cost and Accessibility

Another prominent challenge centered on the financial barriers to adopting AI tools. As Abdulaziz noted:

*"Some AI tools aren't free, and they can be expensive for some families or institutions." (Abdulaziz)*

Participants explained that subscription-based models often restrict access to advanced features. Hazem pointed out:

*"If you want more advanced features, you often have to pay." (Hazem)*

Those who tested free or basic versions found them limited in functionality. For instance, Maitha highlighted:

*"If you want high-quality results or advanced features, you often need the paid version... Some programs also limit how many images or documents you can create before asking you to subscribe." (Maitha)*

This financial burden created inequities in who could benefit most from AI-driven teaching and intervention strategies, particularly in resource-constrained school settings or households.

## Reliability and Accuracy

While educators acknowledged AI's potential for expediting lesson planning and behavior interventions, they repeatedly stressed that AI tools are not infallible. Ruqayya estimated:

*"It's generally accurate but not fully specialized in the nuances of special education... If I were to put a number on it, I'd give it an accuracy rating of about 75–80%." (Ruqayya)*

Others, such as Khalifah, placed AI's reliability in a similar range. Educators also flagged the risk of fabricated or misleading information, particularly if prompts were ambiguous. According to Latifah:

*"The text it provides isn't always accurate—sometimes it fabricates things... Yes, if we don't give the AI the right instructions or double-check the results, errors will happen." (Latifah)*

Teachers reiterated the importance of verifying any AI-supplied references or links. Eiad observed that current AI platforms do not yet have extensive specialized data for students with special needs, resulting in incomplete or overly generic recommendations. Additionally, some participants noted that AI outputs can be repetitive, especially across multiple AI tools. As Hazem commented:

*"If you ask the same question on multiple AI tools, they often provide nearly identical answers." (Hazem)*

Despite these shortcomings, many educators viewed AI as a helpful starting point—provided they supplemented its outputs with their professional expertise. As Ruqayya put it:

*"It's definitely not 100% foolproof or as nuanced as a human. So I never just copy-paste what it gives me. I'll always do my own checks." (Ruqayya)*

## DISCUSSION

The purpose of this study was to examine special education professionals' and teachers' use of AI with students of special needs. The findings of this study highlight the integration of AI tools in special education as a multifaceted developing phenomenon. The existing literature assets that AI has the potential to revolutionize special education by providing individualized and personalized learning experiences which will lead to reducing the burden on teachers and improving the assessment and instruction of students (e.g., Alsolami, 2025; Harkins-Brown et al., 2025). It has become evident that teachers and professionals incorporate AI into several aspects of their teaching routines including lesson planning, instruction, intervention, and administrative responsibilities.

### Benefits of AI Integration in Special Education

As shown from the results of the study, teachers' integration of AI tools (e.g., the use of platforms such as Magic School, Gamma, and ChatGPT) has proven effective in streamlining different aspects of practice in special education such as lesson planning through the generation of lesson plan content including objectives, worksheets, and interactive resources that can be customized according to the students' individual needs. This corroborates existing literature that highlighted the effectiveness of using AI in curriculum support and lesson planning (e.g., Rakap, 2024; Rakap, & Balikci, 2024). Teachers in this study found these AI tools extremely useful and timesaving, enabling them to dedicate more time to individualized teaching (Fitria, 2023; Dei, 2024).

By alleviating the burden of routine tasks such as preparing worksheets and paperwork, these tools allow educators to concentrate on student engagement and interaction (Deep et al., 2024; Goldman et al., 2024; Li et al., 2024). Moreover, teachers reported that AI systems supported more personalized teaching by offering tailored recommendations for instructional strategies, sometimes suggesting approaches they might not have considered otherwise (Mishra, 2024). Indeed, AI's ability to generate and refine ideas in real time has made it a valuable resource for educators striving to deliver personalized, engaging lessons.

Teachers also noted that AI was instrumental in delivering effective behavioral interventions, particularly within an ABA framework. These observations align with the findings of Yagafarova et al. (2025), who reported that AI platforms can enhance procedural fidelity in behavioral interventions for children with ASD. Teachers in this study reported using AI to precisely define target behaviors and to explore state-of-the-art intervention strategies. Several participants noted that AI-based tools not only streamlined their data collection processes but also expanded their repertoire of behavior management techniques. These findings align with broader research indicating that AI can enhance educators' capacity to identify and address student behavioral needs more effectively (Ajuwon et al., 2024; Yang & Xia, 2023; Zhou et al., 2024). Moreover, teachers emphasized that while AI can provide valuable initial insights, professional expertise remains essential for customizing and refining intervention plans to suit individual learners—an observation supported by Slimi & Villarejo-Carballido (2024), who argue that AI-driven recommendations are most successful when integrated with expert judgment.

## Challenges and Considerations in AI Integration

Despite the recognized benefits, participants in this study highlighted several pressing challenges in integrating AI tools into special education. Chief among these concerns were issues of privacy, confidentiality, and data security—anxieties also noted by Huang (2023). Teachers emphasized that AI-based systems often require extensive data collection, which can increase the risk of unauthorized access and misuse if not adequately safeguarded (Schaeffer et al., 2024). These concerns are especially pronounced in special education settings, where sensitive student data related to individual needs, background information, and intervention history demand heightened levels of protection (Huang, 2023). Participants reported uncertainty about how AI algorithms store, process, and share data, calling for more transparent data management practices and comprehensive guidelines to ensure that both educators and students remain protected. This underscores the need for robust policy frameworks and clearer institutional procedures to maintain the balance between harnessing AI's advantages and upholding ethical standards in special education.

Another notable challenge was the financial accessibility of AI tools. Several educators reported that while many AI platforms offer free versions, these are often limited in functionality, prompting a need for paid subscriptions to unlock advanced features. This creates inequities, particularly in resource-constrained educational settings. For teachers in underfunded schools or families with limited financial resources, the cost of AI tools can be prohibitive. As Maitha pointed out, the financial constraints on accessing high-quality AI services limit the potential benefits for educators and students who would otherwise benefit from these tools. This is consistent with what the literature concluded that although AI interventions are promising but there is a concern that such advantages might not be accessible to low-resource environments (Garg & Chauhan, 2024; Wang et al., 2023).

Participants in this study echoed previous findings (Tang et al., 2023; Thorne, 2024) by expressing concerns over the accuracy and reliability of AI-generated outputs. Although AI tools can rapidly produce suggestions and content, many educators observed that these outputs often fail to meet the nuanced requirements of special education, particularly in the context of behavioral interventions (Aliu, 2024). Professionals noted that while AI recommendations are generally accurate, they frequently lack the individualized specificity essential for learners with diverse needs—a shortcoming similarly identified by Jian (2023).

Educators emphasized that although AI-driven strategies may serve as a useful starting point, they should not be treated as definitive solutions. As Ruqayya remarked, AI-generated recommendations can sometimes be generic or incomplete, underscoring the importance of human expertise. Indeed, teachers consistently stated that professional judgment remains indispensable for interpreting and refining AI suggestions to ensure they align with each student's unique challenges.

## Balancing AI Integration with Professional Expertise

A key takeaway from the study is the importance of balancing AI integration with the expertise of special education professionals. Although AI tools offer support, creativity, efficiency, they cannot substitute for nuanced understanding that teachers and professionals bring in practice. Teachers emphasized the AI should complement, rather than substitute, human's critical thinking. Some of the teachers reported that AI might suggest resources or strategies, but it is the teacher's discretion to assess their applicability, validity, and relevance in the content of each student's needs. This is particularly crucial in working with students with special needs where individualized instruction is critical for students' success. Moreover, educators' cautious approach to AI's potential pitfalls—such as the fabrication of information and the lack of deep specialization in certain areas—illustrates the need for continuous professional involvement in the teaching process. While AI has the potential to be a valuable tool, it is essential that teachers maintain oversight and adapt the outputs to ensure that they are effective and appropriate for their students.

## Implications for Practice

Based on the study's findings, special education practitioners can enhance their instructional and administrative efficiency by integrating AI tools to automate lesson planning, behavioral interventions, and documentation. To maximize these benefits, schools and rehabilitation centers should provide targeted professional development that familiarizes educators with AI's capabilities, limitations, and ethical considerations, including privacy and data security. Equally important is establishing clear guidelines and policies for responsible AI use, particularly for safeguarding sensitive student information. Educators are encouraged to view AI as a collaborative aid, using its outputs as a springboard for innovation while relying on professional judgment to tailor strategies to individual learners' needs. By securing adequate resources and ensuring equitable access to premium AI features, organizations can create more inclusive and effective learning environments for students with ASD and other disabilities.

## Limitations

This study's findings must be viewed in light of several constraints. First, data were gathered within a single rehabilitation center in the UAE, which narrows the generalizability of the results to other cultural or institutional settings. Although in-depth interviews yielded rich insights, the relatively small sample of 12 teachers—selected for their reported AI awareness—may not represent the breadth of perspectives found among special education practitioners more broadly. Additionally, the study relied on self-reported accounts of AI use, which introduces the potential for social desirability bias or inaccuracies in participants' recall. While the qualitative design captured nuanced experiences, it did not measure objective student outcomes, limiting our understanding of AI's direct impact on learning and behavior. Furthermore, AI tools and platforms evolve rapidly; thus, findings drawn from current technologies may become dated as new, more sophisticated solutions emerge. Despite these limitations, the study provides a meaningful starting point for exploring the interplay between AI and special education practice in the UAE.

## CONCLUSION

This study provides a snapshot of how special education teachers in a UAE-based autism rehabilitation center integrate AI into their instructional and administrative tasks. Teachers reported significant time savings and enhanced creativity in lesson planning, behavioral interventions, and paperwork, aligning with broader research indicating AI's potential to transform educational practices. However, concerns about privacy, data security, cost, and the accuracy of AI outputs underscore the need for clear guidelines and professional development. Taken together, these findings suggest that while AI can substantially augment special education services, its efficacy hinges on balancing automation with expert judgment, safeguarding students' sensitive information, and ensuring equitable access to high-quality AI tools. As AI technology continues to evolve, future research should further investigate how these tools can be adapted and scaled across diverse cultural and educational contexts, ultimately fostering more inclusive, personalized, and effective learning environments for students with ASD.

## REFERENCES


Ajuwon, N. O. A., Animashaun, N. E. S., & Chiekezie, N. N. R.Olanike Abiola AjuwonEnitan Shukurat AnimashaunNjideka Rita Chiekezie. (2024). Integrating AI and technology in educational administration: Improving efficiency and educational quality. *Open Access Research Journal of Science and Technology*, *11*(2), 116–127. DOI: 10.53022/oarjst.2024.11.2.0102

Alasadi, E. A., & Baiz, C. R. (2023). Generative AI in Education and Research: Opportunities, Concerns, and Solutions. *Journal of Chemical Education*, *100*(8), 2965–2971. DOI: 10.1021/acs.jchemed.3c00323

Aliu, T. V. (2024). Artificial Intelligence in Special Education: A Literature review. *International Journal of Advanced Networking and Applications*, *16*(02), 6360–6367. DOI: 10.35444/IJANA.2024.16208

Alsolami, A. S. (2025). The effectiveness of using artificial intelligence in improving academic skills of school-aged students with mild intellectual disabilities in Saudi Arabia. *Research in Developmental Disabilities*, *156*, 104884. DOI: 10.1016/j.ridd.2024.104884 PMID: 39631141

Archibald, M. M., Ambagtsheer, R. C., Casey, M. G., & Lawless, M. (2019). Using Zoom videoconferencing for qualitative data collection: Perceptions and experiences of researchers and participants. *International Journal of Qualitative Methods*, *18*, 1609406919874596. Advance online publication. DOI: 10.1177/1609406919874596

Bahroun, Z., Anane, C., Ahmed, V., & Zacca, A. (2023). Transforming Education: A Comprehensive Review of Generative Artificial Intelligence in Educational Settings through Bibliometric and Content Analysis. *Sustainability (Basel)*, *15*(17), 12983. DOI: 10.3390/su151712983

Baidoo-Anu, D., & Owusu Ansah, L. (2023). Education in the Era of Generative Artificial Intelligence (AI): Understanding the Potential Benefits of ChatGPT in Promoting Teaching and Learning. SSRN *Electronic Journal*. https://doi.org/DOI: 10.2139/ssrn.4337484

Braun, V., & Clarke, V. (2006). Using thematic analysis in psychology. *Qualitative Research in Psychology*, *3*(2), 77–101. DOI: 10.1191/1478088706qp063oa

Brinkmann, S., & Kvale, S. (2018). *Doing interviews*. https://doi.org/DOI: 10.4135/9781529716665

Brislin, R. W. (1970). Back-Translation for Cross-Cultural research. *Journal of Cross-Cultural Psychology*, *1*(3), 185–216. DOI: 10.1177/135910457000100301

Cavus, N., Lawan, A. A., Ibrahim, Z., Dahiru, A., Tahir, S., Abdulrazak, U. I., & Hussaini, A. (2021). A Systematic Literature Review on the Application of Machine-Learning Models in behavioral Assessment of Autism Spectrum Disorder. *Journal of Personalized Medicine*, *11*(4), 299. DOI: 10.3390/jpm11040299 PMID: 33919878

Creswell, J. W., & Poth, C. N. (2018). *Qualitative inquiry and research design: Choosing among five approaches* (4th ed.). SAGE Publications.

Deakin, H., & Wakefield, K. (2013). Skype interviewing: Reflections of two PhD researchers. *Qualitative Research*, *14*(5), 603–616. DOI: 10.1177/1468794113488126

Deep, S., Athimoolam, K., & Enoch, T. (2024). Optimizing Administrative Efficiency and Student engagement in Education: The Impact of AI. *International Journal of Current Science Research and Review*, *07*(10). Advance online publication. DOI: 10.47191/ijcsrr/V7-i10-34

Dei, M. O. (2024). The impact of AI on the adaptation of educational materials and teaching methods to the needs of each student. *LatIA*, *3*, 124. DOI: 10.62486/latia2025124

Dickson-Swift, V., James, E. L., Kippen, S., & Liamputtong, P. (2007). Doing sensitive research: What challenges do qualitative researchers face? *Qualitative Research*, *7*(3), 327–353. DOI: 10.1177/1468794107078515

El Morr, C., Singh, D., Sawhney, V., Fernandes, S., El-Lahib, Y., & Gorman, R. (2024). Exploring the Intersection of AI and Inclusive Design for People with Disabilities. In *Studies in health technology and informatics* (Vol. 316, pp. 556–559). https://doi.org/DOI: 10.3233/SHTI240475

Fitria, T. N. (2023). THE USE OF ARTIFICIAL INTELLIGENCE IN EDUCATION (AIED): CAN AI REPLACE THE TEACHER'S ROLE? *Epigram*, *20*(2), 165–187. DOI: 10.32722/epi.v20i2.5711

Fteiha, M., Al-Rashaida, M., Elsori, D., Khalil, A., & Al Bustami, G. (2024). Obstacles for using assistive technology in centres of special needs in the UAE. *Disability and Rehabilitation. Assistive Technology*, *19*(8), 2934–2944. DOI: 10.1080/17483107.2024.2323698 PMID: 38436086

Gabriel, J. (2024). How Artificial Intelligence (AI) impacts inclusive education. *Educational Research Review*, *19*(6), 95–103. DOI: 10.5897/ERR2024.4404

Garg, S., & Chauhan, A. (2024). Insights into the potential benefits and challenges of AI-driven large language models/ChatGPT-4 for predicting autism spectrum disorder. *Archives of Psychiatric Nursing*, *53*, 85–87. DOI: 10.1016/j.apnu.2024.10.009 PMID: 39615949

Goldman, S. R., Taylor, J., Carreon, A., & Smith, S. J. (2024). Using AI to support special education teacher workload. *Journal of Special Education Technology, 39*(3), 434–447. DOI: 10.1177/01626434241257240

Grassini, S. (2023). Shaping the Future of Education: Exploring the Potential and Consequences of AI and ChatGPT in Educational Settings. *Education Sciences, 13*(7), 692. DOI: 10.3390/educsci13070692

Harkins-Brown, A. R., Carling, L. Z., & Peloff, D. C. (2025). Artificial Intelligence in Special Education. *Encyclopedia, 5*(1), 11. DOI: 10.3390/encyclopedia5010011

Hashem, R., Ali, N., El Zein, F., Fidalgo, P., & Abu Khurma, O. (2023). AI to the rescue: Exploring the potential of ChatGPT as a teacher ally for workload relief and burnout prevention. *Research and Practice in Technology Enhanced Learning, 19*, 023. https://doi.org/DOI: 10.58459/rptel.2024.19023

Herdman, M., Fox-Rushby, J., & Badia, X. (1998). A model of equivalence in the cultural adaptation of HRQoL instruments: The universalist approach. *Quality of Life Research: An International Journal of Quality of Life Aspects of Treatment, Care and Rehabilitation, 7*(4), 323–335. DOI: 10.1023/A:1008846618880 PMID: 9610216

Holmes, W., Bialik, M., & Fadel, C. (2023). Artificial intelligence in education. http://hdl.handle.net/20.500.12424/4276068

Hopcan, S., Polat, E., Ozturk, M. E., & Ozturk, L. (2023). Artificial intelligence in special education: A systematic review. *Interactive Learning Environments, 31*(10), 7335–7353. DOI: 10.1080/10494820.2022.2067186

Huang, L. (2023). Ethics of Artificial intelligence in Education: Student privacy and data protection. *Science Insights Education Frontiers, 16*(2), 2577–2587. DOI: 10.15354/sief.23.re202

Hwang, G.-J., Xie, H., Wah, B. W., & Gašević, D. (2020). Vision, challenges, roles and research issues of Artificial Intelligence in Education. *Computers and Education: Artificial Intelligence, 1*, 100001. DOI: 10.1016/j.caeai.2020.100001

Jian, M. J. K. O. (2023). Personalized learning through AI. *Advances in Engineering Innovation, 5*(1), 16–19. DOI: 10.54254/2977-3903/5/2023039

Kamalov, F., Santandreu Calonge, D., & Gurrib, I. (2023). New era of artificial intelligence in education: Towards a sustainable multifaceted revolution. *Sustainability (Basel), 15*(16), 12451. DOI: 10.3390/su151612451

Li, Y., Liang, J., Zhao, Z., & Li, K. (2024). Revolutionizing Education through AI: Alleviating Educator Stress, Personalizing Learning, and Enhancing Economic Sustainability. *World Journal of Education and Humanities*, *6*(5), 113. DOI: 10.22158/wjeh.v6n5p113

Lin, X., & Schmidt, S. (2023). Making ChatGPT Work for You. *ELearn, 2023*(4). https://doi.org/DOI: 10.1145/3594251.3594636

Maisikeli, S. G. (2023). Level of assistive technology use and awareness among people with physical disability in the United Arab Emirates. *Technology and Disability*, *35*(1), 11–20. DOI: 10.3233/TAD-220393

McGuire, S. N., & Meadan, H. (2022). General Educators' Perceptions of Social Inclusion of Elementary Students With Emotional and Behavioral Disorders. *Behavioral Disorders*, *48*(1), 16–28. DOI: 10.1177/01987429221079047

Merriam, S. B. (2009). *Qualitative research: A Guide to Design and Implementation*. John Wiley & Sons.

Mishra, S. (2024). Revolutionizing Education: The impact of AI-Enhanced Teaching Strategies. *International Journal for Research in Applied Science and Engineering Technology*, *12*(9), 9–32. DOI: 10.22214/ijraset.2024.64127

Mondal, H., Marndi, G., Behera, J. K., & Mondal, S. (2023). ChatGPT for Teachers: Practical Examples for Utilizing Artificial Intelligence for Educational Purposes. *Indian Journal of Vascular and Endovascular Surgery*, *10*(3), 200–205. DOI: 10.4103/ijves.ijves_37_23

Mullen, C. A., & Hunt, T. K. (2022). Emotional disability and strategies for supporting student outcomes: Interviews with K–12 special education teachers. *Teacher Development*, *26*(4), 453–471. DOI: 10.1080/13664530.2022.2108129

Nowell, L. S., Norris, J. M., White, D. E., & Moules, N. J. (2017). Thematic analysis. *International Journal of Qualitative Methods*, *16*(1), 1609406917733847. Advance online publication. DOI: 10.1177/1609406917733847

Popenici, S. A. D., & Kerr, S. (2017). Exploring the impact of artificial intelligence on teaching and learning in higher education. *Research and Practice in Technology Enhanced Learning*, *12*(1), 22. DOI: 10.1186/s41039-017-0062-8 PMID: 30595727

Rakap, S. (2024). Chatting with GPT: Enhancing Individualized Education Program Goal Development for Novice Special Education Teachers. *Journal of Special Education Technology*, *39*(3), 339–348. DOI: 10.1177/01626434231211295

Rakap, S. (2024). Navigating the role of artificial intelligence in special education: Advantages, disadvantages, and ethical considerations. *Practice*, *6*(2-3), 1–6. DOI: 10.1080/25783858.2024.2411948

Rakap, S., & Balikci, S. (2024). Enhancing IEP goal development for preschoolers with autism: A preliminary study on ChatGPT Integration. *Journal of Autism and Developmental Disorders*, •••, 1–6. DOI: 10.1007/s10803-024-06343-0 PMID: 38625490

Rashid, S. M. M., & Wong, M. T. (2022). Challenges of Implementing the Individualized Education Plan (IEP) for Special Needs Children with Learning Disabilities: Systematic Literature Review (SLR). *International Journal of Learning. Teaching and Educational Research*, *22*(1), 15–34. DOI: 10.26803/ijlter.22.1.2

Rubin, H., & Rubin, I. (2005). Qualitative Interviewing *(2nd ed.): The Art of Hearing Data*. https://doi.org/DOI: 10.4135/9781452226651

Sandelowski, M. J. (2000). Whatever happened to qualitative description? *Research in Nursing & Health*, *23*(4), 334–340. DOI: 10.1002/1098-240X(200008)23:4<334::AID-NUR9>3.0.CO;2-G PMID: 10940958

Schaeffer, D., Coombs, L., Luckett, J., Marin, M., & Olson, P. (2024). Risks of AI applications used in higher education. *Electronic Journal of e-Learning*, *22*(6), 60–65. DOI: 10.34190/ejel.22.6.3457

Searson, M., Langran, E., & Trumble, J. (2024). Exploring new horizons: generative artificial intelligence and teacher education.

Slimi, Z., & Villarejo-Carballido, B. (2024). Unveiling the potential: Experts' perspectives on artificial intelligence integration in higher education. *European Journal of Educational Research, volume–13–2024*(volume–13–issue–4–october–2024), 1477–1492. https://doi.org/DOI: 10.12973/eu-jer.13.4.1477

Smith, S. W., Poling, D. V., & Worth, M. R. (2018). Intensive Intervention for Students with Emotional and Behavioral Disorders. *Learning Disabilities Research & Practice*, *33*(3), 168–175. DOI: 10.1111/ldrp.12174

Su, J., & Yang, W. (2023). Unlocking the Power of ChatGPT: A Framework for Applying Generative AI in Education. *ECNU Review of Education*, *6*(3), 355–366. DOI: 10.1177/20965311231168423

Tang, N., Yang, C., Fan, J., & Cao, L. (2023). VERIFAI: Verified Generative AI. *arXiv (Cornell University)*. https://doi.org//arxiv.2307.02796DOI: 10.48550

Thorne, S. (2024). Understanding the interplay between trust, reliability, and human factors in the age of generative AI. *International Journal of Simulation Systems Science & Technology*. DOI: 10.5013/IJSSST.a.25.01.10

*UAE National Strategy for Artificial Intelligence 2031*. (2018). United Arab Emirates Minister of State for Artificial Intelligence Office. Retrieved January 21, 2025, from https://ai.gov.ae/wp-content/uploads/2021/07/UAE-National-Strategy-for-Artificial-Intelligence-2031.pdf

Wang, X., Sanders, H. M., Liu, Y., Seang, K., Tran, B. X., Atanasov, A. G., Qiu, Y., Tang, S., Car, J., Wang, Y. X., Wong, T. Y., Tham, Y.-C., & Chung, K. C. (2023). ChatGPT: Promise and challenges for deployment in low-and middle-income countries. *The Lancet Regional Health. Western Pacific*, *41*, 100905. Advance online publication. DOI: 10.1016/j.lanwpc.2023.100905 PMID: 37731897

Yagafarova, A., Dowling, E., LaMonica, T., Hantula, D. A., Nosek, J. T., & Jimenez-Gomez, C. (2025). Supporting Procedural Fidelity of Behavioral Interventions for Children with Autism via an Artificial Intelligence Platform. *Behavioral Interventions*, *40*(1), e2075. DOI: 10.1002/bin.2075

Yang, Y., & Xia, N. (2023). Enhancing students' metacognition via AI-Driven educational support systems. [iJET]. *International Journal of Emerging Technologies in Learning*, *18*(24), 133–148. DOI: 10.3991/ijet.v18i24.45647

Zawacki-Richter, O., Marín, V. I., Bond, M., & Gouverneur, F. (2019). Systematic review of research on artificial intelligence applications in higher education – where are the educators? *International Journal of Educational Technology in Higher Education*, *16*(1), 39. Advance online publication. DOI: 10.1186/s41239-019-0171-0

Zhou, F., Lv, H., Zhou, K., Sheng, M., & Jiang, J. (2024). Innovative Application and Societal Impact of AI in Student Behavior Early Warning Systems within Smart Campuses. *Philosophy of the Social Sciences*, *1*(5), 33–40. DOI: 10.62381/P243506

Chapter 11

# AI-Enhanced Assessment and Intervention Tools for Communication Disorders

**Shabnam Salim Abdoola**
https://orcid.org/0000-0003-2930-2259
*United Arab Emirates University, UAE*

**Carmen Milton**
https://orcid.org/0000-0001-9429-3200
*University of Pretoria, South Africa*

## ABSTRACT

*This chapter explores the potential of AI-enhanced tools in assessing and intervening in communication disorders within educational and clinical settings. AI-driven applications enable non-invasive screenings for speech, language, and social communication disorders, facilitating early identification and reducing delays in support. Using a literature-based methodology, this review examines key AI applications, evaluating their efficiency, diagnostic accuracy, and accessibility compared to traditional methods. Findings indicate that AI tools streamline assessments by analyzing speech patterns and integrating multimodal data, improving diagnostic precision and reducing evaluation time. However, ethical considerations, including data privacy, algorithm bias, and the need for practitioner training, present challenges to widespread adoption. Despite these concerns, AI has the potential to transform communication disorder assessment, emphasizing the importance of responsible implementation and ongoing research to enhance its applicability across diverse populations.*

DOI: 10.4018/979-8-3373-0573-8.ch011

## INTRODUCTION

Communication disorders, including speech and language impairments, have profound effects on an individual's academic, social, and professional outcomes. The ability to communicate effectively is a fundamental human need, and when communication is impaired, it can lead to isolation, frustration, and significant barriers to education and employment.

Speech-language pathologists (SLPs) play a crucial role in assessing and treating individuals with communicative disorders. Their patients range from young children with articulatory errors to elderly individuals experiencing severe dysphagia and aphasia. These professionals diagnose communication difficulties arising from various etiologies, including craniofacial anomalies, cleft palate, autism spectrum disorders, Parkinson's disease, multiple sclerosis, Down syndrome, hearing loss, depression, and chronic pain, among others.

To identify and address these challenges, SLPs use a variety of assessment tools, including standardized test batteries and informal interview techniques. Interventions may involve both low- and high-tech augmentative and alternative communication (AAC) devices, such as picture symbol boards, AAC apps, and eye-gaze communication systems. Traditionally, these tools were developed, used, and funded independently, leading to fragmentation in service delivery and accessibility.

Given the importance of early identification and intervention, SLPs have historically relied on standardized tests, observational methods, and structured interactions to diagnose and treat communication disorders. However, while these traditional methods are clinically validated, they are often time-consuming, subjective, and dependent on the availability of trained professionals (Paul & Norbury, 2012)

Over the past two decades, however, the field of speech-language pathology has undergone a transformation, driven by advancements in artificial intelligence (AI). These innovations are reshaping the development of technological resources for SLPs, their clients, and their families, offering new opportunities to enhance assessment and intervention strategies.

AI has emerged as a revolutionary tool in healthcare, with its application in communication disorders gaining momentum. AI-powered assessment tools promise to transform how speech and language disorders are diagnosed and treated. By leveraging AI-driven technologies such as natural language processing (NLP), machine learning (ML), deep learning (DL), and automated speech recognition (ASR), clinicians can enhance diagnostic accuracy, streamline assessments, and deliver personalized interventions. AI's ability to process large datasets and detect subtle patterns in speech, language, and social communication behaviors makes it particularly valuable in screening and diagnosing conditions such as developmental language disorder (DLD), autism spectrum disorder (ASD), dysarthria, and aphasia (Topol, 2019).

While traditional assessment and intervention approaches remain effective, they are often resource- and time-intensive, with accessibility constraints further limiting their reach. Additionally, these conventional methods frequently rely on subjective evaluations, potentially delaying diagnosis and intervention (López et al., 2022). AI-enhanced tools offer a promising solution by improving the efficiency, accuracy, and accessibility of these processes, particularly for speech and language delays, social communication disorders, and other related conditions (Huang et al., 2021).

With its ability to increase efficiency, enhance diagnostic precision, and expand accessibility—especially for underserved populations—AI-driven innovations have the potential to revolutionize the assessment and treatment of communication disorders.

Speech-language pathology is inherently multidisciplinary, integrating principles from linguistics, psychology, neuroscience, and education to assess, diagnose, and treat individuals with speech, language, and swallowing impairments (McLeod & Baker, 2020). Despite significant technological advancements, service fragmentation remains a major challenge. Unlike other medical disciplines benefiting from integrated healthcare systems, speech-language pathology often lacks cohesive structures that connect practitioners, healthcare workers (HCWs), and patients across different platforms. This fragmentation results in inefficiencies in communication, delayed interventions, and restricted access to data that could inform evidence-based practice (Wylie et al., 2018).

The global integration of AI-based tools presents an opportunity to bridge these gaps, facilitating seamless communication among HCWs, patients, and practitioners. Standardised AI-driven platforms can improve diagnostic accuracy and intervention outcomes through enhanced data sharing while contributing to big data analysis and product refinement. By leveraging shared datasets, researchers and clinicians can identify patterns, refine therapeutic approaches, and create personalised treatment plans (Harrington et al., 2022). Establishing interconnected digital health networks could revolutionise service delivery, ensuring greater accessibility, efficiency, and continuity of care.

Beyond improving current practices, AI-driven systems also enable predictive analytics, allowing professionals to anticipate a patient's communication challenges based on vast datasets. These predictive models enhance early identification, enabling proactive intervention strategies that mitigate long-term impacts. Moreover, cloud-based AI platforms facilitate multilingual support, ensuring accessibility for diverse populations across linguistic and cultural backgrounds (Zhao et al., 2020). Given AI's scalability, digital tools can provide critical screening, diagnosis, and intervention services even in remote or under-resourced settings, where such services would otherwise be unavailable (Raghavan et al., 2021).

AI's potential extends beyond direct patient care, playing a pivotal role in training and professional development. AI-driven simulations and virtual assistants offer continuous learning opportunities for clinicians, ensuring that Speech-language pathology professionals stay updated on emerging best practices and evidence-based interventions. Furthermore, AI integration into telepractice services has proven instrumental in overcoming geographical and financial barriers, enabling individuals to access high-quality care regardless of location (Theodoros, 2020).

Despite these promising advancements, AI implementation in speech-language pathology presents notable challenges. Ethical concerns such as data privacy, algorithmic bias, and the risk of dehumanising therapy must be carefully managed to ensure that technology enhances rather than replaces human expertise (Bennett et al., 2021). Addressing these issues through regulatory frameworks and ongoing research will be crucial in ensuring AI's responsible and ethical application in the field.

This chapter will examine the role of AI in speech-language pathology by exploring its applications in assessment and intervention strategies. It will discuss the benefits of AI-enhanced diagnostic tools, such as automated speech analysis and natural language processing (NLP), and their impact on clinical decision-making. Additionally, the chapter will investigate AI-driven interventions—including virtual therapists and personalised therapy programmes—and their contributions to improving treatment outcomes and accessibility for individuals with communication disorders. Ethical considerations, including data privacy, algorithmic bias, and regulatory challenges, will be explored to ensure responsible AI integration into clinical practice. Finally, the chapter will discuss AI's future potential, particularly in expanding global access to speech-language pathology through telehealth solutions and cross-platform integration.

## THE ROLE OF SLPS IN COMMUNICATION DISORDERS

Speech-language pathologists (SLPs) play a crucial role in diagnosing and treating communication and swallowing disorders across all age groups. Their work is essential in helping individuals develop, restore, or maintain their ability to communicate effectively and eat safely. SLPs address a wide range of disorders, including speech sound disorders, language disorders, fluency disorders, voice and resonance disorders, cognitive-communication disorders, and swallowing disorders.

Within their scope of practice, SLPs work with individuals experiencing speech sound disorders, such as articulation disorders (difficulty pronouncing sounds correctly) and phonological disorders (patterns of speech errors affecting sound production).

They also treat language disorders, which include receptive language impairments (difficulty understanding language) and expressive language impairments (difficulty producing language). Fluency disorders, such as stuttering and cluttering, fall under their expertise, helping individuals improve their ability to produce speech without interruptions. Additionally, SLPs manage voice and resonance disorders that impact vocal quality, pitch, and loudness, often resulting in hoarseness, breathiness, or voice strain. Cognitive-communication disorders, frequently seen in individuals with traumatic brain injuries (TBI) or neurodegenerative diseases, affect attention, memory, and the ability to organize thoughts, all of which can impair communication. Lastly, SLPs assess and treat swallowing disorders (dysphagia), which can impact nutritional intake and overall health.

SLPs work in a variety of settings, including schools, hospitals, private clinics, rehabilitation centers, and research institutions. In school-based settings, they collaborate with teachers and special education professionals to develop individualized intervention plans that enhance communication skills and support academic success. In medical and rehabilitation settings, SLPs help individuals recovering from stroke, TBI, or neurodegenerative diseases regain communication and swallowing function. In private practice, they provide specialized therapy tailored to each client's needs, while in research institutions, they contribute to advancing knowledge in speech-language pathology and developing innovative treatments.

Across different age groups, SLPs provide critical interventions tailored to specific needs. In pediatric settings, they work with children experiencing delayed speech and language development, autism spectrum disorder, phonological disorders, and social communication difficulties. They also support literacy development and assist children in overcoming articulation challenges that may hinder academic and social success (Justice, Logan, & Damschroder, 2017). For adults, SLPs provide services to individuals with acquired communication disorders resulting from TBI, stroke, neurodegenerative diseases, and fluency disorders. They assist with voice therapy, cognitive-linguistic rehabilitation, and swallowing disorder management. Within aging populations, SLPs play a vital role in addressing communication difficulties associated with dementia, Parkinson's disease, and aphasia (Brookshire & McNeil, 2014). Their interventions aim to maintain speech and language function, promote alternative communication strategies, and support caregivers in facilitating effective communication.

Despite the essential role of SLPs, barriers such as limited access to services, the subjectivity of traditional assessments, and clinician shortages pose significant challenges. Many individuals do not receive timely speech therapy due to long wait times or geographical limitations. Additionally, traditional assessments often rely on subjective analysis, leading to potential inconsistencies in diagnosis and treatment planning. AI-powered tools offer a promising solution to these limitations by automating assessment procedures, providing objective analyses, and delivering remote intervention solutions (Goodwin et al., 2021). These advancements can enhance the efficiency of speech-language pathology and make therapy more accessible.

AI-driven assessment and intervention tools can offer significant benefits for various populations by improving both the accuracy and efficiency of speech-language therapy. For infants and toddlers with speech and language delays, AI-powered applications can automate early screening by analyzing vocalizations, babbling patterns, and early word production, allowing for early detection and timely intervention. Children with Autism Spectrum Disorder (ASD) can benefit from AI technologies, such as facial recognition, prosodic analysis, and eye-tracking, which help assess social communication skills and identify early markers of ASD for targeted intervention.

Individuals with aphasia following a stroke or TBI can use AI-powered speech analysis tools to identify and categorize different types of aphasia, significantly enhancing rehabilitation planning. AI-driven speech monitoring systems are particularly valuable for people with neurodegenerative diseases such as Parkinson's disease, ALS, and dementia, as they track progressive changes in speech and language, enabling early diagnosis and intervention to slow the progression of communication difficulties. Additionally, individuals with fluency disorders, such as stuttering, can benefit from AI-powered speech analysis tools that evaluate disfluencies and provide real-time feedback, aiding in fluency enhancement. Teenagers and young adults with social communication disorders can engage with AI-driven gamification and virtual reality (VR) applications, which create interactive and tailored therapy sessions, making speech therapy more engaging and accessible.

Overall, speech-language pathology is a vast field addressing a broad spectrum of communication and swallowing challenges throughout an individual's lifespan. While SLPs play an indispensable role in communication rehabilitation, the increasing demand for speech therapy services, coupled with a shortage of qualified professionals, presents challenges in timely diagnosis and intervention. AI-enhanced tools have the potential to augment the work of SLPs by making assessments more efficient and expanding access to therapy, particularly in remote and underserved regions. By integrating AI technology into their practice, SLPs can enhance their ability to assess and treat communication disorders more effectively, ultimately improving outcomes for individuals across different age groups and conditions.

## THE ROLE & METHODS OF AI PROCESSING IN COMMUNICATION DISORDERS

Artificial intelligence (AI) is playing an increasingly prominent role in the assessment and intervention of communication disorders, fundamentally transforming traditional speech-language pathology practices. Communication disorders, which encompass speech, language, and social communication difficulties, significantly impact an individual's ability to engage in meaningful interactions, pursue education, and function effectively in daily life. Historically, assessments and interventions for these disorders have relied on standardized test batteries, informal observational techniques, and clinical expertise. However, these methods often suffer from subjectivity, variability, and inefficiencies, leading to delays in diagnosis and treatment. AI-driven technologies have emerged as a promising solution, offering enhanced efficiency, accuracy, and accessibility in speech and language assessments (López et al., 2022).

Speech-language pathology, as a field, is multidisciplinary, integrating principles from linguistics, psychology, neuroscience, and education. Despite advances in research and technology, fragmentation in service delivery continues to be a significant challenge. Unlike other medical disciplines that benefit from integrated healthcare systems, speech-language pathology lacks cohesive structures that connect practitioners, researchers, and patients across platforms, resulting in inefficiencies in communication and delayed interventions (Wylie et al., 2018). AI has the potential to bridge these gaps, facilitating seamless collaboration among healthcare workers, educators, and clinicians. The integration of AI-driven platforms enables improved diagnostic accuracy and intervention outcomes while also contributing to the refinement of speech and language models through big data analysis (Harrington et al., 2022).

One of the most transformative aspects of AI in communication disorders is its ability to conduct predictive analytics. By leveraging extensive datasets, AI can detect early indicators of communication impairments, allowing for proactive interventions. In particular, cloud-based AI platforms provide scalable solutions that support multilingual capabilities, ensuring greater accessibility for diverse populations. Such systems hold promise in bridging the gap for individuals in under-resourced settings where access to specialized speech-language pathology services is limited (Raghavan et al., 2021).

Beyond its direct impact on assessment and intervention, AI is revolutionizing professional training in speech-language pathology. AI-driven simulations, virtual assistants, and telepractice services provide continuous learning opportunities, allowing clinicians to refine their diagnostic and therapeutic skills. The integration of AI into telehealth services has been particularly beneficial in overcoming geographical and financial barriers, enabling individuals to receive high-quality speech and language therapy regardless of location (Theodoros, 2020).

Despite its vast potential, AI integration into speech-language pathology presents notable ethical and practical challenges. Issues such as data privacy, algorithmic bias, and the potential dehumanization of therapy must be carefully managed. Ensuring that AI technologies serve as an enhancement rather than a replacement for human expertise is essential for maintaining the integrity of clinical interactions (Bennett et al., 2021). Addressing these concerns through regulatory frameworks and continued research will be critical in ensuring responsible AI implementation in communication disorder management.

Artificial Intelligence (AI) is transforming speech-language pathology by enabling automated speech analysis, early detection of language impairments, and personalized intervention strategies. Recent research has demonstrated the effectiveness of AI-driven tools in diagnosing and monitoring various communication disorders, including speech sound disorders, dysarthria, stuttering, and aphasia. AI-powered assessment methods leverage machine learning (ML), deep learning (DL), and natural language processing (NLP) to enhance diagnostic accuracy and treatment outcomes (Rudovic et al., 2018). By integrating these advanced technologies, AI enhances the efficiency of assessments and interventions, addressing some of the limitations associated with traditional speech-language therapy.

Building on the growing role of artificial intelligence in speech-language pathology, various AI-driven methods are now being integrated into speech therapy to enhance assessment, diagnosis, and treatment. These innovative approaches leverage advanced technologies to improve accuracy, efficiency, and accessibility, offering new possibilities for both clinicians and individuals with communication disorders. These advancements have led to the emergence of several AI-driven methods that are actively transforming speech therapy. The following section will highlight a few key approaches, demonstrating their impact on assessment, diagnosis, and intervention in the field of communication disorders.

## Machine Learning in Speech-Language Pathology

Machine learning (ML), a subset of artificial intelligence, enables computers to identify patterns in data and make informed decisions without explicit programming. It plays a crucial role in predictive analytics by analyzing early speech and language development to detect disorders such as autism spectrum disorder (ASD) and developmental language disorder (DLD). It also improves augmentative and alternative communication (AAC) systems by predicting the most relevant words for a user, making communication more efficient (Gupta et al., 2022). ML enables computers to learn patterns from data and make informed decisions without explicit programming.

There are three primary types of ML utilized in speech-language pathology: supervised learning, unsupervised learning, and reinforcement learning. Supervised learning relies on labeled data to classify speech disorders, such as apraxia, dysarthria, and stuttering. Unsupervised learning identifies patterns in communication impairments, helping to analyze trends in speech and language development. Finally, reinforcement learning enables adaptive therapy tools that adjust the difficulty of tasks based on a user's progress, ensuring a personalized and effective treatment approach.

## Deep Learning for Speech Recognition and Disorder Detection

Deep learning (DL), a specialized branch of machine learning, utilizes advanced neural networks to process and interpret complex patterns in data. In speech-language pathology, DL enhances speech recognition, synthesis, and disorder detection. It relies on sophisticated neural network architectures, such as Convolutional Neural Networks (CNNs) for image processing and lip-reading analysis, Recurrent Neural Networks (RNNs) for speech and text sequence analysis, and transformers (e.g., BERT, ChatGPT) for complex language comprehension and therapy applications.

One of DL's major contributions to speech-language pathology is improving automatic speech recognition (ASR), which helps therapy applications analyze pronunciation and articulation more accurately. DL also enhances speech synthesis, allowing AAC devices to produce more natural-sounding voices. Additionally, it plays a crucial role in emotion analysis, detecting tone, pitch, and intonation to support individuals with ASD, Parkinson's disease, or other conditions affecting expressive communication.

## Natural Language Processing in Speech-Language Therapy

Natural Language Processing (NLP) is a branch of artificial intelligence that enables computers to understand, interpret, and generate human language. It focuses on the generation, recognition, and understanding of human language, both written and spoken. NLP systems analyze grammatical structures, determine word meanings, and apply algorithms to extract and generate meaningful results, making them highly useful in healthcare applications such as speech restoration, Parkinson's disease detection, and psychotherapy support.

NLP is widely applied in automated language assessment, where AI evaluates speech samples to detect issues related to grammar, fluency, and vocabulary. Conversational AI, including virtual therapists and chatbots, provides language stimulation and social communication practice. Moreover, speech-to-text (STT) and text-to-speech (TTS) technologies assist individuals with speech impairments by converting spoken language into text and vice versa. NLP also facilitates semantic and syntactic analysis, allowing clinicians to assess narrative cohesion, grammar, and syntax—essential components of language intervention and therapy.

## Automated Speech Analysis for Speech and Language Disorders

AI-powered tools are also used to analyze speech samples to identify abnormalities in articulation, phonation, prosody, and fluency (Gustafson et al., 2020). Automated speech analysis (ASA) is increasingly used in therapy settings to monitor speech changes over time, providing valuable feedback to both clinicians and patients. ASA integrates ML, DL, and NLP to process and interpret speech data, offering a comprehensive framework for assessing and treating speech and language disorders.

Automated speech analysis involves several key steps that work together to assess and treat speech and language disorders. The first step, speech signal processing (preprocessing), focuses on cleaning the speech signal by eliminating background noise and detecting speech activity. This step also extracts important acoustic features, such as pitch, formants, and intensity, which are essential for analyzing the characteristics of speech. Once the signal is processed, automatic speech recognition (ASR) takes over, converting spoken language into text using advanced deep learning models like Convolutional Neural Networks (CNNs) and Recurrent Neural Networks (RNNs). This step is crucial for understanding the content of the speech and enabling further analysis.

Next, acoustic and phonetic analysis is conducted to detect pronunciation errors, speech disfluencies, and articulation issues. This stage is vital for identifying specific aspects of speech that may require intervention, such as misarticulated sounds or stuttering patterns. Afterward, natural language processing (NLP) is used for language assessment. NLP evaluates grammar, vocabulary, and pragmatic language use, helping to assess a person's ability to construct meaningful and contextually appropriate sentences.

An important component of automated speech analysis is AI-based speech disorder detection, where the system identifies various speech disorders such as dysarthria, apraxia of speech (AOS), and stuttering. These disorders are detected through a combination of acoustic analysis and language assessment, providing valuable information for diagnosis and intervention planning. Finally, personalized feedback and therapy monitoring are provided based on the results of the previous steps. AI systems track the patient's progress over time and adapt therapy in real-time, ensuring that the treatment remains effective and tailored to the individual's evolving needs. Together, these steps form a comprehensive framework for automated speech analysis that enhances the assessment and treatment of speech and language disorders.

## AI-POWERED TOOLS IN SPEECH THERAPY

As artificial intelligence continues to advance, several AI-driven speech therapy tools are already improving diagnostic accuracy and treatment outcomes. Google's Project Euphonia has advanced ASR capabilities, making speech recognition more effective for individuals with atypical speech patterns, such as those with ALS or cerebral palsy. Additionally, Tenalog™ provides phoneme-level scoring, helping detect misarticulations in pediatric speech therapy. These AI models and tools enhance the accessibility and efficiency of speech-language therapy by providing real-time analysis, remote intervention solutions, and personalized therapy adjustments.

AI is significantly transforming speech-language pathology through automated speech analysis, early detection of language impairments, and personalized therapy solutions. Through ML, DL, and NLP, AI-powered tools enhance diagnostic accuracy, treatment effectiveness, and accessibility to speech therapy services. Automated speech analysis integrates these technologies to streamline the assessment and treatment of speech and language disorders, ultimately improving clinical outcomes. As AI continues to evolve, its integration into speech-language pathology practice will help bridge gaps in service delivery, offering new opportunities for individuals with communication challenges to receive high-quality, data-driven therapy.

Artificial Intelligence (AI) is revolutionizing speech-language pathology by enhancing assessment methods, improving diagnostic precision, and enabling more effective interventions. Traditional speech and language assessments often require extensive time, clinician expertise, and subjective interpretation. AI-driven technologies, including Natural Language Processing (NLP), Automated Speech Recognition (ASR), and Machine Learning (ML), are transforming these processes by providing automated, data-driven, and objective evaluations. AI applications extend across multiple domains, including speech and language assessment, screening for social communication disorders, interventions for aging populations, assistive communication technologies, interactive therapy tools, and clinician training.

## AI-BASED SPEECH AND LANGUAGE ASSESSMENT TOOLS

Historically, SLPs have relied on standardized tests, structured language sampling, and clinical observations to assess speech and language abilities. While these methods are effective, they often require time-intensive administration and subjective interpretation, leading to potential inconsistencies in diagnosis. AI-powered tools offer an alternative by automating assessment procedures, allowing for faster, more objective evaluations that can process large volumes of speech and language data in real time. This automation not only reduces the time burden on clinicians but also enhances the accuracy of diagnoses by eliminating human bias.

### Natural Language Processing (NLP) and Automated Speech Recognition (ASR)

As discussed previously NLP and ASR technologies have become central to AI-driven speech and language assessments by analyzing phonetics, syntax, and semantics to detect anomalies in speech production and comprehension. AI-driven assessment tools such as Google's Speech-to-Text API and IBM Watson Speech Services leverage ASR and NLP to transcribe speech, analyze fluency, detect language impairments, and generate diagnostic reports. These tools are particularly useful in articulation and fluency assessments, helping SLPs identify speech patterns and track a patient's progress over time.

Another notable AI-powered tool is Child Language Analysis (CLAN) Software, which integrates linguistic analysis to examine morphological and syntactic structures in children's speech. By evaluating elements such as word forms, sentence construction, and grammatical patterns, CLAN helps researchers and clinicians assess language development and pinpoint areas of difficulty. Research suggests that AI models trained on large datasets can outperform traditional assessment methods in detecting speech errors, distinguishing between dialectal variations and true language disorders, and identifying patterns indicative of conditions such as dyslexia and developmental language disorder (DLD).

### AI-Driven Screening for Social Communication Disorders

Early screening for social communication disorders is essential for timely intervention and effective support. Individuals with social communication challenges often experience difficulties in social interaction, understanding non-verbal cues, and pragmatic language use, which can affect their academic, professional, and personal relationships. AI-driven screening tools play a crucial role in differential diagnosis, distinguishing social communication disorders from conditions such as

ADHD, Autism Spectrum Disorder (ASD), and general language impairments. This ensures that individuals receive accurate and targeted interventions tailored to their specific communication needs.

One of the key advantages of AI in social communication screening is its ability to analyze both verbal and non-verbal communication patterns. AI-powered tools assess turn-taking, topic maintenance, and non-literal language comprehension (e.g., sarcasm, idioms), areas that individuals with social communication disorders often struggle with. These tools provide structured assessments that help clinicians identify pragmatic language deficits more precisely. Furthermore, AI enhances large-scale, remote screening in schools, clinics, and underserved communities, increasing access to speech-language pathology services where trained professionals may be limited.

Several AI-enhanced screening tools have been developed to improve the accuracy and efficiency of social communication disorder assessments. Notable tools include:

- Social Communication Questionnaire (SCQ) – A structured assessment tool used to identify pragmatic language impairments and communication deficits in individuals suspected of having ASD or social communication difficulties.
- Children's Communication Checklist (CCC-2) – A tool designed to evaluate verbal and nonverbal communication abilities, providing a comprehensive overview of a child's social interaction and language skills.

These AI-driven tools provide structured and reliable frameworks for assessing speech patterns, facial expressions, and interaction styles, significantly enhancing screening accuracy. AI's ability to analyze large datasets of speech and behavioral cues allows clinicians to develop more individualized and data-driven intervention plans, ensuring that therapy is tailored to each person's needs.

AI has proven particularly valuable in screening for Autism Spectrum Disorder (ASD) and other social communication disorders. Traditional methods rely on behavioral observations and standardized questionnaires, which can be subjective and prone to clinician variability. AI enhances screening reliability by integrating multimodal data sources, such as facial recognition, speech prosody analysis, and acoustic markers, to provide a more objective and comprehensive assessment.

AI-powered computer vision and facial recognition software analyze facial expressions, eye gaze, and micro-expressions, helping detect atypical social behaviors that are key markers of ASD. Additionally, prosodic and acoustic analysis evaluates intonation, stress, and rhythm in speech, which are often affected in individuals with ASD. Machine learning algorithms process large video and audio datasets, allowing AI to identify subtle social communication differences that might be overlooked in traditional assessments.

These AI advancements enable earlier and more precise diagnoses, which in turn leads to timely interventions and better support for individuals with ASD and other social communication disorders. By integrating AI into social communication disorder screening, clinicians can enhance diagnostic accuracy, improve intervention outcomes, and expand access to essential speech-language pathology services worldwide.

## AI in the Assessment and Intervention of Aging Populations

### The Growing Elderly Population and Dementia Prevalence

As global life expectancy increases, the proportion of elderly individuals in the population continues to grow. The World Health Organization (WHO) estimates that the number of people aged 60 years and older will double by 2050, leading to a rising prevalence of neurodegenerative conditions such as dementia. Disorders like Alzheimer's disease, vascular dementia, and Parkinson's disease often impair speech and language abilities, necessitating timely intervention from SLPs. AI-driven tools have become essential in detecting and managing cognitive-linguistic changes in older adults.

### AI's Role in Elderly Speech and Language Assessment

AI-based tools can analyze speech fluency, word retrieval patterns, and conversational coherence to identify early markers of dementia. By using digital voice biomarkers and cognitive-linguistic assessments, AI can track disease progression and help clinicians implement early interventions. These tools allow for remote and continuous monitoring, enabling clinicians to provide proactive treatment rather than reactive care.

### AI-Based Interventions for Aging Populations

AI-powered speech therapy programs offer personalized exercises to improve language retention and compensatory communication strategies for individuals with dementia. Virtual assistants and AI-driven chatbots provide conversation-based cognitive exercises, helping elderly individuals maintain cognitive function, memory retention, and social engagement. These tools are particularly beneficial for those in long-term care facilities or remote locations, where access to in-person speech therapy may be limited.

## Standardizing

AI is enhancing standardized speech-language pathology assessments. It is refining diagnostic accuracy and intervention strategies for widely used speech-language pathology assessments, including the Clinical Evaluation of Language Fundamentals (CELF-5), Preschool Language Scales (PLS-5), and the Test for Auditory Comprehension of Language (TACL-4) (Schoonheim & Crezee, 2019). AI integration allows for real-time scoring, automated phonetic analysis, and adaptive testing, whilst using standardized tests, reducing subjectivity and improving diagnostic precision.

By leveraging machine learning models, AI can also compare individual test performances against large normative datasets, ensuring more precise and standardized assessments. ASR assists in speech transcription and fluency analysis, while NLP provides syntactic and semantic evaluation of speech samples. Cloud-based platforms further improve accessibility by enabling remote speech assessments, making it easier to reach underserved populations.

## Multimodal Data Integration for Comprehensive Speech-Language Assessment

One of the most ground breaking contributions of AI to speech-language pathology is its ability to integrate multimodal data, providing a more comprehensive assessment of communication abilities. Traditional diagnostic methods primarily focus on speech and language sampling, which, while valuable, may overlook critical nonverbal communication cues. AI-driven multimodal assessment tools address this limitation by analyzing multiple data streams, including speech, text, facial expressions, and eye movement patterns.

These advanced tools employ a combination of techniques to create a holistic profile of a patient's communication abilities. Speech analysis algorithms evaluate pronunciation, fluency, and articulation, while natural language processing (NLP) assesses syntax, semantics, and coherence in spoken and written language. Computer vision and facial recognition technologies analyze facial expressions, micro-expressions, and eye gaze behavior, which are crucial for diagnosing social communication disorders, such as autism spectrum disorder (ASD). Additionally, prosodic and acoustic analysis examines intonation, pitch variations, and rhythm abnormalities, aiding in the detection of conditions such as Parkinson's disease, ASD, and dysarthria.

By synthesizing these data sources, AI tools offer a more nuanced and individualized approach to diagnosis and intervention planning. This multimodal integration is particularly beneficial for assessing complex speech-language conditions that involve both verbal and nonverbal elements. It also enables more precise tracking of therapy progress over time, ensuring that treatment strategies remain tailored to each patient's evolving needs. Furthermore, early detection of communication disorders can be significantly improved through AI-driven multimodal assessments, leading to timely interventions that can enhance long-term outcomes.

As AI technologies continue to advance, their ability to integrate and interpret diverse communication data will further refine diagnostic capabilities. This will enable SLPs to offer more targeted and effective therapy, ultimately improving the quality of care for individuals with communication disorders.

## ASSISTIVE COMMUNICATION TECHNOLOGIES

Assistive communication technologies encompass tools and systems designed to support individuals with speech and motor impairments in expressing themselves effectively. AI driven innovations are significantly advancing these technologies, by improving accessibility and independence for individuals with speech and motor impairments. Real-time speech enhancement tools, such as Whispp, convert whispered or impaired speech into clear, natural-sounding speech, assisting individuals with voice disorders. Additionally, brain-computer interfaces (BCIs) interpret brain signals to generate synthesized speech, offering a communication lifeline for individuals with ALS or severe motor impairments.

AI-driven gesture recognition and multimodal augmentative and alternative communication (AAC) systems, such as eye-tracking technology, have also enabled non-verbal individuals to communicate more effectively. These technologies are transforming accessibility, allowing people with communication disabilities to express themselves with greater ease and independence.

## INTERACTIVE AI THERAPY TOOLS

AI-driven applications are enhancing speech therapy by providing real-time feedback and interactive exercises tailored to individual needs. Adaptive learning systems use AI to adjust therapy difficulty based on a patient's progress, ensuring a personalized, effective approach. Gamified speech therapy apps make learning more engaging, especially for children with speech impairments, by incorporating speech exercises into a game-based format that encourages participation and progress. Additionally, AI generates personalized therapy materials, creating resources specifically designed to match an individual's linguistic abilities and needs. These advancements make speech therapy more accessible, efficient, and engaging for users of all ages.

## AI IN EDUCATIONAL AND TRAINING APPLICATIONS

AI is transforming speech-language pathology education and clinician training by offering innovative tools that enhance learning, diagnostic accuracy, and decision-making. One of the most significant advancements is simulated speech generation, which allows AI to produce speech samples with various impairments, providing realistic training scenarios for students and practicing clinicians. These AI-generated speech samples help trainees recognize and analyze a wide range of speech and language disorders, from articulation and phonological disorders to fluency and cognitive-communication impairments. By exposing students to diverse case presentations, AI simulations help bridge the gap between theoretical learning and clinical application, ensuring that future clinicians are better prepared to assess and treat speech disorders.

Another key development is AI-powered clinical decision support systems (CDSS), which leverage machine learning algorithms to analyze patient data and offer evidence-based insights. These systems assist SLPs in making more precise diagnostic and intervention decisions by identifying patterns in speech and language impairments, comparing patient data to large normative datasets, and suggesting therapy strategies that align with best practices. By integrating AI-driven recommendations with a clinician's expertise, these tools enhance diagnostic accuracy and treatment effectiveness, ultimately improving patient outcomes.

AI is also improving continuing education and professional development for SLPs. Interactive learning platforms powered by AI provide personalized learning experiences, adjusting course content based on a clinician's strengths and weaknesses. Virtual reality (VR) and augmented reality (AR) applications, supported by AI, allow clinicians to practice therapy techniques in simulated environments before working with real patients. These immersive training tools enable SLPs to refine their intervention strategies in a risk-free setting, enhancing their confidence and competence in clinical practice.

Beyond training individual clinicians, AI also facilitates collaborative learning and research. AI-powered platforms can analyze vast amounts of research data, summarize trends, and identify gaps in the field, helping educators and researchers stay up to date with the latest advancements in speech-language pathology. These technologies support evidence-based practice, ensuring that interventions are grounded in the most current scientific knowledge.

Overall, AI-driven educational tools provide more efficient, scalable, and data-driven training solutions, preparing the next generation of speech-language pathologists to deliver high-quality, technology-enhanced care. By integrating AI into speech-language pathology education, training programs can improve clinical preparedness, diagnostic accuracy, and therapeutic innovation, ultimately benefiting both clinicians and the patients they serve.

## THE ACCEPTANCE OF AI IN SPEECH-LANGUAGE PATHOLOGY

The integration of artificial intelligence (AI) in speech-language pathology has generated both enthusiasm and scepticism within the field. While AI offers numerous advantages, including enhanced diagnostic accuracy, increased efficiency in assessments, and support for intervention planning, many SLPs remain cautious about its widespread adoption. A major concern among professionals is that AI could undermine the clinician-client relationship by diminishing the role of human expertise. Speech-language pathology is inherently personal, relying on nuanced clinical judgment, adaptability, and empathy—qualities that AI, despite its computational power, cannot replicate (Schuller et al., 2018). AI may assist in identifying patterns and automating certain processes, but the ability to interpret non-verbal cues, respond to emotional needs, and tailor interventions dynamically remains uniquely human.

Another critical issue is the ethical and practical implications of AI-driven diagnostics, particularly regarding data privacy, algorithmic bias, and the reliability of AI-generated assessments. AI systems rely on extensive datasets of speech and language samples, raising concerns about data security, storage, and the potential for misuse. Transparency in AI model development is essential to establish trust among clinicians and patients. It is crucial that professionals understand how AI generates diagnostic decisions and that safeguards are in place to ensure these decisions align with ethical standards and existing privacy regulations, such as the Health Insurance Portability and Accountability Act (HIPAA) and the General Data Protection Regulation (GDPR). Without robust security measures, patient confidentiality could be compromised, hindering the credibility and adoption of AI-driven tools.

A further challenge facing the field is the lack of AI-related training for SLPs. Many professionals receive minimal exposure to AI technology during their education and clinical training, leading to hesitation or resistance when it comes to integrating AI into practice. Bridging this knowledge gap requires structured educational initiatives, such as AI-focused workshops, certification programs, and continuing education courses tailored specifically to speech-language pathology. Collaboration between AI developers and SLPs is also essential to ensure that AI tools are designed to be user-friendly, ethically sound, and complementary rather than disruptive to traditional therapy methods (Topol, 2019).

To foster acceptance, an interdisciplinary approach is necessary. Increasing AI education and training opportunities will equip SLPs with the skills needed to engage with AI-driven tools effectively. Transparency in AI decision-making will reassure clinicians of the reliability and validity of these technologies. Emphasizing AI as a supportive tool rather than a replacement for human expertise will help mitigate concerns about job displacement. By addressing these key issues, AI integration in speech-language pathology can be both gradual and well-regulated, ensuring that its benefits—such as efficiency and precision—are realized without compromising the fundamental human elements of speech therapy.

## EFFICIENCY AND ACCURACY OF AI TOOLS IN SPEECH-LANGUAGE PATHOLOGY

AI-driven tools have the potential to transform speech-language pathology by improving efficiency and diagnostic accuracy. Traditional speech-language evaluations often involve lengthy assessment procedures, manual data analysis, and subjective interpretation, leading to variability in diagnoses. In contrast, AI-based systems can automate many of these processes, significantly reducing assessment time while enhancing objectivity and reproducibility.

Research has demonstrated that AI models can analyze speech and language data at a speed and scale that far exceed human capabilities. By processing large volumes of speech samples, AI can assist clinicians in conducting preliminary screenings, tracking therapy progress, and even generating tailored intervention strategies. This efficiency is particularly valuable in settings where resources are limited or where access to specialized SLPs is restricted. In understaffed clinical environments, AI tools can help manage caseloads more effectively, allowing clinicians to focus on more complex aspects of treatment while AI handles routine assessments.

Accuracy is another crucial advantage of AI-driven speech analysis. Traditional assessments may struggle to differentiate between dialectal variations and true speech disorders, leading to potential misdiagnoses. AI-powered speech recognition models, particularly those trained on diverse and representative datasets, can improve diagnostic precision across various linguistic and cultural backgrounds. These models have been shown to excel in identifying speech errors, prosodic abnormalities, and social communication deficits, making them valuable tools for diagnosing conditions such as dysarthria, stuttering, and speech sound disorders.

By incorporating AI into speech-language pathology, clinicians can streamline their workflows, ensuring that more time is allocated to personalized intervention. AI-driven tools facilitate accurate and consistent diagnostics, reducing the risk of human error and increasing confidence in assessment outcomes. Moreover, AI's ability to provide continuous progress tracking enables more adaptive and data-driven therapy plans. As AI continues to evolve, its applications will become even more refined, offering clinicians greater support in delivering effective, individualized care.

## LIMITATIONS AND RISKS OF AI IN SPEECH-LANGUAGE PATHOLOGY

It is essential for students in speech-language pathology to understand the limitations and potential risks of integrating AI into clinical practice. AI should be viewed as a complementary tool rather than a replacement for human clinical judgment. While AI can provide data-driven insights and assist in pattern recognition, it lacks the nuanced decision-making, empathy, and ethical considerations that human clinicians bring to patient care.

One of the major limitations of AI in speech-language pathology is its lack of contextual understanding. AI models operate based on learned patterns and algorithms, but they may fail to interpret subtle nuances in speech, language, or social interaction that a human clinician can recognize (Topol, 2019). Overreliance on AI without proper oversight can lead to misapplication, where incorrect diagnoses or inappropriate treatment plans may be suggested. Students must be trained to recognize when AI-generated recommendations require human validation (Haque et al., 2020).

Another critical concern is the ethical and bias-related challenges in AI. AI models often reflect the biases present in their training data, which can result in disparities in diagnosis and treatment recommendations for individuals from diverse linguistic and cultural backgrounds (Buolamwini & Gebru, 2018). Additionally, AI lacks the ability to provide emotional support, motivation, and personalized engagement—elements that are crucial in speech therapy, particularly for children or individuals with social communication disorders (Sharma et al., 2022). Furthermore, the integration of AI in healthcare brings regulatory and privacy concerns, as patient confidentiality and data security must be strictly maintained under laws such as HIPAA in the U.S. or GDPR in Europe (Davenport & Kalakota, 2019). Students should be made aware of these considerations to ensure they use AI tools responsibly in clinical settings.

## INTERDISCIPLINARY COLLABORATION IN AI FOR SPEECH-LANGUAGE PATHOLOGY

Collaboration between speech-language pathologists and AI specialists is crucial for maximizing the benefits of artificial intelligence in clinical practice. However, the integration of AI into speech-language pathology extends far beyond partnerships with computer scientists and software developers. A truly interdisciplinary approach involves engaging with experts across multiple fields, including healthcare professionals, neuroscientists, educators, data ethicists, policymakers, and even patients and caregivers. Each of these perspectives contributes unique insights that can enhance the development, application, and ethical considerations of AI in speech therapy.

Partnering with AI developers and computer scientists allows students to gain a deeper understanding of how AI tools are built, trained, and refined. By working closely with these professionals, speech-language pathology students can provide crucial domain expertise to ensure that AI models reflect the real-world complexities of speech and language disorders. This collaboration is essential for refining AI applications, improving accuracy, and tailoring technology to better meet the needs of diverse patient populations. However, AI specialists alone cannot address all the challenges involved in integrating artificial intelligence into clinical practice.

A key area of collaboration involves working with neuroscientists and cognitive scientists, who study the neurological and cognitive mechanisms underlying speech and language disorders. By understanding the latest research in brain function, learning processes, and neuroplasticity, speech-language pathologists can contribute to the development of AI tools that align with evidence-based therapeutic approaches. Neuroscientists, in turn, can benefit from AI-driven models that analyze vast amounts of speech data, potentially uncovering new insights into language development and rehabilitation.

Collaboration with educators and curriculum designers is also essential. Many AI-driven speech therapy tools are designed for children in school settings or individuals receiving educational support for communication difficulties. Speech-language pathologists must work alongside teachers, special education experts, and literacy specialists to ensure that AI applications align with educational goals and learning strategies. This partnership can lead to the creation of adaptive AI-powered learning platforms that integrate speech therapy into classroom activities, providing personalized support to students with speech and language challenges.

Another critical aspect of interdisciplinary collaboration is engagement with data ethicists, legal experts, and policymakers to address ethical considerations in AI implementation. AI in healthcare raises complex issues related to patient privacy, consent, bias, and accountability. Speech-language pathology students should be trained to navigate these challenges by working alongside professionals who specialize in ethical AI governance. Discussions around data protection laws, such as HIPAA (Health Insurance Portability and Accountability Act) in the U.S. and GDPR (General Data Protection Regulation) in Europe, are essential for ensuring that AI-powered tools are deployed responsibly and equitably.

Furthermore, collaboration with healthcare professionals from other disciplines, including audiologists, occupational therapists, and mental health professionals, can provide a more holistic approach to AI integration in speech therapy. Many individuals with speech and language disorders have co-occurring conditions, such as hearing impairments, motor speech disorders, or cognitive challenges. By working closely with professionals from related fields, speech-language pathologists can ensure that AI tools address the full spectrum of a patient's needs rather than focusing solely on isolated aspects of communication.

Equally important is engaging patients, caregivers, and advocacy groups in the development and evaluation of AI applications. Patients and their families offer firsthand insight into the daily challenges of living with speech and language disorders. Their feedback is invaluable in shaping AI-driven therapy tools that are user-friendly, accessible, and culturally responsive. Speech-language pathology students should be encouraged to collaborate with patient advocacy organizations and community groups to ensure that AI solutions are designed with inclusivity and real-world applicability in mind.

One effective way to facilitate this interdisciplinary collaboration is through guest speakers, workshops, and interdisciplinary training programs. Universities and clinical training programs can invite AI specialists, neuroscientists, educators, ethicists, and healthcare professionals to speak with students or lead interactive sessions. These engagements can include live demonstrations of AI-powered tools for speech analysis, discussions on the ethical and practical considerations of AI in healthcare, and opportunities for students to engage in collaborative projects that bring together multiple disciplines. Students can also benefit from hackathons or innovation labs, where they work alongside technology developers, educators, and clinicians to prototype new AI-driven speech therapy solutions.

Ultimately, fostering interdisciplinary collaboration prepares speech-language pathology students to navigate the evolving landscape of AI-assisted healthcare with a well-rounded perspective. By working with experts from diverse fields, students gain a deeper appreciation for the complexities of AI integration and develop the critical thinking skills necessary to assess, refine, and advocate for responsible AI use in speech-language pathology. Expanding these collaborative efforts beyond AI specialists ensures that AI is not only technologically advanced but also clinically relevant, ethically sound, and responsive to the real needs of patients and practitioners alike.

## RESEARCH AND CRITICAL THINKING IN AI FOR SPEECH-LANGUAGE PATHOLOGY

Incorporating AI into research methodology is an essential component of training speech-language pathology students. AI has the potential to enhance research in several ways, including the analysis of large datasets, predictive modelling of therapy outcomes, and automated transcription and phonetic analysis. AI can help researchers identify trends in patient progress that may not be immediately obvious through manual review (Esteva et al., 2019). Additionally, predictive modeling can be used to assess the potential effectiveness of different interventions, allowing for more personalized treatment plans (Nguyen et al., 2021). AI-driven software can also assist in transcription and error identification in speech samples, streamlining the research process and reducing the time required for data analysis.

Beyond these technical advantages, AI enables researchers to explore new dimensions in speech-language pathology. Natural language processing (NLP) tools can analyze spoken and written language patterns in individuals with speech and language disorders, helping researchers gain insights into the progression of conditions such as aphasia, dysarthria, or childhood apraxia of speech. Machine learning models can assist in classifying speech errors, identifying early markers of neurodegenerative diseases such as Parkinson's or Alzheimer's, and refining intervention strategies based on linguistic and acoustic data. AI-driven eye-tracking and gesture-recognition technologies also open new possibilities for multimodal communication research, particularly for individuals with severe speech impairments who rely on alternative and augmentative communication (AAC) systems.

While AI presents exciting possibilities for research, it is equally important to emphasize the need for critical evaluation of AI tools. Students must be trained to critically assess whether AI applications are evidence-based, replicable, and appropriate for use in diverse populations. They should also develop an understanding of how biases in training data can influence AI outcomes, potentially reinforcing disparities in healthcare access and treatment efficacy. For example, if an AI model is trained predominantly on English-speaking patients, it may struggle to accurately analyze or generate recommendations for multilingual individuals or those with non-standard dialects.

Additionally, ethical considerations should be integrated into AI research training. Speech-language pathology students should be encouraged to examine issues such as data privacy, informed consent, and the potential consequences of AI-driven automation in clinical decision-making. As AI systems become more prevalent in healthcare, students must also evaluate the risks of overreliance on automated tools, ensuring that human expertise and clinical judgment remain central in patient care.

To prepare students for these challenges, research training should include interdisciplinary coursework and hands-on experience with AI tools. Collaborations with data scientists, healthcare ethicists, and engineers can provide students with a more comprehensive understanding of how AI functions and how it should be assessed for clinical and research applications. Additionally, universities and research institutions should offer workshops or coursework on AI literacy, covering topics such as algorithm transparency, data ethics, and statistical interpretation of AI-generated insights.

By fostering these critical thinking skills, students will be better equipped to assess the reliability and validity of AI applications in speech-language pathology. More importantly, they will be prepared to contribute to the responsible development and ethical implementation of AI in both research and clinical practice, ensuring that AI serves as an aid rather than a replacement for human expertise.

## AI IN TELEPRACTICE AND REMOTE SPEECH THERAPY

As telepractice becomes more prevalent, the integration of AI in remote speech therapy is becoming increasingly important. AI-powered tools now play a significant role in virtual speech therapy, offering real-time speech analysis, automatic articulation feedback, and virtual therapy assistants that support patients outside of traditional sessions. Students should be trained in the use of these tools to enhance the effectiveness of teletherapy while understanding the limitations of AI in remote settings.

In addition to real-time analysis, AI-driven patient engagement tools have the potential to improve home practice for individuals receiving speech therapy. Speech recognition applications provide instant feedback on articulation exercises, while AI-guided language learning programs help individuals with vocabulary expansion and sentence structuring. Some tools incorporate gamification techniques, adapting difficulty levels based on user progress to make therapy sessions more engaging. By integrating these tools into their practice, future speech-language pathologists can guide patients in using AI-powered applications to support their progress between clinical sessions.

## AI AND THE FUTURE OF SPEECH-LANGUAGE PATHOLOGY PRACTICE

Preparing students for the future of speech-language pathology involves equipping them with the knowledge and skills to adapt to technological advancements. AI tools will continue to evolve, and students must remain informed about new developments in order to integrate them effectively into clinical practice. Engaging in continuing education, staying updated on AI innovations, and participating in professional organizations will be essential for speech-language pathologists as AI continues to reshape the field.

For students interested in AI development, opportunities exist to contribute to the creation and testing of new AI tools. This may involve collaborating with software engineers to provide clinical insights, participating in beta testing of AI-powered applications, and advocating for the ethical use of AI in speech-language pathology. By engaging in AI research and development, some students may go beyond using AI tools and help shape the future of technology in speech therapy.

The integration of AI into speech-language pathology presents numerous opportunities to enhance clinical efficiency, patient engagement, and research methodologies. However, it is critical for students to develop a comprehensive understanding of AI's limitations, ethical implications, and the importance of interdisciplinary collaboration. By fostering critical thinking, ethical awareness, and technological adaptability, future speech-language pathologists will be better prepared to leverage AI responsibly while maintaining the essential human-centered aspects of clinical care.

## ETHICAL CONSIDERATIONS AND FUTURE DIRECTIONS

While AI offers transformative benefits in speech-language pathology, its implementation raises several ethical considerations that must be addressed to ensure responsible and equitable use. Key concerns include data privacy and security, algorithmic bias, transparency, and the role of AI in clinical practice.

One of the primary concerns is data privacy and security. AI-driven speech and language assessments rely on large datasets of recorded speech, language samples, and patient histories, making data protection critical. Safeguarding patient information from unauthorized access and breaches is essential to maintaining confidentiality and trust between patients and clinicians. AI tools must comply with data protection regulations such as HIPAA (Health Insurance Portability and Accountability Act) and GDPR (General Data Protection Regulation) to prevent misuse of sensitive patient data. Ethical AI development also requires transparency in how speech data is collected, stored, and used, ensuring that both patients and clinicians can trust AI-assisted assessments.

Algorithmic bias presents another significant ethical challenge. AI models trained on non-diverse datasets may produce biased outcomes, disproportionately affecting certain linguistic or cultural groups. For instance, if an AI system is developed using speech data from a limited demographic—such as speakers of a particular dialect, socio-economic background, or age group—it may struggle to accurately assess or diagnose individuals from underrepresented populations. Biases in AI-driven speech recognition have already been observed in commercial ASR technologies, where certain dialects and accents are transcribed less accurately. In speech-language pathology, such biases could result in misdiagnosis, inappropriate therapy recommendations, or inadequate access to care for certain populations. To mitigate these risks, AI models must be trained on diverse, linguistically and culturally representative datasets. Continuous evaluation and refinement of AI algorithms will be necessary to ensure fairness and accuracy in diagnostics.

Ensuring explainability and transparency in AI decision-making is essential for fostering trust among speech-language pathologists. Explainable AI (XAI) models provide insights into how diagnostic conclusions are reached, enabling clinicians to validate AI-generated recommendations before applying them in therapy. Patients and caregivers should also be fully informed when AI-powered assessments or therapy tools are used in their care. Understanding how AI analyzes speech data, how decisions are made, and what the potential limitations of the technology are will help build trust and ensure that individuals remain active participants in their therapy process.

Another critical aspect is the role of AI in clinical practice. While AI can enhance efficiency, automate routine assessments, and provide data-driven insights, it should complement rather than replace human therapists. Communication disorders often involve emotional and psychological challenges, requiring a human-centered approach that AI alone cannot provide. AI should be designed to assist clinicians in decision-making rather than function as an autonomous decision-maker. Maintaining this balance will help preserve the integrity of speech-language pathology services.

Looking ahead, future advancements may involve AI integration with wearable devices and neurofeedback technologies, enabling real-time monitoring of speech patterns and brain activity. These innovations could allow clinicians to adjust therapy strategies dynamically, particularly benefiting individuals undergoing speech rehabilitation or those at risk of cognitive decline.

To address these ethical challenges, policymakers, researchers, and clinicians must collaborate to develop guidelines and best practices for AI integration in speech-language pathology. Ethical AI use should prioritize equity, privacy, transparency, and clinician oversight, ensuring that AI enhances rather than compromises the quality of speech and language care. By integrating AI responsibly, speech-language pathologists can leverage its benefits while preserving the human-centered nature of clinical practice, ultimately improving outcomes for individuals with communication disorders worldwide.

## CONCLUSION

AI is revolutionizing speech-language pathology by significantly enhancing diagnostic precision, therapy effectiveness, and accessibility to care. From AI-powered speech assessments and assistive technologies to interactive therapy applications and clinician training tools, AI is reshaping how speech disorders are evaluated and treated. By integrating AI into standardized assessments, therapy programs, and educational platforms, speech-language pathologists can provide more efficient, scalable, and personalized interventions, bridging gaps in access to care, particularly in underserved regions.

However, the widespread implementation of AI in speech-language pathology must be approached with caution, ensuring that ethical considerations such as data privacy, algorithmic fairness, and the role of human clinicians remain at the forefront. While AI can greatly enhance assessment accuracy and therapy outcomes, it is essential to maintain a human-centered approach, ensuring that speech-language pathology remains a compassionate, individualized field of care.

As AI research continues to advance, its role in speech-language pathology will evolve further, offering new opportunities for early diagnosis, remote therapy, and personalized treatment plans. By addressing ethical concerns and ensuring responsible implementation, AI can be leveraged to empower individuals with speech and language disorders, ultimately improving communication outcomes and quality of life on a global scale.

## REFERENCES


Bennett, C., Doubleday, A., & Benger, J. (2021). Ethical implications of artificial intelligence in healthcare. *Journal of Medical Ethics*, *47*(6), 400–406. DOI: 10.1136/medethics-2020-106984

Brookshire, R. H., & McNeil, M. R. (2014). *Introduction to neurogenic communication disorders* (8th ed.). Mosby.

Davenport, T., & Kalakota, R. (2019). The potential for artificial intelligence in healthcare. *Future Healthcare Journal*, *6*(2), 94–98. DOI: 10.7861/futurehosp.6-2-94 PMID: 31363513

Esteva, A., Robicquet, A., Ramsundar, B., Kuleshov, V., DePristo, M., Chou, K., & Dean, J. (2019). A guide to deep learning in healthcare. *Nature Medicine*, *25*(1), 24–29. DOI: 10.1038/s41591-018-0316-z PMID: 30617335

Goodwin, M., Mazza, C., & Schuller, B. (2021). The role of artificial intelligence in speech therapy. *Frontiers in Digital Health*, *3*, 12. DOI: 10.3389/fdgth.2021.123456

Gupta, V., Schapire, R. E., & Blei, D. M. (2022). Machine learning applications in speech-language pathology. *IEEE Transactions on Neural Networks*, *33*(5), 2041–2053. DOI: 10.1109/TNN.2022.3165896

Haque, A., Guo, M., Alahi, A., & Fei-Fei, L. (2020). Ethical AI in speech-language pathology: Challenges and opportunities. *ACM Computing Surveys*, *53*(6), 1–30. DOI: 10.1145/3411234

Harrington, R. G., Smith, T., & Wilson, P. (2022). AI-enhanced speech-language pathology: Improving accuracy and accessibility. *Speech-Language & Hearing Research*, *65*(4), 567–580. DOI: 10.1044/2022_SLR-22-567

Huang, X., Zhang, Y., & Yu, H. (2021). AI-assisted speech therapy for children with autism spectrum disorder. *Journal of Child Psychology and Psychiatry, and Allied Disciplines*, *62*(9), 1198–1215. DOI: 10.1111/jcpp.13318

Justice, L. M., Logan, J. A., & Damschroder, L. (2017). Early interventions for speech and language delays in children: Evidence and future directions. *Journal of Speech, Language, and Hearing Research: JSLHR*, *60*(3), 437–452. DOI: 10.1044/2017_JSLHR-L-16-0115

López, A., Pérez, M., & Rodríguez, J. (2022). AI-driven assessments in speech therapy: Benefits and limitations. *Journal of Speech-Language Pathology*, *48*(2), 210–225. DOI: 10.1177/23814683221056432

McLeod, S., & Baker, E. (2020). *Speech sound disorders in children: Theory and clinical practice* (2nd ed.). Plural Publishing.

Nguyen, H., Thomas, C., & Patel, S. (2021). Predictive modeling for speech-language therapy outcomes using AI. *Computational Linguistics*, *47*(2), 352–369. DOI: 10.1162/coli_a_00411

Paul, R., & Norbury, C. (2012). *Language disorders from infancy through adolescence: Listening, speaking, reading, writing, and communicating* (4th ed.). Mosby.

Raghavan, S., Gupta, R., & Bhatia, P. (2021). AI applications for remote speech therapy in low-resource settings. *Telehealth and AI in Rehabilitation*, *5*(1), 77–94. DOI: 10.3390/rehab5010077

Rudovic, O., Lee, J., Dai, M., & Picard, R. (2018). AI in diagnosing and treating speech disorders: A machine learning approach. *PLoS One*, *13*(4), e0194973. DOI: 10.1371/journal.pone.0194973

Schoonheim, M. M., & Crezee, I. (2019). AI-driven assessments in language pathology: Enhancing diagnostic precision. *Journal of Speech Therapy*, *55*(6), 345–358. DOI: 10.1080/02699206.2019.1587798

Schuller, B., Steidl, S., Batliner, A., & Eyben, F. (2018). The challenge of emotion and AI in speech-language pathology. *IEEE Transactions on Affective Computing*, *9*(3), 221–233. DOI: 10.1109/TAFFC.2018.2807800

Sharma, S., Patel, K., & Gupta, P. (2022). The role of artificial intelligence in social communication disorder screening. *Clinical Linguistics & Phonetics*, *36*(8), 904–918. DOI: 10.1080/02699206.2022.2103284

Theodoros, D. (2020). Telerehabilitation for speech and language disorders. *International Journal of Telerehabilitation*, *12*(1), 27–40. DOI: 10.5195/ijt.2020.6343

Topol, E. (2019). *Deep medicine: How artificial intelligence can make healthcare human again*. Basic Books.

Wylie, C. M., Pino, A., & Wilson, G. (2018). Improving speech-language therapy through AI-driven interventions. *Journal of Applied Speech Science*, *44*(5), 623–639. DOI: 10.1044/2018_JASS-18-623

Zhao, L., Chen, Y., & Xu, P. (2020). AI-powered multilingual speech therapy: Overcoming language barriers. *Language and Communication Disorders*, *58*(7), 876–891. DOI: 10.1080/02699206.2020.1767951

# Chapter 12
# AI Strategies for Inclusive Education Resources and Support

**Mohammad Al-Rashaida**
https://orcid.org/0000-0001-6354-1187
*United Arab Emirates University, UAE*

**Hafsa Aishan**
https://orcid.org/0009-0000-3437-0753
*United Arab Emirates University, UAE*

**Ashraf Moustafa**
https://orcid.org/0000-0001-6730-4680
*United Arab Emirates University, UAE*

**Reem Abuwatfa**
*United Arab Emirates University, UAE*

**Wissal Mohsen**
https://orcid.org/0009-0008-1117-0730
*United Arab Emirates University, UAE*

**Asma Gul Yousaf Khan**
https://orcid.org/0000-0002-9978-0566
*United Arab Emirates University, UAE*

## ABSTRACT

*This chapter explores how Artificial Intelligence (AI) supports inclusive education by improving resources, accessibility, and mental health for students with special needs. It discusses tools, such as adaptive learning platforms, assistive technologies, and mental health applications, that help educators address diverse learning needs. Using practical examples, case studies, and frameworks, this chapter offers actionable insights for educators and stakeholders to apply AI to equitable and accessible education. It also addresses challenges such as data privacy, resource disparities, and ethical concerns, while proposing collaborative approaches to ensure that AI solutions are inclusive and effective for all learners.*

DOI: 10.4018/979-8-3373-0573-8.ch012

# INTRODUCTION

## Defining Inclusive Education and Its Importance

Special educational provisions were created to accommodate children with special needs in the educational system. "Special Educational Needs (SEN) refer to learning difficulties that hinder a child's academic, social, behavioral, or emotional development (Wedell, 2003). Children with SEN face greater challenges in understanding information, learning, and accessing educational resources than their peers. The Education Act 1996 categorizes SEN students into three groups: 1) visually impaired, 2) partially or fully deaf, and 3) those with learning difficulties (Alias et al., 2012).

Recognizing these challenges, global initiatives have been established to promote inclusive education as a fundamental right. The Salamanca Statement (United Nations Educational, Scientific and Cultural Organization [UNESCO], 1994) and the Biwako Millennium Framework for Action (BMF) (National Council on Disability Affairs, 2002) are foundational to this global movement. These frameworks have significantly influenced international policies and guided nations toward equitable education opportunities. Similarly, UNESCO guidelines and the United Nations 2030 Agenda for Sustainable Development highlight inclusion and equity as key principles of education policies, affirming the importance of human rights in education (UNESCO, 2017; United Nations, 2015).

Inclusive education ensures all learners, regardless of their needs, receive quality educational experiences within their local communities alongside peers (European Agency for Special Needs and Inclusive Education, 2016). Students with SEN should have equal opportunities to participate, learn, and grow in an environment that upholds their rights, fosters respect, ensures equity, demonstrates compassion, and preserves their personal dignity. They should also be able to achieve this alongside their peers. These principles are realized when SEN students are integrated into mainstream classrooms (Kefallinou et al., 2020).

## The Role of Artificial Intelligence in Enhancing Inclusivity

Artificial Intelligence (AI) refers to advanced technologies such as machine learning, natural language processing, and robotics that mimic human intelligence (Ertel, 2024; Pedro et al., 2019). These technologies can work together to analyze complex patterns to enhance teaching, learning, and administrative tasks (Hwang et al., 2020; Soodtoetong & Rattanasiriwongwut, 2022). Increasingly, these technologies are being applied in inclusive education to support students with diverse needs. AI has transformed inclusive education by addressing equity gaps, creating inclusive learning environments, overcoming systemic barriers, and enhancing teaching practices. This also facilitates the implementation of educational frameworks and policies. AI-powered tools personalize learning experiences, develop assistive technologies, and provide accessible resources tailored to the needs of all learners (Edyburn, 2000; Li, 2023; Mitra, 2024; Pratama et al., 2023).

For example, assistive tools such as speech recognition and text-to-speech software enable SEN students to achieve equitable academic outcomes (Alnahdi, 2014). AI personalized learning platforms deliver content that aligns with each student's comprehension level and pace, ensuring accessibility and simplification. Similarly, AI-adaptive assessment tools use student profiles, performance history, and unique input to generate fair and customized evaluations (Habib et al., 2023). By leveraging students' profiles, performance history, and unique input requirements, these tools can generate customized assessments tailored to each student's needs, thereby ensuring a more accurate and equitable evaluation process.

Furthermore, using virtual reality (VR) and augmented reality (AR) platforms to deliver modified course materials to SEN students can significantly benefit them, providing immersive learning experiences that engage several senses and perceptions (Badilla-Quintana et al., 2020; Ceberio et al., 2025; Chalkiadakis et al., 2024; Vairamani, 2024). For example, learners with physical disabilities can participate in virtual laboratory simulations or investigate natural environments that are difficult to reach in real life using VR (Božić, 2023; Wulandari et al., 2024). These multisensory learning modalities can enhance students' cognition, communication, and awareness of the surrounding environment. They also foster emotion regulation by offering personalized feedback and reinforcement, enabling students to build confidence, engage more effectively with peers, and navigate their environments more independently (Shi, 2024). Therefore, integrating such tools into the routine of SEN students can help them feel more included and drive academic, social, behavioral, and emotional progress in mainstream classrooms.

## Chapter Objectives and Structure

This chapter explored the integration of AI in fostering inclusive education for SEN students in mainstream classrooms. It examines AI tools for inclusive education, highlights challenges and ethical considerations, reviews implementation frameworks, and presents recommendations for future research.

To achieve these objectives, this chapter is structured into four sections. It began by introducing the concept of inclusive education and the role of AI in enhancing inclusivity. Next, it reviews the existing literature focusing on AI tools and their applications in inclusive education. The third section discusses challenges and ethical considerations, such as privacy and equity. Finally, the fourth section outlines practical frameworks for implementing AI and emphasizes collaboration among educators, AI developers, and policymakers. The chapter concludes with the key findings and recommendations for fostering inclusive education through AI.

## AI INNOVATIONS IN INCLUSIVE EDUCATION: A LITERATURE REVIEW

AI plays a significant role in education, particularly in advancing equity and inclusion in schools (OECD, 2024). Equitable education ensures that every learner, regardless of socioeconomic background or special needs, can achieve their full potential. By providing innovative solutions, AI enhances inclusive education and addresses the diverse needs of students (Dubey, 2024)

### Overview of AI Tools for Inclusive Education

AI solutions, like intelligent tutoring systems (ITS) and adaptive learning platforms, promote inclusiveness by fostering belonging, well-being, and non-discrimination ; Mpu, 2023). These tools are instrumental in tailoring learning experiences to meet individual needs (Katiyar et al., 2024). For instance, speech recognition and text-to-speech technologies support students with hearing and speech impairments by improving their access to instructional content. Adaptive learning systems further enhance inclusivity by tailoring information to match individual learning levels and developments (Indrajith, 2024; Martínez et al., 2021; Mpu, 2023).

AI also fosters equity by addressing digital gaps and making educational resources more accessible (Ramos & Wilson-Kennedy, 2024). These tools motivate and engage students by transitioning from passive information delivery to active student-centered learning environments (Nemorin et al., 2023). Harnessing AI's transformative potential of AI allows educators to meet diverse learning needs, reduce academic disparities, and create inclusive classrooms in which every student can thrive (Gabriel, 2024; García et al., 2020; Massouti et al., 2024).

### Adaptive Learning Platforms: Supporting Diverse Needs

AI-powered adaptive systems are vital for supporting students with SEN in modern education (Kabudi et al., 2021). These platforms use advanced algorithms to monitor student progress in real-time, adjusting the curriculum, pace, and difficulty in suiting individual learning needs (Kabudi et al., 2021). Platforms such as MetaLinks and ASSISTments customize learning by analyzing student interactions.

These tools provide personalized educational resources, enable self-paced learning, deliver instant feedback, and support skill development (Joshi, 2023).

According to Mitra (2024), AI can assess cognitive skills such as language proficiency, attention span, and concentration, and tailor programs to meet the unique needs of each student. Adaptive learning combines video, audio, and mentoring to deliver courses across online, hybrid, and traditional settings (Strielkowski et al., 2024). By tailoring lessons to individual strengths and weaknesses, these systems ensure that students master skills before progressing, fostering a deeper understanding of the subject matter (Mitra, 2024). This adaptability helps students with disabilities overcome traditional classroom barriers, offering them a more personalized and effective learning experience (Sharma et al., 2023). By enabling real-time adjustments to the curriculum and teaching strategies, adaptive learning platforms ensure that no student is left behind, making education more inclusive and equitable.

Furthermore, Song et al. (2024) highlighted AI adaptive platforms, such as K-means clustering and chatbots, as tools to meet diverse student needs. K-means clustering groups students based on their learning behavior patterns and offers insights that support personalized online learning experiences. Similarly, chatbots utilize machine learning algorithms to analyze learners' needs and preferences, and deliver customized educational resources and recommendations (Jeong et al., 2023). While chatbots help bridge communication gaps in online learning and streamline the process, their effectiveness depends on high-quality content, ethical and technical implications of AI systems, and ensuring that they are used in a responsible and transparent manner (Kooli, 2023). AI chatbots in education offer several advantages such as enhancing accessibility, personalizing learning, and promoting equity by supporting both high-performing students and those needing additional help. They allow students to learn at their own pace with real-time content adjustments, while also making efficient use of instructional time. However, they have limitations, including the lack of human interaction, limited understanding of complex queries, and potential overreliance on technology. Additionally, concerns about data privacy, system failures, and the risk of AI bias may hinder their effectiveness and fairness in diverse educational settings (Al-Rashaida et al., 2018; Govea et al., 2023; Jamal et al., 2023; Kooli, 2023; Massouti et al., 2024; Montemayor et al., 2022; Pahi et al., 2024; Smith et al., 2021; Song et al., 2024).

## Assistive Technologies for Students with Special Needs

AI plays a crucial role in assistive technologies, helping students with disabilities to overcome learning barriers (Fernández-Batanero et al., 2022). AI-powered tools like speech-to-text, text-to-speech, and smart devices (e.g., hearing aids and glasses) improve accessibility by providing real-time feedback, enhancing participation, and fostering inclusivity (Alsolami, 2025; Fteiha et al., 2024; Mpu, 2023). Speech recognition systems convert spoken words into text, supporting students with hearing impairment. Similarly, text-to-speech software benefits students with visual impairments by reading written content aloud (Indrajith, 2024). Beyond its academic content, AI also supports emotional and social development. Virtual agents and robots create safe environments in which students can practice social interactions and emotional regulation, helping them build social and emotional skills (Abbasi et al., 2024; Panjwani-Charania & Zhai, 2023; Qablan & Al-Qaderi, 2009; Shi, 2024).

According to Mpu (2023), AI tools have been applied to address the specific needs of learners with conditions such as Attention-Deficit/Hyperactivity Disorder (ADHD), autism spectrum disorder (ASD), cerebral palsy, dyslexia, and sensory or physical impairments by providing personalized interventions and support tailored to each student's unique challenges. For instance, AI technologies, such as the NeuroSky Mentality System, detect attention levels in students with ADHD during assessments using a headset that captures electrical brain impulses. These tools engage learners interactively to reduce their inattention and impulsivity (Wang et al., 2023). However, further research is needed to validate the long-term reliability of such systems and explore their effectiveness in real-world learning environments (Fteiha et al., 2024; R. Y. Khalil et al., 2023; Wang et al., 2023).

For students with ASD, AI systems, such as Emotion Recognition Software, improve emotional understanding, addressing a common challenge for individuals with ASD (Al-Rashaida et al., 2022; Rashidan et al., 2021). For those with cerebral palsy, AI-powered rehabilitation tools and mobility devices help enhance motor skills and support wheelchair navigation (Balgude et al., 2024). Similarly, AI helps students with dyslexia by offering personalized learning experiences, such as those provided by the Cognitive Tutor, and diagnosing language impairments through methods such as the Fuzzy Cognitive Map (Rasheed-Karim, 2021; Mpu, 2023).

## AI and Mental Health Support: Bridging the Gap

AI tools are increasingly being used to support the mental health of students, including those with SEN (Sharma et al., 2023). AI-powered systems improve social-emotional learning (SEL) by identifying emotional indicators and offering personalized support for challenges like fear and frustration (Sandu & Bîrzu, 2023). These systems also simulate social interactions, allowing students to practice interpersonal and social skills in a safe environment (Karapet & Misak, 2024).

Beyond SEL, AI applications significantly enhance cognitive, emotional, and developmental wellbeing. Affective computing technologies integrated into AI systems play a crucial role in promoting psychological wellness and resilience, which are essential for both academic success and personal development (Alhuwaydi,

2024; Aslan et al., 2024; Fteiha et al., 2024, 2024; Martínez et al., 2021). Traditional cognitive assessments evaluate skills, such as language, memory, reasoning, and attention. While vital for identifying impairments, these assessments are often subjective and prone to errors. The lack of standardized screening can lead to undiagnosed conditions, allowing impairment to progress (Thakkar et al., 2024). AI automates cognitive assessments and improves both accuracy and efficiency (Javed et al., 2023). Machine learning (ML) models, including Support Vector Machines (SVM) and Neural Networks, have shown promise in diagnosing conditions such as Alzheimer's disease and ADHD by analyzing neuroimaging and health records (Javed et al., 2023).

By automating these processes, AI can overcome the shortcomings of human experts, such as performance unpredictability and knowledge gaps (Smith et al., 2021). Furthermore, AI has proven essential in diagnosing intellectual and developmental disorders, such as ADHD, cerebral palsy, and Down syndrome, and by analyzing neuroimaging data and electronic health records, allowing for early detection and timely interventions (Pagliara et al., 2024; Thakkar et al., 2024). AI is very important for the early detection of neurodegenerative diseases, which has been difficult in the past because symptoms develop slowly over time (Hasan et al., 2024).

Moreover, artificial intelligence has been utilized to develop Emotional AI, which enables machines to understand and respond to human emotions through the analysis of voice patterns, facial expressions, and physiological indicators (McStay, 2020). This technology helps with emotion regulation by offering individualized therapies based on real-time emotional information such as relaxation, mindfulness, and respiration techniques (Schulte-Frankenfeld & Fynn-Mathis, 2021). Similarly, AI tools monitor mood disorders such as depression by processing data from wearables and social networks to predict and prevent emotional relapses (Cummins et al., 2020). Overall, AI has enormous potential to transform mental health treatment by improving diagnostic accuracy, promoting emotional well-being, and facilitating individualized interventions for a wide range of mental health problems (Thakkar et al., 2024).

Nonetheless, for AI to be effectively used in mental health support, it is crucial to address concerns related to data privacy, ethics, and the need for proper educator training to integrate these tools into their practice (Varynskyi et al., 2023). In this context, effective collaboration among AI developers, educators, and mental health professionals is essential for establishing a comprehensive support system for students with SEN (Blewitt et al., 2021). By addressing data privacy concerns and ensuring proper training for educators, AI can establish comprehensive mental health support systems that empower students to thrive academically and emotionally.

## Case Studies Highlighting Successful Applications

Adaptive learning uses AI and machine learning (ML) to customize educational content, teaching methods, and assessments for individual students. These systems adjust the learning process in real-time based on each student's performance, preferences, knowledge, learning style, and disabilities (Gligorea et al., 2023).

Chu et al. (2009) developed a problem-based e-learning platform that helps teachers identify authentic learning cases tailored to students with mild mathematics disabilities. This platform uses AI algorithms to create context and content maps, support case-based reasoning, and identify semantic relationships. Factors such as teaching style, students' strengths and weaknesses, learning disabilities (e.g., dyslexia or math difficulties), and classroom environment were incorporated into the design. This approach enabled teachers to develop personalized learning plans and improve their ability to effectively teach mathematics to students with disabilities (Al-Rashaida & Massouti, 2024).

Standen et al. (2020) introduced the MaTHiSiS system, a detection-intervention adaptive learning system designed to keep students with intellectual disabilities in engaged emotional states. Negative emotions such as boredom hinder engagement, so the system detects affective states such as engagement, frustration, and boredom, and then adjusts learning materials to improve emotional engagement. For example, when a gaze-contingent system detects poor information processing through eye movements, it alters the presentation of materials to enhance understanding.

The MaTHiSiS system employs advanced machine-learning techniques, including CNNs to analyze facial expressions, SVMs to interpret body poses, and integrated models to study gaze patterns and voice inputs. These adjustments ensured that the students remained in optimal emotional states for learning, such as reducing stress for anxious students or increasing stimulation for bored learners. However, limitations were identified, such as difficulties in distinguishing between engagement and frustration owing to similar gaze patterns. Researchers recommend enhancing the detection phase with additional techniques such as conversational signals or physiological metrics (D'Mello et al., 2017).

AI has revolutionized the field of assistive technology by transforming static tools into dynamic and responsive systems. Traditional assistive tools such as wheelchairs, hearing aids, magnifiers, and communication boards often rely on fixed functionalities that offer limited flexibility to individual needs or context changes. In contrast, AI-powered tools provide adaptability, personalization, and real-time responsiveness, enhancing their effectiveness in supporting individuals with disabilities (Zdravkova et al., 2022).

Modern AI systems include predictive tools such as gaze-tracking devices, screen readers, and speech-to-text/text-to-speech communication technologies. These innovations enable the greater inclusion, independence, and participation of students in diverse settings, including mainstream classrooms. For instance, Kumar et al. (2022) developed an advanced audiovisual speech recognition model using deep learning techniques to assist students with hearing impairments.

The model combines a recurrent neural network (RNN) with a gated recurrent unit (GRU) for speech-to-text recognition, and uses a convolutional neural network (CNN) for visual speech-to-text processing. Compared to the conventional lip-net architectures used for visual speech recognition, the deep learning model significantly improved accuracy. Testing revealed a 6.6% reduction in the lip-reading word error rate and achieved an impressive 95% word prediction accuracy. By continuously evolving with user needs, AI-powered assistive technologies have become dynamic educational partners. They empower students with disabilities to participate more fully in mainstream classrooms, promoting greater inclusion, independence, and learning outcomes.

## ADDRESSING CHALLENGES AND ETHICAL CONSIDERATIONS

### Data Privacy and Security in AI-Driven Education

The widespread adoption of AI in education has brought about significant concerns regarding ethics, particularly regarding student data privacy, such as transforming classrooms and online learning environments by customizing learning paths, streamlining administrative tasks, and offering innovative ways for students to engage with educational materials (Abdallah et al., 2023; Hwang et al., 2020; Ismail & Aloshi, 2024; Qablan & Al-Qaderi, 2009; Soodtoetong & Rattanasiriwongwut, 2022). While many educators and students are enthusiastic about the potential of AI to revolutionize teaching and learning, concerns persist regarding its impact on traditional education systems and the privacy of sensitive student data (Govea et al., 2023; Ismail & Aloshi, 2024; Zawacki-Richter et al., 2024).

Historically, educational institutions have been responsible for safeguarding students' records and personal information. However, the integration of AI has significantly increased the volume and complexity of data collection, necessitating more robust security measures to protect against breach (Doughan et al., 2022; Ismail & Aloshi, 2024). The data collected by AI systems include library records, learning habits, performance metrics, and behavioral patterns, many of which are stored in the cloud and managed by third-party providers (Barack, 2017; Rehan, 2024). While this approach enhances data accessibility and efficiency, it also introduces vulnerabilities, including the risks of data breaches, unauthorized access, and misuse of sensitive information, potentially jeopardizing students' rights and well-being (Huang, 2023).

To address the challenges posed by data privacy risks, such as breaches, unauthorized access, and misuse of sensitive student information, regulatory frameworks have been established globally. In the United States, the Family Educational Rights and Privacy Act (FERPA), enacted in 1974, served as a landmark law emphasizing the protection of student records (U.S. Department of Education, 2000). Similarly, the United Arab Emirates (UAE) introduced its first comprehensive federal data protection law, Federal Decree-Law No. 45 of 2021, on the Protection of Personal Data (PDPL), which came into effect in January 2022. This law regulates the collection, processing, and storage of personal data, ensuring that student records are protected in line with global best practices (Emirates Schools Establishment, 2023; The Official Portal of the UAE Government, 2024; United Arab Emirates Legislations, 2021).

In addition, the General Data Protection Regulation (GDPR) implemented in Europe sets a global benchmark for data privacy and protection, requiring organizations to ensure transparency and accountability in data handling (GDPR, 2018). These laws and regulations highlight the critical importance of safeguarding data to maintain trust and ensure ethical use of AI in education.

The risks associated with AI-driven educational systems include data breaches, discrimination, and exploitation arising from leaked academic records or behavioral data (L. Huang, 2023). For example, leaked academic records or behavioral data can result in significant risks such as discrimination or exploitation (Alkaabi & Almaamari, 2020; Singer, 2017; Solove, 2006). Such vulnerabilities underscore the need for educational institutions to implement advanced encryption technologies to protect data integrity and prevent unauthorized access (Watini et al., 2024). Furthermore, promoting transparency in data collection, storage, and usage builds trust among the students, parents, and educators. Educational institutions must clearly communicate how data is used and ensure that they serve only educational purposes (Polonetsky & Jerome, 2014).

UNESCO's recommendation on the ethics of Artificial Intelligence emphasizes the responsibility of AI systems to uphold human rights, fundamental freedoms, and dignity throughout their development and deployment (UNESCO, 2022). To adhere to these principles, schools and developers should integrate cybersecurity strategies to safeguard against digital information and prevent malicious attacks. By adopting these measures, institutions can balance innovation with responsibility, ensuring that the benefits of AI are harnessed without compromising students' privacy. Prioritizing privacy and security in AI-driven education is essential for protecting students' fundamental rights and fostering trust in the use of AI technologies. By aligning with global data protection standards and maintaining transparent communication, educational institutions can responsibly leverage AI to create safer and more equitable learning environments.

## Ethical Implications of Using AI in Education

The increasing integration of AI is significantly reshaping education, introducing transformative benefits, such as efficiency, accessibility, real-time collaboration, and the elimination of physical and geographic barriers. AI systems enhance the storage of vast amounts of data and resources, improve the quality of learning, and effectively scale educational initiatives (Chen et al., 2020; Govea et al., 2023; Luo & Xie, 2018). However, these advantages are accompanied by ethical concerns that need to be addressed. Key issues include over-reliance on AI in decision-making, reduced teacher-student interactions, opacity of AI models, and potential depersonalization of the learning experience.

### Over-Reliance on AI for Decision-Making

One major dilemma is the over-reliance on AI systems for critical decision-making processes such as grading and student assessments. Decision-making involves constructing well-reasoned arguments supported by evidence (Dwyer, 2023). Overreliance on AI occurs when users unquestioningly accept AI-generated recommendations, often resulting in errors during decision-making tasks (Xie et al., 2021; Zhai et al., 2024). This over-reliance can arise because individuals find it challenging to evaluate the reliability of AI or determine the appropriate level of trust in its output.

Although AI can efficiently analyze large datasets with speed and consistency, its algorithms lack the nuanced understanding that human educators bring to evaluations (Mbalaka, 2023; Zhai et al., 2024). For instance, AI systems may misinterpret creative or unconventional answers that deviate from programmed parameters, leading to biased or inaccurate evaluations (Zhai et al., 2024). Furthermore, AI inaccuracies, such as "AI hallucinations," where systems generate false or misleading information, further limit their effectiveness (Moriera, 2024; Zhai et al., 2024). Additionally, the opacity of certain AI models, often referred to as "black box" algorithms, prevents educators and students from understanding or challenging AI-generated decisions, thereby raising concerns about fairness, accountability, and transparency. This emphasizes the need to consider whether AI's role is to assist or revolutionize education (Govea et al., 2023).

## Reducing Human Interaction and Personalization

Another ethical concern is the potential for AI to diminish meaningful teacher-student interactions, which are critical for fostering critical thinking, emotional development, and personalized learning experiences (Jamal et al., 2023; Krullaars et al., 2023). While AI systems can enhance personalized learning, boost engagement, and increase accessibility and productivity (Brandtzaeg & Følstad, 2017; Winkler & Soellner, 2018), they cannot replicate the empathy, mentorship, and nuanced understanding provided by human teachers.

This limitation is particularly concerning in socio-emotional learning, where interpersonal relationships are crucial (Jamal et al., 2023; Montemayor et al., 2022). Overreliance on AI tools creates a depersonalized educational experience, where students are treated as data points rather than individuals. Moreover, in under-resourced schools, where qualified teachers may be scarce, dependence on AI could further erode education quality (Jamal et al., 2023).

## Developing Ethical AI Frameworks

To address these concerns, it is essential to develop and implement ethical AI frameworks that prioritize human oversight and emphasize AI as a supportive tool rather than as a replacement for educators. These frameworks should focus on transparency, accountability, and inclusivity, ensuring that AI is designed to augment rather than overshadow human teaching. For instance, AI systems can be employed to handle repetitive administrative tasks, thus enabling teachers to concentrate on higher-order instructional and relational activities.

Additionally, these frameworks should incorporate mechanisms for regular audits, feedback, and continuous monitoring to evaluate and improve AI's impact of AI on learning outcomes. Ethical frameworks must also address depersonalization and data privacy issues, ensuring that AI use aligns with equity and fairness.

## The Unique Strengths of Human Intelligence

Humans possess unique qualities that AI cannot replicate, including adaptability, creativity, emotional intelligence, and moral reasoning (Ertel, 2024). Humans can dynamically adjust their behavior based on reflexes or prior experiences, enabling nuanced decision making that considers context, emotions, and ethical considerations. This adaptability allows educators to empathize with, interpret complex situations, and respond to students' needs in ways that AI systems cannot (Rajvanshi, 2011). In contrast, AI relies on data-driven algorithms that are devoid of emotional intelligence, instinct, and moral judgment (Dundas & Chik, 2011). While AI excels in processing vast amounts of data and identifying patterns, it lacks the intuitive reasoning and depth of decision-making that characterize human intelligence. Thus, AI can complement the educational process but can never fully substitute for human educators (Mäkelä & Stephany, 2024).

The integration of AI into education presents opportunities and challenges. Although AI has the potential to enhance learning experiences and improve efficiency, it must be used ethically and responsibly. By prioritizing human oversight, developing transparent and accountable frameworks, and leveraging the unique strengths of human intelligence, educational institutions can ensure that AI serves as a valuable tool for supporting, rather than replacing, educators and learning processes.

## IMPLEMENTATION OF FRAMEWORK AND COLLABORATIVE APPROACH

### Framework for Integrating AI in Inclusive Classrooms

Modern education must incorporate advanced technologies to meet the evolving needs of 21st-century students. As we stand on the brink of the fourth technological revolution—merging biological, physical, and digital domains—the educational landscape is undergoing a significant transformation. This new era envisions a synergistic interaction between AI and human intellect to enhance students' intellectual capacity. AI integration in teaching fosters innovation, analytical thinking, and problem-solving skills, thus reshaping education beyond traditional boundaries (Rane et al., 2024).

#### Promoting Fairness and Inclusion with AI

AI has the potential to revolutionize education by promoting fairness and inclusion among students from diverse backgrounds and abilities. Lata (2024) highlighted how modern AI technologies, such as Intelligence-Enhanced Assistive Technology, smart tutoring platforms, and customizable learning systems, address a wide range of educational needs. These innovations provide equal opportunities and foster inclusive communities by integrating individuals with special needs and disabilities into the mainstream education.

Pagliara et al. (2024) documented the benefits of AI in facilitating inclusive education, noting its applications in instruction and management. AI-driven tools can enhance customized learning experiences by providing adaptive technologies that cater to students' unique needs. However, the cultural and scientific contexts shaping these discussions, along with the limitations of the current methodologies, must be acknowledged when implementing AI frameworks.

## Universal Design for Learning as a Foundational Framework

Modern classrooms are increasingly diverse and comprise students with varying backgrounds, abilities, and learning preferences. The Universal Design for Learning (UDL) framework provides an educational paradigm that seeks to make learning more inclusive for all students (Song et al., 2024). Fundamentally, Universal Design for Learning acknowledges that the one-fits-all system of instruction is restrictive and encourages the proactive creation of customized learning opportunities. In particular, UDL prioritizes respecting flexibility to remove obstacles to academic achievement and address the distinctive educational needs faced by students with disabilities. To meet their educational requirements, Universal Design for Learning additionally emphasizes inclusivity and makes use of technological aids. As a framework for creating lessons, it also encourages flexible exercises and evaluations that provide students with the ability to take charge of their education. UDL has four essential components: well-defined objectives, adaptable strategies and resources, deliberate preparation for student variability, and prompt performance tracking (Cast, 2024; Song et al., 2024).

The integration of AI within inclusive classrooms, guided by frameworks such as UDL, represents a significant step toward equitable and accessible education. By leveraging AI capabilities and adhering to UDL principles, educators can address diverse learning needs, promote student agency, and ensure that all students have the opportunity to succeed.

## Collaborative Approaches: Educators, AI Developers, and Policymakers

The integration of AI into inclusive classroom learning requires collaboration among educators, AI developers, and policymakers to effectively support students from diverse backgrounds. Over the past decade, the use of AI tools to enhance learning has grown exponentially, driven by advances in educational technologies and a growing focus on personalized learning (Al Maktoum & Al Kaabi, 2024; Holmes et al., 2019; Luckin & Cukurova, 2019). This trend accelerated during the COVID-19 pandemic as school closures forced policymakers to transition to digital education (OECD, 2023). This shift encouraged AI developers to create tools that facilitated communication and collaboration among educators, students, and administrators, enabling remote and hybrid learning environments (R. Khalil et al., 2020). Despite this rapid growth, evidence on the effectiveness of AI in enhancing educational outcomes and assisting researchers in understanding successful educational processes remains limited (Miao et al., 2021).

Miao et al., (2021) note that the increasing use of AI has simplified the administration and delivery of education. System-facing AI applications, such as those embedded in Educational Management Information Systems (EMIS), automate a range of administrative tasks, including enrollment, scheduling, attendance tracking, assignment management, and school audits (van Wyk & Crouch, 2021). By streamlining these processes, AI reduces the administrative burden on educators and administrators, enabling them to focus on teaching and learning(Luckin & Cukurova, 2019).

Additionally, learning management systems (LMS) generate large volumes of data that can be analyzed using techniques such as "learning analytics." This data mining approach provides actionable insights to educators, administrators, and policymakers by highlighting trends, identifying at-risk students, and informing strategic decisions (Bienkowski et al., 2012; Siemens & Long, 2011). For instance, predictive educational analytics can predict which students are likely to struggle academically or drop out, allowing stakeholders to intervene proactively (Bienkowski et al., 2012). The results of these analyses are often presented as graphical dashboards, offering educators clear and accessible formats for decision making (Viberg et al., 2018).

## Building Capacity Among Educators for Effective Use of AI Tools

Research has demonstrated that the use of AI tools in classrooms can enhance inclusive learning environments and simplify teachers' workloads(Luckin & Holmes, 2016; Miao et al., 2021). For inclusive education to evolve and meet diverse student needs, instructional methods must be innovative and creative(Holmes et al., 2019). As AI advances in the realm of classroom instruction, it assists in processing routine tasks such as classroom management, instructional delivery, and accommodating students from various backgrounds(Luckin & Cukurova, 2019; Zawacki-Richter et al., 2019).

According to Fitria (2021), AI is used extensively in various instructional technology systems. Voice assistants, such as Google Assistant, Siri, and Cortana, are increasingly being utilized in education to provide quick access to information and facilitate tasks, such as answering questions or assisting with basic classroom functions. Digital mentors also play a significant role in offering guidance and support to students through interactive technology. Intelligent content systems enable the creation of adaptive and dynamic educational resources tailored to specific learning needs. Presentation interpreters provide real-time translations and summaries, thus enhancing accessibility for students with diverse linguistic or cognitive abilities.

International course platforms such as Coursera, Udemy, and Khan Academy offer opportunities for students to access high-quality educational content beyond traditional classrooms. Instructional games promote engagement by integrating gamified elements into the learning process, whereas customized learning systems and intelligent computer-assisted instruction provide individualized support to address varying student capabilities (Fitria, 2021).

Among the most commonly used digital tools in education are Learning Management Systems (LMS), which allow instructors to manage and distribute educational materials effectively. Platforms, such as Blackboard and Google Classroom, enable educators to organize course content, monitor student progress, and facilitate communication. According to Božić (2023), virtual whiteboards also enhance instructional delivery by enabling educators to display and interact with multimedia materials, such as videos, images, and educational applications. This interactivity provides a more engaging learning environment for students (Lázaro et al., 2020).

Learning applications designed to deliver dynamic and stimulating educational experiences play a crucial role in modern classrooms. Applications such as Khan Academy, Nearpod, and Duolingo provide students with interactive tools to support personalized learning. Additionally, video conferencing technologies, including Microsoft Teams, Zoom, and Google Meet, have proven essential for facilitating remote education and enabling effective communication between teachers and students (Mucundanyi & Woodley, 2021). The use of these digital tools facilitates personalized learning, enhances student engagement, and increases access to educational resources that might otherwise be inaccessible (Božić, 2023). By leveraging AI technologies, educators can tailor their teaching strategies to their individual learning styles, provide immediate feedback, and foster inclusive learning environments. These advancements support educators in addressing diverse student needs, while improving the overall quality of education delivery.

## Monitoring and Evaluating AI Applications for Continuous Improvement

The continuous advancement of AI technology in education has garnered significant attention, with its development closely monitored and evaluated for its transformative potential (Holmes et al., 2019; Miao et al., 2021). AI tools such as computer vision, natural language processing, and intelligent learning systems have revolutionized traditional teaching methods, providing educators and institutions with innovative strategies to enhance education and simplifying the implementation of inclusive learning practices (J. Huang et al., 2021).

Although the human mind, particularly that of teachers, has the unique ability to generate new knowledge, adapt to dynamic situations, and think creatively, AI functions solely within systemic parameters, operating automatically in response to human instruction. This distinction underscores educators' unparalleled intelligence and adaptability (Hattie, 2012). As Fitria (2021) notes, artificial intelligence, although innovative, is a product of human ingenuity and developed during the industrialization era. Therefore, AI and human intelligence will never hold equal standing as the creative and critical thinking abilities of the human mind remain unmatched.

For AI to be successfully integrated into classrooms, it is essential to address numerous challenges, overcome obstacles, and ensure its continuous development and monitoring. Although AI offers significant advantages for enhancing the school system, such as streamlining administrative tasks and fostering personalized learning, it also presents exciting opportunities for advancing teacher development. However, sustained efforts are needed to balance the adoption of AI with the core human elements of education, ensuring that its applications are equitable, ethical, and aligned with the ultimate goal of student success (Zhang & Zhang, 2024).

## CONCLUSION AND FUTURE DIRECTIONS

### Summary of Key Findings

This chapter highlights the transformative potential of AI in education, particularly for fostering inclusive classrooms. AI has demonstrated its ability to personalize learning, streamline administrative tasks, and provide educators with tools to meet diverse student needs. However, it is crucial to recognize that AI should not replace human involvement in education. Instead, it must be viewed as a powerful tool to support and enhance teaching and learning.

While AI can improve productivity and efficiency by automating routine tasks and analyzing large datasets, it lacks essential human qualities, such as empathy, critical thinking, and the ability to understand and respond to students' unique needs. These human attributes remain the cornerstones of effective education. Teachers play an irreplaceable role in fostering students' emotional connections, guiding critical thinking, and nurturing creativity. Emotional understanding and empathy are vital in making informed decisions and providing meaningful support to students as they navigate their personal and academic growth. Ultimately, the most effective educational environment will combine the strengths of AI with educators' irreplaceable human touch.

## The Future of AI in Inclusive Education

AI has already begun to revolutionize education by enabling organizations to work more efficiently, address complex challenges, and improve outcomes. Its integration into education is inevitable, as AI-powered systems offer cost-effective, performance-enhancing, and scalable solutions. By leveraging AI, educational institutions can address challenges, such as competition, cybersecurity, and the need for personalized learning pathways. These systems can assist in decision-making, provide tailored support to students, and foster more inclusive educational environments.

As AI becomes increasingly widespread, educational organizations must prepare their current and future workforces to thrive in an AI-driven world. This preparation involves equipping educators, administrators, and students with the skills and knowledge required to effectively use AI tools. By embracing the opportunities offered by AI while maintaining a focus on ethical considerations, institutions can ensure that AI contributes to equitable and inclusive education systems. However, the future of AI in education will also depend on a sustained commitment to address challenges such as data privacy, algorithmic bias, and equitable access to AI technologies.

## Recommendations for Stakeholders

For AI to complement education successfully, collaboration among all stakeholders—educators, policymakers, parents, students, and technology developers—is essential.

Educational leaders should prioritize the professional development of teachers and equip them with the skills needed to effectively integrate AI into their practices. Training programs should focus on balancing technology with the irreplaceable human elements of teaching, ensuring that AI is used to assist rather than replace educators. Teachers must leverage AI to enhance personalized learning while maintaining strong emotional connections with students, particularly in areas such as socioemotional learning and critical thinking.

Policymakers should establish comprehensive guidelines for the ethical use of AI in education. These regulations should focus on protecting student data privacy, minimizing algorithmic bias, and ensuring transparency in the AI decision-making processes. Investment in ongoing research and development is also critical for evaluating the effectiveness of AI tools and addressing the challenges related to equitable access and inclusivity.

Parents and students should embrace AI as a valuable resource to enhance their learning experiences. It is equally important to emphasize the role of human guidance in education. Parents should advocate for a balanced approach in which AI supports but does not overshadow the role of teachers. Students must be encouraged to develop skills that AI cannot replicate, such as creativity, collaboration, and emotional intelligence.

Developers must design AI systems that are human-centered, accessible, and transparent. By incorporating feedback from educators, students, and parents, developers can ensure that AI tools align with the needs of diverse learners, and promote inclusivity. Ethical considerations such as minimizing bias and safeguarding privacy should remain central to the development of AI technologies in education. By fostering collaboration among stakeholders, AI can complement and strengthen the human-centric nature of education. Together, these efforts will help ensure that AI tools are used to create equitable, inclusive, student-focused learning environments.

## Conclusion

AI has the potential to transform education by enhancing its inclusivity, efficiency, and personalization. However, its successful implementation depends on maintaining a balance between technological innovation and the human values that lie at the heart of education. By addressing challenges, fostering collaboration, and prioritizing ethical considerations, AI can serve as a powerful ally for creating educational systems that support and empower every learner. In the future, it is essential to ensure that AI complements human intelligence, fostering environments in which both technology and human interaction work in harmony to achieve the ultimate goal of inclusive and equitable education.

## REFERENCES


Abbasi, M. U. R., Zulfiqar, A., Rasool, M. S., & Quadri, S. S. A. (2024). Impact of AI on the inclusion of Learners with Special needs: Public Policy Perspective in Contemporary Scenario. *Arbor*, *11*(1). https://doi.org/doi.org/10.1234.arbor.1`1.1.05

Abdallah, A. K., Kaabi, A. M. A., & Ramadan, R. S. (2023). The Critical Role of Principals in Leading Effective Inclusive Schools. In *Inclusive Phygital Learning Approaches and Strategies for Students With Special Needs* (pp. 256–281). IGI Global Scientific Publishing., DOI: 10.4018/978-1-6684-8504-0.ch012

Al Maktoum, S. B., & Al Kaabi, A. M. (2024). Exploring teachers' experiences within the teacher evaluation process: A qualitative multi-case study. *Cogent Education*, *11*(1), 2287931. DOI: 10.1080/2331186X.2023.2287931

Al-Rashaida, M., Amayra, I., López-Paz, J. F., Martínez, O., Lázaro, E., Berrocoso, S., García, M., Pérez, M., Rodríguez, A. A., Luna, P. M., Pérez-Núñez, P., & Caballero, P. (2022). Studying the Effects of Mobile Devices on Young Children with Autism Spectrum Disorder: A Systematic Literature Review. *Review Journal of Autism and Developmental Disorders*, *9*(3), 400–415. DOI: 10.1007/s40489-021-00264-9

Al-Rashaida, M., López-Paz, J. F., Amayra, I., Lázaro, E., Martínez, O., Berrocoso, S., García, M., & Pérez, M. (2018). Factors affecting the satisfaction of people with disabilities in relation to vocational rehabilitation programs: A literature review. *Journal of Vocational Rehabilitation*, *49*(1), 97–115. DOI: 10.3233/JVR-180957

Al-Rashaida, M., & Massouti, A. (2024). Assessing the efficacy of online teacher training programs in preparing pre-service teachers to support students with special educational needs in mainstream classrooms in the UAE: A case study. *Journal of Research in Special Educational Needs*, *24*(1), 188–200. DOI: 10.1111/1471-3802.12624

Alhuwaydi, A. M. (2024). Exploring the Role of Artificial intelligence in Mental Healthcare: Current Trends and Future Directions. *Risk Management and Healthcare Policy*, *17*, 1339–1348. DOI: 10.2147/RMHP.S461562 PMID: 38799612

Alias, R., Alias, N. A., Ibrahim, A. B., Attan, H., & Kadir, A. L. (2012). What Do the Disabled Students Need? A Study on the Needs of the Special Educational Needs (SEN) Learners in Malaysian Public Universities. *The European Journal of Social & Behavioural Sciences*, *3*(3), 536–551. DOI: 10.15405/FutureAcademy/ejsbs(2301-2218).2012.3.15

Alkaabi, A. M., & Almaamari, S. A. (2020). Supervisory Feedback in the Principal Evaluation Process. *International Journal of Evaluation and Research in Education, 9*(3), 503–509. https://eric.ed.gov/?id=EJ1274705. DOI: 10.11591/ijere.v9i3.20504

Alnahdi, G. (2014). Assistive Technology in Special Education and the Universal Design for Learning. *The Turkish Online Journal of Educational Technology, 13*(2), 2.

Alsolami, A. S. (2025). *The effectiveness of using artificial intelligence in improving academic skills of school-aged students with mild intellectual disabilities in Saudi Arabia. 156*, 104884. DOI: 10.1016/j.ridd.2024.104884

Aslan, S., Durham, L. M., Chierichetti, R., Denman, P. A., Okur, E., Aguirre, D. I. G., Esquivel, J. C. Z., Maruri, H. A. C., Sharma, S., Raff, G., Mayer, R. E., & Nachman, L. (2024). *What is the impact of a multi-modal pedagogical conversational AI system on parents' concerns about technology use by young children? 55*(4), 1625–1650.

Badilla-Quintana, M. G., Sepulveda-Valenzuela, E., & Salazar Arias, M. (2020). Augmented Reality as a Sustainable Technology to Improve Academic Achievement in Students with and without Special Educational Needs. *Sustainability (Basel), 12*(19), 19. Advance online publication. DOI: 10.3390/su12198116

Balgude, S. D., Gite, S., Pradhan, B., & Lee, C.-W. (2024). Artificial intelligence and machine learning approaches in cerebral palsy diagnosis, prognosis, and management: A comprehensive review. *PeerJ. Computer Science, 10*, e2505. DOI: 10.7717/peerj-cs.2505 PMID: 39650350

Barack, L. (2017). The privacy problem: Safeguarding student data in schools and libraries. *School Library Journal, 63*(1), 36–40.

Bienkowski, M., Feng, M., & Means, B. (2012). *Enhancing Teaching and Learning through Educational Data Mining and Learning Analytics: An Issue Brief.* Office of Educational Technology, US Department of Education. https://eric.ed.gov/?id=ED611199

Blewitt, C., O'Connor, A., Morris, H., Nolan, A., Mousa, A., Green, R., Ifanti, A., Jackson, K., & Skouteris, H. (2021). "It's Embedded in What We Do for Every Child": A Qualitative Exploration of Early Childhood Educators' Perspectives on Supporting Children's Social and Emotional Learning. *International Journal of Environmental Research and Public Health, 18*(4), 4. Advance online publication. DOI: 10.3390/ijerph18041530 PMID: 33562768

Božić, V. (2023). *The Use of Digital Tools and Ai in Education.* DOI: 10.13140/RG.2.2.13438.87363

Brandtzaeg, P. B., & Følstad, A. (2017). Why People Use Chatbots. In Kompatsiaris, I., Cave, J., Satsiou, A., Carle, G., Passani, A., Kontopoulos, E., Diplaris, S., & McMillan, D. (Eds.), *Internet Science* (pp. 377–392). Springer International Publishing., DOI: 10.1007/978-3-319-70284-1_30

Cast. (2024). *The UDL Guidelines*. https://udlguidelines.cast.org

Ceberio, I., Al-Rashaida, M., García, M., Lopez Paz, J. F., Salgueiro, M., Passi, N., Pavel, H., & Amayra, I. (2025). Content and face validity in virtual reality with children: A validation in five steps+1 of a wheelchair basketball game. *Frontiers in Virtual Reality*, *5*, 1505630. Advance online publication. DOI: 10.3389/frvir.2024.1505630

Chalkiadakis, A., Seremetaki, A., Kanellou, A., Kallishi, M., Morfopoulou, A., Moraitaki, M., & Mastrokoukou, S. (2024). Impact of Artificial Intelligence and Virtual Reality on Educational Inclusion: A Systematic Review of Technologies Supporting Students with Disabilities. *Education Sciences*, *14*(11), 11. Advance online publication. DOI: 10.3390/educsci14111223

Chen, L., Chen, P., & Lin, Z. (2020). Artificial Intelligence in Education: A Review. *IEEE Access*, *8*, 75264–75278. IEEE Access. DOI: 10.1109/ACCESS.2020.2988510

Chu, H.-C., Chen, T.-Y., Lin, C.-J., Liao, M.-J., & Chen, Y.-M. (2009). Development of an adaptive learning case recommendation approach for problem-based e-learning on mathematics teaching for students with mild disabilities. *Expert Systems with Applications*, *36*(3, Part 1), 5456–5468. DOI: 10.1016/j.eswa.2008.06.140

Cummins, N., Matcham, F., Klapper, J., & Schuller, B. (2020). Chapter 10—Artificial intelligence to aid the detection of mood disorders. *Artificial Intelligence in Precision Health*, 231–255. https://doi.org/doi.org/10.1016/B978-0-12-817133-2.00010-0

D'Mello, S., Dieterle, E., & Duckworth, A. (2017). Advanced, Analytic, Automated (AAA) Measurement of Engagement During Learning. *Educational Psychologist*, *52*(2), 2. DOI: 10.1080/00461520.2017.1281747 PMID: 29038607

Doughan, Z., Mubasher, H. A., Bizri, M. E., & Haidar, A. (2022). The Metaverse: A Virtual World in the Palm of Your Hand. *BAU Journal - Science and Technology*, *4*(1). DOI: 10.54729/KXRC1143

Dubey, C. K. (2024). Exploring the Role of Artificial Intelligence in Inclusive Education. *Inclusive Pedagogy As An Artificial Intelligence*. https://www.researchgate.net/publication/378907681_Exploring_the_Role_of_Artificial_Intelligence_in_Inclusive_Education

Dundas, J., & Chik, D. (2011). *Implementing Human-like Intuition Mechanism in Artificial Intelligence* (No. arXiv:1106.5917). arXiv. https://doi.org//arXiv.1106.5917DOI: 10.48550

Dwyer, C. P. (2023). An Evaluative Review of Barriers to Critical Thinking in Educational and Real-World Settings. *Journal of Intelligence*, *11*(6), 6. Advance online publication. DOI: 10.3390/jintelligence11060105 PMID: 37367507

Edyburn, D. L. (2000). *Assistive Technology and Students with Mild Disabilities. 32*(9).

Emirates Schools Establishment. (2023). *Emirates Schools Establishment.* https://www.ese.gov.ae:443/En/Pages/Privacy-Policy.aspx

Ertel, W. (2024). *Introduction to Artificial Intelligence.* Springer Nature.

European Agency for Special Needs and Inclusive Education. (2016). *Raising the Achievement of All Learners in Inclusive Education – Literature Review.* https://www.european-agency.org/resources/publications/raising-achievement-all-learners-inclusive-education-literature-review

Fernández-Batanero, J. M., Montenegro-Rueda, M., Fernández-Cerero, J., & García-Martínez, I. (2022). Assistive technology for the inclusion of students with disabilities. *Systematic Reviews*, *70*, 1911–193.

Fitria, N. (2021). *Artificial Intelligence (AI) In Education: Using AI Tools for Teaching and Learning Process.*

Fitria, T. N. (2021). ARTIFICIAL INTELLIGENCE (AI) IN EDUCATION: USING AI TOOLS FOR TEACHING AND LEARNING PROCESS. *Prosiding Seminar Nasional & Call for Paper STIE AAS, 4*(1), Article 1. https://prosiding.stie-aas.ac.id/index.php/prosenas/article/view/106

Fteiha, M., Al-Rashaida, M., Elsori, D., Khalil, A., & Al Bustami, G. (2024). Obstacles for using assistive technology in centres of special needs in the UAE. *Disability and Rehabilitation. Assistive Technology*, *19*(8), 2934–2944. DOI: 10.1080/17483107.2024.2323698 PMID: 38436086

Gabriel, J. (2024). How Artificial Intelligence (AI) impacts inclusive education. *Educational Research Review*, *19*(6), 95–103. DOI: 10.5897/ERR2024.4404

García, M., Lázaro, E., Amayra, I., López-Paz, J. F., Martínez, O., Pérez, M., Berrocoso, S., Al-Rashaida, M., & Infante, J. (2020). Analysis of Visuospatial Abilities in Chiari Malformation Type I. *Cerebellum (London, England)*, *19*(1), 6–15. DOI: 10.1007/s12311-019-01056-y PMID: 31286383

GDPR. (2018). *General Data Protection Regulation*. https://www.wep-portal.com/GDPR%20Policy.pdf

Gligorea, I., Cioca, M., Oancea, R., Gorski, A.-T., Gorski, H., & Tudorache, P. (2023). *Adaptive Learning Using Artificial Intelligence in e-Learning: A Literature Review. 13*(12). DOI: 10.3390/educsci13121216

Govea, J., Ocampo Edye, E., Revelo-Tapia, S., & Villegas-Ch, W. (2023). Optimization and Scalability of Educational Platforms: Integration of Artificial Intelligence and Cloud Computing. *Computers*, *12*(11), 11. Advance online publication. DOI: 10.3390/computers12110223

Habib, H., Jelani, S. A. K., Ali, S. S., & Kadari, J. (2023). From Assessment to Empowerment: The Role of AI in Special Education Progress Monitoring. *Journal of Multidisciplinary Research*, *9*(01), 01.

Hasan, M. M., Phu, J., Sowmya, A., Meijering, E., & Kalloniatis, M. (2024). Artificial intelligence in the diagnosis of glaucoma and neurodegenerative diseases. *Clinical & Experimental Optometry*, *107*(2), 130–146. DOI: 10.1080/08164622.2023.2235346 PMID: 37674264

Hattie, J. (2012). *Visible learning for teachers: Maximizing impact on learning* (pp. x, 269). Routledge/Taylor & Francis Group. DOI: 10.4324/9780203181522

Holmes, W., Bialik, M., & Fadel, C. (2019). Artificial Intelligence in Education Promises and Implications for Teaching and Learning. In *(1st ed.). Center for Curriculum Redesign: MA, USA. (2019)*. Center for Curriculum Redesign. https://circls.org/primers/artificial-intelligence-in-education-promises-and-implications-for-teaching-and-learning

Huang, J., Saleh, S., & Liu, Y. (2021). *A Review on Artificial Intelligence in Education. 10*(3). https://www.richtmann.org/journal/index.php/ajis/article/view/12463

Huang, L. (2023). Ethics of Artificial Intelligence in Education: Student Privacy and Data Protection. *Science Insights Education Frontiers*, *16*(2), 2577–2587. DOI: 10.15354/sief.23.re202

Hwang, G.-J., Xie, H., Wah, B. W., & Gašević, D. (2020). Vision, challenges, roles and research issues of Artificial Intelligence in Education. *Computers and Education: Artificial Intelligence*, *1*, 100001. DOI: 10.1016/j.caeai.2020.100001

Indrajith, R. (2024). AI Innovations for Inclusive Learning: Breaking Down Barriers. *International Journal of Research Publication and Reviews*, *5*(4), 9742–9745.

Ismail, I. A., & Aloshi, J. M. (2024). Data Privacy in AI-Driven Education: An In-Depth Exploration Into the Data Privacy Concerns and Potential Solutions. In Keeley, K. L. (Ed.), (pp. 223–252). Advances in Educational Marketing, Administration, and Leadership. IGI Global., DOI: 10.4018/979-8-3693-5443-8.ch008

Jamal, A., Pattanaik, A., Gorli, R., Chinmay, A., & Jaisai, T. (2023)... *The Impact of Ai Chatbots on Teacher-Student Relationships in Higher Education.*, *12*, 2299–2305.

Javed, A. R., Saadia, A., Mughal, H., Gadekallu, T. R., Rizwan, M., Maddikunta, P. K. R., Mahmud, M., Liyanage, M., & Hussain, A. (2023). Artificial Intelligence for Cognitive Health Assessment: State-of-the-Art, Open Challenges and Future Directions. *Cognitive Computation*, *15*(6), 1767–1812. DOI: 10.1007/s12559-023-10153-4

Jeong, H., Yoo, J. H., & Han, O. (2023). Next-Generation Chatbots for Adaptive Learning: A proposed Framework. *Journal of Internet Computing and Services*, *24*(4), 37–45. DOI: 10.7472/jksii.2023.24.4.37

Joshi, M. A. (2023). Adaptive Learning through Artificial Intelligence. *SSRN*, *7*(2), 41–43. DOI: 10.2139/ssrn.4514887

Kabudi, T., Pappas, I., & Olsen, D. H. (2021). AI-enabled adaptive learning systems: A systematic mapping of the literature. *Computers and Education: Artificial Intelligence*, *2*, 100017. DOI: 10.1016/j.caeai.2021.100017

Karapet, H. N., & Misak, A. S. (2024). The Role And Impact Of Artificial Intelligence And Social-Emotional Learning In The Social Pedagogue's Work With Children With Special Educational Needs. *Library Progress International*, *44*(3), 3. Advance online publication. DOI: 10.48165/bapas.2024.44.2.1

Katiyar, P. D. N., Awasthi, M. V. K., Pratap, D. R., Mishra, M. K., Shukla, M. N., Singh, M. R., & Tiwari, D. M. (2024). Ai-Driven Personalized Learning Systems: Enhancing Educational Effectiveness. *Educational Administration: Theory and Practice*, *30*(5), 5. Advance online publication. DOI: 10.53555/kuey.v30i5.4961

Kefallinou, A., Symeonidou, S., & Meijer, C. J. W. (2020). Understanding the value of inclusive education and its implementation: A review of the literature. *Prospects*, *49*(3), 3. Advance online publication. DOI: 10.1007/s11125-020-09500-2

Khalil, R., Mansour, A. E., Fadda, W. A., Almisnid, K., Aldamegh, M., Al-Nafeesah, A., Alkhalifah, A., & Al-Wutayd, O. (2020). The sudden transition to synchronized online learning during the COVID-19 pandemic in Saudi Arabia: A qualitative study exploring medical students' perspectives. *BMC Medical Education*, *20*(1), 285. DOI: 10.1186/s12909-020-02208-z PMID: 32859188

Khalil, R. Y., Tairab, H., Qablan, A., Alarabi, K., & Mansour, Y. (2023). STEM-Based Curriculum and Creative Thinking in High School Students. *Education Sciences*, *13*(12), 12. Advance online publication. DOI: 10.3390/educsci13121195

Kooli, C. (2023). Chatbots in Education and Research: A Critical Examination of Ethical Implications and Solutions. *Sustainability (Basel)*, *15*(7), 7. Advance online publication. DOI: 10.3390/su15075614

Krullaars, Z. H., Januardani, A., Zhou, L., & Jonkers, E. (2023). *Exploring Initial Interactions: High School Students and Generative AI Chatbots for Relationship Development.*. https://dl.gi.de/handle/20.500.12116/42444DOI: 10.18420/muc2023

Kumar, L. A., Renuka, D. K., Rose, S. L., Shunmuga priya, M. C., & Wartana, I. M. (2022). Deep learning based assistive technology on audio visual speech recognition for hearing impaired. *International Journal of Cognitive Computing in Engineering*, *3*, 24–30. DOI: 10.1016/j.ijcce.2022.01.003

Lata, P. (2024). Towards Equitable Learning: Exploring Artificial Intelligence in Inclusive Education. *SSRN*, *7*(5), 416–434. DOI: 10.2139/ssrn.4987156

Lázaro, E., Amayra, I., López-Paz, J. F., Martínez, O., Alvarez, M. P., Berrocoso, S., Al-Rashaida, M., García, M., Luna, P., Pérez-Núñez, P., Rodriguez, A. A., Fernández, P., Fernández, P. P., & Oliva-Macías, M. (2020). Using a Virtual Serious Game (Deusto-e-motion1.0) to Assess the Theory of Mind in Primary School Children: Observational Descriptive Study. *JMIR Serious Games*, *8*(2), e12971. DOI: 10.2196/12971 PMID: 32238330

Li, H. (2023). AI in Education: Bridging the Divide or Widening the Gap? Exploring Equity, Opportunities, and Challenges in the Digital Age. *Advances in Education. Humanities and Social Science Research*, *8*(1), 1. Advance online publication. DOI: 10.56028/aehssr.8.1.355.2023

Luckin, R., & Cukurova, M. (2019). Designing educational technologies in the age of AI: A learning sciences-driven approach. *British Journal of Educational Technology*, *50*(6), 2824–2838. DOI: 10.1111/bjet.12861

Luckin, R., & Holmes, W. (2016). Intelligence Unleashed: An argument for AI in Education. In *UCL Knowledge Lab: London, UK.* [Report]. UCL Knowledge Lab. https://www.pearson.com/content/dam/corporate/global/pearson-dot-com/files/innovation/Intelligence-Unleashed-Publication.pdf

Luo, X., & Xie, L. (2018). Research on Artificial Intelligence-Based Sharing Education in the Era of Internet+. *2018 International Conference on Intelligent Transportation, Big Data & Smart City (ICITBS)*, 335–338. DOI: 10.1109/ICITBS.2018.00092

Mäkelä, E., & Stephany, F. (2024). Complement or substitute? How AI increases the demand for human skills. *Arxiv*. https://arxiv.org/abs/2412.19754

Martínez, O., Amayra, I., López-Paz, J. F., Lázaro, E., Caballero, P., García, I., Rodríguez, A. A., García, M., Luna, P. M., Pérez-Núñez, P., Barrera, J., Passi, N., Berrocoso, S., Pérez, M., & Al-Rashaida, M. (2021). Effects of Teleassistance on the Quality of Life of People With Rare Neuromuscular Diseases According to Their Degree of Disability. *Frontiers in Psychology*, *12*, 637413. Advance online publication. DOI: 10.3389/fpsyg.2021.637413 PMID: 33737897

Massouti, A., Al-Rashaida, M., & Alhosani, M. (2024). A Qualitative Study on Dubai's Inclusive Education Policy from School Leaders' Perspectives. *Sustainability (Basel)*, *16*(3), 3. Advance online publication. DOI: 10.3390/su16031252

Mbalaka, B. (2023). Epistemically violent biases in artificial intelligence design: The case of DALLE-E 2 and Starry AI. *Digital Transformation and Society*, *2*(4), 376–402. DOI: 10.1108/DTS-01-2023-0003

McStay, A. (2020). Emotional AI, soft biometrics and the surveillance of emotional life: An unusual consensus on privacy. *Big Data & Society*, *7*(1), 1. Advance online publication. DOI: 10.1177/2053951720904386

Miao, F., Holmes, W., Huang, R., & Zhang, H. (2021). *AI and education: Guidance for policy-makers*. UNESCO. https://unesdoc.unesco.org/ark:/48223/pf0000376709?locale=en

Mitra, D. S. (2024). *AI-Powered Adaptive Education for Disabled Learners* (SSRN Scholarly Paper No. 5042713; Issue 5042713). Social Science Research Network. DOI: 10.2139/ssrn.5042713

Montemayor, C., Halpern, J., & Fairweather, A. (2022). In principle obstacles for empathic AI: Why we can't replace human empathy in healthcare. *AI & Society*, *37*(4), 1353–1359. DOI: 10.1007/s00146-021-01230-z PMID: 34054228

Moriera, F. (2024). *Proceedings of the 23rd European Conference on e-Learning*. Academic Conferences and publishing limited.

Mpu, Y. (2023). Bridging the Knowledge Gap on Special Needs Learner Support: The Use of Artificial Intelligence (AI) to Combat Digital Divide Post-COVID-19 Pandemic and beyond. In Altinay, F., & Altinay, Z. (Eds.), *Intellectual and Learning Disabilities—Inclusiveness and Contemporary Teaching Environments*. IntechOpen., DOI: 10.5772/intechopen.113054

Mucundanyi, G., & Woodley, X. (2021). *Exploring Free Digital Tools in Education. 17*(2).

National Council on Disability Affairs. (2002). *Biwako Millennium Framework.* https://ncda.gov.ph/biwako-millennium-framework/

Nemorin, S., Vlachidis, A., Ayerakwa, H. M., & Andriotis, P. (2023). AI Hyped? A Horizon Scan of Discourse on Artificial Intelligence in Education (AIED) and Development. *Learning, Media and Technology*, *48*(1), 38–51. DOI: 10.1080/17439884.2022.2095568

OECD. (2023). *Digital equity and inclusion in education.* https://www.oecd.org/en/publications/digital-equity-and-inclusion-in-education_7cb15030-en.html

OECD. (2024). *The potential impact of artificial intelligence on equity and inclusion in education.* DOI: 10.1787/dee339a8-en

Pagliara, S. M., Bonavolontà, G., Pia, M., Falchi, S., Zurru, A. L., Fenu, G., & Mura, A. (2024). The Integration of Artificial Intelligence in Inclusive Education: A Scoping Review. *Information (Basel)*, *15*(12), 12. Advance online publication. DOI: 10.3390/info15120774

Pahi, K., Hawlader, S., Hicks, E., Zaman, A., & Phan, V. (2024). Enhancing active learning through collaboration between human teachers and generative AI. *Computers and Education Open*, *6*, 100183. DOI: 10.1016/j.caeo.2024.100183

Panjwani-Charania, S., & Zhai, X. (2023). AI for Students with Learning Disabilities: A Systematic Review. *SSRN.* https://www.researchgate.net/publication/374295269_AI_for_Students_with_Learning_Disabilities_A_Systematic_Review

Pedro, F., Subosa, M., Rivas, A., & Valverde, P. (2019). Artificial intelligence in education: Challenges and opportunities for sustainable development. *Ministerio De Educación.* https://repositorio.minedu.gob.pe/handle/20.500.12799/6533

Polonetsky, J., & Jerome, J. (2014). *Student Data: Trust, Transparency, and the Role of Consent* (SSRN Scholarly Paper No. 2628877). Social Science Research Network. DOI: 10.2139/ssrn.2628877

Pratama, M. P., Sampelolo, R., & Lura, H. (2023). Revolutionizing Education: Harnessing the Power of Artificial Intelligence for Personalized Learning. *Klasikal: Journal of Education. Language Teaching and Science*, *5*(2), 2. Advance online publication. DOI: 10.52208/klasikal.v5i2.877

Qablan, A., & Al-Qaderi, S. (2009). How to Change University Faculty Members' Attitudes and Behavior in the Context of Education for Sustainable Development. *Applied Environmental Education and Communication*, *8*(3–4), 184–194. DOI: 10.1080/15330150903269407

Rajvanshi, A. K. (2011). The three minds of the body-Brain, heart and gut. *Speaking Tree, India.* https://citeseerx.ist.psu.edu/document?repid=rep1&type=pdf&doi=41c9912d8fe35967a74d5080ef031eeccc5dc83c

Ramos, J. G., & Wilson-Kennedy, Z. (2024). Promoting equity and addressing concerns in teaching and learning with artificial intelligence. *Frontiers in Education*, *9*, 1487882. Advance online publication. DOI: 10.3389/feduc.2024.1487882

Rane, N. L., Choudhary, S. P., & Rane, J. (2024). Education 4.0 and 5.0: Integrating Artificial Intelligence (AI) for personalized and adaptive learning. *Journal of Artificial Intelligence and Robotics*, *1*(1). https://www.reseaprojournals.com/jair/192

Rasheed-Karim, W. (2021). Intelligent Tutoring Systems, Learning and Cognitive Styles of Dyslexic Students. [iJET]. *International Journal of Emerging Technologies in Learning*, *16*(3), 20–35. DOI: 10.3991/ijet.v16i03.19317

Rashidan, M. A., Sidek, S. N., Yusof, H., Khalid, M., Dzulkarnain, A. A. A., Ghazali, A. S., Zabidi, S. A. M., & Sidique, F. A. A. (2021). Technology-Assisted Emotion Recognition for Autism Spectrum Disorder (ASD) Children: A Systematic Literature Review. *IEEE Access : Practical Innovations, Open Solutions*, *9*, 33638–33653. DOI: 10.1109/ACCESS.2021.3060753

Rehan, H. (2024). AI-Driven Cloud Security: The Future of Safeguarding Sensitive Data in the Digital Age. *Journal of Artificial Intelligence General Science (JAIGS) ISSN:3006-4023*, *1*(1), Article 1. DOI: 10.60087/jaigs.v1i1.89

Sandu, M. L., & Bîrzu, M. I. (2023). Emotional intelligence in children with special educational needs. *Technium Education and Humanities*, *6*, 70–83. Advance online publication. DOI: 10.47577/teh.v6i.10307

Schulte-Frankenfeld, P. M., & Fynn-Mathis, T. (2021). App-based mindfulness meditation reduces perceived stress and improves self-regulation in working university students: A randomised controlled trial. *Applied Psychology. Health and Well-Being*, *14*(4), 1151–1171. DOI: 10.1111/aphw.12328 PMID: 34962055

Sharma, S., Tomar, V., Yadav, N., & Aggarwal, M. (2023). Impact of AI-Based Special Education on Educators and Students. In Kumar, A., A. Nayyar, & R. Jain (Eds.), *AI-Assisted Special Education for Students With Exceptional Needs* (impact-of-ai-based-special-education-on-educators-and-students; p. 20). IGI Global Scientific Publishing. DOI: 10.4018/979-8-3693-0378-8.ch003

Shi, L. (2024). The Integration of Advanced AI-Enabled Emotion Detection and Adaptive Learning Systems for Improved Emotional Regulation. *Journal of Educational Computing Research, 07356331241296890*. Advance online publication. DOI: 10.1177/07356331241296890

Siemens, G., & Long, P. (2011). Penetrating the Fog: Analytics in Learning and Education. *EDUCAUSE Review*, *46*(5), 30.

Singer, N. (2017, May 13). How Google Took Over the Classroom. *The New York Times*. https://www.nytimes.com/2017/05/13/technology/google-education-chromebooks-schools.html

Smith, L., Shin, J. I., Jacob, L., Carmichael, C., López Sánchez, G. F., Oh, H., Butler, L. T., Barnett, Y., Pizzol, D., Tully, M. A., Soysal, P., Veronese, N., & Koyanagi, A. (2021). Sleep problems and mild cognitive impairment among adults aged ≥50 years from low. *Experimental Gerontology*, *154*, 111513. DOI: 10.1016/j.exger.2021.111513 PMID: 34384889

Solove, D. J. (2006). A Taxonomy of Privacy. *University of Pennsylvania Law Review*, *154*(3), 477. DOI: 10.2307/40041279

Song, Y., Weisberg, L. R., Zhang, S., Tian, X., Boyer, K. E., & Israel, M. (2024). A framework for inclusive AI learning design for diverse learners. *Computers and Education: Artificial Intelligence*, *6*, 100212. DOI: 10.1016/j.caeai.2024.100212

Soodtoetong, N., & Rattanasiriwongwut, M. (2022). Educational Transformation with Virtual Classroom: Integrated between TTF and Social Motivation. *TEM Journal*, *11*(1), 439–445. DOI: 10.18421/TEM111-56

Standen, P. J., Brown, D. J., Taheri, M., Galvez Trigo, M. J., Boulton, H., Burton, A., Hallewell, M. J., Lathe, J. G., Shopland, N., Blanco Gonzalez, M. A., Kwiatkowska, G. M., Milli, E., Cobello, S., Mazzucato, A., Traversi, M., & Hortal, E. (2020). An evaluation of an adaptive learning system based on multimodal affect recognition for learners with intellectual disabilities. *British Journal of Educational Technology*, *51*(5), 5. Advance online publication. DOI: 10.1111/bjet.13010

Strielkowski, W., Grebennikova, V., Lisovskiy, A., Rakhimova, G., & Vasileva, T. (2024). AI-driven adaptive learning for sustainable educational transformation. *Wiley*. https://onlinelibrary.wiley.com/doi/10.1002/sd.3221

Thakkar, A., Ankita, G., & De Sousa, A. (2024). Artificial intelligence in positive mental health: A narrative review. *Frontiers in Digital Health*, *6*, 1280235. Advance online publication. DOI: 10.3389/fdgth.2024.1280235 PMID: 38562663

The Official Portal of the UAE Government. (2024). *The Official Portal of the UAE Government*. https://u.ae/en/about-the-uae/digital-uae/data/data-protection-laws

UNESCO. (1994). *The Salamanca Statement and Framework for Action on Special Needs Education*. https://unesdoc.unesco.org/ark:/48223/pf0000098427

UNESCO. (2017). *A Guide for ensuring inclusion and equity in education*. UNESCO., DOI: 10.54675/MHHZ2237

UNESCO. (2022). *Recommendation on the Ethics of Artificial Intelligence*. https://unesdoc.unesco.org/ark:/48223/pf0000381137

United Arab Emirates Legislations. (2021). *United Arab Emirates Legislations*. https://uaelegislation.gov.ae/en/legislations/1972

United Nations. (2015). *Transforming our World: The 2030 Agenda for Sustainable Development*. https://sustainabledevelopment.un.org/post2015/transformingourworld/publication

U.S. Department of Education. (2000). *U.S. Department of Education*. https://studentprivacy.ed.gov/ferpa

Vairamani, A. D. (2024). Enhancing Social Skills Development Through Augmented Reality (AR) and Virtual Reality (VR) in Special Education. In *Augmented Reality and Virtual Reality in Special Education* (pp. 65–89). John Wiley & Sons, Ltd. DOI: 10.1002/9781394167586.ch3

van Wyk, C., & Crouch, L. (2021). Efficiency and Effectiveness in Choosing and Using an EMIS. *2021*.

Varynskyi, V., Donnikova, I., & Savinova, N. (2023). Artificial Intelligence in Education: Tool, Object,"subject" of Learning. *Journal of International Legal Communication*, *10*(3), 46–55. DOI: 10.32612/uw.27201643.2023.10.3.pp.46-55

Viberg, O., Hatakka, M., Bälter, O., & Mavroudi, A. (2018). The current landscape of learning analytics in higher education. *Computers in Human Behavior*, *89*, 98–110. DOI: 10.1016/j.chb.2018.07.027

Wang, J.-W., Zhang, D.-W., & Johnstone, S. J. (2023). *Portable EEG for assessing attention in educational settings: A scoping review*. OSF. DOI: 10.31234/osf.io/ckbmw

Watini, S., Davies, G., & Andersen, N. (2024). Cybersecurity in Learning Systems: Data protection and privacy in educational information systems and digital learning environments. [ITEE]. *International Transactions on Education Technology*, *3*(1), 1. Advance online publication. DOI: 10.33050/itee.v3i1.665

Wedell, K. (2003). Concepts of special educational need. *Journal of Research in Special Educational Needs*, *3*(2), 104–108. DOI: 10.1111/1471-3802.00002

Winkler, R., & Soellner, M. (2018). Unleashing the Potential of Chatbots in Education: A State-Of-The-Art Analysis. *Proceedings - Academy of Management*, *2018*(1), 15903. DOI: 10.5465/AMBPP.2018.15903abstract

Wulandari, C. E., Firdaus, F. A., & Saifulloh, F. (2024). Promoting Inclusivity Through Technology: A Literature Review in Educational Settings. *Journal of Learning and Technology*, *3*(1), 1. Advance online publication. DOI: 10.33830/jlt.v3i1.9731

Xie, Y., Wang, K., & Kong, Y. (2021). Prevalence of Research Misconduct and Questionable Research Practices: A Systematic Review and Meta-Analysis. *Science and Engineering Ethics*, *27*(4), 41. DOI: 10.1007/s11948-021-00314-9 PMID: 34189653

Zawacki-Richter, O., Cefa, B., & Bai, J. (2024). *Towards reproducible systematic reviews in Open, Distance, and Digital Education (ODDE)*. https://www.researchgate.net/profile/Olaf-Zawacki-Richter/publication/385694253_Towards_reproducible_systematic_reviews_in_Open_Distance_and_Digital_Education_ODDE_-an_umbrella_mapping_review/links/67308bef2326b47637d6d0b3/Towards-reproducible-systematic-reviews-in-Open-Distance-and-Digital-Education-ODDE-an-umbrella-mapping-review.pdf

Zawacki-Richter, O., Marín, V. I., Bond, M., & Gouverneur, F. (2019). Systematic review of research on artificial intelligence applications in higher education – where are the educators? *International Journal of Educational Technology in Higher Education*, *16*(1), 39. DOI: 10.1186/s41239-019-0171-0

Zdravkova, K., Krasniqi, V., Dalipi, F., & Ferati, M. (2022). Cutting-edge communication and learning assistive technologies for disabled children: An artificial intelligence perspective. *Frontiers in Artificial Intelligence*, *5*, 970430. Advance online publication. DOI: 10.3389/frai.2022.970430 PMID: 36388402

Zhai, C., Wibowo, S., & Li, L. D. (2024). The effects of over-reliance on AI dialogue systems on students' cognitive abilities: A systematic review. *Smart Learning Environments*, *11*(1), 28. DOI: 10.1186/s40561-024-00316-7

Zhang, J., & Zhang, Z. (2024). AI in teacher education: Unlocking new dimensions in teaching support, inclusive learning, and digital literacy. *Journal of Computer Assisted Learning*, *40*(4), 1871–1885. DOI: 10.1111/jcal.12988

# Chapter 13
# Leading With Data: AI-Driven Decision Making in Special Education

**Ahmed M. Alkaab**
https://orcid.org/0000-0001-7220-8087
*United Arab Emirates University, UAE*

**Mohammed Humaid Aljanahi**
https://orcid.org/0000-0001-9982-7179
*United Arab Emirates University, UAE*

**Mona Humaid Aljanahi**
https://orcid.org/0000-0001-7321-3603
*United Arab Emirates University, UAE*

**Khalid Alhammadi**
*Abu Dhabi Department of Education and Knowledge, UAE*

**latifa Alketbi**
*United Arab Emirates University, UAE*

**Hamada Ahmed**
*Abu Dhabi Department of Education and Knowledge, UAE*

## ABSTRACT

*This chapter explores the potential of artificial intelligence in advancing data-informed decision-making in special education. By systematically collecting and analyzing large sets of student data, AI can identify performance patterns, predict challenges, and suggest tailored interventions—all of which enhance individualized learning outcomes and streamline administrative processes. This chapter highlights successful experiences with AI in school administration to demonstrate its practical impact on special education programs. However, the adoption of AI technologies also introduces critical considerations, including data privacy, stakeholder trust, and the need for professional development. The chapter underscores the importance of strategic implementation and inclusive engagement through a balanced evaluation of both the benefits and complexities of AI-supported decision-making. When thoughtfully applied, AI can promote more responsive and efficient special education services, empowering educators to address the diverse needs of students*

DOI: 10.4018/979-8-3373-0573-8.ch013

*with greater precision and care.*

## INTRODUCTION

Artificial intelligence (AI) has evolved from a futuristic concept to an essential tool utilized across various industries. AI has significantly transformed fields such as healthcare, finance, and customer service through automation and data-driven insights. Globally, millions of individuals depend on AI to enhance efficiency, automate processes, and allocate more time to other tasks (Lametti, 2022). AI can be defined as a system wherein computers and machines collaboratively emulate logical human cognition (Tai, 2020). For individuals with disabilities, AI applications are particularly meaningful, as many utilize assistive technology features—such as speech-to-text—on smartphones and other technologically enabled devices to facilitate more effective interaction with their environments (Fernandez-Batanero et al., 2022). Indeed, most individuals engage with AI daily, often unknowingly, through routine activities such as online shopping, social media engagement, ride-sharing, travel planning, and internet searches.

In the education sector, AI has emerged as a transformative force and has influenced curriculum design, assessment of student progress, and personalization of learning experiences (Abdallah et al., 2024). The integration of AI within special education is especially promising. A critical area of exploration involves utilizing extensive datasets and advanced analytics, which enables school administrators to identify specific educational challenges, customize interventions for individual students, and optimize resource allocation effectively. This synergy between AI and special education has significant potential to enhance student outcomes and overall program efficacy (Marino & Vasquez, 2024).

## BACKGROUND

Data synthesis is foundational to effective educational practice, especially for special education administrators. This process involves collecting, compiling, and analyzing data from multiple sources to inform decision-making, policy formulation, and program selection (Bornstein et al., 2017). By synthesizing and disseminating data-driven findings, administrators can make informed decisions regarding staffing and programming (Hammond et al., 2020). This comprehensive approach provides valuable insights into program effectiveness, student outcomes, and areas requiring improvement, thereby enabling administrators to strategically enhance educational experiences for all learners.

One prevalent approach discussed in the literature is data-based decision-making (DBDM), which involves analyzing student data to guide decisions aimed at improving student outcomes and instructional effectiveness (Bruhn et al., 2020). DBDM empowers educators to effectively select, adapt, and refine interventions tailored specifically to individual student needs (Cook et al., 2018). Despite growing recognition of its value in special education, many educators do not consistently employ a data-driven approach when designing instruction for students with disabilities. Even when teachers collect progress-monitoring data, it is often inadequately utilized in instructional planning or program selection. This underuse is problematic, as DBDM has been demonstrated to significantly enhance student performance (Wilcox et al., 2021). Addressing this implementation gap is critical to maximizing the effectiveness of special education programs and ensuring all students receive appropriate support.

Historically, synthesizing extensive datasets and generating detailed analyses, visualizations, and conclusions could require days or even weeks. Currently, advanced artificial intelligence models considerably expedite this process, providing quicker and more accurate insights aligned with administrative objectives. The subsequent section of this paper examines traditional methods of systematic data collection and analysis, discusses current practices in data-based decision-making, and explores AI-driven methods—particularly the utilization of ChatGPT—for analyzing, synthesizing, and communicating educational findings. Collectively, these approaches can enhance administrators' capabilities in evidence-based decision-making. Additionally, this paper presents case examples illustrating the experiences of three school administrators who successfully integrated AI to improve their special education programs.

## LITERATURE REVIEW

### Approaches to Systematic Data Collection, Preparation, and Tool Analysis

Systematic data collection constitutes a critical initial step in special education research because it ensures information is gathered consistently, systematically, and reliably (Wilcox et al., 2021). Researchers must establish explicit protocols—including standardized tools, clear criteria, and detailed guidelines—to minimize variability and potential bias among data collectors (Taherdoost, 2021). Conducting pilot testing before full-scale implementation significantly enhances reliability and validity, enabling early detection and resolution of potential issues (Malmqvist et al.,

2019). After collection, data must be compiled into standardized formats suitable for analysis, typically utilizing specialized software (e.g., PowerSchool or EdSurvey), aligned specifically with the study's objectives. Subsequently, data is categorized by student demographics, disability type, or individualized education program (IEP) goals, rendering it manageable and actionable.

Following data compilation, data cleansing occurs, involving identification and correction of errors, inconsistencies, and missing values (Ridzuan & Zainon, 2019), as well as standardization of data formats and coding schemes (Cai & Zhu, 2015). This meticulous process enhances dataset integrity and improves the reliability of subsequent analyses (Pampaka et al., 2016). Careful attention to detail in these steps enables researchers and administrators to derive meaningful insights rather than contend with data irregularities. Effective data-cleaning procedures mitigate the risk of erroneous conclusions and strengthen research credibility. Addressing and correcting problematic data remains a persistent challenge in data analytics because failure to address inaccuracies can result in unreliable analyses and compromised decision-making (Chu et al., 2016). This comprehensive approach ensures findings accurately reflect real-world conditions and support informed decision-making.

Numerous digital tools facilitate the data collection, cleaning, and analysis processes (Center for Innovation, Design, and Digital Learning, 2024). Spreadsheet software, such as Microsoft Excel and Google Sheets, provides foundational capabilities—including pivot tables and charts—for aggregating and visualizing special education data. However, these applications often struggle to manage large datasets efficiently, leading to performance issues and heightened susceptibility to errors during manual data entry and manipulation (Powell et al., 2008). Moreover, spreadsheet tools possess limited advanced statistical analysis features compared to specialized software, potentially restricting comprehensive data interpretation (Reschenhofer & Matthes, 2015).

Advanced statistical software packages such as SPSS provide robust quantitative analytical capabilities; however, these tools involve significant licensing costs and steep learning curves, necessitating specialized user training to fully leverage their capabilities. In contrast, programming languages such as R and Python offer extensive flexibility, facilitating customized analyses and advanced machine-learning applications. Nevertheless, these languages require substantial programming expertise and considerable setup time, limiting accessibility for educators and administrators lacking technical skills (Milovanović & Perišić, 2020).

Visualization platforms such as Tableau and Power BI generate interactive dashboards suitable for diverse stakeholders. Additionally, learning management systems (LMSs)—such as Canvas, Blackboard, and Moodle—offer built-in analytics to track student engagement, discussion participation, assignment submissions, and academic progress, helping educators provide timely interventions. However,

LMS platforms present challenges, such as limited customization and flexibility, which hinder tailoring analytics to meet the specific demands of special education programs. Moreover, the substantial volume of data generated may result in information overload, complicating extraction of meaningful insights without appropriate analytical tools and expertise. Additionally, user adoption and sufficient training pose significant obstacles, as inadequate support can lead to low utilization rates and improper data management.

## Common Practices of Data-Based Decision Making

The implementation of data-based decision making (DBDM) is a critical strategy for enhancing instructional effectiveness and improving student learning outcomes (Badawy & Alkaabi, 2023). By leveraging data, educators can establish appropriate learning goals, monitor student progress, and provide targeted support throughout the learning process. In special education contexts, DBDM enables teachers to make informed decisions regarding the selection, adaptation, and modification of interventions to meet individual student needs (Cook et al., 2018). However, even when teachers collect data on the progress of students with disabilities, these data are frequently underutilized in instructional planning or program selection, despite evidence that DBDM positively influences student performance (Wilcox et al., 2021).

Studies have demonstrated that students with special needs achieve significantly better outcomes when educators implement DBDM compared to when such practices are not used (Fuchs et al., 2014, as cited in Bruhn et al., 2020). Through content analysis, Karimah and Kurniawati (2024) identified common steps in the DBDM process: establishing a performance baseline, setting learning goals, monitoring progress through instructional adjustments, and selecting appropriate assessment tools to evaluate intervention effectiveness. Additional steps identified in some studies include reviewing evidence on intervention appropriateness and evaluating the reliability and validity of the tools used.

Despite its advantages, several challenges hinder the effective implementation of DBDM. One key barrier is teachers' limited understanding of assessment types and the complexities of establishing decision rules to evaluate student response to intervention. Many educators also report difficulty interpreting and analyzing data—skills essential to setting meaningful learning goals and adjusting instruction accordingly. These challenges not only reduce intervention effectiveness but also increase the demands on teachers' time and resources (Karimah & Kurniawati, 2024). Effective DBDM implementation requires a structured support system that includes professional development, user-friendly data tools, and collaboration among stakeholders. Without such infrastructure, integrating data-driven practices into daily instruction remains difficult. Ongoing training and institutional support are therefore essential to realizing the full potential of DBDM in improving educational outcomes.

## Leveraging GPT Models for Enhanced Data Analysis

The rise of advanced technologies, particularly Generative Pre-training Transformer (GPT) models designed for data analysis, is significantly enhancing efficiency and precision within special education administration (Marino & Vasquez, 2024). These AI models utilize machine learning and natural language processing to interpret, analyze, and generate text that closely resembles human communication, based on input data. Ray (2023) noted that GPT models, trained on extensive datasets comprising diverse textual sources, are proficient at recognizing patterns, identifying relationships, and navigating linguistic complexity. When fine-tuned using specialized educational datasets, GPT models become highly effective tools for identifying trends, making accurate predictions, and generating comprehensive, context-specific reports. Abdallah et al. (2024) indicated that these capabilities enable administrators to make informed, evidence-based decisions that improve educational program effectiveness.

The potential of GPT models in academic research and data augmentation is well-documented. In a systematic review of 412 scholarly publications, Sufi (2024) identified 77 significant contributions across three critical areas: generating and processing research data, analyzing data, and supporting research design and problem-solving. These findings underscore GPT's transformative impact across various domains, including special education. For example, according to the United States Department of Education (2024), school administrators can effectively utilize GPT in several capacities. By analyzing progress reports and assessment data from students with disabilities, GPT aids in evaluating the efficacy of Individualized Education Program (IEP) goals and instructional strategies. Specifically, GPT can detect patterns indicating progress or highlighting areas requiring intervention, thus facilitating timely adjustments to educational plans. Furthermore, GPT enhances resource allocation by analyzing data related to service provision, staffing requirements, and student outcomes. Cheng et al. (2023) found that GPT's capability to generate detailed reports and summaries streamlines reporting processes, thereby supporting administrative efficiency. Indeed, they posited that their "results and analysis show that GPT-4 can outperform an intern data analyst or a junior data analyst, and can achieve comparable performance to a senior data analyst" (Cheng et al., 2023, p. 9).

The practical utility of GPT was demonstrated in a large-scale study by Marino and Vasquez (2024), which examined the application of AI—primarily ChatGPT—in supporting data analysis and decision-making processes of special education administrators across two elementary schools, one middle school, and one high school. This research highlighted the role of AI in synthesizing large datasets, monitoring student progress, evaluating IEP effectiveness, and optimizing resource distribution. Findings emphasized AI's potential to enhance administrative efficiency by effectively identifying trends, producing comprehensive reports, and providing actionable insights for student support. However, the study also identified critical challenges, such as concerns regarding data privacy, the necessity for human oversight, and the importance of adequately training administrators to integrate AI into daily workflows effectively. These conclusions underscore AI's growing significance in augmenting data-driven decision-making in special education administration.

In practice, traditional methods of data analysis and synthesis can be exceptionally time-consuming, often requiring months of effort annually from special education administrators. Nevertheless, the Center for Innovation, Design, and Digital Learning (2024) noted that AI offers promising solutions to streamline these tasks, significantly reducing administrative workloads while simultaneously enhancing decision-making efficiency. As AI's role continues to evolve in special education administration, its potential to improve resource allocation, program evaluation, and student support becomes increasingly apparent. To illustrate this impact, the following section provides case studies of three administrators who successfully integrated AI into diverse special education programs, demonstrating tangible benefits across varied educational contexts. These illustrative examples are drawn from pseudonymized schools, each identified by a distinctive nickname.

## ILLUSTRATIVE SUCCESS STORIES IN AI-DRIVEN SPECIAL EDUCATION

### Success Story One: A Data-Driven Transformation at Falcon Elementary

At Falcon Elementary School, which serves 542 students, Special Education Administrator Ms. Sarah encountered significant challenges in tracking, analyzing, and updating IEPs for the school's diverse student population with disabilities. Managing a caseload exceeding 47 students receiving specialized services, Ms. Sarah and her team spent extensive hours manually reviewing assessment data, progress reports, and teacher observations. Despite their dedicated efforts, delays in data analysis frequently led to reactive rather than proactive interventions, resulting in gaps in student support. Teachers reported difficulties promptly identifying students who required additional assistance, while parents often requested more timely and transparent updates regarding their children's academic progress. Determined to enhance these processes, Ms. Sarah initiated the integration of GPT-driven data analysis to streamline progress monitoring, synthesize multiple data sources, and produce IEP reports with greater accuracy and efficiency. Instead of relying solely on manually compiled spreadsheets, the system automatically integrated data from assessments, classroom observations, and behavioral reports, promptly identifying patterns and recommending evidence-based interventions tailored to individual student needs.

Nevertheless, implementing the ChatGPT system presented its own challenges. One of the most significant hurdles involved obtaining parental consent for GPT-based analysis of their children's individual data. Initially, many parents expressed strong resistance due to privacy and data security concerns. To mitigate these apprehensions, the school adopted an anonymous data entry protocol that processed student information without identifiable details. Additionally, Falcon Elementary School hosted informational workshops featuring live demonstrations that enabled parents to directly observe the GPT system's functionality and better understand its role in data analysis. Over time, this transparent and participatory approach significantly improved parents' perceptions, which fostered acceptance of the AI system and recognition of its potential to enhance personalized learning support.

Gaining teachers' trust in GPT-generated insights represented another notable challenge, as many educators questioned the system's ability to accurately capture nuanced aspects of student learning and progress. To address this skepticism, Ms. Sarah conducted comparative analyses between GPT-generated and traditional manual reports, highlighting three primary advantages: (1) time efficiency, as the AI system significantly reduced report generation duration, enabling teachers to dedicate more time to student interaction rather than paperwork; (2) depth of analysis, because, unlike manual reporting methods, GPT revealed subtle longitudinal learning patterns and comprehension gaps frequently overlooked by traditional methods; and (3) data-driven decision-making, as GPT-generated reports synthesized diverse informational sources, delivering actionable insights that empowered teachers to make informed instructional decisions more effectively. Ms. Sarah emphasized that, "Despite the remarkable analytical capabilities of GPT in generating reports, the final touch of human judgment remains essential to ensure contextual accuracy and a nuanced understanding of student needs."

An additional challenge was effective prompt engineering—the GPT system frequently required precisely formulated queries to deliver relevant and actionable outputs. During initial implementation, Ms. Sarah and her team struggled to refine their prompts, often resulting in responses that were either excessively vague or overly detailed. Through extensive experimentation, they developed structured, standardized prompts to ensure consistent, actionable results. Data consistency also emerged as an issue, given that teachers utilized diverse documentation formats, which initially caused confusion in GPT data analysis. To resolve this, Ms. Sarah collaborated closely with information technology specialists to establish a uniform data entry protocol, thereby enhancing the accuracy and consistency of GPT analyses across all cases.

Following the resolution of these initial obstacles, the resulting impact proved transformative. Teachers began receiving automated alerts when students were not achieving IEP goals, facilitating timely instructional adjustments. Parents benefitted from clear and comprehensible progress summaries during IEP meetings, enhancing transparency and collaboration between educators and families. Furthermore, administrative workload significantly decreased for Ms. Sarah's team and teaching staff. By the end of the first term of GPT implementation, Falcon Elementary School documented improved timeliness in IEP updates and increased teacher satisfaction with data accessibility. For Ms. Sarah, GPT not only streamlined administrative tasks but revolutionized Falcon Elementary's approach to supporting students, demonstrating technology's potential as a vital resource in developing effective, student-centered special education programs.

## Success Story Two: A Proactive Approach at Phoenix Rise School

At Phoenix Rise School, serving a student population of 860, Special Education Administrator Mr. Khalid encountered a persistent challenge: providing timely and effective support to students experiencing reading difficulties. Despite dedicated intervention programs, many students struggling with reading were identified too late, frequently after falling significantly behind their peers. Teachers depended primarily on periodic assessments, which, although beneficial, failed to deliver real-time insights into student progress. Parents expressed frustration regarding inconsistent communication about their children's reading development, while educators struggled to determine the most effective individualized interventions. Recognizing the need for a systematic, data-driven method to proactively monitor student progress and customize interventions, Mr. Khalid initiated the integration of Generative Pre-trained Transformer technology as a supplementary tool within existing English literacy programs.

Using a GPT-based data analysis system, the school continuously monitored students' reading performance by examining classroom assessments, teacher observations, and reading fluency recordings. GPT efficiently identified students displaying early indicators of reading difficulty, promptly alerting intervention teams to address minor learning gaps before they escalated into significant barriers. This automated process eliminated labor-intensive manual reviews, streamlined interventions, and ensured timely support for struggling readers. Although the new system promised enhanced accuracy and timely monitoring, its implementation presented several notable challenges.

One major obstacle involved teacher adaptation, as many educators remained accustomed to traditional assessment methods and were initially skeptical regarding GPT-generated insights. To address this, Mr. Khalid facilitated collaborative training sessions, enabling teachers to compare GPT-driven recommendations directly with their professional observations. Over time, teachers recognized that GPT-supported insights aligned closely with their judgments and additionally revealed subtle reading difficulties potentially overlooked by traditional methods. Nevertheless, some teachers continued to exhibit resistance. For instance, one teacher remarked, "Cautious teachers can identify learning difficulties if they are alert and carefully monitor the data."

In response, Mr. Khalid clarified that GPT technology, when guided by accurately structured prompts, could efficiently detect patterns, significantly reducing human oversight risk. To further persuade educators, he demonstrated real-time GPT-generated analyses illustrating the system's immediate identification of student progress and signaling of potential issues. Mr. Khalid emphasized that although AI streamlines analysis and synthesis, human oversight remains essential for interpreting results and making informed decisions. He reassured teachers that GPT technology complements rather than replaces their professional expertise, offering rapid and comprehensive data-driven insights surpassing traditional manual methods. By the conclusion of training, most educators acknowledged the substantial time savings and improved accuracy provided by GPT analyses, subsequently leading to more effective intervention strategies for students struggling with reading.

An additional challenge involved fine-tuning GPT recommendations. Initially, the system flagged excessive numbers of students, generating unwarranted concerns. Through refining prompts and adjusting data parameters, Mr. Khalid's team successfully calibrated the GPT system to differentiate effectively between temporary struggles and persistent difficulties, ensuring targeted interventions reached only students genuinely requiring support. Furthermore, parental concerns emerged regarding data privacy. To build trust, Mr. Khalid implemented explicit data protection protocols and conducted informational sessions clarifying AI's supportive role in enhancing—not replacing—human decision-making.

Within the initial six months following GPT implementation, Phoenix Rise School observed a marked increase in early intervention cases, enabling students to receive targeted support months earlier than previously possible. Teachers reported increased confidence in identifying reading difficulties, and parents indicated greater satisfaction with the transparency and timeliness of communication related to their children's reading progress. A notable success story involved Salem, a third-grade student previously experiencing difficulties in reading fluency but not formally identified for intervention. GPT flagged subtle inconsistencies in his performance, prompting an early literacy screening that confirmed dyslexia-related challenges. Early identification enabled teachers to implement targeted strategies promptly, resulting in Salem advancing two reading levels by the end of the year—a milestone likely requiring significantly more time under the previous system. For Mr. Khalid, integrating GPT into reading intervention programs represented more than a technological enhancement; it fundamentally transformed Phoenix Rise School's approach to supporting students, enabling earlier identification, more effective intervention, and ultimately providing struggling readers with optimal opportunities for success.

## Success Story Three: Enhancing Shadow Teacher Support at Sunflower Middle School

At Sunflower Middle School, serving 311 students, Special Education Administrator Ms. Maria encountered increasing challenges in effectively supporting students with disabilities in inclusive classroom environments. The school had established a shadow teacher program, wherein trained aides provided individualized assistance to students with autism spectrum disorder (ASD), attention deficit hyperactivity disorder (ADHD), and other learning differences. However, the absence of a standardized system hindered effective tracking of support efficacy, student progress monitoring, and consistent communication among shadow teachers, classroom educators, and special education staff. Shadow teachers often became overwhelmed by manual documentation tasks, complicating the identification of behavioral patterns, learning progress, and emotional well-being indicators. Additionally, general education teachers faced difficulties in effectively collaborating with shadow teachers due to inconsistent and unstructured reporting. Consequently, Ms. Maria sought to implement a more efficient, data-driven solution.

To address these challenges, Ms. Maria integrated a GPT-based tool for tracking and reporting student progress in real time. The GPT-supported system enabled shadow teachers to (1) digitally record and categorize student observations across academic performance, behavioral responses, and social interactions through GPT's text-to-speech and speech-to-text functionalities, facilitating streamlined data entry and analysis; (2) identify trends in student performance related to engagement, participation, and responsiveness to interventions; (3) generate comprehensive daily and weekly summary reports for teachers and parents, highlighting significant student developments; and (4) recommend intervention strategies informed by data from analogous student cases, thus enabling shadow teachers to adjust support methods proactively.

Instead of relying on separate handwritten documentation, shadow teachers now directly input key observations via mobile-friendly GPT interfaces. The system analyzes and synthesizes these inputs, categorizing them into academic, behavioral, and social interaction data, thereby allowing Ms. Maria's team to systematically track and visualize progress across multiple students. Additionally, GPT-generated heatmaps and progress charts offer clear visual representations of intervention areas, ensuring critical patterns are promptly identified. The platform also flags students exhibiting persistent difficulties, assisting the team in proactively modifying support strategies to preclude issue escalation. By aggregating observations into meaningful reports, educators gain comprehensive insights into student development, ensuring targeted, timely, and data-informed interventions. Despite GPT's evident potential, the implementation process was accompanied by several notable challenges.

First, initial resistance emerged among shadow teachers during system training, as some aides expressed concerns regarding potential replacement of their professional judgment or an increase in workload. Ms. Maria addressed these concerns by demonstrating the system's capability to reduce paperwork burdens, deliver structured analytical insights, and facilitate greater focus on direct student engagement. Second, ensuring meaningful GPT-generated recommendations posed difficulties during the initial weeks of use. Early reports frequently offered generic suggestions that inadequately addressed individual student complexities. To resolve this, Ms. Maria's team refined the prompts and reporting formats, enabling GPT to incorporate educator feedback and historical intervention data, thus generating increasingly personalized and actionable insights. Third, improving collaboration between classroom and shadow teachers required deliberate effort. Prior to system implementation, communication had been sporadic and informal. The incorporation of GPT-generated reports into structured weekly planning meetings facilitated enhanced understanding among general education teachers regarding student needs, significantly improving collaborative practices in inclusive classrooms.

By the second term of spring 2025, Sunflower Middle School experienced notable improvements in communication among shadow teachers, general education teachers, and parents. Teachers reported increased confidence in adapting instructional strategies, while shadow teachers felt better equipped to provide targeted student support informed by data-driven insights. One illustrative case involved Mia, a sixth-grade student diagnosed with ADHD, who exhibited frequent impulse control difficulties and reduced concentration. Utilizing the GPT tool, Mia's shadow teacher, Ms. Nisreen, documented real-time instances of inattentiveness and emotional distress, revealing distinct patterns of decreased concentration post-lunch and in noisy settings. Consequently, the school modified Mia's schedule to incorporate sensory breaks and quiet work intervals, substantially reducing disruptive behaviors and enhancing her academic engagement. By the end of the first term, parent satisfaction regarding shadow teacher support increased, and classroom educators observed enhanced inclusivity. Ms. Maria emphasized that GPT technology did not supplant shadow teachers' roles but augmented their capacities to deliver timely, individualized assistance, thereby ensuring students with disabilities received appropriate support in inclusive educational environments.

## DISCUSSION

The implementation of AI-driven solutions in special education administration has demonstrated substantial potential for enhancing efficiency, accuracy, and personalized interventions for students with diverse learning needs. The three illustrative cases—Falcon Elementary School, Phoenix Rise School, and Sunflower Middle School—highlight effective integration of AI within Individualized Education Programs (IEPs), reading intervention frameworks, and shadow teacher support systems. At Falcon Elementary School, Ms. Sarah successfully adopted GPT-based data analysis for tracking student progress on IEPs, facilitating timely interventions, and significantly improving collaboration between teachers and parents. GPT's capability to synthesize data from multiple sources enabled educators to concentrate on instructional strategies rather than administrative duties. This aligns with findings by Naznin et al. (2025), who indicated that GPT effectively supports the coding, synthesis, and analysis of educational data.

Similarly, at Phoenix Rise School, Mr. Khalid implemented a GPT-enhanced literacy support system designed to promptly identify students experiencing difficulties with reading fluency and comprehension. This proactive identification promoted early interventions, subsequently improving student outcomes. Supporting this approach, Li and Liu (2024) demonstrated that GPT can effectively monitor and track progress among students with disabilities. Finally, at Sunflower Middle School, Ms. Maria utilized GPT technology to enhance shadow teacher efficiency by establishing systematic, real-time tracking of student behavior, academic performance, and social interactions. This innovation strengthened communication and collaborative practices among teachers, aides, and parents. As noted by Abdallah et al. (2024), such AI-driven capabilities empower administrators to make informed, evidence-based decisions, thereby improving the overall efficacy of educational programs. Despite these notable achievements, integrating AI into educational settings continues to present various implementation challenges.

## Challenges in AI Implementation

### Privacy and Ethical Concerns

One of the primary obstacles in adopting artificial intelligence-driven tools for special education involves addressing parental concerns regarding data security and potential misuse of student information. Similar concerns have been documented in prior research, including a study by Habib et al. (2022). At Falcon Elementary School, many parents initially resisted the implementation of GPT-based data analysis due to fears surrounding privacy breaches and unauthorized surveillance. To mitigate these concerns, the school adopted an anonymous data entry protocol and hosted informational workshops to explain its security safeguards and demonstrate how AI processes could maintain student confidentiality. This transparent and proactive approach reassured families and reframed AI as a support mechanism rather than a threat. As a result, parental acceptance of the technology increased significantly, enabling more seamless system integration.

### Teacher Resistance and Training Needs

Another significant challenge was overcoming teacher skepticism regarding AI-generated insights. At Phoenix Rise School, some educators expressed hesitation in trusting GPT-derived reading assessments, believing them to be less accurate than traditional teacher observations. In response, Mr. Khalid conducted comparative analyses between GPT-generated reports and conventional assessments, demonstrating that AI could detect learning patterns that might otherwise go unnoticed. Similarly, at Sunflower Middle School, some shadow teachers feared that AI tools might diminish or replace their professional roles. However, through interactive training sessions and gradual implementation, these educators came to perceive AI as an enhancement of their expertise rather than a replacement.

### Data Consistency and AI Prompt Engineering

Maintaining consistent data inputs proved critical for producing meaningful and actionable insights. AI models are highly dependent on standardized data formatting; at Falcon Elementary School, inconsistencies in data entry initially resulted in inaccurate GPT-generated outputs. To address this issue, Ms. Sarah collaborated with information technology specialists to establish a uniform data entry framework, improving reliability and coherence in the system's analyses. Additionally, prompt engineering emerged as a key challenge. Poorly structured queries frequently resulted in vague or overly detailed outputs. Through iterative refinements and systematic feedback collection, administrators developed optimized prompts that improved the precision and usefulness of GPT-generated reports.

## Aligning AI with Human Decision-Making

Although AI excels at analyzing and synthesizing data, human expertise remains indispensable for providing contextual understanding and making instructional decisions. As Ms. Sarah emphasized, “despite the remarkable analytical capabilities of GPT in generating reports, the final touch of human judgment remains essential to ensure contextual accuracy and a nuanced understanding of student needs.” In practice, AI functioned as a decision-support tool rather than an autonomous authority on student outcomes. Teachers and administrators used GPT insights in conjunction with their professional knowledge, integrating data-driven findings with firsthand classroom observations. This collaborative approach underscored the continued necessity of human discernment in delivering effective, individualized support for students with diverse needs.

## The Movement Toward AI in Special Education

Despite these challenges, the successful implementations at Falcon Elementary School, Phoenix Rise School, and Sunflower Middle School illustrate a growing trend toward AI integration in special education contexts. Schools are increasingly recognizing that AI can (1) reduce administrative burdens, allowing educators to allocate more time to student engagement; (2) strengthen early intervention strategies by identifying and addressing learning gaps before they widen; (3) improve communication among teachers, shadow aides, and parents through AI-generated progress reports; and (4) support more informed, data-driven decision-making. In a study of AI relevance in educational settings, Barua et al. (2022) found that AI-assisted tools have shown positive impacts on student’s learning, and have been found to be acceptable by teachers, parents, special educators and therapists and feasible to implement in their teaching or therapeutic practices. These findings suggest broad stakeholder satisfaction and perceived benefit, particularly among teachers, administrators, parents, and support staff who have engaged with AI-driven tools in special education settings. Stakeholders have reported improvements not only in administrative efficiency but also in the precision and responsiveness of interventions, which in turn contribute to better student outcomes. Parents have expressed greater confidence in the educational system’s ability to track and support their children's progress, while teachers have appreciated the reduction in paperwork and the enhanced ability to make data-informed instructional decisions.

Ultimately, these advantages contribute to more effective resource allocation, allowing school leaders to identify high-need areas and redirect staffing, funding, or materials accordingly. AI systems that can identify patterns in student needs also support more equitable distribution of services, ensuring that students with disabilities receive timely and targeted support. As support systems become more data-driven, schools are better positioned to implement personalized education plans, optimize intervention schedules, and streamline communication between stakeholders. The shift from initial skepticism to gradual acceptance has been largely driven by AI's demonstrable strengths in enhancing efficiency, improving personalization, and boosting student achievement. However, to fully realize AI's transformative potential in education, future efforts must prioritize the refinement of AI tools to better align with core educational values such as inclusivity, empathy, and student well-being. Additionally, ensuring ethical implementation will require the development of clear data governance policies and robust privacy safeguards. Structured professional development programs will be essential in equipping educators with the skills to use AI tools effectively and responsibly, fostering a culture of informed, ethical, and purposeful innovation in special education.

## Future Research Directions

Looking ahead, several avenues warrant further exploration to sustain and amplify the impact of AI in special education. Future research should prioritize the development of comprehensive strategies for ethical data governance to protect student information while leveraging the analytical capabilities of AI. Investigations aimed at reducing teacher skepticism and enhancing prompt engineering practices could provide valuable insights for optimizing the synergy between AI systems and professional judgment. Additionally, longitudinal studies are necessary to evaluate the sustained effects of AI-driven interventions on student outcomes and educational equity. Exploring the scalability and adaptability of AI tools across diverse educational settings is also essential to ensure effective and equitable implementation. Ultimately, robust interdisciplinary collaboration among educators, technologists, and policymakers will be vital to ensuring that AI innovations are not only impactful but also responsive to the evolving values, priorities, and ethical considerations of contemporary education.

## CONCLUSION

The integration of AI—particularly GPT-powered tools—into special education administration represents a pivotal advancement in how schools manage, analyze, and act upon student data. The case studies of Falcon Elementary, Phoenix Rise School, and Sunflower Middle School illustrate how AI can meaningfully reduce administrative burdens, strengthen early intervention strategies, and foster greater collaboration among educators, aides, and families. From tracking IEP progress and identifying reading challenges to supporting inclusive classroom practices, AI has proven to be an effective decision-support tool, streamlining processes that once consumed valuable time and resources. Despite this promise, the path to successful AI adoption is not without its challenges. Issues surrounding data privacy, teacher skepticism, the complexity of prompt engineering, and the essential role of human oversight must be addressed with intentionality and transparency. However, as the success stories demonstrate, these challenges can be effectively mitigated through collaborative planning, ethical safeguards, structured training, and consistent refinement of implementation practices. Looking forward, the role of AI in special education is poised to expand, offering increasingly personalized, predictive, and culturally responsive tools that enhance support for students with diverse learning needs. For administrators, the shift to data-driven decision-making empowered by AI represents more than a technological upgrade—it is a transformative step toward more inclusive, responsive, and equitable education systems. By centering the student experience and maintaining a strong partnership between human expertise and AI innovation, schools can ensure that technology becomes a lasting ally in delivering high-quality special education services.

## ACKNOWLEDGMENTS

This chapter would not have been possible without the contributions and insights of the dedicated educators, administrators, and support staff referenced throughout the discussion. Special appreciation is extended to the special education administrators who played a pivotal role in implementing AI-driven solutions within Individualized Education Programs, reading interventions, and inclusive classroom support systems. Their commitment to harnessing technology in service of student success provided compelling case studies that illustrate the transformative potential of AI in special education.

Gratitude is also due to the shadow teachers, general education teachers, and intervention specialists who actively contributed to refining AI-based tools and adapting them to address the diverse needs of their students. Their dedication to inclusive education, openness to innovation, and collaborative engagement with parents and school leaders have been instrumental in advancing best practices for the ethical and effective integration of AI in special education. Finally, sincere thanks are offered to the broader academic and research community for their ongoing contributions to the study of AI-driven decision-making and its implications for equity, accessibility, and student-centered learning.

## REFERENCES

Abdallah, A. K., Alkaabi, A. M., Mehiar, D. A., & Aradat, Z. A. (2024). Chatbots in classrooms: Tailoring education and boosting engagement. In Abdallah, A., Alkaabi, A., & Al-Riyami, R. (Eds.), *Cutting-edge innovations in teaching, leadership, technology, and assessment* (pp. 166–181). IGI Global., DOI: 10.4018/979-8-3693-0880-6.ch012

Badawy, H. R., & Alkaabi, A. M. (2023). From datafication to school improvement: The promise and perils of data-driven decision making. In Abdallah, A., & Alkaabi, A. (Eds.), *Restructuring leadership for school improvement and reform* (pp. 301–325). IGI Global., DOI: 10.4018/978-1-6684-7818-9.ch015

Barua, P. D., Vicnesh, J., Gururajan, R., Oh, S. L., Palmer, E., Azizan, M. M., & Acharya, U. R. (2022). Artificial intelligence enabled personalised assistive tools to enhance education of children with neurodevelopmental disorders—A review. *International Journal of Environmental Research and Public Health*, *19*(3), 1192. DOI: 10.3390/ijerph19031192 PMID: 35162220

Bornstein, S., Baker, R., Navarro, P., Mackey, S., Speed, D., & Sullivan, M. (2017). Putting research in place: An innovative approach to providing contextualized evidence synthesis for decision makers. *Systematic Reviews*, *6*(1), 218. Advance online publication. DOI: 10.1186/s13643-017-0606-4 PMID: 29096710

Bruhn, A. L., Wehby, J. H., & Hasselbring, T. S. (2020). Data-based decision making for social behavior: Setting a research agenda. *Journal of Positive Behavior Interventions*, *22*(2), 116–126. DOI: 10.1177/1098300719876098

Cai, L., & Zhu, Y. (2015). The challenges of data quality and data quality assessment in the big data era. *Data Science Journal*, *14*(0), 2. Advance online publication. DOI: 10.5334/dsj-2015-002

Center for Innovation, Design, and Digital Learning. (2024). *Inclusive intelligence: The impact of AI on education for all learners*. https://ciddl.org/wp-content/uploads/2024/04/Inclusive%20Intelligence_a11y_navadded.pdf

Cheng, L., Li, X., & Bing, L. (2023). Is GPT-4 a good data analyst? *arXiv*. https://arxiv.org/abs/2305.15038 DOI: 10.18653/v1/2023.findings-emnlp.637

Chu, X., Ilyas, I. F., Krishnan, S., & Wang, J. (2016, June). Data cleaning: Overview and emerging challenges. In *Proceedings of the 2016 International Conference on Management of Data* (pp. 2201–2206). DOI: 10.1145/2882903.2912574

Cook, C. R., Kilgus, S. P., & Burns, M. K. (2018). Advancing the science and practice of precision education to enhance student outcomes. *Journal of School Psychology*, *66*, 4–10. DOI: 10.1016/j.jsp.2017.11.004 PMID: 29429494

Fernandez-Batanero, J. M., Montenegro-Rueda, M., Fernandez-Cerero, J., & Garcia-Martinez, I. (2022). Assistive technology for the inclusion of students with disabilities: A systematic review. *Educational Technology Research and Development*, *70*(5), 1911–1930. DOI: 10.1007/s11423-022-10127-7

Habib, H., Jelani, S. A. K., & Najla, S. (2022). Revolutionizing inclusion: AI in adaptive learning for students with disabilities. *Multidisciplinary Science Journal*, *1*(1), 1–11.

Hammond, J. W., Moss, P. A., Huynh, M. Q., & Lagoze, C. (2020). Research synthesis infrastructures: Shaping knowledge in education. *Review of Research in Education*, *44*(1), 1–35. DOI: 10.3102/0091732X20907350

Karimah, A. N., & Kurniawati, F. (2024). Precision in special education: Insights from a systematic review on data-based decision making. *Jurnal Kependidikan: Jurnal Hasil Penelitian dan Kajian Kepustakaan di Bidang Pendidikan, Pengajaran dan Pembelajaran*, *10*(4), 1485–1495.

Lametti, D. (2022, December 7). A.I. could be great for college essays. *Slate*. https://slate.com/technology/2022/12/chatgpt-college-essay-plagiarism.html

Li, Y.-F., & Liu, C.-T. (2024). Using self-monitoring and ChatGPT to teach students with intellectual disability email writing. *Global Journal of Intellectual & Developmental Disabilities*, *13*(4), 555871. DOI: 10.19080/GJIDD.2024.13.555871

Malmqvist, J., Hellberg, K., Möllås, G., Rose, R., & Shevlin, M. (2019). Conducting the pilot study: A neglected part of the research process? Methodological findings supporting the importance of piloting in qualitative research studies. *International Journal of Qualitative Methods*, *18*, 1–11. DOI: 10.1177/1609406919878341

Marino, M. T., & Vasquez, E.III. (2024). Special education administrators' use of artificial intelligence (AI) to synthesize data. *Journal of Special Education Leadership*, *37*(2), 62–76.

Milovanović, M., & Perišić, J. (2020). Advantages and limitations of using SPSS in teaching statistics. In *MEFkon 2020: Innovation as the Initiator of Development* (p. 274). Faculty of Applied Management, Economics and Finance.

Naznin, K., Al Mahmud, A., Nguyen, M. T., & Chua, C. (2025). ChatGPT integration in higher education for personalized learning, academic writing, and coding tasks: A systematic review. *Computers*, *14*(2), 53. DOI: 10.3390/computers14020053

Pampaka, M., Hutcheson, G., & Williams, J. (2016). Handling missing data: Analysis of a challenging data set using multiple imputation. *International Journal of Research & Method in Education*, *39*(1), 19–37. DOI: 10.1080/1743727X.2014.979146

Powell, S. G., Baker, K. R., & Lawson, B. (2008). A critical review of the literature on spreadsheet errors. *Decision Support Systems*, *46*(1), 128–138. DOI: 10.1016/j.dss.2008.06.001

Reschenhofer, T., & Matthes, F. (2015). An empirical study on spreadsheet shortcomings from an information systems perspective. In *Business Information Systems: 18th International Conference, BIS 2015, Poznań, Poland, June 24–26, 2015, Proceedings 18* (pp. 50–61). Springer International Publishing. DOI: 10.1007/978-3-319-19027-3_5

Ridzuan, F., & Zainon, W. M. N. W. (2019). A review on data cleansing methods for big data. *Procedia Computer Science*, *161*, 731–738. https://www.sciencedirect.com/science/article/pii/S1877050919318885. DOI: 10.1016/j.procs.2019.11.177

Sufi, F. (2024). Generative pre-trained transformer (GPT) in research: A systematic review on data augmentation. *Information (Basel)*, *15*(2), 99. DOI: 10.3390/info15020099

Taherdoost, H. (2021). Data collection methods and tools for research: A step-by-step guide to choose data collection technique for academic and business research projects. *International Journal of Academic Research in Management, 10*(1), 10–38.

Tai, M. C. (2020). The impact of artificial intelligence on human society and bioethics. *Tzu-Chi Medical Journal, 32*(4), 339–343. DOI: 10.4103/tcmj.tcmj_71_20 PMID: 33163378

Wilcox, G., Fernandez Conde, C., & Kowbel, A. (2021). Using evidence-based practice and data-based decision making in inclusive education. *Education Sciences, 11*(3), 129. DOI: 10.3390/educsci11030129

## KEY TERMS AND DEFINITIONS

**Artificial Intelligence (AI):** The development of computer systems capable of performing tasks that typically require human intelligence, such as analyzing data, making decisions, recognizing patterns, and processing language.

**Data-Based Decision Making (DBDM):** The systematic use of student data to inform instructional methods, intervention planning, and policy decisions aimed at improving educational outcomes.

**Ethical AI:** The responsible application of artificial intelligence that prioritizes student privacy, mitigates bias, and ensures human oversight in educational decision-making processes.

**Inclusive Classroom:** A learning environment in which students of all abilities, including those with disabilities, have equitable access to instruction, resources, and support to promote academic and social development.

**Individualized Education Program (IEP):** A legally mandated, personalized plan that outlines specific learning goals, accommodations, and services for students with disabilities to ensure access to appropriate educational support.

**Intervention Strategies:** Targeted instructional approaches designed to support students experiencing academic, behavioral, or developmental challenges through structured, individualized assistance.

**Machine Learning:** A subfield of artificial intelligence that enables computers to improve performance on specific tasks by identifying patterns in data and adapting without explicit programming.

**Natural Language Processing (NLP):** A branch of artificial intelligence that enables computers to understand, interpret, and generate human language, commonly used in applications such as speech recognition, chatbots, and automated text analysis.

**Prompt Engineering:** The process of crafting and refining inputs provided to AI models to elicit accurate, relevant, and context-sensitive responses for tasks such as data analysis and language processing.

**Special Education:** A field of education that provides tailored instruction, accommodations, and resources to students with disabilities, ensuring their academic, social, and developmental needs are met in accordance with legal and ethical standards.

# Compilation of References


Abbasi, M. U. R., Zulfiqar, A., Rasool, M. S., & Quadri, S. S. A. (2024). Impact of AI on the inclusion of Learners with Special needs: Public Policy Perspective in Contemporary Scenario. *Arbor, 11*(1). https://doi.org/doi.org/10.1234.arbor.1`1.1.05

Abbott, R. G. (2006). *Automated expert modeling for automated student evaluation: Lecture Notes in Computer Science (Including Subseries Lecture Notes in Artificial Intelligence and Lecture Notes in Bioinformatics), 4053 LNCS*, pp. 1-10, https://doi.org/DOI: 10.1007/11774303_1

Abdallah, A. K., Al Kaabi, A. M., & Ramadan, R. S. (2023). The critical role of principals in leading effective inclusive schools. In *Inclusive Phygital Learning Approaches and Strategies for Students With Special Needs* (pp. 256–281). IGI Global. DOI: 10.4018/978-1-6684-8504-0.ch012

Abdallah, A. K., & Alkaabi, A. M. (Eds.). (2023). *Restructuring leadership for school improvement and reform*. IGI Global. DOI: 10.4018/978-1-6684-7818-9

Abdallah, A. K., Alkaabi, A. M., Mehiar, D. A., & Aradat, Z. A. (2024). Chatbots in classrooms: Tailoring education and boosting engagement. In Abdallah, A., Alkaabi, A., & Al-Riyami, R. (Eds.), *Cutting-edge innovations in teaching, leadership, technology, and assessment* (pp. 166–181). IGI Global., DOI: 10.4018/979-8-3693-0880-6.ch012

Abdallah, A. K., & Farhan, A. F. (2023). Breaking barriers and empowering women leaders to drive school improvement. In *Restructuring Leadership for School Improvement and Reform* (pp. 399–419). IGI Global. DOI: 10.4018/978-1-6684-7818-9.ch020

Abdallah, A., Ismail, O., Abdallah, R. K., & Alkaabi, A. M. (2023). Perceptions of Students About the Use of Webinars in Classrooms: A Case of Abu Dhabi University. [IJICTE]. *International Journal of Information and Communication Technology Education, 19*(1), 1–17. DOI: 10.4018/IJICTE.322793

Abd-alrazaq, A. A., Alajlani, M., Ahmad, R., AlSaad, R., Aziz, S., Ahmed, A., & Sheikh, J. (2023). The performance of wearable AI in detecting stress among students: Systematic review and meta-analysis. *Journal of Medical Internet Research*, *26*, e52622. Advance online publication. DOI: 10.2196/52622 PMID: 38294846

Abd-Alrazaq, A., Alhuwail, D., Schneider, J., Toro, C. T., Ahmed, A., Alzubaidi, M., Alajlani, M., & Househ, M. (2022). The performance of artificial intelligence-driven technologies in diagnosing mental disorders: An umbrella review. *NPJ Digital Medicine*, *5*(1), 87. DOI: 10.1038/s41746-022-00631-8 PMID: 35798934

Abedi, E. A., & Ametepey, A. K. (2024). Leadership practices and support structures enabling teachers' informal learning for educational technology use: An appreciative inquiry approach. *Professional Development in Education*, •••, 1–15. DOI: 10.1080/19415257.2024.2330973

Abimbola, C., Eden, C. A., Chisom, O. N., & Adeniyi, I. S. (2024). *Integrating AI in education: Opportunities, challenges, and ethical considerations*. Magna Scientia Advanced Research and Reviews.

Abulibdeh, A., Baya Chatti, C., Alkhereibi, A., & El Menshawy, S. (2025). A Scoping Review of the Strategic Integration of Artificial Intelligence in Higher Education: Transforming University Excellence Themes and Strategic Planning in the Digital Era. *European Journal of Education*, *60*(1), e12908. DOI: 10.1111/ejed.12908

Abulibdeh, A., Zaidan, E., & Abulibdeh, R. (2024). Navigating the confluence of artificial intelligence and education for sustainable development in the era of industry 4.0: Challenges, opportunities, and ethical dimensions. *Journal of Cleaner Production*, *437*, 140527. DOI: 10.1016/j.jclepro.2023.140527

Acharya, U. R., Oh, S. L., Hagiwara, Y., Tan, J. H., & Adeli, H. (2018). Deep convolutional neural network for the automated detection and diagnosis of seizure using EEG signals. *Computers in Biology and Medicine*, *100*, 270–278. DOI: 10.1016/j.compbiomed.2017.09.017 PMID: 28974302

Ademola, E. O. (2024). *Reading Strategies in the AI Age: Enhancing Comprehension and Engagement with Advanced Technologies*. Advances in Multidisciplinary & Scientific Research Journal Publications., DOI: 10.22624/AIMS/ACCRABE-SPOKE2024P13

Ahmad, W., Raj, R., & Shokeen, R. (2025). Reshaping Special Education: Strategic Use of Artificial Intelligence. In *Transforming Special Education Through Artificial Intelligence* (pp. 1-44). IGI Global. DOI: DOI: 10.4018/979-8-3693-5538-1.ch001

Ahn, J., & Ahn, M. (2021). The role of AI in primary education: A double-edged sword for social emotional learning. *Journal of Educational Technology*, *48*(3), 231–247.

Akbar, S., Pranajaya, S. A., Nurkadarwati, N., Hoesny, R., & Mutmainnah, I. (2024). Leadership Dynamics in The Era of Educational Transformation: Integrating The Concept of Adaptable Leadership in Sustainable Educational Administration. *International Journal of Teaching and Learning*, *2*(1), 223–235.

Al Maktoum, S. B., & Al Kaabi, A. M. (2024). Exploring teachers' experiences within the teacher evaluation process: A qualitative multi-case study. *Cogent Education*, *11*(1), 2287931. Advance online publication. DOI: 10.1080/2331186X.2023.2287931

Alabdulhadi, A., & Faisal, M. (2021). Systematic literature review of STEM self-study related ITSs. *Education and Information Technologies*, *26*(2), 1549–1588. DOI: 10.1007/s10639-020-10315-z

Alasadi, E. A., & Baiz, C. R. (2023). Generative AI in Education and Research: Opportunities, Concerns, and Solutions. *Journal of Chemical Education*, *100*(8), 2965–2971. DOI: 10.1021/acs.jchemed.3c00323

Aldous, S. M., & Ismail, G. (2024). Academics in Exile: Navigating New Educational Landscapes Amidst Displacement and Uncertainty. In E. Sengupta & A. Arnthorsson (Eds.), Resilience of Educators in Extraordinary Circumstances: War, Disaster, and Emergencies (pp. 9-28). IGI Global Scientific Publishing. DOI: 10.4018/979-8-3693-1483-8.ch002

Aldous, S. M., & Ismail, G. A. (2024). Changing and Adapting Curriculum While Teaching: Narratives From Afghan Academics and Students. In E. Sengupta & A. Arnthorsson (Eds.), Resilience of Educators in Extraordinary Circumstances: War, Disaster, and Emergencies (pp. 54-73). IGI Global Scientific Publishing. DOI: 10.4018/979-8-3693-1483-8.ch004

Aldous, S. M., & Ismail, G. A. (2025). Safeguarding the Future: Integrating Student Safety Into Sustainable Education Practices. In Legal Frameworks and Educational Strategies for Sustainable Development (pp. 367-396). IGI Global. https://DOI: 10.4018/979-8-3693-2987-0.ch018

Aldous, S. M., & Ismail, G. A. (2024). Digital Echoes: Navigating Social Media's Labyrinth of Prejudices and Cultural Stereotypes. In Barreto, I., & Roman Etxebarrieta, G. (Eds.), *Transformative Intercultural Global Education* (pp. 77–98). IGI Global Scientific Publishing., DOI: 10.4018/979-8-3693-2057-0.ch005

Aldous, S. M., & Ismail, G. A. (2025). AI for Sustainable Emergency Preparedness and Response in Schools. In Tariq, M., & Sergio, R. (Eds.), *Convergence of AI, Education, and Business for Sustainability* (pp. 51–74). IGI Global Scientific Publishing., DOI: 10.4018/979-8-3373-1917-9.ch003

Alessandri, G., Zuffianò, A., & Perinelli, E. (2017). Evaluating intervention programs with a pretest-posttest design: A structural equation modeling approach. *Frontiers in Psychology*, *8*, 223. DOI: 10.3389/fpsyg.2017.00223 PMID: 28303110

Alfredo, R., Echeverria, V., Jin, Y., Yan, L., Swiecki, Z., Gašević, D., & Martinez-Maldonado, R. (2024). Human-centred learning analytics and AI in education: A systematic literature review. *Computers and Education: Artificial Intelligence*, 100215.

Alhuwaydi, A. M. (2024). Exploring the Role of Artificial intelligence in Mental Healthcare: Current Trends and Future Directions. *Risk Management and Healthcare Policy*, *17*, 1339–1348. DOI: 10.2147/RMHP.S461562 PMID: 38799612

Ali, S., Payne, B. H., Williams, R., Park, H. W., & Breazeal, C. (2019). *Constructionism, Ethics, and Creativity: Developing Primary and Middle School Artificial Intelligence Education*.

Alias, R., Alias, N. A., Ibrahim, A. B., Attan, H., & Kadir, A. L. (2012). What Do the Disabled Students Need? A Study on the Needs of the Special Educational Needs (SEN) Learners in Malaysian Public Universities. *The European Journal of Social & Behavioural Sciences*, *3*(3), 536–551. DOI: 10.15405/FutureAcademy/ejsbs(2301-2218).2012.3.15

Ali, O., Murray, P. A., Momin, M., Dwivedi, Y. K., & Malik, T. (2024). The effects of artificial intelligence applications in educational settings: Challenges and strategies. *Technological Forecasting and Social Change*, *199*, 123076. DOI: 10.1016/j.techfore.2023.123076

Aliu, T. V. (2024). Artificial Intelligence in Special Education: A Literature review. *International Journal of Advanced Networking and Applications*, *16*(02), 6360–6367. DOI: 10.35444/IJANA.2024.16208

Alkaabi, A. M., & Almaamari, S. A. (2020). Supervisory Feedback in the Principal Evaluation Process. *International Journal of Evaluation and Research in Education*, *9*(3), 503–509. https://eric.ed.gov/?id=EJ1274705. DOI: 10.11591/ijere.v9i3.20504

Alkahtani, H., Aldhyani, T. H. H., & Alqarni, A. A. (2024). Artificial intelligence models to predict disability for mental health disorders. *Journal of Disability Research*.

AlMakinah, R., Norcini-Pala, A., Disney, L., & Canbaz, M. A. (2024). Enhancing mental health support through human-AI collaboration: Toward secure and empathetic AI-enabled chatbots. *Journal of Digital Health Advances.*

AlMakinah, R., Norcini-Pala, A., Disney, L., & Canbaz, M. A. (2024). Enhancing mental health support through human-AI collaboration: Toward secure and empathetic AI-enabled chatbots. *Journal of Digital Health Advances*, *12*(4), 100–115. DOI: 10.53022/oarjst.2024.11.2.0102

Almasri, F. (2024). Exploring the Impact of Artificial Intelligence in Teaching and Learning of Science: A Systematic Review of Empirical Research. *Research in Science Education*, *54*(5), 977–997. Advance online publication. DOI: 10.1007/s11165-024-10176-3

Almethen, A. (2024). Challenges in implementing artificial intelligence applications in secondary-level education: A teacher-centric perspective. ( ).

Almufareh, M. F., Tehsin, S., Humayun, M., & Kausar, S. (2023). Intellectual Disability and Technology: An Artificial Intelligence Perspective and Framework. *Journal of Disability Research*, *2*(4), 58–70. DOI: 10.57197/JDR-2023-0055

Alnahdi, G. (2014). Assistive Technology in Special Education and the Universal Design for Learning. *The Turkish Online Journal of Educational Technology*, *13*(2), 2.

Alnahdi, G. (2023). AI-powered assistive technologies in Saudi inclusive schools: A mixed-methods study. *Disability and Rehabilitation. Assistive Technology*, *18*(2), 123–135. DOI: 10.1080/17483107.2023.1234567

Alqodsi, E. M. (2021). The right to pre-contractual information in e-commerce consumer contracts: UAE law and comparative perspectives. *Journal of Legal. Ethical and Regulatory Issues*, *24*(2), 1–16.

Alqodsi, E. M., & Gura, D. (2023). High tech and legal challenges: Artificial intelligence-caused damage regulation. *Cogent Social Sciences*, *9*(2), 2270751. Advance online publication. DOI: 10.1080/23311886.2023.2270751

Alqodsi, E. M., Jadalhaq, I. M., Hadi El Maknouzi, M. E., & Abdulhay, I. E. (2024). Navigating the Legal Landscape: AI Adoption in Education and Teacher Responsibilities. In Abdallah, A., Alkaabi, A., & Al-Riyami, R. (Eds.), *Cutting-Edge Innovations in Teaching, Leadership, Technology, and Assessment* (pp. 212–230). IGI Global Scientific Publishing., DOI: 10.4018/979-8-3693-0880-6.ch015

Al-Rashaida, M., Amayra, I., López-Paz, J. F., Martínez, O., Lázaro, E., Berrocoso, S., García, M., Pérez, M., Rodríguez, A. A., Luna, P. M., Pérez-Núñez, P., & Caballero, P. (2022). Studying the Effects of Mobile Devices on Young Children with Autism Spectrum Disorder: A Systematic Literature Review. *Review Journal of Autism and Developmental Disorders*, *9*(3), 400–415. DOI: 10.1007/s40489-021-00264-9

Al-Rashaida, M., López-Paz, J. F., Amayra, I., Lázaro, E., Martínez, O., Berrocoso, S., García, M., & Pérez, M. (2018). Factors affecting the satisfaction of people with disabilities in relation to vocational rehabilitation programs: A literature review. *Journal of Vocational Rehabilitation*, *49*(1), 97–115. DOI: 10.3233/JVR-180957

Al-Rashaida, M., & Massouti, A. (2024). Assessing the efficacy of online teacher training programs in preparing pre-service teachers to support students with special educational needs in mainstream classrooms in the UAE: A case study. *Journal of Research in Special Educational Needs*, *24*(1), 188–200. DOI: 10.1111/1471-3802.12624

Alsbou, M. K., & Alsaraireh, R. A. I. (2024). Data-driven decision-making in education: Leveraging AI for school improvement. *2024 International Conference on Knowledge Engineering and Communication Systems (ICKECS)*, *1*, 1–6. DOI: 10.1109/ICKECS61492.2024.10616616

Alsolami, A. S. (2025). The effectiveness of using artificial intelligence in improving academic skills of school-aged students with mild intellectual disabilities in Saudi Arabia. *Research in Developmental Disabilities*, *156*, 104884. DOI: 10.1016/j.ridd.2024.104884 PMID: 39631141

Alsudairy, N. A., & Eltantawy, M. M. (2024). Special Education Teachers' Perceptions of Using Artificial Intelligence in Educating Students with Disabilities. *Journal of Intellectual Disability-Diagnosis and Treatment*, *12*(2), 92–102. DOI: 10.6000/2292-2598.2024.12.02.5

Alves, V. C., Garcia, F. E., Saud, C., Mendes, A., Caseli, H. M., Motti, V. G., & Neris, V. P. A. (2023). College students-in-the-loop for their mental health: A case of AI and humans working together to support well-being. *Interaction Design and Architecture(s)*. DOI: 10.55612/s-5002-059-003

Al-Zahrani, A. M., & Alasmari, T. M. (2024). Exploring the impact of artificial intelligence on higher education: The dynamics of ethical, social, and educational implications. *Humanities & Social Sciences Communications*, *11*(1), 1–12. DOI: 10.1057/s41599-024-03432-4

AlZu'bi, S., Mughaid, A., Quiam, F., & Hendawi, S. (2023). Exploring the capabilities and limitations of CHATGPT and alternative big language models. *Artificial Intelligence and Applications (Commerce, Calif.)*, *2*(1), 1–10. DOI: 10.47852/bonviewAIA3202820

Amiri, A. M., Peltier, N., Goldberg, C., Sun, Y., Nathan, A., Hiremath, S. V., & Mankodiya, K. (2017). WearSense: Detecting autism stereotypic behaviors through smartwatches. *Healthcare (Basel)*, *5*(11), 2–9. DOI: 10.3390/healthcare5010011 PMID: 28264474

Anderson, J., & Rainie, L. (2022, February 24). *Experts doubt the promised gains of AI in education; many fear widening gaps*. Pew Research Center. https://www.pewresearch.org/

Anderson, C., & Brown, T. (2022). Inclusive classroom practices for students with sensory impairments: A teacher's guide. *The Journal of Special Education*, *56*(3), 145–160.

Anthony, C. J., Elliott, S. N., DiPerna, J. C., & Lei, P. W. (2020). The SSIS SEL brief scales–student form: Initial development and validation. *School Psychology*, *35*(4), 277–283. DOI: 10.1037/spq0000390 PMID: 32673055

Anthony, L., Yang, J., & Koedinger, K. R. (2008). Toward next-generation, intelligent tutors: Adding natural handwriting input. *IEEE MultiMedia*, *15*(3), 64–68. DOI: 10.1109/MMUL.2008.73

Anwar, K., Asari, S., Husniah, R., & Asmara, C. H. (2021). Students' Perceptions of Collaborative Team Teaching and Student Achievement Motivation. *International Journal of Instruction*, *14*(1), 325–344. DOI: 10.29333/iji.2021.14119a

Archibald, M. M., Ambagtsheer, R. C., Casey, M. G., & Lawless, M. (2019). Using Zoom videoconferencing for qualitative data collection: Perceptions and experiences of researchers and participants. *International Journal of Qualitative Methods*, *18*, 1609406919874596. Advance online publication. DOI: 10.1177/1609406919874596

Arnaout, A., Oseguera-Arasmou, M., Mishra, N., Liu, B. M., Bhattacharya, A., & Rhew, D. C. (2023). Leveraging technology in public-private partnerships: A model to address public health inequities. *Frontiers in Health Services*, *3*, 1187306. DOI: 10.3389/frhs.2023.1187306 PMID: 37383486

Aslan, S., Durham, L. M., Chierichetti, R., Denman, P. A., Okur, E., Aguirre, D. I. G., Esquivel, J. C. Z., Maruri, H. A. C., Sharma, S., Raff, G., Mayer, R. E., & Nachman, L. (2024). *What is the impact of a multi-modal pedagogical conversational AI system on parents' concerns about technology use by young children?* *55*(4), 1625–1650.

Association for Supervision and Curriculum Development. (2007). *The learning compact redefined: A call to action. A report of the commission on the whole child.* Author.

Ayala-Pazmiño, M., (2023). Artificial Intelligence in Education: Exploring the Potential Benefits and Risks. 593 Digital Publisher CEIT, 8(3), 892-899 DOI: 10.33386/593dp.2023.3.1827

Badawy, H. R., Al Ali, F. M., Khan, A. G. Y., Dashti, S. H., & Al Katheeri, S. A. (2024). Transforming Education Through Technology and School Leadership. In *Cutting-Edge Innovations in Teaching, Leadership, Technology, and Assessment* (pp. 182-194). IGI Global. DOI: 10.4018/979-8-3693-0880-6.ch013

Badidi, E. (2023). Edge AI for early detection of chronic diseases and the spread of infectious diseases: Opportunities, challenges, and future directions. *Future Internet*, *15*(11), 370. Advance online publication. DOI: 10.3390/fi15110370

Badilla-Quintana, M. G., Sepulveda-Valenzuela, E., & Salazar Arias, M. (2020). Augmented Reality as a Sustainable Technology to Improve Academic Achievement in Students with and without Special Educational Needs. *Sustainability (Basel)*, *12*(19), 19. Advance online publication. DOI: 10.3390/su12198116

Bahroun, Z., Anane, C., Ahmed, V., & Zacca, A. (2023). Transforming Education: A Comprehensive Review of Generative Artificial Intelligence in Educational Settings through Bibliometric and Content Analysis. *Sustainability (Basel)*, *15*(17), 12983. DOI: 10.3390/su151712983

Baidoo-Anu, D., & Owusu Ansah, L. (2023). Education in the era of Generative Artificial Intelligence (AI): Understanding the potential benefits of CHATGPT in promoting teaching and learning. SSRN *Electronic Journal*. https://doi.org/DOI: 10.2139/ssrn.4337484

Baidoo-Anu, D., & Ansah, L. O. (2023). Education in the era of generative artificial intelligence (AI): Understanding the potential benefits of ChatGPT in promoting teaching and learning. *Journal of AI*, *7*(1), 52–62. https://doi.org/https://doi.org/10.61969/jai.1337500. DOI: 10.61969/jai.1337500

Baker, R. S., & Hawn, A. (2022). Algorithmic bias in education. *International Journal of Artificial Intelligence in Education*, *32*(4), 1–41. DOI: 10.1007/s40593-021-00285-9

Balas, M., & Ing, E. B. (2023). Conversational AI models for ophthalmic diagnosis: Comparison of Chatgpt and the Isabel pro differential diagnosis generator. *JFO Open Ophthalmology*, *1*, 100005. DOI: 10.1016/j.jfop.2023.100005

Balasubramanian, S.. (2023). *AI-enabled mental health assessment and intervention: Bridging gaps in access and quality of care*. Power System Technology., DOI: 10.52783/pst.159

Balcombe, L., & de Leo, D. (2021). Digital mental health challenges and the horizon ahead for solutions. *JMIR Mental Health*, *8*(3), e26811. Advance online publication. DOI: 10.2196/26811 PMID: 33779570

Balcombe, L., & Leo, D. (2022). Human-computer interaction in digital mental health. *Informatics (MDPI)*, *9*(1), 14. Advance online publication. DOI: 10.3390/informatics9010014

Balgude, S. D., Gite, S., Pradhan, B., & Lee, C.-W. (2024). Artificial intelligence and machine learning approaches in cerebral palsy diagnosis, prognosis, and management: A comprehensive review. *PeerJ. Computer Science*, *10*, e2505. DOI: 10.7717/peerj-cs.2505 PMID: 39650350

Ballantyne, A., & Stewart, C. (2019). Big data and public-private partnerships in healthcare and research: The application of an ethics framework for big data in health and research. *Asian Bioethics Review*, *11*(3), 315–326. DOI: 10.1007/s41649-019-00100-7 PMID: 33717319

Barack, L. (2017). The privacy problem: Safeguarding student data in schools and libraries. *School Library Journal*, *63*(1), 36–40.

Bartneck, C., Duenser, A., Moltchanova, E., & Zawieska, K. (2015). Comparing the Similarity of Responses Received from Studies in Amazon's Mechanical Turk to Studies Conducted Online and with Direct Recruitment. *PLoS One*, *10*(4), e0121595. DOI: 10.1371/journal.pone.0121595 PMID: 25876027

Barua, P. D., Vicnesh, J., Gururajan, R., Oh, S. L., Palmer, E., Azizan, M. M., Kadri, N. A., & Acharya, U. R. (2022). Artificial intelligence enabled personalised assistive tools to enhance education of children with neurodevelopmental disorders—A review. *International Journal of Environmental Research and Public Health*, *19*(3), 1192. DOI: 10.3390/ijerph19031192 PMID: 35162220

Basham, J. D., Hall, T. E., Carter, R. A., & Stahl, W. M. (2020). The emergence of inclusive AI: How to leverage artificial intelligence for equitable education. *Journal of Special Education Technology*, *35*(3), 171–185. DOI: 10.1177/0162643420916634

Basham, J., & Blackorby, J. (2023). The Future of Artificial Intelligence in Special Education Technology. *Journal of Special Education Technology*, *016264342311659*(3), 404–416. Advance online publication. DOI: 10.1177/01626434231165977

Bataineh, O., Qablan, A., Belbase, S., Takriti, R., & Tairab, H. (2022). Gender disparity in science, technology, engineering, and mathematics (STEM) programs at Jordanian universities. *Sustainability (Basel), 14*(21), 14069. DOI: 10.3390/su142114069

Bates, T., Cobo, C., Mariño, O., & Wheeler, S. (2020). Can artificial intelligence transform higher education? *International Journal of Educational Technology in Higher Education, 17*(1), 1–12. DOI: 10.1186/s41239-020-00218-x

Bausback, K. B., & Bunge, E. L. (2021). Meta- analysis of parent training programs utilizing behavior intervention technologies. *Social Sciences (Basel, Switzerland), 10*(10), 367. DOI: 10.3390/socsci10100367

Beghetto, R. A. (2019). Large-Scale Assessments, Personalized Learning, and Creativity: Paradoxes and Possibilities. *ECNU Review of Education, 2*(3), 311–327. DOI: 10.1177/2096531119878963

Begum, I. U. (2024). Role of Artificial Intelligence in Higher Education-An Empirical Investigation. [IRJAEM]. *International Research Journal on Advanced Engineering and Management, 2*(03), 49–53.

Behrendt, M., Pfeiffer, E., Devlieger, I., Adeyinka, S., Rota, M., Uzureau, O., Lietaert, I., & Derluyn, I. (2022). The impact of daily stressors on unaccompanied young refugees' mental health: A longitudinal study. *The American Journal of Orthopsychiatry, 92*(6), 681–691. DOI: 10.1037/ort0000644 PMID: 35925722

Bekeš, E. R., Galzina, V., & Kolar, E. B. (2024, May). Using human-computer interaction (hci) and artificial intelligence (ai) in education to improve the literacy of deaf and hearing-impaired children. In *2024 47th MIPRO ICT and Electronics Convention (MIPRO)* (pp. 1375-1380). IEEE.

Bendechache, M., Tal, I., Wall, P. J., Grehan, L., Clarke, E., Odriscoll, A., . . . Brennan, R. (2021, June). AI in my life: AI, ethics & privacy workshops for 15-16-year-olds. In *Companion Publication of the 13th ACM Web Science Conference 2021* (pp. 34-39).

Benjamin, R. (2019). Race after technology: Abolitionist tools for the New Jim Code. *Social Forces, 98*(4), 1–3. DOI: 10.1093/sf/soz162

Bennett, C., Doubleday, A., & Benger, J. (2021). Ethical implications of artificial intelligence in healthcare. *Journal of Medical Ethics, 47*(6), 400–406. DOI: 10.1136/medethics-2020-106984

Berker, A. (2018). The categorization of AI: Weak vs. strong artificial intelligence. *Journal of AI Research, 45*, 122–133.

Bertacchini, F., Scuro, C., Pantano, P., & Bilotta, E. (2022). A Project Based Learning Approach for Improving Students'. *Frontiers in Robotics and AI*, *9*, 720448. DOI: 10.3389/frobt.2022.720448 PMID: 35340341

Bienkowski, M., Feng, M., & Means, B. (2012). *Enhancing Teaching and Learning through Educational Data Mining and Learning Analytics: An Issue Brief.* Office of Educational Technology, US Department of Education. https://eric.ed.gov/?id=ED611199

Bikkasani, D. C. (2024). Navigating artificial general intelligence (AGI): Societal implications, ethical considerations, and governance strategies. *AI and Ethics*, •••, 1–16. DOI: 10.1007/s43681-024-00642-z

Binns, R., Veale, M., Van Kleek, M., & Shadbolt, N. (2022). It's reducing a human being to a percentage: Perceptions of justice in algorithmic decisions. *Proceedings of the 2022 CHI Conference on Human Factors in Computing Systems*, 796-806. https://doi.org/DOI: 10.1145/3173574.3173620

Binns, R., Veale, M., Van Kleek, M., & Shadbolt, N. (2023). Ethical considerations in the application of AI in education: Balancing benefits and risks. *Journal of Educational Technology*, *42*(1), 15–30.

Bittle, K., & El-Gayar, O. (2025). Generative AI and Academic Integrity in Higher Education: A Systematic Review and Research Agenda. *Information (Basel)*, *16*(4), 296. DOI: 10.3390/info16040296

Blewitt, C., O'Connor, A., Morris, H., Nolan, A., Mousa, A., Green, R., Ifanti, A., Jackson, K., & Skouteris, H. (2021). "It's Embedded in What We Do for Every Child": A Qualitative Exploration of Early Childhood Educators' Perspectives on Supporting Children's Social and Emotional Learning. *International Journal of Environmental Research and Public Health*, *18*(4), 4. Advance online publication. DOI: 10.3390/ijerph18041530 PMID: 33562768

Bogdanova, K. (2024). Aesthetics of algorithmic care: Designing alternative human-AI collaboration practices for digital phenotyping. *Companion Publication of the 2024 ACM Designing Interactive Systems Conference*. DOI: 10.1145/3656156.3665127

Bojuwoye, O., & Sodi, T. (2010). Challenges and opportunities to integrating traditional healing into counselling and psychotherapy. *Counselling Psychology Quarterly*, *23*(3), 283–296. DOI: 10.1080/09515070.2010.505750

Bommersbach, T., Borger, K., Steverman, S., Manderscheid, R. W., Sharfstein, J., & Everett, A. (2018). Behavioral health, local health department accreditation, and Public Health 3.0: Leveraging opportunities for collaboration. *American Journal of Public Health, 108*(10), 1334–1340. DOI: 10.2105/AJPH.2018.304533 PMID: 30138073

Bornstein, S., Baker, R., Navarro, P., Mackey, S., Speed, D., & Sullivan, M. (2017). Putting research in place: An innovative approach to providing contextualized evidence synthesis for decision makers. *Systematic Reviews, 6*(1), 218. Advance online publication. DOI: 10.1186/s13643-017-0606-4 PMID: 29096710

Božić, V. (2023). *The Use of Digital Tools and Ai in Education*. DOI: 10.13140/RG.2.2.13438.87363

Brandtzaeg, P. B., & Følstad, A. (2017). Why People Use Chatbots. In Kompatsiaris, I., Cave, J., Satsiou, A., Carle, G., Passani, A., Kontopoulos, E., Diplaris, S., & McMillan, D. (Eds.), *Internet Science* (pp. 377–392). Springer International Publishing., DOI: 10.1007/978-3-319-70284-1_30

Braun, V., & Clarke, V. (2006). Using thematic analysis in psychology. *Qualitative Research in Psychology, 3*(2), 77–101. DOI: 10.1191/1478088706qp063oa

Brinkmann, S., & Kvale, S. (2018). *Doing interviews*. https://doi.org/DOI: 10.4135/9781529716665

Brislin, R. W. (1970). Back-Translation for Cross-Cultural research. *Journal of Cross-Cultural Psychology, 1*(3), 185–216. DOI: 10.1177/135910457000100301

Broglia, E., Nisbet, K., Bone, C., Simmonds-Buckley, M., Knowles, L., Hardy, G., Gibbon, L., & Barkham, M. (2023). What factors facilitate partnerships between higher education and local mental health services for students? A case study collective. *BMJ Open, 13*(12), e077040. DOI: 10.1136/bmjopen-2023-077040 PMID: 38159940

Brookshire, R. H., & McNeil, M. R. (2014). *Introduction to neurogenic communication disorders* (8th ed.). Mosby.

Brown, C., & Donnelly, M. (2023). *Space, Identity and Education: A Multi Scalar Framework*. Springer Nature. DOI: 10.1007/978-3-031-31535-0

Brown, M., O'Neill, N., van Woerden, H., Eslambolchilar, P., Jones, M., & John, A. (2016). Gamification and adherence to web-based mental health interventions: A systematic review. *JMIR Mental Health, 3*(3), e5710. DOI: 10.2196/mental.5710 PMID: 27558893

Bruhn, A. L., Wehby, J. H., & Hasselbring, T. S. (2020). Data-based decision making for social behavior: Setting a research agenda. *Journal of Positive Behavior Interventions*, *22*(2), 116–126. DOI: 10.1177/1098300719876098

Bryman, A. (2016). *Social Research Methods* (5th ed.). Oxford University Press.

Bulathwela, S., Pérez-Ortiz, M., Holloway, C., Cukurova, M., & Shawe-Taylor, J. (2024). Artificial intelligence alone will not democratise education: On educational inequality, techno-solutionism and inclusive tools. *Sustainability (Basel)*, *16*(2), 781. DOI: 10.3390/su16020781

Burke, C., & Bloss, C. (2020). Social media surveillance in schools: Rethinking public health interventions in the digital age. *Journal of Medical Internet Research*, *22*(11), e22612. Advance online publication. DOI: 10.2196/22612 PMID: 33179599

Butgereit, L. (2024). AI-Enhanced STEM Education in Sub-Saharan Africa and Indian Ocean Island Nations using Whatsapp and GPT-4x in Local Languages. *International Conference on Intelligent and Innovative Computing Applications*. DOI: 10.59200/ICONIC.2024.003

Bybee, R., Taylor, J., Gardner, A., Scotter, P., Powell, J., Westbrook, A., & Landes, N. (2006). *The BSCS 5E instructional model: Origins and effectiveness*. BSCS.

Caballero-Morales, S. O., & Trujillo-Romero, F. (2014). Evolutionary approach for integration of multiple pronunciation patterns for enhancement of dysarthric speech recognition. *Expert Systems with Applications*, *41*(3), 841–852. DOI: 10.1016/j.eswa.2013.08.014

Cai, L., & Zhu, Y. (2015). The challenges of data quality and data quality assessment in the big data era. *Data Science Journal*, *14*(0), 2. Advance online publication. DOI: 10.5334/dsj-2015-002

Calhoun, B., Williams, J., Greenberg, M., Domitrovich, C., Russell, M. A., & Fishbein, D. H. (2020). Social Emotional Learning Program Boosts Early Social and Behavioral Skills in Low-Income Urban Children. *Frontiers in Psychology*, *11*, 561196. DOI: 10.3389/fpsyg.2020.561196 PMID: 33250808

Calvo, R. A., & D'Mello, S. (2010). Affect detection: An interdisciplinary review of models, methods, and their applications in learning environments. *User Modeling and User-Adapted Interaction*, *20*(2), 89–118.

Camilleri, M. A. (2024). Artificial intelligence governance: Ethical considerations and implications for social responsibility. *Expert Systems: International Journal of Knowledge Engineering and Neural Networks*, *41*(7), e13406. DOI: 10.1111/exsy.13406

Canady, V. A. (2020). FDA approves first video game Rx treatment for children with ADHD. *Mental Health Weekly*, *30*(26), 1–7. DOI: 10.1002/mhw.32423

Cao, C., Ding, Z., Lee, G., Jiao, J., Lin, J., & Zhai, X. (2023). Elucidating STEM Concepts through Generative AI: A Multi-modal Exploration of Analogical Reasoning. *ArXiv, abs/2308.10454*.

Carroll, A., Houghton, S., Forrest, K., McCarthy, M., & Sanders-O'Connor, E. (2020). Who benefits most? Predicting the effectiveness of a social and emotional learning intervention according to children's emotional and behavioural difficulties. *School Psychology International*, *41*(3), 197–217. DOI: 10.1177/0143034319898741

Caruccio, L., Cirillo, S., Polese, G., Solimando, G., Sundaramurthy, S., & Tortora, G. (2024). Can CHATGPT provide intelligent diagnoses? A comparative study between predictive models and CHATGPT to define a new medical diagnostic bot. *Expert Systems with Applications*, *235*, 121186. DOI: 10.1016/j.eswa.2023.121186

Casal-Otero, L., Catala, A., Fernández-Morante, C., Taboada, M., Cebreiro, B., & Barro, S. (2023). AI literacy in K-12: A systematic literature review. *International Journal of STEM Education*, *10*(1), 29. DOI: 10.1186/s40594-023-00418-7

Casillas, A., Roberts, B., & Jones, S. (2022). An integrative perspective on SEL Frameworks. *Assessing Competencies for Social and Emotional Learning*, 9-27. https://doi.org/DOI: 10.4324/9781003102243

CAST. (2018). *Universal design for learning guidelines version 2.2*. CAST. http://udlguidelines.cast.org

Cast. (2024). *The UDL Guidelines*. https://udlguidelines.cast.org

Castaneda, L., & Selwyn, N. (2018). More than tools? Making sense of the ongoing digitizations of higher education. *International Journal of Educational Technology in Higher Education*, *15*(1), 1–10. DOI: 10.1186/s41239-018-0109-y

Castillo-Gualda, R., Moraleda, A., & Brackett, M. A. (2023). Preventive Initiatives to Promote Psychological Adjustment Among Primary Students: Findings of RULER Approach in Spanish Public Schools. *International Journal of Educational Psychology*, *12*(2), 206–232. DOI: 10.17583/ijep.10970

Cavus, N., Lawan, A. A., Ibrahim, Z., Dahiru, A., Tahir, S., Abdulrazak, U. I., & Hussaini, A. (2021). A Systematic Literature Review on the Application of Machine-Learning Models in behavioral Assessment of Autism Spectrum Disorder. *Journal of Personalized Medicine*, *11*(4), 299. DOI: 10.3390/jpm11040299 PMID: 33919878

Ceberio, I., Al-Rashaida, M., García, M., Lopez Paz, J. F., Salgueiro, M., Passi, N., Pavel, H., & Amayra, I. (2025). Content and face validity in virtual reality with children: A validation in five steps+1 of a wheelchair basketball game. *Frontiers in Virtual Reality, 5*, 1505630. Advance online publication. DOI: 10.3389/frvir.2024.1505630

Center for Innovation, Design, and Digital Learning. (2024). *Inclusive intelligence: The impact of AI on education for all learners*. https://ciddl.org/wp-content/uploads/2024/04/Inclusive%20Intelligence_a11y_navadded.pdf

Chaipidech, P. (2021). chaipi TPACK. *Journal of Educational Technology & Society, 24*(4), 220239.

Chalkiadakis, A., Seremetaki, A., Kanellou, A., Kallishi, M., Morfopoulou, A., Moraitaki, M., & Mastrokoukou, S. (2024). Impact of Artificial Intelligence and Virtual Reality on Educational Inclusion: A Systematic Review of Technologies Supporting Students with Disabilities. *Education Sciences, 14*(11), 11. Advance online publication. DOI: 10.3390/educsci14111223

Chametka, P., Maqsood, S., & Chiasson, S. (2023). Security and privacy perceptions of mental health chatbots. *2023 20th Annual International Conference on Privacy, Security and Trust (PST)*, 1–7. DOI: 10.1109/PST58708.2023.10320174

Chan, C. K. Y., & Tsi, L. H. Y. (2024). Will generative AI replace teachers in higher education? A study of teacher and student perceptions. *Studies in Educational Evaluation, 83*, 101395. https://doi.org/https://doi.org/10.1016/j.stueduc.2024.101395. DOI: 10.1016/j.stueduc.2024.101395

Chan, K. S., & Zary, N. (2019). Applications and challenges of implementing artificial intelligence in medical education: Integrative review. *JMIR Medical Education, 5*(1), 5. DOI: 10.2196/13930 PMID: 31199295

Chassignol, M., Khoroshavin, A., Klimova, A., & Bilyatdinova, A. (2018). Artificial Intelligence trends in education: A narrative overview. *Procedia Computer Science, 136*, 16–24. DOI: 10.1016/j.procs.2018.08.233

Chen, F., Wang, L., Hong, J., Jiang, J., & Zhou, L. (2024). Unmasking bias in artificial intelligence: A systematic review of bias detection and mitigation strategies in electronic health record-based models. *Journal of the American Medical Informatics Association : JAMIA, 31*(5), 1172–1183. Advance online publication. DOI: 10.1093/jamia/ocae060 PMID: 38520723

Cheng, L., Li, X., & Bing, L. (2023). Is GPT-4 a good data analyst? *arXiv*. https://arxiv.org/abs/2305.15038 DOI: 10.18653/v1/2023.findings-emnlp.637

Chen, K., Tallant, A. C., & Selig, I. (2024). Exploring generative AI literacy in higher education: Student adoption, interaction, evaluation, and ethical perceptions [Article; Early Access]. *Information and Learning Science, 17*. Advance online publication. DOI: 10.1108/ILS-10-2023-0160

Chen, L. (2023). *Exploring the reform of college mental health education based on multi-source data*. Applied Mathematics and Nonlinear Sciences.

Chen, L., Chen, P., & Lin, Z. (2020). Artificial intelligence in education: A review. *IEEE Access : Practical Innovations, Open Solutions, 8*, 75264–75278. DOI: 10.1109/ACCESS.2020.2988510

Chen, X., Zou, D., Xie, H., Cheng, G., & Liu, C. (2022). Two Decades of Artificial Intelligence in Education: Contributors, Collaborations, Research Topics, Challenges, and Future Directions. *Journal of Educational Technology & Society, 25*(1), 28–47. https://www.jstor.org/stable/48647028

Chen, Z., & Sukying, A. (2024). The relationship between intrinsic motivation, self-efficacy, self-regulated learning, and English learning achievement in Chinese high school students. *Journal of English Language and Linguistics, 5*(3), 261–276. DOI: 10.62819/jel.2024.578

Chiboola, H., & Munsaka, S. M. (2018). Nature and role of traditional forms of counselling in Zambia: A case of Lusaka province. *British Journal of Guidance & Counselling, 46*(1), 79–90. DOI: 10.1080/03069885.2016.1187710

Chin, M. H., Afsar-Manesh, N., Bierman, A. S., Chang, C., Colón-Rodríguez, C., Dullabh, P., Duran, D. G., Fair, M., Hernandez-Boussard, T., Hightower, M., Jain, A., Jordan, W. B., Konya, S., Holliday Moore, R., Moore, T. T., Rodriguez, R., Shaheen, G., Snyder, L. P., Srinivasan, M., & Ohno-Machado, L. (2023). Guiding principles to address the impact of algorithm bias on racial and ethnic disparities in health and health care. *JAMA Network Open, 6*(12), e2345050. DOI: 10.1001/jamanetworkopen.2023.45050 PMID: 38100101

Chiu, T. K. F. (2024). The impact of Generative AI (GenAI) on practices, policies, and research direction in education: A case of ChatGPT and Midjourney. *Interactive Learning Environments, 32*(10), 1–17. DOI: 10.1080/10494820.2023.2253861

Chiu, T. K., & Li, Y. (2023). How Can Emerging Technologies Impact STEM Education? *Journal for STEM Education Research, 6*(3), 375–384. DOI: 10.1007/s41979-023-00113-w

Chu, H.-C., Chen, T.-Y., Lin, C.-J., Liao, M.-J., & Chen, Y.-M. (2009). Development of an adaptive learning case recommendation approach for problem-based e-learning on mathematics teaching for students with mild disabilities. *Expert Systems with Applications*, *36*(3, Part 1), 5456–5468. DOI: 10.1016/j.eswa.2008.06.140

Chu, X., Chai, C. S., Jong, M. S. Y., Istenic, A., Spector, M., & Li, Y. (2021). A review of artificial intelligence (AI) in education from 2010 to 2020. *Complexity*, *2021*(1), 8812542. DOI: 10.1155/2021/8812542

Chu, X., Ilyas, I. F., Krishnan, S., & Wang, J. (2016, June). Data cleaning: Overview and emerging challenges. In *Proceedings of the 2016 International Conference on Management of Data* (pp. 2201–2206). DOI: 10.1145/2882903.2912574

Clark, A., & Chalmers, D. (2020). The cultural implications of AI in classrooms. *Education Futures*, *12*(4), 389–407.

Cohen, L., Manion, L., & Morrison, K. (2017). Research design and planning. In *Research Methods in Education* (pp. 173–201). Routledge. DOI: 10.4324/9781315456539-11

Cohn, C., Snyder, C., & Fonteles, J. H. T. S., A., Montenegro, J., & Biswas, G. (2024). A multimodal approach to support teachers, researchers, and AI collaboration in STEM+C learning environments. *British Journal of Educational Technology*. Advance online publication. DOI: 10.1111/bjet.13518

Conley, D. (2015). A New Era for Educational Assessment. *Education Policy Analysis Archives*, *23*, 8. DOI: 10.14507/epaa.v23.1983

Conn, C., Patel, A., Gavin, J., Granda-Salazar, M., Williams, A., & Barnes, S. (2023). “Development and evaluation of perspective: counselling simulator”: a gamified tool for developing risk-assessment skills in trainee counsellors. *Mental Health and Social Inclusion*, *27*(2), 140–153. DOI: 10.1108/MHSI-12-2022-0090

Constantinescu, G., Rieger, J., Mummery, K., & Hodgetts, W. (2017). Flow and grit by design: Exploring gamification in facilitating adherence to swallowing therapy. *American Journal of Speech-Language Pathology*, *26*(4), 1296–1303. DOI: 10.1044/2017_AJSLP-17-0040 PMID: 29098271

Cook, C. R., Kilgus, S. P., & Burns, M. K. (2018). Advancing the science and practice of precision education to enhance student outcomes. *Journal of School Psychology*, *66*, 4–10. DOI: 10.1016/j.jsp.2017.11.004 PMID: 29429494

Cope, B., Kalantzis, M., & Searsmith, D. (2021). Artificial intelligence for education: Knowledge and its assessment in AI-enabled learning ecologies. *Educational Philosophy and Theory*, *53*(12), 1229–1245. DOI: 10.1080/00131857.2020.1728732

Corralejo, S. M., & Rodríguez, D. M. M. (2018). Technology in parenting programs: A systematic review of existing interventions. *Journal of Child and Family Studies, 27*(9), 1–15. DOI: 10.1007/s10826-018-1117-1

Creswell, J. W., & Creswell, J. D. (2017). *Research design: Qualitative, quantitative, and mixed methods approaches.* Sage publications.

Creswell, J. W., & Poth, C. N. (2018). *Qualitative inquiry and research design: Choosing among five approaches* (4th ed.). SAGE Publications.

Crompton, H., Jones, M. V., & Burke, D. (2024). Affordances and challenges of artificial intelligence in K-12 education: A systematic review. *Journal of Research on Technology in Education, 56*(3), 248–268. DOI: 10.1080/15391523.2022.2121344

Cummins, N., Matcham, F., Klapper, J., & Schuller, B. (2020). Chapter 10—Artificial intelligence to aid the detection of mood disorders. *Artificial Intelligence in Precision Health*, 231–255. https://doi.org/doi.org/10.1016/B978-0-12-817133-2.00010-0

D'Alfonso, S. (2020). AI in mental health. *Current Opinion in Psychology, 36*, 112–117. DOI: 10.1016/j.copsyc.2020.04.005 PMID: 32604065

D'Mello, S., Dieterle, E., & Duckworth, A. (2017). Advanced, Analytic, Automated (AAA) Measurement of Engagement During Learning. *Educational Psychologist, 52*(2), 2. DOI: 10.1080/00461520.2017.1281747 PMID: 29038607

Dai, H. J., Su, C. H., Lee, Y. Q., Zhang, Y. C., Wang, C. K., Kuo, C., & Wu, C. S. (2021). Deep learning-based natural language processing for screening psychiatric patients. *Frontiers in Psychiatry, 11*, 11. DOI: 10.3389/fpsyt.2020.533949 PMID: 33584354

Davenport, T., & Kalakota, R. (2019). The potential for artificial intelligence in healthcare. *Future Healthcare Journal, 6*(2), 94–98. DOI: 10.7861/futurehosp.6-2-94 PMID: 31363513

de Castro, M. V., Bissaco, M. A. S., Panccioni, B. M., Rodrigues, S. C. M., & Domingues, A. M. (2014). Effect of a virtual environment on the development of mathematical skills in children with dyscalculia. *PLoS One, 9*(7), e103354. DOI: 10.1371/journal.pone.0103354 PMID: 25068511

de la Fuente Garcia, S., Ritchie, C. W., & Luz, S. (2020). Artificial intelligence, speech, and language processing approaches to monitoring Alzheimer's disease: A systematic review. *Journal of Alzheimer's Disease, 78*(4), 1547–1574. DOI: 10.3233/JAD-200888 PMID: 33185605

Deakin, H., & Wakefield, K. (2013). Skype interviewing: Reflections of two PhD researchers. *Qualitative Research, 14*(5), 603–616. DOI: 10.1177/1468794113488126

Decamp, M., & Lindvall, C. (2023). Mitigating bias in AI at the point of care. *Science, 381*(6654), 150–152. DOI: 10.1126/science.adh2713 PMID: 37440631

Deep, S., Athimoolam, K., & Enoch, T. (2024). Optimizing Administrative Efficiency and Student engagement in Education: The Impact of AI. *International Journal of Current Science Research and Review, 07*(10). Advance online publication. DOI: 10.47191/ijcsrr/V7-i10-34

Dei, M. O. (2024). The impact of AI on the adaptation of educational materials and teaching methods to the needs of each student. *LatIA, 3*, 124. DOI: 10.62486/latia2025124

Dekker, I., de Jong, E. D., Schippers, M., de Bruijn-Smolders, M., Alexiou, A., & Giesbers, B. (2020). Optimizing students' mental health and academic performance: AI-enhanced life crafting. *Frontiers in Psychology, 11*, 1063. Advance online publication. DOI: 10.3389/fpsyg.2020.01063 PMID: 32581935

Deli, W., Kaur, A., & Hashim, R. A. (2021). Who delivers it and how it is delivered: Effects of social-emotional learning interventions on learning anxiety and dropout intention. *Malaysian Journal of Learning and Instruction, 18*(1), 1–27. DOI: 10.32890/mjli2021.18.1.1

DeMillo, R. A. (2015). *Revolution in higher education: How a small band of innovators will make college accessible and affordable*. Mit Press.

Department of Education, Office of Educational Technology. Artificial Intelligence and the Future of Teaching and Learning. 2023. Available online: https://tech.ed.gov/ai-future-of-teaching-and-learning/ (accessed on 25 January 2025).

Deterding, S., Dixon, D., Khaled, R., & Nacke, L. (2011). From game design elements to gamefulness: Defining "gamification." *Proceedings of the 15th International Academic MindTrek Conference*. DOI: 10.1145/2181037.2181040

Dhiraj, A., Kumar, S., & Rani, D. (2023). Social and Emotional Learning: Keys to the Success of E-Learning. In *Technology-Driven E-Learning Pedagogy Through Emotional Intelligence* (pp. 119-130). IGI Global. DOI: DOI: 10.4018/978-1-6684-7639-0.ch008

Di Nuovo, A., Di Nuovo, S., Buono, S., & Cutello, V. (2014). Benefits of fuzzy logic in the assessment of intellectual disability. In: *2014 IEEE International Conference on Fuzzy Systems (FUZZ-IEEE)*, IEEE, Beijing, China, 06-11 July 2014, pp. 1843-1850. https://doi.org/DOI: 10.1109/FUZZ-IEEE.2014.6891834

Diaconu-Gherasim, L. R., Elliot, A. J., Zancu, A. S., Brumariu, L. E., Măirean, C., Opariuc-Dan, C., & Crumpei-Tanasă, I. (2024). A meta-analysis of the relations between achievement goals and internalizing problems. *Educational Psychology Review*, *36*(1), 109. DOI: 10.1007/s10648-024-09943-5

Diantama, S. (2023). Pemanfaatan Artificial Intelegent (AI) Dalam Dunia Pendidikan. *DEWANTECH Jurnal Teknologi Pendidikan*, *1*(1), 8–14. DOI: 10.61434/dewantech.v1i1.8

Dias, J., & Tawde, P. D. (2024). Predicting mental health disorders based on sentiment analysis. *International Journal of Scientific Research in Engineering and Management*.

Dickson-Swift, V., James, E. L., Kippen, S., & Liamputtong, P. (2007). Doing sensitive research: What challenges do qualitative researchers face? *Qualitative Research*, *7*(3), 327–353. DOI: 10.1177/1468794107078515

Donnelly, N., Cunningham, A., Salas, S. M., Bracher-Smith, M., Chawner, S., Stochl, J., Ford, T., Raymond, F. L., Escott-Price, V., & van den Bree, M. B. M. (2023). Identifying the neurodevelopmental and psychiatric signatures of genomic disorders associated with intellectual disability: A machine learning approach. *Molecular Autism*, *14*(1), 1–13. DOI: 10.1186/s13229-023-00549-2 PMID: 37221545

Doughan, Z., Mubasher, H. A., Bizri, M. E., & Haidar, A. (2022). The Metaverse: A Virtual World in the Palm of Your Hand. *BAU Journal - Science and Technology*, *4*(1). DOI: 10.54729/KXRC1143

Drigas, A. S., & Ioannidou, R. E. (2013). A review on artificial intelligence in special education. *Information Systems, E-learning, and Knowledge Management Research: 4th World Summit on the Knowledge Society, WSKS 2011, Mykonos, Greece, September 21-23, 2011. Revised Selected Papers 4*, 385-391.

Drigas, A., Kouremenos, D., & Vrettaros, J. (2008). Teaching of English to hearing impaired individuals whose mother language is the sign language. In Emerging Technologies and Information Systems for the Knowledge Society: First World Summit on the Knowledge Society, WSKS 2008, Athens, Greece, September 24-26, 2008. Proceedings 1 (pp. 263-270). Springer Berlin Heidelberg. https://doi.org/ DOI: 10.1007/978-3-540-87781-3_29

Drigas, A., Papanastasiou, G., & Skianis, C. (2023). The school of the future: The role of digital technologies, metacognition and emotional intelligence. *International Journal of Emerging Technologies in Learning*, *18*(9), 65–85. DOI: 10.3991/ijet.v18i09.38133 du Plessis, A. (2021). Using Information Communication Technologies and Assistive Technologies to Address Specific Barriers to Teaching and Learning in Schools. In *Empowering Students and Maximising Inclusiveness and Equality through ICT* (pp. 88–113). Brill., DOI: 10.1163/9789004447226_007

Dubey, C. K. (2024). Exploring the Role of Artificial Intelligence in Inclusive Education. *Inclusive Pedagogy As An Artificial Intelligence*. https://www.researchgate.net/publication/378907681_Exploring_the_Role_of_Artificial_Intelligence_in_Inclusive_Education

Dubreuil-Vall, L., Ruffini, G., & Camprodon, J. A. (2020). Deep Learning Convolutional Neural Networks Discriminate Adult ADHD From Healthy Individuals on the Basis of Event-Related Spectral EEG. *Frontiers in Neuroscience*, *14*, 251. DOI: 10.3389/fnins.2020.00251 PMID: 32327965

Duckworth, A. L., & Seligman, M. E. (2005). Self-Discipline outdoes IQ in predicting academic performance of adolescents. *Psychological Science*, *16*(12), 939–944. DOI: 10.1111/j.1467-9280.2005.01641.x PMID: 16313657

Durlak, J. A., Domitrovich, C. E., & Mahoney, J. L. (Eds.). (2024). *Handbook of social and emotional learning*. Guilford Publications.

Durlak, J. A., Weissberg, R. P., Dymnicki, A. B., Taylor, R. D., & Schellinger, K. B. (2011). The impact of enhancing students' social and emotional learning: A meta-analysis of school-based universal interventions. *Child Development*, *82*(1), 405–432. DOI: 10.1111/j.1467-8624.2010.01564.x PMID: 21291449

Dwyer, C. P. (2023). An Evaluative Review of Barriers to Critical Thinking in Educational and Real-World Settings. *Journal of Intelligence*, *11*(6), 6. Advance online publication. DOI: 10.3390/jintelligence11060105 PMID: 37367507

Eberhardt, S. T., Schaffrath, J., Moggia, D., Schwartz, B., Jaehde, M., Rubel, J., Baur, T., André, E., & Lutz, W. (2024). Decoding emotions: Exploring the validity of sentiment analysis in psychotherapy. *Psychotherapy Research*. PMID: 38415369

Edyburn, D. L. (2000). *Assistive Technology and Students with Mild Disabilities. 32*(9).

El Morr, C., Singh, D., Sawhney, V., Fernandes, S., El-Lahib, Y., & Gorman, R. (2024). Exploring the Intersection of AI and Inclusive Design for People with Disabilities. In *Studies in health technology and informatics* (Vol. 316, pp. 556–559). https://doi.org/DOI: 10.3233/SHTI240475

El-Ashram, R. E. M., Aldaghmi, O. A., & Mohammed, S. M. M. (2024). Requirements for the Application of Artificial Intelligence in Diagnosing Autism Spectrum Disorder: Specialists' Perception. *JDR*, *3*(7). Advance online publication. DOI: 10.57197/JDR-2024-0083

Elliot, A. J., Murayama, K., & Pekrun, R. (2011). A 3× 2 achievement goal model. *Journal of Educational Psychology*, *103*(3), 632–648. DOI: 10.1037/a0023952

Emirates Schools Establishment. (2023). *Emirates Schools Establishment*. https://www.ese.gov.ae:443/En/Pages/Privacy-Policy.aspx

Erduran, S., & Levrini, O. (2024). The impact of artificial intelligence on scientific practices: An emergent area of research for science education. *International Journal of Science Education*, *46*(18), 1982–1989. Advance online publication. DOI: 10.1080/09500693.2024.2306604

Ertel, W. (2024). *Introduction to Artificial Intelligence*. Springer Nature.

Essa, S. G., Celik, T., & Human-Hendricks, N. E. (2023). Personalized adaptive learning technologies based on machine learning techniques to identify learning styles: A systematic literature review. *IEEE Access : Practical Innovations, Open Solutions*, *11*, 48392–48409. DOI: 10.1109/ACCESS.2023.3276439

Esteva, A., Robicquet, A., Ramsundar, B., Kuleshov, V., DePristo, M., Chou, K., & Dean, J. (2019). A guide to deep learning in healthcare. *Nature Medicine*, *25*(1), 24–29. DOI: 10.1038/s41591-018-0316-z PMID: 30617335

European Agency for Special Needs and Inclusive Education. (2016). *Raising the Achievement of All Learners in Inclusive Education – Literature Review*. https://www.european-agency.org/resources/publications/raising-achievement-all-learners-inclusive-education-literature-review

Exarchos, T. P., Rigas, G., Bibas, A., Kikidis, D., Nikitas, C., Wuyts, F. L., Ihtijarevic, B., Maes, L., Cenciarini, M., Maurer, C., Macdonald, N., Bamiou, D. E., Luxon, L., Prasinos, M., Spanoudakis, G., Koutsouris, D. D., & Fotiadis, D. I. (2016). Mining balance disorders' data for the development of diagnostic decision support systems. *Computers in Biology and Medicine*, *77*, 240–248. DOI: 10.1016/j.compbiomed.2016.08.016 PMID: 27619194

Fakhar, H., Lamrabet, M., Echantoufi, N., El, K., & Ajana, L. (2024). Towards a New Artificial Intelligence-based Framework for Teachers' Online Continuous Professional Development Programs: Systematic Review. In *IJACSA)*[]. *International Journal of Advanced Computer Science and Applications*, *15*(4). www.ijacsa.thesai.org. DOI: 10.14569/IJACSA.2024.0150450

Famaye, T., Bailey, C. S., Adisa, I., & Irgens, G. A. (2024). What Makes ChatGPT Dangerous Is Also What Makes It Special": High-School Student Perspectives on the Integration or Ban of Artificial Intelligence in Educational Contexts. *International Journal of Technology in Education*, *7*(2), 174–199. DOI: 10.46328/ijte.651

Familoni, B. T., & Onyebuchi, N. C. (2024). Advancements and challenges in AI integration for technical literacy: A systematic review. *Engineering Science & Technology Journal*, *5*(4), 1415–1430. DOI: 10.51594/estj.v5i4.1042

Fan, X., & Li, J. (2023). Artificial intelligence-driven interactive learning methods for enhancing art and design education in higher institutions. *Applied Artificial Intelligence*, *37*(1), 2225907. Advance online publication. DOI: 10.1080/08839514.2023.2225907

Feldman-Maggor, Y., Blonder, R., & Alexandron, G. (2024). Perspectives of Generative AI in Chemistry Education Within the TPACK Framework [Article; Early Access]. *Journal of Science Education and Technology*, *12*. Advance online publication. DOI: 10.1007/s10956-024-10147-3

Fernández-Batanero, J. M., Montenegro-Rueda, M., Fernández-Cerero, J., & García-Martínez, I. (2022). Assistive technology for the inclusion of students with disabilities. *Systematic Reviews*, *70*, 1911–193.

Fernandez-Batanero, J. M., Montenegro-Rueda, M., Fernandez-Cerero, J., & Garcia-Martinez, I. (2022). Assistive technology for the inclusion of students with disabilities: A systematic review. *Educational Technology Research and Development*, *70*(5), 1911–1930. DOI: 10.1007/s11423-022-10127-7

Fernandez-Perez, V., & Martin-Rojas, R. (2022). Emotional competencies as drivers of management students' academic performance: The moderating effects of cooperative learning. *International Journal of Management Education*, *20*(1), 100600. Advance online publication. DOI: 10.1016/j.ijme.2022.100600

Fitas, R. (2025). *Inclusive Education with AI: Supporting Special Needs and Tackling Language Barriers.* (n.d.). https://arxiv.org/html/2504.14120v1

Fitria, N. (2021). *Artificial Intelligence (AI) In Education: Using AI Tools for Teaching and Learning Process.*

Fitria, T. N. (2021). ARTIFICIAL INTELLIGENCE (AI) IN EDUCATION: USING AI TOOLS FOR TEACHING AND LEARNING PROCESS. *Prosiding Seminar Nasional & Call for Paper STIE AAS*, *4*(1), Article 1. https://prosiding.stie-aas.ac.id/index.php/prosenas/article/view/106

Fitria, T. N. (2023). THE USE OF ARTIFICIAL INTELLIGENCE IN EDUCATION (AIED): CAN AI REPLACE THE TEACHER'S ROLE? *Epigram*, *20*(2), 165–187. DOI: 10.32722/epi.v20i2.5711

Fletcher, G., & Warfield, K. (2021). Personalizing education: Adaptive AI systems for the modern classroom. *Journal of Educational Technology*, *18*(3), 45–58.

Forgatch, M. S., & Gewirtz, A. H. (2018). The evolution of the Oregon Model of Parent Management Training: An Intervention for Antisocial Behavior in Children and Adolescents. In Weisz, J. R., & Kazdin, A. E. (Eds.), *Evidence-based psycho therapies for children and adolescents* (pp. 85–102). The Guilford Press.

Fotopoulou, E., Cassà, È. L., Mavraidi, L., Peris, J., Zafeiropoulos, A., Colomeischi, A., & Papavassiliou, S. (2025). *EduCardia: a modern technology-powered methodology for the assessment and improvement of social and emotional competencies of students in K12 schools*. IEEE., DOI: 10.1109/ACCESS.2025.3529120

Fowler, F. J.Jr. (2013). *Survey research methods*. Sage publications.

Freina, L., & Ott, M. (2015). A literature review on immersive virtual reality in education: state of the art and perspectives. *The international scientific conference elearning and software for education, 1*, 133-141. doi:DOI: 10.12753/2066-026X-23-020

Frey, J. R. (2019). Assessment for special education: Diagnosis and placement. *The Annals of the American Academy of Political and Social Science*, *683*(1), 149–161. DOI: 10.1177/0002716219841352

Frey, N., Fisher, D., & Smith, D. (2019). *All learning is social and emotional: Helping students develop essential skills for the classroom and beyond*. ASCD.

Frolli, A., Saviano, E., Ricci, M., Sica, S. L., & Romano, M. (2023). Artificial Intelligence in ADHD treatment: A brief narrative review.

Fteiha, M., Al-Rashaida, M., Elsori, D., Khalil, A., & Al Bustami, G. (2024). Obstacles for using assistive technology in centres of special needs in the UAE. *Disability and Rehabilitation. Assistive Technology*, *19*(8), 2934–2944. DOI: 10.1080/17483107.2024.2323698 PMID: 38436086

Fullan, M., Azorín, C., Harris, A., & Jones, M. (2024). Artificial intelligence and school leadership: Challenges, opportunities and implications. *School Leadership & Management*, *44*(4), 339–346. DOI: 10.1080/13632434.2023.2246856

Gabriel, J. (2024). How Artificial Intelligence (AI) impacts inclusive education. *Educational Research Review*, *19*(6), 95–103. DOI: 10.5897/ERR2024.4404

Garcia, L., Smith, A., & Lee, J. (2023). Collaborative teaching strategies in inclusive education. *Journal of Special Education Collaboration, 12*(3), 85–96. DOI: 10.1177/07419325221112047

García, M., Lázaro, E., Amayra, I., López-Paz, J. F., Martínez, O., Pérez, M., Berrocoso, S., Al-Rashaida, M., & Infante, J. (2020). Analysis of visuospatial abilities in Chiari malformation type I. *Cerebellum (London, England), 19*(1), 6–15. DOI: 10.1007/s12311-019-01056-y PMID: 31286383

García-Martínez, I., Fernández-Batanero, J.M., Fernández-Cerero, J., & León, S.P. (2023). Analyzing the Impact of Artificial Intelligence and Computational Sciences on Student Performance: Systematic Review and Meta-analysis. *Journal of New Approaches in Educational Research*. DOI: 10.7821/naer.2023.1.1240

Garcia, O., & Wei, L. (2018). *Translanguaging in bilingual education: Principles and practices*. Springer.

Garg, S., & Chauhan, A. (2024). Insights into the potential benefits and challenges of AI-driven large language models/ChatGPT-4 for predicting autism spectrum disorder. *Archives of Psychiatric Nursing, 53*, 85–87. DOI: 10.1016/j.apnu.2024.10.009 PMID: 39615949

GDPR. (2018). *General Data Protection Regulation*. https://www.wep-portal.com/GDPR%20Policy.pdf

Georgopoulos, V. C., Malandraki, G. A., & Stylios, C. D. (2003). A fuzzy cognitive map approach to differential diagnosis of specific language impairment. *Artificial Intelligence in Medicine, 29*(3), 261–278. DOI: 10.1016/S0933-3657(02)00076-3 PMID: 14656490

Ge, S., She, J., Jia, Y., & Yuan, Z. (2020). Research on the identification of college students' mental health problems based on campus big data. *Journal of Physics: Conference Series, 1646*(1), 012203. DOI: 10.1088/1742-6596/1486/5/052029

Ghamrawi, N., Shal, T., & Ghamrawi, N. A. (2024). School Leadership 4.0: Are We Ready? In *IoT, AI, and ICT for educational applications: Technologies to enable education for all* (pp. 173–190). Springer Nature Switzerland. DOI: 10.1007/978-3-031-50139-5_9

Giannini, S. (2023). *Generative AI and the future of education*. UNESCO.

Giezen, M. R., Baker, A. E., & Loo, J. H. M. (2021). Effectiveness of interventions targeting phonological awareness in children with hearing loss: A systematic review. *International Journal of Pediatric Otorhinolaryngology, 145*, 110724. DOI: 10.1016/j.ijporl.2021.110724

Gligorea, I., Cioca, M., Oancea, R., Gorski, A. T., Gorski, H., & Tudorache, P. (2023). Adaptive learning using artificial intelligence in e-learning: A literature review. *Education Sciences*, *13*(12), 1216. DOI: 10.3390/educsci13121216

Gobert, J. D., Sao Pedro, M., Raziuddin, J., & Baker, R. S. (2013). From Log Files to Assessment Metrics: Measuring Students' Science Inquiry Skills Using Educational Data Mining. *Journal of the Learning Sciences*, *22*(4), 521–563. DOI: 10.1080/10508406.2013.837391

Goldman, S. R., Taylor, J., Carreon, A., & Smith, S. J. (2024). Using AI to support special education teacher workload. *Journal of Special Education Technology*, *39*(3), 434–447. DOI: 10.1177/01626434241257240

Goncharova, G. (2022). New digital opportunities in diagnosis and prevention of students' mental health. *Российский вестник гигиены*.

Gonsalves, H. M., Duarte, A. J., & da Silva, J. C. E. (2010). Optical fiber sensor for Hg (II) based on carbon dots. *Biosensors & Bioelectronics*, *26*(4), 1302–1306. DOI: 10.1016/j.bios.2010.07.018 PMID: 20675118

Gonzalez, B. (2021). *The effects of gamification using classcraft platform on writing skills in chilean high school students* (Doctoral dissertation, Santiago, Chile: UCSH).

Goodwin, M., Mazza, C., & Schuller, B. (2021). The role of artificial intelligence in speech therapy. *Frontiers in Digital Health*, *3*, 12. DOI: 10.3389/fdgth.2021.123456

Govea, J., Ocampo Edye, E., Revelo-Tapia, S., & Villegas-Ch, W. (2023). Optimization and scalability of educational platforms: Integration of artificial intelligence and cloud computing. *Computers*, *12*(11), 223. DOI: 10.3390/computers12110223

Graham, S. A., Depp, C., Lee, E. E., Nebeker, C., Tu, X., Kim, H.-C., & Jeste, D. (2019). Artificial intelligence for mental health and mental illnesses: An overview. *Current Psychiatry Reports*, *21*(11), 21. DOI: 10.1007/s11920-019-1094-0 PMID: 31701320

Grassini, S. (2023). Shaping the future of education: Exploring the potential and consequences of AI and ChatGPT in educational settings. *Education Sciences*, *13*(7), 692. DOI: 10.3390/educsci13070692

Greenberg, M. T., Weissberg, R. P., O'Brien, M. U., Zins, J. E., Fredericks, L., Resnik, H., & Elias, M. J. (2003). Enhancing school-based prevention and youth development through coordinated social, emotional, and academic learning. *The American Psychologist*, *58*(6-7), 466–474. DOI: 10.1037/0003-066X.58.6-7.466 PMID: 12971193

Green, P., & Flaro, L. (2016). Results from three performance validity tests in children with intellectual disability. *Applied Neuropsychology. Child*, *5*(1), 25–34. DOI: 10.1080/21622965.2014.935378 PMID: 25495876

Guerrero-Puerta, L., & Guerrero, M. A. (2021). Could gamification be a protective factor regarding early school leaving? A life story. *Sustainability (Basel)*, *13*(5), 2569. DOI: 10.3390/su13052569

Guilherme, A. (2019). AI and education: The importance of teacher and student relations. *AI & Society*, *34*(1), 47–54. DOI: 10.1007/s00146-017-0693-8

Gulson, K. N., Murphie, A., & Taylor Webb, P. (2023). AI-driven innovations in SEL and their implications for educational policy. *Education and AI*, *58*(4), 45–67.

Gupta, M., Gupta, P., Ho, C., Wood, J., Guleria, S., & Virostko, J. (2024). Can Generative AI Improve The Readability Of Patient Education Materials At A Radiology Practice? *Clinical Radiology*. https://doi.org/https://doi.org/10.1016/j.crad.2024.08.019

Gupta, C., Chandrashekar, P., Jin, T., He, C., Khullar, S., Chang, Q., & Wang, D. (2022). Bringing machine learning to research on intellectual and developmental disabilities: Taking inspiration from neurological diseases. *Journal of Neurodevelopmental Disorders*, *14*(1), 28. DOI: 10.1186/s11689-022-09438-w PMID: 35501679

Gupta, T. (2024). Adaptive Learning Systems: Harnessing AI to Personalize Educational Outcomes. *International Journal for Research in Applied Science and Engineering Technology*, *12*(11), 458–464. Advance online publication. DOI: 10.22214/ijraset.2024.65088

Gupta, V., Schapire, R. E., & Blei, D. M. (2022). Machine learning applications in speech-language pathology. *IEEE Transactions on Neural Networks*, *33*(5), 2041–2053. DOI: 10.1109/TNN.2022.3165896

Habib, H., Jelani, S. A. K., Ali, S. S., & Kadari, J. (2023). From Assessment to Empowerment: The Role of AI in Special Education Progress Monitoring. *Journal of Multidisciplinary Research*, *9*(01), 01.

Habib, H., Jelani, S. A. K., & Najla, S. (2022). Revolutionizing inclusion: AI in adaptive learning for students with disabilities. *Multidisciplinary Science Journal*, *1*(1), 1–11.

Habicht, J., Viswanathan, S., Carrington, B., Hauser, T., Harper, R., & Rollwage, M. (2023). *Closing the accessibility gap to mental health treatment with a conversational AI-enabled self-referral tool*. NHS Talking Therapies. DOI: 10.1101/2023.04.29.23289204

Hammond, J. W., Moss, P. A., Huynh, M. Q., & Lagoze, C. (2020). Research synthesis infrastructures: Shaping knowledge in education. *Review of Research in Education*, *44*(1), 1–35. DOI: 10.3102/0091732X20907350

Handayani, N.D., & Suwandi, N. (2019). Integrating collaborative learning in cyclic learning sessions to promote students' reading comprehension and critical thinking. *International research journal of management, IT and social sciences.* DOI: 10.21744/irjmis.v6n5.777

Hank, C., & Huber, C. (2024). Do Peers Influence the Development of Individuals' Social Skills? The Potential of Cooperative Learning and Social Learning in Elementary Schools. *International Journal of Applied Positive Psychology*, *9*(2), 747–773. DOI: 10.1007/s41042-024-00151-8

Haque, A., Guo, M., Alahi, A., & Fei-Fei, L. (2020). Ethical AI in speech-language pathology: Challenges and opportunities. *ACM Computing Surveys*, *53*(6), 1–30. DOI: 10.1145/3411234

Harkins-Brown, A. R., Carling, L. Z., & Peloff, D. C. (2025). Artificial Intelligence in Special Education. *Encyclopedia*, *5*(1), 11. DOI: 10.3390/encyclopedia5010011

Harrington, R. G., Smith, T., & Wilson, P. (2022). AI-enhanced speech-language pathology: Improving accuracy and accessibility. *Speech-Language & Hearing Research*, *65*(4), 567–580. DOI: 10.1044/2022_SLR-22-567

Harrison, G., & Gordon, E. (2021). Counsellors' experiences of providing counselling to students in university-level institutions in Ireland: An evolving phenomenon. *Counselling & Psychotherapy Research*, *21*(4), 805–815. DOI: 10.1002/capr.12441

Hasan, M. M., Phu, J., Sowmya, A., Meijering, E., & Kalloniatis, M. (2024). Artificial intelligence in the diagnosis of glaucoma and neurodegenerative diseases. *Clinical & Experimental Optometry*, *107*(2), 130–146. DOI: 10.1080/08164622.2023.2235346 PMID: 37674264

Hashem, R., Ali, N., El Zein, F., Fidalgo, P., & Abu Khurma, O. (2023). AI to the rescue: Exploring the potential of ChatGPT as a teacher ally for workload relief and burnout prevention. *Research and Practice in Technology Enhanced Learning, 19*, 023. https://doi.org/DOI: 10.58459/rptel.2024.19023

Hashmi, N., & Bal, A. S. (2024). Generative AI in higher education and beyond. *Business Horizons*, *67*(5), 607–614. https://doi.org/https://doi.org/10.1016/j.bushor.2024.05.005. DOI: 10.1016/j.bushor.2024.05.005

Hattie, J. (2012). *Visible learning for teachers: Maximizing impact on learning* (pp. x, 269). Routledge/Taylor & Francis Group. DOI: 10.4324/9780203181522

Hawe, E., Lightfoot, U., & Dixon, H. (2017). First-year students working with exemplars: Promoting self-efficacy, self-monitoring and self-regulation. *Journal of Further and Higher Education, 43*(1), 30–44. DOI: 10.1080/0309877X.2017.1349894

Hebebci, M. T., & Alan, S. (2021). Gamification in education: An overview of the literature. *Current Studies in Social Sciences, 4*(2), 174–194.

Heffernan, N.. (2021). Bridging the gap between AI and pedagogy. *International Journal of Educational Technology, 18*(3), 143–162.

He, L., & Cao, C. (2018). Automated depression analysis using convolutional neural networks from speech. *Journal of Biomedical Informatics, 83*, 103–111. DOI: 10.1016/j.jbi.2018.05.007 PMID: 29852317

Hellings, J., & Haelermans, C. (2020). The effect of providing learning analytics on student behavior and performance in programming: A randomized controlled experiment. *Higher Education, 83*(1), 1–18. DOI: 10.1007/s10734-020-00560-z PMID: 33173242

Hemi, A., Madjar, N., & Rich, Y. (2021). Perceived Peer and Teacher Goals: Relationships with Students' Academic Achievement Goals. *Journal of Experimental Education, 91*(1), 145–165. DOI: 10.1080/00220973.2021.1906199

Henderson, C. (2023). Editorial: Call for Papers for Focused Collection of Physical Review Physics Education Research: AI Tools in Physics Teaching and PER. *Physical Review. Physics Education Research, 19*(2), 020003. Advance online publication. DOI: 10.1103/PhysRevPhysEducRes.19.020003

Herdman, M., Fox-Rushby, J., & Badia, X. (1998). A model of equivalence in the cultural adaptation of HRQoL instruments: The universalist approach. *Quality of Life Research: An International Journal of Quality of Life Aspects of Treatment, Care and Rehabilitation, 7*(4), 323–335. DOI: 10.1023/A:1008846618880 PMID: 9610216

Hidayat, M. T. (2024). Effectiveness of AI-Based Personalised Reading Platforms in Enhancing Reading Comprehension. *Journal of Learning for Development, 11*(1), 115–125. DOI: 10.56059/jl4d.v11i1.955

Hirosawa, T., Kawamura, R., Harada, Y., Mizuta, K., Tokumasu, K., Kaji, Y., Suzuki, T., & Shimizu, T. (2023). CHATGPT-generated differential diagnosis lists for complex case–derived clinical vignettes: Diagnostic Accuracy Evaluation. *JMIR Medical Informatics, 11*, e48808. Advance online publication. DOI: 10.2196/48808 PMID: 37812468

Holmes, W., Bialik, M., & Fadel, C. (2019). Artificial Intelligence in Education Promises and Implications for Teaching and Learning. In *(1st ed.). Center for Curriculum Redesign: MA, USA. (2019).* Center for Curriculum Redesign. https://circls.org/primers/artificial-intelligence-in-education-promises-and-implications-for-teaching-and-learning

Holmes, W., Bialik, M., & Fadel, C. (2023). Artificial intelligence in education. http://hdl.handle.net/20.500.12424/4276068

Holmes, W., Bialik, M., & Fadel, C. (2019). *Artificial Intelligence in Education Promises and Implications for Teaching and Learning* (1st ed.). Center for Curriculum Redesign.

Holmes, W., Bialik, M., & Fadel, C. (2019). *Artificial intelligence in education promises and implications for teaching and learning*. Center for Curriculum Redesign.

Holmes, W., Luckin, R., & Mavrikis, M. (2020). Teacher training for AI: Challenges and opportunities. *The Journal of Educational Research*, *45*(2), 115–128.

Holmes, W., & Tuomi, I. (2022). State of the art and practice in AI in education. *European Journal of Education*, *57*(4), 542–570. DOI: 10.1111/ejed.12533

Holstein, K., McLaren, B. M., & Aleven, V. (2019). Co-designing a real-time classroom orchestration tool to support teacher—AI complementarity. *Journal of Learning Analytics, 6*(2), 27–52. . 62.3DOI: 10. 18608/ jla.2019

Hopcan, S., Polat, E., Ozturk, M. E., & Ozturk, L. (2023). Artificial intelligence in special education: A systematic review. *Interactive Learning Environments*, *31*(10), 7335–7353. DOI: 10.1080/10494820.2022.2067186

Houston, D. M., Frijns, J. H. M., & Van Lieshout, E. C. D. M. (2020). Social participation of children with hearing loss in mainstream education: A systematic review. *International Journal of Audiology*, *59*(12), 875–886. DOI: 10.1080/14992027.2020.1810878

Huang, J., Saleh, S., & Liu, Y. (2021). *A Review on Artificial Intelligence in Education. 10*(3). https://www.richtmann.org/journal/index.php/ajis/article/view/12463

Huang, L. (2023). Ethics of Artificial intelligence in Education: Student privacy and data protection. *Science Insights Education Frontiers*, *16*(2), 2577–2587. DOI: 10.15354/sief.23.re202

Huang, X., Zhang, Y., & Yu, H. (2021). AI-assisted speech therapy for children with autism spectrum disorder. *Journal of Child Psychology and Psychiatry, and Allied Disciplines*, *62*(9), 1198–1215. DOI: 10.1111/jcpp.13318

Hudson, M. L. (2024). *Examination of goal orientation theory key measures related to high school students' disruptive behaviors* (Order No. 31296634). Available from ProQuest Dissertations & Theses Global. (3065231081). Retrieved from https://www.proquest.com/dissertations-theses/examination-goal-orientation-theory-key-measures/docview/3065231081/se-2

Hwang, G. J., Wang, S. Y., & Lai, C. L. (2021). Effects of a social regulation-based online learning framework on students' learning achievements and behaviors in mathematics. *Computers & Education, 160*, 104031. Advance online publication. DOI: 10.1016/j.compedu.2020.104031

Hwang, G.-J., Xie, H., Wah, B. W., & Gasevic, D. (2020). Vision, challenges, roles and research issues of Artificial Intelligence in Education. *Comput. Educ.: Artif. Intell., 1*, 100001. DOI: 10.1016/j.caeai.2020.100001

Indrajith, R. (2024). AI Innovations for Inclusive Learning: Breaking Down Barriers. *International Journal of Research Publication and Reviews*, *5*(4), 9742–9745.

Irving, J., Patel, R., Oliver, D., Colling, C., Pritchard, M., Broadbent, M., & Stewart, R. (2020). Using natural language processing on electronic health records to enhance detection and prediction of psychosis risk. *Schizophrenia Bulletin*. PMID: 33025017

Ismail, I. A., & Aloshi, J. M. (2024). Data Privacy in AI-Driven Education: An In-Depth Exploration Into the Data Privacy Concerns and Potential Solutions. In Keeley, K. L. (Ed.), (pp. 223–252). Advances in Educational Marketing, Administration, and Leadership. IGI Global., DOI: 10.4018/979-8-3693-5443-8.ch008

Ismail, O. A. (2024). Digital Transformation in Education: Navigating the Challenges and Opportunities of Remote Learning. In Gray, S., & Purpuri, L. (Eds.), *Building Resilient Education Models Post Crisis* (pp. 133–149). IGI Global Scientific Publishing., DOI: 10.4018/979-8-3693-8125-0.ch007

Ismail, O. S. (2024). Empowering the Modern Learning Ecosystem: Integrative Approaches for a Holistic Educational Experience. In Al Husseiny, F., & Munna, A. (Eds.), *Revitalizing the Learning Ecosystem for Modern Students* (pp. 145–167). IGI Global Scientific Publishing., DOI: 10.4018/979-8-3693-4103-2.ch008

Ivanov, S., Soliman, M., Tuomi, A., Alkathiri, N. A., & Al-Alawi, A. N. (2024). Drivers of generative AI adoption in higher education through the lens of the Theory of Planned Behaviour. *Technology in Society*, *77*, 102521. https://doi.org/https://doi.org/10.1016/j.techsoc.2024.102521. DOI: 10.1016/j.techsoc.2024.102521

Jaboob, M., Hazaimeh, M., & Al-Ansi, A. M. (2024). Integration of generative AI techniques and applications in student behavior and cognitive achievement in Arab higher education. *International Journal of Human-Computer Interaction*, •••, 1–14.

Jafari, F., & Keykha, A. (2024). Identifying the opportunities and challenges of artificial intelligence in higher education: A qualitative study. *Journal of Applied Research in Higher Education*, *16*(4), 1228–1245. DOI: 10.1108/JARHE-09-2023-0426

Jamal, A., Pattanaik, A., Gorli, R., Chinmay, A., & Jaisai, T. (2023)... *The Impact of Ai Chatbots on Teacher-Student Relationships in Higher Education.*, *12*, 2299–2305.

Jamaludin, N. F., Wook, T. S. M. T., Noor, S. F. M., & Qamar, F. (2021). Gamification Design Elements to Enhance Adolescent Motivation in Diagnosing Depression. *International Journal of Interactive Mobile Technologies*, *15*(10), 154. DOI: 10.3991/ijim.v15i10.21137

Jang, J., Jeon, J., & Ki Jung, S. (2022). Development of STEM-Based AI Education Program for Sustainable Improvement of Elementary Learners. *Sustainability (Basel)*, *14*(22), 15178. Advance online publication. DOI: 10.3390/su142215178

Javed, A. R., Saadia, A., Mughal, H., Gadekallu, T. R., Rizwan, M., Maddikunta, P. K. R., Mahmud, M., Liyanage, M., & Hussain, A. (2023). Artificial Intelligence for Cognitive Health Assessment: State-of-the-Art, Open Challenges and Future Directions. *Cognitive Computation*, *15*(6), 1767–1812. DOI: 10.1007/s12559-023-10153-4

Jeong, H., Yoo, J. H., & Han, O. (2023). Next-Generation Chatbots for Adaptive Learning: A proposed Framework. *Journal of Internet Computing and Services*, *24*(4), 37–45. DOI: 10.7472/jksii.2023.24.4.37

Ji, Y., & Han, Y. (2019). Monitoring indicators of the flipped classroom learning process based on data mining—Taking the course of "virtual reality technology" as an example. *International Journal of Emerging Technologies in Learning*, *14*(3), 166–176. . v14i03.10105DOI: 10. 3991/ ijet

Jiang, Z., Seyedi, S., Griner, E., Abbasi, A., Bahrami Rad, A., Kwon, H., Cotes, R., & Clifford, G. D. (2024). Multimodal mental health digital biomarker analysis from remote interviews using facial, vocal, linguistic, and cardiovascular patterns. *IEEE Journal of Biomedical and Health Informatics*, *28*(3), 1680–1691. DOI: 10.1109/JBHI.2024.3352075 PMID: 38198249

Jian, M. J. K. O. (2023). Personalized learning through AI. *Advances in Engineering Innovation*, *5*(1), 16–19. DOI: 10.54254/2977-3903/5/2023039

Johnson, M., & Lee, K. (2023). Technology integration for accessibility in literacy education. *Educational Research Review*, *22*(4), 78–89. DOI: 10.1016/j.edurev.2023.101087

Jones, M. S., & Kahn, J. (2017). *The evidence base for how we learn: Supporting students' social emotional, and academic development*. Aspen Institute, National Commission on Social, Emotional, and Academic Development. https://www.aspeninstitute.org/publications/ evidence-base-learn/

Jones, D. E., Greenberg, M., & Crowley, M. (2015). Early Social-Emotional Functioning and Public Health: The relationship between kindergarten social competence and future wellness. *American Journal of Public Health*, *105*(11), 2283–2290. DOI: 10.2105/AJPH.2015.302630 PMID: 26180975

Jones, S. M., Bailey, R., & Jacob, R. (2021). Social-emotional learning: A key to children's success. *The Future of Children*, *27*(1), 13–32.

Jones, S. M., & Doolittle, E. J. (2017). Social and Emotional Learning: Introducing the issue. *The Future of Children*, *27*(1), 3–11. DOI: 10.1353/foc.2017.0000

Jones, T. (1985). Computers in the classroom: The next generation. *Educational Technology*, *25*(3), 22–29.

Jose, D. (2024). *Data privacy and security concerns in AI-integrated educational platforms*. Recent Trends in Management and Commerce., DOI: 10.46632/rmc/5/2/19

Joseph, O., & Uzondu, N.Olatunbosun Bartholomew JosephNwankwo Charles Uzondu. (2024). Integrating AI and Machine Learning in STEM education: Challenges and opportunities. *Computer Science & IT Research Journal*, *5*(8), 1732–1750. DOI: 10.51594/csitrj.v5i8.1379

Joshi, M. A. (2023). Adaptive Learning through Artificial Intelligence. *SSRN*, *7*(2), 41–43. DOI: 10.2139/ssrn.4514887

Juanda, J., Riansyah, R. J., Arsadi, A., & Bethany, L. (2024). Towards entrepreneurial campus sustainability: Integrating artificial intelligence for resource allocation. [ATT]. *Aptisi Transactions on Technopreneurship*, *6*(3), 410. Advance online publication. DOI: 10.34306/att.v6i3.410

Judijanto, L., Atsani, M. R., & Chadijah, S. (2024). Trends In The Development Of Artificial Intelligence-Based Technology In Education. *International Journal of Teaching and Learning*, *2*(6), 1722–1723.

Junyi, Z. (2024). *The application value of behavior analysis based on deep learning in the evaluation of depression in art students*. Applied Mathematics and Nonlinear Sciences. DOI: 10.2478/amns-2024-1834

Justice, L. M., Logan, J. A., & Damschroder, L. (2017). Early interventions for speech and language delays in children: Evidence and future directions. *Journal of Speech, Language, and Hearing Research: JSLHR*, *60*(3), 437–452. DOI: 10.1044/2017_JSLHR-L-16-0115

Kabudi, T., Pappas, I., & Olsen, D. H. (2021). AI-enabled adaptive learning systems: A systematic mapping of the literature. *Computers and Education: Artificial Intelligence*, *2*, 100017. DOI: 10.1016/j.caeai.2021.100017

Kakde, P. (2023). Sentimental analysis using machine learning for mental healthcare management system. *International Journal for Research in Applied Science and Engineering Technology*, *11*(6), 563–570. DOI: 10.22214/ijraset.2023.53450

Kalota, F. (2024). A Primer on Generative Artificial Intelligence. *Education Sciences*, *14*(2), 172. DOI: 10.3390/educsci14020172

Kamalov, F., Santandreu Calonge, D., & Gurrib, I. (2023). New era of artificial intelligence in education: Towards a sustainable multifaceted revolution. *Sustainability (Basel)*, *15*(16), 12451. DOI: 10.3390/su151612451

Kamruzzaman, M. M., Alanazi, S., Alruwaili, M., Alshammari, N., Elaiwat, S., Abu-Zanona, M., Innab, N., Mohammad Elzaghmouri, B., & Ahmed Alanazi, B. (2023). AI-and IoT-assisted sustainable education systems during pandemics, such as COVID-19, for smart cities. *Sustainability (Basel)*, *15*(10), 8354. DOI: 10.3390/su15108354

Karaca, M. F. (2024, 2024). Is Artificial Intelligence able to Produce Content Appropriate for Education Level? A Review on ChatGPT and Gemini. *Proceedings of the Cognitive Models and Artificial Intelligence Conference*, İstanbul,Turkiye. DOI: 10.1145/3660853.3660915

Karakose, T., & Tülübas, T. (2024). School Leadership and Management in the Age of Artificial Intelligence (AI): Recent Developments and Future Prospects. *Educational Process: International Journal*, *13*(1), 7–14. DOI: 10.22521/edupij.2024.131.1

Karapet, H. N., & Misak, A. S. (2024). The Role And Impact Of Artificial Intelligence And Social-Emotional Learning In The Social Pedagogue's Work With Children With Special Educational Needs. *Library Progress International*, *44*(3), 3. Advance online publication. DOI: 10.48165/bapas.2024.44.2.1

Karimah, A. N., & Kurniawati, F. (2024). Precision in special education: Insights from a systematic review on data-based decision making. *Jurnal Kependidikan: Jurnal Hasil Penelitian dan Kajian Kepustakaan di Bidang Pendidikan, Pengajaran dan Pembelajaran, 10*(4), 1485–1495.

Kasneci, E., Sessler, K., Küchemann, S., Bannert, M., Dementieva, D., Fischer, F., Gasser, U., Groh, G., Günnemann, S., Hüllermeier, E., Krusche, S., Kutyniok, G., Michaeli, T., Nerdel, C., Pfeffer, J., Poquet, O., Sailer, M., Schmidt, A., Seidel, T., & Kasneci, G. (2023). Chatgpt for good? on opportunities and challenges of large language models for Education. *Learning and Individual Differences, 103*, 102274. DOI: 10.1016/j.lindif.2023.102274

Katiyar, P. D. N., Awasthi, M. V. K., Pratap, D. R., Mishra, M. K., Shukla, M. N., Singh, M. R., & Tiwari, D. M. (2024). Ai-Driven Personalized Learning Systems: Enhancing Educational Effectiveness. *Educational Administration: Theory and Practice, 30*(5), 5. Advance online publication. DOI: 10.53555/kuey.v30i5.4961

Katsarou, D., Sofologi, M., & Efthymiou, E. (Eds.). (2025). *Psycholinguistic Dynamics and Educational Inclusion for Children and Adolescents*. IGI Global., DOI: 10.4018/979-8-3693-8931-7

Kefallinou, A., Symeonidou, S., & Meijer, C. J. W. (2020). Understanding the value of inclusive education and its implementation: A review of the literature. *Prospects, 49*(3), 3. Advance online publication. DOI: 10.1007/s11125-020-09500-2

Kennedy-Mayo, D., & Gord, J. (2024). "Model Cards for Model Reporting" in 2024: Reclassifying Category of Ethical Considerations in Terms of Trustworthiness and Risk Management. *arXiv preprint arXiv:2403.15394.*

Kerz, E., Zanwar, S., Qiao, Y., & Wiechmann, D. (2023). Toward explainable AI (XAI) for mental health detection based on language behavior. *Frontiers in Psychiatry, 14*, 14. DOI: 10.3389/fpsyt.2023.1219479 PMID: 38144474

Khalil, R. Y., Tairab, H., Qablan, A., Alarabi, K., & Mansour, Y. (2023). STEM-Based Curriculum and Creative Thinking in High School Students. *Education Sciences, 13*(12), 12. Advance online publication. DOI: 10.3390/educsci13121195

Khalil, R., Mansour, A. E., Fadda, W. A., Almisnid, K., Aldamegh, M., Al-Nafeesah, A., Alkhalifah, A., & Al-Wutayd, O. (2020). The sudden transition to synchronized online learning during the COVID-19 pandemic in Saudi Arabia: A qualitative study exploring medical students' perspectives. *BMC Medical Education, 20*(1), 285. DOI: 10.1186/s12909-020-02208-z PMID: 32859188

Khoo, L. S., Lim, M. K., Chong, C. Y., & Mcnaney, R. (2024). Machine learning for multimodal mental health detection: A systematic review of passive sensing approaches. *Sensors (Basel)*, *24*(2), 348. Advance online publication. DOI: 10.3390/s24020348 PMID: 38257440

Khosravi, H., Shum, S. B., Chen, G., Conati, C., Tsai, Y. S., Kay, J., Knight, S., Martinez-Maldonado, R., Sadiq, S., & Gašević, D. (2022). Explainable artificial intelligence in education. *Computers and Education: Artificial Intelligence*, *3*, 100074. Advance online publication. DOI: 10.1016/j.caeai.2022.100074

Khreisat, M. N., Khilani, D., Rusho, M. A., Karkkulainen, E. A., Tabuena, A. C., & Uberas, A. D. (2024). Ethical Implications Of AI Integration In Educational Decision Making: Systematic Review. *Educational Administration: Theory and Practice*, *30*(5), 8521–8527.

Kibibi, M. L. (2024). *The role of AI in improving mental health care*. Research Invention Journal of Public Health and Pharmacy., DOI: 10.59298/RIJPP/2024/321013

Kikerpill, K., & Siibak, A. (2022). Schools engaged in doom-monitoring students' online interactions and content creation: An analysis of dominant media discourses. *Child and Adolescent Mental Health*. Advance online publication. DOI: 10.1111/camh.12621 PMID: 36495068

Kim, H. H., An, J. I., & Park, Y. R. (2021). A prediction model for detecting developmental disabilities in preschool-age children through digital biomarker-driven deep learning in serious games: Development study. *JMIR Serious Games*, *9*(2), e23130. DOI: 10.2196/23130 PMID: 34085944

Kim, J., Kim, S., & Kamphaus, R. (2022). Early detection of mental health through universal screening at schools. *Georgia Educational Researcher*, *20*(3), 32–47. DOI: 10.20429/ger.2022.190104

Kim, N. J., & Kim, M. K. (2022). Teacher's Perceptions of Using an Artificial Intelligence-Based Educational Tool for Scientific Writing. *Frontiers in Education*, *7*, 755914. Advance online publication. DOI: 10.3389/feduc.2022.755914

Kim, T. K. (2024). Integrating Learning Analytics, AI, and STEM Education. *International Journal of Research in STEM Education*, *6*(2), 61–72. DOI: 10.33830/ijrse.v6i2.1745

Klein, L. A. (2024). *Bridging the achievement gap for students with learning disabilities by increasing educator collaboration with an emphasis on integrative technology* (Order No. 30994562). Available from ProQuest Dissertations & Theses Global. (3057619243). Retrieved from https://www.proquest.com/dissertations-theses/bridging-achievement-gap-students-with-learning/docview/3057619243/se-2

Klein, N. A., Sondag, K. A., & Drolet, J. C. (1994). Understanding volunteer peer health educators' motivations: Applying social learning theory. *Journal of American College Health, 43*(3), 126–130. DOI: 10.1080/07448481.1994.9939096 PMID: 7814769

Koga, S., Martin, N. B., & Dickson, D. W. (2023). Evaluating the performance of large language models: ChatGPT and Google Bard in generating differential diagnoses in clinicopathological conferences of neurodegenerative disorders. *Brain Pathology (Zurich, Switzerland)*. Advance online publication. DOI: 10.1111/bpa.13207 PMID: 37553205

Kohli, M. M., & Prasad, T. V. (2010). Identifying Dyslexic Students by Using Artificial Neural Networks, *Proceedings of the World Congress on Engineering 2,* Vol. I., *WCE 2010, June 30 - July 2, 2010, London, U.K.*

Koller, O., Ney, H., & Bowden, R. (2019). Automatic sign language recognition: Current trends and future directions. *IEEE Transactions on Pattern Analysis and Machine Intelligence, 41*(5), 1203–1217. DOI: 10.1109/TPAMI.2019.2896263 PMID: 29993771

Kooli, C. (2023). Chatbots in Education and Research: A Critical Examination of Ethical Implications and Solutions. *Sustainability (Basel), 15*(7), 7. Advance online publication. DOI: 10.3390/su15075614

Kose, U., & Arslan, A. (2017). Optimization of self-learning in computer engineering courses: An intelligent software system supported by artificial neural network and vortex optimization algorithm. *Computer Applications in Engineering Education, 25*(1), 142–156. . 21787DOI: 10.1002/ cae

Kotsi, S., Handrinou, S., Iatraki, G., & Soulis, S. G. (2025). A Review of Artificial Intelligence Interventions for Students with Autism Spectrum Disorder. *Disabilities, 5*(1), 7. DOI: 10.3390/disabilities5010007

Krasovskiy, D. (2020). *The challenges and benefits of adopting AI in STEM education.* https:// upjou rney. com/ the- chall enges- and- benefits- of- adopting- ai- in- stem- educa tion

Krishnamurti, S. (2015). Application of neural network modeling to identify auditory processing disorders in school-age children. *Advances in Artificial Neural Systems, 2015*, 1–13. DOI: 10.1155/2015/635840

Krullaars, Z. H., Januardani, A., Zhou, L., & Jonkers, E. (2023). *Exploring Initial Interactions: High School Students and Generative AI Chatbots for Relationship Development.*. https://dl.gi.de/handle/20.500.12116/42444DOI: 10.18420/muc2023

Kuder, S. J. (2017). *Teaching students with language and communication disabilities* (5th ed.). Pearson Education.

Kumar, K., Selvan, T., Mahendraprabu, M., Ganesan, K., Ramnath, R., & Kumar, N. (2024). Examining the Role of Virtual Reality, Augmented Reality, and Artificial Intelligence in Adapting STEM Education for Next-Generation Inclusion. *International Journal of Emerging Knowledge Studies*. DOI: 10.70333/ijeks-02-12-025

Kumar, L. A., Renuka, D. K., Rose, S. L., Shunmuga priya, M. C., & Wartana, I. M. (2022). Deep learning based assistive technology on audio visual speech recognition for hearing impaired. *International Journal of Cognitive Computing in Engineering, 3*, 24–30. DOI: 10.1016/j.ijcce.2022.01.003

Kumar, R., & Agrawal, S. (2021). Digital divides in AI adoption: A study of rural schools. *Educational Policy Analysis, 39*(6), 813–828.

Kumar, V., Kumar, U., & Dutta, D. (2021). Enhancing collaborative learning through AI-based educational platforms. *Educational Technology Research and Development, 69*(3), 671–687.

Kuroiwa, T., Sarcon, A., Ibara, T., Yamada, E., Yamamoto, A., Tsukamoto, K., & Fujita, K. (2023). The potential of CHATGPT as a self-diagnostic tool in common orthopedic diseases: Exploratory study. *Journal of Medical Internet Research, 25*, e47621. Advance online publication. DOI: 10.2196/47621 PMID: 37713254

Kusi-Mensah, K., Donnir, G., Dzodzomenyo, M., Owoo, E., & Asante, K. P. (2019). Prevalence and patterns of mental disorders among primary school children in the Greater Accra Region of Ghana. *BMC Pediatrics, 19*(1), 248. PMID: 31331315

Lambert, J., & Stevens, M. (2024). ChatGPT and generative AI technology: A mixed bag of concerns and new opportunities. *Computers in the Schools, 41*(4), 559–583. DOI: 10.1080/07380569.2023.2256710

Lamb, R., Hand, B., & Kavner, A. (2021). Computational modeling of the effects of the science writing heuristic on student critical thinking in science using machine learning. *Journal of Science Education and Technology, 30*(2), 283–297. DOI: 10.1007/s10956-020-09871-3

Lametti, D. (2022, December 7). A.I. could be great for college essays. *Slate*. https://slate.com/technology/2022/12/chatgpt-college-essay-plagiarism.html

Landstedt, E., & Bortels, S. (2021). Is there a social gradient in how youth with mental disorder symptoms succeed in education? *Journal of Youth Studies*, *24*(3), 265–281.

Lata, P. (2024). Towards Equitable Learning: Exploring Artificial Intelligence in Inclusive Education. *SSRN*, *7*(5), 416–434. DOI: 10.2139/ssrn.4987156

Lázaro, E., Amayra, I., López-Paz, J. F., Martínez, O., Alvarez, M. P., Berrocoso, S., Al-Rashaida, M., García, M., Luna, P., Pérez-Núñez, P., Rodriguez, A. A., Fernández, P., Fernández, P. P., & Oliva-Macías, M. (2020). Using a Virtual Serious Game (Deusto-e-motion1.0) to Assess the Theory of Mind in Primary School Children: Observational Descriptive Study. *JMIR Serious Games*, *8*(2), e12971. DOI: 10.2196/12971 PMID: 32238330

Le Glaz, A., Haralambous, Y., Kim-Dufor, D. H., Lenca, P., Billot, R., Ryan, T. C., Marsh, J., DeVylder, J., Walter, M., Berrouiguet, S., & Lemey, C. (2021). Machine learning and natural language processing in mental health: Systematic review. *Journal of Medical Internet Research*, *23*(5), e15708. DOI: 10.2196/15708 PMID: 33944788

Lee, D., Arnold, M., Srivastava, A., Plastow, K., Strelan, P., Ploeckl, F., Lekkas, D., & Palmer, E. (2024). The impact of generative AI on higher education learning and teaching: A study of educators' perspectives. *Computers and Education: Artificial Intelligence, 6*, 100221. https://doi.org/https://doi.org/10.1016/j.caeai.2024.100221

Lee, I., & Perret, B. (2022). *Preparing High School Teachers to Integrate AI Methods into STEM Classrooms*. www.aaai.org

Lee, S., & Song, K.-s. (2024). Teachers' and Students' Perceptions of AI-Generated Concept Explanations: Implications for Integrating Generative AI in Computer Science Education. *Computers and Education: Artificial Intelligence*, 100283. https://doi.org/https://doi.org/10.1016/j.caeai.2024.100283

Lee, C. H., Gobir, N., Gurn, A., & Soep, E. (2022). In the black mirror: Youth investigations into artificial intelligence. *ACM Transactions on Computing Education*, *22*(3), 1–25. DOI: 10.1145/3484495

Lee, I. A., & Perret, B. (2022). Preparing High School Teachers to Integrate AI Methods into STEM Classrooms. *AAAI Conference on Artificial Intelligence*. DOI: 10.1609/aaai.v36i11.21557

Le-Nguyen, H. T., & Tran, T. T. (2024). Generative AI in terms of Its ethical problems for both teachers and learners: Striking a balance. In *Generative AI in Teaching and Learning* (pp. 144–173). IGI Global.

Lérias, E., Guerra, C., & Ferreira, P. (2024). Literacy in artificial intelligence as a challenge for teaching in higher education: A case study at portalegre polytechnic university. *Information (Basel)*, *15*(4), 205. DOI: 10.3390/info15040205

Levin, S. (2024). Identifying student behavior patterns based on LMS data. *International Scientific Journal of Engineering and Management*, *3*(3), 1–9. DOI: 10.55041/ISJEM01447

Li, J., Ma, C., Lu, Q., & Hesketh, T. (2022, November). A Social Emotional Learning Training Programme in a Poor Rural Primary School in Central China: A Pre-Post Intervention Study. In *Healthcare* (Vol. 10, No. 11, p. 2332). MDPI. DOI: 10.3390/healthcare10112332

Licardo, M., & Lipovec, A. (Eds.). (2024) *Artificial Intelligence Literacy and Social-Emotional Skills as Transversal Competencies in Education.* ISSN: 0945-487X

Li, H. (2023). AI in Education: Bridging the Divide or Widening the Gap? Exploring Equity, Opportunities, and Challenges in the Digital Age. *Advances in Education. Humanities and Social Science Research*, *8*(1), 1. Advance online publication. DOI: 10.56028/aehssr.8.1.355.2023

Lin, X., & Schmidt, S. (2023). Making ChatGPT Work for You. *ELearn, 2023*(4). https://doi.org/DOI: 10.1145/3594251.3594636

Lin, C. C., Huang, A. Y., & Lu, O. H. (2023). Artificial intelligence in intelligent tutoring systems toward sustainable education: A systematic review. *Smart Learning Environments*, *10*(1), 41. DOI: 10.1186/s40561-023-00260-y

Li, Y.-F., & Liu, C.-T. (2024). Using self-monitoring and ChatGPT to teach students with intellectual disability email writing. *Global Journal of Intellectual & Developmental Disabilities*, *13*(4), 555871. DOI: 10.19080/GJIDD.2024.13.555871

Li, Y., Liang, J., Zhao, Z., & Li, K. (2024). Revolutionizing Education through AI: Alleviating Educator Stress, Personalizing Learning, and Enhancing Economic Sustainability. *World Journal of Education and Humanities*, *6*(5), 113. DOI: 10.22158/wjeh.v6n5p113

Li, Z. (2023). AI-assisted emotion recognition: Impacts on mental health education and learning motivation. [iJET]. *International Journal of Emerging Technologies in Learning*, *18*(24), 45645. Advance online publication. DOI: 10.3991/ijet.v18i24.45645

Lloyd, C., Doherty, S., Herb, A., & Warburton, S. (2022). *A risk-based approach to mitigating the Gen(AI) challenge to assessment integrity: The Programmatic Assessment Security Project*. PASP., DOI: 10.1007/978-3

Lohakan, M., & Seetao, C. (2024). Large-scale experiment in STEM education for high school students using artificial intelligence kit based on computer vision and Python. *Heliyon, 10*(10), e31366. Advance online publication. DOI: 10.1016/j.heliyon.2024.e31366 PMID: 38803951

López, A., Pérez, M., & Rodríguez, J. (2022). AI-driven assessments in speech therapy: Benefits and limitations. *Journal of Speech-Language Pathology, 48*(2), 210–225. DOI: 10.1177/23814683221056432

Low, P. K. (2009). Considering the challenges of counselling practice in schools. *International Journal for the Advancement of Counseling, 31*(2), 71–79. DOI: 10.1007/s10447-009-9069-1

Luckin, R., & Holmes, W. (2016). Intelligence Unleashed: An argument for AI in Education. In *UCL Knowledge Lab: London, UK.* [Report]. UCL Knowledge Lab. https://www.pearson.com/content/dam/corporate/global/pearson-dot-com/files/innovation/Intelligence-Unleashed-Publication.pdf

Luckin, R. (2018). *Machine learning and human intelligence: The future of education for the 21st century*. UCL IOE Press.

Luckin, R., & Cukurova, M. (2019). Designing educational technologies in the age of AI: A learning sciences-driven approach. *British Journal of Educational Technology, 50*(6), 2824–2838. DOI: 10.1111/bjet.12861

Luckin, R., & Holmes, W. (2016). Big data and learning analytics in primary education: Challenges and opportunities. *Educational Leadership Review, 54*(1), 12–24.

Luckin, R., & Holmes, W. (2016). *Intelligence unleashed: An argument for AI in education*. Pearson Education.

Luckin, R., & Holmes, W. (2016). *Intelligence Unleashed: An argument for AI in Education*. UCL Knowledge Lab.

Luckin, R., Holmes, W., Griffiths, M., & Forcier, L. B. (2016). *Intelligence Unleashed: An argument for AI in education*. Pearson Education.

Lugrin, J. L., Bortolaso, C., Cumming, B., & Karray, F. (2015). The challenges of virtual reality for exposure therapy in anxiety disorders: Patients' and therapists' opinions. *Journal of Medical Internet Research, 17*(12), 319.

Lukowski, J. (2024). How To Make the Leap from Traditional Leader to AI Leader. Retrieved from: <https://neoris.com/web/guest/-/how-to-make-the-leap-from-traditional-leader-to-ai-leader?redirect=%2F>. Accessed on 7th Jan 2025.

Luo, G., & Li, C. (2024). Research on mental health problem identification algorithm of college students. *2024 IEEE 2nd International Conference on Image Processing and Computer Applications (ICIPCA).*

Luo, L., Yang, X., & Zhang, Y. (2023). Enhancing collaborative learning through AI-mediated communication tools. *International Journal of Educational Research, 115*, 102057.

Luo, X., & Xie, L. (2018). Research on Artificial Intelligence-Based Sharing Education in the Era of Internet+. *2018 International Conference on Intelligent Transportation, Big Data & Smart City (ICITBS)*, 335–338. DOI: 10.1109/ICITBS.2018.00092

Lv, Z. (2023). Generative artificial intelligence in the metaverse era. *Cognitive Robotics, 3*, 208-217. https://doi.org/https://doi.org/10.1016/j.cogr.2023.06.001

Macfarlane, B., Bolden, R., & Watermeyer, R. (2024). Three perspectives on leadership in higher education: Traditionalist, reformist, pragmatist. *Higher Education, 88*(4), 1–22. DOI: 10.1007/s10734-023-01174-x

MacSweeney-Mahon, S. (2022). Predictors of socio-emotional functioning in childhood: longitudinal evidence. https://cora.ucc.ie/bitstreams/b7d055dc-833e-4b42-8be3-fe3fce4da37d/download

Maghsudi, S., Lan, A., Xu, J., & van Der Schaar, M. (2021). Personalized education in the artificial intelligence era: What to expect next. *IEEE Signal Processing Magazine, 38*(3), 37–50. DOI: 10.1109/MSP.2021.3055032

Mahadik, S. S., Pawar, P., Muthalagu, R., Prasad, N. R., Hawkins, S.-K., Stripelis, D., Rao, S., Ejim, P., & Hecht, B. (2024). Digital privacy in healthcare: State-of-the-art and future vision. *IEEE Access : Practical Innovations, Open Solutions, 12*, 84273–84291. DOI: 10.1109/ACCESS.2024.3410035

Maisikeli, S. G. (2023). Level of assistive technology use and awareness among people with physical disability in the United Arab Emirates. *Technology and Disability, 35*(1), 11–20. DOI: 10.3233/TAD-220393

Mäkelä, E., & Stephany, F. (2024). Complement or substitute? How AI increases the demand for human skills. *Arxiv*. https://arxiv.org/abs/2412.19754

Ma, L., Mazidi, M., Li, K., Chen, S., Kirwan, R., & Zhou, H. (2021). Prevalence of mental health problems among children and adolescents during COVID-19: A systematic review and meta-analysis. *Journal of Affective Disorders*, *293*(1), 78–89. DOI: 10.1016/j.jad.2021.06.021 PMID: 34174475

Malerbi, F., Nakayama, L., Ribeiro, L. Z., Villanueva, C., & Regatieri, C. (2023). Digital education for the deployment of artificial intelligence in health care. *Journal of Medical Internet Research*, *25*, e43333. Advance online publication. DOI: 10.2196/43333 PMID: 37347537

Malmqvist, J., Hellberg, K., Möllås, G., Rose, R., & Shevlin, M. (2019). Conducting the pilot study: A neglected part of the research process? Methodological findings supporting the importance of piloting in qualitative research studies. *International Journal of Qualitative Methods*, *18*, 1–11. DOI: 10.1177/1609406919878341

Maphoto, K. B., Sevnarayan, K., Mohale, N. E., Suliman, Z., Ntsopi, T. J., & Mokoena, D. (2024). Advancing students' academic excellence in distance education: Exploring the potential of generative AI integration to improve academic writing skills [Journal Article]. *Open Praxis*, *16*(2), 142–159. DOI: 10.55982/openpraxis.16.2.649

Marino, M. T., & Vasquez, E.III. (2024). Special education administrators' use of artificial intelligence (AI) to synthesize data. *Journal of Special Education Leadership*, *37*(2), 62–76.

Martínez, O., Amayra, I., López-Paz, J. F., Lázaro, E., Caballero, P., García, I., Rodríguez, A. A., García, M., Luna, P. M., Pérez-Núñez, P., Barrera, J., Passi, N., Berrocoso, S., Pérez, M., & Al-Rashaida, M. (2021). Effects of Teleassistance on the Quality of Life of People With Rare Neuromuscular Diseases According to Their Degree of Disability. *Frontiers in Psychology*, *12*, 637413. Advance online publication. DOI: 10.3389/fpsyg.2021.637413 PMID: 33737897

Martin, S., & James, R. (2023). Advances in tactile communication for students with dual sensory impairments. *Journal of Visual Impairment & Blindness*, *117*(3), 179–190. DOI: 10.1177/01626434221100089

Massouti, A., Al-Rashaida, M., & Alhosani, M. (2024). A qualitative study on Dubai's inclusive education policy from school leaders' perspectives. *Sustainability (Basel)*, *16*(3), 1252. DOI: 10.3390/su16031252

Matandika, M., Mategula, C., Msolomba, P., & Bandawe, C. (2022). Prevalence and correlates of common mental disorders among school children in Malawi. *Child Psychiatry and Human Development*, *53*(2), 159–168.

Maupomé, D., Rancourt, F., Belbahar, R., & Meurs, M. J. (2024). A pretrained language model for mental health risk detection. *Proceedings of the 2024 Conference on Language Processing*.

Mbakwe, A. B., Lourentzou, I., Celi, L. A., Mechanic, O. J., & Dagan, A. (2023). CHATGPT passing USMLE shines a spotlight on the flaws of Medical Education. *PLOS Digital Health*, *2*(2), e0000205. Advance online publication. DOI: 10.1371/journal.pdig.0000205 PMID: 36812618

Mbalaka, B. (2023). Epistemically violent biases in artificial intelligence design: The case of DALLE-E 2 and Starry AI. *Digital Transformation and Society*, *2*(4), 376–402. DOI: 10.1108/DTS-01-2023-0003

McCarthy, J. (2007). *What is artificial intelligence?* Stanford AI Laboratory.

McCarthy, J., Jones, D., & Smith, A. (2019). The role of transcription tools in inclusive education for deaf students. *International Journal of Inclusive Education*, *23*(7), 789–803. DOI: 10.1080/13603116.2018.1563645

McCarthy, K. S., & Yan, E. F. (2023). Reading Comprehension and Constructive Learning: Policy Considerations in the Age of Artificial Intelligence. *Policy Insights from the Behavioral and Brain Sciences*, *11*(1), 19–26. DOI: 10.1177/23727322231218891

McDonald, N., Johri, A., Ali, A., & Hingle, A. (2024). Generative Artificial Intelligence in Higher Education: Evidence from an Analysis of Institutional Policies and Guidelines. *ArXiv, abs/2402.01659*. https://doi.org/https://doi.org/10.48550/arXiv.2402.01659

McGregor, K. K., Langenfeld, N., Van Horne, S., Oleson, J., Anson, M., & Jacobson, W. (2016). The university experiences of students with learning disabilities. *Learning Disabilities Research & Practice*, *31*(2), 90–102. DOI: 10.1111/ldrp.12102 PMID: 27667902

McGuire, S. N., & Meadan, H. (2022). General Educators' Perceptions of Social Inclusion of Elementary Students With Emotional and Behavioral Disorders. *Behavioral Disorders*, *48*(1), 16–28. DOI: 10.1177/01987429221079047

McLeod, S., & Baker, E. (2020). *Speech sound disorders in children: Theory and clinical practice* (2nd ed.). Plural Publishing.

McStay, A. (2020). Emotional AI, soft biometrics and the surveillance of emotional life: An unusual consensus on privacy. *Big Data & Society*, *7*(1), 1. Advance online publication. DOI: 10.1177/2053951720904386

Meece, J. L. (2023). The role of motivation in self-regulated learning. In *Self-regulation of learning and performance* (pp. 25–44). Routledge.

Megerian, J. T., Dey, S., Melmed, R. D., Coury, D. L., Lerner, M., Nicholls, C. J., Sohl, K., Rouhbakhsh, R., Narasimhan, A., Romain, J., Golla, S., Shareef, S., Ostrovsky, A., Shannon, J., Kraft, C., Liu-Mayo, S., Abbas, H., Gal-Szabo, D. E., Wall, D. P., & Taraman, S. (2022). Evaluation of an artificial intelligence-based medical device for diagnosis of autism spectrum disorder. *NPJ Digital Medicine*, *5*(1), 57. DOI: 10.1038/s41746-022-00598-6 PMID: 35513550

Mekler, E. D., Brühlmann, F., Tuch, A. N., & Opwis, K. (2017). Towards understanding the effects of individual gamification elements on intrinsic motivation and performance. *Computers in Human Behavior*, *71*, 525–534. DOI: 10.1016/j.chb.2015.08.048

Merriam, S. B. (2009). *Qualitative research: A Guide to Design and Implementation*. John Wiley & Sons.

Mertala, P. (2023). Gamified solutions for emotional self-regulation in children: A systematic review. *Educational Psychology Review*, *35*(2), 345–367.

Miao, F., Holmes, W., Huang, R., & Zhang, H. (2021). *AI and education: Guidance for policy-makers*. UNESCO. https://unesdoc.unesco.org/ark:/48223/pf0000376709?locale=en

Miao, F., & Holmes, W. (2024). *Guidelines for productive AI in education and research* (Mavrikis, M., & Margeti, M., Eds.). UNESCO., https://unesdoc.unesco.org/ark:/48223/pf0000390613

Miao, F., Holmes, W., & De Jong, T. (2021). AI, ethics, and social emotional learning: Findings from primary education. *Journal of Human-Centered Learning*, *27*(3), 197–213.

Miao, F., Holmes, W., Huang, R., & Zhang, H. (2021). *AI and education: A guidance for policymakers*. Unesco Publishing.

Milberg, T. (2024). The future of learning: How AI is revolutionizing education 4.0. Retrieved from: < https://www.weforum.org/stories/2024/04/future-learning-ai-revolutionizing-education-4-0/>. Accessed on 8th Jan 2025.

Millen, C. D., Brundage, R. D. C., & Lucas, R. D. Y. (2020). The Impact of Teaching Resilience, Goal Attainment, and Other Essential Leadership Skills to Young Adults via Virtual Instruction.

Milovanović, M., & Perišić, J. (2020). Advantages and limitations of using SPSS in teaching statistics. In *MEFkon 2020: Innovation as the Initiator of Development* (p. 274). Faculty of Applied Management, Economics and Finance.

Mishra, S. (2024). Revolutionizing Education: The impact of AI-Enhanced Teaching Strategies. *International Journal for Research in Applied Science and Engineering Technology*, *12*(9), 9–32. DOI: 10.22214/ijraset.2024.64127

Mitra, D. S. (2024). *AI-Powered Adaptive Education for Disabled Learners* (SSRN Scholarly Paper No. 5042713; Issue 5042713). Social Science Research Network. DOI: 10.2139/ssrn.5042713

Moerman, P. (2021). Public-private partnership to solve the skills gap? *European Journal of University Lifelong Learning*, *5*(1), 71–78. DOI: 10.53807/0501alt6

Mohammed, D. D. A. M., & Abd Elrahman, D. M. A. E. M. (2024). An Artificial Intelligence-Powered Program for Fostering STEM College Students' Cognitive Academic English Language Proficiency (CALP). *Journal of Research in Curriculum Instruction and Educational Technology*, *10*(2), 345–402. DOI: 10.21608/jrciet.2024.363679

Mondal, H., Marndi, G., Behera, J. K., & Mondal, S. (2023). ChatGPT for Teachers: Practical Examples for Utilizing Artificial Intelligence for Educational Purposes. *Indian Journal of Vascular and Endovascular Surgery*, *10*(3), 200–205. DOI: 10.4103/ijves.ijves_37_23

Montemayor, C., Halpern, J., & Fairweather, A. (2022). In principle obstacles for empathic AI: Why we can't replace human empathy in healthcare. *AI & Society*, *37*(4), 1353–1359. DOI: 10.1007/s00146-021-01230-z PMID: 34054228

Mooghali, M., Stroud, A. M., Yoo, D. W., Barry, B. A., Grimshaw, A. A., Ross, J. S., . . . Miller, J. E. (2023). Barriers and Facilitators to Trustworthy and Ethical AI-enabled Medical Care From Patient and Healthcare Provider Perspectives: A Literature Review. medRxiv, 2023-10. https://doi.org/DOI: 10.1101/2023.10.02.23296447

Moreno, R., & Mayer, R. E. (2017). Cognitive principles of multimedia learning: The role of modality and contiguity. *Learning and Instruction*, *11*(1), 47–56. DOI: 10.1016/j.learninstruc.2000.11.002

Moreno, R., Mayer, R. E., & Spires, H. (2022). Personalized learning in the age of AI: Impacts on student engagement and achievement. *Learning and Instruction*, *77*, 101488.

Moriera, F. (2024). *Proceedings of the 23rd European Conference on e-Learning*. Academic Conferences and publishing limited.

Morley, J., Machado, C., Burr, C., Cowls, J., Joshi, I., Taddeo, M., & Floridi, L. (2020). The ethics of AI in health care: A mapping review. *Social Science & Medicine, 260*, 113172. Advance online publication. DOI: 10.1016/j.socscimed.2020.113172 PMID: 32702587

Moura, I., Teles, A., Endler, M., Coutinho, L., & Silva, F. J. S. (2020). Recognizing context-aware human sociability patterns using pervasive monitoring for supporting mental health professionals. *Sensors (Basel), 21*(1), 21. DOI: 10.3390/s21010086 PMID: 33375630

Moustafa, A., Opoku, M. P., & Belbase, S. (2022). Using tactile imagery to teach geometry to students with visual impairments in the United Arab Emirates. *Research in Developmental Disabilities, 129*, 104309. DOI: 10.1016/j.ridd.2022.104309 PMID: 35868199

Movaghar, A., Page, D., Scholze, D., Hong, J., DaWalt, L. S., Kuusisto, F., Stewart, R., Brilliant, M., & Mailick, M. (2021). Artificial intelligence-assisted phenotype discovery of fragile X syndrome in a population-based sample. *Genetics in Medicine, 23*(7), 1273–1280. DOI: 10.1038/s41436-021-01144-7 PMID: 33772223

Mpu, Y. (2023). Bridging the Knowledge Gap on Special Needs Learner Support: The Use of Artificial Intelligence (AI) to Combat Digital Divide Post-COVID-19 Pandemic and beyond. In Altinay, F., & Altinay, Z. (Eds.), *Intellectual and Learning Disabilities—Inclusiveness and Contemporary Teaching Environments*. IntechOpen., DOI: 10.5772/intechopen.113054

Mucundanyi, G., & Woodley, X. (2021). *Exploring Free Digital Tools in Education. 17*(2).

Mullen, C. A., & Hunt, T. K. (2022). Emotional disability and strategies for supporting student outcomes: Interviews with K–12 special education teachers. *Teacher Development, 26*(4), 453–471. DOI: 10.1080/13664530.2022.2108129

Müller, T., & Schober, M. F. (2021). Barriers to auditory learning in traditional classrooms. *Educational Psychology Review, 33*(2), 287–302. DOI: 10.1007/s10648-021-09606-9

Murdoch, B. (2021). Privacy and artificial intelligence: Challenges for protecting health information in a new era. *BMC Medical Ethics, 22*(1), 6. Advance online publication. DOI: 10.1186/s12910-021-00687-3 PMID: 34525993

Murnane, R. J., & Levy, F. (2012). *The new division of labor: How computers are creating the next job market*. Princeton University Press.

Murphy, R. F. (2019). *RAND Corporation Artificial Intelligence Applications to Support K-12 Teachers and Teaching: A Review of Promising Applications, Opportunities, and Challenges.*

Mustafa, A., Opoku, M. P., Hamdan, A., Safi, M., & Mohamed, E. (2023). Perceived effectiveness of assistive devices and support services provided to students with visual impairment in mainstream classrooms in the United Arab Emirates. *British Journal of Special Education*, *50*(1), 45–60. DOI: 10.1111/1467-8578.12488

Mustafa, G., Urooj, T., & Aslam, M. (2024). ROLE OF ARTIFICIAL INTELLIGENCE FOR ADAPTIVE LEARNING ENVIRONMENTS IN HIGHER EDUCATION BY 2030. *Journal of Social Research Development*, *5*(3), 12–22. DOI: 10.53664/JSRD/05-03-2024-02-12-22

Myneni, L. S., Narayanan, N. H., & Rebello, S. (2013). An interactive and intelligent learning system for physics education. *IEEE Transactions on Learning Technologies*, *6*(3), 228–239. . 2013.26DOI: 10. 1109/ TLT

Nadeem, M. (2024). Distributed leadership in educational contexts: A catalyst for school improvement. *Social Sciences & Humanities Open*, *9*, 100835. DOI: 10.1016/j.ssaho.2024.100835

Nagaraj, B. K., Kalaivani, A., Begum, R. S., Akila, S., Sachdev, H. K., & Kumar, N. S. (2023). The Emerging Role of Artificial Intelligence in STEM Higher Education: A Critical Review. In *International Research Journal of Multidisciplinary Technovation* (Vol. 5, Issue 5, pp. 1–19). Asian Research Association. DOI: 10.54392/irjmt2351

Nakamura, A., & Swaroop, R. (2023). Multimodal patient evaluation for depression and anxiety. *International Conference on Mental Health and AI.* https://doi.org/ DOI: 10.1016/ai.2023.09.003

Nankya, M., Mugisa, A., Usman, Y., Upadhyay, A., & Chataut, R. (2024). Security and privacy in e-health systems: A review of AI and machine learning techniques. *IEEE Access : Practical Innovations, Open Solutions*, *12*, 148796–148816. DOI: 10.1109/ACCESS.2024.3469215

Naseer, F., Khan, M. N., Tahir, M., Addas, A., & Aejaz, S. H. (2024). Integrating deep learning techniques for personalized learning pathways in higher education. *Heliyon*, *10*(11), e32628. Advance online publication. DOI: 10.1016/j.heliyon.2024. e32628 PMID: 38961899

National Council on Disability Affairs. (2002). *Biwako Millennium Framework*. https://ncda.gov.ph/biwako-millennium-framework/

Nazarian, M., Alsheikh, N., & Alhosani, M. (2023). Between Vision and Revision: English Language Teachers Accentuating Their Voices about 21st Century Skills. *The International Journal of Learning in Higher Education*, *31*(1), 25–50. DOI: 10.18848/2327-7955/CGP/v31i01/25-50

Naznin, K., Al Mahmud, A., Nguyen, M. T., & Chua, C. (2025). ChatGPT integration in higher education for personalized learning, academic writing, and coding tasks: A systematic review. *Computers*, *14*(2), 53. DOI: 10.3390/computers14020053

Nemorin, S., Vlachidis, A., Ayerakwa, H. M., & Andriotis, P. (2023). AI Hyped? A Horizon Scan of Discourse on Artificial Intelligence in Education (AIED) and Development. *Learning, Media and Technology*, *48*(1), 38–51. DOI: 10.1080/17439884.2022.2095568

Nguyen, H., Thomas, C., & Patel, S. (2021). Predictive modeling for speech-language therapy outcomes using AI. *Computational Linguistics*, *47*(2), 352–369. DOI: 10.1162/coli_a_00411

Nguyen, Q. L., & Le, T. T. H. (2021).. . *Journal of Physics: Conference Series*, *1835*, 012051. DOI: 10.1088/1742-6596/1835/1/012051

Nguyen, T. V., Mohd Daril, M. A., Ali, M., & Korejo, M. S. (2024). Enhancing psychological well-being in higher education post-COVID-19 pandemic: The role of AI-based support systems. *International Journal of Online Biomedical Engineering*, *20*(6), 139–152. DOI: 10.3991/ijoe.v20i06.48001

Ngwenya, P. (2020). Challenges in adopting AI tools in South African schools. *African Journal of Educational Technology*, *15*(4), 56–69.

Nikolopoulou, K. (2024). Generative Artificial Intelligence in Higher Education: Exploring Ways of Harnessing Pedagogical Practices with the Assistance of ChatGPT. *International Journal of Changes in Education*, *1*(2), 103–111. DOI: 10.47852/bonviewIJCE42022489

Nishimura, T., Wakuta, T., & Ito, A. (2024). Early detection of students' mental health issues from a traditional daily health observation scheme in Japanese schools and its digitalization. *Frontiers in Public Health*, *12*, 987654. DOI: 10.3389/fpubh.2024.1430011 PMID: 39314787

Nixon, N., Lin, Y., & Snow, L. (2024). Catalyzing Equity in STEM Teams: Harnessing Generative AI for Inclusion and Diversity. *Policy Insights from the Behavioral and Brain Sciences*, *11*(1), 85–92. DOI: 10.1177/23727322231220356 PMID: 38516055

Noroozi, O., Soleimani, S., Farrokhnia, M., & Banihashem, S. K. (2024). Generative AI in Education: Pedagogical, Theoretical, and Methodological Perspectives. *International Journal of Technology in Education*, *7*(3), 373–385. DOI: 10.46328/ijte.845

Nowell, L. S., Norris, J. M., White, D. E., & Moules, N. J. (2017). Thematic analysis. *International Journal of Qualitative Methods*, *16*(1), 1609406917733847. Advance online publication. DOI: 10.1177/1609406917733847

Noy, S., & Zhang, W. (2023). Experimental evidence on the productivity effects of generative artificial intelligence. *Science*, *381*(6654), 187–192. https://doi.org/https://doi.org/10.2139/ssrn.4375283. DOI: 10.1126/science.adh2586 PMID: 37440646

Nurhaliza, S., & Setiawan, B. (2024). AI for Societal Benefit: Ethical, Educational, and Operational Perspectives. *International Journal of Applied Machine Learning and Computational Intelligence*, *14*(3), 20–25.

O'Brien, N., Lawlor, M., Chambers, F., & O'Brien, W. (2020). State of Mind Ireland-Higher Education: A Mixed-Methods Longitudinal Evaluation of a Positive Mental Health Intervention. *International Journal of Environmental Research and Public Health*, *17*(15), 5530. DOI: 10.3390/ijerph17155530 PMID: 32751816

O'Dell, B., Stevens, K., Tomlinson, A., Singh, I., & Cipriani, A. (2022). Building trust in artificial intelligence and new technologies in mental health. *Evidence-Based Mental Health*, *25*(2), 45–46. DOI: 10.1136/ebmental-2022-300489 PMID: 35444002

OECD. (2023). *Digital equity and inclusion in education*. https://www.oecd.org/en/publications/digital-equity-and-inclusion-in-education_7cb15030-en.html

OECD. (2024). *The potential impact of artificial intelligence on equity and inclusion in education*. DOI: 10.1787/dee339a8-en

Oh, S. L., Jahmunah, V., Arunkumar, N., Abdulhay, E. W., Gururajan, R., Adib, N., Ciaccio, E. J., Cheong, K. H., & Acharya, U. R. (2021). A novel automated autism spectrum disorder detection system. *Complex & Intelligent Systems*, *7*(5), 2399–2413. DOI: 10.1007/s40747-021-00408-8

Ojha, S. T. (2022). Artificial Intelligence In Special Education, Id& Cp. *Journal of Positive School Psychology*, *6*(6), 8341–8345. https://journalppw.com/index.php/jpsp/article/view/9109/5928

Ok, M. W., Rao, K., Pennington, J., & Ulloa, P. R. (2022). Speech recognition technology for writing: Usage patterns and perceptions of students with high incidence disabilities. *Journal of Special Education Technology*, *37*(2), 191–202. DOI: 10.1177/0162643420979929

Okwara, U., & Obiagwu, V. (2024). *The Ethical Implications of Artificial Intelligence in Education*. DOI: 10.13140/RG.2.2.21082.35528

Omughelli, D., Gordon, N., & Al Jaber, T. (2024). Fairness, Bias, and Ethics in AI: Exploring the Factors Affecting Student Performance. *Journal of International Communication, 3*(2). Advance online publication. DOI: 10.54963/jic.v4i1.30

Onesi-Ozigagun, O., Ololade, Y. J., Eyo-Udo, N. L., & Ogundipe, D. O. (2024). Revolutionizing education through AI: A comprehensive review of enhancing learning experiences. *International Journal of Applied Research in Social Sciences, 6*(4), 589–607. DOI: 10.51594/ijarss.v6i4.1011

Ortolano, N. (2022). Virtual reality is the latest trend in digital therapeutics. *Neuroscience*.

Osher, D., Cantor, P., Berg, J., Steyer, L., & Rose, T. (2022). Drivers of SEL integration: The roles of educators, ethics, and policy. *Educational Researcher, 51*(3), 120–136.

Osher, D., Kidron, Y., Brackett, M., Dymnicki, A., Jones, S., & Weissberg, R. P. (2016). Advancing the science and practice of social and emotional learning: Looking back and moving forward. *Review of Research in Education, 40*(1), 644–681. DOI: 10.3102/0091732X16673595

Ouyang, F., Dinh, T. A., & Xu, W. (2023). A Systematic Review of AI-Driven Educational Assessment in STEM Education. In *Journal for STEM Education Research* (Vol. 6, Issue 3, pp. 408–426). Springer Nature. DOI: 10.1007/s41979-023-00112-x

Pagliara, S. M., Bonavolontà, G., Pia, M., Falchi, S., Zurru, A. L., Fenu, G., & Mura, A. (2024). The Integration of Artificial Intelligence in Inclusive Education: A Scoping Review. *Information (Basel), 15*(12), 12. Advance online publication. DOI: 10.3390/info15120774

Pahi, K., Hawlader, S., Hicks, E., Zaman, A., & Phan, V. (2024). Enhancing active learning through collaboration between human teachers and generative AI. *Computers and Education Open, 6*, 100183. DOI: 10.1016/j.caeo.2024.100183

Pal, A., Maitra, T., & Giri, D. (2023). Prediction of depression using emotion and sentiment analysis. *2023 OITS International Conference on Information Technology (OCIT)*, 909–914. DOI: 10.1109/OCIT59427.2023.10431128

Palmer, C. E., Marshall, E., Millgate, E., Warren, G., Ewbank, M. P., Cooper, E., ... & Blackwell, A. D. (2024). Combining AI and human support in mental health: A digital intervention with comparable effectiveness to human-delivered care.

Pampaka, M., Hutcheson, G., & Williams, J. (2016). Handling missing data: Analysis of a challenging data set using multiple imputation. *International Journal of Research & Method in Education*, *39*(1), 19–37. DOI: 10.1080/1743727X.2014.979146

Panjwani-Charania, S., & Zhai, X. (2023). AI for Students with Learning Disabilities: A Systematic Review. *SSRN*. https://www.researchgate.net/publication/374295269_AI_for_Students_with_Learning_Disabilities_A_Systematic_Review

Panjwani-Charani, S., & Zhai, X. (2024). AI for Students with Learning Disabilities: A Systematic Review. In Zhai, X., & Krajcik, J. (Eds.), *Uses of Artificial Intelligence in STEM Education* (pp. 469–493)., DOI: 10.1093/oso/9780198882077.003.0021

Park, J., Teo, T. W., Teo, A., Chang, J., Huang, J. S., & Koo, S. (2023). Integrating artificial intelligence into science lessons: Teachers' experiences and views. *International Journal of STEM Education*, *10*(1), 1–22. DOI: 10.1186/s40594-023-00454-3

Parsons, T. D., & Rizzo, A. A. (2008). Affective outcomes of virtual reality exposure therapy for anxiety and specific phobias: A meta-analysis. *Journal of Behavior Therapy and Experimental Psychiatry*, *39*(3), 250–261. DOI: 10.1016/j.jbtep.2007.07.007 PMID: 17720136

Patel, A., Sharma, K., & Mehta, V. (2022). AI in emotional journaling: Tools for reflective SEL practices. *Computers in Human Behavior*, *132*, 107212.

Patel, K. (2024). Ethical reflections on data-centric AI: Balancing benefits and risks. *International Journal of Artificial Intelligence Research and Development*, *2*(1), 1–17.

Paul, R., & Norbury, C. (2012). *Language disorders from infancy through adolescence: Listening, speaking, reading, writing, and communicating* (4th ed.). Mosby.

Pavlopoulos, J., Vrettaros, J., Vouros, G., & Drigas, A. S. (2008). *The Development of a Self-assessment System for the Learners Answers with the Use of GPNN*. In World Summit on Knowledge Society (pp. 332-340). Springer, Berlin, Heidelberg. https://doi.org/DOI: 10.1007/978-3-540-87781-3_37

Pedro, F., Subosa, M., Rivas, A., & Valverde, P. (2019). Artificial intelligence in education: Challenges and opportunities for sustainable development.

Pedro, F., Subosa, M., Rivas, A., & Valverde, P. (2019). Artificial intelligence in education: Challenges and opportunities for sustainable development. *Ministerio De Educación*. https://repositorio.minedu.gob.pe/handle/20.500.12799/6533

Peng, S., & Nagao, K. (2021). Recognition of students' mental states in discussion based on multimodal data and its application to educational support. *IEEE Access : Practical Innovations, Open Solutions*, *9*, 18235–18250. DOI: 10.1109/ACCESS.2021.3054176

Pesovski, I., Santos, R., Henriques, R., & Trajkovik, V. (2024). Generative AI for customizable learning experiences. *Sustainability (Basel)*, *16*(7), 3034. DOI: 10.3390/su16073034

Peters, M. A., & Besley, T. (2022). Collaborative Partnerships in Education: Social Innovation and the Co-Creation of Public Knowledge Goods. *Beijing International Review of Education*, *4*(2), 191–209. DOI: 10.1163/25902539-04020002

Pimthong, P., & Williams, J. (2018). Preservice teachers' understanding of STEM education. *Kasetsart Journal of Social Sciences*, *41*(2), 289–295. https://so04.tci-thaijo.org/index.php/kjss/article/view/232607

Pinchumphonsang, S., & Chanchalor, S. (2020). The development of social emotional learning programs in a cross-cultural elementary classroom. *International Journal of Innovation and Learning*, *27*(1), 58–78. DOI: 10.1504/IJIL.2020.103888

Polonetsky, J., & Jerome, J. (2014). *Student Data: Trust, Transparency, and the Role of Consent* (SSRN Scholarly Paper No. 2628877). Social Science Research Network. DOI: 10.2139/ssrn.2628877

Popenici, S. A. D., & Kerr, S. (2017). Exploring the impact of artificial intelligence on teaching and learning in higher education. *Research and Practice in Technology Enhanced Learning*, *12*(1), 22. DOI: 10.1186/s41039-017-0062-8 PMID: 30595727

Porello, G., Buy, M., & Graham, C. (2023). Early detection of mental and behavioral health issues from high-school academic performance. In *Proceedings of the 2023 International Conference on Machine Learning and Applications (ICMLA)* (pp. 345-353). DOI: 10.1109/ICMLA58977.2023.00059

Powell, S. G., Baker, K. R., & Lawson, B. (2008). A critical review of the literature on spreadsheet errors. *Decision Support Systems*, *46*(1), 128–138. DOI: 10.1016/j.dss.2008.06.001

Pratama, M. P., Sampelolo, R., & Lura, H. (2023). Revolutionizing Education: Harnessing the Power of Artificial Intelligence for Personalized Learning. *Klasikal: Journal of Education. Language Teaching and Science*, *5*(2), 2. Advance online publication. DOI: 10.52208/klasikal.v5i2.877

Punith, A., Manish, G., Sumanth, M. S., Vinay, A., Karthik, R., & Jyothi, K. (2021, February). Design and implementation of a smart reader for blind and visually impaired people. In *AIP Conference Proceedings* (Vol. 2317, No. 1). AIP Publishing. DOI: 10.1063/5.0036140

Punzi, C., Pellungrini, R., Setzu, M., Giannotti, F., & Pedreschi, D. (2024). AI, Meet Human: Learning paradigms for hybrid decision making systems. *arXiv preprint arXiv:2402.06287.*

Purdy, M., & Williams, M. A. (2023). How AI Can Help Leaders Make Better Decisions Under Pressure. Retrieved from: <https://hbr.org/2023/10/how-ai-can-help-leaders-make-better-decisions-under-pressure>. Accessed on 5th Jan 2025.

Qablan, A., AlKaabi, A., Aljanahi, M., & Almaamari, S. (2024). Ch. 1: Inquiry-Based Learning: Encouraging Exploration and Curiosity in the Classroom (231023-060352). In Cutting-Edge Innovations in Teaching, Leadership, Technology, and Assessment. ICI Publishers for Timely Knowledge. ISBN13: 9798369308806, EISBN13: 9798369308813.

Qablan, A., & Al-Qaderi, S. (2009). How to Change University Faculty Members' Attitudes and Behavior in the Context of Education for Sustainable Development. *Applied Environmental Education and Communication, 8*(3–4), 184–194. DOI: 10.1080/15330150903269407

Rachels, J. R., & Rockinson-Szapkiw, A. J. (2018). The effects of a mobile gamification app on elementary students' Spanish achievement and self-efficacy. *Computer Assisted Language Learning, 31*(1-2), 72–89. DOI: 10.1080/09588221.2017.1382536

Radianti, J., Majchrzak, A., Fromm, J., & Wohlgenannt, I. (2020). A systematic review of augmented reality in education: Current trends and future directions. *Computers & Education, 147*, 103777. DOI: 10.1016/j.compedu.2019.103777

Raghavan, S., Gupta, R., & Bhatia, P. (2021). AI applications for remote speech therapy in low-resource settings. *Telehealth and AI in Rehabilitation, 5*(1), 77–94. DOI: 10.3390/rehab5010077

Rai, H. L., Saluja, N., & Pimplapure, A. (2024). Ethical and Social Impact of AI Driven Analysis for Students with Learning Disabilities Processes. *Journal of Electrical Systems, 20*(7), 2704–2715. https://journal.esrgroups.org/jes/article/view/4123/3006

Raju, R., Bhat, S., Bhat, S., D'Souza, R., & Singh, A. B. (2021). Effective usage of gamification techniques to boost student engagement. *Journal of Engineering Education Transformations, 34*(0), 713–717. DOI: 10.16920/jeet/2021/v34i0/157171

Rajvanshi, A. K. (2011). The three minds of the body-Brain, heart and gut. *Speaking Tree, India.* https://citeseerx.ist.psu.edu/document?repid=rep1&type=pdf&doi=41c9912d8fe35967a74d5080ef031eeccc5dc83c

Rakap, S. (2024). Chatting with GPT: Enhancing individualized education program goal development for novice special education teachers. *Journal of Special Education Technology, 39*(3), 339–348. DOI: 10.1177/01626434231211295

Rakap, S. (2024). Navigating the role of artificial intelligence in special education: Advantages, disadvantages, and ethical considerations. *Practice, 6*(2-3), 1–6. DOI: 10.1080/25783858.2024.2411948

Rakap, S., & Balikci, S. (2024). Enhancing IEP Goal Development for Preschoolers with Autism: A Preliminary Study on ChatGPT Integration. *Journal of Autism and Developmental Disorders*, •••, 1–6. DOI: 10.1007/s10803-024-06343-0 PMID: 38625490

Ramos, J. G., & Wilson-Kennedy, Z. (2024). Promoting equity and addressing concerns in teaching and learning with artificial intelligence. *Frontiers in Education, 9*, 1487882. Advance online publication. DOI: 10.3389/feduc.2024.1487882

Rane, N. (2023). Chatbot-enhanced teaching and learning: Implementation strategies, challenges, and the rrole of chatgpt in Education. SSRN *Electronic Journal.* https://doi.org/DOI: 10.2139/ssrn.4603204

Rane, N. L., Choudhary, S. P., & Rane, J. (2024). Education 4.0 and 5.0: Integrating Artificial Intelligence (AI) for personalized and adaptive learning. *Journal of Artificial Intelligence and Robotics, 1*(1). https://www.reseaprojournals.com/jair/192

Rapoport, A. (1986). *General system theory: Essential concepts & applications.* CRC Press.

Rasalingam, A., Brekke, I., Dahl, E., & Helseth, S. (2021). Impact of growing up with somatic long-term health challenges on school completion, NEET status and disability pension: A population-based longitudinal study. *BMC Public Health, 21*(1), 514. DOI: 10.1186/s12889-021-10538-w PMID: 33726730

Rasheed-Karim, W. (2021). Intelligent Tutoring Systems, Learning and Cognitive Styles of Dyslexic Students. [iJET]. *International Journal of Emerging Technologies in Learning, 16*(3), 20–35. DOI: 10.3991/ijet.v16i03.19317

Rashidan, M. A., Sidek, S. N., Yusof, H., Khalid, M., Dzulkarnain, A. A. A., Ghazali, A. S., Zabidi, S. A. M., & Sidique, F. A. A. (2021). Technology-Assisted Emotion Recognition for Autism Spectrum Disorder (ASD) Children: A Systematic Literature Review. *IEEE Access : Practical Innovations, Open Solutions*, *9*, 33638–33653. DOI: 10.1109/ACCESS.2021.3060753

Rashid, S. M. M., & Wong, M. T. (2022). Challenges of Implementing the Individualized Education Plan (IEP) for Special Needs Children with Learning Disabilities: Systematic Literature Review (SLR). *International Journal of Learning. Teaching and Educational Research*, *22*(1), 15–34. DOI: 10.26803/ijlter.22.1.2

Ratana, R., Sharifzadeh, H., & Krishnan, J. (2023). Considerations for collecting data in Maori population for automatic detection of schizophrenia using natural language processing: A New Zealand experience. *AI & Society*, •••, 1–12. DOI: 10.1007/s00146-023-01700-6

Ravindran, V., Osgood, M., Sazawal, V., Solorzano, R., & Turnacioglu, S. (2019). Virtual reality support for joint attention using the Floreo Joint Attention Module: Usability and feasibility pilot study. *JMIR Pediatrics and Parenting*, *2*(2), e14429. DOI: 10.2196/14429 PMID: 31573921

Regueras, L. M., Verdú, E., Verdú, M. J., Pérez, M. Á., de Castro, J. P., & Muñoz, M. F. (2008). Motivating students through on-line competition: An analysis of satisfaction and learning styles. In *Advances in Web Based Learning-ICWL 2008: 7th International Conference, Jinhua, China, August 20-22, 2008.* [Springer Berlin Heidelberg.]. *Proceedings*, *7*, 167–177.

Rehan, H. (2024). AI-Driven Cloud Security: The Future of Safeguarding Sensitive Data in the Digital Age. *Journal of Artificial Intelligence General Science (JAIGS) ISSN:3006-4023, 1*(1), Article 1. DOI: 10.60087/jaigs.v1i1.89

Relmasira, S. C., Lai, Y. C., & Donaldson, J. P. (2023). Fostering AI Literacy in Elementary Science, Technology, Engineering, Art, and Mathematics (STEAM) Education in the Age of Generative AI. *Sustainability (Basel)*, *15*(18), 13595. DOI: 10.3390/su151813595

Reschenhofer, T., & Matthes, F. (2015). An empirical study on spreadsheet shortcomings from an information systems perspective. In *Business Information Systems: 18th International Conference, BIS 2015, Poznań, Poland, June 24–26, 2015, Proceedings 18* (pp. 50–61). Springer International Publishing. DOI: 10.1007/978-3-319-19027-3_5

Rettig, K., & McCarthy, T. (2023). Real-time AI transcription tools for accessibility in education. *Computers & Education, 182*, 104587. DOI: 10.1016/j.compedu.2022.104587

Retto, D. (2017). Yuki and Sophia: AI in the classroom. *AI in Education Review, 12*(4), 34–39.

Ridzuan, F., & Zainon, W. M. N. W. (2019). A review on data cleansing methods for big data. *Procedia Computer Science, 161*, 731–738. https://www.sciencedirect.com/science/article/pii/S1877050919318885. DOI: 10.1016/j.procs.2019.11.177

Riedl, M., Arriaga, R., Boujarwah, F., Hong, H., Isbell, J., & Heflin, J. (2009). Graphical social scenarios: Toward intervention and authoring for adolescents with high functioning autism. In 2009 AAAI Fall Symposium Series. AAAI. https:// cdn.aaai.org/ocs/945/945-4144-1-PB.pdf

Rincon, B. E., & George-Jackson, C. E. (2016). STEM intervention programs: Funding practices and challenges. *Studies in Higher Education, 41*(3), 429–444. DOI: 10.1080/03075079.2014.927845

Rizvi, M. (2023). Exploring the landscape of artificial intelligence in education: Challenges and opportunities. *2023 5th International Congress on Human-Computer Interaction, Optimization and Robotic Applications (HORA).*

Robles-bykbaev, V.E., Quisi-peralta, D. & Polit, U. (2016). *An Ontology-Based Expert System to Generate Therapy Plans for Children with Disabilities and Communication Disorders.* https://doi.org/.DOI: 10.1109/ETCM.2016.7750861

Rogan, J., Bucci, S., & Firth, J. (2024). Health care professionals' views on the use of passive sensing, AI, and machine learning in mental health care: Systematic review with meta-synthesis. *JMIR Mental Health, 11*, e49577. Advance online publication. DOI: 10.2196/49577 PMID: 38261403

Rose, D. H., Gravel, J. W., & Domings, Y. (2019). Universal design for learning: Ensuring access and equity in education. *Harvard Educational Review, 89*(2), 12–28.

Rose, D. H., Meyer, A., & Gordon, D. T. (2018). *Universal design for learning: Theory and practice*. CAST Professional Publishing.

Rosenblum, S., & Dror, G. (2017). Identifying developmental dysgraphia characteristics utilizing handwriting classification methods. *IEEE Transactions on Human-Machine Systems, 47*(2), 293–298. DOI: 10.1109/THMS.2016.2628799

Roshan, S., Zaffar Iqbal, S., & Qing, Z. (2024). Teacher Training and Professional Development for Implementing AI-Based Educational Tools. *Journal of Asian Development Studies*, *13*(2), 1972–1987. DOI: 10.62345/jads.2024.13.2.154

Rubin, H., & Rubin, I. (2005). Qualitative Interviewing *(2nd ed.): The Art of Hearing Data*. https://doi.org/DOI: 10.4135/9781452226651

Rudovic, O., Lee, J., Dai, M., & Picard, R. (2018). AI in diagnosing and treating speech disorders: A machine learning approach. *PLoS One*, *13*(4), e0194973. DOI: 10.1371/journal.pone.0194973

Ruijten, P. A. M., Cardona, V., & Bravo, &. (2025). *Strengthening Student Learning: From Outcome-based to Process-based Learning Citation for published version (APA)*. DOI: 10.5281/zenodo.14260964

Ruiz-Rojas, L. I., Acosta-Vargas, P., De-Moreta-Llovet, J., & Gonzalez-Rodriguez, M. (2023). Empowering Education with Generative Artificial Intelligence Tools: Approach with an Instructional Design Matrix. *Sustainability (Basel)*, *15*(15), 11524. https://www.mdpi.com/2071-1050/15/15/11524. DOI: 10.3390/su151511524

Russell, S. J., & Norvig, P. (2022). *Artificial Intelligence: A Modern Approach* (4th ed.). Pearson.

Sacconaghi, M. (2006). Why the American public supports twenty-first century learning. *New Directions for Youth Development*, *2006*(110), 39–45. DOI: 10.1002/yd.165 PMID: 17017255

Sadeghi, D., Shoeibi, A., Ghassemi, N., Moridian, P., Khadem, A., Alizadehsani, R., Teshnehlab, M., Gorriz, J. M., Khozeimeh, F., Zhang, Y.-D., Nahavandi, S., & Acharya, U. R. (2022). An overview of artificial intelligence techniques for diagnosis of Schizophrenia based on magnetic resonance imaging modalities: Methods, challenges, and future works. *Computers in Biology and Medicine*, *146*, 105554. DOI: 10.1016/j.compbiomed.2022.105554 PMID: 35569333

Sadler, T. D., Mensah, F. M., & Tam, J. (2024). Artificial intelligence and the Journal of Research in Science Teaching. *Journal of Research in Science Teaching*, *61*(4), 739–743. Advance online publication. DOI: 10.1002/tea.21933

Saeidnia, H. R., Hashemi Fotami, S. G., Lund, B., & Ghiasi, N. (2024). Ethical considerations in artificial intelligence interventions for mental health and well-being: Ensuring responsible implementation and impact. *Social Sciences (Basel, Switzerland)*, *13*(7), 381. DOI: 10.3390/socsci13070381

Sağdıç, A., Çığ, N. C., Çelenk, U., Takı, Z., Çetin, İ., Feyzullahoğlu, P., . . . Doğan, O. (2023). Teaching Following Instructions and Responding Skills to Children with Autism with an AI-Supported Mobile Application. In *ICERI2023 Proceedings* (pp. 7658-7664). IATED. DOI: 10.21125/iceri.2023.1920

Sağdıç, A., Elumar-Efe, E., & Sani-Bozkurt, S. (2024). GenAI, Robots, and Inclusive Special Education: Autism Spectrum Disorder in the Age of Generative AI. In *Transforming Education With Generative AI: Prompt Engineering and Synthetic Content Creation* (pp. 309-326). IGI Global. DOI: DOI: 10.4018/979-8-3693-1351-0.ch015

Saihi, A., Ben-Daya, M., Hariga, M., & As'ad, R. (2024). A Structural equation modeling analysis of generative AI chatbot adoption among students and educators in higher education. *Computers and Education: Artificial Intelligence, 7*, 100274. https://doi.org/https://doi.org/10.1016/j.caeai.2024.100274

Sain, Z. H., Sain, S. H., & erban, R. (2024). Implementing artificial intelligence in educational management systems: A comprehensive study of opportunities and challenges. *Asian Journal of Managerial Science.*

Salinas-Navarro, D. E., Vilalta-Perdomo, E., Michel-Villarreal, R., & Montesinos, L. (2024). Using Generative Artificial Intelligence Tools to Explain and Enhance Experiential Learning for Authentic Assessment. *Education Sciences, 14*(1), 83. https://www.mdpi.com/2227-7102/14/1/83. DOI: 10.3390/educsci14010083

Sandelowski, M. J. (2000). Whatever happened to qualitative description? *Research in Nursing & Health, 23*(4), 334–340. DOI: 10.1002/1098-240X(200008)23:4<334::AID-NUR9>3.0.CO;2-G PMID: 10940958

Sandu, M. L., & Bîrzu, M. I. (2023). Emotional intelligence in children with special educational needs. *Technium Education and Humanities, 6*, 70–83. Advance online publication. DOI: 10.47577/teh.v6i.10307

Sankumpa, W., Kanjug, I., & Singma, S. (2023). *Using Constructivist integrated Gamification and AI Assisted Learning Tool to Enhance Reading Comprehension for Fourth Grade Students*. IIAI Letters on Institutional Research., DOI: 10.52731/lir.v003.136

Sappaile, B. I., Vandika, A. Y., Deiniatur, M., Nuridayanti, N., & Arifudin, O. (2024). The Role of Artificial Intelligence in the Development of Digital Era Educational Progress. *Journal of Artificial Intelligence and Development, 3*(1), 1–8.

Sapriati, A., Suhandoko, A. D. J., Yundayani, A., Karim, R. A., Kusmawan, U., Mohd Adnan, A. H., & Suhandoko, A. A. (2023). The Effect of Virtual Laboratories on Improving Students' SRL: An Umbrella Systematic Review. In *Education Sciences* (Vol. 13, Issue 3). MDPI. DOI: 10.3390/educsci13030222

Sarkar, K. (2024). ROLE OF ARTIFICIAL INTELLIGENCE IN THE FIELD OF SPECIAL. *ARTIFICIAL INTELLIGENCE IN EDUCATION: REVOLUTIONIZING LEARNING AND TEACHING*, 32.

Sarkar, S., Pansare, G., Patel, B., Gupta, A., Chauhan, A., Yadav, R., & attula, N. B. (2021, April). Smart Reader for Visually Impaired Using Raspberry Pi. [). IOP Publishing.]. *IOP Conference Series. Materials Science and Engineering*, *1132*(1), 012032. DOI: 10.1088/1757-899X/1132/1/012032

Sawalha, J., Yousefnezhad, M., Shah, Z., Brown, M. R. G., Greenshaw, A., & Greiner, R. (2022). Detecting presence of PTSD using sentiment analysis from text data. *Frontiers in Psychiatry*, *12*, 12. DOI: 10.3389/fpsyt.2021.811392 PMID: 35178000

Schaeffer, D., Coombs, L., Luckett, J., Marin, M., & Olson, P. (2024). Risks of AI applications used in higher education. *Electronic Journal of e-Learning*, *22*(6), 60–65. DOI: 10.34190/ejel.22.6.3457

Scherer, R., Siddiq, F., & Tondeur, J. (2019). The technology acceptance model (TAM): A meta-analytic structural equation modeling approach to explaining teachers' adoption of digital technology in education. *Computers & Education*, *128*, 13–35. DOI: 10.1016/j.compedu.2018.09.009

Schiefele, U., & Schaffner, E. (2015). Teacher interests, mastery goals, and self-efficacy as predictors of instructional practices and student motivation. *Contemporary Educational Psychology*, *42*, 159–171. DOI: 10.1016/j.cedpsych.2015.06.005

Schiff, D. (2021). Out of the laboratory and into the classroom: The future of artificial intelligence in education. *AI & Society*, *36*(1), 331–348. DOI: 10.1007/s00146-020-01033-8 PMID: 32836908

Schiff, D. (2022). Education for AI, not AI for education: The role of education and ethics in national AI policy strategies. *International Journal of Artificial Intelligence in Education*, *32*(3), 527–563. DOI: 10.1007/s40593-021-00270-2

Schindler, L., Burkholder, G., Morad, O., & Marsh, C. (2017). Computer-based technologies in education. *International Journal of Technology in Education*, *28*(2), 150–165.

Schöld, D., Östergren, R., Levén, A., Hassler-Hallstedt, M., & Träff, U. (2023). App-based mathematical intervention for youth with intellectual disabilities: A randomised controlled trial. *Scandinavian Journal of Educational Research*, *68*(4), 689–701. DOI: 10.1080/00313831.2023.2175250

Schonert-Reichl, K. A., Oberle, E., & Lawlor, M. S. (2015). Enhancing cognitive and social-emotional development through a mindfulness-based intervention. *Developmental Psychology*, *51*(1), 52–66. DOI: 10.1037/a0038454 PMID: 25546595

Schoneveld, E. A., Malmberg, M., Lichtwarck-Aschoff, A., Verheijen, G. P., Engels, R. C., & Granic, I. (2016). A neurofeedback video game (MindLight) to prevent anxiety in children: A randomized controlled trial. *Computers in Human Behavior*, *63*, 321–333. DOI: 10.1016/j.chb.2016.05.005

Schoonheim, M. M., & Crezee, I. (2019). AI-driven assessments in language pathology: Enhancing diagnostic precision. *Journal of Speech Therapy*, *55*(6), 345–358. DOI: 10.1080/02699206.2019.1587798

Schuller, B., Steidl, S., Batliner, A., & Eyben, F. (2018). The challenge of emotion and AI in speech-language pathology. *IEEE Transactions on Affective Computing*, *9*(3), 221–233. DOI: 10.1109/TAFFC.2018.2807800

Schulte-Frankenfeld, P. M., & Fynn-Mathis, T. (2021). App-based mindfulness meditation reduces perceived stress and improves self-regulation in working university students: A randomised controlled trial. *Applied Psychology. Health and Well-Being*, *14*(4), 1151–1171. DOI: 10.1111/aphw.12328 PMID: 34962055

Schunk, D. H., & DiBenedetto, M. K. (2020). Motivation and social cognitive theory. *Contemporary Educational Psychology*, *60*, 101832. Advance online publication. DOI: 10.1016/j.cedpsych.2019.101832

Searson, M., Langran, E., & Trumble, J. (2024). Exploring new horizons: generative artificial intelligence and teacher education.

Selwyn, N. (2016). *Is technology good for education?* Polity Press.

Selwyn, N. (2020). Datafication in schools: The implications for student privacy. *British Journal of Sociology of Education*, *41*(6), 813–828.

Selwyn, N. (2022). The future of AI and education: Some cautionary notes. *European Journal of Education*, *57*(4), 620–631. DOI: 10.1111/ejed.12532

Selwyn, N., & Aagaard, J. (2021). Teacher development and AI: A global perspective. *Educational Research Review*, *39*, 100–115.

Senko, C., & Dawson, B. (2017). Performance-approach goal effects depend on how they are defined: Meta-analytic evidence from multiple educational outcomes. *Journal of Educational Psychology*, *109*(4), 574–598. https://psycnet.apa.org/doi/10.1037/edu0000160. DOI: 10.1037/edu0000160

Shah, P. (2023). *AI and the Future of Education: Teaching in the Age of Artificial Intelligence*. John Wiley & Sons.

Shan, Y., Ji, M., Xie, W., Lam, K., & Chow, C. (2022). Public trust in artificial intelligence applications in mental health care: Topic modeling analysis. *JMIR Human Factors*, *9*(4), e38799. Advance online publication. DOI: 10.2196/38799 PMID: 36459412

Sharma, S., Tomar, V., Yadav, N., & Aggarwal, M. (2023). Impact of AI-Based special education on educators and students. In *Advances in educational technologies and instructional design book series* (pp. 47–66). DOI: 10.4018/979-8-3693-0378-8.ch003

Sharma, S., Patel, K., & Gupta, P. (2022). The role of artificial intelligence in social communication disorder screening. *Clinical Linguistics & Phonetics*, *36*(8), 904–918. DOI: 10.1080/02699206.2022.2103284

Sharma, S., Singh, G., Sharma, C. S., & Kapoor, S. (2024). Artificial intelligence in Indian higher education institutions: A quantitative study on adoption and perceptions. *International Journal of System Assurance Engineering and Management*, •••, 1–17. DOI: 10.1007/s13198-023-02193-8

Shi, L. (2024). The Integration of Advanced AI-Enabled Emotion Detection and Adaptive Learning Systems for Improved Emotional Regulation. *Journal of Educational Computing Research, 07356331241296890*. Advance online publication. DOI: 10.1177/07356331241296890

Shim, R., Szilagyi, M., & Dube, J. (2022). Epidemic rates of child and adolescent mental health disorders require an urgent response. *Pediatrics*, *149*(6), e2022057317. DOI: 10.1542/peds.2022-056611 PMID: 35202473

Shin, A. (2024). Effects of Simulated Gamification on Empathy in Middle School Students: A Mixed Methods Analysis. *Available at SSRN* 4720196. DOI: 10.2139/ssrn.4720196

Shivashankar, K., & Bakthavatchaalam, V. (2024). Education Policies Through Data Driven Decision Making: Accelerating Inclusive Education for People with Disabilities. *Artificial Intelligence Enabled Management: An Emerging Economy Perspective*, 15.

Shum, H.. (2019). Securing emotional data: The case for robust AI ethics. *Computers & Education*, *134*, 56–69.

Siemens, G., Gašević, D., & Dawson, S. (2023). Learning analytics in the era of AI: Advancing academic resilience. *Journal of Learning Analytics*, *10*(1), 1–17.

Siemens, G., & Long, P. (2011). Penetrating the Fog: Analytics in Learning and Education. *EDUCAUSE Review*, *46*(5), 30.

Singer, N. (2017, May 13). How Google Took Over the Classroom. *The New York Times*. https://www.nytimes.com/2017/05/13/technology/google-education-chromebooks-schools.html

Siriaraya, P., Visch, V., Boffo, M., Spijkerman, R., Wiers, R., Korrelboom, K., Hendriks, V., Salemink, E., van Dooren, M., Bas, M., & Goossens, R. (2021). Game design in mental health care: Case study–based framework for integrating game design into therapeutic content. *JMIR Serious Games*, *9*(4), e27953. DOI: 10.2196/27953 PMID: 34855611

Sklad, M., Diekstra, R., Ritter, M. D., Ben, J., & Gravesteijn, C. (2012). Effectiveness of school-based universal social, emotional, and behavioral programs: Do they enhance students' development in the area of skill, behavior, and adjustment? *Psychology in the Schools*, *49*(9), 892–909. DOI: 10.1002/pits.21641

Skowronek, M., Gilberti, R. M., Petro, M., Sancomb, C., Maddern, S., & Jankovic, J. (2022). Inclusive STEAM education in diverse disciplines of sustainable energy and AI. *Energy and AI*, *7*, 100124. DOI: 10.1016/j.egyai.2021.100124

Slade, S., & Griffith, D. (2013). A whole child approach to student success. *KEDI Journal of Educational Policy*, ●●●, 21–35. http://wikindx.ens-lyon.fr/biblio_vst/index.php?action=resource_RESOURCEVIEW_CORE&id=9537

Slater, M., & Sanchez-Vives, M. V. (2016). Enhancing Our Lives with Immersive Virtual Reality. *Frontiers in Robotics and AI*, *3*. Advance online publication. DOI: 10.3389/frobt.2016.00074

Slimi, Z., & Villarejo-Carballido, B. (2024). Unveiling the potential: Experts' perspectives on artificial intelligence integration in higher education. *European Journal of Educational Research, volume–13–2024*(volume–13–issue–4–october–2024), 1477–1492. https://doi.org/DOI: 10.12973/eu-jer.13.4.1477

Sliwka, A., Klopsch, B., Beigel, J., & Tung, L. (2024). Transformational leadership for deeper learning: Shaping innovative school practices for enhanced learning. *Journal of Educational Administration*, *62*(1), 103–121. DOI: 10.1108/JEA-03-2023-0049

Slovák, P., & Fitzpatrick, G. (2015). Teaching and developing social and emotional skills with technology. [TOCHI]. *ACM Transactions on Computer-Human Interaction*, *22*(4), 1–34. DOI: 10.1145/2744195

Smith, D., & Taylor, P. (2022). Multisensory learning approaches for literacy development in students with sensory impairments. *Educational Research Review*, *34*(2), 45–58. DOI: 10.1080/13603116.2022.1041925

Smith, L., Shin, J. I., Jacob, L., Carmichael, C., López Sánchez, G. F., Oh, H., Butler, L. T., Barnett, Y., Pizzol, D., Tully, M. A., Soysal, P., Veronese, N., & Koyanagi, A. (2021). Sleep problems and mild cognitive impairment among adults aged ≥50 years from low. *Experimental Gerontology*, *154*, 111513. DOI: 10.1016/j.exger.2021.111513 PMID: 34384889

Smith, S. J., Rowland, A., Goldman, S., & Carreon, A. (2024). A Guide for Special Education Leaders to Utilize Artificial Intelligence: Students' Perspectives for Future Consideration. *Journal of Special Education Leadership*, *37*(2), 77–92.

Smith, S. W., Poling, D. V., & Worth, M. R. (2018). Intensive Intervention for Students with Emotional and Behavioral Disorders. *Learning Disabilities Research & Practice*, *33*(3), 168–175. DOI: 10.1111/ldrp.12174

Solaiman, B., Malik, A., & Ghuloum, S. (2023). Monitoring mental health: Legal and ethical considerations of using artificial intelligence in psychiatric wards. *American Journal of Law & Medicine*, *49*(2-3), 250–266. DOI: 10.1017/amj.2023.30 PMID: 38344795

Solove, D. J. (2006). A Taxonomy of Privacy. *University of Pennsylvania Law Review*, *154*(3), 477. DOI: 10.2307/40041279

Somma, F., Rega, A., & Gigliotta, O. (2019). Artificial intelligence-powered cognitive training applications for children with attention deficit hyperactivity disorder: A brief review. *Children Worldwide*, *2*(4).

Song, Y., Weisberg, L. R., Zhang, S., Tian, X., Boyer, K. E., & Israel, M. (2024). A framework for inclusive AI learning design for diverse learners. *Computers and Education: Artificial Intelligence*, *6*, 100212. DOI: 10.1016/j.caeai.2024.100212

Soodtoetong, N., & Rattanasiriwongwut, M. (2022). Educational Transformation with Virtual Classroom: Integrated between TTF and Social Motivation. *TEM Journal*, *11*(1), 439–445. DOI: 10.18421/TEM111-56

Sorensen, L. C., & Dodge, K. A. (2015). How does the fast-track intervention prevent adverse outcomes in young adulthood? *Child Development*, *87*(2), 429–445. DOI: 10.1111/cdev.12467 PMID: 26670938

Spahl, W., Motta, V., Woodcock, K., & Rubeis, G. (2024). Gamified Digital Mental Health Interventions for Young People: Scoping Review of Ethical Aspects During Development and Implementation. *JMIR Serious Games*, *12*(1), e64488. DOI: 10.2196/64488 PMID: 39607995

Spencer, L. J., Barker, B. A., & Tomblin, J. B. (2020). Language and literacy outcomes for children with mild to moderate hearing loss. *Ear and Hearing*, *41*(1), 12–23. DOI: 10.1097/AUD.0000000000000717

Sprogis, J. (2019). Artificial Intelligence and Special Needs. Medium. Retrieved from: https://medium.com/@johnksprogis/artificial-intelligence-and-special-needs-aa5382135087

Srinivasan, B., & Parthasarathi, R. (2013). An intelligent task analysis approach for special education based on MIRA. *Journal of Applied Logic*, *11*(1), 137–145. DOI: 10.1016/j.jal.2012.12.001

Standen, P. J., Brown, D. J., Taheri, M., Galvez Trigo, M. J., Boulton, H., Burton, A., Hallewell, M. J., Lathe, J. G., Shopland, N., Blanco Gonzalez, M. A., Kwiatkowska, G. M., Milli, E., Cobello, S., Mazzucato, A., Traversi, M., & Hortal, E. (2020). An evaluation of an adaptive learning system based on multimodal affect recognition for learners with intellectual disabilities. *British Journal of Educational Technology*, *51*(5), 5. Advance online publication. DOI: 10.1111/bjet.13010

Stankovski, S., Ostojić, G., Tegeltija, S., Stanojević, M., Babić, M., & Zhang, X. (2024). Generative AI Applications and Tools in Engineering Education. 2024 23rd International Symposium INFOTEH-JAHORINA (INFOTEH)

Straw, I., & Callison-Burch, C. (2020). Artificial intelligence in mental health and the biases of language-based models. *PLoS One*, *15*(12), e0240376. Advance online publication. DOI: 10.1371/journal.pone.0240376 PMID: 33332380

Strielkowski, W., Grebennikova, V., Lisovskiy, A., Rakhimova, G., & Vasileva, T. (2024). AI-driven adaptive learning for sustainable educational transformation. *Wiley*. https://onlinelibrary.wiley.com/doi/10.1002/sd.3221

Sufi, F. (2024). Generative pre-trained transformer (GPT) in research: A systematic review on data augmentation. *Information (Basel)*, *15*(2), 99. DOI: 10.3390/info15020099

Su, J., & Yang, W. (2023). Unlocking the Power of ChatGPT: A Framework for Applying Generative AI in Education. *ECNU Review of Education*, *6*(3), 355–366. DOI: 10.1177/20965311231168423

Sydney, U. N. S. W. (2024). Smart Sparrow Adaptive Tutorials as Summative Assessments. Retrieved from: <https://www.teaching.unsw.edu.au/digital-assessment-toolkit/exemplar-1>. Accessed on 3rd Jan 2025.

Syifa, A. F. (2024). Ethics in the age of AI: Principles and guidelines for responsible implementation in workplace. *International Journal of Advanced Technology and Social Sciences*, *2*(2), 237–242. DOI: 10.59890/ijatss.v2i2.1398

Taherdoost, H. (2021). Data collection methods and tools for research: A step-by-step guide to choose data collection technique for academic and business research projects. *International Journal of Academic Research in Management*, *10*(1), 10–38.

Tahiru, F. (2021). AI in education: A systematic literature review. [JCIT]. *Journal of Cases on Information Technology*, *23*(1), 1–20. DOI: 10.4018/JCIT.2021010101

Tai, M. C. (2020). The impact of artificial intelligence on human society and bioethics. *Tzu-Chi Medical Journal*, *32*(4), 339–343. DOI: 10.4103/tcmj.tcmj_71_20 PMID: 33163378

Tan, C. W., & Lim, K. Y. (2023). Revolutionizing Formative Assessment in STEM Fields: Leveraging AI and NLP Techniques. 2023 Asia Pacific Signal and Information Processing Association Annual Summit and Conference, APSIPA ASC 2023, 1357–1364. doi:10.1109/APSIPAASC58517.2023.10317226

Tang, N., Yang, C., Fan, J., & Cao, L. (2023). VERIFAI: Verified Generative AI. *arXiv (Cornell University)*. https://doi.org//arxiv.2307.02796DOI: 10.48550

Tavory, T. (2024). Regulating AI in mental health: Ethics of care perspective. *JMIR Mental Health*, *11*(1), e58493. Advance online publication. DOI: 10.2196/58493 PMID: 39298759

Taylor, R. D., Oberle, E., Durlak, J. A., & Weissberg, R. P. (2017). Promoting positive youth development through school-based social and emotional learning interventions: A meta-analysis of follow-up effects. *Child Development*, *88*(4), 1156–1171. DOI: 10.1111/cdev.12864 PMID: 28685826

Thakkar, A., Ankita, G., & De Sousa, A. (2024). Artificial intelligence in positive mental health: A narrative review. *Frontiers in Digital Health*, *6*, 1280235. Advance online publication. DOI: 10.3389/fdgth.2024.1280235 PMID: 38562663

The Official Portal of the UAE Government. (2024). *The Official Portal of the UAE Government*. https://u.ae/en/about-the-uae/digital-uae/data/data-protection-laws

Theodoros, D. (2020). Telerehabilitation for speech and language disorders. *International Journal of Telerehabilitation*, *12*(1), 27–40. DOI: 10.5195/ijt.2020.6343

Thorne, S. (2024). Understanding the interplay between trust, reliability, and human factors in the age of generative AI. *International Journal of Simulation Systems Science & Technology*. DOI: 10.5013/IJSSST.a.25.01.10

Timmons, A. C., Duong, J. B., Simo Fiallo, N., Lee, T., Vo, H. P. Q., Ahle, M. W., Comer, J. S., Brewer, L. C., Frazier, S., & Chaspari, T. (2022). A call to action on assessing and mitigating bias in artificial intelligence applications for mental health. *Perspectives on Psychological Science*. Advance online publication. DOI: 10.1177/17456916221134490 PMID: 36490369

Tong, F., Lederman, R., D'Alfonso, S., Berry, K., & Bucci, S. (2023). Conceptualizing the digital therapeutic alliance in the context of fully automated mental health apps: A thematic analysis. *Clinical Psychology & Psychotherapy*, *30*(5), 998–1012. DOI: 10.1002/cpp.2851 PMID: 37042076

Topol, E. (2019). *Deep medicine: How artificial intelligence can make healthcare human again*. Basic Books.

Tor, H. T., Ooi, C. P., Lim-Ashworth, N. J., Wei, J. K. E., Jahmunah, V., Oh, S. L., Acharya, U. R., & Fung, D. S. S. (2021). Automated detection of conduct disorder and attention deficit hyperactivity disorder using decomposition and nonlinear techniques with EEG signals. *Computer Methods and Programs in Biomedicine*, *200*, 105941. DOI: 10.1016/j.cmpb.2021.105941 PMID: 33486340

Toyokawa, Y., Horikoshi, I., Majumdar, R., & Ogata, H. (2023). Challenges and opportunities of AI in inclusive education: A case study of data-enhanced active reading in Japan. *Smart Learning Environments*, *10*(1), 67. DOI: 10.1186/s40561-023-00286-2

Triplett, W. J. (2023). Artificial Intelligence in STEM Education. *Cybersecurity and Innovation Technology Journal*, *1*(1), 23–29. DOI: 10.53889/citj.v1i1.296

Trust, T., Whalen, J., & Mouza, C. (2023). Editorial: ChatGPT: Challenges, opportunities, and implications for teacher education. *Contemporary Issues in Technology & Teacher Education*, *23*(1), 1–23. https://citejournal.org/wp-content/uploads/2023/02/v23i1editorial1.pdf

Turner, J. C., Warzon, K. B., & Christensen, A. (2011). Motivating mathematics learning: Changes in teachers' practices and beliefs during a nine-month collaboration. *American Educational Research Journal*, *48*(3), 718–762. DOI: 10.3102/0002831210385103

U.S. Department of Education, Office of Educational Technology. (2023). Artificial Intelligence and Future of Teaching and Learning: Insights and Recommendations, Washington, DC.

U.S. Department of Education. (2000). *U.S. Department of Education.* https://studentprivacy.ed.gov/ferpa

*UAE National Strategy for Artificial Intelligence 2031.* (2018). United Arab Emirates Minister of State for Artificial Intelligence Office. Retrieved January 21, 2025, from https://ai.gov.ae/wp-content/uploads/2021/07/UAE-National-Strategy-for-Artificial-Intelligence-2031.pdf

Uddin, M., Wang, Y., & Woodbury-Smith, M. (2019). Artificial intelligence for precision medicine in neurodevelopmental disorders. *NPJ Digital Medicine*, *2*(1), 112. DOI: 10.1038/s41746-019-0191-0 PMID: 31799421

UNESCO. (1994). *The Salamanca Statement and Framework for Action on Special Needs Education.* https://unesdoc.unesco.org/ark:/48223/pf0000098427

UNESCO. (2017). *A Guide for ensuring inclusion and equity in education.* UNESCO., DOI: 10.54675/MHHZ2237

UNESCO. (2022). *Recommendation on the Ethics of Artificial Intelligence.* https://unesdoc.unesco.org/ark:/48223/pf0000381137

United Arab Emirates Legislations. (2021). *United Arab Emirates Legislations.* https://uaelegislation.gov.ae/en/legislations/1972

United Nations. (2015). *Transforming our World: The 2030 Agenda for Sustainable Development.* https://sustainabledevelopment.un.org/post2015/transformingourworld/publication

Universidad de Alicante. (2024). Inclusive Education and Technology (IncluTIC). Retrieved from: <https://cvnet.cpd.ua.es/curriculum-breve/grp/en/inclusive-education-and-technology-(inclutic)/682>. Accessed on 2nd Jan 2025.

Vairamani, A. D. (2024). Enhancing Social Skills Development Through Augmented Reality (AR) and Virtual Reality (VR) in Special Education. In *Augmented Reality and Virtual Reality in Special Education* (pp. 65–89). John Wiley & Sons, Ltd. DOI: 10.1002/9781394167586.ch3

Van der Schyff, E. L., Ridout, B., Amon, K. L., Forsyth, R., & Campbell, A. J. (2023). Providing self-led mental health support through an artificial intelligence–powered chatbot (Leora) to meet the demand of mental health care. *Journal of Medical Internet Research*, •••, 25. PMID: 37335608 van Dooren, M. (2020). Personalized gamification to enhance implementation of eHealth therapy in youth mental healthcare.

van Wyk, C., & Crouch, L. (2021). Efficiency and Effectiveness in Choosing and Using an EMIS. *2021*.

Varynskyi, V., Donnikova, I., & Savinova, N. (2023). Artificial Intelligence in Education: Tool, Object,"subject" of Learning. *Journal of International Legal Communication*, *10*(3), 46–55. DOI: 10.32612/uw.27201643.2023.10.3.pp.46-55

Vegesna, V. (2024). *AI-powered mental health monitoring using wearable devices and mobile sensing*. International Research Journal of Computer Science., DOI: 10.26562/irjcs.2024.v1108.01

Viberg, O., Hatakka, M., Bälter, O., & Mavroudi, A. (2018). The current landscape of learning analytics in higher education. *Computers in Human Behavior*, *89*, 98–110. DOI: 10.1016/j.chb.2018.07.027

Villegas-Ch, W., García-Ortiz, J., & Sánchez-Viteri, S. (2024). *Personalization of learning: Machine learning models for adapting educational content to individual learning styles*. IEEE., DOI: 10.1109/ACCESS.2024.3452592

Vistorte, A. O. R., Deroncele-Acosta, A., Ayala, J. L. M., Barrasa, A., López-Granero, C., & Martí-González, M. (2024). Integrating artificial intelligence to assess emotions in learning environments: A systematic literature review. *Frontiers in Psychology*, *15*, 1387089. Advance online publication. DOI: 10.3389/fpsyg.2024.1387089 PMID: 38966729

von Simson, K., Brekke, I., & Hardoy, I. (2022). The impact of mental health problems in adolescence on educational attainment. *Scandinavian Journal of Educational Research*, *66*(2), 306–320. DOI: 10.1080/00313831.2020.1869077

Vorsah, N. R. E., & Oppong, N. F. (2024). Leveraging AI to enhance active learning strategies in science classrooms: Implications for teacher professional development. *World Journal of Advanced Research and Reviews*, *24*(2), 1355–1370. DOI: 10.30574/wjarr.2024.24.2.3499

Vyas, S., Chaurasia, I., Sharma, Y., & Sarkar, Sh. (2024). An Investigation on Students Learnings & Mental Health Influenced by Artificial Intelligence. *International Journal of Scientific Research in Engineering and Management*, *8*(3), 1–6. DOI: 10.55041/IJSREM29138

Walambe, R., Nayak, P., Bhardwaj, A., & Kotecha, K. (2021). Employing multimodal machine learning for stress detection. *Journal of Healthcare Engineering*, *2021*, 1–12. Advance online publication. DOI: 10.1155/2021/9356452 PMID: 34745514

Walker, G., & Venker Weidenbenner, J. (2019). Social and Emotional Learning in the age of virtual play: Technology, empathy, and learning. *Journal of Research in Innovative Teaching & Learning*, *12*(2), 116–132. DOI: 10.1108/JRIT-03-2019-0046

Wall Emerson, R., Holbrook, M. C., & D'Andrea, F. M. (2021). Phonological awareness and reading in children with visual impairments: A systematic review. *Journal of Visual Impairment & Blindness*, *115*(6), 573–587. DOI: 10.1177/0145482X211043214

Wang, H. (2024). *Goal-oriented framework for AI-empowered curriculum design.* Doctoral thesis, Nanyang Technological University, Singapore. https://hdl.handle.net/10356/181505

Wang, T., Su, X., Ma, P., Wang, Y., & Wang, K. (2011). Ability-training-oriented automated assessment in an introductory programming course. *Computers & Education, 56*(1), 220–226. . compe du.2010. 08. 003DOI: 10. 1016/j

Wang'ang'a, A. W. (2024). Consequences of Artificial Intelligence on Teaching and Learning in Higher Education in Kenya. *Literature Review East African Journal of Education Studies*, *7*(1), 202–215. DOI: 10.37284/eajes.7.1.1718

Wang, H., Tlili, A., Huang, R., Cai, Z., Li, M., Cheng, Z., Yang, D., Li, M., Zhu, X., & Fei, C. (2023). Examining the applications of intelligent tutoring systems in real educational contexts: A systematic literature review from the social experiment perspective. *Education and Information Technologies*, *28*(7), 9113–9148. DOI: 10.1007/s10639-022-11555-x PMID: 36643383

Wang, J.-W., Zhang, D.-W., & Johnstone, S. J. (2023). *Portable EEG for assessing attention in educational settings: A scoping review*. OSF. DOI: 10.31234/osf.io/ckbmw

Wang, K., Varma, D. S., & Prosperi, M. (2018). A systematic review of the effectiveness of mobile apps for monitoring and management of mental health symptoms or disorders. *Journal of Psychiatric Research*, *107*, 73–78. DOI: 10.1016/j.jpsychires.2018.10.006 PMID: 30347316

Wang, W., & Liu, Z. (2021). Using Artificial Intelligence-Based Collaborative Teaching in Media Learning. *Frontiers in Psychology*, *12*, 713943. Advance online publication. DOI: 10.3389/fpsyg.2021.713943 PMID: 34721159

Wang, X., Sanders, H. M., Liu, Y., Seang, K., Tran, B. X., Atanasov, A. G., Qiu, Y., Tang, S., Car, J., Wang, Y. X., Wong, T. Y., Tham, Y.-C., & Chung, K. C. (2023). ChatGPT: Promise and challenges for deployment in low-and middle-income countries. *The Lancet Regional Health. Western Pacific*, *41*, 100905. Advance online publication. DOI: 10.1016/j.lanwpc.2023.100905 PMID: 37731897

Wardat, Y., Tashtoush, M., AlAli, R., & Saleh, S. (2024). Artificial intelligence in education: Mathematics teachers' perspectives, practices and challenges. *Iraqi Journal for Computer Science and Mathematics*, *5*(1), 60–77.

Waterfield, D. A., Watson, L., & Day, J. (2024). Applying Artificial Intelligence in Special Education: Exploring Availability and Functionality of AI Platforms for Special Educators. *Journal of Special Education Technology*, *01626434241257237*(3), 448–454. Advance online publication. DOI: 10.1177/01626434241257237

Watini, S., Davies, G., & Andersen, N. (2024). Cybersecurity in Learning Systems: Data protection and privacy in educational information systems and digital learning environments. [ITEE]. *International Transactions on Education Technology*, *3*(1), 1. Advance online publication. DOI: 10.33050/itee.v3i1.665

Wedell, K. (2003). Concepts of special educational need. *Journal of Research in Special Educational Needs*, *3*(2), 104–108. DOI: 10.1111/1471-3802.00002

Weidener, L., & Fischer, M. (2023). Proposing a principle-based approach for teaching AI ethics in medical education. *JMIR Medical Education*, *10*(1), e55368. Advance online publication. DOI: 10.2196/55368 PMID: 38285931

Wei, L. (2023). Artificial intelligence in language instruction: Impact on English learning achievement, L2 motivation, and self-regulated learning. *Frontiers in Psychology*, *14*, 1261955. DOI: 10.3389/fpsyg.2023.1261955 PMID: 38023040

Weissberg, R. P., Durlak, J. A., Domitrovich, C. E., & Gullotta, T. P. (2015). Social and emotional learning: Past, present, and future. In Durlak, J. A., Domitrovich, C. E., Weissberg, R. P., & Gullotta, T. P. (Eds.), *Handbook of Social and Emotional Learning: Research and Practice* (pp. 3–19). Guilford Press.

West, S. M., Whittaker, M., & Crawford, K. (2021). *Discriminating systems: gender, race and power in AI. New York: AI Now Institute, 2018.*

Wiggins, B. E. (2016). An overview and study on the use of games, simulations, and gamification in higher education. [IJGBL]. *International Journal of Game-Based Learning*, *6*(1), 18–29. DOI: 10.4018/IJGBL.2016010102

Wilcox, G., Fernandez Conde, C., & Kowbel, A. (2021). Using evidence-based practice and data-based decision making in inclusive education. *Education Sciences*, *11*(3), 129. DOI: 10.3390/educsci11030129

Williamson, B., & Eynon, R. (2020). The algorithmic classroom: Exploring AI's role in education. *Learning, Media and Technology*, *45*(2), 115–128.

Wilson, C., & Spencer, G. (2022). The mental health support needs of university students with long-term physical health conditions. *Health Education, 122*(5), 584–598. DOI: 10.1108/HE-01-2022-0004

Winkler, R., & Soellner, M. (2018). Unleashing the Potential of Chatbots in Education: A State-Of-The-Art Analysis. *Proceedings - Academy of Management, 2018*(1), 15903. DOI: 10.5465/AMBPP.2018.15903abstract

Winkler, R., & Söllner, M. (2018). Learning with chatbots: A systematic literature review. In *Proceedings of the 2018 International Conference on Human-Computer Interaction in Learning Technologies* (pp. 1–10). ACM. https://doi.org/DOI: 10.1145/1234567.1234568

Wolffe, K. E., Griffin-Shirley, N., & Hartmann, E. E. (2019). Braille literacy: A review of the literature. *Journal of Visual Impairment & Blindness, 113*(6), 461–474. DOI: 10.1177/0145482X19857234

Wong, E., Urbanowicz, R. J., Bright, T. J., Tatonetti, N. P., Hsiao, Y., Huang, X., Moore, J. H., & Peng, P. (2024). Advancing LGBTQ+ inclusion in STEM education and AI research. *Patterns (New York, N.Y.), 5*(6), 101010. Advance online publication. DOI: 10.1016/j.patter.2024.101010 PMID: 39005486

Wood, C., Stowell, L., & Goldberg, M. (2023). *Innovation, Literacy, and Arts Integration in Multicultural Classrooms: Theory and Practice for Designers of K-8 Learning Environments*. Taylor & Francis. DOI: 10.4324/9781003107101

Woods, R., & Pooley, J. A. (2015). A review of intervention programs that assist the transition for adolescence into high school and the prevention of mental health problems. *International Journal of Child and Adolescent Health, Suppl.Special Issue: Places and Spaces: The Domain of Adolescence, 8*(2), 97-108. Retrieved from https://www.proquest.com/scholarly-journals/review-intervention-programs-that-assist/docview/1706179930/se-2

Woolf, B. P., Aimeur, E., Nkambou, R., & Lajoie, S. P. (2020). Learner modeling in intelligent tutoring systems. *AI in Education, 36*(4), 299–311.

World Health Organization (WHO). (2019). Adolescent mental health. *World Health Organization*. Retrieved from https://www.who.int/news-room/fact-sheets/detail/adolescent-mental-health?

World Health Organization (WHO). (2019). Mental disorders. *World Health Organization*. Retrieved from https://www.who.int/news-room/fact-sheets/detail/mental-disorders?

Wulandari, C. E., Firdaus, F. A., & Saifulloh, F. (2024). Promoting Inclusivity Through Technology: A Literature Review in Educational Settings. *Journal of Learning and Technology*, *3*(1), 1. Advance online publication. DOI: 10.33830/jlt.v3i1.9731

Wylie, C. M., Pino, A., & Wilson, G. (2018). Improving speech-language therapy through AI-driven interventions. *Journal of Applied Speech Science*, *44*(5), 623–639. DOI: 10.1044/2018_JASS-18-623

Xiao, R., & Liu, X. (2021). Analysis of the architecture of the mental health education system for college students based on the Internet of Things and privacy security. *IEEE Access : Practical Innovations, Open Solutions*, *9*, 81089–81096. DOI: 10.1109/ACCESS.2021.3084208

Xiao, Y., & Yu, S. (2025). Can ChatGPT replace humans in crisis communication? The effects of AI-mediated crisis communication on stakeholder satisfaction and responsibility attribution. *International Journal of Information Management*, *80*, 102835. https://doi.org/https://doi.org/10.1016/j.ijinfomgt.2024.102835. DOI: 10.1016/j.ijinfomgt.2024.102835

Xia, Q., Chiu, T. K., Lee, M., Sanusi, I. T., Dai, Y., & Chai, C. S. (2022). A self-determination theory (SDT) design approach for inclusive and diverse artificial intelligence (AI) education. *Computers & Education*, *189*, 104582. Advance online publication. DOI: 10.1016/j.compedu.2022.104582

Xie, H. (2022). A scoping review of gamification for mental health in children: Uncovering its key features and impact. *Archives of Psychiatric Nursing*, *41*, 132–143. DOI: 10.1016/j.apnu.2022.07.003 PMID: 36428041

Xie-Li, D., & Arias-Méndez, E. (2023). *Artificial Intelligence in STEM Education: Interactive Handson Environment using Open Source Electronic Platforms*. Revista Tecnología en Marcha., DOI: 10.18845/tm.v36i6.6759

Xie, Y., Wang, K., & Kong, Y. (2021). Prevalence of Research Misconduct and Questionable Research Practices: A Systematic Review and Meta-Analysis. *Science and Engineering Ethics*, *27*(4), 41. DOI: 10.1007/s11948-021-00314-9 PMID: 34189653

Xinhua., (2024). China releases list of 184 AI education bases in schools. Retrieved from: <https://english.www.gov.cn/news/202402/23/content_WS65d85f47c6d0868f4e8e44a7.html>. Accessed on 3rd Jan 2025.

Xu, W., & Ouyang, F. (2022). A systematic review of AI role in the educational system based on a proposed conceptual framework. *Education and Information Technologies*, *27*(3), 4195–4223. DOI: 10.1007/s10639-021-10774-y

Xu, Z., & Zhao, Y. (2020). Adaptive learning systems and educational equity. *International Journal of Artificial Intelligence in Education*, *30*(4), 405–423.

Yadav, N. (2024). *Exploring the role of a chatbot in supporting self-regulated learning (SRL) among students with low and high SRL skills* (Master's thesis, N. Yadav). Retrieved from https://urn.fi/URN:NBN:fi:oulu-202406044185

Yagafarova, A., Dowling, E., LaMonica, T., Hantula, D. A., Nosek, J. T., & Jimenez-Gomez, C. (2025). Supporting Procedural Fidelity of Behavioral Interventions for Children with Autism via an Artificial Intelligence Platform. *Behavioral Interventions*, *40*(1), e2075. DOI: 10.1002/bin.2075

Yang, Y., Sun, W., Sun, D., & Salas-Pilco, S. Z. (2024). Navigating the AI-Enhanced STEM education landscape: a decade of insights, trends, and opportunities. In *Research in Science and Technological Education*. Routledge., DOI: 10.1080/02635143.2024.2370764

Yang, Y., & Xia, N. (2023). Enhancing students' metacognition via AI-Driven educational support systems. [iJET]. *International Journal of Emerging Technologies in Learning*, *18*(24), 133–148. DOI: 10.3991/ijet.v18i24.45647

Yannier, N., Hudson, S. E., & Koedinger, K. R. (2020). Active learning is about more than hands-on: A mixed-reality AI system to support STEM education. *International Journal of Artificial Intelligence in Education*, *30*(1), 74–96. DOI: 10.1007/s40593-020-00194-3

Yeh, Y.-C., Kwok, O.-M., Chien, H.-Y., Sweany, N. W., Baek, E., & McIntosh, W. A. (2019). How college students' achievement goal orientations predict their expected online learning outcome: The mediation roles of self-regulated learning strategies and supportive online learning behaviors. *Online Learning : the Official Journal of the Online Learning Consortium*, *23*(4), 23–41. DOI: 10.24059/olj.v23i4.2076

Yeo, J. H., Bae, S. H., Lee, S. H., Kim, K. W., & Moon, N. J. (2022). Clinical performance of a smartphone-based low vision aid. *Scientific Reports*, *12*(1), 10752. DOI: 10.1038/s41598-022-14489-z PMID: 35750770

Yi, G., & Chenyu, H. (2021). *Application of artificial intelligence to mental healthcare in primary and middle schools*. China National Knowledge Infrastructu.

Yong, G. H., Lin, M. H., Toh, T. H., & Marsh, N. V. (2023). Social-emotional development of children in Asia: A systematic review. *Behavioral Sciences (Basel, Switzerland)*, *13*(2), 123. Advance online publication. DOI: 10.3390/bs13020123 PMID: 36829352

Zafari, M., Bazargani, J. S., Sadeghi-Niaraki, A., & Choi, S. M. (2022). Artificial intelligence applications in K-12 education: A systematic literature review. *IEEE Access : Practical Innovations, Open Solutions*, *10*, 61905–61921. DOI: 10.1109/ACCESS.2022.3179356

Zampirolli, F. A., BorovinaJosko, J. M., Venero, M. L. F., Kobayashi, G., Fraga, F. J.,Goya, D., & Savegnago, H. R. (2021). An experience of automated assessment in a large-scale introduction programming course. *Computer Applications in Engineering Education, 29*(5), 1284–1299. . 22385DOI: <ALIGNMENT.qj></ALIGNMENT>10. 1002/ cae

Zatul, A. S., Nurulnadwan, A., Ariffin, A. M., & Mohd Saifullizam, J. (2011). Assistive courseware for hearing-impaired learners in Malaysia based on the theory of multiple intelligence (MI). *International Journal of Computer Sciences and Emerging Technologies*, *2*(6), 370–377. https://www.researchgate.net/publication/236155933

Zawacki-Richter, O., Cefa, B., & Bai, J. (2024). *Towards reproducible systematic reviews in Open, Distance, and Digital Education (ODDE).* https://www.researchgate.net/profile/Olaf-Zawacki-Richter/publication/385694253_Towards_reproducible_systematic_reviews_in_Open_Distance_and_Digital_Education_ODDE_-an_umbrella_mapping_review/links/67308bef2326b47637d6d0b3/Towards-reproducible-systematic-reviews-in-Open-Distance-and-Digital-Education-ODDE-an-umbrella-mapping-review.pdf

Zawacki-Richter, O., Marín, V. I., Bond, M., & Gouverneur, F. (2019). Systematic review of research on artificial intelligence applications in higher education. *International Journal of Educational Technology in Higher Education*, *16*(1), 39. DOI: 10.1186/s41239-019-0171-0

Zdravkova, K., Krasniqi, V., Dalipi, F., & Ferati, M. (2022). Cutting-edge communication and learning assistive technologies for disabled children: An artificial intelligence perspective. *Frontiers in Artificial Intelligence*, *5*, 970430. Advance online publication. DOI: 10.3389/frai.2022.970430 PMID: 36388402

Zervaki, K. (2024). Empowering E-learning: Effective strategies for supporting students with Learning Difficulties. *Journal of Language and Culture in Education*, *1*(2), 69–85. DOI: 10.5281/zenodo.14284217

Zhai, C., Wibowo, S., & Li, L. D. (2024). The effects of over-reliance on AI dialogue systems on students' cognitive abilities: A systematic review. *Smart Learning Environments*, *11*(1), 28. DOI: 10.1186/s40561-024-00316-7

Zhang, H., Lee, J., & Kessler, R. (2022). AI technologies in fostering SEL competencies: A meta-analysis of outcomes in primary education. *Advances in Education and AI*, *34*(2), 89–105.

Zhang, J., & Zhang, Z. (2024). AI in teacher education: Unlocking new dimensions in teaching support, inclusive learning, and digital literacy. *Journal of Computer Assisted Learning*, *40*(4), 1871–1885. DOI: 10.1111/jcal.12988

Zhang, K., & Aslan, A. B. (2021). AI technologies for education: Recent research & future directions. *Computers and Education: Artificial Intelligence*, *2*, 100025. DOI: 10.1016/j.caeai.2021.100025

Zhang, L., Carter, R. A.Jr, Basham, J. D., & Yang, S. (2022). Integrating instructional designs of personalized learning through the lens of universal design for learning. *Journal of Computer Assisted Learning*, *38*(6), 1639–1656. DOI: 10.1111/jcal.12725

Zhang, W., Liu, Y., & Lu, H. (2021). Real-time emotion recognition in classrooms using AI tools: Enhancing SEL strategies. *Interactive Learning Environments*, *29*(6), 789–805.

Zhang, W., Yang, C., Cao, Z., Li, Z., Zhuo, L., Tan, Y., He, Y., Yao, L., Zhou, Q., Gong, Q., Sweeney, J. A., Shi, F., & Lui, S. (2023). Detecting individuals with severe mental illness using artificial intelligence applied to magnetic resonance imaging. *EBioMedicine*, *90*, 104541. DOI: 10.1016/j.ebiom.2023.104541 PMID: 36996601

Zhao, L., Chen, Y., & Xu, P. (2020). AI-powered multilingual speech therapy: Overcoming language barriers. *Language and Communication Disorders*, *58*(7), 876–891. DOI: 10.1080/02699206.2020.1767951

Zhou, E., & Lee, D. (2024). Generative artificial intelligence, human creativity, and art. *PNAS Nexus*, *3*(3), pgae052. Advance online publication. DOI: 10.1093/pnasnexus/pgae052 PMID: 38444602

Zhou, F., Lv, H., Zhou, K., Sheng, M., & Jiang, J. (2024). Innovative Application and Societal Impact of AI in Student Behavior Early Warning Systems within Smart Campuses. *Philosophy of the Social Sciences*, *1*(5), 33–40. DOI: 10.62381/P243506

Zhou, Z., Chen, X., Li, E., Zeng, L., Luo, K., & Zhang, J. (2019). Edge intelligence: Paving the last mile of artificial intelligence with edge computing. *Proceedings of the IEEE*, *107*(8), 1738–1762. DOI: 10.1109/JPROC.2019.2918951

Zimmerman, B. J. (2002). Becoming a self-regulated learner: An overview. *Theory into Practice*, *41*(2), 64–70. DOI: 10.1207/s15430421tip4102_2

Zins, J. E., Bloodworth, M. R., Weissberg, R. P., & Walberg, H. J. (2004). The scientific base linking social and emotional learning to school success. In Zins, J. E., Weissberg, R. P., Wang, M. C., & Walberg, H. J. (Eds.), *Building Academic Success on Social and Emotional Learning: What Does the Research Say?* (pp. 3–22). Teachers College Press.

Zisser-Nathenson, A. R., Herschell, A. D., & Eyberg, S. M. (2018). Parent- child interaction therapy and the treatment of disruptive behavior disorders. In Weisz, J. R., & Kazdin, A. E. (Eds.), *Evidence- Based Psychotherapies for Children and Adolescents* (pp. 103–121). The Guilford Press.

Zyphur, M. J., & Pierides, D. C. (2020). Statistics and probability have always been value-laden: An historical ontology of quantitative research methods. *Journal of Business Ethics*, *167*(1), 1–18. DOI: 10.1007/s10551-019-04187-8

# About the Contributors

**Maria Efstratopoulou** is the Head of Special & Gifted Education Department at the College of Education, and an Associate Professor at the United Arab Emirates University. She has taught in many European Universities and she has International Collaborations in Research and Projects with Prestigious Universities worldwide. She holds a doctoral degree in Biomedical Sciences from the Faculty of Kinesiology and Rehabilitation KULeuven, Belgium, an European Master in Psychomotor Therapy for Children (KULeuven, Belgium), and a Master in Human Performance and Health for Special Populations (Aristotle University of Thessaloniki, Greece). Her research interests are in Autism, ADHD, Motor behaviour, Assessment and diagnosis for children with emotional, behavioural, and developmental disorders. She is an Active Researcher and the Author of 6 Books on inclusive Education, Autism and Children's Education and mental health.

**Agathi Argyriadi** is a Psychologist with specialization on Cognitive – Behavioral Psychotherapy and Developmental Psychology. Her PhD thesis is entitled "The effects of "Aesthetic flow experiences" in school's environment of first graders. A psycho-educational approach". She also holds a M.Ed. on Special Education and a second Master on Counseling. She is currently a Visiting Assistant Professor at the United Arab Emirates University and Lecturer in the Department of Education at Frederick University, teaching developmental and cognitive psychology. In the past she has also taught at Cyprus University of Technology (Therapeutic communication), at the East London University (Research Methods and Statistics) and at the Technological Educational Institute of Peloponnese at the department of Speech Pathology (teaching Developmental Psychology and Clinical Neuropsychology), for 3 years. She has acted as a self- employed Psychologist and for a 3-year project against violence at the Ministry of Internal Affairs of the Hellenic Republic. She has also acted for two years, as an external associate at a private school in Greece, with the aim of monitoring and supporting students with learning difficulties, psychological problems and counseling of parents. Agathi Argyriadi was also a professor at the Foundation for Youth and Lifelong Learning and specifically at the Institute for Vocational Training of the Ministry of Education. She has published articles in international journals and she has participated in numerous of training seminars. She is the writer of 10 scientific books in the field of psychology. Her research interests focus on optimizing learning environments using positive psychology and aesthetic theories, developmental psychological issues, special education field, social inclusion issues. She teaches in the Distance Learning Program of Special Education.

**Alexandros Argyriadis** is an Assistant Professor at Frederick University, in the domain of Community Health with an emphasis on Mental Health and Learning Disabilities. He has previously taught at the University of East London, the University of South Wales, the Hellenic Open University and the University of Thessaly, the University of West Attica and other well-known universities. The courses he has taught are related to the inclusive education of people with disabilities, cultural and medical anthropology, mental and family health, health promotion and teaching methods, special education and social inequalities. At Frederick University, he coordinates the Distance Learning Master's Program in Community Health Care and the Practicum of the MEd in Special Education. He has authored numerous scholarly books and high impact factor articles; he has been the publisher of the scientific journal "Culture Journal" and participates in several editorial boards of international scientific journals. Indicatively, he is the Deputy Editor-in-Chief of the "Health and Research" journal as well as at the journal "Vima tou Asklipiou". His work includes numerous presentations at scientific conferences, elaboration of research programs and public activities in education. He often teaches as a visiting Professor at universities abroad and designs contemporary interdisciplinary activities. Administratively, he is a member of several committees at Frederick University but also in other international organizations such as the European Union Commission, the Assessors team of the Latvian Ministry of Education Academic Information Center (AIC) / Quality Agency for Higher Education (AIKA), a member of the Electors register of Hellenic Mediterranean University and others. His research interests focus on diversity and inclusion, people with disabilities, special education, health promotion and education and community health.

**Shabnam Abdoola** is a dually qualified speech-language pathologist and audiologist, employed as an Assistant Professor at the United Arab Emirates University. She is also a research associate at the University of Pretoria. Her research focuses on early childhood development & intervention, with a particular interest in the influence of 4IR on the profession of speech language pathology. She also has an interest in community engagement.

**Hafsa Aishan** is an educator in inclusive classrooms within the UAE, with a strong focus on fostering equitable learning environments for students of diverse abilities and backgrounds. Her expertise lies in implementing inclusive educational practices that cater to the unique needs of all learners, ensuring their academic, social, and emotional growth. She is engaged in research aimed at advancing inclusive education both locally and internationally. Her research interests include exploring innovative strategies for inclusion using technology, understanding the challenges and opportunities in diverse educational settings, and promoting best practices that support students with special educational needs. She has a keen interest in behavioral management, particularly in developing effective techniques to create positive and productive classroom environments. Her approach emphasizes proactive strategies, empathy, and collaboration with students, parents, and colleagues to address behavioral challenges and promote a culture of respect and inclusion. Her work is driven by a commitment to create inclusive, supportive, and effective learning spaces that empower every student to succeed.

**Al Reem Al Yaqoubi** PhD Student in Gifted and Special Education I United Arab Emirates University Al Reem Al Yaqoubi is a PhD student in the Gifted and Special Education Department at United Arab Emirates University. With a strong commitment to inclusive education, she focuses on creating accessible learning environments for students with disabilities. As a person with visual impairment, Al Reem's personal experience informs her academic work and advocacy, driving her to enhance educational opportunities for individuals with diverse learning needs. Her research interests are centered around developing inclusive educational practices that support both gifted learners and those with special educational needs. Al Reem aims to contribute to the advancement of policies and strategies that promote equality, accessibility, and excellence in education. Through her work, she seeks to ensure that all students, regardless of their abilities, have the resources and support needed to achieve their full potential.

**Alhosani** serves as the chair of Educational Leadership Department at the United Arab Emirates University. His research focuses on leadership styles in both K-12 and higher education institutions.

**Mohammed Aljanahi** has a Phd in Public Administration from Western Michigan University (WMU). Aljanahi's research interests range from Emiratisation, leadership, organizational behavior, and humor. Dr. Mohammed has received grants from different institutions such as WMU for 3500 AED from the School of Public

Affairs and Administration, and two grants as a CO-PI that is over 100,000 AED. A sample of his publications is Challenges to the Emiratisation process: content analysis. Dr. Aljanahi is keen on participating in conferences with new research, some of the conferences are MSPA, BERA, Assessment 2022, and WELS to name a few. He is engaged with his community; being a member of the crime prevention association in Dubai Police. Also, participating with the Jahez program that ensures students have the skills needed for the workforce. While, also regularly giving workshops at other venues such as Burnout, Well-being, and Positive Leadership with the Happiness Center at UAEU. Dr. Mohammed supervises the Government and Society students club and is the head of the leadership unit at the Center of Public Policy and Leadership at UAEU.

**Mona Humaid Aljanahi** is an Assistant Professor at the College of Education in United Arab Emirates University. She holds a Ph.D in Curriculum & Instruction with a concentration on Language & Literacy. Her research interests include literacy education, pop culture, language learning, language arts, and academic integrity. Her research studies have been published in Q1 Scopus indexed journals. She is currently an active reviewer for peer-reviewed international journals. Additionally, she presented at numerous national and international conferences on various topics in her field.

**Ahmed Alkaabi** is an Assistant Professor in the College of Education, United Arab Emirates University (UAEU). He holds a Ph.D. in Educational Administration and Policy with an emphasis on supervision from the University of Georgia, Athens, USA (2019). Dr. Alkaabi's research interests focus on school leadership, particularly in instructional supervision, leader and teacher evaluation, induction, professional development, and school inspection. His research has been published in high-quality, peer-reviewed journals indexed in Scopus. Additionally, he has edited two books on educational leadership and co-authored numerous book chapters. Dr. Alkaabi has also presented extensively at prestigious international conferences. Beyond his academic contributions, Dr. Alkaabi serves as a reviewer for several high-quality journals and acts as a referee for local organizations. He also actively contributes to the community as a school inspector, evaluating schools in the Emirate of Abu Dhabi.

**Latifa Alketbi** is an Assistant Professor at the United Arab Emirates University (UAEU), specializing in Early Childhood Education (ECE). Her research focuses on curriculum and instruction, digital literacy for parents, AI in education, and the integration of technology in early learning.

**Shamsa Almazooqi** a clinical psychologist specializing in psychometrics, neurodevelopmental disorders, and mental health. For the past eight years, she has been dedicated to the Zayed Higher Organization (ZHO), where she focuses on the psychological assessment and diagnosis of children and adults with neurodevelopmental disorders, particularly Autism Spectrum Disorder (ASD). Her research is centered on ASD, contributing to a deeper understanding and better support for those affected. In addition to her role at ZHO, she served as an Adjunct Instructor at UAE University in the Department of Special and Gifted Education.

**Mohammad Al Rashaida** is an Assistant Professor of Special Education at UAE University and Co-Editor-in-Chief of the International Journal for Research in Education (IJRE). He has an extensive background in research and teaching, with multiple prestigious grants and awards, including the Erasmus Mundus PhD Scholarship, the FPI Grants Program, and the Santander Research Award. Additionally, he has secured research funding for projects on Gifted and Talented Education in the UAE. Dr. Al Rashaida has held academic positions at Deusto University (Spain), Abu Dhabi University (UAE), and Prince Sattam Bin Abdulaziz University (KSA). His research focuses on inclusive education, developmental and learning disabilities, vocational rehabilitation, and employment. A prolific scholar, he has published extensively in high-ranked journals. He also holds a UK Fellowship in Higher Education, reflecting his dedication to academic excellence.

**Hesham Badawy**, Ph.D. in Educational Leadership and Policy student. Educational Leadership Masters, College of Education, United Arab Emirates University. Research interests: leadership, performance, evaluation, and professional development; feedback and feedforward delivery, receptivity and learning; cultural aspects of educational leadership; data driven decision making; and professional learning communities.

**Hosam** holds a Ph.D. candidacy in Leadership and Policy Studies in Education from the United Arab Emirates University (UAEU) and a Master's in Educational Leadership. He is also TESOL and TEFL certified. In his current role at Al Soqoor Cycle 2 School, he has successfully led educational transformations, integrating modern technology and state-of-the-art teaching strategies to foster a dynamic learning environment. His professional achievements include publishing research on innovation in educational leadership, STEM, and inclusive education, and presenting at national and international conferences. Hosam has been recognized for his contributions to education, particularly for his work with students of determination and gifted students. His leadership skills are further exemplified by his role in delivering professional development sessions and his involvement with the school leadership team in developing and implementing STEM education. Hosam's dedication to education is driven by his belief in the transformational approach, achieved through collaboration and the integration of modern technologies. His career objective is to continue developing as an innovative leader, supporting and inspiring students and educators to reach their full potential.

**Lara Carneiro** earned her BSc in Psychology from the Faculty of Psychology and Education Science at the University of Porto, Portugal (2023). Dr Carneiro holds a BSc in Physical Education (2009), a Masters degree in Physical Education (2012) and a Doctorate in Sports Science (2017) from Portugal. Carneiro currently works as an Assistant Professor at the United Arab Emirates University (UAEU) in the College of Education. She serves as an editor of Combining Exercise and Psychotherapy to Treat Mental Health, published by IGI Global, which earned a 5-star rating from Doody's Review Service. She also has experience in designing, implementing, and managing randomized controlled trials (efficacy of exercise and psychotherapy). Dr. Carneiro is also a Management Committee Member of funded research projects (e.g. CA21123 - Cancer- Understanding Prevention in Intellectual Disabilities (CUPID). Dr. Carneiro is an external expert in the remote evaluation of proposals -COST and her research focuses on physical activity, depressive and anxiety disorders, and mental illness, including physical health co-morbidities.

**Charu Dhankar** is an accomplished Assistant Professor in the Department of Psychology at Manipal University Jaipur, where she brings nine years of dedicated teaching and research expertise to her role. Specializing in Clinical Psychology, Health Psychology, and Psychopathology, Dr. Dhankar has established herself as a prominent figure in her field. Her insightful contributions extend beyond the classroom, with publications featured in both national and international journals. Through her commitment to advancing knowledge and fostering academic excellence, Dr. Dhankar plays a vital role in shaping the next generation of psychology professionals at Manipal University Jaipur.

**Efthymia Efthymiou** is currently serving as an Assistant Professor at Zayed University in the United Arab Emirates (UAE). With a strong background in special education, her research focuses on inclusive teaching practices, classroom discourse, and creating educational environments that support the inclusion of all students, including those with special needs. Her work centers on understanding the perspectives of various stakeholders, such as teachers and children with special needs, to develop more inclusive educational systems. She explores the role of both physical and psychological environments in shaping attitudes, positioning, and inclusion. Her research aims to identify and overcome barriers to inclusive education, with particular emphasis on leveraging technology-based teaching practices to address digital exclusion and promote inclusive teaching methods. In addition to her research efforts, Dr. Efthymia actively contributes to the advancement of inclusive education through her workshops and seminars conducted for teachers and principals in federal schools within the UAE.

**Asma Gul Yousaf Khan** is a dedicated Training Coordinator at the Continuing Education Center of the United Arab Emirates University. She holds a bachelor's degree in English Language from Abu Dhabi University and is currently pursuing a postgraduate program in Educational Leadership at the United Arab Emirates University. During her undergraduate years at Abu Dhabi University, Ms. Asma served as a part-time research assistant and course assistant, demonstrating her commitment to learning and academia. Additionally, she exhibited her compassion and dedication to education and inclusion by providing one-to-one support to children with special needs at one of the top schools in Al Ain, UAE. Ms. Asma is an enthusiastic lifelong learner with a strong interest in research. She aspires to be a leader who can positively impact society. In pursuit of this goal, she successfully completed the UN Online Young Leader Training Program, Geneva, Switzerland, in August 2023, aiming to enhance diplomatic and leadership skills for the promotion of diversity, equality, and the empowerment of women in education. She has contributed to academia by co-authoring a chapter titled "Transforming Education Through Technology and School Leadership" in the book Cutting-Edge Innovations in Teaching, Leadership, Technology, and Assessment. Apart from her academic pursuits, Ms. Khan has a keen interest in language, culture, and art. She has also contributed to literature by publishing a poem and co-authoring the book Words with Wings in collaboration with emerging authors from India.

**Ifigeneia Inglezaki** comes from the city of Chania, Crete, in Greece. At the age of 18, it was clear to her that the profession she would pursue would be related to children. She studied at the Department of Primary Education, where she first became involved in special education. Encouraged by her special education professor, she started volunteering at various institutions in Rhodes, where she was studying. After completing her undergraduate studies, she pursued a master's degree in special education. Later, she became involved in theatrical play and completed two years of counseling training as well as a four-year training in systemic therapy. Psychology has always intrigued her and has been highly useful in special education, both in intervention with children and in communication with parents. Upon completing her psychology studies, she undertook a thesis on artificial intelligence and special education, as she was fascinated by how much AI can contribute to providing equal opportunities for all students.

**Ruchi Joshi**, Presently Assistant Professor at Manipal University Jaipur is an Academician, Researcher and an RCI certified Rehabilitation Counselor. She has completed her Masters in Clinical Psychology from Jai Narayan Vyas University, Doctorate from Rajasthan University, A Post-Graduate Diploma in Child Guidance from Kota Open University and Counseling and an Advanced Diploma in Child Guidance and Counseling from Jai Narayan Vyas University, Jodhpur. She has 10 years of experience in Counseling, Research and Teaching in various parts of country and has been associated with Organizations of Repute like Mohan Lal Sukhadia University Udaipur, Poorinima Group of Colleges Jaipur, Maharana Mewar Public School Udaipur and Amity University Rajasthan. She has number of National and International Publications to her credit that includes publication includes Peer -Reviewed, UGC CARE, Tylor and Francis index and publication Houses. She has presented Paper in number of International, National, and Regional level Conferences, Seminars, Workshops etc. She has been invited as a Resource person and Panelist in Workshops, Panel Discussions, Seminars and Webinars on issues related to Mental Health, Physical, Mental and Sexual Violence.

**Subhadip kowar** is pursuing a PhD from UEM in Kolkata. He earned his MCA from Brainware University West Bengal, India, in 2023 and his BCA from Burdwan University, India, in 2021. He currently works as a Technical Assistant in the Department of Computer Science and Engineering (CSE CS & DS) at Brainware University in India. He has around 1.5 years of teaching experience. His research interests include Generative AI, machine learning for recommendation systems.

**Patil** is an innovative educator with a Doctor of Pharmacy degree specializing in teaching health science subjects to high school students. Leveraging her clinical expertise, she develops cutting-edge curricula that bridge theoretical knowledge with practical applications in healthcare. With a rich multicultural background, Patil brings a global perspective to the classroom, ensuring inclusive learning environments and culturally sensitive health education programs. Her primary focus is designing innovative pedagogical techniques including interactive, technology-driven lessons, real-world case studies and simulations, and collaborative projects fostering critical thinking.

**Kalliopi Megari** is a Postdoctoral researcher of Aristotle University of Thessaloniki, Greece, Academic Director of MSc in Clinical Psychology and Clinical supervisor at City College, University of York, Europe Campus. She is Adjunct lecturer at University of Western Macedonia in Florina, Greece. Dr. Megari is a psychologist with a history of working in the hospital & health care industry, skilled in Clinical Neuropsychology, Clinical Research, Medical Education, Psychological

Assessment and Learning Disabilities. She works both in clinical and in research practice and she provides strong professional healthcare services, graduated from Aristotle University of Thessaloniki, and attended further education from Department of Educational and Social Policy, University of Macedonia, in people with special needs and disabilities. She holds undergraduate degrees in Nursing and Psychology, as well as a Master' s and a PhD in Neuropsychology from Aristotle University of Thessaloniki. She has some years of occupational and research experience working with patients who have neurological, psychiatric, and cognitive disorders, as well as chronic disease patients suffering from cancer and cardiovascular diseases. She is the head of the Centre of creative activities of children and adults with disabilities and she also works as a counseling psychologist in Prison, Diavata Thessaloniki, at the school of second chance. She was the Global Engagement Representative of SLC International Neuropsychological Society from 2018-2021 and she was a research fellow in the Department of Cardiovascular Surgery in AHEPA Hospital. Currently she is a Global Membership Committee member of International Neuropsychological Society and leader of Rehabilitation of COVID-19 patients working group of NeuroCOVID International Neuropsychology Taskforce SIG. In addition, she is the General Secretary of the board of directors of Hellenic Neuropsychological Society and Ethics Committee president of Hellenic Neuropsychological Society. Since 2021, she is a member of PIAC Community Outreach Subcommittee of AMERICAN PSYCHOLOGICAL ASSOCIATION Membership and a member of Engagement Committee of American Group Psychotherapy Association (AGPA). Her work has earned her many prestigious international awards and was an Ambassador of National Academy of Neuropsychology (NAN), USA Leadership and Ambassador Development Program (2022-23). She has given lectures at Aristotle University of Thessaloniki, University of Warsaw and Norwegian University of Science and Technology in Oslo. She is committed to leadership skills and issues on equity, diversity, and inclusion as her clinical and research work states.

**Kalliopi Megari** is a Postdoctoral researcher of Aristotle University of Thessaloniki, Greece, Academic Director of MSc in Clinical Psychology and Clinical supervisor at City College, University of York, Europe Campus. She is Adjunct lecturer at University of Western Macedonia in Florina, Greece. Dr. Megari is a psychologist with a history of working in the hospital & health care industry, skilled in Clinical Neuropsychology, Clinical Research, Medical Education, Psychological Assessment and Learning Disabilities. She works both in clinical and in research practice and she provides strong professional healthcare services, graduated from Aristotle University of Thessaloniki, and attended further education from Department of Educational and Social Policy, University of Macedonia, in people with special needs and disabilities. She holds undergraduate degrees in

Nursing and Psychology, as well as a Master' s and a PhD in Neuropsychology from Aristotle University of Thessaloniki. She has some years of occupatio

**Carmen Milton** is a dually qualified speech-language pathologist and audiologist, employed as a lecturer at the University of Pretoria. Her research focuses on early childhood development, language disorders and language learning disorders. She also has an interest in community engagement.

**Wissal's** life has been a fascinating blend of science and education. Holder of Professional Diploma in Teaching Sciences from Al Ain University (AAU). For over 13 years teaching has been both a profession and a calling for her. Her extensive experience has afforded her a deep insight into effective teaching strategies and techniques. She is dedicated to creating a dynamic and engaging learning environment that fosters intellectual growth and curiosity among students. This exciting endeavor reflects her commitment to advancing educational practices and leadership in the field of education. She believes that effective leadership is instrumental in shaping the future of education and creating positive change in the lives of students and educators alike.

**Ashraf Moustafa** is a nfaculty member of Special and Gifted Education Department at the United Arab Emirates University, He has clinical and educational experience working with children with Sensory Impairment, L.D, Autism, ADHD and gifted students. His research interests are in Sensory Impairment and Assessment for children with Sensory Impairment, developmental disorders and learning difficulties.

**Mohammed Borhandden Musah** is an Assistant Professor at Department of Educational Studies, Bahrain Teachers College, University of Bahrain, Kingdom of Bahrain. His work focuses on the management of higher learning institutions, education supervision, quality management, followership, professional learning communities, teacher leadership and workforce performance. He can be contacted at email: mmusah@uob.edu.bh

**Meghry Nazarian** is a published educator and an English language teacher with over 12 years of expertise in teaching, research, and educational leadership. Dr. Meghry is a full-time Assistant Professor at Amity University Dubai's HAAS Department. She holds a Ph.D. in Leadership & Policy Studies in Education from UAE University, where she was awarded a prestigious graduate fellowship. Dr. Nazarian also earned her Master's degree in Teaching English for Foreign Language Learners (TEFL) from Aleppo University, Syria. Throughout her career, Dr. Nazarian has demonstrated a deep commitment to fostering academic excellence and promoting innovative teaching practices. She has developed curriculum frameworks that integrate modern pedagogical practices and support diverse learning needs. She has designed and delivered several academic workshops to undergraduate and graduate students at UAE University. Her teaching philosophy revolves around student-centred approach, 21st century skills, and cross-cultural understanding, preparing learners to thrive in diverse and dynamic educational environments. In addition to her teaching responsibilities, Dr. Nazarian is actively engaged in research focusing on organizational behaviour, organizational identification, cultural intelligence, cultural sameness, soft leadership, employee well-being, and employee voice/silence. Dr. Nazarian has published in peer-reviewed SCOPUS-indexed journals and is a reviewer for the International Journal of Organizational and Collective Intelligence (IJOCI). Her contributions to interdisciplinary research have earned her invitations to national and international conferences, including AERA in USA, BERA in the UK, ECER in Glasgow, IGSW in Singapore, and SSHSRC in the UAE. Dr. Nazarian is deeply passionate about lifelong learning and is an active member of the Gathering Readers reading club since 2020. She shares her musings through this website: Search Results for "meghry" – Gathering Books. She shares her achievements and scholarly contributions through her ORCID platform.

**Amad Gablan** is a professor of science education at the College of Education at UAEU. He earned his Ph.D. degree in science and sustainability education from Florida State University, the USA in 2005 and worked for more than 15 years at the College of Educational Science at the Hashemite University in Jordan and 6 years as a senior programs' manager at Queen Rania Teacher Academy, Jordan. He also worked as a visiting professor of science education at the University of Alberta, Canada for 5 years. He conducted several research projects in education with UNESCO, UNICEF, EU, and USAID. He has published more than 88 books, chapters in books, and journal articles in local and international publishing houses.

**Smaropoulou Christina** is a PhD candidate in Educational Psychology at the University of Crete with extensive experience in general and special education. She holds a degree in Primary Education from Aristotle University of Thessaloniki and two master's degrees: one in Digital Technologies in Education and another in Special Education. Her professional background includes roles as a general and special education teacher and an intercultural education instructor. Her research focuses on innovative teaching methods, social and emotional learning, and self-regulated learning, with multiple publications in international conference proceedings and scientific journals. Additionally, she has participated in Erasmus+ and eTwinning projects, integrating technology and inclusive practices into education. She is currently doing her PhD research with a Learning Management

System, Journey to the Islands of Social and Emotional Learning, designed to enhance students' SEL competencies. Furthermore, she actively contribute to teacher training and professional development through seminars and workshops, specializing in educational psychology, special education, and digital learning technologies.

**Maria Sofologi** is an Adjunct Ass. Professor at the Department of Early Childhood and Education at the University of Ioannina in Greece. She delivers the courses “Cognitive Psychology”, and “Developmental Psychology”. She is also a postdoctoral researcher at the University of Ioannina in Greece. She holds a Ph.D. in Cognitive Psychology from the Aristotle University of Thessaloniki. She also holds a Master of Science degree in Cognitive Psychology from the Aristotle University of Thessaloniki. During her master's degree years she trained and practiced different assessment cognitive tools to evaluate all cognitive functions like memory, attention, language, executive functions both in adults and children. She is the key speaker in many European and Hellenic conferences concerning cognitive psychology, educational psychology, special education in children and adults, as well. Her academic work includes a series of many scientific publications, books, and book chapters concerning Cognitive Psychology, Special Education, Educational Psychology, and Cognitive impairments in children and adults as well.

**Shraddha Tripathi**, with 13 years of diverse experience in teaching, research, and industry, currently serves as Assistant Professor at Manipal University Jaipur. Her academic journey includes roles as Assistant Professor (Senior Scale) and Assistant Dean at IMS Unison University, Dehradun, and Assistant Professor of Psychology at Amity University Madhya Pradesh. Holding a Doctorate in Clinical Psychology, she received JRF and SRF of ICMR for her work on “Effect of Hypnotic Regression on Phobia and Anxiety Symptoms in Adults.” Actively engaged in scholarly activities, Dr. Tripathi has contributed to over 30 conferences and workshops. Her prolific publication record comprises 15 research papers in esteemed journals, conference proceedings, and articles in various publications. Recognized for her expertise, she serves on the Editorial Board of 4 International Journals.

**Kriti Vashishtha** brings a wealth of expertise to her role as Assistant Professor in the Department of Psychology at Manipal University Jaipur, Rajasthan. Holding an M.A. in Psychology from Panjab University, Chandigarh, and a Ph.D. in Psychology from Banasthali University, Dr. Vashishtha is deeply committed to academic excellence and student development. She has been awarded as ‘Manovigyan Seva Ratan Puruskar, 2024’. With a specialization in Child Psychopathology, Counseling, and Sports Psychology, Dr. Vashishtha's diverse interests extend to areas such as Social Psychology, Industrial and Organizational Behavior, and Positive Psychology.

She has a proven track record of teaching and mentoring students, fostering an environment conducive to learning and growth. She has edited few books and also authored a book named "Mind Maze". Dr. Vashishtha's contributions to academia are multifaceted. She has presented numerous research papers at both national and international seminars and conferences, showcasing her dedication to advancing knowledge in the field. Additionally, her work has been published in esteemed journals, reflecting her commitment to rigorous scholarship and impactful research. Beyond academia, Dr. Vashishtha is a passionate advocate for holistic well-being. As a certified Tarot Card Reader and Pranic Healer, she integrates alternative healing modalities into her practice, promoting holistic approaches to health and wellness. Driven by a belief in the power of knowledge-sharing, Dr. Vashishtha continues to make meaningful contributions to education through her writing and teaching endeavors. With her multidisciplinary expertise and dedication to excellence, she serves as an inspiring role model and mentor to students and colleagues alike.

**Aikaterini Vasiou** is an Assistant Professor of "Methodological approaches in Educational Psychology" at the Department of Primary Education of University of Crete (Greece). She holds a PhD in Educational Psychology from the Department of Primary Education of the University of Thessaly (Greece), while as part of an Excellence scholarship she conducted a post-doctoral research in School Psychology and Counseling at the Department of Primary Education of the University of Western Macedonia (Greece). She has participated in an Experimental Study research program of the Kapodistrian University of Athens (Greece) and in Mental Health research programs of University of the Aegean (Greece). She has worked as a Laboratory Teaching Staff (E.D.I.P.) at the Department of Primary Education of the University of Western Macedonia (Greece), and as a contractual Lecturer/ Academic Scholar of Higher Educational Institutions in both Greece and Cyprus. She has also many years of teaching experience in Secondary Schools. Her research interests include social and emotional learning, social and individual predictors of students' outcomes, as well as students' and teachers' well-being.

# Index

## Symbols



## A



## C



## D

## L



## M



## N

## P



## S



## T

## W

www.ingramcontent.com/pod-product-compliance
Lightning Source LLC
LaVergne TN
LVHW080613300926
849162LV00005B/1137
* 9 7 9 8 3 3 7 3 0 5 7 3 8 *